Cognitive-Behavioral
Marital Therapy

BRUNNER/MAZEL COGNITIVE THERAPY SERIES
CONSULTING EDITOR
Arthur Freeman, Ed.D.

Cognitive-Behavioral Therapy with Families
Edited by *Norman Epstein,* Ph.D.,
Stephen E. Schlesinger, Ph.D.,
and *Windy Dryden,* Ph.D.

Cognitive-Behavioral Marital Therapy
by *Donald H. Baucom,* Ph.D.,
and *Norman Epstein,* Ph.D.

Cognitive-Behavioral Marital Therapy

by
Donald H. Baucom, Ph.D.
and
Norman Epstein, Ph.D.

BRUNNER/MAZEL COGNITIVE THERAPY SERIES

CONSULTING EDITOR:
Arthur Freeman, Ed.D.

BRUNNER/MAZEL, *Publishers* • **New York**

To our wives,
Linda and Carolyn

Library of Congress Cataloging-in-Publication Data

Baucom, Donald H.
    Cognitive-behavioral marital therapy / by Donald H. Baucom and
Norman Epstein
       p.   cm. — (Brunner/Mazel cognitive therapy series)
    Bibliography: p.
    Includes index.
    ISBN 0-87630-558-3
    1. Marital psychotherapy. 2. Cognitive therapy. I. Epstein,
Norman, –   . II. Title. III. Series.
    [DNLM: 1. Behavior Therapy. 2. Cognition. 3. Marital Therapy—
-methods.   WM 55 B337c]
RC488.5B37   1989
616.89'156 – dc20
DNLM/DLC
for Library of Congress   89-7279
                                        CIP

Published by
BRUNNER/MAZEL, INC.
19 Union Square
New York, New York 10003

Manufactured in the United States of America

10 9 8 7 6 5 4 3 2 1

Contents

Foreword

The current volume by Baucom and Epstein demonstrates the product that can result when two individuals, both of whom are skilled therapists, creative theoreticians, and experienced researchers, combine their efforts. No other two individuals have the depth of understanding and the breadth of knowledge needed to write a book of this magnitude on cognitive behavioral therapy for marital distress. As a result, the best of the scientist-practitioner is revealed in *Cognitive-Behavioral Marital Therapy*.

Too often, there are significant gaps among theory, basic research, applied clinical research, and clinical practice in the real world. Baucom and Epstein have bridged those gaps in a way that is rarely seen. They share with us the theoretical bases for their treatment approach. In a detailed manner, they demonstrate the empirical grounding that supports their theoretical notions. And most importantly, they clarify the implications of these empirical findings for clinical practice. Thus, theory, research, and clinical practice are interwoven in a way that epitomizes the advancement of psychotherapy as a science as well as an art.

But let it be clearly stated: this is a book for clinicians. Cognitive behavioral marital therapy is a treatment approach which incorporates a fair amount of structure into the clinical setting. Consequently, it is easy for the novice to believe that it is a cookbook approach with a set of routinized treatment procedures. The authors reveal throughout the text that nothing could be further from the truth. Whereas they detail a wide range of specific treatment procedures, they also clarify the numerous

vii

decisions regarding intervention which must be made within each session. Instead of relying upon the ubiquitous, ill-defined, clinical judgment of the clinician, these therapists take us much further, providing us with the logic and algorithms which they employ in making these critical treatment decisions. These decisions are brought to life through the numerous examples that the authors provide from their own clinical experience. For heuristic purposes, the authors provide separate coverage of couples' behaviors, cognitions, and emotions. Yet, they continually explain the interrelationships among these variables and their reciprocal influences upon each other. Among their many useful recommendations, they clarify when to focus on each of these classes of variables, and when and how to make a transition from a focus on one of these to another. Thus, the reader will find here a more detailed guide to conducting cognitive behavioral marital therapy than can be found anywhere else.

In order to arrive at the point where they could provide the field with this contribution, these authors needed numerous skills and experiences: a detailed understanding of the cognitive theory of maladaptive behavior and cognitive interventions; a firm grasp of behavioral principles and their application to clinical phenomena; insight into the multifaceted phenomena classified under the rubric of marital distress; and an empirical perspective on all of the above. Epstein worked for a number of years as Director of Research at the Center of Cognitive Therapy. His ongoing interests in marital distress and his knowledge of cognitive therapy for individuals placed him in a unique position to clarify the similarities and differences between marital distress and individual disorders such as depression from a cognitive perspective.

Baucom had been conducting research on marital distress for a number of years from a behavioral perspective and gradually came to recognize the importance that couples' cognitions have in their relationships. It is not surprising, then, that in the early 1980s, these two individuals began to work together to propel the field forward in its attempts to understand and treat marital discord. They have both been active researchers in exploring the foundations of marital discord as well as its treatment. They have developed some of the few existing measures of spouses' cognitions, which are critical for basic research in this area. In addition, they are both experienced researchers in the area of treating marital discord. Baucom is one of the field's major researchers in evaluating the effectiveness of behavioral marital therapy.

Between the two of them, Baucom and Epstein have conducted the majority of the existing outcome research studies on cognitive therapy for marital distress. Furthermore, they both maintain active clinical practices in treating maritally distressed couples. It is important that in the field of psychotherapy, we write no book before its time: before the underlying theory can be articulated; before basic research is conducted to evaluate the phenomena of interest; before applied research is completed to clarify the effectiveness of the treatment strategies; before the authors have had years of experience to convey what they have learned in the clinic as well as in the laboratory. These authors have waited until the time was right for them and the field was sufficiently mature to receive a major contribution. *Cognitive-Behavioral Marital Therapy* is just such a contribution — a work that significantly expands our understanding of the phenomenon and treatment of marital distress.

AARON T. BECK, M.D.
Center for Cognitive Therapy
University of Pennsylvania, Philadelphia

Preface

This book is intended for individuals who wish to understand marital discord and treat couples with relationship problems. It is hoped that professionals from a wide range of disciplines who having been working with distressed couples will find something new and useful to them in the text. At the same time, it is appropriate for graduate students who have little experience in the field. Thus, we have attempted to provide appropriate background material, but the intent was to go beyond an introductory level of discussion of material.

As the title indicates, this book provides a cognitive-behavioral, skills-oriented approach to understanding and treating couples. A cognitive-behavioral therapist is concerned with how the couple thinks, experiences emotions, and behaves. The skills-oriented emphasis prepares couples to address not only their current concerns, but also future difficulties when they arise. Whereas the domains of behavior, cognition, and affect are integrally related, for the purposes of presentation and focus of intervention, it is appropriate to differentiate among them. Thus, the text is organized around these three constructs. Each of the constructs is considered in each of the three major sections of the book: (a) theoretical issues and research findings concerning marital discord; (b) assessment; and (c) intervention. Thus, there are chapters focusing on cognitive factors in marital dysfunction, assessment of cognitions, etc.

In an attempt to limit the scope of discussion, certain parameters were introduced. Therefore, issues rather generic to the field of marital therapy, such as establishing rapport, the use of cotherapists, and responding to confidential information from one spouse are not addressed as general topics. They are discussed only to the extent that a cognitive-behavioral marital therapist would be expected to respond to these issues in a unique way. Consequently, the role of the therapist, the structuring of the sessions, and decision making are described, specific to the cognitive-behavioral model. In addition, several specialty areas, such as behavioral treatment of sexual dysfunctions and spouse abuse, have become popular in recent years. Owing to the large volume of materials already published on these topics, they are not dealt with in detail in this book.

There are many current books on the treatment of marital discord. Unfortunately, most of the theoretical notions on which these treatments are based have not been empirically investigated, and there have been few studies evaluating the effectiveness of these other theoretical approaches in treating distressed couples. Behavioral and cognitive-behavioral approaches are rather distinct in this regard. In the past 20 years, there have been a large number of investigations attempting to understand the cognitive, emotional, and behavioral components of marital discord. Skills-oriented approaches comprise the majority of well-controlled studies evaluating the effectiveness of treatment for marital discord.

Several excellent books already exist on the behavioral treatment of marital discord. However, they give only minimal attention to interventions focusing on cognitions and emotions. The research in these areas and clinical developments have now reached a point where a more in-depth discussion of cognitions and emotions in marital distress is needed. The current volume differs from other behavioral marital therapy books by providing equal attention to cognitions, emotions, and behaviors in marital distress.

This text has a stronger research focus than many texts describing the treatment of marital discord. We hope that this has not translated into a dry presentation of the material. This book is intended for clinicians, and working with distressed couples is anything but dry and boring. The goal of presenting research findings is to provide a sound research basis for clinical practice. Even where there is substantial research supporting the effectiveness of a particular technique, that research base typically has been rather general. For example, many investigations have demonstrated that teaching problem-solving skills to distressed couples can benefit them a great deal. While teaching the problem-solving process to couples, the therapist must make many decisions. How these specific decisions are made by the therapist has not been investigated empirically. At present, all we know is that couples often benefit from learning problem-solving techniques. Yet, these and numerous other decisions must be made by the therapist throughout treatment. Therefore, the treatment of distressed couples is not presented merely as a set of routinized techniques. Instead, various decision points for the therapist and guidelines for making decisions are described throughout the book, although there is no empirical support for many of these specific guidelines, owing to a lack of investigation at this detailed level.

A skills-oriented approach to marital therapy involves a number of techniques for addressing specific cognitions, emotions, and behaviors. Therefore, some of our students with different theoretical orientations have approached these different interventions with skepticism, concerned that the approach is too structured and routinized. Most of them have been pleased to find that the treatment is individualized for each couple. In addition, they have found that they can use many of the strategies described in this book, even though they maintain their primary allegiance to another theoretical orientation. For example, it is hard to argue against the value of learning to express emotions adaptively and becoming a good listener in a marriage. Thus, we hope that this discussion of marital therapy will be of assistance to clinicians from varying orientations.

This volume was truly a collaborative effort, and the order of authorship merely reflects an alphabetical listing of our names. We both made unique and equally important contributions to the book, and it would have been difficult, if not impossible, for either of us to have accomplished this task alone. We hope the reader will enjoy reading it as much as we have enjoyed working together to prepare it.

We would like to give special thanks to the many researchers who have devoted their careers to investigating marital discord from a cognitive-behavioral perspective and thus laying the empirical basis for this volume. A number of our graduate students have read earlier drafts of chapters and provided us with useful feedback; a special thanks to Tamara Sher for her feedback. Most important, our sincere appreciation goes to our wives, Linda and Carolyn, and our children, Brian, Jennifer, Anna, and Meredith. They have helped us to maintain a realistic perspective on families and to realize that it can look great on paper, but if it does not fly at home, it is not worth much.

This book is about understanding and helping couples. It is about caring, loving, dealing with disappointment, and having fun—not only for the couple, but also for the therapist. If we have succeeded in describing how that can occur, we have met our goals.

SECTION I

THEORETICAL AND EMPIRICAL FOUNDATIONS

This book focuses on the roles that behaviors, cognitions, and emotions play in determining couples' levels of marital satisfaction or distress, and consequently on the roles that they play in the treatment of marital problems. This first section of the book describes both the theoretical conceptualizations and empirical research findings that have identified a variety of specific behavioral, cognitive, and affective factors differentiating distressed from nondistressed couples. In our cognitive-behavioral approach to marital therapy, the assessment of couples' relationship strengths and problems, as well as the design of therapeutic interventions, is tied closely to these theoretical and empirical foundations. The assessment and intervention procedures described in the following sections of the book are organized around the behavioral, cognitive, and affective factors reviewed in the four chapters of this section.

Chapter 1 provides an overview of the manner in which spouses' behaviors, cognitions, and affects interact in functional and dysfunctional ways. It begins with a case example that illustrates the interplay of behavioral factors such as communication patterns, cognitive factors such as arbitrary inferences that spouses make about each other's behavior, and affective factors such as high levels of anger. The case example is followed by an outline of the ways in which a spouse's behaviors, cognitions, and affects can influence either his or her own or the partner's subsequent behaviors, cognitions, and affects. All of these potential links among the three types of factors are described in detail in the subsequent three chapters.

1

Chapter 2 begins with a description of the social learning and social exchange theories that underlie behavioral approaches to understanding marital and other intimate relationships. Empirical findings bearing on the relevance of these theoretical views of relationship dysfunctions are reviewed. Furthermore, cognitive factors that may mediate couples' behavioral exchanges are noted. The chapter then describes behavioral discrimination skills, communication skills, problem-solving skills, and behavior-change skills that are important if a relationship is to meet the needs of both partners and if a couple is to resolve marital conflicts that may arise.

Chapter 3 presents a cognitive view of marital distress, including a discussion of five types of cognitive phenomena that can influence spouses' behavioral and affective responses to events in their relationship: perceptions (particularly selective attention), attributions, expectancies, assumptions, and standards. Theoretical and empirical support for the importance of these types of cognitions in intimate relationships is reviewed. In addition, the systematic information-processing errors (i.e., cognitive distortions) identified in the cognitive therapy literature (e.g., Beck et al., 1979) and in social cognition research are described as they apply to dysfunctional marital interaction. Finally, possible causal relationships among perceptions, attributions, expectancies, assumptions, and standards are proposed, and a case example is offered to illustrate the contributions of all five types of cognitions to a marital problem.

Chapter 4 describes four aspects of spouses' affective experiences within their marriages: (a) the degrees of various positive and negative emotions experienced by each spouse, (b) each individual's ability to recognize his or her emotions and the factors that elicit them, (c) the degree to which the individual expresses emotions overtly, and (d) the presence of specific emotional responses that interfere with constructive interaction between spouses. Cognitive factors that can influence the experience and expression of emotions are discussed, as are clinical and empirical data concerning specific communication skill deficits that impede affective expression. Deficits in listening skills also are examined as potential blocks to the communication of affect in marital relationships. Furthermore, special attention is paid to the nature and determinants of four types of affect that can be both causes and results of negative marital cognitions and behaviors: anger, depression, anxiety, and jealousy.

The behavioral, cognitive, and affective factors that influence mar satisfaction and distress are presented in separate chapters for heurist purposes, but throughout this book it is stressed that behavior, cognition and affect exert mutual influences on each other. Each chapter in this section describes this interdependence, and this integrative model is extended through the assessment and treatment sections of the book.

1

The Interplay of Behavior, Cognition, and Affect in Marital Interaction

Therapists and researchers who are interested in understanding intimate relationships such as marriage are faced with the challenge of taking into account both the interpersonal behavioral interactions that occur between two people and the individuals' intrapsychic cognitive and affective experiences. On the whole, the predominant theoretical approaches to marital relationships and therapy (e.g., psychoanalytic, systems, behavioral) traditionally have tended to emphasize either the interpersonal or the intrapsychic aspects of marriage (Segraves, 1982). For the most part, separate research literatures have developed concerning behavior, cognition, and affect in close relationships (Bradbury & Fincham, 1987). Recently, there have been promising efforts to construct theoretical models that integrate components of marital interaction (e.g., Bradbury & Fincham, 1987; Segraves, 1982). Furthermore, the clinical marital literature increasingly has described interventions that address links among behaviors, cognitions, and emotions (see, for example, Neidig & Friedman's [1984] book on spouse abuse), and a growing body of empirical studies on the association between marital interaction and depression (e.g., Hooley, 1986) is representative of researchers' concerns with integrating intra- and interpersonal processes.

It is a premise of this book that when a couple is experiencing difficulties in their relationship, the problems are likely to include behavioral, cognitive, and affective components, and that these three types of factors exert mutual influences on one another. Although the three factors might not have equivalent impact on dysfunction in a particular marriage

5

(e.g., a couple's distress might be determined primarily by a chronic deficit in basic problem-solving skills rather than by cognitions or emotional states), most often it is important to alter all three of them in therapy. The following case example illustrates the complex interplay of behavioral, cognitive, and affective factors in a couple's marital problems.

KEN AND SUE: A CASE OF MARITAL DISTRESS

Ken (age 36) and Sue (age 35) sought marital therapy after eight years of marriage, due to increasingly bitter arguments. Both were highly distressed about the deterioration of their relationship and remarked to their therapist that they had not experienced such strife in their earlier years together, or in any dating relationships with other people prior to their marriage. Their concerns were not only for themselves, but also for their six-year-old and four-year-old daughters, who clearly were upset by their parents' conflict.

During an initial interview with the couple, the therapist learned that both spouses were college graduates and had moderately stressful and time-consuming, white collar jobs. At present, their work and family commitments left them little leisure time, and they reported few pleasant shared activities. In fact, both spouses complained that they felt neglected by their partner, and that the other person did not seem to care about the marriage any longer. During the session, the therapist noticed that at times each spouse appeared quite sad when describing the marriage, and at other times they became angry when debating who was more at fault for their problems.

When the therapist asked each spouse to describe the marital problem as he or she viewed it, the following exchange occurred:

Sue: Ken is so preoccupied with himself and what he's doing, whether it's his job or his projects with the house. So much of the time, he seems like he's in another world.

Ken (interrupting): Oh, come on! You're as busy and distracted with things as I am.

Therapist: Ken, I can see that you don't agree with what Sue is saying, but right now it is important for me to get an idea about how each of you views the problems in your relationship. My goal is not to see who is right or wrong, but to understand how the relationship looks to each of you and what about it makes each of you upset. So, it is very important that you do not interrupt each other now. I'd like you to just listen carefully to what Sue has to say, and if your views of things are different, you will have an opportunity to describe how you see it in a few minutes. Now, Sue would you please tell me a little more about what the difficulties seem to be from your perspective?

Sue: Well, as I was saying, he seems so self-centered. After the children are in bed and the dishes are washed, he just goes off and reads something for work or works on the house. Sometimes I'm just seething, because I've been upset about something, maybe something that happened at work, and he's so insensitive that he ignores me and heads off for other things.

Therapist: If you are upset about something, how do you tend to let Ken know about it?

Sue: Sometimes I start to talk about it, maybe during dinner, but at other times it just has to show, because I'm so upset inside, but he doesn't pay any attention.

Therapist: And when he doesn't seem to pay any attention, what do you do next?

Sue: I've learned that there isn't much I *can* do. Whenever I tell him that I want him to pay attention to me, he gets defensive and we have a fight. Most of the time I sit on my feelings now. Sometimes I get so frustrated that I blow up and scream or call him names, and I really don't like what I've become at times like that. I'm generally a pretty reasonable person, but he makes me go wild.

Therapist: When you blow up, how does Ken react?

Sue: Well, I get his attention that way. It seems like the only way to get through to him. But, he usually walks out of the room and I really get nowhere. Once in a while, if I yell enough he actually seems to feel guilty and tries to soothe me. It doesn't take him long to get distracted again though.

Therapist: So, one thing that really seems to upset you is when Ken doesn't seem to notice how you are feeling or pay more attention when you want him to. Is there anything else that goes on between you two that is upsetting to you?

Sue: Yes. When I described our hectic evening before, I didn't mention that I'm the one who does most of the cooking, dishwashing, and other chores. Ken talks a good game about having a balanced and fair relationship, but with both of us working full time, somehow I still get stuck with a lot more of the housework.

Therapist: Is that something that the two of you have discussed?

Sue: Many times. There's a big difference between the excuses and promises that Ken makes at those times and his actual lack of follow-through.

Therapist: When Ken doesn't do things that he said he would do, what goes through your mind?

Sue: That he's selfish and doesn't care how much stress I have to handle. What really upsets me is that I've seen the kind of relationship that his parents have, and his father has taken advantage of his mother for years and years. She doesn't complain, but I can tell that she's had to tolerate a lot while her husband expects her to take care of him. I didn't realize this for a long time, but Ken seems to take after his father a lot. I guess if you see that kind of thing for years as you are growing up, it must seem like the natural way of things.

Therapist: When you thought about coming to meet with me about these issues, what were you thinking I might be able to help you with?

Sue: I can't say that I feel like there's much chance that you can do anything about this, but I guess that I had enough hope to make the appointment. It's just

that these seem to be such ingrained patterns on Ken's part. He isn't
motivated to change, and I don't know if he could if he wanted to do it.
To be honest, I was hoping that you knew some way to get him more
involved in our relationship and more sensitive to my needs.

Therapist: O.K., I've begun to get an idea about some of your concerns, Sue, and
I would like to shift now and get some of your views, Ken. I'd like to hear
about your impressions of the things that Sue said, but first I would prefer
that you tell me a little about the aspects of the marriage that have been
of greatest concern to *you.*

Ken: Well, it's sure interesting hearing Sue talking about my not listening to her,
because she makes it sound like it's my fault. Since the day I met her, she's
always been introverted and I had to take the lead to get conversations going.
If I don't baby her and almost plead with her to tell me what's on her mind,
I don't hear about it. Then, out of the blue, she blows her top and starts
screaming. I don't want any part of her when she's like that. Most of the
time, I don't know what she's upset about.

Therapist: You said "most of the time." Can you give me an example of a time
when you did know what was upsetting Sue?

Ken: Yes. When she expects me to do something like wash the dishes and I haven't
gotten around to doing it, she makes it *very* clear how angry she is about
it. I think that I should do my fair share, because we both work, but when
Sue tries to run the show and be the big director, I'm not going to be
ordered around and treated like a child. When she gets like that, it's clear
that she wants to cut me down to size, and I can tell that there's nothing
that will get her to back off once she's started to go after me. I just get myself
away from her. I don't know if it's just her reaction to me in particular, or maybe she has a need to dominate a man. Well, she picked the
wrong one!

As the therapist explored the spouses' concerns further, a number of
other factors emerged. The couple was asked to provide a brief history of
the development of their relationship, including how they met, what
attracted them to each other initially, how they decided to get married,
and what significant events (e.g., moves, job changes, major illnesses)
seemed to affect their marriage. Both reported that they had been very
attracted to each other physically and had enjoyed spending time pursuing
mutual interests such as dancing, bicycling, and hiking. Sue said that she
was attracted by Ken's stability, his ambition about getting ahead in his
career, and his being more serious and mature than some other men she
had known. Ken noted that he had been attracted by Sue's sense of humor,
her knowing what she wanted out of life, and her easygoing nature; she
didn't seem to like to fight.

The couple's account of the developmental history of their relationship
indicated that there was little conflict or distress during the year that they
dated or for the first few years of marriage. However, as their careers and

the births of their daughters increasingly placed significant demands on their coping abilities as individuals and as a dyad, arguments such as those described above increased, and both spouses experienced a drop in marital satisfaction. Both spouses reported that during the past year their distress had progressed to the point where merely seeing the other person made them feel discouraged and irritated. Ken and Sue claimed that they made attempts from time to time to do nice things for the other, but neither was able to recall receiving such favors.

BEHAVIOR, COGNITION, AND AFFECT IN MARITAL DISTRESS

The case of Ken and Sue illustrates how behavioral, cognitive, and affective factors all can contribute to dysfunction in a couple's relationship, and how these factors tend to be intertwined.

Behaviorally, their communication with each other about the sources of their dissatisfaction consists of mutual criticism, interruptions, and yelling. Other problematic behavioral patterns include Ken's tendency to withdraw when Sue yells and the couple's overall low rate of pleasant shared activities.

In terms of cognitions, both spouses tend to see the other as responsible for the marital problems, and they attribute each other's negative behaviors to traits that are unlikely to change (e.g., Sue sees Ken as self-centered and insensitive; Ken sees Sue as having a need to dominate men). Their descriptions of the qualities that initially attracted them to each other suggest that to some extent their partners' actual behaviors might have remained constant over the years, but that their attention is focused on the negative aspects of these behaviors now, whereas initially they focused on the positive aspects. For example, when they met, Ken labeled some of Sue's behavior as indicative that she "knew what she wanted" (which he valued), but now he has come to attribute the same behavior to a negative characteristic of "needing to dominate men."

Both spouses appear to have perceptual biases, whereby they fail to notice each other's positive acts, and this selective attention might be linked to their tendencies to have global negative emotional responses to the other's mere presence, independent of the partner's current behaviors. Thus, their strong and consistent emotional responses to each other not only are the result of their negative behavioral interactions and their negative cognitions about each other, but the emotions in turn influence their perceptions and behaviors toward each other.

Up to this point in the assessment interview, Sue also has provided some clues concerning some of her other cognitions about the marital problems. It appears that she may apply a general standard to their relationship whereby Ken should be able to "mindread" her thoughts and feelings without her having to express these directly, and she also may have developed an expectancy (prediction) that screaming is the only behavior that is effective in drawing Ken's attention. Ken also appears to be pessimistic about the potential for altering the couple's interaction pattern; he has indicated that he has a general expectancy that there is nothing he can do to influence Sue's behavior once she has started to criticize him.

Thus, as this couple was faced with coping with some major developmental life stresses (demands of careers and children), deficits in their behavioral relationship skills such as communication and problem solving seem to have produced a negative interaction pattern. Their exchanges of negative behavior, in conjunction with the decline in pleasant shared activities, produced emotional distress, and the distress seems to have been exacerbated by the spouses' tendencies to attribute each other's unpleasant behaviors to negative traits. In a reciprocal manner, their negative appraisals of each other elicited more emotional distress and more negative behavioral responses toward each other. Rather than expressing their distress to each other in a direct but nonattacking manner, and communicating empathy for each other's frustration and pain, both spouses focused on expressing their own complaints in an aversive manner.

Furthermore, Ken and Sue's global negative emotions regarding their relationship tended to bias their perceptions, such that they selectively noticed each other's negative rather than positive behaviors. In other words, there was an upward spiral of negativity comprised of behaviors, cognitions, and emotions.

This case example is not intended to illustrate a comprehensive model integrating behavioral, cognitive, and affective components of marital dysfunction. Rather, its purpose is to demonstrate that the three aspects of marital interaction are interrelated in a complex manner, and that ignoring any of these components leads to an incomplete conceptualization of a couple's relationship.

The next three chapters review specific behavioral, cognitive, and affective factors derived from theory and empirical research concerning marital dysfunction. The following are brief overviews of each of these three types of factors and the ways in which they can influence one another.

Behavioral Factors in Marital Dysfunction

As described in Chapter 2, theory and research on behavioral aspects of marital interaction have identified several forms of behavior that can facilitate or detract from marital satisfaction. In general, distressed couples tend to (a) exchange higher rates of negative behavior and lower rates of positive behavior, (b) use less effective (i.e., indirect, unclear) and more aversive (i.e., critical) communication to express their thoughts and feelings, (c) attempt to solve relationship problems with less effective problem-solving skills, and (d) use more coercive methods for attempting to change their partners' behavior than do nondistressed couples. Each spouse's behaviors can influence both the partner's and his or her own subsequent behaviors, cognitions, and affective states. The following is a summary of the impacts that one spouse's behaviors can have.

One spouse's behaviors can influence the other's behaviors directly, without cognitive mediation. For example, consistent with reinforcement principles, verbally and nonverbally rewarding some aspects of the partner's behavior but not other aspects can influence the relative frequencies of those acts. Furthermore, research studies reviewed in Chapter 2 have indicated that distressed couples are more likely than nondistressed couples to engage in negative behavioral reciprocity, in which one spouse's negative behavior is followed by a negative response from the partner.

An individual's behaviors can influence his or her own subsequent behavior by creating an environment that limits stimuli and contingencies. For example, an individual who consistently avoids spending time with his or her partner eliminates opportunities for expressing thoughts and feelings to the partner. If the avoidant behavior produces general isolation, the individual's lack of exposure to any reinforcement from the partner or other sources may lead to overall inactivity (and perhaps an affective response of depression).

A significant way in which *one spouse's behavior can alter the partner's cognitions about the relationship* involves very aversive acts that are so potent (emotionally significant) they become the foci of the recipient's future thinking about the marriage. For example, acts that involve physical or psychological abuse and those that involve the violation of a basic tenet of the relationship (e.g., a sexual affair that breaks an explicit or implicit vow of fidelity and trust) can alter the partner's basic assumptions about the nature of the relationship. After the revelation of an affair, it is common for a partner to attend selectively to those of the spouse's behaviors that might be signs of further infidelity.

Because individuals perceive and interpret their own behavior as well as those of their partners, *a spouse's behavior can influence his or her own cognitions about the marriage.* For example, an individual who finds himself or herself engaging in a behavior inconsistent with his or her view of the marriage may alter that view. A spouse who is flirting with an acquaintance might conclude, "I must be losing interest in my spouse, or else I wouldn't be acting this way." Furthermore, poor communication skills (e.g., arguing and interpreting a partner's messages instead of listening carefully) can reduce an individual's awareness of the partner's thoughts and emotions, thereby either producing or maintaining a biased view of the partner. Other behaviors that absorb the spouse and channel his or her attention (e.g., watching television during a discussion with the partner) can have a similar effect.

A spouse's behavior can elicit affective responses in a partner, in the absence of cognitive mediation. As described in Chapter 2, research studies have supported the behavior exchange model of marital interaction (cf., Jacobson & Margolin, 1979), which postulates that an individual's marital distress increases as the ratio of pleasant to unpleasant behaviors received from the partner decreases. Although spouses' appraisals of partner behaviors as positive or negative can be influenced by idiosyncratic cognitive factors (see Chapter 3), many behaviors appear to have direct effects in eliciting pleasant or unpleasant emotions in the recipients.

Also, by means of a process of classical conditioning, the pairing of particular partner behaviors with particular emotional experiences can produce conditioned responses to those partner behaviors. Clinical reports (e.g., Kaplan, 1974) suggest that such a process often occurs in the development of sexual problems that involve anxiety. Once an individual experiences strong anxiety in a sexual interaction with a partner, future benign sexual behavior by the partner may elicit anxiety.

As already noted, *an individual's behavior can influence his or her own emotions* by creating a pleasant or unpleasant environment for the self. Just as a person's avoidance of a partner can produce social isolation and depression, initiation of shared leisure activities with a partner may increase the likelihood of pleasant marital interactions and an associated improvement in marital satisfaction. Furthermore, some behaviors can decrease an individual's *awareness* of his or her own emotions. For example (and in some cases this may be an intentional means of coping with marital distress), some spouses keep themselves so involved in daily activities that they lose awareness of their emotions concerning their marriages.

Cognitive Factors in Marital Interaction

Clinical writers such as Beck (1976) have noted particular themes in the content of cognitions associated with particular emotional states (e.g., themes of loss in depression, danger in anxiety, and violated personal rights in anger). Consequently, cognitive therapy for disorders involving affective states such as depression and anxiety focus on altering specific cognitions that elicit those emotions (Beck & Emery, 1985; Beck et al., 1979). Chapters 3 and 4 describe types of cognitions that can elicit emotions such as anger, depression, anxiety, and jealousy in marital interactions.

As detailed in Chapter 3, five major types of cognitions play roles in marital interaction: *assumptions* about the nature of spouses and marriage, *standards* about how spouses and marriage "should" be, *attributions* about the causes of positive and negative marital events, *expectancies* about the likelihood that particular marital events will occur in the future, and *perceptions* (notably, selective attention) of the information available when observing one's interactions with a partner. These forms of cognition can influence the type and intensity of either the individual's own or the partner's behaviors, cognitions, and emotions. The following are examples of these impacts of marital cognitions.

An individual's cognitions can influence his or her emotions and behavior toward a partner. For example, some individuals mistakenly interpret physiological and behavioral manifestations of their anger toward their partners as signs that they will lose control (e.g., "go crazy"; become physically abusive). Consequently, they experience anxiety due to the perceived danger and may avoid discussions with the partner concerning important issues that anger them.

Similarly, *a spouse's cognitions can influence his or her other cognitions concerning marital interactions.* An individual's standards about individual or marital functioning can bias his or her perceptions of marital events. For example, a husband who believes "To feel anger means that you are a bad person" may selectively ignore cues of his own anger. In contrast, a wife who holds the standard "A good spouse should not anger a mate" may be hypervigilant for cues of anger from her husband.

As described in cognitive consistency theories (e.g., Abelson et al., 1968; Cooper & Fazio, 1984; Zanna & Cooper, 1976), when an individual becomes aware of having inconsistent cognitions, one way of resolving this dilemma is to alter one of the cognitions in order to increase consistency. For example, a woman's life experiences may have led her to develop an assumption that men primarily want to control women in relationships, but she also may have tended to attribute her husband's doing favors for her as a sign that "he is trying to make life easier for me." One possible way in which she may reconcile the apparent inconsistency between her assumption and her attribution would be to alter the attribution to "he is trying to win my confidence and make me vulnerable to his influence."

When an individual expresses his or her cognitions explicitly (i.e., verbally) or even implicitly through behaviors toward the partner, the *cognitions can influence the partner's cognitions, behaviors, and emotions*. A spouse's expressed assumptions and standards concerning marriage (e.g., "Disagreement is destructive to a relationship," "You should always support your partner's views in public") can strengthen a similar belief held by the partner. In terms of effects on a partner's behavior, when a spouse expresses negative trait attributions (e.g., "You forgot to call because you are selfish and self-centered"), the partner may respond defensively or aggressively, perhaps even behaving in ways that seem consistent with the spouse's negative attribution. In such a situation, not only can the expressed cognition elicit particular behaviors from the partner, but it also can provoke particular emotions, such as anger.

Affective Factors in Marital Interaction

Although popular literature emphasizes the strong pleasant and unpleasant emotions that commonly occur in intimate relationships, less systematic attention has been paid by marital researchers and therapists to identifying specific ways in which affect influences marital interaction. Chapter 4 describes four aspects of affect in marital relationships: (a) each spouse's degrees of positive and negative emotions toward the partner and marriage, (b) spouses' awareness of their emotions and the causes of their emotional states, (c) the degrees to which spouses express their emotions and respond to each other's emotional expressions with empathic listening, and (d) forms and intensities of affect that can interfere with good marital functioning. The following are some ways in which affective factors can influence marital interaction.

A spouse's affective states can influence his or her own cognitions and behaviors. For example, Weiss (1980) has described a process of "sentiment override" by which an individual's perception and evaluation of a partner's behaviors are colored by the person's overall affect toward the partner rather than by the partner's current behavior. Thus, a spouse who is generally very angry toward his or her partner may perceive the partner's behavior as negative even when the partner attempts to communicate caring messages. As Beck et al. (1979) note, individuals also tend to use their affective experiences as "data" in making inferences about events. For example, it is common for distressed spouses to conclude, "If I don't have loving feelings toward my partner, the relationship must be dead." Clearly, the degree to which an individual is *aware* of his or her emotions will determine whether affective information can influence his or her judgments about the marriage.

Chapter 4 also describes how particular affective states can influence the manner in which an individual interacts with a partner. For example, depression may decrease a spouse's overall activity in interacting with his or her partner, anxiety may lead to either avoidance or clinging to the partner, and anger may contribute to abusive behavior toward the partner.

Furthermore, the degrees to which spouses possess good expressive and empathic listening skills can determine whether emotions such as anger, depression, and anxiety lead to constructive or destructive marital interaction. When a spouse is able to express anger (and information about its cause) to his or her partner in a clear and nonattacking manner, and the spouse achieves and communicates good empathic understanding of the affective messages, there is potential for subsequent joint problem solving to resolve the anger-eliciting circumstances. In contrast, if the angry person blames and criticizes the partner, and the partner reciprocates criticism rather than responding empathically, problems of negative escalation described in Chapter 2 are more likely than problem solving.

A spouse's expression of affect can influence the partner's cognitions, affect, and behavior. Just as individuals use cues about their own emotions as "data," their cognitions about their partners can be shaped by verbal and nonverbal cues about the partner's emotions. Thus, a wife who observes her husband's frequent mood fluctuations may conclude that he is "an unstable, unreliable person." Research on empathic processes has indicated that an individual may experience a contagious induction of emotions exhibited by another person (such as a marital partner), and that emotional empathy for the other person's distress can produce less aggression and more helping behavior toward that person (Eisenberg & Miller, 1987). In contrast to empathic responses, there is evidence that partners of depressed individuals often exhibit hostile as well as supportive responses toward the depressed spouses.

In terms of the escalation of marital conflict, Schaap (1984) found that among both distressed and nondistressed couples an expression of negative affect (e.g., an angry facial expression) by one spouse was likely to be followed by an expression of negative affect by the partner.

Schaap also found evidence of reciprocity sequences in which an expression of negative affect by one spouse was likely to elicit negative verbal communication by the partner.

Implications for the Assessment and Treatment of Marital Problems

Because behaviors, cognitions, and emotions are so intertwined in marital interaction, it is important that the assessment of a couple's problems include evaluations of all three types of factors, as well as the ways in which the factors influence each other. Furthermore, the complex interplay of behavior, cognition, and affect in influencing spouses' marital satisfaction necessitates that therapeutic interventions address each of the three areas.

In this section of this book, the specific behavioral, cognitive, and affective factors that theory and empirical research have implicated in marital dysfunction are described. The following section provides detailed descriptions of strategies and instruments for assessing behavioral, cognitive and affective components of marital dysfunction. The final section covers specific therapeutic interventions for modifying behavioral, cognitive, and affective aspects of couples' problems, as well as guidelines for integrating the three types of interventions. The book concludes with a survey of research findings concerning the effectiveness of cognitive-behavioral marital therapy.

2

Behavioral Factors in Marital Dysfunction

The behaviors that are the foci of a cognitive-behavioral approach to marital dysfunction are those that have become the standard targets of behavioral marital therapy (BMT): namely, (a) excesses of displeasing acts and deficits in pleasing acts exchanged by members of a couple, (b) general communication skills, (c) problem-solving skills, and (d) behavior change skills. This chapter describes the basic theoretical concepts and empirical findings underlying therapeutic attention to these forms of marital behavior, as well as an overview of the specific types of behaviors that the cognitive-behavioral marital therapist attempts to assess and modify.

SOCIAL LEARNING AND SOCIAL EXCHANGE VIEWS OF MARITAL DISTRESS

Because there are a number of detailed reviews available concerning the theoretical models underlying BMT (e.g., Epstein & Williams, 1981; Jacobson & Margolin, 1979; Stuart, 1980; Weiss, 1978), the present discussion is a brief summary of the major concepts that guide therapists' assessments of potential problems in marital interaction.

The two major theoretical models underlying behavioral marital therapy are social learning theory and social exchange theory. Both models postulate that an individual's behavior both influences and is influenced by his or her environment. As applied to marital relationships, these models suggest that in order to understand an individual spouse's behaviors

17

one must determine how that person's actions are influenced by the partner's responses. A reciprocal process of mutual influence develops between two spouses, and each spouse's behavior in the marital context may differ from the behavior that he or she has learned to exhibit with other people.

SOCIAL LEARNING VIEW OF MARRIAGE

Among the basic tenets of social learning theory (Bandura, 1977; Rotter, 1954) are the concepts that (a) behavior is controlled by its consequences (i.e., operant conditioning) and antecedent discriminative stimuli that signal to the individual that particular reinforcement contingencies are operating, (b) much human behavior (especially complex behavior patterns) is learned through the imitation of observed models, and (c) the learning and performance of behaviors commonly are mediated by cognitive processes.

Operant conditioning shapes marital interaction when spouses provide reinforcement for some of each other's responses and punishment for other responses. This process begins with the earliest interactions that the couple has when they first meet (e.g., he suggests that they see a horror movie, and she expresses her displeasure; in the future he is less likely to make such a suggestion). Each person learns about discriminative stimuli that signal the likelihood that particular responses will elicit reinforcement or punishment from the partner (e.g., she learns that when they reunite at the end of a workday, if he looks preoccupied it is likely that he will rebuff any attempts she might make to talk about problems of any sort). The internalized expectancies that each person has about probabilities of particular outcomes under particular circumstances are important cognitions in the learning process.

A common example of the reciprocal nature of reinforcement processes in couple interaction occurs when one spouse complies with the other in order to terminate the other's aversive behavior. Thus, if a husband nags his wife about not paying attention to him when he finds her working on her personal hobby and she turns her attention to him in order to stop his nagging, she receives negative reinforcement for shifting attention to him. In turn, he receives positive reinforcement for nagging. Her paying attention to him rather than to her individual interests may be more likely to occur in the future because that behavior effectively terminates unpleasant stimulation (nagging), whereas his nagging may be more likely to occur in the future because it apparently elicits desirable consequences (her attention). Such an interactional dynamic is powerful because the spouses' reinforcement contingencies are so interdependent.

Patterson and his colleagues (cf. Patterson, 1982) have demonstrated reciprocal coercion patterns in family interactions, whereby each individual's behaviors serve as antecedents (i.e., elicit) and reinforcers for the other family members' aversive acts. On the one hand, an individual's aversive behavior can be maintained or increased by positive reinforcement (e.g., attention) or negative reinforcement (e.g., termination of another person's nagging). On the other hand, Patterson (1982) notes that many parents attempt to suppress their children's unpleasant behavior with ineffective forms of punishment. The parents offer (a) insults, threats, and scolding that are not backed up by more serious punishment (e.g., consistent deprivation of privileges) or (b) physical assault that suppresses the child's behavior only temporarily. These patterns are similar to the aversive exchanges of distressed couples, which are described later in this chapter.

Observational learning plays a major role in marital interaction because many of an individual's patterns of behavior toward his or her partner are based on imitation of behaviors exhibited by a variety of other people, including the individual's parents, couples portrayed in movies and other mass media, and any other available models of intimate relationships. It is highly unlikely that complex interpersonal skills such as communication and dyadic problem solving can be learned solely through trial-and-error reinforcement processes. Thus, if an individual has observed repeatedly that people seem to gain compliance from their intimate partners by acting aversively (e.g., the models obtain positive reinforcement for using threats and criticism), he or she may imitate such behavior with a partner. Spouses also may imitate their own partners' behaviors that have produced desired outcomes for the partners in the past.

A SOCIAL EXCHANGE VIEW OF MARRIAGE

Social exchange theory (Thibaut & Kelley, 1959) views social relationships such as marriage in economic terms; that is, the involved parties engage in an exchange of "goods," and each person's satisfaction with the relationship is a function of his or her ratio of benefits received to costs incurred. This model meshes well with the social learning model, in which partners provide each other with varying amounts of reinforcement.

Marital Satisfaction and the Exchange of Noncommunication Behaviors

Based on social exchange theory, a number of studies have investigated the degree to which spouses' levels of marital satisfaction are associated with frequencies or ratios of pleasant and unpleasant behaviors received from their partners during their daily interactions. In contrast to the communication behaviors such as expressive and listening skills discussed later in this chapter, these "noncommunication" behaviors include a wide variety of affectional and instrumental behaviors (e.g., companionship, household management), most commonly assessed in marital research by means of the Spouse Observation Checklist (SOC) developed by Weiss and his associates (Weiss, Hops, & Patterson, 1973; Weiss & Perry, 1983). Each spouse is asked to complete the SOC at the end of each day, indicating which of the 408 behaviors he or she received from the partner (although some items describe joint activities; e.g., "We listened to music on the radio or stereo"). The respondent categorizes each behavior as pleasing or displeasing and also provides an overall Daily Satisfaction Rating concerning the relationship, using a nine-point Likert scale (see Chapter 5 for a more detailed description of this instrument).

Studies using the SOC have provided considerable support for the social exchange model of marriage. First, distressed spouses report significantly more displeasing and fewer pleasing partner behaviors than nondistressed spouses (Barnett & Nietzel, 1979; Birchler, Weiss, & Vincent, 1975; Jacobson, Follette, & McDonald, 1982; Margolin, 1981). Second, daily marital satisfaction ratings have been found to be correlated with daily frequencies of pleasing and displeasing behaviors (Christensen & Nies, 1980; Jacobson et al., 1982; Jacobson, Waldron, & Moore, 1980; Margolin, 1981; Wills, Weiss, & Patterson, 1974).

Given the importance that daily exchanges of various affectional and instrumental behaviors have for spouses' levels of marital satisfaction, it is important that treatments for distressed couples include procedures for alleviating deficits in pleasing behaviors and decreasing excesses of displeasing behaviors. Several strategies for helping couples alter their exchanges of noncommunication behavior are described in Chapter 8.

Reciprocity in marital behavioral exchanges.

Social exchange theory also postulates that in ongoing relationships the exchange of goods is characterized by *reciprocity*, such that the reinforcements that one partner provides to the other depend on the level of reinforcement received from the other person. The result of this "you give what you get" process is a fairly equal exchange of rewards and punishments between partners.

As research studies have investigated the degree to which reciprocity operates in marital interactions, it has become clear that reciprocity can be defined in a number of ways. First, although studies have demonstrated that members of distressed couples direct more negative behaviors and fewer positive behaviors toward each other than do nondistressed spouses (e.g., Billings, 1979; Birchler et al., 1975; Gottman, Markman, & Notarius, 1977; Jacobson et al., 1982; Margolin, 1981; Vincent, Weiss, & Birchler, 1975), these differences in base rates do not demonstrate that partners are engaging in reciprocity (i.e., giving positives and negatives because they receive them). Reciprocity is more accurately defined in terms of *contingencies*, whereby one spouse's giving the other a negative or a positive behavior increases the probability that the other partner will subsequently reciprocate with a similar type of behavior.

Some studies (e.g., Vincent, Cook, & Messerly, 1980) have examined groups of couples and found that husbands' reports of frequencies of pleasant and unpleasant behaviors received from their wives are correlated with the wives' reports of pleasant and unpleasant behaviors received from the husbands. However, Vincent et al. note that such correlational results do not indicate whether or not *temporal reciprocity* has occurred; e.g., whether a wife's negative act elicits a negative act from her husband, and vice versa.

A number of studies (e.g., Billings, 1979; Gottman et al., 1977; Margolin & Wampold, 1981; Raush, Barry, Hertel, & Swain, 1974; Revenstorf, Hahlweg, Schindler, & Vogel, 1984; Schaap, 1984) have investigated temporal or contingency-based reciprocity (Gottman, 1979) by coding *sequences* of behaviors exchanged by spouses in a laboratory discussion task. Reciprocity is defined as the conditional probability that one spouse's positive (negative) behavior will be followed immediately by a positive (negative) behavior from the partner, taking into account the overall base rates of these behaviors. Although the results of these studies have varied somewhat, overall they have revealed that reciprocity of negative behavior is more characteristic of distressed than of nondistressed couples, whereas reciprocity of positive behavior is comparable in distressed and nondistressed couples. Revenstorf et al. (1984) have examined longer interactional sequences, up to five alternating husband and wife behaviors. They have identified sequential patterns such as "problem escalation" (more common in distressed than nondistressed couples) in which spouses alternate, with one describing a problem and the other responding negatively.

Based on theory and research concerning reciprocity in marital interactions, behavioral marital therapists focus on couples' tendencies to reciprocate positive and negative behaviors on a moment-to-moment basis. The importance of focusing on immediate temporal reciprocity is underscored by Jacobson et al.'s (1982) finding that distressed spouses are more reactive to the immediate events in their interactions than are nondistressed spouses. Jacobson et al. found significantly higher correlations between spouse reports of both daily positive and negative partner behaviors and the spouses' daily ratings of their marital satisfaction among distressed than among nondistressed couples. Thus, not only do distressed spouses exchange more negative and fewer positive behaviors than nondistressed spouses, but their daily marital satisfaction also is influenced more by the daily quality of their interactions. Gottman, Notarius, Markman, Bank, Yoppi, and Rubin (1976) have suggested that distressed couples react to immediate positive and negative partner behaviors, "keep score," and get even with negative reciprocity. However, nondistressed couples tend to operate according to a "bank account" principle whereby they "deposit" (give) positives based on good faith that at some point their partners will reciprocate. Similarly, the trust that one will receive future positives from one's partner allows the individual to tolerate negatives received from the partner without reciprocating.

Stuart (1980) also has stressed that reciprocity does not imply symmetry or equality in couples' behavior exchanges, but rather it refers to equity. In other words, in a relationship characterized by reciprocity there need not be an immediate and equal exchange of goods, but over time the exchange is balanced enough to be seen as fair by both people. It is not uncommon for a marital therapist to note that a couple has an unequal exchange of reinforcements but that both members of the couple are satisfied overall with their relationship (whereas the therapist might view that relationship as undesirable by his or her own personal standards). Weiss (1978) notes that relationships become dysfunctional when the partners work less toward achieving mutual rewards and more toward minimizing their own costs. A common pattern in distressed relationships is for each partner to attempt to elicit rewards from the other by means of coercion (i.e., providing negatives in order to receive positives).

The social exchange model of relationships has led to behavioral interventions for distressed couples that emphasize increasing exchanges of positive behaviors and decreasing negative exchanges. Beginning with

Stuart's (1969) "operant interpersonal" approach, behavioral marital therapists have included a variety of behavioral contracting procedures that are designed to alter couples' ratios of positive to negative exchanges (Epstein & Williams, 1981; Jacobson & Margolin, 1979; O'Leary & Turkewitz, 1978; Stuart, 1980). Methods for applying such behavior-exchange procedures in clinical practice, including the advantages and disadvantages of alternative approaches, are described in Chapter 8.

Comparison level and marital satisfaction.

Another important concept in the social exchange model is *comparison level*, whereby an individual's satisfaction with a relationship depends on the degree to which the ratio of benefits to costs is better or worse than the ratios that might be received in alternative situations (e.g., another relationship; no relationship). This concept suggests a role for cognitive processes in social exchanges, because the benefit/cost ratios that an individual perceives in alternative situations often involve expectancies that are untested until he or she substitutes the alternative for the present situation. For example, a married individual who predicts that being single would produce a better ratio of benefits to costs may find that in practice this is not so in his or her case.

Cognitions as mediators of couples' social exchanges.

Although there are some behaviors that virtually all spouses would find pleasant or unpleasant, to a significant degree the extent to which an individual experiences pleasure from his or her partner's actions is idiosyncratic. Behaviorists have long recognized that this is so by defining reinforcement in terms of whether or not providing a consequence for an individual's behavior affects the future frequency of the behavior, not in terms of the apparent pleasant quality of the consequence. In other words, one cannot assume that praising a child for cleaning his or her room serves as a positive reinforcement for cleaning behavior merely on the basis that praise seems to be a pleasant consequence. Some children may find praise very pleasurable and thus work hard to obtain more of it, but others may, for a variety of reasons, experience praise as neutral or even unpleasant. Therefore, an observer can determine that praise has served as a positive reinforcer only by noting that it does in fact lead a child to clean his or her room more frequently.

Thus, it is important that behavioral assessment and treatment procedures be guided by such learning principles that take into account the degree to which spouses' experiences of their partners' behaviors are subjective. Weiss and Perry's (1983) modification of the Spouse Observation Checklist is a good example of this point. In the original SOC, the items were categorized a priori as pleasing or displeasing by the scale constructors. In contrast, the revised SOC asks spouses to provide their own categorization of their partners' behaviors as pleasing or displeasing. Similarly, when using standardized observational systems for coding spouses' behaviors (see Chapter 5), caution should be exercised in using codes for verbal and nonverbal behaviors that were defined solely on the basis of the developers' intuitive conceptions of definitions of positive and negative behavior.

Furthermore, when couples are taught to increase particular behaviors that are presumed to be more satisfying, clinicians should be sensitive to the possibility that some spouses might not find the behavior changes pleasing. Even when spouses increase specific behaviors that their partners have *requested*, this does not guarantee that the partners will be pleased by the change, because partners may discount the new behavior (e.g., because they interpret it as insincere). As emphasized in Chapter 1 and detailed in Chapter 3, it was the recognition of the extent to which spouses' idiosyncratic cognitive appraisals influence the impact of each other's behaviors that has led to the integration of cognitive variables into behavioral theoretical models, assessment techniques, and therapeutic interventions for couples.

Thus, when applying a social exchange model of marriage, clinicians must take into account (a) rates of behaviors exchanged by a couple, (b) each spouse's subjective appraisal of how desirable or pleasant each of the partner's behaviors is, (c) the spouses' standards for what constitutes an equitable exchange, (d) their attributions about *why* the partner gives what he or she does give (e.g., "She only gives to me out of a sense of duty, not because she cares"), and (e) their expectancies about future exchanges (e.g., "If I request any further changes, he'll stop giving me anything"). In cognitive-behavioral marital therapy, spouses' subjective cognitions about their behavior exchanges are at least as important as the behaviors themselves. These cognitions are described in detail in Chapter 3.

Limitations of the social exchange model.

Although social exchange theory does seem to capture part of the dynamics of close personal relationships, and research studies have produced evidence of reciprocity between spouses, a pure economic model does not seem to account fully for marital interaction and satisfaction. First, the tendency for distressed spouses to be more reactive to immediate behavior exchanges than nondistressed spouses suggests that members of the two types of couples have developed *qualitatively different views of their relationships.* The implicit view of nondistressed spouses seems to be "I can give freely to my partner, because I know that my partner is committed to my needs as well and will give to me, if not now then soon" (the "bank account" model). Thus, during periods when the individual is receiving a low ratio of benefits to costs in the relationship, he or she does not interpret it as a reflection of an unsatisfactory marriage. In contrast, the distressed spouse seems to view his or her relationship in terms such as "I cannot trust my partner to meet my needs because my partner is unreliable, uncaring, insensitive, etc." Consequently, when this individual receives a low ratio of benefits to costs, he or she interprets it as characteristic of an unsatisfactory relationship. Of course, a benefit-to-cost ratio that becomes chronically inconsistent with a nondistressed or distressed spouse's basic view of the relationship might alter that view and the person's level of marital satisfaction.

Some basic views about one's relationship and partner, such as those described here, reflect ideas about reciprocity. Spouses whose standards concerning a "good" relationship emphasize equitable exchanges are likely to be distressed when they do not receive favorable ratios of benefits to costs. It also seems likely that such spouses would be especially distressed if they attribute the poor benefit-to-cost ratio to negative traits in their partners (e.g., insensitivity, lack of caring). Research findings about trait attributions that spouses make for negative partner behaviors (reviewed in Chapter 3) are consistent with this prediction, although they have not addressed spouses' cognitions about behavior exchanges per se.

Other standards about intimate relationships may make some spouses *more* tolerant of low ratios of benefits to costs. For example, an individual may hold to a standard such as, "If you have committed yourself to a marriage, you live with what it brings." Such a person's marital satisfaction may decrease to some extent due to an unfavorable current exchange ratio, but because of that relationship standard he or she may continue to provide benefits to the partner and accept the circumstances to some extent. Additional standards about relationships such as (a) "No one else really can make you happy in life; your happiness comes from rewarding yourself," (b) "It is selfish to focus on meeting your own needs," and (c) "My pleasure comes from making others in my life happy" (an altruistic model) also differ from the reciprocity concept of the behavior exchange model that has been applied to couples' relationships. Consequently, it is important to consider spouses' basic relationship standards and other cognitions when considering interventions to shift the couple's behavioral exchanges toward a more equitable balance.

Finally, some spouses may not approach their relationships with prosocial values and ethics. For example, they may not establish positive reciprocity in their marriages owing to the fact that fairness and nurturance are not salient dimensions for them in thinking about a relationship with another person. In such cases, their partners' negative attributions about these individuals' characteristics may be accurate. Under such circumstances, appropriate therapeutic interventions might include (a) problem-solving training and negotiation training to help a couple agree on a pattern of exchange acceptable to both spouses, without altering their basic relationship standards, or (b) modifying the spouses' basic standards about intimate relationships (e.g., increasing the value that a nonnurturant spouse places on engaging in pleasant acts for a partner). In some cases, therapy may lead distressed spouses to decide to end their relationship, based on their realization that their partners do not share their prosocial values about being in a relationship with another person.

THE ROLE OF SKILLS IN MARITAL INTERACTION

In a well-functioning relationship, a couple is able to meet a variety of needs of each spouse (e.g., affection, self-esteem, companionship) and also accomplish a number of joint goals (e.g., raising children, running a household, sharing leisure activities). Consequently, many of the existing marital adjustment questionnaires (see Chapter 7) assess the degree to which spouses experience conflict and distress in these areas. At times a couple's failure to achieve individual and dyadic goals is determined to a significant degree by deficits in particular relationship skills. In social exchange terms, it is unlikely that spouses' interactions will provide them with satisfying benefit-to-cost ratios when they lack certain abilities to produce individual and joint rewards for each other. Thus, it is important for therapists to devote considerable effort to identifying and modifying skill deficits that appear to be impeding couples from having satisfying interactions.

In order to maximize positive individual and joint outcomes and minimize negative outcomes, a couple needs to have skills for (a) discriminating specific positive and negative behaviors that affect marital satisfaction,

(b) communicating preferences and emotions, (c) solving problems, and (d) changing chronic behavior patterns (Weiss, 1978). In addition to these general skills that can be used in any area of a couple's relationship, couples need a variety of other specific skills that are involved in particular aspects of daily life such as sexual interaction, time management, and money management. The remainder of this chapter describes the nature of these general and specific relationship skills that are the foci of assessment and modification in behavioral marital therapy.

Behavioral Discrimination Skills

Many couples who enter therapy do not conceptualize their relationship problems in behavioral terms, and they are not accurate observers of their own dyadic interactions. In other words, they do not (a) think about their problems as excesses and deficits in specific observable behaviors, or (b) notice the causal connections whereby each spouse's behaviors influence the other's actions. Weiss (1978) stresses that spouses need to be able to discriminate specific behaviors that occur between them concerning the positive and negative behaviors exchanged, the specific situations that control each spouse's behavior, and the communication options available at any point. Weiss notes that spouses commonly do not "track" (monitor) events between them and identify what behaviors produce which consequences under which conditions. Spouses are more likely to attribute global traits to their partners (e.g., "She's inconsiderate") than to identify specific excesses or deficits in the partners' behaviors (e.g., "She doesn't call me on the phone when she is going to get home late, and she rarely asks my opinion before buying things for our house"). Within a social learning model, it is crucial for therapists and their client couples to identify specific behaviors that occur too seldom or too often, as well as reinforcement contingencies that influence the rates of those behaviors. Therefore, a marital therapist must conduct an assessment of a couple's behavior exchange pattern *and* an assessment of the degree to which the spouses have the skills necessary to evaluate their own behavioral interactions.

As noted by Weiss, it is important that spouses be able to translate their global impressions of their partners into excesses and deficits of objective behaviors. Behavioral discrimination or objectification skills apply to both noncommunication behaviors and communication behaviors (described in detail later in this chapter). Concerning noncommunication behaviors, therapists need to inquire about specific acts that each spouse experiences as pleasing or displeasing, and they need to ask each person to define global complaints in behavioral terms. When an individual does not produce clear operational definitions of complaints and preferences, it is important for the therapist to determine whether this is due to a behavioral discrimination skill deficit or a conscious decision by the individual to focus on global characteristics rather than concrete behaviors. For example, Bornstein and Bornstein (1986) note that some spouses who have romanticized views of intimate relationships may find it distasteful to translate relationship dynamics into specific pleasing and displeasing behaviors, even if they are capable of doing so. Thus, understanding couples' deficits in the use of objectification skills involves assessing both the observational skills and the cognitions of each spouse.

Concerning communication behaviors, it is important for therapists to determine the degree to which spouses are able to identify (a) that their distress and related difficulties at a particular point in their interactions are due to deficits in the communication process and (b) which specific expressive, listening, and problem-solving behaviors should be used at what times. Although many couples complain, "We can't (or don't) communicate," very often they are referring only to global unpleasant interactions rather than deficits in specific expressive and listening skills. Spouses need to be adept at noticing circumstances when particular communication behaviors would be likely to improve the quality of their interactions; for example, "I need something from you right now, and I am not getting it. I think that the problem is that I am not expressing my needs clearly and specifically enough. I'll try to do that now."

Objectification skills concerning behavioral sequences.

Even when spouses are able to define their relationship problems in terms of specific behaviors that occur in their marital interactions, they commonly take a unidirectional causal view of these events. As emphasized by systems-oriented marital and family therapists (e.g., Watzlawick, Beavin, & Jackson, 1967), clients who observe their own family interactions typically "punctuate" them in a manner that portrays their own behaviors as results of other family members' actions. Punctuation refers to the point in an ongoing sequence of interaction where an observer assumes that causation originates. Thus, even though an outside observer may notice a repetitive pattern in which one spouse's nagging alternates with the other spouse's withdrawal, the person who nags may report, "I nag *because* she withdraws," and the person who withdraws may report, "I withdraw *because* he nags." The unidirectional causal explanations offered by both spouses do not capture the circular causality that has developed in their relationship. Because a deficit in a spouse's ability to see mutual causality in marital inter-action sequences can interfere with his or her willingness to collaborate in behavior change efforts, it is important that therapists determine the extent of such deficits and remediate them as quickly as possible. As discussed in Chapter 3, a spouse's tendency to blame the partner for relationship prob-lems may be due to cognitive factors such as biased attributional processes (which may serve the purpose of preserving the individual's own self-esteem), and it may be necessary to alter such cognitions before the individual will be able to exercise good behavioral discrimination skills.

In essence, objectification skills are concerned with behavior but are themselves cognitive (perceptual) processes. Chapter 3 includes a discussion of research studies (e.g., Christensen & Nies, 1980; Jacobson & Moore, 1981) that have indicated low rates of agreement between spouses concerning the occurrence of specific behaviors in their daily interactions. These studies appear to reflect spouses' tendencies to attend selectively to events in their relationship, noticing some and overlooking others. Clearly, it is important to determine the degree to which spouses have difficulty with behavioral discrimination owing to systematic selective attention that may require cognitive as well as behavioral interventions.

Communication Skills

Geiss and O'Leary (1981) found that both couples and marital therapists identify communication problems as the most frequent and destructive problems in distressed marriages. Although it is common for couples to tell marital therapists, "We cannot communicate" or "We do not communicate," these tend to be imprecise descriptions for communication problems, because in fact there are always messages sent between partners, even through silence (Lederer & Jackson, 1968). Consequently, a behavioral approach to couples' communication involves focusing on (a) the amount of information (facts, emotions, thoughts) that is communicated, (b) its specificity and clarity, and (c) its tendency to decrease or escalate marital conflict and distress.

Skill deficits versus performance deficits.

The quantity and quality of messages sent between spouses appear to be influenced by the degree to which spouses have particular communication skills in their behavioral repertoires and by situational variables that determine whether or not spouses employ the skills they possess. Although some spouses show evidence that they lack skill in expressing their thoughts and emotions effectively (e.g., their messages directed to a therapist are as unclear as those to their partners), others exhibit an ability to communicate well with people other than their partners. Studies by Vincent et al. (1975) and Birchler et al. (1975) indicated that distressed spouses did not communicate in negative ways with strangers, as they did with their partners. This contrast may be due to deficits in communication skills that are properties of couples rather than individuals, but it also may be due to *choices* that some spouses make to behave negatively with their partners. Such factors that may lead spouses to fail to use skills that they possess when interacting with their partners are covered more extensively in the discussion of behavioral assessment in Chapter 5. The important issue is that in order to understand problematic communication between spouses, a therapist must consider both actual skill deficits and the possibility that other factors (particularly negative cognitions) may block the use of existing skills. Consequently, the assessment of both behaviors and cognitions is crucial in preparation for therapeutic interventions with couples' communication patterns.

Quantity of communication.

Deficits in the amount of information that spouses disclose to one another (particularly regarding their subjective thoughts and emotions) are among the major targets of communication skill training. Such deficits are considered important because it is widely assumed that spouses who do not exchange much information about their preferences, attitudes, perceptions, and emotions are less likely to feel intimate and to resolve whatever conflicts they may have. This view has been reinforced by research findings indicating significant positive correlations between measures of marital satisfaction and self-report measures of communication that assess the amount of expressiveness between spouses (e.g., Navran, 1967; Snyder, 1981). There also is some evidence from behavioral observations of couples' communication interactions (Hahlweg, Reisner, Kohli, Vollmer, Schindler, & Revenstorf, 1984) that distressed spouses exchange fewer statements disclosing emotions, wishes, and needs than do nondistressed spouses. In addition, Noller (1982) found that distressed wives were more likely than nondistressed wives to want their husbands to increase their initiation of conversations and their expression of emotions.

On the other hand, Guerney (1977) reports that clients' abilities to express their emotions and thoughts subjectively (coded observationally) were not correlated with self-reports of communication quality and relationship satisfaction. Also, Raush et al. (1974) found that couples who actively avoided discussing their conflicts were not necessarily distressed. Furthermore, there is evidence that uncensored communication is more common in distressed than nondistressed relationships (Bornstein & Bornstein, 1986), and Stuart (1980) stresses the need for tact and "measured honesty" when spouses discuss material that may hurt or alienate each other. Thus, although the quality of communication between spouses has been found to differentiate distressed from nondistressed couples, there is less direct evidence that deficits in the *amount* of information exchanged is problematic. However, it is evident that in order for couples to exchange a satisfying level of positives and to engage in constructive problem solving they must express their thoughts and emotions. Consequently, marital therapists need to coach relatively unexpressive spouses to disclose more information to their partners about their thoughts and emotions. Procedures for improving expressiveness skills are described in Chapter 10. Also, because some spouses fail to express themselves owing to inhibiting cognitions (e.g., an anxiety-eliciting expectancy that the partner will react very negatively to such disclosures), it is important for therapists to determine whether a lack of disclosure is due to a skill deficit or conscious choice. Cognitive restructuring procedures (Chapter 9) will be needed to modify any cognitions that interfere with spouses' expressiveness.

Even when spouses do not have deficits in the *amount* of information that they express to one another about their behaviors, cognitions, and affects, the *specificity* and *clarity* of their messages may be problematic. Clinicians consistently have noted that couples and families frequently make vague statements that do not specify particular behaviors and emotions (Falloon, Boyd, & McGill, 1984; Gottman, Notarius, Gonso, & Markman, 1976; Guerney, 1977; Stuart, 1980). A lack of specificity can be especially limiting when a spouse wants to express dissatisfaction with a partner's behaviors, because vague descriptions of problems give the partner little information about behavioral changes that would please the other person. Furthermore, when spouses describe their complaints in global terms (e.g., attributing negative personality traits to their partners rather than specifying particular displeasing behaviors), their partners commonly respond with anger and defensiveness to the pejorative labeling. Consequently, it is important for therapists to determine the degree to which each spouse uses concrete descriptions of behaviors and specific labels for his or her emotions when expressing messages to the partner. Brevity and specificity are emphasized in clinicians' guidelines for clear communication, such as Gottman, Notarius, Gonso, and Markman's (1976) formula, "When you do X in situation Y, I feel Z." The person expressing such a message should describe the "X" in terms of specific observable behaviors, the "Y" in terms of specific circumstances (e.g., time of day, setting, particular people present), and the "Z" in terms of the specific quality of emotion (e.g., angry, depressed, anxious) rather than imprecise global emotional labels such as "I felt bad."

Lack of clarity can also result from a variety of other communication problems, such as poor logic in a spouse's statements, dysfluencies, frequent topic shifts, overgeneralized statements, and inconsistencies between verbal and nonverbal communication channels (Bornstein & Bornstein, 1986; Falloon et al., 1984; Stuart, 1980; Thomas, 1977). Concerning verbal-nonverbal inconsistencies (e.g., a spouse says, "I am not angry!" through clenched teeth), recipients of such mixed messages commonly give greater weight to the nonverbal behavior (Mehrabian, 1972). Nevertheless, it often is difficult for spouses to interpret inconsistent messages clearly. This problem is even more serious when the members of a couple fail to "meta-communicate" about inconsistent messages; that is, they do not tell each other that an inconsistent message has been sent and ask for clarification.

Although misunderstandings between spouses often are due to unclear expression of messages, it also is important to determine whether the confusion may arise at the recipient's end. Noller (1984) notes that inaccuracies in communication can be divided into those involved in *encoding* (the sender does not express his or her intended message clearly) and those involved in *decoding* (the receiver does not recognize the message's cues accurately). In Noller's marital nonverbal communication research, spouses were videotaped while sending each other specific messages. In each case, the sender was given standardized verbal content (e.g., "I'm cold, aren't you?"), plus instructions to convey a positive, neutral, or negative message with those words. Thus, the accurate communication of a message depended on the vocal qualities and nonverbal behaviors (e.g., facial expressions) used by the sender and "read" by the receiver. Each message sent was considered to be "good communication" if at least two-thirds of a group of independent raters correctly identified the message intended by the sender, or "bad communication" if less than two-thirds of the judges identified it correctly. Consequently, an encoding error by a couple was defined as a sender's bad communication that was decoded incorrectly by the partner, and a decoding error was a sender's good communication that was decoded incorrectly by the partner.

Among Noller's (1984) findings with this methodology were that (a) the tendency for more inaccuracies in the communication of messages among distressed than among nondistressed couples was due more to encoding than to decoding errors; (b) wives (distressed as well as nondistressed) tended to be better encoders than husbands, especially when sending positive messages; (c) more decoding errors occurred with neutral than with positive or negative messages; (d) wives' decoding errors tended to involve seeing their husbands' messages as more positive than intended, whereas husbands' decoding errors tended to involve seeing their wives' messages more negatively; and (e) distressed husbands made more encoding and decoding errors than nondistressed husbands, whereas distressed and nondistressed wives' encoding and decoding were comparable. Noller (1984) provides an extensive discussion of this marital communication research, as well as related studies by herself and other investigators. Findings concerning spouses' encoding and decoding errors can be useful in guiding marital therapists' assessments of deficits in couples' exchanges of information about their thoughts and emotions. For example, it is important to determine whether a particular husband tends to decode his wife's communications as more negative than she intends, and if so, to plan interventions that can reduce his perceptual bias.

In regard to factors that might interfere with accurate decoding of messages, Guerney (1977) has emphasized that effective communication requires a receptive and attentive listener as well as an individual who expresses clear, specific messages to the listener. There can be incomplete or distorted communication if a listener is distracted or has a biased "filter" for understanding incoming messages. For example, Guerney stresses that in order to listen well an individual must refrain from expressing opinions, judgments, and advice while attempting to receive messages from another person. Aside from the fact that such responses would disrupt the expresser's train of thought, it is unlikely that the listener would be capable of assimilating information at the same time that he or she was thinking and talking about other matters.

Gottman, Notarius, Markman, Bank, Yoppi, and Rubin (1976) found that whereas distressed and nondistressed couples did not differ in how positive versus negative they intended their messages to be, distressed spouses rated the *impact* of their partners' messages as more negative than did nondistressed spouses. Floyd and Markman (1983) found that distressed wives rated the impact of their husbands' messages more negatively than did independent observers, whereas distressed husbands rated the impact of their wives more positively than did the observers. Separate objective coding of the couples' communication samples indicated that the distressed wives actually exhibited more negative communication behaviors than their husbands. Thus, it appears that the distressed husbands were engaging in selective inattention to their spouses' negative behavior, whereas the distressed wives' negative perceptions of their spouses' behaviors were influenced by their *own* negative feelings about the husbands.

Although there are some discrepancies in the findings about sex differences in decoding biases between the Noller (1984) and Floyd and Markman (1983) studies, taken together they indicate that there may be processes occurring in listeners that color their perceptions of their partners' messages. Weiss (1980) has described a process of "sentiment override" (discussed further in Chapter 3) by which an individual's perception of the positive or negative quality of a partner's messages depends on the recipient's overall positive or negative feelings about the partner and relationship. Consistent with this view, Weiss, Wasserman, Wieder, and Summers (1981) found that even after they controlled statistically for objectively coded positive versus negative couple communication behaviors, 25% to 50% of spouses' positive versus negative ratings of their partners' communication were due to their own satisfaction with their marriages.

Markman (1979, 1981, 1984) conducted a longitudinal study that indicates that communication problems are predictive of future marital distress. He assessed premarital couples' intent and impact ratings of their communication and found that the impact ratings (but not initial intent ratings or relationship satisfaction) significantly predicted marital satisfaction both 2½ and 5½ years later. Unlike the Weiss et al. (1981) study, there was no significant correlation between relationship satisfaction and communication impact ratings at the initial premarital testing session. However, this may have been due to the fact that Markman's initial assessment was conducted at the premarital stage, when the couples may not have developed the type of pervasive "sentiment" about their relationships that Weiss (1980) describes acting as a perceptual filter when spouses view their partners' current communication.

In summary, research findings regarding the encoding and decoding of marital communication indicate that when attempting to understand a couple's misunderstandings, it is important to investigate the degree to which it is a problem of unclear expressiveness by one party or ineffective listening by the other party. Spouses' errors in decoding their partners' messages might be due to their own systematic perceptual biases that may need modification if the couple's communication process is to be improved.

Constructive and destructive forms of communication.

Marital theorists and clinicians have for many years proposed that particular types of communicative behaviors are constructive, whereas others are distressing and exacerbate conflict. Consequently, marital researchers have conducted many studies intended to identify which behaviors truly are associated with marital distress. Two major strategies have been used to identify specific behaviors that may detract from or enhance marital satisfaction: (a) comparison of base rates of particular behaviors in groups of distressed and nondistressed couples, and (b) sequential analyses for identifying any dyadic interaction *patterns* that distinguish distressed from nondistressed couples (Baucom & Adams, 1987). The first strategy involves simple frequency counts of the behaviors of interest, whereas the second involves calculating conditional probabilities that certain behaviors by one spouse will be followed by particular behaviors by the partner. Most commonly, the data used for both types of analyses have been generated by having couples engage in a structured discussion (e.g., with the goal of solving a specific problem in their relationship) and having trained observers code each spouse's responses according to a standard system such as the Marital Interaction Coding System (MICS; Hops, Wills, Patterson, & Weiss, 1972; Weiss & Summers, 1983) and the Couples Interaction Scoring System (CISS; Gottman, 1979; Notarius & Markman, 1981).

Base rate studies generally have indicated that distressed couples exhibit more of the negative communication behaviors and fewer of the positive communication behaviors tapped by the observational coding systems (Birchler et al., 1975; Gottman, 1979; Gottman et al., 1977; Revenstorf et al., 1984; Schaap, 1984; Vincent, Friedman, Nugent, & Messerly, 1979; Vincent et al., 1975). Gottman et al.'s (1977) finding that nonverbal affect codes differentiated distressed from nondistressed couples more strongly than did verbal content codes indicated the importance of including nonverbal behaviors in such studies of marital communication. Margolin and Wampold (1981) found that nondistressed couples exhibited significantly more MICS positive behaviors than distressed couples, but the groups did not differ on negative behaviors. Robinson and Price (1980) examined only positive behaviors and found no difference between distressed and nondistressed couples. Any inconsistencies among studies using the MICS are difficult to interpret, because investigators employed different combinations of individual behavioral codes in their investigations.

Although the studies cited indicate overall differences between distressed and nondistressed couples in positive and negative communication, their use of summary categories for various positive and negative behaviors fails to identify specific constructive and problematic communication behaviors. However, when studies have examined the associations of individual behavioral codes with levels of marital distress (e.g., Haynes, Follingstad, & Sullivan, 1979; Resnick, Welsh, & Zitomer, 1979; Revenstorf et al., 1984; Schaap, 1984), the codes that are found to be related to marital distress (e.g., put downs, criticism, problem descriptions, disagreement) vary from one study to another. This may not be a limitation of coding systems such as the MICS, but rather may indicate that distressed couples may each have a unique pattern of negative communication, which is lost when behaviors of a number of couples are combined for group analyses (Baucom & Adams, 1987). Unfortunately, at this point it is not possible to determine whether or not there are some specific common constructive and destructive forms of communication that should be targets of marital communication training.

A number of studies have involved *sequential analyses* that examined whether certain behaviors by one spouse are likely to be followed by particular behaviors by the partner. As described earlier, one of the major purposes of those studies has been to investigate whether the process of *reciprocity* hypothesized in social exchange theory does indeed characterize marital interactions. Sequential analyses have indicated that there is greater negative reciprocity among distressed than nondistressed couples (Billings, 1979; Gottman, Notarius, Markman, Bank, Yoppi & Rubin, 1976; Margolin & Wampold, 1981; Raush et al., 1974; Revenstorf et al., 1984). Positive reciprocity has been found to be more characteristic of nondistressed than distressed couples (Revenstorf et al., 1984) or comparable in the two groups (Margolin & Wampold, 1981; Gottman, Notarius, Gonso, & Markman, 1976).

Gottman (1979) examined sequences of couples' behaviors coded with the CISS in order to determine whether distressed couples are less egalitarian (i.e., have a dominant partner) than nondistressed couples. A spouse was considered dominant if his or her behaviors predicted the partner's subsequent behaviors, but his or her own behaviors were not predicted by those of the partner. Gottman found egalitarian patterns among nondistressed couples (either the dominance shifted back and forth between the spouses, or neither spouse's behaviors predicted the other's), whereas dominance by the husband was more common among distressed couples. This pattern occurred in high-conflict situations but not in low- or no-conflict situations. Clearly, caution should be exercised in drawing conclusions about couples' dominance patterns from this one study, but Gottman's work demonstrates that sequential analyses can be used to explore a variety of aspects of marital interaction. Alternative approaches to defining power and dominance in marital relationships are reviewed by Gray-Little and Burks (1983).

Analyses of longer sequences have identified a number of interactional patterns that differentiate distressed from nondistressed couples. Revenstorf et al. (1984) examined sequences of spouses' behaviors that had been coded into four MICS summary categories (problem solving, positive, negative, and validation). As described earlier, they investigated sequences of up to five behaviors exchanged between partners (statistically, it is not feasible to study longer behavioral chains, for which the number of possible sequences becomes very high), and they identified some patterns that differentiated distressed from nondistressed couples. For example, a "yes, but" sequence was found to be more common in distressed couples and decreased after marital therapy.

Revenstorf et al. (1984) focused on four major summary categories of couples' behavioral sequences. *Problem escalation* (e.g., problem solving by spouse 1, negative by spouse 2, negative by spouse 1) was found to be more common in distressed couples; however, after therapy treated couples exhibited a level even lower than nondistressed couples. *Distancing* (alternating negatives) was more common in distressed couples and continued for longer sequences than in nondistressed couples. In contrast, *attraction* sequences (alternating positive responses) were shorter among distressed couples, but after therapy these were more common and lasted for longer sequences than among nondistressed couples. Marital therapy also was helpful in increasing the frequency and length of *problem acceptance* sequences among distressed spouses (e.g., problem solving by spouse 1, positive by spouse 2, positive or problem solving by spouse 1), although not to the level found among nondistressed couples. Although Revenstorf et al. found a higher probability that a negative will follow a negative and a lower probability that a positive will follow a positive among distressed than among nondistressed couples, they did not examine longer sequences of negative or positive reciprocity.

Gottman et al. (1977) conducted sequential analyses on couples' communication, as coded with the CISS, during the initial, middle, and final stages of a problem-solving discussion. Nondistressed couples commonly began with problem statements that were followed by agreements, avoided negative escalation during the middle phase, and ended with problem solutions followed by agreement. In contrast, the distressed couples began with "cross-complaining" (a problem statement by one spouse, followed by a problem statement by the other), reciprocated disagreements during the middle phase, and commonly did not reach agreement during the final phase of their discussion.

Clinical implications of research on constructive and destructive communication.

As described in the previous section, the most consistent research findings have been that distressed couples exhibit more negative nonverbal communication, more negative verbal communication such as criticism and put-downs, and fewer forms of positive communication such as acknowledgment than nondistressed couples. Initial studies of communication sequences indicate that distressed couples engage in patterns such as problem escalation and distancing which are likely to impede conflict resolution. However, most studies have used summary categories of positive and negative behaviors rather than individual behavioral codes, and those studies that have compared distressed and nondistressed couples on specific behaviors have produced inconsistent results. Consequently, existing research results can only serve as general guidelines for clinical practice (e.g., reducing negative reciprocity and helping distressed couples "short-circuit" sequences of problem escalation).

Also, cross-sectional studies on communication and marital distress have yielded correlational data that indicate an association between specific behaviors and distress but do not identify the causal relationship between the behaviors and the distress. Such studies do not show whether (a) particular behaviors cause distress, (b) distress leads spouses to exhibit more negative communication behaviors, or (c) some third variable leads to both negative communication and distress. However, Markman's (1979, 1981, 1984) longitudinal study demonstrated that communication problems can precede marital distress, and the studies by Birchler et al. (1975) and Vincent et al. (1975) indicate that marital distress can elicit dysfunctional communication between spouses who are effective communicators with other people. It seems likely that all three of the causal processes noted here exist to some extent and have contributed to the research findings, but the prevalence of each process has yet to be demonstrated.

Problematic and constructive forms of communication identified in clinical practice.

In the absence of clear empirical evidence that specific communication behaviors are constructive or problematic for most couples, it is necessary to base clinical practice on common clinical observations of positive and negative marital interaction. Although there are less consistent research findings regarding the following types of communication, there appears to be a good deal of consensus among clinical writers that they commonly play roles in constructive and dysfunctional marital interaction. These forms of communication are described briefly here and are detailed in the discussion of communication training in Chapter 8.

As noted earlier, negative reciprocity is a common phenomenon in the interactions of distressed couples. One common form of negative reciprocity is *fault finding*, in which each spouse blames the other for problems in the marriage. Rather than observing patterns of mutual causality for problems, each person's perceptual "punctuation" of the dyadic interaction focuses on blaming the partner. Gottman, Notarius, Gonso, and Markman (1976) have described how mutual fault finding leads to a pattern of *cross-complaining*, in which the spouses reciprocate each other's criticisms and do not acknowledge each other's concerns and desires. Cross-complaining is similar to *problem escalation* (Revenstorf et al., 1984) wherein one spouse's statement of a problem is followed by a negative response from the partner. Similarly, *debating the truth* concerning events, opinions, and emotions involves each spouse attempting to establish the validity (and thus the superiority) of his or her views, and neither validating the other's position. Furthermore, as distressed spouses propose solutions to their problems, they have a tendency to counter each other's proposals with a different solution, rather than attempting to compromise and take each other's interests into account. This pattern leads to couples' frequent complaints that as they attempt to resolve problems, they reach *stalemates*, wherein each person takes an unyielding position regarding the solution. Revenstorf et al.'s research indicates that distressed couples have difficulty terminating these escalation patterns.

Interruptions commonly have been described as problematic, because they may reflect that the person who interrupted was focused more on his or her own thoughts than on listening to the speaker, or because they break the flow of communication. However, research has not shown consistently that distressed couples interrupt each other more than nondistressed couples do, and some interruptions can be constructive (e.g., providing the speaker with useful information to clarify his or her own position). Thus, interruptions must be evaluated in terms of their impact on the couple's interactions.

A number of other forms of communication commonly are cited as problematic when an individual is expressing his or her thoughts and feelings to a partner. For example, the use of the terms *always* and *never* tends to make a listener defensive and thus polarize the couple's positions on an issue. *Sidetracking*, whereby the speaker frequently shifts from one topic to another, commonly results in neither the speaker nor the listener paying enough attention to any one topic.

Many aspects of *constructive communication* consist of the converse of the negative patterns described here. For example, rather than engaging in fault finding, cross-complaining, and problem escalation, it is helpful to state problems in terms of positive requests and to communicate empathy for the partner's position. Thus, instead of stating, "You don't pay attention to me or show interest in our relationship," a spouse might say, "I know that you enjoy your personal interests, but I feel lonely and sad when you make plans without me, and I would enjoy it a lot if you would ask me to join you more often."

Rather than debating the truth of memories, opinions, and feelings, it is considered constructive for spouses to attain an *empathic understanding* of their partner's subjective experiences, and to provide *acknowledgment* and *validation* for each other's positions. Gottman, Notarius, Gonso, and Markman (1976) emphasize the importance of validating a partner's messages by communicating that one can see how the partner's views make sense within the partner's frame of reference (e.g., his or her assumptions about the nature of relationships), even if one does not agree with those views. The goal of empathic listening is to place oneself into the partner's frame of reference as much as possible, understanding his or her thoughts and emotions *without evaluating them* (Guerney, 1977; Stuart, 1980). Chapter 4 of this volume describes the nature of empathic listening in detail (including the use of reflections or paraphrasing of the partner's messages), Chapter 7 addresses the assessment of listening skills, and Chapter 10 provides guidelines for teaching couples these skills.

Hahlweg, Reisner, Kohli, Vollmer, Schindler, and Revenstorf's (1984) system for coding couples' communication includes the category Acceptance of the Other, which includes (a) paraphrasing, (b) open question (i.e., asking for more information), and (c) positive feedback (e.g., "It was helpful when you explained your feelings"). They found that nondistressed couples exhibited significantly more acknowledgment than did distressed couples, and that behavioral marital therapy increased distressed spouses' frequencies of these acknowledgments, whereas there was no change for couples in a waiting-list control group.

Although empathic listening by a receptive partner is necessary for accurate communication, it also is important that the spouse who is sending messages structure them in particular ways. A speaker who uses *"I" statements* clearly states what his or her own thoughts and emotions are concerning specific situations. Thus, the individual is taking responsibility for describing his or her subjective experiences. In contrast, statements that begin, "You . . ." tend to accuse the partner and elicit defensiveness rather than empathy. Partners also are more likely to be receptive listeners when the spouses who are expressing thoughts and feelings (a) *note any positives in a situation* as well as describing negatives, (b) *avoid using absolute terms* such as "always" and "never," and (c) *focus on one topic at a time* rather than sidetracking from one topic to another (Guerney, 1977; Hahlweg, Reisner, Kohli, Vollmer, Schindler, & Revenstorf, 1984).

Furthermore, spouses need to negotiate in a manner that minimizes coercive power plays. In this regard, it is helpful to distinguish between *assertion* and *aggression* in marital interactions. An assertive spouse clearly states his or her position but is willing to accept it if the partner does not agree or comply, but an aggressive spouse uses coercion (verbal and nonverbal threats, criticism, and other aversive behaviors) to force compliance (DeGiovanni & Epstein, 1978; Epstein, 1981). Some spouses use more indirect *passive aggressive* means of coercing their partners, such as inducing guilt (e.g., "If you love me, you would . . .") and engaging in obstructionistic behavior (e.g., repeatedly failing to follow through after agreeing to do something requested by the partner). Epstein, DeGiovanni, and Jayne-Lazarus (1978) found that conjoint assertiveness training for couples significantly increased marital satisfaction. Methods for assessing and modifying assertiveness and other aspects of marital communication are described in Chapters 5 and 8.

Spouses who are in the role of listener also can maximize the match between intent and impact of a speaker's messages by *metacommunicating* —in particular, telling the speaker when there are any perceived inconsistencies between verbal and nonverbal messages and asking for clarification of the speaker's intended messages. Metacommunication can be used to clarify the "report" and "command" aspects of messages (Lederer & Jackson, 1968). The term "report" is used to denote the literal content of the words spoken (e.g., "Let's not stay late at the party tonight; you have had us scheduled for social events every week for months. We haven't had much time alone in days"). In contrast, the term "command" concerns the *implied* way in which the speaker is trying to define or influence his or her relationship with the partner (e.g., "I want to share the decision-making power in our relationship"). The command aspect of a message may be signified by nonverbal cues (e.g., a smile, a pat on the arm) or may be a subtle message that the listener receives by "reading between the lines" of the words spoken.

Because the command aspects of messages can be ambiguous, listeners may misinterpret them. Consequently, it is important for spouses to be aware of the multiple levels of communication and to use meta-communication to clarify any ambiguities and inconsistencies that occur.

Notarius, Markman, and Gottman (1983) conclude from their investigations that metacommunication is typical of both distressed and nondistressed couples, but the impact of metacommunication statements appears to be different in the two types of couples. Among nondistressed couples, metacommunication sequences are short and the couple returns to the problem being discussed. However, among distressed couples, metacommunication sequences become extended, for example, including long discussions about whether the wife just interrupted the husband.

Problem-Solving Skills

Because it is virtually impossible for two individuals in an intimate relationship to have compatible desires at all times, any couple will experience some degree of conflict from time to time. Distressed couples who enter therapy usually have some major unresolved conflicts that continue to erode the quality of their relationships. Unfortunately, distressed couples tend to rely heavily on aversive control strategies (e.g., threats, punishment) to attempt to resolve their conflicts by coercing compliance from their partners. In contrast, nondistressed couples exhibit more positive problem-solving behaviors (e.g., proposing a compromise, acknowledging the partner's position, agreeing) than do distressed spouses (Schaap, 1984).

Effective problem solving is a cognitive-behavioral *process* that involves a series of logical steps which can be applied to any problem content (Bornstein & Bornstein, 1986; Jacobson & Margolin, 1979; Stuart, 1980). Good communication skills such as those described previously in this chapter are likely to be prerequisites for using the components of problem solving that are outlined below. For example, Koren, Carlton, and Shaw

(1980) coded the behaviors of couples who were engaged in conflict resolution tasks and found that the behaviors of responsiveness, criticism, and solution proposal were predictive of whether or not the couples successfully resolved their conflicts.

Problem-solving steps.

Although the clinical literature reflects some variations in the problem-solving steps that therapists teach to couples, for the most part there is consensus regarding the major components of the process and the skills that spouses need. The two major phases of problem solving are (a) identifying/defining the problem and (b) solving the problem (Bornstein & Bornstein, 1986). Because the specific behavioral components of problem solving and the procedures for training couples in these skills are detailed in Chapter 8, the present discussion is limited to an overview of the steps in the problem-solving process.

Problem solving begins with a clear *statement of the problem*, in terms of specific behavioral excesses or deficits that are of concern to the couple. Consequently, spouses must be skilled at translating global complaints into "operational definitions," as described earlier in our discussion of behavioral specification and discrimination skills. Stuart (1980) stresses that an incorrect initial definition of a problem will bias all subsequent steps of problem solving.

The first major step in solving a problem is *generating alternative solutions*. Many couples are ineffective problem solvers because they foreclose their options by quickly committing themselves to the first palatable solution that occurs to them. Such a process reduces creativity and the opportunity for the couple to compare relative costs and benefits of alternative solutions.

Creative generation of solutions involves an ability to view a problem from a variety of perspectives and a flexible (i.e., open-minded) attitude toward considering the merits of alternatives to one's preferred solution. Clearly, this involves cognitive factors at least as much as behavioral skills. For example, spouses who are threatened or angered by their partners' proposed solutions to problems are likely to block the process of generating creative alternative solutions. Although spouses may be fortunate enough to identify solutions that are equally attractive to each of them, often there will be a need for the couple to *compromise on a solution*. A compromise can involve a true combination of the two individuals' preferences, or it can be a decision to adopt one person's favorite solution on one occasion and the other person's solution at another time or for another problem. In either case, the couple must be able to exercise *negotiation skills*, taking into account the costs and benefits that each alternative solution poses for each party. Compromises are shaped when couples adopt a "two winners" approach, attempting to maximize the benefits and minimize the costs that a solution will produce for each partner (Bornstein & Bornstein, 1986; Stuart, 1980).

Even the best conceived solutions will be ineffective if couples lack the abilities to (a) implement them in their daily lives and (b) evaluate their impact on the defined problems. On the one hand, as described earlier with respect to the generation of solutions, a failure to *implement* a solution might be due to either deficits in behavioral skills (e.g., time management that permits the scheduling of "trial runs" with the solution; mastery of new behaviors that are needed to carry out a solution) or the interference of cognitive factors (e.g., a fear that a better solution could be found if only the couple would wait and think more). On the other hand, failure to *evaluate* the impact of a solution on an identified problem may occur if spouses lack skills for defining desirable outcomes in terms of specific, observable events, and for observing and recording those events (Bornstein & Bornstein, 1986). It is important that therapists consider potential impediments to both implementing and evaluating solutions.

Behavior Change Skills

As described earlier, when members of a couple are dissatisfied with the balance of positives and negatives exchanged in their relationship or are faced with some other sort of problem for which there is no immediately apparent solution (e.g., how to deal with a child's negative behavior), problem-solving skills can help them generate new options. However, solutions that "look good on paper" may not be implemented if a couple lacks constructive ways of structuring behavior changes. As described previously, many distressed couples attempt to change each other's behavior through the use of aversive control (e.g., threats, punishment). Furthermore, when distressed spouses fail to reinforce each other for positive acts, there is the danger that they will develop learned helplessness and make fewer constructive gestures toward each other over time (Weiss, 1978). Consequently, although many couples do not need additional strategies for implementing behavior changes once they have developed good communication and problem-solving skills (Weiss, 1978), others clearly need the structure of specific *positive behavior change skills* in order to produce real shifts in their interactions.

Beginning with Stuart's (1969) initial work, behavioral marital therapists have taught distressed couples to use behavioral contracting to structure changes in their interaction patterns. A few different forms of contracting have been developed, ranging from the *quid pro quo* contract (Azrin, Naster, & Jones, 1973; Lederer & Jackson, 1968) in which each spouse's behavior change serves as the reinforcement for the other's change, to the *holistic contract* (Stuart, 1980) in which each spouse agrees to enact some of the list of changes requested by the partner, with no specific contingencies attached to keeping or not adhering to the agreement. Chapter 8 provides a detailed description of the procedures, appropriate application, and limitations of teaching couples contracting skills as a behavior change strategy.

Although there are some specific behavioral skills associated with contracting, the process also calls for many of the other skills already discussed in this chapter. For example, in order for spouses to devise lists of behavioral changes that they would like their partners to enact, they must have good behavioral discrimination and communication skills. When contingencies are used in contracts, the couple must be able to generate attractive and feasible reinforcers to exchange. Furthermore, there are cognitive factors that can influence whether a couple will carry out contracts. For example, spouses who see their relationship as adversarial and adopt a "win-lose" orientation to behavior exchanges (Stuart, 1980) are unlikely to participate in such agreements unless their views of their relationship and the potential benefits of behavior change can be shifted somewhat. Also, as discussed in Chapter 3, when spouses make negative attributions about their partners' positive behavior changes (e.g., "She just did it because we had this written contract, not because she cares about me"), therapists need to structure the contracts to minimize such interpretations.

CONCLUSION

Social learning and social exchange models of close relationships provide important concepts for understanding how the behaviors of two spouses are intertwined. Their emphasis on the empirical study of human behavior has led to the systematic investigation of marital behavior patterns that enhance or detract from a relationship's ability to meet the needs of the two partners. As methods for studying marital behavior have advanced (e.g., the shift to analyzing interaction sequences), research results have demonstrated that processes such as negative reciprocity and conflict escalation differentiate distressed from nondistressed couples. These findings can serve as guidelines for the clinical assessment and treatment of dysfunctional marriages. It is clear from the research to date that spouses' overt behavioral exchanges and skills have significant impacts on their daily satisfaction with their relationships; furthermore, outcome research on behavioral marital therapy (reviewed in Chapter 12) has demonstrated that altering negative behavioral patterns can increase relationship satisfaction significantly. As methods for studying couples' behavioral interactions develop further, it is likely that even more refined assessment and treatment approaches will evolve.

Early marital assessment and treatment methods which were derived from social learning and social exchange models tended to focus on concepts and interventions regarding spouses' overt behavioral interactions, such as cost-benefit ratios and behavioral contracting (e.g., Stuart, 1969). More recently, there has been increased attention to internal cognitive factors in social learning theory such as perceptions, expectancies, and performance standards (Bandura, 1977). In the areas of marital research and therapy, this trend is reflected in a view of marital distress as a product of both destructive behavioral patterns and distorted or inappropriate cognitions. The next chapter describes several types of cognitive factors involved in marital dysfunction which have been identified in theory and research.

3

Cognitive Factors in Marital Dysfunction

A COGNITIVE VIEW OF MARITAL DISTRESS

This chapter describes theory, research, and clinical evidence concerning the major cognitive phenomena that play roles in marital conflict and distress. The cognitive variables that have become the foci of cognitive-behavioral marital therapy have their roots in cognitive models of individual psychopathology (e.g., Beck 1976; Beck et al., 1979; Ellis, 1962; Meichenbaum, 1977) and in social psychological models of social cognition. The existing empirical evidence implicating these variables in marital dysfunction will be reviewed, and the conceptualization of particular marital problems in terms of such cognitive phenomena will be illustrated.

In this chapter, five types of interrelated cognitive phenomena that appear to play important roles in the development and maintenance of marital dysfunction will be described: *perceptions* (about *what* events occur), *attributions* (about *why* events occur), *expectancies* (predictions of what *will* occur), *assumptions* (about the nature of the world and correlations among events), and *beliefs or standards* (about what "should" be). All of these cognitive phenomena are natural aspects of the information processing that is necessary in order for individuals to understand their environments and make decisions about how they will interact with other people. However, perceptions, attributions, expectancies, assumptions, and standards also are susceptible to distortion, such that they may be inaccurate or extreme.

We have found it most useful to evaluate these forms of cognition in terms of how *appropriate* they are in contributing to a satisfying marital relationship. Appropriateness of a cognition can refer to (a) how *valid* it is as a representation of objective reality or (b) how *reasonable* it is as a standard or as an explanation for relationship events when there are no clear objective criteria available for determining "reality." For example, the validity of a man's expectancy "My wife will refuse to attend a business party with me" can be tested by observing her actual behavior when he asks her to accompany him, whereas one must judge how *reasonable* it is for the man to live by a standard such as "A good wife always cooperates with requests that her husband considers important."

A major premise of cognitive-behavioral approaches to both intrapersonal and interpersonal problems is that people's dysfunctional emotional and behavioral responses to life events often are influenced by inappropriate information processing, whereby cognitive appraisals of the life events are either invalid or are evaluated according to unreasonable standards. Research on social cognition, on cognitive factors in individual psychopathology, and on the role of cognition in marital distress, which is cited in this chapter, has provided support for this model. A second premise of cognitive-behavioral therapies is that individuals commonly fail to evaluate the appropriateness of their cognitions. Beck and his associates (Beck, 1976; Beck et al., 1979; Beck & Emery, 1985) use the term "automatic thoughts" to describe an individual's stream-of-consciousness thoughts and visual images that are elicited by any internal event (e.g., a pain in one's chest) or external event (e.g., a scowl on a spouse's face). These cognitions have been labeled "automatic" because they tend to occur instantaneously, with no forethought, and seem highly plausible to the individual at the time. The individual's emotional and behavioral responses to an event tend to be logical responses to reality *as the person's automatic thoughts portray it,* but that view of reality may be distorted or inappropriate.

Just as individuals usually do not question their moment-to-moment thoughts about events in their lives, they generally do not question their longstanding assumptions and standards about the nature of the world. There is considerable evidence from social psychology research that people cling to basic attitudes and beliefs quite strongly, even in the face of contradictory evidence (Nisbett & Ross, 1980; Slusher & Anderson, in press). Consequently, a major task of the cognitive-behavioral therapist is to help clients become more active observers and evaluators of their own stream-of-consciousness cognitions as well as their longstanding assumptions and standards.

The following are descriptions of the nature of the perceptions, attributions, expectancies, assumptions, and standards that can play roles in the development and maintenance of marital conflict and distress. Ways in which these types of cognitive phenomena appear to be interrelated also are discussed.

ASSUMPTIONS AND STANDARDS

This survey of marital cognitions begins with a discussion of assumptions and standards that an individual holds about the nature of close relationships, because these tend to serve as "templates" by which a person processes the ongoing events in his or her marriage. Both assumptions and standards are within the realm of what cognitive theorists have labeled "cognitive structures," "knowledge structures," or "schemata" (Nisbett & Ross, 1980; Seiler, 1984; Turk & Speers, 1983). Seiler (1984) notes that at a general level, cognitive structures are the internalized representations that a person has regarding rules for categorizing things and events, for solving problems, and for taking action toward particular goals. The infant is born with some complex sensorimotor reflexes (e.g., the sucking reflex), but then through repeated experiences with events in the world he or she develops more extensive concepts about the characteristics of objects and how one relates to them. A cognitive structure is the representation of the sum of one's experiences with a particular class of objects or events.

Once established, a cognitive structure serves as a reference point for understanding objects and situations. Cognitive structures have important survival value, in that they allow people to learn to understand and interact with the complexities of events in their lives. For example, Schank and Abelson (1977) describe how children gradually learn the complex "scripts" involved in routine behaviors such as eating in a restaurant, including sequences of appropriate behaviors of the diners and restaurant personnel. Once established, this cognitive structure guides the perceptions and behaviors of the individual each time he or she enters that particular type of situation. Thus, on the one hand a person's cognitive structures are shaped by past experiences, and on the other hand they influence future experiences by controlling the processing of new information.

Turk and Speers (1983) and Seiler (1984) also note that cognitive structures are not emotion-free; rather, based on the circumstances that existed when a structure was developed, it is likely to be associated with a pleasant or unpleasant emotional state. For example, the child's cognitive structures regarding eating in restaurants may now elicit unpleasant emotions if the child's earlier experiences in such settings were aversive. This link between cognitive structures and emotions is quite relevant for our understanding of the role that cognition plays in marital distress. As we discuss in this and later chapters, longstanding assumptions and standards that individuals hold about the nature of marital relationships can elicit powerful emotional reactions, both pleasant and unpleasant, to events in their relationships.

Because cognitive theorists have used a variety of terms to describe types of cognitive structures (and two theorists' terms for similar concepts may be quite different), we will strive for consistency in our own usage and will note when our usage departs from any widely used terms. For example, Nisbett and Ross (1980) have distinguished between "beliefs" as cognitive structures that involve simple propositional statements (e.g., an individual's belief that "if a person had particular experiences in his or her childhood, then those experiences have a permanent imprint on the person's personality") and "schemata" that refer to more complex conceptions of the dynamic interrelationships among a number of characteristics or objects (e.g., a person's schema about the complex decision-making process that family members go through when they make a group decision about vacation plans). Although we believe that the distinction between these two forms of cognitive structures is useful when one attempts to map the cognitive "filters" through which people interpret their experiences, we tend to include both simple propositional statements and more complex dynamic concepts under the term "schemata." What they have in common is that they are relatively stable cognitive structures that people have developed over time and which provide frameworks by which an individual makes sets of assumptions that go considerably beyond the data that he or she perceives in a situation (Nisbett & Ross, 1980; Turk & Speers, 1983).

We consider assumptions and standards to be two related forms of schemata. *Assumptions* concern a person's conception of the characteristics of objects and events that *do* exist, whereas *standards* concern the person's conception of those characteristics that *should* exist. Our definitions of these terms may differ from others found in the social psychology and cognitive therapy literatures, but we find them to be useful labels for the two types of schemata.

Assumptions

Based on past experiences, which themselves may have been colored by distortions in information processing (which will be described in later discussions of perceptions, attributions, and expectancies), an individual comes to believe that particular objects and events in the world have certain qualities and are related to one another in certain ways. For example, in the realm of marital interaction, an individual develops basic assumptions about the characteristics of a person who fills the role of "husband," as well as assumptions about how such a person relates to a person who is in the role of "wife." The assumptions about a husband's characteristics involve not only a set of traits, but also a set of correlations among those traits. In other words, first an individual may assume that husbands tend to be at least moderately loving, emotionally strong, cooperative, and responsible. In addition, whereas the individual may assume that the degree to which a husband is cooperative is highly correlated with the degree to which he is responsible, the person may assume that the degrees to which a husband is loving and responsible are only slightly related.

A common consequence of such assumptions is that when an individual assigns a person or object to a particular category based on an observed characteristic, he or she then makes many inferences about unseen characteristics of the person or object (Nisbett & Ross, 1980; Turk & Speers, 1983). For example, once one assigns an individual to the category "member of a dual-career couple," one may make assumptions about that person's personality traits, daily behaviors, and attitudes about sex roles. As Nisbett and Ross also note, although such inferences may be fairly safe with concrete objects (e.g., characteristics of oak trees), they are susceptible to considerable error with characteristics and events concerning people. Stereotyped preconceptions about the degrees of association among characteristics of people can produce biased estimates of such associations in a particular person, as well as biased attributions about the causes of a certain characteristic and biased expectancies about an unobserved characteristic based on an observed characteristic or behavior. For example, if one mistakenly assumes a high correlation between wives' degrees of love for their spouses and their degrees of cooperation with their husbands' wishes, one might attribute a particular wife's lack of cooperation to a lack of love (whereas it actually may be due to her ethical opposition to the course of action that her husband wants to pursue). Similarly, based on the same biased assumption, one might hear a wife voice a lack of loving feelings for her spouse and mistakenly have an expectancy that she will not cooperate with him (whereas she in fact does cooperate, in capitulation to pressure from in-laws). Thus, as will be described in greater detail later, assumptions are fairly stable cognitive structures that form the bases of the moment-to-moment inferences that comprise the attributions and expectancies that spouses make about each other's behavior.

Functions of assumptions.

Assumptions serve a major function of allowing an individual to extract meaningful information from the vast array of stimuli confronting him or her in any situation (Beck et al., 1979; Nisbett & Ross, 1980). For example, when a person's spouse arrives home upset about a problem that occurred at work, his or her perception of what might be helpful to do for the spouse at that moment (e.g., offer advice, be affectionate, leave the spouse alone) may be shaped by a number of his or her assumptions relevant to such a situation. These may include assumptions about the roles that marital partners play as helpers of each other, as well as assumptions about what people who are having work problems of this sort find helpful. Because the person makes assumptions about the correlations among various aspects of the situation, when he or she notices a particular aspect of the spouse's behavior, this will lead to specific expectancies about other characteristics. For example, if a spouse assumes that the more a person is upset about a problem, the more the person will benefit from talking about it, when he or she notices signs of agitation in the partner, this leads to an expectancy that the partner will appreciate a series of questions about the problem.

In general, the function that assumptions serve in screening out irrelevant stimuli in a situation and focusing a person's attention on a range of stimuli relevant to a particular need or task is quite valuable. It allows people to benefit from knowledge gained from prior experiences and to adapt quickly to new situations. As will be described in Chapters 6 and 9 concerning cognitive assessment and restructuring, most often even the assumptions that elicit significant dysfunction in clients' marital interactions have advantages as well as disadvantages. Commonly they provide the individual with a sense of order and predictability in his or her life, and even when they are distorted, assumptions usually contain at least some valid information about the nature of people and their interpersonal relationships. In spite of the fact that particular assumptions are distorted and have clear disadvantages for an individual's marital relationship, they tend to be parts of the person's basic world view and therefore can be quite resistant to change. Strategies for modifying such entrenched assumptions are described in Chapter 9.

Types of assumptions.

One useful way of categorizing assumptions, which has been described by Nisbett & Ross (1980), involves event schemata or "scripts" and person schemata or "personae." *Scripts* involve sequences of events among social objects (with the individual as an actor or observer). For example, an individual's script for "a sexual encounter with my spouse" is likely to include a sequence of events (e.g., who begins flirting, and under what circumstances of time and place; who eventually overtly initiates sexual interaction, through words or actions). Scripts can vary along a number of dimensions, such as the following. First, they can vary from abstract to highly concrete (e.g., a person's undefined sense of seeking a spiritual unity with a spouse, versus concrete assumptions about how a couple shares specific kinds of leisure activities in order to promote intimacy). Second, they may vary from being widely shared in one's culture to being quite idiosyncratic (e.g., commonly held scripts about how a couple spends a major religious holiday with their family, versus an individual's fairly unique script about how two partners balance shared activities with independent "private time" so that each person will feel comfortable in the relationship). Finally, scripts may vary from (a) those directly tied to one's prior experiences to (b) those that developed without direct personal experience (e.g., a person's script in which open disagreement between two spouses leads to the dissolution of their relationship may be based on painful prior conflicts in a present or former relationship, or it may be based only on the person's assumption that love must be a fragile state that would not be able to withstand conflict). Scripts also include estimates about the probabilities that certain events in the sequence will occur (Turk & Speers, 1983).

Personae are schemata or cognitive structures that include the characteristics and typical behaviors of certain types of people (Nisbett & Ross, 1980; Turk & Speers, 1983). Like scripts, personae can be widely shared in a culture (e.g., the "henpecked husband") or idiosyncratic to a particular individual (e.g., John's own conception of the typical wife as domineering, monopolizing the children, dedicated to the family, and not very interested in romantic "escapes" with her husband). Personae also can be based on one's own experiences with people, or they can have other sources such as one's own imagination, popular fiction (e.g., TV's bigoted Archie Bunker), metaphors drawn from the animal kingdom and occupational roles (e.g., "He's a real mule!"; "She's your typical unfeeling engineer!"), and even popularized psychology (e.g., "He's a Type A personality").

Once a characteristic or behavior of an observed individual has elicited a particular persona, the observer then makes a variety of assumptions about other characteristics and behaviors of that person. On the one hand, inferences (attributions) are made about the causes of the person's behavior, in terms of unseen characteristics and motives, and on the other hand, inferences (expectancies) are made about the person's future behavior. Thus there are links between the personae (or stereotypes) that an individual holds and that person's attributions and expectancies regarding his or her spouse and other people to whom the personae are applied. We will elaborate on the links among these types of cognitions later in this chapter.

A particular type of persona that includes the characteristics that a person has come to attribute to himself or herself based on past experience is the *self-schema* (Markus, 1977; Turk & Speers, 1983). Research findings have indicated that people tend to ignore and have less recall of information inconsistent with their self-schemata (Goldfried & Robins, 1983). Cognitive biases due to self-schemata can take the form of "self-serving bias" (seeing oneself as responsible for successes but not failures) (Greenwald, 1980) or a "self-disparaging bias" in which the individual discounts successes and takes personal responsibility for negative outcomes (Goldfried & Robins, 1983). Turk and Speers (1983) note that an individual also may use a self-schema to evaluate other people, making inappropriate inferences that people who are similar to the self on a particular characteristic will share others of one's characteristics. Thus, the persona that an individual develops about the self can shape the personae that he or she applies to others (including a marital partner).

Among the most common assumptions that people hold which influence how they interpret each other's behaviors are those regarding *causes of human behavior.* Nisbett and Ross (1980) review a number of culturally shared assumptions, including the ideas that rewards and punishment for behaviors influence the future frequencies of the behaviors, that people's actions are guided by plans and goals (particularly the goals of maximizing pleasure and minimizing pain), and that people's actions across a variety of situations are determined by stable traits. They note that in spite of considerable empirical evidence regarding the situation specificity of behavior, people in our culture are taught a highly dispositional view of the causes of human behavior. Therefore, when an individual observes his or her spouse's behavior and assumes that it is correlated with an unseen characteristic, the observer also is likely to assume that the associated characteristic is a stable trait that cannot be changed. Clearly, such underlying assumptions can have a major effect on the moment-to-moment attributions that spouses make about causes of each other's behavior during their ongoing marital interactions. In addition, assumed stability of personal characteristics is likely to influence people's expectancies and perceptions regarding their spouses' future behaviors. For example, an individual who expects "the same old thing" from his or her partner across a variety of situations may fail to notice variations in the partner's behavior, as well as the circumstances associated with those variations.

Beck and his associates (Beck, 1976; Beck et al., 1979) have described assumptions commonly associated with individual psychopathology such as depression. In particular, they argue that depressed individuals are likely to have fairly stable negative schemata about themselves, the world, and the future. Beck et al. (1979) suggest that in severe depression the individual's thinking is dominated by such negative schemata rather than by objective perceptions and interpretations of changes in his or her environment. A number of studies (e.g., Eaves & Rush, 1984; Rholes, Riskind, & Neville, 1985) have provided evidence of relatively stable schemata that persist even when individuals' depressive symptoms abate and that predict future depression. However, another set of studies have demonstrated reductions in negative attitudes when patients' levels of depression were reduced with interventions that were not focused on cognitive restructuring (Coyne & Gotlib, 1983, 1986); consequently, the empirical status of the causal role of schemata in depression remains somewhat unclear. Although the debate among depression researchers tends to become polarized in terms of whether cognitive schemata cause depression or whether depression includes negative cognitions as symptoms, it seems plausible that both processes occur. Clearly, more research is needed to refine knowledge about the role of relatively stable schemata in depression.

The concept of negative assumptions is quite relevant to marital distress when the individual includes aspects of his or her marriage in the negative views of the self, world, and future. For example, the degree to which individuals assume that spouses cannot change a relationship (i.e., hopelessness about relationships) has been found to be significantly correlated with marital distress (Eidelson & Epstein, 1982; Epstein & Eidelson, 1981). Epstein (1985b) has suggested that part of the documented link between depression and marital distress may be due to cognitive factors such as hopelessness that are components of both problems.

Assumptions that spouses hold about the nature of intimate relationships can detract from the quality of their marriages by contributing to a negative cognitive set about coping with relationship problems. For example, Epstein and Eidelson (1981) found that the more that strongly distressed spouses assumed that partners cannot change a relationship and that overt disagreement is destructive to a relationship, the more likely they were to prefer individual to marital therapy, and the lower were their estimates that their own marital problems would improve with treatment. It also seems reasonable to hypothesize that spouses who make such assumptions would engage in less problem-solving communication with each other, but as yet no studies have investigated such links between assumptions and actual behavioral interactions in couples.

The development of inappropriate assumptions.

There seem to be a few ways in which faulty assumptions about people and intimate relationships can be learned. First, one may be exposed to models who are not representative of larger populations of people and couples. For example, if one grows up in a family where every time that the parents have an overt disagreement the father leaves the house for days, one might develop an assumption that disagreement is destructive to a relationship. This assumption is inappropriate to the extent that it does not apply to other marriages that one did not have an opportunity to observe, and to the extent that it would not apply in practice with one's own marital relationship as an adult. Other potential sources of unrepresentative role models are the mass media (e.g., movies, books, news reports) that often portray colorful characters and relationships which may be quite unlike the average person or marriage. Similarly, one's assumptions about the characteristics of people and relationships may have been developed from information provided by significant others, such as parents and friends, who themselves have biased concepts.

Second, an individual's assumptions may be based on inaccurate perceptions of events that have occurred in his or her life. For example, if a man has observed a number of people in their "husband" roles but has only noticed some of their characteristics and not others, he may develop a persona about the role "husband" that has an incomplete set of characteristics and an incomplete set of correlations among the characteristics. He may not have noticed that many husbands who are high on the characteristic "committed to the marriage" also are high on the characteristic "compromises with his spouse when there is conflict." On the other hand, he may have noticed that many husbands who are high on commitment are high on the characteristic "takes an active part in disciplining the children." The result may be that as he views himself as a committed husband he is quite invested in raising the children, but becomes defensive when his wife disagrees with him about certain discipline techniques. In other words, his own selective perceptions of other people have produced assumptions that do not fit his current relationship in some important ways.

Third, both lay observers and professionals are susceptible to the operation of "illusory correlation" (Chapman & Chapman, 1969), whereby the correlation that one assumes between two characteristics or events is based on the semantic association those characteristics have for the observer, rather than their actual correlation in the world. For example, Mr. Jones has noticed changes in two of his wife's characteristics: Increasingly she has disagreed with him regarding decisions involving their family, and two months ago she was promoted to a position of greater authority at work. He sees a link between her being "in a position where she calls the shots at work" and her "trying to take over the family." He has linked her behavior change with her job promotion because he holds an assumption that people are motivated by traits which permeate many aspects of their lives. In this case, he sees a semantic similarity in the two events, viewing both as involving the exercise of power, so he assumes that one has caused the other. An interview with Mr. Jones reveals his thought that his wife "likes power, and now that she's gotten a taste of it at work, she wants to push me around at home too." However, further inquiry with the couple indicates that Mr. Jones's resulting attribution that his wife's assertive behavior represents her attempt to take over the family (which followed from the illusory correlation he assumed concerning "power") is inaccurate. In fact, interviews with the two spouses reveal that Mrs. Jones's behavior changes at home preceded her promotion by several months, and that she had decided to voice her opinions about family issues after she and her husband received a negative report about their daughter's behavior at school. Mr. Jones had not noticed the real correlations among events because he assumed the existence of a correlation based on the theme of power.

Standards

In contrast to the assumptions that a person makes about the way people and relationships *are*, standards constitute the person's views about the way people and relationships *should be*. For example, whereas an individual may have an assumption that the more time a couple spends together the more happy they will be, he or she also may have a standard that spouses *should* spend as much time together as possible in order to have a good marriage.

A person's standard about an aspect of marriage may be similar to his or her assumption about that aspect (as in the preceding example), or it may be in contrast to the assumption. For example, a person may assume that for many couples a major contributor to their feeling of intimacy with each other is the substantial amount of time they spend together. However, this person may hold a standard that such involvement stifles individual growth and that spouses *should not* spend large amounts of time together.

In the conceptual models underlying Beck's cognitive therapy (Beck et al., 1979) and Ellis's rational-emotive therapy (RET; Ellis, 1962; Wessler & Wessler, 1980), a distinction is made between perceptions and interpretations of events, on the one hand, and evaluation of such cognitions according to basic beliefs or standards, on the other hand. The RET model acknowledges that an individual's perceptions and interpretations may be distorted, but the emphasis is on the distress that results when the person compares the perceived events to internalized standards, judges the events as failing to meet the standards, and evaluates this failure in a negative manner. Consequently, when the RET model is applied to marital problems, a distinction is made between marital *dissatisfaction*, which occurs when a person's desires are not fully met by the relationship, and marital *disturbance* (dysfunctional emotions such as hostile anger and dysfunctional behaviors such as verbal abuse), which occurs when the individual refuses to accept or tolerate any dissatisfaction with his or her marriage (Dryden, 1985; Ellis, 1986). The disturbance results from the application of extreme, unrealistic standards for judging one's marriage *and* extreme evaluations (e.g., it is *awful*) when the marriage does not meet the standards.

For example, a man might perceive that his wife spends a considerable amount of time involved in independent activities, and he may feel some dissatisfaction because he prefers more shared activity. If he evaluates this situation as unfortunate but one that may be tolerated or improved with effort, his emotions are unlikely to be more than mildly negative. In addition, his behavior is likely to include some constructive efforts toward building a more satisfying marriage (e.g., talking with his wife about ways to schedule more time doing mutually enjoyable things together). However, if he instead evaluates the situation as "awful" or intolerable, he is likely to experience strong negative emotions and to behave in destructive ways (e.g., verbally attacking his wife about her behavior). From the RET viewpoint, it is underlying extreme evaluations attached to rigid standards, such as "It is *terrible* for a person to do things that result in any neglect of a spouse's needs" and "I *cannot tolerate it* if *any* of my needs go unmet" that produce marital disturbance. These basic beliefs or standards about what the nature of the world and one's place in it "should" be are seen as the primary cause of marital problems, as well as other kinds of intrapersonal and interpersonal problems (Ellis, 1986). In the RET model, perceptions and interpretations of stimuli are cognitive components of the "A" or activating event, which is subjected to evaluation according to the "B" or belief system, leading to the "C" or emotional and behavioral consequences (Wessler & Wessler, 1980). As part of the activating event, the perceptions and interpretations (e.g., causal attributions) do not play a direct role in dysfunctional responses to life situations. Rather, they merely stimulate the evaluative process involving realistic or unrealistic standards, and it is the evaluations that determine the degree of dysfunction.

Although Beck's cognitive model (cf., Beck, 1976; Beck et al., 1979) also stresses the importance of extreme standards in generating distress and inappropriate behavior, it also includes misperceptions and misinterpretations themselves as significant sources of dysfunctional emotional and behavioral responses to life events. For example, an event that would be judged by most people as positive, neutral, or perhaps slightly negative may be perceived as highly negative by a particular individual, and the perceiver may then become as upset as if a truly aversive event had occurred. Similarly, an individual who has an expectancy that losing his job will lead to his wife losing all respect for him may experience severe anxiety even when the wife actually is extremely unlikely to respond in that manner. Thus, in this model a person's dysfunctional negative emotional and behavioral responses can result directly from an inappropriate perception, attribution, or expectancy, as well as from evaluations based on extreme standards. We will discuss the nature of such problematic perceptions, attributions, and expectancies later in this chapter.

It is important to note that standards per se need not be problematic. In fact, widely shared moral and ethical principles (e.g., people "should not" abuse their spouses physically or psychologically; you "should" take other people's needs into account as well as your own) involve standards that tend to be quite functional. Standards tend to be dysfunctional when they are inflexible, unattainable, or so extreme that meeting them takes a significant toll on a person. As an example of the last circumstance, an individual may hold the standard "You should do your best at everything you do." Although a person might meet this standard in all of the roles he or she plays in life, attempting to do so might produce exhaustion, lack of pleasure in any activities, and alienation from other people in the individual's life. Thus, marital therapy need not be designed to eliminate all of a person's standards related to marriage, but rather to identify and modify those standards and extreme evaluations that contribute to marital distress.

The term "irrational belief" is used extensively in the RET literature to denote extreme standards and evaluations about the way things *should be.* However, because the term "belief" can be confused easily with the term "assumption" (used to denote cognitive structures about the way things *are*), we will use the term "standard" rather than "belief" to refer to the "shoulds" in this book.

Functions of standards.

As is the case with assumptions, standards serve a major function of providing an individual with a sense of order in the world. However, standards go beyond acceptance of the world as it is, to the extent of proposing (and even demanding) how the world *should* be. As described in the RET literature, standards (labeled as irrational by those authors) commonly involve themes of justice, fairness, and right versus wrong. Those who apply the principles of RET to marital problems focus on how the irrational standards and evaluations held by each spouse make him or her intolerant of the often unavoidable conflicts and dissatisfactions that arise when two people live in close proximity over a period of time (Ellis, 1977, 1986). Ellis proposes that spouses commonly enter a relationship with unrealistic (extreme) standards about marriage (e.g., that one's partner should always be supportive of all one's actions). Each spouse then reacts with dysfunctional emotions (e.g., anger) and behavior (e.g., fighting, withdrawal) when he or she applies such standards (e.g., "It is *awful* if my partner doesn't support me in all situations, as I desire") to the realities of a marriage that does not match them.

In spite of the negative impact of extreme standards on marital interaction, spouses commonly cling to them. Again, one function of such standards appears to be the order that they impose on the often confusing complexities of human experiences such as intimate relationships. In addition, as part of the world view that a person has developed over his or her lifetime, they are likely to be tied to the individual's self-concept and self-esteem. For example, the woman who holds the standard that her husband "should" support all of her actions may have a related standard that her self-worth depends on others' approval of her. To give up her standards regarding approval would be to alter her definition of herself in a major way. Spouses whose standards involve extremes of right and wrong often seem to judge issues in an all-or-nothing manner, concluding that "If I am not completely right about this, then I must be completely wrong (i.e., *bad*)." Unfortunately, just as standards can give an individual a sense of security that he or she *knows* how something should be, they set the stage for a precipitous drop in the person's perceived security and self-esteem if the world does not fit the standard.

Types of standards.

Epstein (1986) has noted that unrealistic standards about the nature of close relationships can erode marital satisfaction even when the spouses do not apply irrational, extreme evaluations (e.g., "This is *awful*; I can't stand it") to the violation of those standards. As described earlier, it is important to differentiate between the standard itself (which can be reasonable or unrealistic) and the evaluation (which can be reasonable or extreme) when one's experiences do not meet the standard. For example, a person who holds an unrealistic standard that in a "good" relationship the partners should be able to mind-read each other's feelings and needs is likely to experience repeated disappointments as his or her spouse fails to do so. Even though this individual may never evaluate this problem in an extremely negative manner (i.e., the person sees it as mildly unpleasant, but certainly tolerable), his or her satisfaction with the relationship is likely to decrease as the number of disappointing experiences accumulates. As we know from the research findings that support the behavior-exchange model of marital satisfaction (cf., Jacobson & Margolin, 1979), marital distress increases with the proportion of marital events experienced as negative. Consequently, cognitive-behavioral marital therapists assess and work to modify unrealistic standards that spouses hold about the nature of close relationships, so that such standards will not contribute to the accumulation of dissatisfying experiences between the partners.

However, this is not to say that extreme evaluations of dissatisfying experiences are neglected in this approach. Given that even spouses who hold the most realistic standards about marriage are likely to experience disappointments in their relationships, it is important that the extreme evaluations (e.g., "I can't stand it if. . .") emphasized in rational-emotive therapy be identified and modified when they exist.

Epstein and Eidelson (1981) found that spouses' marital distress and their lack of involvement in marital therapy were more strongly associated with their scores on a questionnaire measure of specific unrealistic standards about marriage (Eidelson & Epstein, 1982) than with scores on Jones's (1968) Irrational Beliefs Test, which was designed to assess irrational beliefs about individual functioning proposed by Ellis (1962). The results of that study suggest that cognitive content specific to aspects of relationships (e.g., the standard that mind reading should occur between spouses) is more important than broadly applicable extreme standards concerning individual functioning (e.g., demanding perfection in everything one does) in determining marital dysfunction. Similarly, Jordan and McCormick (1987) found that unrealistic standards about relationships were much stronger predictors of marital distress than were extreme standards about couple sexual functioning.

To date, Eidelson and Epstein's (1982) Relationship Belief Inventory (RBI) is the only validated standardized measure of unrealistic schemata that tend to be associated with marital dysfunction. In fact, according to our present distinction between assumptions and standards, the RBI subscales assessing expected mind reading and sexual perfectionism are the only ones that measure unrealistic standards. The scales assessing the ideas that disagreement is destructive (rather than a standard that partners *should not* disagree), that partners cannot change their relationship, and that the two sexes have major differences in personality and needs appear to measure unrealistic *assumptions* about the nature of relationships rather than extreme standards. This mixture of the two types of schemata in the RBI does not detract from its usefulness as an index of unrealistic cognitions that can play a role in marital problems, but it is clear that a total score for the set of five subscales does not provide a pure index of either unrealistic assumptions or standards. The RBI also does not assess the degree to which an individual evaluates violations of these assumptions and standards in an extreme manner.

Cognitive-behavioral marital therapists assume that the variety of potentially unrealistic standards that may exist among distressed spouses is much wider than those assessed by the RBI. Unrealistic standards can be concerned with adequate role performance (e.g., the behaviors that a "good" husband or wife should exhibit), the qualities that should exist in the experience of love (e.g., what emotions should exist initially and over the years), and the nature of good marital interaction (e.g., what "good communication" between spouses should be like) (Epstein, 1986). An individual's standards about relationships are likely to include idiosyncratic standards developed from his or her unique set of life experiences, including those in the family of origin and those due to exposure to various mass media representations of relationships. Consequently, it is difficult to provide a comprehensive scheme for categorizing all unrealistic relationship standards, and the marital therapist is faced with conducting a careful assessment of potentially problematic idiosyncratic standards with each member of a distressed relationship.

Problematic combinations of partners' relationship standards.

Identifying the relationship standards held by each individual spouse does not always provide the full picture of the role that such standards play in a marital problem. At times a particular unrealistic standard (or assumption) may be especially potent because two partners both adhere to it and reinforce each other's belief in it. Another problematic situation sometimes arises when the standards of two spouses are different but complementary. For example, a husband might believe that loving partners should focus on the positives in their relationship and not criticize each other, as in the honeymoon stage of most relationships. His wife may believe that in a close relationship partners should be able to mind-read each other's needs and desires. Although an absence of open communication between these spouses might be partly consistent with this combination of standards, over time it also would be likely to leave each partner dissatisfied. The husband may be pleased with the absence of overt conflict, but he may be quite frustrated about (a) the inaccurate assumptions that his mind-reading wife makes about his desires and (b) his inability to confront her about her errors. The wife may be pleased that her husband does not correct her mind-reading efforts but may feel frustrated when he indirectly expresses dissatisfaction with what he receives from her, perhaps by exhibiting passive aggression and by failing to meet her needs.

In the absence of unrealistic or extreme standards, marital problems still can result if two spouses have fairly reasonable but *incompatible standards*. It is important that the clinician assess whether marital distress is based on extreme "shoulds" or is due to the failure of two people who each hold flexible standards to engage in effective negotiation. For example, two partners may have different *preferences* regarding the amount of emotional expression in their relationship, or they may place different values on the role of religion in family life. In either case, if the partners do not hold rigidly to their standards, they may need assistance in developing their skills for negotiation and problem solving, rather than cognitive restructuring.

PERCEPTIONS, ATTRIBUTIONS, AND
EXPECTANCIES

Although unrealistic standards about relationships can play an important role in the development and maintenance of marital distress, distortions in spouses' perceptions and interpretations of each other's behavior also can lead to significant increases in distress, independent of any extreme standards and evaluations. This can occur because the individual's distorted views serve as his or her reality. Even though that reality may not involve unrealistic standards for relationships or include irrational evaluations (e.g., that events are intolerable), experiencing the relationship in a negative manner can contribute to a gradual deterioration in the person's levels of affection and good will in the marriage (Epstein, 1986). For example, a woman may accurately perceive that whenever she and her husband argue, he asks to take her out to dinner or he buys her a gift. If she routinely infers that his behavior reflects "trying to humor me" and "not taking me seriously," when in fact it reflects his attempt to communicate the idea "in spite of our differences, I still value our relationship and want to symbolize that with a special gesture," she is likely to be distressed rather than pleased on each such occasion. Unless the discrepancy between his intent and the message she receives is clarified, she may experience a significant number of unpleasant exchanges with her husband. Although she may evaluate none of these events as awful or intolerable, the accumulation of negative experiences can detract from the level of satisfaction she experiences. Her husband may not have violated a standard that she holds about how a husband "should" behave (i.e., she may acknowledge a wide variety of appropriate ways that husbands might behave), but she may perceive him as failing to behave in ways that she *enjoys* or *prefers*. As proposed in social exchange theory and supported by research evidence (e.g., Birchler et al., 1975; Jacobson et al., 1982; Jacobson, Waldron, and Moore, 1980), the higher the proportion of exchanges in a relationship that are experienced by each partner as negative, the lower that person's subjective satisfaction with the relationship will be.

One of the common clinical findings of behavioral marital therapists that increasingly has led them to pay attention to clients' cognitions is that distressed spouses often do not feel more satisfied after their partners produce desired behaviors in the context of communication training or behavioral contracting procedures. When questioned about the failure of the behavior changes to increase marital satisfaction, these clients frequently reveal negative interpretations of the partner's actions (e.g., "She did it just to impress you [the therapist], not because she really cares about behaving better"). Not only might such interpretations maintain or increase a spouse's sense of hopelessness about ever improving the marriage, but they may lead the individual to punish rather than reinforce positive acts by his or her partner.

Wessler and Wessler (1980) note that practitioners of rational-emotive therapy (RET) acknowledge that perceptions and inferences can influence people's responses to life events, but they focus more of their therapeutic efforts on the identification and modification of irrational standards and evaluations. This practice is based on the idea that no matter how an individual perceives or interprets an event, it is the extreme evaluation (e.g., "This is *awful*") that produces the person's dysfunctional emotional and behavioral responses. Our own approach is more similar to the cognitive therapy procedures used by Beck and his associates (Beck et al., 1979), wherein fairly equal attention is paid to perceptions, attributions, expectancies, assumptions, and standards.

Theory and research on social cognition (cf., Nisbett & Ross, 1980) have pointed to an important link between cognitive structures, such as assumptions and standards, and the ways that individuals process current information available to them in their daily experiences. As applied to marital interaction, a person is likely to assimilate information about his or her spouse based on the former's preexisting assumptions and standards concerning the spouse, spouses in general, and marriage. There is a growing body of evidence that people's preconceptions bias (a) what they notice about situations they encounter, (b) their inferences about causes of events, and (c) their predictions about one characteristic or event from their knowledge about another characteristic or event (Nisbett & Ross, 1980).

Research on cognition in marital interaction has only begun to investigate such theoretical links between spouses' fairly longstanding standards and assumptions on the one hand and their perceptions, attributions, and expectancies about ongoing marital events on the other hand. Significant positive correlations have been found between spouses' self-reported negative expectancies and attributions about causes of their marital problems (e.g., low expectancy of improvement in the relationship, attribution of marital problems to the partner's personality, malicious intent, and lack of love), on the one hand, and their unrealistic assumptions and standards about relationships, on the other hand (Epstein, Pretzer, & Fleming, 1987; Pretzer, Fleming, & Epstein, 1983). Similarly, Fincham and Bradbury (1987) found that both causal attributions (e.g., attributing a spouse's negative behavior to a global or stable characteristic of that individual) and responsibility attributions (e.g., the degree to which the individual thought that the partner had negative intentions, was selfish, and deserved to be blamed) were positively related to unrealistic assumptions and standards about relationships. These preliminary findings are consistent with our clinical observations that couples' perceptions, attributions, and expectancies regarding their relationships generally seem to reflect their basic assumptions about spousal roles and the nature of marital interaction (i.e., personae and scripts). For example, a man might have a longstanding assumption that "actions speak louder than words," namely, that a person's behavior is a more accurate reflection of his or her "true" attitudes and feelings than are the words the person speaks. Consequently, when his wife forgets about his birthday but tells him "I can't believe that I did that! I love you so much!" he makes inferences that her behavior was due to a lack of love and that her words were due to her trying to maintain a facade about their marriage.

Later in this chapter, we will describe how cognitive structures such as assumptions and standards in turn may be shaped by perceptions, attributions, and expectancies. For now, it is important to keep two points in mind when considering the following descriptions of the perceptions, attributions, and expectancies that can play roles in marital problems: (a) a spouse's perceptions, attributions, and expectancies about marital events can contribute to relationship problems even when the individual does not hold unrealistic or irrational *standards* about the way spouses and marriages *should be,* but (b) perceptions, attributions, and expectancies are likely to be linked to longstanding *assumptions* about the way spouses and marriages *are.*

Perceptions

A variety of theorists who have described how people perceive their social environments have emphasized that perception is an active process rather than a passive reception of stimuli. Writers such as Kelly (1955) and Heider (1958) portrayed the actively perceiving individual as an "intuitive scientist" who attends to stimuli selectively and attaches meanings to events that he or she notices. Consistent with this view, we define *perceptions* as those aspects of the information available in a situation which in fact an individual notices and fits into categories that have meaning to him or her.

The results of a number of recent studies have suggested that a process of selective perception probably operates when spouses view the events in their relationships. These studies have found low levels of agreement between spouses about the occurrence of particular communication acts and other behaviors in their marital interactions and low correlations between behaviors reported by spouses versus outside observers (Christensen, Sullaway, & King, 1983; Elwood & Jacobson, 1982; Floyd & Markman, 1983; Jacobson & Moore, 1981; Margolin, Hattem, John, & Yost, 1985). The rates of agreement between spouses concerning the occurrence of specific behaviors (recorded on a daily basis) commonly are no higher than 50%, and Elwood and Jacobson (1982) found only a 38.6% overall interspouse agreement rate. Floyd and Markman's (1983) results suggested that the discrepancies between behavioral ratings by spouses and outside observers were due to perceptual biases on the part of the couples rather than the outside observers.

Clinically oriented writers who emphasize the role of cognition in mediating people's emotional and behavioral responses to life events (e.g., Beck et al., 1979; Wessler & Wessler, 1980) have noted that perceptions are vulnerable to selective attention due to a variety of factors such as emotional states, fatigue, and the cognitive structures that an individual has available for classifying information. An individual who is experiencing a high level of emotional arousal, such as anger or anxiety, may have a narrowing of perception or "tunnel vision," thereby noticing a limited amount of what there is available to notice in a particular situation. This selective perception can be quite systematic, with the person mostly noticing aspects of a situation that are related to an event that produced his or her emotional arousal. For example, a person who is experiencing anxiety following a "failure" to satisfy his or her sexual partner then may pay almost exclusive attention to cues of the partner's sexual responsiveness when they attempt to engage in sex again, thereby failing to notice other aspects of the partner's behavior (e.g., verbal expressions of love and understanding) in that situation. Similarly, spouses who attempt to communicate about important matters when they are fatigued may fail to notice certain verbal and nonverbal messages that are sent by their partners. Finally, as noted in Kelly's (1955) landmark work on personal constructs, the concepts that one has available (due to past life experiences) for categorizing people and events channel what one notices in situations. A person for whom the characteristics "intelligence," "education," and "sophistication" are salient for evaluating other people (perhaps because of the way this person was socialized in his or her family of origin) may quickly notice a stranger's vocabulary and manners, while failing to notice whether or not the stranger is friendly.

In regard to the cognitive structures described earlier that can influence marital distress, the aspects that a spouse notices about his or her marriage may be constrained by the *assumptions* that he or she holds about marriage, including "husband" and "wife" *personae* and *scripts* about sequences of events that occur between spouses. Similarly, what is perceived may be influenced by one's *standards* about how husbands, wives, and marriages "should" be. Beck and his associates (Beck et al., 1979; Beck & Emery, 1985) use the term *selective abstraction* to refer to such a cognitive bias in which an individual tends to notice particular aspects of a situation and ignore others. As applied to marital problems, a spouse who assumes that intimate relationships are very fragile may be likely to engage in selective abstraction, noticing signs of even minor conflict in his or her relationship and ignoring signs of harmony that most people would consider significant. Perceptual biases can have powerful influences on the quality of a relationship because individuals normally are unaware that the information they perceive is only a subset of all the information available in a situation. Consequently, a number of the cognitive and behavioral intervention procedures described in this book are intended to increase spouses' discrimination of the varied data available to them during their marital interactions, so that they can minimize skewed perceptions of those interactions.

Dysfunctional Attributions

Beginning with seminal work by Heider (1958), Jones and Davis (1965), and Kelley (1967) in social psychology, there has been a rapidly growing theoretical and empirical literature examining how people search for explanations for the events that occur in their daily lives. Attributions are the basic explanations that people devise regarding the factors that cause a particular event. Because the attributional process involves observing an event (e.g., the behavior of one's spouse) and making inferences about its possible causes, there is considerable potential for cognitive distortion in the process.

Functions of attributions.

Both clinical and empirical evidence indicates that people do make attributions spontaneously (Baucom, 1987; Holtzworth-Munroe & Jacobson, 1985). Baucom (1987) has described several important functions that attributions serve for members of intimate relationships, including the following. First, making attributions about the causes of a partner's behavior can increase one's sense of understanding and intimacy with that person (whether or not the attributions are accurate). Second, making attributions can give an individual a sense of control over his or her life. On the one hand, if one knows the causes of a partner's behavior, one can plan ways to change the partner's negative behaviors or to maintain positive ones. A dissatisfied spouse also can exercise some control over the marriage by communicating his or her attributions to the partner, thereby inducing the person to behave otherwise. For example, when a husband fails to complete a task at home and his wife expresses the attribution, "You didn't do it because you are such a lazy person," her message may be intended in part to induce guilt in her partner and motivate him to behave differently. Similarly, expressing positive attributions (e.g., "You are such a thoughtful person!") can provide strong reinforcement to maintain a partner's desirable behaviors. In addition, when an individual has been involved in a long-term distressing relationship, he or she can exercise what has been labeled "secondary control" to minimize future hurt and disappointment. This process involves attributing stable negative traits to one's partner, thereby setting up an expectancy that he or she will continue to behave in negative ways. In the words of one wife from a chronically distressed relationship, "Because I know my husband is an ungiving person, I don't expect much and I don't set myself up for disappointment."

A third function of attributions involves protecting and enhancing one's own self-esteem. Members of distressed relationships commonly blame each other for marital problems (Gottman, 1979) and often attempt to justify their own negative behaviors. Frequently, an individual justifies his or her own behavior by attributing its cause to external factors, especially actions of the partner. As described by systems theorists (e.g., Watzlawick et al., 1967), although interactions between two people tend to occur in a circular process, each party is likely to "punctuate" the sequence of interaction, arbitrarily dividing it into segments. Commonly, each distressed spouse punctuates the sequence of events that occurred between the two partners in a manner that portrays his or her own negative behavior as being caused by preceding behaviors of the other person. By making such causal attributions, each spouse maintains his or her self-esteem. Baucom (1987) has suggested that members of nondistressed relationships may have less need to make self-enhancing attributions because they feel more secure in the relationship.

Another function that attributions may serve is to enhance one's image of one's partner or marriage. When the nature of the partner or the marriage does not match what one desires, some spouses make distorted attributions for problematic events which create a less distressing picture.

For example, one husband repeatedly declined his wife's invitations to join her in a variety of leisure activities. Although eventually she was faced with his disclosure that he no longer wanted to be married to her, for some time she attributed his behavior to fatigue and stress from his job.

Types of attributions.

It is only recently that attribution theory has been applied to the issue of marital problems, and the early work in this area has borrowed heavily from the reformulated learned helplessness model of depression developed by Abramson, Seligman, and Teasdale (1978). Extending Abramson et al.'s attributional model of depression to marital distress has a considerable amount of face validity, because the two types of problems have many affective, behavioral, and cognitive components in common (Epstein, 1985b). Learned helplessness theory proposes that the symptoms of depression (e.g., decreased instrumental behavior; negative affect) will be greater to the extent that the individual attributes uncontrollable negative life outcomes to global, stable, and internal factors. First, attributing lack of control in a particular situation to internal factors (e.g., one's level of intelligence) lowers self-esteem. Second, attributing it to stable factors produces an expectancy that one will be helpless to control that situation in the future. Third, attributing it to global factors (i.e., those that affect a variety of life situations) creates an expectation that one will not be able to control many different life events in the future. In contrast, attributing lack of control in a particular situation to external factors (e.g., another person's actions), unstable factors (those that may not exist in the future), and specific factors (those that do not apply to other life situations) is not expected to produce chronic depression.

As this model has been applied to marital distress, it has been hypothesized that spouses will be distressed about their relationships when they attribute marital problems to global and stable factors (Baucom, Bell, & Duhe, 1982; Doherty, 1981a; Fincham & O'Leary, 1983; Holtzworth-Munroe & Jacobson, 1985). Attributions regarding global, stable factors (e.g., a partner's negative personality trait) are expected to be associated with marital distress because (as in depression) they suggest little hope for improvement of current problems. For example, one wife forgot to buy her husband a birthday present, and he attributed this behavior to a lack of love on her part. When asked to describe the nature of his wife's lack of love, he reported that it was global, affecting most aspects of their relationship, and stable, not likely to change in the future. Consequently, he felt hopeless about the future of their relationship and helpless to effect any positive changes in the marriage.

In contrast to the attributional model of depression, in which depressed individuals tend to blame themselves for their problems, distressed spouses are hypothesized to attribute marital problems to sources other than themselves, most commonly blaming their partners. An exception to this pattern noted by Baucom (1987) is when a distressed marriage includes a depressed member, and both spouses blame that person for the marital problems. Fincham (1985) has noted that when spouses rate causes of relationship events in terms of "internal" and "external" factors, a single bipolar internal-external dimension is not appropriate, because it does not specify whether "internal" refers to within the person making the attribution or within that person's relationship (which could include factors concerning the spouse). Consequently, questionnaires used in recent studies have asked participants to rate causes of marital events on separate scales for self, partner, and factors outside the relationship.

A number of studies have been conducted to test whether marital distress is associated with the systematic patterns of attributions described here. In some studies (e.g., Baucom et al., 1982; Fincham, Beach, & Baucom, 1987, Study 1; Fincham, Beach, & Nelson, 1987; Fincham & O'Leary, 1983; Kyle & Falbo, 1985) distressed and nondistressed spouses have been asked to rate hypothetical partner behaviors on internal-external, global-specific, and stable-unstable dimensions. In other studies (e.g., Camper, Jacobson, Holtzworth-Munroe, & Schmaling, 1988; Fichten, 1984; Fincham, 1985; Fincham, Beach, & Baucom, 1987, Study 2; Holtzworth-Munroe & Jacobson, 1985; Jacobson, McDonald, Follette, & Berley, 1985) spouses have been asked to make attributional ratings regarding the causes of actual recent marital events.

Although not all of these studies asked participants to make ratings on all of the internal-external, global-specific, and stable-unstable dimensions, and there have been some inconsistent results among the various studies, there have been common patterns found for attributions to stable causes, and especially for attributions to global causes. Distressed spouses tend to rate the causes of negative behaviors by their partners as more global and stable than do nondistressed spouses, and nondistressed spouses tend to rate causes of positive partner behaviors as more global and stable than do distressed individuals. The attributions made by distressed spouses have been referred to as "distress-maintaining," and those made by nondistressed spouses have been labeled "relationship-enhancing"

(Holtzworth-Munroe & Jacobson, 1985). On the one hand, when distressed individuals assume that negative partner behaviors are due to global, stable factors (i.e., bad traits) and that positive spouse behaviors are due to fleeting specific and unstable factors (i.e., "Something must have gotten into her today; she's just not like that"), the results are likely to be responses such as anger, despair, blaming, and helpless behavior, as noted earlier. On the other hand, when nondistressed spouses discount negative behaviors as due to more specific and unstable factors and attribute positive spouse behaviors to global and stable factors, they are likely to feel good about the relationship and to reward their partners for the positive behavior. The results of studies that have used "internal versus external" rating scales that distinguish between attribution to the self and attribution to the partner also commonly have revealed a tendency for distressed spouses to blame their partners for marital problems, a tendency likely to maintain distress by creating the mutual "cross-complaining" described by Gottman (1979).

   Although attributional ratings on the dimensions derived from the learned helplessness model of depression have been found to be associated with level of marital distress, Fincham (1985) has suggested that in intimate relationships the level of distress is even more likely to be associated with what he has labeled "responsibility" attributions, those that identify the degree and type of *motivation* involved in a person's actions. For example, to say that a partner's negative behavior was due to a global, stable cause does not indicate whether or not the partner had any purposeful negative intent. Fincham, Beach, and Nelson (1987) assessed spouses' attributions of blameworthiness, positive versus negative intent, and selfish motivation concerning positive and negative partner behaviors, in addition to internal-external (self versus partner), global-specific, and stable-unstable attributions. Their sample of distressed spouses rated hypothetical negative partner behaviors as more due to global causes, negative intent, and selfish motivation, and more worthy of blame than did nondistressed spouses. Nondistressed spouses rated the causes of hypothetical positive partner behaviors as more global, stable, due to positive intent and unselfish motivation, and praiseworthy than did distressed spouses. Also, only the "responsibility" attributions significantly predicted participants' ratings of how positive or negative the partner's behavior made them feel and how punishing or rewarding their response to the partner's behavior would be. Thus, attributions concerning the individual's view of the partner's attitudes and intentions regarding the marriage appear to be quite important in understanding marital distress.

In contrast to Fincham, Beach, and Nelson's (1987) results, Fincham and Bradbury (1987) found that attributional dimensions based on the learned helplessness model and attributions concerning partner motives were *equally* associated with marital distress. They conclude that the difference in results between the two studies may be due to the fact that the Fincham, Beach, and Nelson study compared extreme groups (samples of nondistressed and highly distressed couples), whereas the Fincham and Bradbury study used a sample of couples who primarily were recruited with a newspaper advertisement concerning a study of marriage, and whose mean marital satisfaction score was in the very mildly distressed range. It may be that attributions about negative intentions and responsibility are especially relevant for highly distressed spouses.

In a review of attribution research concerning couples, Thompson and Snyder (1986) stress that attributional processes are complex, and that it is important to differentiate and assess various types of attributions (e.g., responsibility, intentions) that spouses make about each other's (and their own) behaviors. In addition, Thompson and Snyder (1986) and Fincham and Bradbury (1987) note that spouses' attributions about determinants of events in their relationships are likely to vary according to the types of behaviors for which attributions are made. For example, attributions about a partner's intentions and regard for his or her spouse might be more salient when that person has exhibited violent behavior than when he or she has voiced disagreement about childrearing philosophies.

The correlational nature of the studies linking attributions and marital distress has not allowed us to determine the direction of causality between these two aspects of marriage. In other words, the statistically significant correlations between attributions and marital distress may be due to attributions causing distress, distress causing attributions, or even a third factor causing both attributions and distress. Fincham and Bradbury (1987) have provided an initial test of causality by assessing both attributions and marital distress at two points, 12 months apart. In their longitudinal study, they found that (a) for wives, but not for husbands, both causal and responsibility attributions at the first testing predicted marital satisfaction scores 12 months later (controlling for initial satisfaction levels), but that (b) initial satisfaction scores did not predict attributions 12 months later for either sex. Although this study had limitations ([a] it did not rule out the possibility that a "third variable" accounted for both attributions and marital satisfaction; [b] data were collected at only two points in time; and [c] no data are available to clarify why the prediction of satisfaction level over time from attributions only was found for females), its longitudinal nature represents an important step toward identifying the roles that cognitions such as attributions play in the *development* of marital problems.

The major clinical implications of these research findings regarding attributions and marital distress appear to be as follows. First, marital therapists need to determine whether spouses are making inaccurate attributions that exacerbate the impact of negative partner behaviors, that discount positive partner behaviors, or that elicit a negative response to an objectively neutral or positive partner behavior. Second, therapists need to assist spouses in challenging the validity of such dysfunctional attributions in order to promote more constructive and satisfying behavioral interactions between distressed spouses. Specific guidelines and procedures for conducting such cognitive assessments and interventions are described in Chapters 5 and 8, respectively.

Inaccurate Expectancies

Rotter's (1954) social learning model of behavior included a central cognitive concept of expectancies that people hold about the probabilities of outcomes in particular life situations. According to Rotter's model, the probability that an individual will exhibit a behavior depends on his or her subjective expectancies about the outcomes that would follow from such behavior, as well as the values that he or she attaches to those outcomes. For example, an individual might be faced with a choice of whether to disagree with a spouse assertively or to conform to the spouse's wishes. The individual's decision might be shaped by an expectancy that it is highly likely that assertiveness will elicit scathing criticism from the spouse and the person's view that such criticism is quite aversive.

Rotter (1954) differentiated between *specific expectancies*, which concern situation-specific predictions (e.g., "If I disagree with my spouse when he has had a bad day, all I'll get is criticism"), and *generalized expectancies*, which are more global and stable (e.g., "There's no way I can have any influence on the people close to me"). In Rotter's model, both the expectancies and the reinforcing values of outcomes are determined by a person's earlier learning history.

Bandura (1977) has emphasized the important role of cognition in learning by describing how people come to anticipate probable consequences of different actions and thereby vary their behavior in order to produce or avoid particular consequences. In general, this is a highly adaptive ability that allows people to use environmental cues to choose actions that will produce the most favorable outcomes for them. An individual will inhibit certain actions that he or she anticipates will produce unpleasant consequences in a particular situation, and will act in other ways that are anticipated to produce pleasant outcomes in that situation. Bandura (1977) argues that the learning that takes place is not a direct stimulus-response connection, as in a strict behavioral model, but instead is due to cognitive representations in the form of expectancies. Expectancies often are not learned through a person's direct experience with particular response-consequence contingencies, but through instruction and modeling by other people. For example, an individual may have learned to anticipate unpleasant consequences of self-disclosure to other people by hearing his or her mother say, "Don't expose your weak points to other people, or they'll take advantage of you."

Bandura (1977) notes that expectancies that were formed through a person's own direct experiences can be more difficult to alter by means of cognitive interventions than expectancies learned indirectly. For example, fear and avoidance responses to particular stimuli which were developed through actual aversive experiences with those stimuli may be quite persistent even when the individual is given accurate information that future contact with the stimuli will no longer produce unpleasant results. In such circumstances, the most effective treatment involves repeated powerful new experiences in which the person observes first-hand that the contingencies have changed. Unfortunately, people often create negative self-fulfilling prophecies by acting in accord with their expectancies and thus eliciting the anticipated unpleasant consequences from other people. The person who anticipates being hurt by romantic partners may act in defensive ways that elicit the rejection they fear.

One can conceptualize marital interactions as influenced by an ongoing sequence of decisions that the two partners make about the ways in which they will and will not behave toward each other, based on their subjective expectancies about the probable outcomes of particular actions. Once the spouses' expectancies have been established, these decisions often may be almost instantaneous and not necessarily even fully within the person's awareness. Using Rotter's (1954) distinction, some of these expectancies are likely to be quite specific (restricted to certain situations), whereas others may be relatively generalized and guide the individual's responses across a wide range of situations in the marriage.

Functions of expectancies.

As is the case with attributions, expectancies commonly serve the functions of giving people perceptions that they can understand, predict, and control events in their lives. As described earlier, expectancies also play a role in an active decision-making process by which an individual chooses which of the responses available to him or her is the most likely to produce desired outcomes. Clearly, the human ability to develop such cognitive maps based on previous experiences and other sources of information allows us to avoid trial-and-error learning in each new encounter with people and events in life. Therefore, the accurate development and application of expectancies is a highly adaptive process that allows efficient and effective interaction in human relationships. However, as we emphasize about cognitive processes throughout this book, when expectancies are based on faulty data or are applied in an illogical manner, they easily can lead spouses to make faulty decisions about their actions toward each other. Also, within our cognitive mediation model, an inaccurate expectancy can elicit not only inappropriate behavior toward a marital partner, but inappropriate emotional responses as well. For example, an individual who inaccurately expects her spouse's wrath any time she makes any "mistake" not only may withdraw from him behaviorally, but also may experience fairly chronic anxiety or anger.

Types of expectancies.

Bandura (1977) distinguishes between *outcome expectancies* and *efficacy expectancies*. An outcome expectancy is a person's estimate that a particular action will lead to particular consequences in a certain situation. In contrast, an efficacy expectancy is the person's estimate of the probability that he or she will be *able* to carry out the action that would produce those consequences.

Three major forms of *outcome expectancies* of the type described by Bandura seem to be common when spouses make predictions about events in their relationships. These three forms of outcome expectancies can be categorized in terms of the particular forms of "if-then" statements that comprise them. First, regarding *reactions of the partner,* the logical form of the expectancy is "if I do X in situation A, my partner will have a probability (p) of doing Y." For example, one wife whose husband often fell asleep on the sofa after dinner had the expectancy that "if I don't wake him up and get him to bed, he'll most certainly blame me if he gets a sore back from the sofa, and he'll also sleep poorly and fall asleep on the sofa again tomorrow night."

Second, regarding *reactions of the self*, the expectancy has the form "If my partner does X in situation A, I will have the probability (p) of doing Y." For example, a husband we interviewed stated that if his wife expressed anger toward him, he definitely would sleep poorly that night and also have trouble getting his work done the next day; so he avoided overt conflict as much as possible.

The third type of expectancy involves *outcomes of a joint event*, where the form of the expectancy is "If my partner and I do X in situation A, the probability is (p) that outcome Y will occur." An example of this form of expectancy is a wife who reported that any arguments between herself and her husband that occurred openly in front of their children would harm the children psychologically. Expectancies about outcomes of joint events might be shared by both spouses or held by only one of them.

Doherty (1981a, 1981b) has proposed that spouses' *efficacy expectancies* are important determinants of marital and family conflict resolution. According to Doherty, the lower the individual's expectation that one or both spouses will be able to carry out actions that are likely to solve marital problems, the more he or she will exhibit learned helplessness responses (Seligman, 1975). Due to a history of painful experiences in the marriage and unsuccessful attempts to resolve the problems, the individual develops a perception that escalation of conflict is uncontrollable, gives up trying to solve the problems, fails to learn any new information that might increase ability to improve the situation, actively avoids the issues, and decreases his or her commitment to the relationship (Doherty, 1981b). Doherty's model also proposes that low-efficacy expectancies are more likely to develop when spouses attribute the causes of their marital problems to global and stable factors, as well as to negative intentions on their partner's parts.

Pretzer, Epstein, and Fleming (1985), using a self-report questionnaire assessing spouses' attributions and expectancies about their marital problems, produced results consistent with Doherty's (1981a, 1981b) hypotheses linking low-efficacy expectancies with relationship distress, a depressive cognitive set (part of learned helplessness), and attributions regarding traits and negative partner intentions. First, they found that the degree to which spouses reported an expectancy that the couple would improve their relationship was positively associated with their level of marital satisfaction, and with the degree to which the individual attributed marital problems to his or her own behavior. In contrast to those findings, the higher the expectancy of improvement in the relationship, the lower the individual's level of depression, and the lower the attribution of causality for relationship problems to the partner's behavior, personality traits, malicious intent, and lack of love.

Doherty (1981a, 1981b) has emphasized those efficacy expectations that involve a couple or family's success in problem solving as a group. It is the lack of such joint efficacy expectations that Doherty sees as contributing most to the breakdown or absence of the collaborative efforts needed to resolve interpersonal conflicts.

Another useful way to categorize expectancies is in terms of Rotter's *generalized* versus *specific* distinction. Clinically, this distinction suggests that the kinds and amounts of new data needed to challenge and modify more generalized versus more specific expectancies (in reality, these probably represent a continuum rather than a dichotomy) may differ.

On the one hand, the validity of relatively specific expectancies may be challenged by generating data about exceptions to the prediction the person has made about the specific consequences that will result from particular actions taken in a specific situation. For example, if a man has predicted that if he makes suggestions about weekend plans with his wife she almost certainly will reject his ideas, then the expectancy can be challenged with information indicating that when he makes such suggestions a few days in advance rather than at the last minute his wife fairly often does *not* respond with criticism.

On the other hand, when a person has a generalized expectancy such as "I cannot have any influence on the people close to me," the same disconfirming information described above might lead the person to conclude that the outcome in a particular situation (or even a few situations) was the exception rather than the rule, thereby maintaining the general expectancy that attempts to influence others will be futile. It seems likely that cognitive interventions such as those described later in this book would have to be applied in a more broad manner in order to modify more generalized expectancies.

COGNITIVE DISTORTIONS

Throughout our discussions of assumptions, standards, perceptions, attributions, and expectancies, we have emphasized that these normal cognitive phenomena generally are highly adaptive, and in fact are essential in order for humans to understand and learn from their experiences. However, we also have stressed that these cognitions all are susceptible to distortion, such that they may be inaccurate or inappropriate representations of events in a person's life. Those who have studied cognitive factors in psychopathology and those who have investigated social cognition have identified a number of systematic distortions that can bias individuals' assumptions, standards, perceptions, attributions, and expectancies. These cognitive distortions are errors in the *process* of collecting and using information, independent of the particular *content* of that information. This distinction between information content and information processing will be described further in the following survey of the major types of cognitive distortions that commonly contribute to dysfunctional cognitions in marital interaction.

Beck and his associates (Beck, 1976; Beck & Emery, 1985; Beck et al., 1979) have described systematic information-processing errors common in the thinking of persons with affective and anxiety disorders. In marital interactions, such cognitive distortions can lead spouses to have biased perceptions of one another and to draw faulty conclusions about the causes and meanings of each other's behavior (Epstein, 1982). For example, Beck et al. (1979) define an *arbitrary inference* as an inference about an unobserved characteristic or event from an observed one, without adequate evidence of such a connection. A person who makes an arbitrary inference about the cause of her husband's teasing ("He doesn't respect my opinion") may feel quite angry when in fact her spouse had a very different intent (e.g., an attempt, perhaps misguided, to cheer her up after she had a stressful day at work). Arbitrary inferences are commonly the basis of inaccurate attributions (as in the preceding example) and inaccurate expectancies. In the case of expectancies, an individual may make an inference, based on little or no valid data, that a particular behavior on the part of his or her spouse is a signal that disagreeing with the spouse's opinions at that moment will elicit verbal abuse from the spouse.

The distortion of *personalization*, a second type of inferential error, involves an overestimate of the degree to which particular events are related to oneself (e.g., when the husband in the above example concludes that he must cheer up his wife because her distress with her job must be his fault, owing to the pressure he had put on her to accept a promotion). Not only can personalization contribute to inaccurate attributions and expectancies about events between partners, but the egocentric process of relating marital events to oneself can permeate an individual's basic assumptions and standards about relationships. For example, the set of characteristics that a man assumes constitute the role "wife" may be restricted to those that involve the ways in which a woman in that role would relate to him (e.g., "is nurturant to me," "likes to share leisure time together," "takes my views into account in making decisions"). Characteristics that do not relate to the self (e.g., "is interested in political causes," "enjoys periods of solitude for creative work") may not be included in this man's "wife" persona, and therefore he will not make inferences from characteristics within the persona to those other characteristics that do not "fit." As a specific example, if the characteristic "is nurturant to me" falls within the man's "wife" persona but "is interested in political causes" does not, he will not assume any correlation between the two characteristics, when in fact the two may be associated owing to their common root in the wife's concern with the needs of other people. Thus, personalization can shape cognitive structures such as assumptions that are incomplete representations of the ways that objects and events actually are associated in the world.

Emotional reasoning is another inferential error that involves equating subjective experiences such as emotions with facts. A common example of emotional reasoning among distressed spouses occurs when an individual makes the attribution, "I must not care about my spouse any longer, because I don't feel the warm feelings for him/her that used to be there." This conclusion might be accurate, but the decrease in positive affect also might reflect reversible effects of having unpleasant rather than pleasant daily experiences with the partner. Emotional reasoning also commonly produces inaccurate expectancies, such as when an individual feels anxiety in the presence of his or her spouse and essentially concludes, "I *feel* like he is going to do something awful, so he probably *will* do something awful if I keep talking with him." Relevant to this concept of emotional reasoning, Nisbett and Ross (1980) have noted that the importance that an individual attaches to various characteristics when making inferences about a person or event depends on how "vivid" each characteristic is for the person. Vividness of information is a function of how familiar, concrete, intense, and emotionally interesting it is. Consequently, an individual might make broad assumptions about the nature of events and interpersonal relationships solely on the basis of his or her own limited experiences. Those experiences may be quite atypical of people's relationships in general, but for the individual they are "vivid" and memorable.

As described earlier, a similar type of inferential error that can contribute to inaccurate attributions and expectancies, and can be at the core of inaccurate or inappropriate assumptions and beliefs, involves the phenomenon of *illusory correlation* (Chapman & Chapman, 1969). Illusory correlation exists when a person sees a common meaning in two characteristics or events and then concludes that the two are causally linked, when in fact they are unrelated. For example, a husband may choose not to disclose feelings to his wife, such as anxiety regarding his career and his ability to fulfill certain aspects of his roles as husband and father, because he expects that such disclosures would lower her esteem for him. However, his expectancy may be based on an illusory correlation in his mind between earning the respect of one's wife and demonstrating one's competence and strength. He associates these two characteristics because he sees the same theme of "strength" in them. Unfortunately, the correlation that he assumes between being "the strong, silent type" and gaining his wife's respect may have either no relationship to the actual association between self-disclosure and respect in their marriage, or it may even be the opposite of what is true. His wife actually may value self-disclosure as a means of achieving intimacy, and she may lose respect for her husband when he withdraws from her.

In *dichotomous thinking,* the individual views the world in all-or-nothing terms. A common example of this distortion occurs when spouses who disagree about an issue such as childrearing techniques each view the self as "right" and the partner as "wrong." By failing to notice or acknowledge areas of overlap in their positions, the spouses may "polarize" themselves into more extreme positions. Thus, the man who views his wife as "harsh" with their children may then go out of his way to behave in a more solicitous manner toward them, whereas the wife views her spouse as "totally lax" with the children and therefore becomes more strict with them in order to compensate for the perceived laxness.

Just as dichotomous thinking can bias spouses' perceptions of one another, as in the preceding example, it often is involved in unrealistic assumptions and standards from which spouses draw inferences about each other's behavior. For example a woman's internal "script" about independence versus dependence in a relationship may include a dichotomy: "When someone allows himself or herself to become dependent on a spouse, the spouse takes over the person's life; maintaining one's own identity calls for avoiding any emotional and financial dependence on one's spouse." Such an assumption about the nature of close relationships does not allow moderate degrees of interdependence between partners and might contribute to spouses leading parallel lives with little intimacy or commitment. When an individual turns the assumption into a rigid standard about how spouses "should not" allow themselves any dependence on one another, he or she may react dysfunctionally (e.g., strong anger, leaving the house for periods of time) when the partner attempts to be nurturant or directive.

Furthermore, dichotomous thinking can contribute to biased attributions and expectancies by restricting the possible inferences that can be drawn from the information that one notices. For example, if a man notices that his wife has avoided talking with him about an issue that is important to him, dichotomous thinking may lead him to make an attribution that she does not care about the way he feels, because in his mind there are only two possibilities: either someone cares or does not care. He has not taken into account that his wife may have a good deal of concern for him but finds the topic threatening and difficult to discuss. Expectancies can be biased in a similar manner by dichotomous thinking, such that the predictions that one makes about a partner's future responses are severely restricted. In the preceding example, the man may predict that if he asks his wife to sit and talk about the issue that concerns him, she either will spend a long period of time in mutual self-disclosure with him or will refuse to talk with him at all. Because he sees these as the only options and does not want to face the total rejection in the latter case, he chooses to avoid mentioning the important topic to his wife in the future.

Beck et al.'s (1979) concept of *selective abstraction* is comparable to the biased perceptual process of selective attention described previously in this chapter. It involves paying attention to only part of the information available in a situation and drawing conclusions based only on that limited information.

The cognitive distortion of *overgeneralization* occurs when an individual draws a broad conclusion based on a limited number of incidents. A common example of this cognitive distortion is when a spouse incorrectly concludes that a specific aversive act by his or her partner reflects a broad negative personality trait or other general characteristic. In the example just cited, the wife made an overgeneralization that her husband's placing limitations on certain types of shared time and activities meant that he had no interest in sharing other types of activities with her as well. She seems to have formed a "persona" concerning her husband, shaped by the assumption many people hold (Nisbett & Ross, 1980) that human behavior is due to underlying traits. The persona then influenced her attributions and expectancies regarding her husband's behavior. On the one hand, her overgeneralization produced an attribution that her husband's behavior was due to a general lack of interest in her, and on the other hand, it produced an expectancy that he would not share leisure time with her in the future.

Concerning overgeneralization, Nisbett and Ross (1980) review social cognition research that indicates that lay "intuitive scientists" tend to make strong inferences based on small and often biased samples of data. People generally make poor use of statistical sampling theory, as it would be applied by a scientist conducting a systematic experiment. For example, in an experiment, the scientist attempts to draw a random sample so that his or her data are not biased in any particular way. To the extent that the sample is not random, the scientist restricts how much he or she makes generalizations concerning findings to larger populations. As noted earlier, lay observers also tend to assign heavy weights to "vivid" personal experiences (the concept of the "testimonial") in drawing general conclusions. In distressed relationships, the spouses often overgeneralize about unpleasant experiences they have with one another, for example, concluding, "He's an inconsiderate person" rather than "He behaves in an inconsiderate manner with me under particular circumstances." As described in Chapter 2, marital researchers have demonstrated that distressed spouses who communicate in negative ways with their partners often communicate in more positive and effective ways with strangers (e.g., Birchler et al., 1975), but the partners may fail to consider such situation specificity of behavior when they make overgeneralized inferences from a limited number of unpleasant events.

Magnification and *minimization* are cognitive distortions in which the significance of an event is overestimated or underestimated, respectively, to a notable degree. A man who forms the expectancy that his first big argument with his wife means that "our marriage probably won't last" is likely to be magnifying the significance of the argument. In contrast, the woman who concludes that success in asserting herself with intrusive in-laws "really means nothing, because they have run our lives for years" may be minimizing the importance of that event, thereby attributing her success to an unstable, specific cause (in some sense, a fluke). Both magnification and minimization can contribute to unrealistic assumptions (personae and scripts) by inflating or attenuating the correlations that an individual assumes exist among various characteristics and events. For example, most people might assume that there is at least a mild positive correlation between the degree to which a person criticizes his or her mate and the overall level of dissatisfaction that person feels about the relationship. However, the individual whose thinking tends to be characterized by maximization may inflate that correlation and assume that any level of criticism indicates that a spouse is likely to be very dissatisfied and uncommitted to his or her relationship.

The essence of all of the above cognitive distortions is that they involve inaccurate processing of the information available to a person. The determination of whether or not an individual has engaged in a cognitive distortion rests on a careful examination of evidence regarding the accuracy of the resulting perceptions and inferences. Procedures for evaluating evidence regarding possible cognitive distortions in spouses' thoughts are described in Chapters 6 and 9.

The information-processing errors involved in the cognitive distortions described by cognitive therapists (e.g., Beck et al., 1979; Burns, 1980) are not assumed to be instances of "pathological thinking" that are somehow qualitatively different from the thought processes of individuals who do not experience psychological and interpersonal problems. Rather, these perceptual and inferential errors appear to be quite common in the general population (as demonstrated by research on social cognition), and it may be the frequency with which they occur or the degree to which individuals test the validity of such cognitions that differentiates nonclinical from clinical groups of individuals.

THE RELATIONSHIPS AMONG PERCEPTIONS, ATTRIBUTIONS, EXPECTANCIES, ASSUMPTIONS, AND STANDARDS

Throughout this discussion of cognitions that can influence the development and maintenance of relationship problems, there have been references to links among perceptions, attributions, expectancies, assumptions, and standards. At this point, marital researchers have just begun to examine such associations (e.g., between assumptions and attributions), so future research will be needed in order to determine the degree to which these theoretical assumptions are valid. As a way of summarizing the present working model, the major relationships that seem likely among the five types of cognitions in this model will be listed. Subsequently, a hypothetical case example will illustrate how all of these cognitions can play roles in a specific marital problem.

As described earlier, *assumptions* (personae and scripts) serve as templates with which people organize and interpret information. The correlations that a person assumes among the characteristics and events in interpersonal relationships influence the inferences that he or she makes from observed to unobserved data. On the one hand, these assumed correlations lead the person to make *causal attributions* about a spouse's characteristics and behaviors, and on the other hand, they lead the person to form *expectancies* about the spouse's future behavior on the basis of current observed characteristics and behaviors.

Assumptions also can channel a person's *perceptions,* because they make particular information in a situation more relevant than other information. In other words, people notice data relevant to their preconceptions about people and situations. The individual who assumes that there is a high correlation between a person's degree of love for his or her partner and the degree to which that person makes personal sacrifices for that partner is likely to pay special attention to behaviors of his or her own spouse that do or do not indicate personal sacrifice.

Assumptions may lead to the development of *standards* about how people and relationships "should" be. The shift from an assumption about the way things are to a firm standard may occur when the individual attaches a good-versus-bad evaluation to an assumption about the nature of people or relationships. For example, based on personal learning experience, an individual may have developed the assumption described above that love is correlated with personal sacrifice. If the person then evaluates the association between love and sacrifice as a highly desirable aspect of close relationships, it becomes a standard against which spouses' behaviors toward one another are evaluated. When the standard becomes extreme and rigid (i.e., relationships "must" be this way), the original assumption has been transformed into what Ellis and his associates (cf. Ellis & Grieger, 1977) have labeled irrational beliefs.

A standard may not only be a rigidified version of an assumption, but it also may be the converse of an assumption. In other words, an individual may have come to assume that close relationships have a particular characteristic, but he or she may evaluate that characteristic quite negatively and develop a standard that a good relationship should *not* have that quality.

It also seems that standards can shape assumptions. Because we develop many of our standards about people and relationships indirectly (e.g., by being told by parents, teachers, books, and movies how things should be) rather than through first-hand life experiences, some of our assumptions about the way things *are* may follow from our preconceptions about the way things *should be.*

Standards can channel *perceptions* as a person scans situations for data that fit or do not fit his or her standard. For example, when a person holds to a standard that a loving spouse should make personal sacrifices for a partner whenever possible, he or she is likely to "track" instances of sacrifice or lack thereof by anyone with whom he or she has a close relationship. It also seems likely that a person's preconceptions about "good" versus "bad" relationships will bias his or her *attributions* about causes of marital events and *expectancies* about future events. For example, once a person's spouse has violated one aspect of the former's standards for a "good" partner, the individual may assume that the partner has other characteristics of "bad" spouses (whatever this individual conceives these to be). The person whose standard was violated then may attribute spouse behaviors to a variety of negative motives and traits and may predict a variety of negative behaviors from the spouse in the future.

Perceptions provide the data from which a person's assumptions and standards develop and are maintained. As noted earlier, an assumption or standard may be formed from an individual's own life experiences, or it can be learned from what other people tell the individual (Bandura, 1977). Any biases in a person's perceptions, due to the cognitive distortion of selective abstraction, to emotional states such as anger, to other conditions such as fatigue, or in childhood to limited cognitive development, may produce assumptions and standards that are inaccurate or inappropriate representations of people and intimate relationships. Fortunately for cognitive therapists, social cognition research also has indicated that people's basic assumptions can be modified through direct exposure to discrepant information and by inducing individuals to devise causal explanations for events that are consistent with a *new* assumption (Nisbett & Ross, 1980; Slusher & Anderson, in press).

Inferential errors such as those that occur in *attributions* and *expectancies* can produce assumptions and standards that are idiosyncratic to the individual and inappropriate as descriptions of the dynamics of either the person's own relationship or relationships in general. For example, one man formed a relationship with a woman who was an accountant. When his partner seemed insensitive to his feelings about important events in his life on two separate occasions, he not only attributed it to her background ("She cares about numbers, not people!"), but he also overgeneralized from the event, concerning both his wife and accountants in general ("She's a typical accountant. All they care about is numbers and logic, not the human side of relationships. You can't ever count on them when you have any emotional needs"). Because in fact his wife was an emotionally sensitive person who had failed to respond to her husband's needs due to extenuating circumstances, he had made inferential errors that included arbitrary inferences and overgeneralization. Unfortunately, his biased attributions had contributed to a basic assumption about members of a particular profession. Consequently, improvement in the relationship required modification not only of his biased attributions but also of this assumption.

Inaccurate *expectancies* and *attributions* also can shape assumptions when they become self-fulfilling prophecies (i.e., elicit the outcomes they predict). In the preceding example, if the man now predicts that his partner will fail to be emotionally supportive, he may behave toward her in a manner that blocks any urges she has to be supportive and instead elicits rejection from her. Over time, the man will receive fairly consistent "data" that will reinforce an assumption about insensitivity in his wife or accountants in general.

These examples are not meant to cover all of the possible links among perceptions, attributions, expectancies, assumptions, and standards, but they are meant to illustrate how all five types of cognition can influence the others. Given the theoretical interdependence of these cognitive phenomena, it is important that our assessment and treatment procedures take all of them into account. On the one hand, interventions aimed at one type of dysfunctional cognition might produce therapeutic changes in other types of cognition, but clinicians also should be concerned about the possibility that efforts to modify one form of cognition (e.g., attributions) will have limited effects if specific efforts are not made to change other dysfunctional cognitions (e.g., extreme standards). With the current lack of empirical knowledge about such issues, it seems prudent for therapists to examine the full range of cognitions that might be contributing to a couple's problems and to plan interventions to modify all forms of inappropriate cognitions that have been identified.

Multiple Dysfunctional Cognitions: A Case Example

The following is a brief example of how perceptions, attributions, expectancies, assumptions, and standards all may play a role in a relationship problem. A heterosexual couple (both aged 50) presented for therapy with a complaint that the male had periodic erectile dysfunction that had increased in frequency over the past year. Medical assessment had produced no indication of organic factors, but a careful cognitive assessment revealed that both spouses' cognitions seemed to play a role at least in the maintenance, if not the etiology, of the problem.

In regard to *perceptions*, over time the male selectively noticed his own sexual arousal cues, as well as any signs of distress from his partner. He increasingly failed to notice signs of pleasure from his partner, as well as pleasurable sensations from touching his partner. Over time, the female selectively noticed whenever her partner did not respond with signs of pleasure and arousal to her touching, and she failed to notice pleasurable sensations from touching her partner.

The male's *attributions* about the causes of his sexual problem primarily involved the idea that it was a symptom of general physical and mental decline associated with aging. He saw decline in his athletic abilities as another sign of such a decline. In contrast to the male's views, the female tended to attribute her partner's erectile dysfunction to a loss of sexual interest (and perhaps even love) for her. When she asked him about his feelings for her and he responded affirmatively, she still was not reassured, owing to their chronic unpleasant sexual experiences.

The male developed negative *expectancies* regarding the couple's sexual interactions, such as "If she wants sex and approaches me, I won't get aroused (get an erection)." The female also developed negative expectancies, such as "If I touch him, he won't find it interesting or pleasurable." Over time, as the couple's sexual interactions became more tense and dominated by self-consciousness, these expectancies became more accurate. As the partners elicited negative responses from one another, the expectancies became self-fulfilling prophecies.

The male's responses to his sexual problem were influenced by his *assumption* that a normal, healthy male becomes aroused automatically by his sexual partner. His partner's responses to the problem were shaped by her assumption that sexual arousal is a reliable sign of love.

Both members of the couple were influenced by their *standards* about the way sex "should" be. The male had long held to a standard that a good sexual partner always satisfies his partner, and the female believed that a lovable, sexually desirable person always should be able to elicit sexual interest from a partner.

This example was not intended to suggest that in any relationship problem all five types of cognition are bound to be distorted and play roles in the couple's difficulties. However, it is important that clinicians assess all five forms and develop treatment plans that are designed to modify dysfunctional cognitions of any sort that contribute to the couple's problems.

THE STATUS OF RESEARCH ON MARITAL COGNITIONS

The bulk of recent research on the role of cognitions in marital dysfunction has focused on the identification of biased attributions that differentiate distressed from nondistressed couples. As noted earlier, a substantial body of evidence is accumulating that links particular types of attributions to marital distress, and those findings have had important implications for identifying treatment targets in clinical practice. At this point, initial research also has demonstrated links between unrealistic relationship assumptions and standards, on the one hand, and marital problems, on the other hand (Eidelson & Epstein, 1982; Epstein & Eidelson, 1981; Fincham & Bradbury, 1987), but there is a need for additional research to investigate the range of dysfunctional assumptions and standards further and to develop ways of measuring the more complex "dynamic" interpersonal schemata such as personae and scripts which are described in the social cognition literature (cf., Arias & Beach, 1987; Nisbett & Ross, 1980). Further attention to such cognitive structures is warranted owing to the important roles that they play in cognitive models of intra- and interpersonal problems.

Baucom, Epstein, Sayers, and Sher (1989) have argued that theory, research, and practice concerning cognitive factors in marital dysfunction have lacked clear direction because of the narrow focus on attributions. Consequently, it is important that all five types of cognitions described in this chapter (perceptions, attributions, expectancies, assumptions, and standards) be considered in the development of (a) theoretical models concerning marital interaction, (b) measures of marital cognitions, and (c) marital cognitive restructuring procedures. As described in Chapter 6, the few existing questionnaires for assessing spouses' cognitions focus on attributions and schemata (assumptions and standards). Furthermore, the existing treatment outcome studies that have evaluated the effectiveness of cognitive restructuring with distressed couples (see Chapter 12) have used interventions focused only on attributions and schemata as well (Baucom et al., 1989; Epstein & Baucom, 1988). There is a clear need for more basic research concerning what cognitive variables influence marital functioning and what specific types of interventions are most effective in altering each form of cognition.

Efforts to refine our understanding of marital cognitions should also investigate variations *within* each category of cognition (e.g., attributions, assumptions). For example, attributions can be assessed in terms of *dimensions* (e.g., global-specific, stable-unstable) with which spouses describe causes of marital events, or in terms of *content* (e.g., malicious intent, lack of love). Also, spouses may hold standards and assumptions that apply specifically to their own relationships, or more broadly to marriages in general. Thus, refined conceptualizations and assessments of marital cognitions are needed in order to (a) select specific cognitions to be modified, (b) provide adequate evaluation of cognitive changes that occur due to therapy, and (c) make comparisons among empirical studies. Because the research studies reviewed in this chapter and Chapter 12 used varied cognitive measures and the treatment studies focused on various types of cognitions, it is difficult to account for different results. The preliminary studies of marital cognitions have been encouraging, but clinicians should apply cognitive assessment and intervention techniques with caution until theoretical models and empirical knowledge catch up to the enthusiasm for practical applications.

CONCLUSION

Clinical and research findings regarding distorted and inappropriate perceptions, attributions, expectancies, assumptions, and standards demonstrate how people commonly make particular types of errors in processing the information available to them. As noted earlier, these do not constitute pathological processes, but most often represent poor use of human information-processing capacities that at other times are used to produce sophisticated and impressive accomplishments. In other words, humans have the potential to make more accurate observations and inferences than they often do make, and the limitations seem to be due at least in part to underdevelopment and underutilization of cognitive skills. The identification of specific cognitive errors by social psychological researchers and by clinicians such as Beck et al. (1979) points to particular targets for therapeutic intervention. The cognitive assessment and intervention procedures that are described in this book are intended to identify and alter clients' information-processing errors, so that spouses as lay intuitive scientists can maximize accuracy in their perceptions and interpretations of the events in their intimate relationships.

4

Affective Factors in
Marital Dysfunction

The family is the setting where people are most likely to have negative as well as positive emotional experiences in their lives, and where they are likely to have their most intense emotional experiences (Berscheid, 1983). As described in Chapter 1, a cognitive-behavioral approach to marital and other intimate relationships views emotion as a major component of functional and dysfunctional relationships, which simultaneously influences and is influenced by cognitive and behavioral factors. On the one hand, emotions constitute part of the happiness or distress that leads spouses to be satisfied with their relationship or to desire change. A great deal of cognitive-behavioral marital therapy is devoted to identifying and modifying cognitive and behavioral aspects of a couple's interaction that have typically elicited unpleasant emotional responses and that have decreased positive emotions.

On the other hand, as will be described below, emotional states can influence spouses' cognitions about each other, as well as their actions toward each other. Consequently, a therapist's ability to understand and modify the sources of a couple's distress depends on a careful assessment of the range and intensities of emotional responses the partners have regarding marital interactions, as well as the impacts that emotions have on those interactions.

This chapter describes four interrelated aspects of affect in intimate relationships which should be the foci of the marital therapist: (a) the overall degrees of positive and negative emotions that an individual experiences toward his or her partner and their marriage, (b) the degree of difficulty an individual has in recognizing his or her emotions and their causes, (c) the degree to which each spouse overtly expresses emotions of which he or she is aware, and (d) the presence of emotional reactions that interfere with adaptive functioning between partners. The roles that cognitive and behavioral factors appear to have in these aspects of marital emotions also are noted.

AMOUNT AND INTENSITY OF POSITIVE AND NEGATIVE AFFECT

Popular conceptions of close relationships tend to emphasize that intimacy is correlated with more frequent and more intense positive emotions between the partners, as well as fewer and less intense negative emotions. Berscheid (1983) notes that this view also has been shared by many marital researchers, who measure the intensities of positive versus negative emotion as an important index of marital adjustment. Although the positive and negative emotions experienced by spouses often can be valid indicators of their satisfaction with their relationships (e.g., measures of affect tend to differentiate clinical from nonclinical couples [Sade & Notarius, 1985]), relying solely on emotion as an index of intimacy (versus a lack of involvement) has a number of limitations. As described by Berscheid, couples who experience a high magnitude of *positive* affect probably have close relationships by any definition. However, there also are many clinical reports of couples who have stable relationships in which there is a high level of *negative* affect, and in which the spouses grieve if their relationship is ended by death or separation. Furthermore, the absence of any strong positive or negative emotion between two partners may reflect a relationship wherein daily interactions run quite smoothly and thus produce few events that would be expected to elicit emotional reactions.

According to the model proposed by Berscheid and her colleagues (Kelley et al., 1983), emotion occurs when an event interrupts an individual's typical chain of behaviors in a particular situation. For example, one spouse routinely may engage in a sequence of behaviors on Sunday mornings, including getting out of bed early, going jogging, taking a shower, and eating breakfast while watching a particular news program on television. Typically, the partner's behaviors may "mesh" well with this sequence; that is, the partner also gets out of bed early and then reads the Sunday newspaper until the couple has breakfast together. However, on a particular Sunday morning, when the alarm clock awakens the couple, the partner might interrupt the other person's routine behavioral sequence by asking him or her to help with a task instead of going jogging. The person whose behavioral sequence was interrupted is then likely to have an emotional response.

Berscheid (1983) proposes that couples who have established interaction patterns in which there is much interdependence but few interruptions of each other's behavioral chains (which necessitates a considerable degree of involvement and coordination between the parties) would be expected to have quiescent relationships rather than high levels of positive emotion. Thus, the absence of strong positive emotion might reflect a relationship devoid of caring and intimacy, but it also might reflect a smoothly running relationship between two people who are involved intimately in each other's lives. Consequently, when a marital therapist examines the degrees of positive and negative emotion in a couple's relationship, it is important to take into account other factors as well in evaluating the status of that relationship.

Berscheid (1983) notes that the popular assumption that close relationships are characterized by frequent and strong positive emotions, as well as by an absence of negative emotions, leads many people to make unfavorable appraisals of relationships that do not have these qualities. On the one hand, an individual might conclude that a quiescent relationship lacks depth of involvement, and on the other hand, a relationship characterized by a mixture of positive and negative emotion might be viewed as being in danger of disintegration.

Another popular assumption about affect in close relationships is that intimacy allows the strong emotions of courtship to persist indefinitely. Clinical evidence that passionate emotions naturally decline over time to a milder "afterglow" is consistent with Berscheid's model in which spouses interrupt each other's behavioral chains less as they get to know each other better and sources of novelty in the relationship decrease. Unfortunately, some individuals become quite distressed when they observe such a shift in the intensity of emotion in their relationships. Their distress may involve sadness (or even depression) at the perceived decline in the relationship or anxiety associated with a perception that the entire relationship might be in jeopardy.

One of the hallmarks of "marital enrichment" programs that have been designed primarily to strengthen nondysfunctional relationships (see reviews by Hof & Miller, 1981; L'Abate & McHenry, 1983) is a focus on increasing intimacy between spouses through the facilitation of awareness and sharing of feelings (especially positive ones). A large percentage of the millions of couples who have attended such programs have reported experiencing emotional "highs" in which strong positive feelings about their partners and marriages were rekindled. Although such experiences no doubt are quite pleasant, often the changes appear to be short-term. In the absence of the conditions that produced the high (e.g., very enthusiastic program leaders, the presence of other highly motivated couples, often a very pleasant atmosphere in a resort setting, removal from the stresses of daily life), there is great potential for a precipitous drop in warm, intimate feelings between spouses at some point following their participation in the program (Hof, Epstein, & Miller, 1980). If couples have come to value strong positive feelings as an index of growth and health in their marriages, they may become quite distressed when the high wears off after a marital enrichment experience (Doherty, McCabe, & Ryder, 1978). In fact, Lester and Doherty (1983) found that almost 1 in 10 couples who had participated in marriage encounter weekends (an average of four years previously) reported that the experience had negative effects on their relationships, particularly frustration when needs identified during the weekend were not fulfilled when the couple returned to their daily life together. Doherty and Walker (1982) also documented "casualties" of marriage encounter programs; couples whose relationships deteriorated after their participation. Hof, Epstein, and Miller (1980) suggested that leaders of enrichment programs prepare couples carefully for such shifts in their emotions, but they also stressed the potential for using enrichment experiences as an adjunct to marital therapy, to help increase motivation in clinical couples whose typical interactions include few positive behaviors and emotions.

Thus, possible cognitive distortions regarding the significance of particular emotions (or lack of emotions) have the potential to add negative emotional experiences to a couple's marriage. In addition, the resulting distress might lead spouses to behave in dysfunctional ways (e.g., pressing a partner for reassurances of love; seeking more intense emotional experiences through an extramarital affair). Consequently, marital therapists and their clients must carefully evaluate both the current levels of positive and negative emotion between two partners *and* any shifts in those emotions over the course of the relationship.

In addition to examining the *frequency* and *intensity* of spouses' negative emotional reactions, it is important for the clinician to differentiate among various *kinds* of negative emotions that clients may be experiencing. The emotional aspects of marital distress can differ markedly among individuals who seek marital therapy. For example, two people may have equal scores on questionnaires assessing global distress (reviewed in

Chapter 7), but one person's distress may consist primarily of anger toward the partner whereas the other individual's distress may be a mixture of depression regarding the perceived failure of the marriage and anxiety regarding an expectancy that a stressful divorce lies ahead.

In a cognitive-behavioral evaluation of a couple's marital problems, it is quite important to determine the specific nature of the emotions experienced by each spouse, for at least two reasons. First, cognitive theorists (e.g., Beck, 1976) have proposed that there are different factors associated with different emotions (e.g., in Beck's model thoughts of loss lead to sadness or depression, thoughts concerning the danger of future harm produce anxiety, and thoughts of injustice produce anger). Recent research (e.g., Beck, Brown, Steer, Eidelson, & Riskind, 1987) has indicated that emotions such as depression and anxiety are indeed associated with different cognitive themes, although further work is needed to establish whether there is actually a causal link between the cognitions and emotions. Whether or not the link is causal, therapists need to be aware of the specific factors associated with the emotions experienced by each individual spouse, so that therapeutic interventions can be tailored to the particular type of distress each person presents. For example, if an individual's marital distress consists primarily of anger, cognitive interventions would be more likely to be focused on ways in which the person perceives the partner as acting unfairly and unjustly. In contrast, the person whose distress is primarily depression may need special attention to cognitions that focus on failure and hopelessness regarding the marriage.

Second, different emotions may lead to different behaviors toward a partner. For example, an individual who feels strong anger toward his or her partner may be likely to behave in aggressive and vengeful ways. In contrast, a person who experiences strong anxiety regarding marital interactions may be more likely to *avoid* the partner if the anxiety involves an expectation of aversive interaction, or to *cling* to the partner if he or she anticipates losing the partner. Thus, not only are different emotions associated with different behaviors, but the same emotion can be associated with different behaviors, depending on the cognitions involved. In cases such as these, different interventions would be needed to alter aggressive, avoidant, and dependent behavior patterns.

RECOGNITION OF EMOTIONS AND THEIR DETERMINANTS

Individuals vary considerably in the degrees to which they are *aware* of their emotions, able to differentiate among various emotions, and aware of cognitions and behaviors that elicit particular emotional states. Consequently, when one spouse fails to communicate to the other about emotions, one possible source of the problem can be a lack of awareness, rather than a deficit in communication skills. Also, when an individual *is* aware of his or her emotional reactions during interactions with the partner but is unaware of their causes, the result can be a sense of helplessness and pessimism about the potential for reducing the unpleasant experiences. Spouses entering marital therapy commonly have a very diffuse view of the thoughts and behaviors that elicit their strong negative emotions, and their resulting sense that their lives are out of control can lead them to use very limited and inappropriate approaches for stopping the negative feelings. For example, some individuals who experience unpleasant levels of anger toward their partners and who do not understand either the specific actions of the partner or their own cognitive appraisals of those actions that produce the anger decide to withdraw from most interactions with the partner. In other words, in order to remove themselves from whatever might be causing their anger, they distance themselves from all possible sources of the emotion. However, in so doing, they fail to change the upsetting behaviors or thoughts, and they create a new problem of alienation in the relationship.

Factors That Reduce Awareness of Emotions

Several factors appear to reduce spouses' awareness of their emotions and their causes. When an assessment of a couple indicates that an individual lacks such awareness, identification of the causal factors can help in the planning of appropriate interventions.

Level of cognitive complexity.

Based on Kelly's (1955) pioneering work on cognitive complexity, theorists who focus on interpersonal relationships (e.g., Duck, 1977; Markman, 1984) have proposed that marital dysfunction may result when two individuals have different sets of constructs for conceptualizing aspects of their life together, or if one partner's set of constructs is more complex (e.g., varied) than the other's. Kelly described how an individual's "personal constructs" include the dimensions with which he or she categorizes and understands life events. For example, based on past experiences with people, one individual may use dimensions such as "friendly-unfriendly," "talkative-quiet," and "disclosing-private" to categorize others, whereas another individual might apply dimensions such as "assertive-inhibited," "powerful-weak," and "decisive-indecisive." The former person tends to notice and base evaluations on characteristics that deal with affiliative tendencies, and the latter person focuses more on aspects of interpersonal power. If these two people form a relationship, their different views of interactions might be an important source of misunderstanding and conflict.

People appear to vary in how differentiated their constructs are concerning emotional experiences. Some people tend to make few distinctions among emotions other than a gross pleasant-versus-unpleasant judgment, whereas other individuals apply a rich set of dimensions for describing varieties of emotion. For example, the former person might conceptualize his or her response to unwittingly revealing a family secret at a party as "I felt lousy about it." In contrast, the latter person might describe an emotional state of "mild shame, pretty guilty, anxious about how others would react, irritated with myself, and resentful that we have 'skeletons in our closet.' "

When one spouse tends to apply a complex set of constructs* regarding emotions and the partner does not, the former may voice complaints such as, "My husband/wife doesn't deal with his/her feelings." The spouse who is more cognitively complex also may experience a lack of empathy from the partner, who seems insensitive to the nuances of the former individual's emotional experiences. On the other hand, the person who has fewer constructs available for categorizing emotions may experience his or her partner as making obsessive distinctions among mood states and making unreasonable demands for mutual emotional expression and empathy. The therapist who is faced with two partners who have a notable discrepancy in cognitive complexity regarding emotions most likely will need to attend to it in some manner, either by helping the couple adjust to their differences in processing emotional data or by decreasing the "gap" between them. Chapter 10 describes some interventions, such as emotional expressiveness training, that can expand individuals' constructs for differentiating various emotions and communicating such distinctions to their partners.

---

*The number of constructs is not the only definition used for cognitive complexity, but a description of alternative definitions is beyond the scope of this chapter. For current purposes, examining differences in the numbers and content of two spouses' constructs concerning emotion generally is sufficient for identifying sources of misunderstanding between the two people.

Assumptions about emotions and their causes.

A second factor that can reduce awareness of emotions involves popular assumptions about the determinants of emotion which often differ markedly from the assumptions of a cognitive mediation model. One common assumption is that emotions are caused directly by events (e.g., "My wife made me angry by what she said"). Although spouses may have conditioned emotional responses to each other's behaviors, when individuals assume that the causes of all or most of their emotions reside outside themselves, they are likely to overlook highly relevant internal cognitive data. A second common assumption is that emotions build inside a person and must be released in some manner in order to maintain the person's well-being (an hydraulic model of emotion). Such an assumption may lead an individual to vent emotions indiscriminately in an attempt to achieve catharsis. For example, one husband in marital therapy stated that he needed to vent his anger at his wife by screaming, so that he would not develop ulcers or high blood pressure. However, research evidence indicates that ventilation of anger sometimes produces temporary decreases in arousal but tends to increase rather than decrease future anger and aggression toward other people (Patterson, 1982). Similarly, clinical data suggest that continued ventilation of depressed and anxious feelings can maintain those states, and active interventions are needed to reduce them (Beck et al., 1979).

Another assumption often associated with the catharsis model is the idea that the expression of emotions cannot be controlled. For example, Neidig and Friedman (1984) describe how many verbally and physically abusive individuals assume that once they begin to experience anger they cannot control the degree or manner of its expression. However, as noted by Stuart (1980), even though initial anger responses to frustrating stimuli may be at least partly reflexive, the continuation and escalation of an individual's anger to a high level generally involves a *decision* to commit oneself to the anger, for any of a number of reasons (e.g., to inflict pain in retribution for past wrongs committed by the partner). Except for individuals who have severe impulse control disorders, most people exercise considerable control over their emotions in order to avoid undesirable consequences. For example, many individuals who vent anger at their spouses choose to inhibit expressing their anger at their employers, in order to protect their jobs. However, many spouses are not aware of such patterns and truly believe that they are provoked by their partners into expressing their emotions. Thus, this is another assumption that can impede spouses' abilities to identify the actual causes of their emotions during marital interactions.

The previously described assumption that a decrease in positive emotion between partners is due to a loss of love or caring in the relationship also can contribute to a lack of awareness of the actual causes of such emotional shifts. Marital therapists often need to stress to couples that decreases in positive emotion between partners commonly result from chronic negative behavioral interactions, and that it is important to see whether more positive emotions return as the spouses substitute more positive behaviors for the distressing ones.

Standards about the appropriateness and usefulness of emotions.

Some individuals' standards about what constitutes "good" behavior include the belief that the experience or expression of emotions is neither useful nor appropriate. Much has been written about the differential socialization of males and females that might account for the tendency of males to be less expressive of emotion and to desire their female partners to be less emotional (Sade & Notarius, 1985; Sloan & L'Abate, 1985). Traditional sex roles tend to lead many men to see emotion as interfering with logical problem-solving efforts, and many women to see a male partner's task-oriented behavior as detracting from intimacy in their relationships.

Gottman and Levenson (1986) cite research on autonomic nervous system reactivity as a basis for suggesting that males may find it more adaptive to inhibit emotional expression because they tend to have stronger autonomic responses to stressful events (such as marital conflict) and recover from stresses more slowly than females. Although much more research is needed to identify the bases of individual differences in emotionality, clinicians are likely to encounter individuals of both sexes who believe that attending to emotions has serious drawbacks. Such individuals may pay little attention to the range and intensity of their emotions, or to factors that elicit emotions. In order to encourage these individuals to focus more on affect, therapists are likely to need to modify their clients' standards about emotion.

For some individuals, past unpleasant experiences are an important source of standards regarding the inappropriateness of feeling and expressing emotions. For example, some people fear an aversive and maladaptive loss of control (e.g., "going crazy," harming another person) if they allow themselves to experience emotional arousal. These fears sometimes result from memories of past instances in which the individual either lost some degree of emotional or behavioral control in some way that had unpleasant consequences or observed negative consequences when other people lost control in some manner. Such individuals may exhibit selective inattention to cues of their own emotional arousal.

A history of relationship tranquility.

As described by Berscheid (1983), spouses whose two individual chains of behaviors have become well "meshed" (i.e., synchronized) may experience few strong positive or negative emotions within their relationship, because emotional arousal is most likely when one person's behavior interrupts the other's ingrained behavioral sequence. To the extent that this is the case for a couple, the spouses may have had few opportunities to sharpen their abilities to differentiate types of emotion and identify their causes. Therefore, when an incident finally occurs that does elicit emotion, these individuals may be ill prepared to understand and express their mood states.

INADEQUATE AND DYSFUNCTIONAL EXPRESSION OF EMOTION

As is evident from the preceding discussion, many factors can affect the awareness of emotions, thereby accounting for an individual's failure to express feelings to a partner. When a clinician has determined that a spouse is indeed aware of his or her emotions (perhaps by means of systematic interviewing that probes for the person's affective responses to various life events), but has observed that the person fails to express emotions to the partner, the next question that must be answered is whether this represents a communication skill deficit or a *choice* not to share the feelings.

One clue for determining whether a client has a skill deficit or whether he or she has chosen not to be expressive is whether or not the individual who does not express emotion to the partner can do so with the therapist and other people. Research studies such as those by Birchler et al. (1975) and Vincent et al. (1975) have demonstrated that although distressed spouses behave more negatively with their partners than do nondistressed spouses, they behave as positively as nondistressed spouses when talking with strangers. Consequently, it is important to determine whether an individual's problematic communication with his or her partner is part of a broader difficulty for the individual or whether it is specific to interactions with the partner. This aspect of the assessment of emotional expression is discussed in Chapter 7.

Several of the factors that can inhibit the expression of emotion are similar to those that can impede a person's awareness of emotion. First, some individuals devalue emotion and prefer rational thought; therefore, they do not consider it worthwhile to spend time talking about feelings. Second, an individual who expects that emotional expression will have harmful consequences (due to memories of first-hand negative experiences or to messages conveyed by parents and other people) may decide not to share feelings. For example, if an individual's self-disclosure about personal feelings had been used as "ammunition" by another person during a past argument, the former may decide that it is too dangerous to be so expressive and vulnerable. Similarly, a person may be unexpressive because of an expectancy that expressing *any* emotion will lead to a total loss of control over his or her emotions or behavior.

Basic assumptions and standards such as those described in Chapter 2 also can lead spouses to choose not to express emotions. For example, an individual who holds the standard that loving partners should be able to read each other's mind may refuse to describe feelings to his or her partner which the partner "should" be able to sense.

Deficits in Expressive Skills

The communication training provided in most behaviorally oriented marital therapy (e.g., Baucom, 1985; Emmelkamp, van der Helm, MacGillavry, & van Zanten, 1984; Gottman, Notarius, Gonso, & Markman, 1976; Jacobson & Margolin, 1979; Stuart, 1980) as well as in programs designed for marital enrichment (e.g., Guerney, 1977; Hof & Miller, 1981; L'Abate, 1977; Markman, Floyd, Stanley, & Jamieson, 1984; Miller, Nunnally, & Wackman, 1975) includes a focus on specific skills for expressing emotions. This emphasis on emotional expression follows from research findings that distressed spouses exchange more negative affect than nondistressed spouses (Schaap, 1984) and from a basic theoretical assumption that the sharing of feelings facilitates intimacy in a relationship.

Although at times marital therapists have taken the "communication produces intimacy" assumption to an extreme (i.e., the more emotional the expression, the better), a number of important cautions have been noted concerning appropriate kinds and degrees of feeling expression. Stuart (1980) stresses that unbridled expression of thoughts and feelings can hurt and alienate a partner, and he recommends that spouses use "measured honesty" (tact regarding what, when, and how to express thoughts and feelings) with each other. Sloan and L'Abate (1985) note that members of couples tend to find the expression of hurt feelings and vulnerability more intimate than the expression of anger. Guerney (1977) stresses that whenever an individual expresses negative feelings to a partner, he or she also should include a statement of any positive feelings about the situation. The goal of this approach is to communicate acceptance and caring for the partner, and to maximize the partner's receptivity to the entire message.

Another caution concerning the promotion of emotional expressiveness concerns the issue of whether maximal intimacy is a reasonable or desirable goal for all couples (L'Abate & McHenry, 1983). On the one hand, it is not clear that all couples *can* achieve a high level of intimacy if given competent assistance, and on the other hand, it is not clear that all couples *want* to achieve a high level of emotional intimacy. Raush et al. (1974) identified a group of couples who reported satisfaction in their marriages in spite of the fact that their communication patterns included a good deal of avoidance of direct expression. Therapists should be aware of their own personal values about emotional intimacy and should try to avoid imposing those values on couples who find alternative ways of relating satisfactory.

Criteria for effective expression.

Programs designed to foster effective expression of emotion (as well as thoughts) typically focus on specific target communication behaviors assumed to be functional and others assumed to be dysfunctional. For example, Guerney's (1977) Relationship Enhancement program presents a set of guidelines for expressing messages, including stating one's emotions as subjective rather than the absolute truth, describing emotions as specifically as possible, and making brief statements that one's partner will be likely to remember. (A detailed description of these guidelines and the procedures of Guerney's program is provided in Chapter 10.)

Both negative verbal and nonverbal behaviors have been found to be more characteristic of communication in distressed than in nondistressed couples, with nonverbal behavior providing the stronger discrimination of the two groups (Sade & Notarius, 1985; Schaap, 1984). The nonverbal communication of distressed couples has been found to be more negative than that of nondistressed couples even when the spouses were instructed to fake positive interaction (Vincent et al., 1979), a finding that has been attributed to the greater difficulty of masking nonverbal cues of emotion (Sade & Notarius, 1985). Consequently, the roles of nonverbal behaviors such as voice tone, body gestures, posture, eye contact, and facial expressions in the accurate communication of emotion between spouses have been investigated, and communication training programs typically coach spouses in the use of nonverbal behavior to express emotions.

Stuart (1980) also stresses the importance of identifying inconsistencies between verbal and nonverbal expressions of emotion (e.g., when an individual tells his spouse through clenched teeth, "I am *not* angry"). Communication training programs commonly assist spouses in reducing discrepancies between their verbal and nonverbal messages by coaching them in producing behaviors that best reflect their subjective emotional experiences. For example, in the above example, a therapist might point out to the husband that his facial expression conveyed some negative affect, which did not appear to be compatible with his verbal denial of anger. The therapist and client then could explore whether the nonverbal behavior might reflect subtle feelings of which the client had been unaware, or whether the facial expression seemed to reflect another emotion (e.g., anxiety) which had been apparent to the client. This process tends to make clients more sensitive to cues of their emotional states and more accountable in communicating emotions to others.

Compared to nondistressed spouses, distressed spouses have been found to exhibit higher frequencies of a number of nonverbal behaviors considered to be expressions of negative emotion (e.g., staccato voice, arms akimbo) and lower frequencies of nonverbal behaviors considered to reflect positive emotion (e.g., warm voice, empathic facial expression, open posture, sitting closer together) (Schaap, 1984). Gottman and Levenson (1986) note that recent technological advances in the assessment of voice qualities and facial expressions, including Ekman and Friesen's (1978) Facial Action Coding System, permit reliable nonverbal identification of emotional states.

Noller (1980, 1981, 1984) conducted a series of studies of the encoding (sending) and receiving (decoding) of nonverbal behavior between spouses. Using trained coders to determine whether or not messages were encoded correctly by one partner and decoded correctly by the other partner, Noller found that the communications of couples low in marital adjustment were rated as good less often than those of better-adjusted couples. This difference was due primarily to the poor encoding and decoding by males in the low-marital-adjustment group. Wives in both groups were better at encoding messages than were husbands, particularly when sending positive messages. Studies by Noller (1981) and Gottman and Porterfield (1981) indicated that the relatively poor decoding by distressed males was specific to interactions with their wives. The fact that these men decoded nonverbal behavior as well as nondistressed men when receiving messages from strangers suggests that they do not lack decoding skills, and that some other factor is likely to be impeding effective use of their communication skills. This again raises the issue that improvement of couples' communication of emotion often calls for more than skill training. In particular, it has been proposed (Revenstorf, 1984; Sade & Notarius, 1985) that strong emotional arousal elicited in the interactions of distressed couples can interfere with effective sending and receiving of messages about thoughts and emotions. To the extent that this process does occur, marital therapists would need to focus on reducing disruptive levels of emotion in couples' interactions, as well as teaching them better expressive and listening skills.

Inappropriate expressiveness.

As noted earlier, some spouses tend to use little or no tact in expressing thoughts and feelings. Such individuals commonly need assistance in choosing what and when (or *if*) to share particular feelings with their partners. They also may tend to express emotions in an aggressive rather than an assertive manner (e.g., expressing anger through criticism and threats rather than noncoercive statements of feeling). Consequently, it often is as important to identify *excesses* of dysfunctional emotional expression as it is to identify deficits in effective communication. Procedures for assessing positive and negative communication behaviors and for altering them are described in Chapters 7 and 10, respectively.

Revenstorf (1984) notes that the expression of emotion can have instrumental value for the expresser, in that it can produce changes in the individual's environment. A common example of this phenomenon is when an individual vents anger, and another family member then complies with his or her wishes. Spouses either knowingly or unknowingly may continue to express particular emotions because their partners' responses reinforce them for doing so. Commonly it is not the partner's intention to reinforce the expression of negative emotions, but the process occurs nevertheless. Therefore, it is important that the marital therapist determine the degree to which problematic expression of emotion might be due to reinforcement patterns within a couple rather than to skill deficits.

Deficits in Listening Skills

The communication of emotion between spouses requires not only effective expression by one partner, but also effective listening by the other.

Listening is an active process in which an individual must concentrate his or her attention on incoming verbal and nonverbal messages, interpret the meanings of those messages (including any inconsistencies between verbal and nonverbal "channels"), and determine what would be an appropriate response to the partner. Consequently, good listening cannot be taken for granted, and many members of distressed couples exhibit deficits in listening skills.

One spouse's failure to listen well to the other's expressions of emotion can have a negative impact on the couple's interactions, because it can lead the listener to respond inappropriately to the partner who has expressed emotions. For example, if one spouse expresses a great deal of hurt and also some anger at the partner, but the partner focuses on the anger and responds in a nasty manner, the expresser may then retaliate with more anger, and an argument may escalate quickly between the two people. However, if the listener had paid more attention to the hurt feelings and discussed those empathically with the expresser, the expresser may have felt accepted and the anger may not have escalated. Thus, the partner's poor listening not only failed to address the other's needs (e.g., some form of support to ease the hurt), but it also shifted the emotional tone of the couple's interaction in a negative direction.

Guerney's (1977) Relationship Enhancement program focuses on a set of behaviors assumed to be characteristic of good listening. In Guerney's approach, a good listener exhibits behaviors similar to those that Rogers (1957) stressed in empathic, nondirective therapy. The empathic listener's goals are (a) to gain an accurate understanding of the expresser's subjective thoughts and feelings, (b) to communicate that understanding by summarizing and restating the partner's thoughts and feelings, and (c) to communicate acceptance of the partner's right to have those thoughts and emotions by means of nonverbal behaviors (e.g., concerned and accepting voice tone). The behaviors expected of an empathic listener are detailed in Chapter 10 and in Guerney's (1977) book. These include a number of behaviors that the listener should *not* exhibit (e.g., making suggestions and judgments about the speaker's messages), because they interfere with the ability to listen, communicate a lack of acceptance to the speaker, or shift the speaker's attention away from the thoughts and emotions that he or she was expressing.

Factors that impede listening.

It often is difficult for an individual to pay close, unbiased attention to messages from a partner because of thoughts, emotions, and behaviors that interfere with listening. Among the *cognitions* that impede objective listening are basic assumptions (e.g., "There's a right way and a wrong way to deal with this issue, and if I'm right, then he must be wrong"), standards (e.g., "She has no right to be sad about our day together, because I did everything I could to make it a good day"), attributions (e.g., "She's crying just to make me look bad"), and expectancies (e.g., "His jealousy will make him pressure me into being no more than a prisoner in our own home, so I won't listen to how he feels"). Concerning *emotions*, Revenstorf (1984) has described how once spouses become aroused by negative emotions during an interaction their arousal often triggers ingrained dysfunctional behavioral patterns (e.g., withdrawal, escalation of aggression) that are incompatible with listening to each other's messages. In such circumstances, any good listening skills that the partners possess are abandoned.

Among the *behaviors* that can interfere with listening, many couples try to carry on a variety of tasks at the same time that they are discussing important emotional material. When spouses are working on household chores, taking care of their children, or watching television, their attention simply cannot be focused fully on either expressing feelings clearly or listening well enough to understand each other's subjective experiences and communicate their understanding. As noted earlier, Guerney (1977) has identified other behaviors (e.g., expressing one's own opinions when listening to those of one's partner) that a listener should avoid.

Thus, in order to understand the sources of difficulty that a couple is having regarding the expression of emotions, one needs to take into account cognitive, affective, and behavioral aspects of the couple's relationship. These three aspects of marital interaction are interrelated in complex ways, and to overlook any of them is to form an incomplete picture of marital dysfunction.

EMOTIONS THAT INTERFERE WITH ADAPTIVE FUNCTIONING

Among the varied emotions that spouses experience in their daily interactions, several stand out as having the potential to disrupt the functioning of a relationship: anger, depression, anxiety, and jealousy. This section describes empirical and clinical evidence regarding the roles that these emotions can play in marital dysfunction.

Anger

Anger is such a common characteristic of distressed relationships that in many cases therapists do not consider it a problem in itself, but rather a barometer of the need to address other aspects of a relationship (e.g., conflicts about childrearing, finances, and in-laws) that are eliciting the emotional upset. However, some spouses enter therapy with chronic, severe anger responses to interactions with their partners, and their emotional arousal and its expression have become contributing factors to the couples' failure to resolve areas of conflict and dissatisfaction. At its worst, uncontrolled anger can produce verbal and physical abuse between spouses. Because strong anger can impede the use of constructive communication skills and other positive behaviors that might resolve a couple's conflicts, therapists must determine whether each spouse's anger is likely to abate as procedures such as communication training are used, or whether the initial therapeutic efforts should be focused on reducing the anger itself.

Characteristics of dysfunctional anger.

Although some clinicians propose that it is healthy for spouses to experience and vent anger (Bach & Wyden, 1968) whereas others consider it irrational to do so (Ellis, 1976), there are a number of aspects of the anger exhibited by some spouses that clearly contribute to marital dysfunction. First, anger is likely to be dysfunctional when it is so *intense* that it activates abusive behavior. Second, it is problematic when an individual reacts with anger in a nondiscriminating way to almost anything the partner does. Weiss's (1980) concept of "sentiment override" describes such a process whereby an individual's reactions to a partner's actions depend on his or her general feelings about the partner rather than the positive or negative qualities of the partner's behaviors. A major drawback of indiscriminate anger is that it provides punishment for many positive behaviors emitted by the person's partner, a process likely to block improvement in the relationship.

As described by Revenstorf (1984), anger can *interfere with constructive behavioral skills*, such as communication and problem solving, by producing dysfunctional reflexive "overlearned" behavioral responses, such as withdrawal or attack. In the course of working on communication skills with some couples, it quickly becomes clear that they are unable to interact positively with each other in spite of the fact that they are able to behave positively with other people (with whom they are less emotionally involved).

In such cases, further work on skill training might be fruitless until the disruptive anger is reduced.

For example, Margolin, John, and Gleberman (1988) assessed affective communication, emotional states, and physiological arousal in couples whose typical patterns of dealing with marital conflicts were identified as primarily (a) physically aggressive, (b) verbally aggressive, (c) withdrawing, or (d) nondistressed/nonaggressive. Although the sample of physically aggressive couples had not been identified by themselves or by social agencies as battering cases, and the couples engaged in fairly benign discussions of their relationship problems during the study, the husbands exhibited more negative emotional experiences and affective behavior than did husbands from the other groups. Margolin et al. suggest that the physically aggressive husbands' often subtle but nonconstructive responses (negative voice qualities such as sarcasm, nagging, mocking, whining; behaviors such as signs of dismissal, finger pointing, mimicking; emotional responses such as sadness, anger, fear, feeling attacked) easily could escalate into more severe forms of aggression.

Margolin et al. (1988) also found that wives from physically aggressive couples escalated their negative behavior toward their spouses during the middle of their discussions and then decelerated it, whereas wives from verbally aggressive and withdrawing couples exhibited a more gradual but steady escalation of negative behavior over the course of the discussions. Margolin et al. suggest that this pattern might reflect the wives' backing down in an attempt to avoid more severe aggression by their husbands, but they also note that the deceleration of negative behavior by the wives paradoxically may negatively reinforce the husbands' aggression.

When spouses have *little sense of control* over their anger, owing to factors such as sentiment override, they are likely to need assistance both in achieving an expectancy that they can control the emotion (its intensity and/or its expression) and in developing cognitive and behavioral skills for implementing the control. Neidig and Friedman (1984) note that physically abusive individuals commonly lack a sense of control over their anger and the destructive manner in which it is expressed, and these clinicians use a variety of cognitive and behavioral interventions to develop anger control in their abusive clients. Until spouses achieve a sense of control over their anger, they are likely to be pessimistic about the chances of improvement in their relationship, often realistically so.

As described earlier, strong emotions such as anger can take on *instrumental value*, in that they allow the individual to manipulate his or her environment and produce rewarding outcomes. Anger is likely to be dysfunctional and difficult to change if it has become an established means by which one spouse influences the other, especially when the individual has no alternative interpersonal skills in his or her repertoire.

One common function that expressed anger serves is to motivate a partner to comply with the individual's wishes in order to terminate the aversive stimulation (i.e., negative reinforcement). Another function that anger sometimes appears to serve is to increase distance between two partners when they have become too intimate for the comfort level of one or both individuals. Whether or not the spouses are aware of the pattern, they may have been reinforced for expressing anger at times when they were experiencing anxiety about intimacy with each other and by having the anxiety abate as the anger interrupted the intimate interactions. Unfortunately, there is a danger that the use of anger expression to control the degree of intimacy can escalate, especially because anger in one partner often begets anger in the other. This escalation can produce a steady decrease in intimacy, thereby disrupting the homeostasis in the relationship and eventually leaving the spouses quite alienated from each other. Although psychodynamic explanations commonly have been offered for such patterns (e.g., Kaplan, 1979), behavioral reinforcement principles seem quite useful in accounting for the phenomenon. The clinical implication is that unless the instrumental value of anger expression can be reduced and the spouses can be taught to use more constructive means of controlling their interactions, anger responses are likely to be maintained in the couple's relationship.

The experience and expression of anger can be dysfunctional if it *masks other emotions* (Neidig & Friedman, 1984). As noted by Sloan and L'Abate (1985), the sharing of feelings associated with vulnerability (e.g., hurt, sadness) tends to promote a sense of intimacy between spouses more than the expression of anger, but some distressed couples tend to express the former types of emotions much less than they share their anger. Consequently, it is important to determine whether an individual who focuses on anger toward his or her partner is aware of experiencing other emotions as well. If so, the therapist needs to identify factors that are leading the individual to express only the anger, such as an assumption that "my spouse won't understand how wrong his behavior is unless I keep letting him know how angry it makes me." Also, some individuals report that they feel more comfortable expressing anger than expressing emotions such as hurt and sadness. Their discomfort with the more "vulnerable" feelings often stems from embarrassment or fear that the partner will use the opportunity to hurt them further.

Sources of dysfunctional anger.

One source of chronic and global anger is an individual's upset about a partner's past behaviors which were painful or abusive (e.g., sexual affairs, physical abuse, substance abuse). Even when the partner's negative behavior has ended, the individual who had been the recipient may dwell on memories of the past wrongs and continue to feel quite angry. The continued anger may result from an expectancy that the partner's negative behavior is likely to recur (i.e., the past is blended with the present and future). Some chronically angry spouses report that they fear that "letting go" of the anger will give the partner the impression that he or she no longer needs to work on improving the relationship.

Schlesinger (1984) and Schlesinger and Epstein (1986) have noted three desires often experienced by an abused individual. These concern themes of (a) retribution, (b) restitution, and (c) refuge. The person who has been hurt in the past wants the other person to be punished in return, wants the offender to repay him or her in some way for the wrongs committed, and wants some guarantee that further abuse will not occur in the future. The continued expression of anger is a common means by which the spouse who experienced abuse exacts retribution and tries to coerce the partner into providing restitution and at least some promises of refuge.

Many spouses who have been abusive do feel some remorse and share the abused individual's belief that restitution should be made. Consequently, when they make overt attempts to provide restitution, they may reinforce the abused person's belief in "evening the score." With both parties holding to an unrealistic assumption that somehow the score *can* be evened (whereas usually there truly is nothing the former abuser can do that will compensate for painful past events), the couple can develop a pattern where the abused presses for restitution and the abuser continues trying to provide it, with both individuals resentful about the chronic lack of resolution of the problem.

The *attributions of blame* for marital problems that spouses make (see Chapter 3) commonly seem to be associated with cognitions about retribution and restitution, and the accompanying anger. Blaming one's partner tends to lead a spouse to take a unidirectional causal view of marital interactions (i.e., "My partner causes the problems, and any negative behavior on my part is just a reaction to his/her provocation"). The individual who construes the relationship in this manner is likely to experience anger that might be more appropriate if, in fact, he or she was consistently the helpless victim of the partner's negative actions. However, marital inter-action research (e.g., Revenstorf et al., 1984) has indicated that the inter-actions of distressed couples commonly are characterized by escalations of conflict in which *both* partners reciprocate negative behavior. It is rare for spouses to perceive mutual, circular causality in their interactions, probably because they are not accustomed to viewing interpersonal events in this manner; in addition, blaming one's partner can serve the function of main-taining one's own self-esteem (Baucom, 1987).

For some individuals, anger arises when their partners' behaviors violate the *standards* that the person holds about proper behavior in a close relationship. As described in Chapter 3, the degree to which these stand-ards are reasonable can vary considerably, but the more unrealistic they are, the more likely the person is to be distressed about the marriage (Epstein & Eidelson, 1981). Violation of standards that a person holds about what is "fair" commonly elicits anger (Burns, 1980; Ellis, 1977), and the degree to which the person chooses to ventilate the anger to the partner often depends on the degree to which he or she also holds to a standard that people who behave unfairly deserve to be punished (Neidig & Friedman, 1984).

As described earlier, anger can become a *learned response* that has been reinforced in the past by allowing the individual to exercise some control over his or her environment. In operant conditioning terms, particular circumstances involving the two spouses may become discriminative stimuli for a response of anger expression, resulting in reinforcement. For example, the stimulus "partner making a request of me" may signal to the person that an expression of anger is likely to result in the spouse backing off. Because expressions of anger have been negatively reinforced in the past by terminating what the individual experiences as aversive behavior from the partner, they are likely to be used in the future in similar situations.

A *lack of skills for assertion, negotiation, and problem solving* can contribute to anger because the individual does not have the ability to counter unwanted behaviors and requests from his or her partner. The anger results from feeling put-upon and having no sense of control over the situation. In contrast to anger that is instrumental (influenced by its positive consequences), these anger experiences are due more to the frustration of not having instrumental responses in one's repertoire that can achieve one's goals. Clearly, the two sources of anger can coexist: The individual lacks constructive skills for influencing a partner, feels helpless and angry, and learns to express anger in order to influence the partner.

External sources of stress such as the spouses' jobs also can contribute to a general level of tension in a relationship and thereby increase the likelihood that an individual will respond to frustration by becoming angry. Consequently, it is important for marital therapists to evaluate aspects of a couple's life beyond their dyadic interactions. Procedures for surveying such sources of stress are described in Chapter 7.

Depression

A number of research studies (e.g., Bothwell & Weissman, 1977; Coleman & Miller, 1975; Heins, 1978; Hinchliffe, Hooper, & Roberts, 1978; Weiss & Aved, 1978) have shown that marital distress and depression coexist quite often. Both Beach, Jouriles, and O'Leary (1985) and Birchler (1986) report that over half of the distressed couples attending their outpatient clinics had at least one depressed member. Conversely, Rounsaville, Weissman, Prusoff, and Herceg-Baron (1979) found that more than half of the individuals seeking treatment for depression in their sample also reported marital dysfunction.

There still is little known about the degree to which depression causes marital problems or the degree to which marital problems cause depression, but there have been research results suggesting that both of these processes occur. Studies by Brown and Harris (1978) and Weissman and Paykel (1974) indicated that the presence of supportive family members is associated with more improvement in depressive symptoms over the course of treatment, as well as less relapse. In the Weissman and Paykel study, marital problems such as poor communication persisted even after treatment for depression reduced depressive symptoms. Rounsaville et al. (1979) found that depressed women with marital distress who resolved their marital problems (without marital therapy) during treatment for depression showed improvement in depression equal to that exhibited by individuals who entered treatment with no marital problems.

Recent research on high "expressed emotion" (EE) (i.e., high levels of criticism and emotional overinvolvement) in families has indicated that depressed individuals who have high EE spouses have less positive interaction with their partners, are more distressed about their marriages, and have greater relapse of depressive symptoms than those with spouses rated low in EE (Hooley, 1985; Hooley & Hahlweg, 1986; Hooley, Orley, & Teasdale, 1986). Also, studies by Friedman (1975) and Beach and O'Leary (1986) have provided preliminary evidence that marital therapy can produce reduction in spouses' depressive symptoms. Birchler (1986) notes that there is clinical evidence that individual psychotherapy or drug therapy for depression can produce deterioration in clients' marriages.

The potential for depression to cause marital problems has been stressed by Coyne (1976), who found that people who interacted with depressed individuals evaluated them negatively and had increases in their own levels of negative moods such as depression and hostility. Coyne argues that whereas people initially respond in sympathetic and supportive ways to individuals who exhibit depressive symptoms, over time they become frustrated and hostile toward the depressed person's chronic negativity and other symptoms. Repeated exposure to a partner's depressive symptoms, such as self-deprecation, crying, sleep disturbances, loss of energy, loss of motivation for work and leisure activities, physical complaints, diminished sexual interest, loss of appetite, inability to experience pleasure in life activities, and suicidal ideation (Beck et al., 1979; Klerman, Weissman, Rounsaville, & Chevron, 1984), can make one quite aversive to other people.

In studies by Coyne (1976) and Howes and Hokanson (1979), people who interacted with depressed individuals exhibited a combination of supportive and rejecting responses, reflecting *ambivalent* reactions. Thus, it often is difficult for people to avoid sympathetic responses to another's depressive symptoms, even when feeling hostility. Arkowitz, Holliday, and Hutter (1982) found that spouses of depressed women felt hostility toward their partners, but expressed it in subtle ways. The indirect expression of hostility by the partners of the depressed individuals seems consistent with the ambivalence that the partners feel; that is, they feel frustrated and angry but also experience sympathy for the depressive's plight.

In addition to the various symptoms of depression that can become aversive for an individual's partner, depressed individuals also tend to express critical, hostile behavior toward their partners and thus may contribute to an escalation of marital conflict. Arkowitz et al. (1982) found that depressed women in their study also felt hostility toward their partners, and Baucom and Sher (1986) found a great deal of *mutual* criticism in the communication between depressed individuals and their spouses.

Hinchliffe et al. (1978) found that when communicating with their partners, depressed individuals were more negative, less responsive to the partners, and more self-occupied than a comparison group of surgical patients.

Hops et al. (1987) found evidence of a "coercive interactive system" in the families of depressed women, whether or not the couples in the families also were maritally distressed. In this study, families' behavioral interactions were coded during home observations, and *sequences* of behaviors among the family members were examined in order to identify the probabilities that particular responses by one member would be followed by particular responses by other members. On the one hand, depressed women exhibited higher rates of dysphoric affect (sadness and despondency), as well as lower rates of happy affect, than nondepressed women, and their dysphoric affect tended to lower the probability that their husbands and children would respond with aggressive affect. Hops et al. (1987) suggest that the expression of dysphoric affect is functional for the depressed women, producing brief periods of respite from aggression by other family members.

On the other hand, expressions of aggression by other family members tended to reduce the probability of immediate expressions of dysphoric affect by the depressed wives/mothers. Again, Hops et al. (1987) propose that the aggressive behaviors serve a function for the nondepressed family members, temporarily reducing the depressed women's aversive emotional expressions. The limited short-term relief provided by this interaction pattern serves as negative reinforcement, strengthening aversive exchanges in the family.

Thus, in the marriages of depressed individuals, a circular pattern tends to develop, in which negativity and a lack of positive responsiveness on the depressed spouse's part elicit hostility and withdrawal from the partner, which in turn elicits anxiety, more depression, and demands for reassurance by the depressed person (Birchler, 1986; Hinchliffe et al., 1978; Klerman et al., 1984). Because quite often the clinician will see couples in which both the individual's depression and the conflictual marital interaction pattern are firmly established, both problems should be taken into account when planning therapeutic interventions.

Because depression and marital distress have a number of similarities (e.g., low rates of positive experiences and high rates of negative experiences, a sense of low self-efficacy and hopelessness, selective perceptual tracking of negative events, biased attributions that focus on global and stable causes of unpleasant events, unrealistic standards, deficits in communication and problem-solving skills), it seems likely that the two problems can be addressed simultaneously by means of cognitive and behavioral interventions designed to address such factors (Epstein, 1985b). For example, by teaching a couple more effective communication skills, a therapist could modify their dysfunctional dyadic interactions *and* improve deficits in a depressed spouse's communication skills. Similarly, modification of spouses' tendencies to attribute unpleasant events to global, stable causes can reduce both the tendencies of spouses to see little chance for improving aspects of their relationship and a depressed spouse's tendency to believe that negative events in his or her life are due to unchangeable personality traits.

In order to determine whether such "dual treatment" is feasible with a particular couple, the clinician must evaluate the extent to which each of the factors listed above is involved in both the depression and marital distress of this dyad. When there is evidence that the factors influencing one of the two problems differ from those influencing the other problem, at least somewhat separate treatment plans may be needed. This is not to say that the treatments for depression and marital distress would be distinct, but particular interventions primarily focused on one of the presenting problems may be needed. For example, medication may be administered to one spouse in order to control large mood swings in bipolar disorders, or to reduce severe "vegetative" symptoms (e.g., insomnia, loss of appetite, fatigue) during major depressive episodes.

Some therapists conduct individual cognitive therapy with a depressed spouse concurrently with conjoint marital therapy, in cases where it is clear that the severity of the individual's negative thinking and self-absorption are impeding his or her ability to collaborate with the partner in marital therapy (Epstein, 1985a; Jacobson, 1984b). Special attention to the individual depressed spouse also may be needed when there is evidence that his or her symptoms are being elicited or exacerbated by life stresses external to the couple's relationship, such as job pressures.

Anxiety

Aside from the emphasis placed on anxiety as a factor in couples' sexual dysfunctions, little has been written about the role of anxiety in marital interaction. However, some clinical and empirical evidence suggests that dysfunctional relationships can be a source of significant anxiety in individuals' lives, and conversely, that anxiety can disrupt marital functioning. Consequently, it is important to evaluate whether members of a couple are experiencing significant amounts of anxiety, and to identify how anxiety symptoms and marital interaction patterns are influencing each other.

Anxiety as a response to relationship problems.

There have been few specific hypotheses in the marital literature concerning relationship dynamics that might elicit significant anxiety in spouses. Beginning with Masters and Johnson's (1966, 1970) pioneering work, anxiety has been implicated in the development and maintenance of sexual dysfunctions, primarily in the form of "performance anxiety." Although less has been proposed about aspects of sexual interaction that can elicit anxiety, there are a number of possibilities. First, Kaplan (1974) has described how an individual can develop conditioned anxiety responses to sexual stimuli (e.g., foreplay; merely being naked in bed with one's partner) if these stimuli have been paired with anxiety-provoking stimuli such as criticism and rejection by the partner. Second, if a couple's inter-actions include repetitive tests of each other's caring (e.g., asking for reassurance, criticizing the partner for not demonstrating caring), the sexual aspects of the relationship can become a focal point for such tests. Spouses may experience considerable anticipatory "performance anxiety" due to their concerns that they must behave the "right" way sexually in order to avoid upsetting their partners. Third, if a couple disagrees about a decision to have a child, the more reluctant partner may experience anxiety about engaging in sex, especially if the other spouse presses for no birth control. Fourth, if a couple has experienced conflict in their overall relationship and a spouse does not feel inclined to share sexual intimacy with the partner, he or she may feel anxiety (and perhaps anger as well) at the prospect of rejecting the partner's advances.

Michelson (1987) notes that there is some clinical evidence that marital dysfunction can contribute to the development and maintenance of *agoraphobia*. Studies by Hudson (1974) and Milton and Hafner (1979) indicated that treatment for agoraphobia was less successful for individuals with distressed marital and family relationships. Marital distress was positively related to relapse in a study by Bland and Hallam (1981). Although the treatment of choice for agoraphobia is behavioral intervention (particularly exposure), increasingly clinicians (e.g., Chambless & Goldstein, 1982) are including spouses in treatment programs. However, Mathews, Gelder, and Johnston (1981) caution that existing studies have not provided any clear evidence that marital problems cause or maintain agoraphobia. They suggest that marital tensions might contribute to the occurrence of the panic attacks that lead to agoraphobia, and that spouses' responses to agoraphobics' symptoms (e.g., solicitous attention) might reinforce the symptoms, but that as yet such processes have not been documented.

Panic disorders consist of frequent, sudden attacks of extreme fear, with no obvious cause (Ley, 1987). Ley reviews a variety of psychological and physiological theories of the etiology of panic disorders, including his own view that people who have a predisposition to hyperventilate under stress and who experience significant life stresses eventually have a panic attack produced by the effects of hyperventilation (e.g., heart palpitations, shortness of breath, fatigue, anxiety, dizziness, chest pain). He notes that conceptualizations such as the hyperventilation theory assume the presence of life stresses but do not specify the nature of such "problems of personal and social living that predispose the individual to hyperventilate" (p. 210). It seems likely that marital and family conflict could be major factors in this process.

The syndrome of *post-traumatic stress disorder* (PTSD) has received increasing attention since it became clear that large numbers of Vietnam veterans were exhibiting symptoms that interfered significantly with intrapersonal and interpersonal functioning, often many years after traumatic war experiences. Although PTSD has been documented with a range of traumatic experiences (e.g., automobile accidents, rape), the majority of research studies have investigated the aftermath of combat experiences. The results of recent studies have indicated that the occurrence and intensity of PTSD symptoms are not a simple function of exposure to combat trauma, but depend on the combination of combat trauma and the quality of social support the individual receives after the experience (Barrett & Mizes, 1985; Foy, Resnick, Sipprelle, & Carroll, 1987). The importance of the presence of supportive individuals such as spouses has been stressed by writers such as Foy, Donahoe, Carroll, Gallers, and Reno (1987). Thus, it seems reasonable to expect that trauma victims whose intimate relationships such as marriages are characterized by conflict and low levels of emotional support would be at greater risk for the development of PTSD. At this point, further research is needed to test this hypothesis.

The preceding review of anxiety disorders that might be influenced by relationship dynamics is not meant to be comprehensive. It seems prudent for the marital therapist to be aware of any other anxiety disorders exhibited by members of distressed couples (e.g., generalized anxiety disorder) and to evaluate whether the occurrence of symptoms is associated with variations in marital interactions.

Effects of anxiety on marital interaction.

Again, the most attention has been paid to the impact of anxiety on the sexual aspects of couples' relationships. Anxiety has been proposed as a major contributing factor to a variety of sexual dysfunctions (e.g., erectile dysfunction, inhibited ejaculation, female inorgasmic dysfunction, vaginismus), and standard sex therapy procedures include a number of techniques designed to reduce anxiety concerning sexual behavior (Friedman & Chernen, 1987; Kaplan, 1974; Masters & Johnson, 1970). For example, sensate focus exercises in which partners engage in progressively intimate nondemand touching provide an opportunity for systematic desensitization of anxiety responses to intimate contact (Friedman & Chernen, 1987).

Kaplan (1974) has proposed that anxiety contributes to sexual dysfunctions by disrupting autonomic nervous system functioning that controls arousal and orgasm responses. However, Barlow (1986) reviews clinical and empirical evidence that suggests a more complex situation: namely, that anxiety can increase sexual arousal in sexually functional individuals but decreases arousal in dysfunctional individuals. The mechanism for this difference which is suggested by the research is that dysfunctional individuals tend to focus on performance-related stimuli and are thereby distracted from attending to sexually arousing stimuli. Anxiety tends to intensify their attention to nonarousing stimuli, whereas it increases sexually functional individuals' tendencies to focus on (and be aroused by) performance-related sexual stimuli. Barlow (1986) notes that the reasons why some people may learn to attend to distracting thoughts such as expectancies about the consequences of inadequate sexual performance have not yet been identified. He also stresses that only preliminary support for his model concerning the interaction of cognitive interference and anxiety has been provided by existing studies, and further research is needed.

Because individuals who suffer from *agoraphobia* often require the presence of a spouse or other person in order to spend time in public places without experiencing panic attacks, the symptoms of this disorder have the potential to affect marital functioning as well as the individual's own ability to carry out normal daily tasks. In addition, the panic attacks themselves are likely to be distressing for the partner as well as for the individual who experiences them. Buglass, Clarke, Henderson, Kreitman, and Presley (1977) found that the symptoms of agoraphobic women had negative effects on their husbands, but Mathews et al. (1981) argue that there has been no evidence that agoraphobia has a substantial negative impact on family life. It seems likely that the degree of marital and family disruption would depend on the severity of the symptoms and the degree to which they alter normal family activities.

Several of the common symptoms of *post-traumatic stress disorder* affect the individual's relationships with family members and others. These include a feeling of detachment or estrangement from other people, loss of interest in activities, constricted affect, exaggerated startle responses, and difficulty concentrating (DSM-III-R; American Psychiatric Association, 1987). It has been suggested (Foy, Resnick, Sipprelle, & Carroll, 1987) that the poor social support in the lives of many war veterans with PTSD symptoms might be accounted for, at least in part, by their own difficulties in relating to people and accepting support.

Foy, Donahoe, Carroll, Gallers, and Reno (1987) note that problems have been identified consistently in the marital and family relationships of PTSD victims. It has been our own experience in working with families that include war veterans who exhibit PTSD symptoms that some of the family members' complaints (e.g., communication problems, anger outbursts by the veteran) appeared to be associated with the syndrome. However, the family members frequently did not even mention the individual's war experience until the therapist uncovered it in the course of gathering information about the family history, because they did not conceptualize such a link between the war experiences and the current problems.

Thus, the symptoms of anxiety disorders have the potential to disrupt marital interactions in a variety of ways. Consequently, it is important to assess the forms and levels of anxiety experienced by spouses and to evaluate whether specific treatment of anxiety disorders may be needed in order to improve marital interactions. When anxiety symptoms appear to be disrupting marital interactions, specific cognitive and behavioral interventions (e.g., Beck & Emery, 1985; Michelson & Ascher, 1987) can be used to reduce them.

Jealousy

Although jealousy commonly is thought of as a response to a perceived threat that one's partner is attracted to another individual, it can be elicited by the partner's involvement with any interest or activity that may be seen as competing for his or her attention. Although mild jealousy probably occurs sporadically in a large percentage of relationships and is not dysfunctional, some couples are plagued by intense jealous reactions that have profound effects on their interactions and satisfaction.

Jealousy is not merely an emotional response, but consists of three components: (a) *cognitions* concerning potential loss of the partner (in entirety or some significant aspects such as sexual exclusivity or leisure time together), (b) *affect,* including a strong component of anxiety and often a degree of anger, and (c) *behavior,* including overt expression of emotion and attempts to control or punish the partner (Constantine, 1976, 1987; Jacobson & Margolin, 1979). In order to understand the role of jealousy in a particular couple's relationship, it is important to evaluate all three of its components.

Factors influencing jealousy.

Although it is easy for therapists to focus their attention on jealous spouses who exhibit outbursts of emotion and intrude into their partners' privacy, it is important to determine the extent to which an individual's jealousy is due to his or her own dispositional characteristics and to what extent it is elicited by specific situations in the couple's interactions. On the one hand, some studies have found moderate correlations between jealousy and trait measures of characteristics such as self-criticism, anxiety, external locus of control, and sex-role-stereotyped attitudes (Constantine, 1987). Jealousy also can be associated with fairly consistent tendencies to base one's self-worth on love and approval from others (Jacobson & Margolin, 1979). In addition, past traumatic events (e.g., having a former partner suddenly leave one for another person) can produce chronic fear and vigilance in future relationships.

On the other hand, there often is at least a grain of truth in the concerns of jealous individuals, and specific aspects of a partner's behavior (as well as the interaction pattern between the spouses) may be eliciting jealous responses in an individual who has not felt jealous in other intimate relationships. For example, in a couple one of us treated, the husband complained bitterly about his wife's "snooping" into his belongings, but he also kept photographs of himself and past girlfriends in his office and left a slip of paper with the name and address of a former lover (who he insisted was now only a friend) on his desk at home. Thus, in evaluating situational factors that may play a role in jealousy, a therapist should determine the degree to which actual events provide a reality base for the response. In devising treatment plans, the therapist also must take into account the degree to which situational factors that elicit or reinforce jealousy can (or should) be modified. For example, it became clear that the jealousy of the husband in one couple was elicited primarily by the amount of time his wife spent involved in her career. When it became equally clear that the wife derived great satisfaction from her career and was unlikely to reduce the time she spent working, other factors such as the husband's cognitions about marital roles, alternative ways of expressing commitment, and ways in which the couple could schedule time together more effectively became central foci of the therapy.

A variety of *cognitive factors* can influence jealousy. First, although jealousy can reflect the degree to which a partner is valued, it also can be based on an unrealistic standard in which an individual bases his or her self-worth on the love and attention of a partner. As noted by Jacobson and Margolin (1979), the degree to which one bases self-worth on a partner is not equivalent to love and caring for the partner. Therefore, caution should be exercised in "reframing" jealousy as a positive reflection on a relationship.

Jealousy can arise from a variety of other extreme, unrealistic standards and harsh evaluations when those standards are not followed. A whole series of beliefs related to how one should get one's personal needs met within a marriage can contribute to jealousy. One wife was extremely jealous based primarily on the belief that she should be able to meet all of her husband's needs. When he developed platonic relationships with other women, she perceived it as very threatening. Similar standards that one should not be attracted to other persons or that caring about other people means that the spouse is loved less also can elicit jealousy. Evaluating violations of standards in extreme ways, as in telling oneself that it is "awful" for one's partner to dance with other people, can result in strong negative emotional reactions and maladaptive behavior.

Unreasonable *assumptions* also can contribute to jealousy. For example, a woman may have developed a generalized persona that men are untrustworthy, always interested in other women, and likely to be unfaithful if they can. Many jealous individuals hold negative assumptions about whether they are lovable and appealing to others. Assumptions about the correlations among various behaviors also can be problematic. For example, a husband may assume a strong correlation between finding members of the opposite sex attractive and having an affair. Understandably, based on this assumption, the husband is likely to become concerned if his wife expresses that she finds certain men to be handsome. Similarly, some husbands assume that if a wife flirts with another man in public, it is a reflection of a lack of respect for her spouse, and furthermore they assume that other persons present make the same associations. These husbands therefore view themselves as publicly ridiculed, and they become angry.

In terms of *perceptions*, the jealous person may be attuned to the positive comments and behaviors which the partner shows toward other persons and ignores the partner's loving behavior toward the jealous individual. Often these skewed perceptions result from related cognitions, such as faulty *attributions* for the partner's behavior. For example, if a spouse spends time with members of the opposite sex at a party, this is attributed to a lack of love. Questionable *expectancies* can be based on overgeneralizations from earlier times in an individual's life. For example, a husband who was abandoned in a previous marriage may conclude that his current wife will do the same thing, and consequently his perceptual "filter" leads him to notice her behaviors that seem to indicate disappointment with him and to ignore signs of her commitment to their relationship. Such an expectancy might serve the functions of providing him a sense of predictability (no future surprises) and eliciting reassurance from his wife when he expresses his fear.

When a negative expectancy has developed from an earlier event in the current relationship (e.g., a partner had an affair), constructive ways of coping with broken trust become the central foci of therapy. In such cases, cognitions concerning retribution, restitution, and refuge usually play a role in the anger and anxiety components of the jealousy.

Just as understanding the bases for the emotional component of jealousy is important, so too is understanding the functions served by behavior stemming from jealous feelings. One goal of much jealous behavior is to punish the partner who is viewed as violating some standard. Thus, screaming at the partner and avoiding affectionate and sexual behavior can be a way of saying, "You can't have your cake and eat it too! If you show interest in other people, don't expect me to be receptive to you." Such persons have learned to use punishment to stop their partners from engaging in undesired behaviors.

A second major goal of jealous behavior (whether or not the jealous person is aware of this dynamic) is to prompt statements of reassurance or caring behaviors from the partner. Understandably, when a person feels threatened by the potential loss of a partner, that individual wants some type of reassurance that the partner is dedicated to their relationship. Thus, statements such as "You don't love me" can be viewed as attempts to elicit statements of caring from the partner. Some jealous persons are willing to endure the negative interactions and arguments stemming from jealous behavior because they have learned that afterward there is a reconciliation in which their partners comfort them.

Because extreme feelings of jealousy involve a high level of arousal, often the subsequent behavior (e.g., pressuring the partner for reassurance, making phone calls to check on the partner's activities) is an attempt to lower an uncomfortable drive state. However, the reduction in the individual's level of tension commonly is short-lived, because the consequences of the jealous behavior do not alter the individual's expectancy that sooner or later the partner will be involved with such a threatening person or activity.

For example, one wife interrogated her husband each day concerning his activities at work, because she felt anxiety regarding fantasies that he was having affairs with women at the office. She reported that she felt a marked drop in her tension when her husband would reassure her of his fidelity and would give her a detailed report of all his interactions with women at the office (e.g., when he stated other people were present when he met with a female co-worker). However, these reassurances and evidence about his daily activities did not alter the wife's *persona* concerning her husband, which portrayed him as easily bored with familiar things (such as herself), sexually attracted to a variety of women, and only moderately committed to her. Therefore, any sense of security that she experienced at the moment when she heard his reassurances was transitory.

Effects of jealousy on marital interaction.

The cognitive, emotional, and behavioral aspects of jealousy can take their toll on a relationship in several ways. First, unrealistic perceptions, attributions, expectancies, assumptions, and standards can create such a negative view of the relationship for the jealous individual that he or she becomes highly distressed about the relationship. As unrealistic cognitions feed mistrust, the jealous person may not only act aversively toward the partner, but also may decide not to take any chances on compromising with the partner or permitting intimacy.

Frequent crying and requests for reassurance may at times motivate the partner to provide reassurance, more time together, and other attempts to reduce the jealous spouse's feelings and behavior. However, on the one hand, if the partner provides excessive reassurance (e.g., "I really love you more than anything, and I promise that I'll spend less time at the office and more time with you"), he or she may be creating a context for broken promises which will only intensify the jealousy (Jacobson & Margolin, 1979). On the other hand, as a partner finds that "bending over backward" to satisfy a jealous spouse never seems to provide enough reassurance to reduce the jealousy, the partner is likely to become quite resentful and withdraw. This process can produce a marital interaction pattern similar to that found in couples with a depressed member. Specifically, the jealous person exhibits unremitting jealous behavior, which elicits *ambivalent* responses from the partner, including positive attempts to soothe and reassure the jealous individual and negative responses such as hostility and withdrawal. The partner's withdrawal then elicits more jealous behavior. This pattern has the potential to escalate to a point where one or both parties may choose to end the relationship.

SUMMARY

As this chapter demonstrates, affect is a factor of considerable importance in a cognitive-behavioral approach to marital problems. Of major concern are (a) the types and intensities of emotions spouses experience about their partners and relationships, (b) deficits that spouses may have in recognizing the nature of their emotions and the factors that elicit and maintain them, (c) skill deficits, emotions, and cognitions that interfere with spouses' expression of emotions within their awareness, and (d) types of emotion that can impede constructive marital functioning.

Consideration of any of these emotional aspects of the relationship between two people makes it clear that affect is complexly intertwined with cognitions and behavioral patterns. On the one hand, one cannot alter spouses' cognitions or behaviors without having some impact on the emotional quality of the relationship. On the other hand, emotions can have either facilitative or detrimental effects on cognitive and behavioral processes in the relationship. Consequently, for the sake of planning treatments that will assist spouses in achieving more satisfaction, therapists need to assess all of the above aspects of emotion in a couple and apply interventions carefully designed to have a positive impact on the interplay of affect, cognition, and behavior. Procedures for assessing aspects of affect in marriage are described in Chapter 7, and techniques for modifying problems associated with affect are detailed in Chapter 10.

SECTION II

ASSESSMENT

This section is devoted to a detailed description of interview, questionnaire, and behavioral observation methods used in the assessment of behavioral, cognitive, and affective components of marital interaction. Consistent with the social learning tradition in which assessment is a necessary prerequisite for therapeutic intervention, these chapters outline a variety of methods for collecting specific data concerning behaviors, cognitions, and emotions that are the targets of the structured cognitive-behavioral interventions described in the treatment chapters of this book.

Chapter 5 covers methods and instruments for assessing (a) problem content areas of a relationship (e.g., childrearing, sex, decision making), (b) excesses and deficits in spouses' exchanges of pleasing and displeasing behaviors (i.e., instrumental and affectional "noncommunication" behaviors), (c) communication skills, (d) problem-solving skills, and (e) behavior change skills. Guidelines for integrating any inconsistencies between self-report and observational sources of behavioral data are discussed.

Chapter 6 surveys interview, self-report, and behavioral observation approaches to the assessment of perceptions, attributions, expectancies, assumptions, and standards. Because standardized clinical instruments for cognitive assessment still are in an early stage of development, the systematic use of interviews for the collection of data regarding cognitions is emphasized. The importance and therapeutic implications of differentiating between distorted cognitions and spouses' accurate appraisals of negative marital interactions are discussed.

Chapter 7 describes methods for assessing (a) the amount and intensity of spouses' positive and negative affect regarding their marriage, (b) the degree to which spouses recognize and differentiate their emotions and the aspects of marital interactions that elicit emotional states, (c) excesses and deficits in the expression of emotion, and (d) types of affect (anger, depression, anxiety, and jealousy) that impede adaptive marital functioning. Interview, questionnaire, and behavioral observation approaches to assessment in each of these areas are surveyed. Finally, strategies are proposed for integrating affective data from all of these sources.

Throughout these three chapters, there is a basic premise that assessment is necessary in order to plan appropriate interventions, and that assessment is an ongoing process during the course of treatment. Some assessment strategies are designed primarily for use in a pretherapy evaluation of behavioral, cognitive, and affective factors, but others can be used repeatedly to identify targets for treatment on a session-by-session basis.

The assessment strategies concerning marital behaviors, cognitions, and emotions are covered in three separate chapters primarily for the sake of clarity of presentation. In practice, all three domains are assessed simultaneously, and the therapist integrates data concerning all three factors when planning types and sequences of interventions.

5

Assessment of Behavior

Within the past decade, several excellent reviews have been written focusing on the current behavioral marital therapy assessment strategies available to the clinician and researcher (e.g., Margolin & Jacobson, 1981; Weiss & Margolin, 1977). Overall these works have provided a thorough review of the theoretical, conceptual, and empirical status of these techniques. However, they have not emphasized the clinical utility of these techniques to the same degree. We are committed to a strong empirical basis for clinical work and believe that gaps between the researcher and clinician can be bridged only by making clear the clinical implications of research findings. At the same time, many basic research findings on assessment techniques do not have direct clinical implications, and some of the seemingly most useful clinical applications of behavioral assessment techniques have not been well researched. Therefore, marital therapists are in the same position as assessors in other areas in the mental health field of having to rely to a large extent on clinical experience to provide guidance in how to apply various techniques, interpret findings from single instruments, and combine information gathered from different assessment techniques. Given the complexity of the task and somewhat limited state of the assessment field, the clinician's task is to identify the presence and absence of important behaviors and behavioral sequences that are contributing to marital distress. Once these behaviors are identified, the clinician uses this information along with data from the cognitive and affective realms to develop an appropriate intervention strategy.

127

INITIAL INTERVIEW

The initial interview serves as the medium for organizing the various assessment strategies to be employed. This interview can easily require two to three hours, and at times will be spaced over more than one session. Some clinicians limit the couple's sessions to 50 to 60 minutes and conduct the initial assessment over a period of several weeks. Whenever possible, it is preferable to complete the evaluation more quickly by conducting longer sessions or seeing the couple more than once a week during the evaluation. Often couples have struggled with the idea of coming to therapy for a long time and are eager to begin remedying their problems. Completing the initial assessment during a one- or two-week period can help to maintain the couple's initial enthusiasm.

The initial assessment as we conduct it consists of four major phases. During each of these phases, behavior, cognition, and affect are all assessed. First, a marital history is obtained in order to place current concerns in some meaningful perspective. Second, a discussion of current concerns and strengths of the relationship ensues. Third, the couple is asked to provide a sample of different types of communication. Finally, the clinician has a discussion with the couple and provides feedback regarding his or her perception of the couple's problems and proposed interventions. The feedback portion of the assessment will be discussed in Chapter 7, after the assessment of behavior, cognitions, and emotions is addressed.

During this initial assessment, several types of behaviors are of concern to the clinician. First, the clinician is interested in behaviors that have occurred throughout the marriage. Past behaviors are important for at least two reasons. Often behaviors that are no longer occurring continue to serve as a major source of distress for the couple. Thus, an affair one person had several years ago may still be very distressing to the partner. Simply focusing on present behavior might result in a total omission of discussion of this behavior. Also, understanding past behavior and relationship patterns helps to put current behaviors into a meaningful context. For example, a husband's concern about his wife's current part-time job may be hard to understand on the surface. However, a discussion of their relationship history might clarify that the wife for many years had stayed home full time, focusing primarily on the needs of the husband and the children. The part-time job might, thus, entail a significant shift in family roles which is difficult for the husband to adjust to, and he may conclude that his wife no longer loves him. Because behavior occurs in a context and derives meaning from that context, a clinician who focuses only on current concerns may overlook important issues from the past and therefore will not adequately understand the meaning of current behaviors.

In addition to focusing on past marital behaviors, the clinician will be attuned to current relationship behaviors in several domains. On a general level, the clinician will want to obtain some sense of the overall rate with which meaningful positive and negative exchanges are occurring in the relationship. Some distressed couples rarely do nice things for each other, engage in few rewarding joint activities, and frequently behave negatively toward one another. On the other hand, other distressed couples are rarely hostile toward each other, are polite at least superficially, but feel that there is "something lacking" in their marriages. Therefore, obtaining a measure of the overall rate of positive and negative behaviors can help to provide a sense of the atmosphere of the relationship. Whereas this type of information has been widely advocated by behavioral marital therapists, the clinician must recognize that the information obtained is typically rather global. Alone it usually does not provide the level of detail needed to clarify what specific behaviors might most effectively be changed, in what order, or how this change is to be brought about.

Consequently, the clinician needs to obtain information on the specific current behaviors that are of concern to the couple. For heuristic purposes, these behaviors can be divided into (a) instrumental and (b) affiliative, recreational, and affectionate behaviors—those behaviors which focus on the pleasure-seeking aspects of the individual's and couple's life. Similarly, the therapist has to identify the relationship strengths in these areas. At times these positive aspects of the relationship can be strengthened even further. In addition, positive aspects of the relationship often can provide guidance as to what the couple wants to accentuate in the relationship and thus give direction as the couple and therapist attempt to alter more problematic aspects of the relationship.

Finally, the clinician focuses on the couple's communication behavior. By the time that couples seek intervention, most of them have significant difficulty communicating with their partners. Therefore, their communication is evaluated so that this important behavior, which in itself can be very rewarding or punishing, can be changed to the degree necessary. Also, effective communication is necessary so that couples can profitably discuss other noncommunication aspects of their relationship that need intervention.

TABLE 5-1
Outline of Marital History

I. Initial encounter
  A. How did you meet?
    1. Where?
    2. Who was present?
    3. Circumstances?
  B. What attracted you to your partner?
  C. Are those characteristics still present?
II. Relationship development
  A. What happened next?
  B. What were the major events from the time you met to when you decided to get married?
  C. How did you get along during that time period—arguments, affection, communication, fun together, etc.?
III. Marriage
  A. What were the circumstances surrounding your decision to get married?
  B. Did any major changes occur in your relationship when you got married?
  C. What are the major events, both positive and negative, that have occurred since you married?
IV. Relationship and personal difficulties
  A. When did each of you first think that your relationship was experiencing significant difficulties?
  B. How did you decide to seek counseling at this time?
    1. Whose idea was it?
    2. Are both of you in favor of being here?
  C. Have you previously or are you currently in individual or marital therapy?
    1. If so, what is or was it like?
    2. What do or did you find more helpful and less helpful?
  D. Has either of you been married previously?
    1. If so, how did that or those relationship(s) end?
    2. What do you perceive as your contribution to the difficulties in the prior relationship(s)?

Marital History

Table 5-1 provides a brief outline of the issues typically included in the marital history. The usual beginning point is to discuss how the couple met. This includes where they met, who they were with, who said what to whom, and so forth. These questions are asked because they are a logical place to begin a history. In addition, it is often rather nonthreatening for a couple who may be nervous seeing a therapist for the first time to begin by providing this type of historical information. The therapist often can help the couple to enjoy recalling some of those early moments together. For many couples, the initial encounter was exciting, adventuresome, or at least humorous, although for some it was disastrous or rather mundane. In most instances, a discussion of a couple's meeting often elicits an enjoyable discussion but rarely provides critical information other than an initial sense of how the couple's relationship developed.

"What about the other person attracted you to him or her?" is another question that can assist the therapist in coming to an understanding of what was important to each person during the development of the relationship. Again, the responses here are tremendously varied but usually provide the opportunity for a continued positive focus on the relationship. Some individuals discuss the personal qualities of the other, commenting on the other's thoughtfulness, and so forth. Others focus on the partner's physical attractiveness. On such occasions, the therapist does not minimize the importance of finding the other person physically appealing but continues by asking, "In addition to the way that Bill looked, what about him as a person attracted you to him? What qualities or characteristics in him did you find that you liked?" Most persons will comment on personal characteristics when encouraged, but some spouses have remained resolute that it was really only the other's physical appearance that was appealing in their courtship. Although data about this issue are lacking, such an emphasis is suggestive of future discord because physical attractiveness often seems inadequate to sustain a couple through the difficult times which many couples encounter. When describing the factors that attracted them to one another, still other couples emphasize the environment or situation in which they found themselves.

Husband: Actually, I think we were both just available. I mean we both were lonely, and I'm not sure, well we might very well have gotten together if we were any two people. It's not that we disliked each other, we didn't or we wouldn't have gotten married, but I think we were two lonely and frightened kids away from home in the Army in Europe. Mainly, I think we were in the same place at the same time.

Again, if the husband's memory and report of their early attraction are accurate, then one must wonder about the long-term prognosis for a relationship based on being in the same place at the same time. However, the therapist must be cautious in accepting such pessimistic descriptions. Some spouses who are uncertain of maintaining their relationship attempt to justify leaving it by convincing the therapist that the marriage should never have occurred in the first place.

Still other spouses comment on attributes of the other person that were appealing initially, such as the partner's wit, concern for others, and high level of energy. When these descriptions of the partner emerge, the therapist might continue by inquiring whether the person believes that the partner still has these qualities or whether the person has changed in some major way. Often responses to this question provide meaningful information about the individual's feelings about why the relationship is now experiencing difficulties. That is, frequently the individual will comment on how the spouse has changed in some significant ways and how this has led to major conflict in their marriage. Conversely, as noted in Chapter 3, some individuals conclude that the partner has not really changed, but many of the qualities that initially were appealing now create problems in their relationship. Thus, the high energy level which initially led to fun and creative endeavors now is interpreted as an inability to sit still and simply enjoy life. When such responses occur, the therapist is likely to plan for two types of intervention once therapy gets underway: (a) from a cognitive perspective, clarifying how the interpretational aspect of the individual's perception is of major importance because the partner has not actually changed in energy level, and (b) from a behavioral perspective, helping the couple capitalize on the positive aspects of the partner's high level of energy.

After the therapist has an understanding of how the couple met and what attracted them to each other, the therapist continues the focus on the early relationship by asking how it proceeded after the initial encounter. The therapist is interested not only in the events that occurred but also in the ways in which the couple interacted with each other. This is helpful in putting the couple's current relationship in proper perspective. Thus the therapist might learn that the couple argued with each other frequently from the early stages of their relationship, and the current pattern reflects a chronic interaction style for the couple; again, although data are not available on this issue, the interaction patterns of such couples would probably be more difficult to alter. Such chronic patterns of interaction stand in contrast to couples who describe a warm, loving early relationship which deteriorated after the husband took a new job that required many hours of night work. In the latter case, the couple's problem may have resulted less from skill deficits and more from an environmental complication, the demands of the husband's job. Thus, understanding long-term interaction patterns as well as major events in the couple's history can be helpful in conceptualizing the couple's problems and planning interventions.

After a discussion of the major developmental events, the therapist might inquire about the couple's decision to get married, "What were the circumstances surrounding your decision to get married?" Some couples will respond that the decision was based on mutual love and a strong desire to spend the rest of their lives together, but a significant number of couples provide other explanations. These include such reasons as: (a) the parents applied pressure because the couple were living together; (b) the partners completed college and were faced with either returning to their homes in distant cities or getting married; (c) the female became pregnant; and (d) the partners both were ready to get married to someone, and the current partner was the obvious choice. This type of information can be useful in helping the therapist evaluate whether the couple seemed to have made a reasonable initial decision regarding marriage.

For some couples, major changes occur with the initiation of the marriage. Some spouses suddenly perceive significantly more responsibility, have a desire to upgrade their standards of living, and develop different expectations of the partner. For these reasons, it is helpful to inquire whether any significant changes occurred soon after the couple married.

The next major phase of the relationship history is focused on the time between marriage and the present. The therapist's goal is to understand the major events that occurred during various times in the couple's relationship, for example, birth of children, wife's affair, and so forth. In addition to a discussion of historical events that occurred, the therapist will want to know when either member of the couple first felt that their relationship was experiencing significant difficulties, whether this was discussed between the spouses, what efforts they made to deal with their difficulties, and which strategies were helpful and which were not. This information provides some sense of how the spouses have dealt with their marital problems as a couple, and it can offer ideas as to what strategies work best for this particular couple. Also, the therapist will want to know how the couple made the decision to come for assistance at this time. This is helpful because it often makes clear whether both persons are motivated to improve the marriage or whether one person has finally succumbed to pressure from the other to seek treatment.

If the couple has sought marital therapy in the past, it is important to clarify what treatment was like, what was helpful, and what was not. If couples have been in a particular type of treatment in the past, then they may have expectancies about the nature of the current treatment. For example, if they previously were involved in a more psychodynamically oriented marital therapy, they might expect to spend a great deal of time focusing on childhood and unconscious motivations of the two partners; in addition, they might not expect to be learning skills and practicing new interaction patterns at home. Consequently, clarifying differences between past therapies and the present approach may prevent disappointment or confusion about the current therapy. Also, identifying what the couple found useful about therapy and what they did not like can suggest some ways of working with the couple and possible strategies to avoid or minimize.

Many individuals have had not only previous marital therapy but also previous marriages. If so, some conversation about how those relationships proceeded and ended can be useful. Of particular importance, the therapist can look for similar patterns of difficulty in the previous relationship as in the current marriage. At times the individual him- or herself will be aware of such patterns and openly share them. However, at other times existent patterns are not obvious to the individual but can be observed in terms of presenting complaints, perceptions of what the partner is like and should be like, and similar complaints raised by the spouse concerning the previous partner. For example, a man may report that both wives have complained that he is unwilling to share his feelings and thoughts, and that this concern was a major factor in the termination of his first marriage. Again, it is possible that both wives have unrealistic standards of how much the husband should share, but this information also provides the hypothesis that it is an area of particular difficulty for the husband.

Discussion of Current Concerns, Behaviors, and Relationship Strengths

After the marital history is completed, the session focuses on the couple's current concerns, individual and relationship strengths, and relationship behaviors. Whereas the discussion of the marital history is rather unstructured in terms of which spouse provides answers to which questions, the discussion of current concerns and strengths can be handled much more profitably by structuring the discussion in a particular manner. More specifically, the therapist discusses each person's concerns with that individual while the partner listens. Thus the conversation is between one spouse and the therapist, not between the two partners. Otherwise, there is a strong tendency for the two partners to argue about what the problems *really* are, whose fault they are, and so forth. This negative, argumentative tone can be almost totally averted by the therapist's directing the conversation to one spouse at a time. At this point in the session, the goal is to obtain a clarification of what behaviors are occurring and not occurring which are of concern to the individual.

In order to conduct this phase of the interview, it is helpful for the therapist to have available a list of concerns provided by each spouse. To accomplish this goal, the therapist can mail to the couple a packet of self-report inventories which are to be completed and returned prior to the initial session. This will probably include a demographic sheet and some of the inventories described below. Although data are lacking on the subject, clinical observation suggests that the therapist is likely to get a much more complete picture of a couple's concerns by providing self-report inventories that focus on numerous content areas rather than by waiting and merely asking the couple in the session what their concerns are. The latter approach often results in the presentation of a few major concerns. However, providing the stimuli on paper to direct the couple's attention to various areas of interaction seems to result in a more comprehensive picture of a couple's concerns. Also, some individuals appear more likely to acknowledge concerns privately on a self-report inventory that is returned to the therapist than to raise the concerns verbally with the spouse present. Because this means that the self-report inventories may provide more data, the couple needs to know before they complete the inventories that the answers will be discussed in the session with both partners present.

The therapist's introduction to the discussion of current concerns might be phrased as follows:

Therapist: Now I would like to get a better sense of your current concerns as well as strong points in your relationship. And I would like to do that in a certain way. Joe, we will start with you. I'm going to read what I understood to be your major concerns when I looked through the questionnaires you completed. I want to spend literally just a minute or so on each one. What I want you to do is to clarify for me exactly what your concern is in that area.

How are Alice and/or you behaving or not behaving that is troubling you? Just clarify what your concern is. Is that clear? Also I want to obtain some understanding of the areas that you feel are working well in your relationship.

Alice, what I want you to do during this time is to listen quietly. You may have heard many of these concerns before, but often people say that they learn something about their partners during this time. Also, you should know that when I hear one person's point of view, I take it for just that — that person's point of view on the issue. We will have a chance to talk in just a few minutes. O.K., Joe, you mentioned that you would like Alice to get together with your friends more often. Clarify what you mean there.

Several inventories exist which provide useful information for structuring a discussion of current concerns.

Areas-of-Change Questionnaire (A-C; Weiss et al., 1973).

The A-C consists of two parts, each composed of the same 34 items. The two parts differ only in terms of whose behavior is being discussed. In Part I, the respondent specifies whether he or she would like to see the partner behave more, less, or offer no change in a particular area of marital interaction. For example, Item 1 states, "I want my partner to participate in decisions about spending money." The responses range from much less (-3) to much more $(+3)$. The content of the items includes such areas as housekeeping and meals, finances, communication, relatives, friends, sex, work habits, children, leisure time, physical abuse, and so forth. In many research applications, the items are summed to arrive at an overall measure of how much change an individual desires across these content areas. This summary score has been found to be correlated with global measures of marital adjustment (Margolin, 1978), and A-C scores have shown expected changes in response to BMT (e.g., Baucom, 1982).

Whereas a summary score may provide the clinician with a global index of the amount of change desired, it provides little information about the particular areas requiring intervention. For the latter purpose, using the A-C on the item level is much more useful. That is, the clinician can merely note the content of the items in which the respondent wishes behavioral change from the partner and ask for clarification of these concerns during the initial interview. Another helpful feature of the A-C is that for each item, the respondent indicates whether the issue is one of major importance in the relationship. Thus, amount of change desired in a content area and importance of that area are assessed separately.

Isolating aspects of the relationship that are successful is also important in order to help the couple recognize their strengths and clarify what behaviors could be maintained to promote satisfaction. Part I of the A-C also provides an opportunity to focus on areas that are working smoothly in the marriage. That is, the therapist can comment on the specific areas in which the respondent did not desire any change on the partner's part and follow these observations by an inquiry about what behaviors from the spouse contribute to satisfaction in that area.

At times, the A-C has been described as if it provides an assessment of actual behaviors (Jacobson, Elwood, & Dallas, 1981). Therefore, when the couple has altered their A-C scores from the beginning to the end of therapy, this is interpreted as indicating behavioral change in these particular content areas. However, the A-C actually assesses each partner's desire for behavior change in the partner. Changes with treatment could be indicative of behavior changes in the partner; however, lower requests for change also could reflect only the respondent's *perception* that the partner has changed his or her behavior, or lower A-C scores could reflect a change in *standards* of how the partner should behave. Thus a lower request for change might not be indicative of a behavior change on the partner's part so much as a cognitive shift from the respondent.

Part II of the A-C includes the same 34 items but worded in terms of how much the respondent believes the partner wants the respondent to change in these areas. For example, Item 1 is phrased, "It would please my partner if I participated in decisions about spending money . . . much less (−3) to much more (+3). By comparing Part II of one person's answers with Part I of the other person's form, it is possible to obtain some indication of whether each person understands what the partner wants from him or her. In some cases, merely providing a clarification of what the two persons want from each other can be all that is needed to promote behavior change. Also, these comparisons across forms can point out to the couple the importance of communication and how difficulties arise when the two persons do not clearly communicate their desires.

On other occasions, the partner's perception in Part II of the A-C matches the other's response on Part I. That is, the husband may correctly perceive in Part II of his form that his wife would like him to pay more attention to his appearance. Such concordance in perceptions suggests that a spouse's request for behavioral changes does not result from a history of poor communication between the spouses regarding what is desired from one another. Instead, it probably results from a difference in the partners' opinions about what is appropriate or acceptable behavior, or from differences in how the two partners want their relationship to be in a given area. This calls for a different kind of intervention, focused either on shifting incompatible standards or on teaching the couple to problem-solve and compromise in areas where they have different preferences for behavior.

It is important during the assessment phase to stress to the couple that each person will not be focusing solely on requesting the partner to change. Each person also will be asked to evaluate changes that he or she can make to improve the relationship. An alteration in the wording of the A-C can also provide this opportunity. A Part III can be added which is phrased, "I want to. . ." This wording allows the respondent to think about how he or she can behave differently in order to benefit the marriage.

Dyadic Adjustment Scale (DAS; Spanier, 1976).

The DAS is a self-report inventory which has been used extensively in the past decade to provide an overall indicator of marital adjustment. The DAS has been shown to discriminate between divorced and married couples; in addition, DAS scores correlate .93 (Spanier, 1976) with the frequently used Locke-Wallace Marital Adjustment Scale (Locke & Wallace, 1959). Also, as would be expected, DAS scores have been shown to increase in response to BMT (cf., Baucom & Lester, 1986).

Whereas numerous terms such as level of adjustment, satisfaction, and happiness have been used in the literature to describe a couple's general status, the use of the term adjustment with the DAS has a particular meaning which reflects the content of the scale's items. The DAS is composed of 32 items which have been factor-analyzed, resulting in four factors: "Dyadic Consensus (the degree to which the couple agrees on matters of importance to the relationship); Dyadic Cohesion (the degree to which the couple engages in activities together); Dyadic Satisfaction (the degree to which the couple is satisfied with the present state of the relationship and is committed to its continuance); and Affectional Expression (the degree to which the couple is satisfied with the expression of affection and sex in the relationship)" (Spanier & Filsinger, 1983, p. 157). Thus, the DAS assesses more than whether or not the couple is satisfied with the overall relationship, although a summary score across all items on the inventory is the most frequent score provided. Spanier and Filsinger (1983) advocate the use of this summary score for research and clinical purposes, but the specificity of information provided from the summary is limited.

In addition to this total score, additional useful clinical information can be obtained from the DAS. On the item level, the consensus items can be evaluated to clarify which particular content areas of the marriage (e.g., religion, career decisions, amount of time spent together) are perceived by the individual as areas of disagreement for the couple. Rather than focusing on requests for behavior change in the partner, the DAS consensus items focus on the degree of agreement as a couple, and one person is not singled out. This format provides an easy opportunity for the therapist to inquire about how the respondent thinks each person might change to assist the marriage. In addition, the consensus items on which the individuals report little disagreement provide an opportunity to point out and clarify areas of the relationship that may be more satisfactory for the couple.

A description of the historical development of the DAS as well as other suggestions for its clinical use are provided by Spanier and Filsinger (1983).

Marital Satisfaction Inventory (MSI; Snyder, 1979).

The MSI is a 280-item true-false inventory consisting of 11 scales and can be completed in approximately 30 minutes. The 11 scales include one validity scale, a global distress scale, and nine scales focusing on specific areas: affective communication, problem-solving communication, time together, disagreement about finances, sexual dissatisfaction, role orientation (traditional versus nontraditional attitudes toward marital and parental roles), family history of distress, dissatisfaction with children, and conflict over childrearing. Snyder, Wills, and Keiser (1981) have provided evidence for the convergent and discriminant validity of the scales based on correlations between scale scores and clinicians' ratings of areas of difficulty for couples entering marital therapy.

One of the strengths of the MSI is the norms that have been developed which allow for a profile of the scores on the various scales. In form, the profile resembles that obtained with the Minnesota Multiphasic Personality Inventory (Hathaway & McKinley, 1967). The two spouses' scores are placed on the same profile sheet, which allows for a direct comparison of their responses in order to clarify where they have overlapping concerns and where they differ in their perceptions of the marital problems. Snyder and his colleagues are engaged in an impressive series of investigations to provide actuarial interpretations of various profile configurations on the MSI. However, at present the main use of the MSI for behavioral assessment is again a clarification of the couple's specific areas of concern.

All of the above inventories provide information focal to the specific areas of concern to the couple. Using all three with each couple would probably be too time consuming for the couple and would provide redundant information. At present there are no data to lead the clinician to favor any single one or combination of these instruments over the others. Given our current state of knowledge, it is appropriate for the clinician to become familiar with these various inventories and to decide which to use after trying various combinations with couples. In any case, the instruments identify content areas of concern which the therapist will then clarify with the couple during interviews, as described earlier.

Regardless of which inventories are selected, there are often concerns of couples which are not included on any inventory. Therefore, after discussing the problem areas which have been isolated on the questionnaires, the clinician is wise to ask the individual if there are other areas of concern which have not been discussed. After discussing the various areas of concern, the clinician also might ask the individual to rank his or her top two or three concerns. Likewise, the clinician can maintain some balance between positives and negatives by asking each individual to state the aspects of the relationship with which he or she is most satisfied or least dissatisfied.

Spouse Observation Checklist (SOC; Weiss et al., 1973).

None of the above inventories asks the respondent to focus on a particular time period for evaluating the relationship or to report specific behaviors that occurred. Instead the respondent is to think back over the relationship and make summary evaluations in each area addressed. The SOC, one of several assessment instruments developed at the University of Oregon and Oregon Research Institute, is different in that regard. The SOC describes 408 behaviors that might occur in a relationship on a daily basis. The couple is asked to select an agreed-upon 24-hour period and at the end of that time to check the behaviors that occurred during that period. Thus, the SOC was developed from the behavioral premise that the couple's satisfaction with the relationship on a given day will be, to an extent, a function of the behaviors that occur during that day. As noted in Chapter 2, this hypothesis has obtained considerable support when couples have been asked to gather SOC data for a number of consecutive days along with ratings of relationship satisfaction. In addition to the more summary evaluative statements provided by the previously described inventories, the clinician might want to use the SOC to obtain a report of the behaviors in which the partners are engaging on a daily basis.

As indicated in its title, the SOC focuses on the spouse's behavior; that is, the husband reports the behavior of the wife, and vice versa. In addition, some items focus on the couple as a unit, for example, "We went jogging or bicycle riding." The items have been grouped on an a priori basis into 12 content areas: (a) affection; (b) companionship; (c) consideration; (d) sex; (e) communication process; (f) coupling activities; (g) child care and parenting; (h) household management; (i) financial decision making; (j) employment-education; (k) personal habits and appearance; (l) self and spouse independence. The respondent checks that a given behavior occurred by placing it into one of the two categories of "pleasing" or "displeasing," depending on how the behavior affected him or her. At the end of the checklist, the respondent marks how he or she felt about the marital relationship *for that one day* on a nine-point scale. Weiss and Perry (1983) recommend that the couple be asked to complete the SOC each 24 hours for two weeks during the initial assessment period. However, the therapist must be prepared for the reality that many couples are unlikely to cooperate in systematic data gathering for this lengthy time period.

Various types of information can be obtained from the SOC. Because recent investigations indicate that frequently there are significant discrepancies between the spouses in their reporting of the same events (see Chapter 3), the clinician cannot assume that the SOC provides a veridical report of behaviors that actually occurred. In fact, determining whether the couple perceives similarly what is and is not occurring in the relationship is important. For example, if the therapist were to help one spouse increase a given behavior which was expected to benefit the relationship, it might serve little purpose if the partner did not notice or track that behavior. Thus, discrepancies in reporting can alert the clinician to significant cognitive factors which may be filtering the spouses' experience of their encounters.

In addition to observing discrepancies in reporting, the clinician can identify any behaviors or events that would be expected to be important to the couple but are not reported on the SOC as having occurred; yet, concern about the absence of these behaviors has not been reported on other forms. For example, the therapist might conclude from the SOC reports that the couple has had no sexual interaction during the assessment period, yet they have not complained of sexual concerns on other inventories. It may be that the spouses were embarrassed or for some other reason reluctant to raise sexual concerns; however, the behavioral absence of sexual interaction can bring the issue to the therapist's attention and initiate a conversation.

In other cases, a couple might have fallen into such a routinized pattern of interaction that they have become oblivious to the presence or absence of other behaviors. For example, some couples have a rather routine evening schedule which includes preparing and eating dinner, cleaning the house, getting the children to bed, and watching television. A look at their SOC might indicate that they are engaging in few joint recreational or coupling activities. Because the couple rarely engages in such behaviors, they may have lost perspective and not even realize that such activities are missing from the marriage.

A third way of evaluating the SOC is in terms of the average frequency of overall pleasures and displeasures that occur during a given day, disregarding the content of the behavior. There are not well-defined norms for the SOC, and they will be difficult to obtain because the frequencies and types of behaviors will vary according to the amount of time a couple spends together. Yet, continued experience allows the clinician to develop some informal norms for what is a high and low rate of positive and negative behaviors. Then the clinician can note whether a given distressed couple seems to engage in a high rate of negative behaviors, a low rate of positive behaviors, or some combination of these. This can lead the clinician to develop a treatment strategy that focuses on either increasing positives or decreasing negatives. Alternatively, the clinician might note that a couple's behaviors resemble those of most nondistressed couples. In such cases, one plausible hypothesis is that the spouses have unrealistic standards for each other, a situation calling for cognitive intervention.

Self and spouse monitoring.

The SOC is intended as a device to monitor a wide range of behaviors of the partner. However, the clinician is often interested in learning about *sequences* of behavior that occur during a given interaction, in order to understand some issue more completely. In such cases, the clinician might want to obtain additional information by asking spouses to monitor their own, their partner's, or both persons' behavior in a given area of the relationship.

For example, one couple complained that their sexual interactions were extremely awkward, resulting in both partners' feeling anxious and tense. They were unable to describe clearly the sequence of behaviors that contributed to this discomfort. Therefore, the therapist asked them to observe carefully who did and said what, and what their thoughts and feelings were during that time. By the next week, they had had only one sexual encounter, but the behaviors they observed allowed them to clarify their typical interaction pattern. The husband would tentatively initiate physical contact by rubbing the wife's arm or shoulder with his hand. The wife wanted little to do with his advances and would attempt to lie perfectly still in the bed when he touched her. However, she had trouble not moving at all. The husband attempted to read these cues, wondering whether they were a positive response to his initiation or merely symptoms of anxiety. He would continue his caressing further in order to obtain some clarification. When his wife did not respond demonstratively, he would finally stop initiating and would roll over angrily. Understanding this series of behaviors, thoughts, and feelings was extremely important in designing an appropriate intervention strategy.

By combining the information from such self and spouse monitoring with findings from the SOC and the self-report inventories described above, the clinician can gain a good understanding of a couple's perceptions of areas of disagreement, specific behaviors that the spouses would like changed in the partner and self, the couple's perceptions of events occurring and not occurring on a daily basis and their relation to daily satisfaction, important behavioral sequences, and a delineation of aspects of the relationship that appear to be functioning more smoothly.

EVALUATION OF COMMUNICATION

After the above information is obtained in a structured manner by having each spouse speak directly to the clinician, the next phase of the assessment focuses on evaluating the spouses' interaction with each other. Obtaining a behavioral sample of the couple's communication in the clinician's office is not difficult. However, even here one must be cautious concerning the generalizations made about the couple's interaction in their home setting based on observations made in the office. For example, Gottman (1979) found that both husbands and wives were more negative in their communication at home than in a laboratory, and they were more likely to reciprocate negative affect at home. Consequently, after observing a couple's interaction, it is useful to ask them the extent to which that interaction was typical of the way they frequently talk to each other.

In assessing communication, several decisions must be made in structuring the task. First the type of communication or the goal of the communication must be specified. Consistent with the differentiation between problem solving and emotional expressiveness, couples are typically asked to communicate at different times with both of these goals in mind. (In this chapter, assessment of problem-solving communication will be the focus because emotional expressiveness will be addressed in Chapter 7, on affective assesssment.) Second, the content of the communication must be specified. In problem solving, couples typically are asked to spend about 10 minutes attempting to resolve a moderate-size problem of their choice which exists in their relationship. A problem of moderate intensity is suggested so that it will have enough importance to involve the couple but will not overwhelm them if they lack the skills to resolve it at this time. Many couples become distraught when focusing on major problems without the skills to approach them.

Third, in addition to concerns about the effects of the setting, other issues related to generalizability of the observations must be considered. The content of the particular topic discussed might influence the communication process. Therefore, asking the couple to attempt to problem-solve on at least two different problems can help isolate common patterns across the two conversations. Also, it is somewhat risky to assess problem-solving ability during a single session. After assessing couples' problem-solving communication on two occasions a week apart without any intervening treatment, Wieder and Weiss (1980) concluded that although meaningful information about the couple could be obtained from a single occasion, assessment on two occasions was preferable. Similarly, Haynes et al. (1979) found that across three evenings, there was high stability on only 5 of 10 selected coding categories of communication.

Finally, the person(s) to provide the evaluation of the communication must be chosen based on what the clinician wants to learn. Most researchers have asked a couple to interact and then had tapes of the interaction coded by a trained observer who has learned a particular coding system, thus having an "outsider" evaluate the communication. Similarly, in clinical settings the therapist often directly observes the couple interacting and, using some informal or formal system, evaluates the communication. Alternatively, the couple can be asked to interact with each other, and the spouses are asked to evaluate the interaction themselves, an "insider's approach."

Outsiders' Evaluation of Communication

Consistent with the importance given to problem-solving skills in BMT, an assessment of problem solving is essential for treatment planning.

If the clinician is planning to evaluate the interaction, then an introduction to the task might be as follows:

Therapist: Next, what I would like to do is to get a glimpse of your interaction with each other. So, I'd like you to pick what you consider to be a moderate-size problem in your relationship. While you talk to each other, I am going to sit here quietly and just watch and listen. If you would, pick a topic to discuss and then spend about 10 minutes trying to reach a solution to it. I'll tell you when that time is up.

Once the couple has discussed a problem, then the communication must be evaluated. Several comprehensive coding systems have been developed to rate couples' verbal and nonverbal interactions. Some of the more widely used systems include (a) the Marital Interaction Coding System, now in its third version (MICS III; Weiss & Summers, 1983); (b) the Couples Interaction Scoring System (CISS; Gottman, 1979; Notarius & Markman, 1981); and (c) the Kategoriensystem fur Partnerschaftliche Interaktion (KPI; Hahlweg, Reisner, Kohli, Vollmer, Schindler, & Revenstorf, 1984), created in West Germany but now translated into English. Although these coding systems have been used in numerous research investigations, they are not applicable on a wide-scale clinical basis because of the time and expense involved in utilizing them. Consequently, some alternative strategies are needed for assessing communication on a routine clinical basis.

One such strategy is for the therapist to become intimately familiar with one or more of the comprehensive coding systems and apply it to the interaction informally. Once a therapist has a categorization system to apply, it becomes rather apparent when a couple or spouse is engaging in a high rate of a specific type of negative communication or seems to lack certain types of positive communication. Even without detailed knowledge of the specific coding systems, the therapist can become familiar with the couple communication literature in order to become aware of the types of communication that seem to be problematic for couples and then recognize them when they occur in a particular couple. Consequently, the therapist can informally note specific types of communication that are problematic for a couple.

The experienced clinician should simply keep these problematic communications in mind when he or she is integrating assessment information for treatment planning. However, it is often useful to record communication information in some form so that the clinician can study it more carefully and/or provide feedback to the couple at the end of the assessment phase. Thomas and his associates (Thomas, 1977; Thomas, Walter, & O'Flaherty, 1974) have developed the Verbal Problem Checklist, which can be useful for this purpose. The clinician directly observes the couple interacting and then rates them on 49 categories of verbal behavior. This rating includes both an evaluation of the frequency with which each behavior occurs and the degree to which that category appears to be a problem area for the couple. One limitation of the checklist is that it is restricted to verbal behavior and does not include nonverbal behavior. However, it would not be difficult for the clinician to supplement the checklist with ratings of important nonverbal behaviors. Also, if the clinician has learned on of the more comprehensive coding systems such as the MICS, CISS, or KPI, adapting the format of Thomas's checklist to the categories of another coding system is not difficult. For example, Table 5-2 presents an adaptation of the checklist for use with the MICS III coding system.

TABLE 5-2
Checklist Version for the Marital Interaction Coding
System III* and for Communication Sequences

Code	Frequency†	Degree of Problem/Facilitation§
	MICS III	
Description		
Problem description external	_____	_____
Problem description internal	_____	_____
Blame		
Complain	_____	_____
Criticize	_____	_____
Negative mind-read	_____	_____
Put-down	_____	_____
Propose change		
Positive solution	_____	_____
Negative solution	_____	_____
Compromise	_____	_____
Irrelevant		
Normative	_____	_____
Talk	_____	_____

*See Weiss and Summers (1983) for detailed explanations of the communication codes.

† 1—not at all, 2—slight amount, 3—moderate amount, 4—large amount.

§1—presence of problem, 2—no problem, 3—facilitates communication, 4—rater uncertain.

Validation

Agree	_____	_____
Approve	_____	_____
Accept responsibility	_____	_____
Compliance	_____	_____

Invalidation

Disagree	_____	_____
Deny responsibility	_____	_____
Excuse	_____	_____
Interrupt	_____	_____
Noncompliance	_____	_____
Turn-off	_____	_____

Facilitation

Paraphrase/reflection	_____	_____
Positive mind-read	_____	_____
Humor	_____	_____
Positive physical contact	_____	_____
Smile/laugh	_____	_____
Assent	_____	_____

COMMUNICATION SEQUENCES

Yes-but	_____	_____
Problem escalation and cross complaining	_____	_____
Distancing	_____	_____
Stalemating	_____	_____
Metacommunication	_____	_____
Attraction	_____	_____
Problem acceptance	_____	_____

Whereas the above approach will isolate single communication acts, the clinician also will want to assess the important communication sequences discussed in Chapter 2: (a) yes-but; (b) problem escalation and cross-complaining; (c) distancing; (d) stalemating; (e) metacommunication; (f) attraction; (g) problem acceptance. A sequential analysis would be necessary to isolate these patterns precisely. However, just as when assessing individual communications, the clinician can informally evaluate these sequences as the spouses interact with each other. Therefore, these sequences are included at the bottom of Table 5-2.

Once the above specific communications and patterns are clarified, the clinician must interpret this information for treatment planning. The typical behavioral approach has been to interpret such patterns as resulting from skill deficits. However, as noted in Chapter 2, the findings from Vincent et al. (1975) and Birchler et al. (1975) showing that married individuals communicate differently with other people compared to how they communicate with their partners cast suspicion on an automatic interpretation of a skill deficit as the basis for a couple's interaction pattern. In fact, this difference in communication often can be observed in the therapy session, where a spouse speaks constructively with the therapist and then immediately enters into a negative interaction cycle with the partner. One plausible interpretation of this discrepancy is that communication patterns are not so much an individual skill but rather are a *couple's* skill, and the couple as a unit has not learned how to interact effectively with each other. Or perhaps the couple has been able to communicate effectively with each other in the past, but owing to other stresses in their marriage they have now developed bad habits which are maintained. All of these interpretations would put primary emphasis on a communications skills-oriented approach to remedy the couple's problems.

However, at times the therapist may attempt to teach the couple problem-solving and communication skills for a number of weeks and be unsuccessful. This can be particularly perplexing when the spouses seem to be bright and articulate. In this situation, a reasonable hypothesis is that the clinician has "missed something" important in the assessment and conceptualization of the couple. On many occasions, one or both members of the couple do not appear to be *trying* to communicate effectively. Even more problematic, at times one or both persons seem to be actively attempting to disrupt the couple's progress toward reaching solutions to their problems. As Notarius, Markman, and Gottman (1983) suggest, on many such occasions the couple may have *hidden agendas* which are interfering with their interaction in other realms, including communication. A hidden agenda refers to a problem, concern, or feeling which has not been made explicit but which is affecting the couple's relationship. At times the individual with the hidden agenda seems to know clearly what the issue is about; at other times the person has only a vague feeling or sense that something is wrong and that he or she does not want to cooperate. Clearly, the clinician wants to uncover any hidden agendas whenever possible during the initial assessment phase so that they can be taken into account in treatment planning. Cues that there may be hidden agendas include extreme emotional responses to seemingly minor issues or emotional responses that the individual cannot relate to any issue: "I just know I feel depressed when we are together, but I don't know why." As suggested earlier, hidden agendas also are suggested by a pattern of communication that seems highly discrepant from a person's level of education or highly discrepant from the individual's communication pattern with others.

Unfortunately, it is not always possible to recognize the existence of a hidden agenda or to clarify its contents during the initial assessment. At times these become obvious only as therapy proceeds. For example, one wife seemed quite motivated to improve her communication with her husband and talked about her desire to improve the relationship. As therapy proceeded, she did work hard to communicate more positively, but the therapist and husband became confused because none of the solutions she offered seemed to be oriented toward increasing togetherness or cooperative long-term plans. After several discussions, the wife acknowledged that she was in love with another man and intended to terminate her current marriage. However, she had wanted to improve her communication with her husband before telling him about her plans, in the hope that they would be able to terminate the relationship on more friendly terms and with maximum cooperation regarding decisions about the children. Because she wanted the communication to be improved before telling her husband about her plans regarding divorce, it is quite unlikely that the therapist could have uncovered this issue during the initial assessment.

At the same time, the therapist should not automatically assume that troubled communication is indicative of some other issue or hidden agenda. Although there may be unacknowledged issues that are interfering with the couple's functioning, this is not always the case. We have used communication training to treat a number of couples who demonstrated communication difficulties and found this treatment to be successful without hidden agendas ever entering into the picture.

Insiders' Evaluation of Communication

The preceding strategies for assessing communication all rely on the clinician or some trained observer to evaluate the couple's interaction. A great deal of empirical evidence exists to validate the utility of such information. However, as noted in Chapter 2, the couple's own perception of their communication has been shown to be predictive of their marital adjustment up to five years later (Markman, 1979, 1981). Also, evidence to date indicates that couples' perceptions of their communication do not correlate well with outsiders' perceptions of the same interaction (Floyd & Markman, 1983; Margolin, 1978; Robinson & Price, 1980; Weiss et al., 1981). Which of these two perspectives is more important is unclear at this point, but it might be quite useful for the clinician to know whether the couple perceives the communication in the same way that the clinician does. Otherwise, the clinician may be asking the couple to change certain communications which appear to be destructive to the clinician but which the spouses perceive as positive. Also, a couple may have their own private form of communication, and the clinician may be unable to recognize the private meanings given to certain communications. For example, owing to the couple's past history, certain terms that may appear neutral to outsiders may have a negative connotation to the couple. Therefore, an outsider might view the communication as positive, whereas the couple is aware through their private communication system that a negative communication has transpired.

At least two major strategies have been employed for having a couple evaluate a specific interaction between them. One approach has the couple evaluate each communication as it occurs (e.g., Gottman, Notarius, Markman, Bank, Yoppi, & Rubin, 1976; Markman & Poltrock, 1982). The couple is asked to problem-solve (or have some other type of conversation) and pause after each person speaks. During that pause, two ratings occur. The speaker rates whether he or she *intended* the message just delivered to be positive, neutral, or negative. Similarly, the listener rates whether the *impact* of the message was positive, neutral, or negative. If the two ratings are discrepant, then the communication system is faulty or ineffective. Of particular importance is how the communication is perceived by the listener because Markman (1979, 1981) has found that this impact rating predicts marital adjustment in the future. Consequently, the clinician should be attuned particularly to discrepancies between the two spouses' evaluations of a message and the negativity of the impact ratings. After the ratings have occurred for a given communication, the couple continues with the other person speaking. Whereas various devices have been constructed to assist the couple in making ratings that can be recorded and evaluated for research purposes, the task can be simplified for clinical purposes. Each person can be handed three cards, one marked neutral, one marked negative, and one marked positive. Each person can hold up the appropriate card for the clinician to observe after each communication. These cards should be held up in such a way that the partner does not see the rating from the spouse.

An alternative strategy has been employed by Weiss et al. (1981) to obtain couples' evaluations of their interactions. They asked couples to problem-solve and videotaped the interaction. Then they replayed the interaction to the spouses separately and asked the spouses to rate each communication. At present there has been no direct comparison of these two strategies, but there are potential difficulties with each. Video reconstruction techniques such as that used by Weiss et al. rely on the couple's memory of how they perceived the interaction as it was occurring. Also, ratings of communication early in the interaction could be influenced by communication later in the interaction. For example, a couple might have started an interaction in a positive manner but begun to argue near the end of the interaction. When the spouse is asked to observe the tape, his or her perception of the early part of the tape could be influenced by the knowledge that the conversation ended in an argument. Using Markman's approach of having the couple rate each communication as it occurs could influence the subsequent communication in at least two ways. First, the couple is focused on how positive or negative the communication appears to them, something to which they might not otherwise be attending. Second, the interaction is stopped after each person speaks, an unnatural state of affairs. Although each strategy has some potential problems, the only two alternatives appear to be to have the couple rate the communication as it occurs or at some later point.

The strategies described here ask the couple to rate a specific interaction, evaluating each communication in it. Another approach to obtaining the spouses' perceptions of their communication is to ask them to complete communication self-report inventories. However, these differ from their ratings of a given interaction sequence in several ways and thus provide different information (Glick & Gross, 1975). Whereas the rating systems described above focus on a specific interaction, communication self-report inventories do not specify a given interaction on which to base an evaluation of the communication. Instead, the respondent is to think back and evaluate the communication across situations. Thus a summary type of evaluation is provided for each question. Also, the self-report inventories typically do not ask the respondent to evaluate the communication in a specific context, in terms of either the setting for the interaction or the type of conversation that is occurring. The inventories seem to assume a fair amount of constancy of communication across situations, which may or may not be characteristic of a specific couple.

These differences between the self-report inventories and ratings of specific interactions do not imply the superiority of either strategy; this is an empirical question which surprisingly has been rarely addressed. The ratings from one or two interactions may not generalize well to most of the couple's interactions at home. Also, the couple's more global evaluation of their interaction through self-report inventories may provide a good over-all picture of how the couple is likely to interact or at least perceive that they interact with each other. Because the self-report communication inventories do not focus the spouse on specific occasions for rating communication but instead rely on rather global evaluations, the self-report measures may maximize the opportunity for cognitive appraisals of the relationship to influence the reports of communication. Consequently, it is not surprising that Epstein et al. (1987) found that self-reports of marital communication were correlated with spouses' dysfunctional patterns of cognitions regarding marital relationships; in addition, the dysfunctional cognitions largely, but not totally, accounted for the often reported correlations between marital communication and marital distress.

There are a number of self-report communication scales, including the Marital Communication Inventory (MCI; Bienvenu, 1970), the Primary Communication Inventory (PCI; Navran, 1967), the self-report form of the Verbal Problems Checklist (VPC; Chavez, Samuel, and Haynes, 1981), and the Problem-Solving Communication (PSC) and Affective Communication (AFC) scales from the Marital Satisfaction Inventory (MSI; Snyder, 1981). A more detailed description of each of these scales, comparisons among them, along with a discussion of the various observational coding systems and related marital communication research, is available in Baucom and Adams (1987). At present, the MCI will be presented as an example of one such scale and how it might be used clinically.

The MCI consists of 48 items answered in terms of frequency of occurrence, ranging from "usually" to "never." The MCI typically has been scored to obtain a single global index of communication effectiveness. As expected, scores on the MCI have typically been very highly correlated (r = .80 and above) with global measures of marital adjustment and satisfaction (i.e., DAS and MAS) (Costa, 1981; Lumpkin, 1981; Murphy & Mendelson, 1973). However, the lack of adequate norms for the MCI and the general level of information provided by such an index limits its clinical utility. On the basis of a number of factor analytic studies, Schumm, Anderson, and Griffin (1983) make a convincing argument that it is more useful to look at the MCI in terms of several subscales. The content of the regard subscale of the MCI assesses the extent to which the respondent perceives that he or she receives positive communication and general support from the partner. The empathy subscale measures the extent to which the respondent believes that the partner is willing and able to listen attentively to the respondent. Conversely, the self-disclosure subscale focuses on the respondent's comfort in expressing feelings to the partner. The level of hostility and aversive control tactics that the respondent believes the couple displays in their communication is tapped by the aversive communication scale. Finally, the discussion scale measures the respondent's perception of the amount of communication shared by the couple. Although these perceptions cannot be assumed to be veridical reports, they can focus the clinician on particular areas of communication difficulty for the couple.

In addition to utilization of the MSI on the subscale level, potentially important information can be obtained by scrutinizing individual item responses. For example, the MCI asks for the respondent's perception of the number of compliments given by the partner and whether the couple discusses pleasant events that occurred during the day. Responses to these items can serve as stimuli for discussions of these specific areas which are important for treatment planning. Thus, inventories such as the MCI can help to ensure that communication in a broad range of contexts has been considered by the couple and brought to the therapist's attention.

SELECTING ASSESSMENT STRATEGIES

Attempting to employ all the possible assessment strategies discussed in this and the next two chapters is neither possible nor necessary. Instead, the clinician must be selective and, to an extent, must tailor the assessment to the particular couple. Yet, certain types of information are useful to gather for all couples. With regard to behavior, both communication and noncommunication behavior is of interest. Mailing the DAS and A-C to the couple prior to the initial session and having them returned before the session can result in a delineation of specific areas of concern to the couple as well as an assessment of overall level of marital adjustment. During the initital assessment sessions, the marital history, discussion of current relationship concerns and strengths, evaluation of communication from an outsider's perspective, and feedback to the couple are routinely included. The remaining assessment instruments are used on a supplemental basis when needed. For example, if the couple has an unclear picture of what behaviors occur on a daily basis or if they greatly disagree about what behaviors occur, then the couple might be asked to monitor these behaviors with the SOC. Similarly, if the spouses agree that a specific aspect of their relationship is problematic but have difficulty describing the behavioral sequences involved, the clinician might ask them to monitor the behavioral interaction in that domain. Thus, the couple might agree that they do not enjoy their evenings out together but are not certain why.

The clinician might ask them to write down what each person says and how each responds when they go out together for entertainment. The monitoring by spouses at home occurs not only during the initial assessment; the clinician continually asks the couple to monitor changes at home that were agreed upon during therapy.

Having the couple evaluate their own communication can be particularly useful on certain occasions. When either or both spouses are having an unexpected reaction to the partner's communication, that reaction is often a function of how the partner's communication is being interpreted. To clarify whether this is the case, it can be useful to have the couple rate the intent and impact of a communication sequence. Furthermore, when couples explain that they often do not understand each other, it can be helpful to evaluate whether certain types of communication or topics are difficult for them to discuss clearly, again by having them rate their own communication.

INTEGRATING ASSESSMENT INFORMATION

The strategies described here provide a wealth of data for the clinician and the couple to consider. In addition, extensive information about the cognitive and affective aspects of the relationship is gathered during the initial assessment sessions. Obviously the clinician will attempt to integrate the behavioral, cognitive, and affective information. However, this chapter focuses on the integration of the various items of information regarding the couple's behaviors.

Given that a variety of behaviors are being assessed, the clinician is likely to want to profile the couple's behavioral strengths and weaknesses. Thus, on a global level the clinician should evaluate whether the couple appears to be engaging in a surfeit of negative behaviors which typifies many distressed couples. Similarly, the frequency of positive behaviors also is important. Because the couple is distressed, it is easy to focus on the destructive aspects of the relationship which are so apparent, neglecting the absence of positives. Important among these is the extent to which the couple engages in pleasurable activities together, such as recreation and relaxation activities. As couples' lives become increasingly complex with job and family demands, the first thing to be forfeited for many couples is joint leisure activities.

In addition to the overall rates with which positive and negative behaviors seem to occur for the couple, the clinician will want to note the specific areas of married life about which the couple disagrees or has arguments. At times these various content areas may seem unrelated and will serve as separate topics for discussion, perhaps during problem solving. On other occasions, the content areas of concern will revolve around one or more general themes which may typify the couple's interaction. For example, one wife responded with extreme jealousy if her husband sat next to another woman at a dinner party. This same wife had panic attacks if she went outside to help her husband work in the yard but did not see him immediately when she got outside. These and several other presenting problems centered around the themes of unrealistic fear of losing her husband and the desire to control even trivial aspects of her family members' lives. Noting the themes can be useful for bringing coherence to the couple's problems as well as guiding the direction for treatment.

The couple's communication strengths and weaknesses also are important. The communication difficulties may seem somewhat independent of other noncommunication problems, but at times the major communication patterns reflect broader patterns that affect other aspects of the relationship. For example, a wife may state that her husband treats her like a child, attempting to take care of her and not allowing her to be an adult. This may be evident in the way that he makes arrangements for trips, takes care of all financial investments, and so forth. This same pattern also may be evident in their problem-solving communication, in which he listens to what she says politely but then seems to ignore it in making his response. Thus, looking for continuity of patterns across communication and other behaviors will assist the clinician in conceptualizing the couple's difficulties.

As with all assessment strategies, the integration of information becomes more complex when inconsistencies seem to arise. Within the responses of a single spouse, there may be seeming inconsistencies when discussing a single issue. This may reflect that the spouse's behavioral preferences are situation-specific, and *seeming* inconsistencies may result when there is not enough detail elicited to clarify when a given behavior is desired and not desired. For example, one wife commented that she wanted her husband to help her more in the preparation of the evening meals. Later, during the assessment, she stated that she would prefer that he stay out of the kitchen and watch the children while she was cooking. However, when the issue was pursued further, the wife clarified that when their children were playing outside with neighborhood children, she wanted her husband to help her in the kitchen. When the weather was bad and the children were inside, she preferred that her husband assist by keeping everyone out of the kitchen. Thus, when such discrepancies appear to exist, the clinician can attempt to obtain additional information, stating that he or she is unclear about what the respondent means because on one assessment device the person is asking for more of a given behavior but on a different instrument appears to be requesting less of the same behavior.

Seeming inconsistencies also might reflect ambivalence on the spouse's part. For example, one husband complained that he felt suffocated by his wife and demanded more time for himself. Yet he stated that his wife did not spend enough time with him and that he needed her approval. Further exploration clarified that this husband was caught in a major autonomy/ dependence conflict. In this case, his two conflicting requests represented the two sides of the conflict he was experiencing. A useful strategy in such instances is to legitimize the existence of ambivalent feelings and help the couple decide how to respond to them.

In addition to inconsistencies in reporting by one spouse, the two partners often present somewhat different pictures of the relationship, behaviors that occur, and requests for behavioral changes. These differences can be due to several factors. If one partner really does not want to be in marital therapy, that person might minimize the extent of problems in the relationship. This minimization can be intended to convince the therapist that therapy is not needed. The minimization can produce noticeable discrepancies in the two spouses' reports. Often it is possible to note a response set in the self-report inventories, in which one person rates major conflict or a desire for a great deal of change in several behavioral areas whereas the spouse acknowledges concerns in the same areas but generally states the need for only minor changes in those areas.

Differing presentations of the relationship may reflect that the two persons actually perceive what is occurring in the relationship differently. Different reports of behaviors by the two spouses might suggest that one person is not tracking certain behaviors that occur. For example, many spouses seem to be unaware of certain communications they are using; for example, they may not realize that they interrupt their partners frequently.

Differential reports from the two partners also might result from the meanings that are given to certain behaviors by the two spouses. Because many of the self-report inventories ask for an evaluation of the behaviors (e.g., desire for amount of change in partner, etc.), these cognitive factors become important when people report behavioral concerns. For example, the couple may differ in their evaluations of what happens when they attend a party. The husband may be upset, reporting that his wife flirts with other men. On the other hand, she may believe that she is only being friendly, trying to make a good impression on his business associates. Thus, the two might actually agree on the specific behaviors in which she engages, but the meaning given to these behaviors can result in different concerns about the relationship. Cognitive factors that can produce such idiosyncratic interpretations of marital events were described in Chapter 2.

Closely related to differences in perceptions and interpretations of what specific behaviors mean, differential behavioral concerns between the spouses can result from what each person believes a marriage should be like. Again the interface between behavior and cognitions becomes evident. Thus, both persons may agree on what behaviors are occurring and even what the particular behaviors mean, but they may disagree about the *appropriateness* of those behaviors. For example, they both might acknowledge that the wife goes out with her female friends about once a week and that it merely represents her desire to have some time alone with her friends. However, they may disagree about the role of individual friends in marriage. The husband might believe that the couple should engage in all their socializing together. On the other hand, the wife may believe that it is important to maintain personal friendships which are not shared with the spouse. Thus, different standards about how a person should behave or what relationships should be like can result in discrepancies regarding behavioral concerns.

Differentiating between the bases for these discrepancies is important because they suggest different types of interventions. If the couple is not tracking behaviors similarly, then a first step is to assist them in tracking more accurately so that they can then decide whether a given behavior occurs, with what frequency it occurs, and in what context it occurs. Then they are in a better position to discuss behavior change. If the couple disagrees on the meaning of a given behavior, having them discuss possible meanings of the behavior and increasing their awareness of the different meanings they attach to it is a beginning point in dealing with the behavior. On many occasions, once one person realizes the meaning that a given behavior has for a partner, he or she is more willing to change that behavior. Of course, another possible outcome is that they can come to an agreement regarding the meaning of the behavior. Similarly, if the two disagree about the appropriateness of a given behavior for a married couple, then the discussion likely turns to the standards the two people have about what they want their marriage to be like. Consequently, some of the behavioral concerns mentioned by couples will result in interventions focusing on behavioral tracking and problem solving. However, other behavioral concerns will result in cognitive interventions, again demonstrating the interwoven nature of behavior and cognitions.

6

Assessment of Cognition

The strategies for assessing couples' cognitions all hold one common characteristic: The spouses in one way or another must tell the clinician what they are thinking. That is, the clinician must not attempt to read the spouses' minds; instead, the clinician should elicit the important thoughts from the couple. Even though the clinician will focus on the couple's self-reports in order to assess cognitions, the ways in which those cognitions are elicited can vary substantially. This chapter will discuss several approaches to obtaining this information in order to assess the important perceptions, attributions, expectancies, assumptions, and standards occurring within the marriage.

PERCEPTIONS

Although an almost steady stream of behaviors is occurring within a marital relationship, it is not possible for spouses to attend to all behaviors and events that transpire. Instead, all persons selectively attend to events of relevance in their environment, and what they focus upon shapes their perception of reality. Thus, if spouses ignore the positive behaviors of their partners and instead focus on the negative behaviors that occur, such a focus is likely to contribute to a feeling of dissatisfaction with the relationship. On the other hand, some spouses ignore negative behaviors from their partners in order to avoid recognizing some painful truth, such as an extramarital affair, or in order to preserve a certain image of their relationship.

158

Such distortions can be equally destructive to the relationship. Consequently, one focus of cognitive assessment is to evaluate whether either spouse is selectively attending to certain events and behaviors such that the perceptual process leads to a skewed view of the nature of the relationship, the partner, or oneself within the marriage.

Perception Self-Report Inventories

Spouse Observation Checklist (SOC; Weiss et al., 1973).

Establishing what behaviors do and do not *actually* occur within a relationship is difficult and often impossible. Instead, the clinician more often relies on whether or not the two spouses *agree* on what behaviors are and are not occurring on a daily basis. The SOC can be a useful device for this purpose. The SOC is described in detail in Chapter 5 because it typically is viewed as a behavioral assessment technique. To briefly reiterate, each spouse marks the behaviors that occurred during a 24-hour period from among the 408 behaviors listed on the SOC. Whereas most of the items focus on the partner's behaviors, a number of items do ask about the couple. Thus, comparing the husband's and wife's responses on these latter items can help to clarify whether or not they have similar perceptions of the events that have occurred (actually this strategy confounds *perception* of the event when it occurred with *memory* for the event, but no attempt will be made to separate the process into these components). In addition, the wording of the SOC can be altered such that each spouse notes not only the partner's behavior, but also his or her own behavior. Having this information from both spouses allows the clinician to note differences in the ways that each spouse perceives both persons' behavior. Because the SOC is already quite long, an abbreviated list of items must be selected for such purposes, as has been done in the formation of the Partner Observation/Attribution Questionnaire (POAQ), described later in this chapter.

When discrepancies in reporting do occur, it is difficult for the clinician to evaluate what did and did not actually occur. One approach is to report to the couple any distinguishable differences in patterns of reporting and ask for their understanding of the differences. At times, one spouse is able to acknowledge that he or she has a tendency not to notice when the partner helps with housework, for example. However, many spouses merely reconfirm their differences in perceptions by clinging to the view that their perceptions accurately mirror reality. In such cases, the clinician can at least retain such information and form hypotheses regarding selective attention from one or both spouses, which must be confirmed with other data.

Love days (Weiss et al., 1973).

As described in Chapter 8, love days is a behavioral technique in which each spouse is asked to engage in one special positive behavior toward the partner on designated days. This is typically viewed as an intervention technique, but it also can be used during the assessment period to evaluate whether the two individuals are tracking the positive behaviors of the other person. For example, if a wife prepares breakfast one day, a task that is typically her husband's responsibility, she writes down her behavior. The husband also can be asked to write down what his wife did that day to please him. Because she selected making breakfast for him as a special treat, more confidence can be placed in the likelihood that it actually occurred if she reports it. Having both persons return their lists to the therapy session the next week can help to clarify whether one or both persons have a tendency to ignore the positive behavior of their partner.

Interview

There are numerous opportunities during the assessment interviews to observe whether the partners have different perceptions and memories of events in their marriage. During the history portion of the interview, the spouses frequently offer differing opinions of what has occurred during their marriage in the past. Similarly, when discussing current problems, the two partners often describe events very differently from each other. If each partner does not spontaneously offer his or her perceptions regarding a given problem area, the clinician can ask one partner for his or her perceptions of what events occur in a problem area, after the other spouse has completed describing his or her concerns. When the couple is describing problem areas in the interview, their descriptions of events are not likely to be limited to single behaviors; instead, sequences of behaviors often become the focus of discussion. Noting whether each person is able to observe and report his or her own role in creating or maintaining the problem is important because such self-focus and reflection are important in order for each person to change his or her own behavior to improve the problem area. If such information is not offered spontaneously, the therapist at times might directly ask each person how his or her behavior contributes to the problem.

Couple's interaction and communication.

During the initial assessment, the clinician is interested in both communication and other behavior. In order to assess communication, spouses typically are asked to interact with each other. A frequent complaint of many spouses is, "You don't listen to me." Although the spouses might provide a special effort when given instructions, the clinician can evaluate whether the two persons do tend to listen to each other accurately or whether (a) one person does not listen to the other or (b) one person does listen but tends to distort what the other says. This particular perceptual problem obviously can lead to severe communication problems as well as more general marital discord if one person is unaware of much of what the other is saying. Distorted listening can deprive the listener of many positive statements and compliments from the partner as well as making it difficult for the couple to conduct a meaningful conversation. Evaluations of listening difficulties can be accomplished by asking each spouse to reflect or rephrase what the other says during a segment of the communication assessment period.

Selective attention as described above not only can contribute to the development and maintenance of marital discord, but it also can interfere with successful intervention. If one spouse is successful in making meaningful behavioral changes but the partner does not notice these changes, then the partner is unlikely to feel more satisfied with the marriage. Similarly, the person making the behavior changes is likely to feel discouraged or angry that his or her efforts have gone unrewarded and even unacknowledged.

ATTRIBUTIONS

Although there have been hundreds of studies conducted that investigate the attributions people make in various contexts, an important issue has been whether people often make attributions in their ongoing lives. This issue surfaced as investigators realized that research subjects are usually able to provide attributions when asked to do so, but investigators typically have directed the subjects to give explanations. For example, subjects might be asked, "To what extent are you responsible for what occurred in this situation?" However, would subjects seek such explanations on their own if not directed to do so? That is, in assessing cognitions, directing an individual to think about certain issues can alter that individual's thoughts. Therefore, the clinician must be aware of the extent to which he or she is directing or channeling the spouse's thoughts toward making attributions or other cognitions. Attributions resulting from a very directive assessment strategy might or might not reflect the thought processes that the individual displays on a day-to-day basis.

Employing a range of assessment strategies can allow the clinician to vary the extent to which the couple is directed toward making attributions. Various assessment strategies lend themselves easily to different degrees of directing couples to make attributions. Perhaps most directive are the self-report attribution inventories. Most of these inventories provide the respondent with attributional dimensions that are to be rated. Thus, a spouse may be asked to rate, "To what extent was your partner responsible for the argument that occurred?" Second, during the initial assessment interview, the couple often spontaneously provides attributions for various marital events; however, the clinician can direct the interview and at times probes for attributions. Thus, the interview might be seen as providing an intermediate degree of directiveness in asking the couple to make attributions. Finally, during the initial assessment, the couple is asked to communicate with each other about both positive and negative aspects of the relationship without intervention from the therapist. During these discussions with each other, spouses frequently discuss their explanations for marital problems and positive aspects of the marriage. Thus, the couple's interaction involves the least direction from the therapist in eliciting attributions.

Attribution Self-Report Inventories

Recently several self-report inventories have been developed for assessing couples' attributions. All of these measures are in early validational stages, and much more empirical evidence is needed to substantiate what is and is not measured by each of these inventories. With this caution in mind, these inventories are presented with a description of how each might be employed in a clinical setting.

One major difference among these scales is whether they focus on hypothetical marital events or events that have actually occurred in the couple's relationship. That is, the respondent may be asked to imagine that a particular event just occurred in his or her relationship; then, the respondent is asked to provide explanations for why that event might happen. Conversely, the respondent might be asked to check, from a list provided, those events which actually have occurred in the couple's relationship during a specified time period; the respondent then provides explanations for those events.

There are potential assets and liabilities in using either actual or hypothetical events. Actual events, by definition, have the asset of being directly relevant to the couple. Thus, the clinician can have some confidence in generalizing from questionnaire responses to the couple's actual life. At the same time, there may be a number of specific aspects of any one actual situation that influence an individual's attributions for that situation. Unless a wide range of situations is sampled, the overall response pattern may be influenced greatly by idiosyncrasies of the specific situations sampled. For example, a wife might report that she was primarily responsible for the couple's disagreement the previous night because she had not slept well and was grouchy. However, if her fatigue was infrequent, her scores might not be representative of her typical attributions. Of course, adequate sampling is a concern with all measurement instruments, but instruments which focus on specific events that have occurred have the particular risk that those events may not be representative of the typical way in which the events occur in a person's life. Another possible psychometric liability of using actual events in a couple's life is that different couples will have different events occurring in their lives. Consequently, different respondents may describe different situations or items on an inventory, and comparing across couples and developing norms becomes difficult. Thus, one couple may provide attributions for events 1 and 4 whereas another will respond to events 2 and 3, depending on what events occurred in their lives.

Using hypothetical marital events as items also has assets and liabilities. Perhaps the major concern with such a strategy is generalizing from attributions for hypothetical events to attributions for events in the person's actual life. The person can provide explanations for the event, assuming the event were to happen. However, if the hypothetical events do not typically occur in the person's life, it is risky to assume that the person makes similar attributions for actual events. If the scale constructor has chosen hypothetical events which have meaning for the respondent, such inventories have the advantage that all respondents make attributions for the same events, and the development of scale norms is simplified.

The use of hypothetical events may help to clarify the person's attributional patterns, if such patterns exist. Because the person is not responding to a particular event on a given day with the idiosyncrasies that accompany that event, the respondent might be providing his or her more typical explanations for why events occur in the marriage. That is, if the respondent is asked to imagine that his or her partner forgot to buy the respondent a birthday present, the respondent is likely to explain this event according to what he or she believes is the spouse's most likely reason for behaving this way rather than being influenced by some atypical aspects of a specific situation.

Dyadic Attributional Inventory (DAI; Baucom, Sayers, & Duhe, 1987) (See Appendix).

The DAI is a 24-item self-report inventory which employs hypothetical marital events. The respondent reads an item (a single sentence describing a marital situation) and is asked to imagine that the event has occurred. The respondent writes down one major reason for the *partner's* behavior in that situation, and then the respondent rates that reason on several attributional dimensions: source, stable/unstable, global/specific. Source actually receives three separate ratings—the extent to which each of the following factors influences the cause: self, partner, and outside circumstances. In an earlier version of the DAI, respondents made a single source rating from internal to external (Baucom et al., 1982). However, what is internal or external when a dyad is considered becomes a complex issue. Respondents seem more comfortable making three separate ratings for source, and the resultant data have been much more interpretable. The format of the DAI was modeled after the Attributional Style Questionnaire (Seligman et al., 1979) designed for use in depression research, with the major difference being that the DAI focuses on marital events only. The clinician also should note that the DAI focuses on attributions for the partner's behavior only, not attributions for the respondent's own behavior. Clearly, how one explains one's own behavior and one's partner's behavior may be very different (Fincham et al., 1987).

In addition to the attributional ratings, the respondent answers two other questions about each item. First, because hypothetical situations are employed, the respondent evaluates how important the situation would be if it actually occurred. This item is to assist in evaluating the relevance of the item for the respondent. Second, the respondent rates how he or she would feel (ranging from extremely bad to extremely good) if the situation occurred. The scale constructors divided the items on a rational basis into situations that probably would be perceived as negative and those that would be perceived as positive. The mood rating by the respondent confirms that a particular individual evaluated the item as expected.

The 24 items are divided into a grouping of 12 negative items and 12 positive items because attributions for a partner's negative behaviors often are different from attributions for his or her positive behaviors. Using the DAI, 14 summary scores are created. For the positive items, the ratings across the 12 items are averaged and result in the following subscales: Pos-Me, Pos-Partner, Pos-Outside Circumstances, Pos-Stable, Pos-Global, Pos-Important, Pos-Feeling. Seven similar scores are produced for the negative items.

Each of the attribution subscales has shown moderate internal consistency with alpha coefficients ranging from .88 to .71. These alpha coefficients suggest that individuals do have somewhat general patterns in the attributions that they make for their partners' behavior; however, the coefficients are not so high that the content of the specific items can be totally ignored. Furthermore, Baucom et al. (1987) found that some spouses show extreme consistency in the attributions they provide regardless of the situation described, whereas other individuals display great variability in their attributions depending on the situation. Greater situation specificity in making attributions was correlated with greater marital adjustment; that is, spouses who have a standard way of interpreting their partners' behavior regardless of the situation seem more distressed. The initial validational evidence for the DAI is promising. The findings indicate that the scores on the various attributional dimensions correlate with marital adjustment, such that distressed spouses provide attributions that tend to maximize the significance of negative spouse behaviors whereas nondistressed spouses provide attributions to minimize negative behaviors. Consistent with the communication literature, the negative aspects of the relationship (in this case attributions for negative behavior) are more highly related to marital adjustment than are positive aspects of the marriage. (See Baucom et al., 1987, for a detailed description of current validational evidence.)

In using the DAI clinically, it is recommended that the clinician calculate the 14 subscale scores. From such scores, the clinician can obtain a picture of the extent to which the respondent tends to discount or minimize the positive behaviors of the spouse. This can be found in such patterns of scores as not believing that the partner is reponsible for the partner's positive behaviors, seeing the partner as responsible for the positive behaviors but viewing the attribution as unstable and specific, or viewing the situations as unimportant and not making the respondent feel good if the event were to occur. A blaming pattern which maximizes negative behaviors would be indicated by viewing the spouse as largely responsible for negative events, not viewing oneself or outside circumstances as important, seeing the cause as stable and global, viewing the situation as important, and feeling bad if the situation were to occur.

Examining individual item scores can be useful when the mean subscale score is in the midrange, 3–5. Such a score could result from giving midrange scores to all or most items. A midrange score also could result from giving very high scores to some items and very low scores to other items. If there is substantial variability in responding, the clinician can search for patterns of responding based on the content of the items. For example, several items focus on communication, several focus on fulfilling responsibilities, and several deal with closeness, affection, and sexual behavior. Perhaps the repondent sees the attributions for only certain of these areas as being primarily influenced by one partner, as being particularly stable, or as being specific.

Compared to nondistressed spouses, distressed spouses do make more blaming, pessimistic attributions for their partners' behavior. Based on the DAI alone, it is unclear how accurate or distorted these attributions are. After viewing the partner's behavior over a long time period, perhaps it is reasonable for the respondent to view that behavior as resulting from global, stable causes. Assessment of whether the attributions seem reasonable or distorted is important for treatment planning, as will be discussed later. None of the existing self-report inventories allow for an assessment of the appropriateness of the attributions spouses make. This determination generally must be made from information gathered in interviews with the couple.

Attribution Questionnaire (Fincham & O'Leary, 1983).

Fincham and O'Leary constructed the first published marital attribution questionnaire, which is similar to the DAI just described. It consists of 12 hypothetical marital scenes, six describing positive behaviors and six describing negative behaviors by the spouse. The respondent provides the major cause for the spouse's behavior and then rates the cause on internal/external, global/specific, and stable/unstable dimensions. As a fourth attribution dimension, the respondent rates how controllable he or she believes the cause is. In addition, the respondent rates (a) how certain he or she is about the cause provided, (b) how the respondent would feel as a result of the spouse's behavior, (c) how the respondent would behave in response to the spouse's behavior, and (d) how the respondent would view his or her own response, rated from extemely punishing to extremely rewarding. Alpha coefficients assessing the internal consistency of the attribution dimensions ranged from .79 to .58. Comparison of the six common alpha coefficients on Fincham and O'Leary's scale with the alphas obtained on the DAI shows that the DAI has consistently higher internal consistency. This probably results from the DAI being twice as long as Fincham and O'Leary's scale and suggests that the six-item subscales on Fincham and O'Leary's inventory might be too short. Also, on the DAI, internal/external attributions (source) were meaningfully related to level of marital discord. However, Fincham and O'Leary did not find level of marital distress to be related to their internal/external dimension. Their lack of findings probably resulted from their method of measuring the internal/external dimension. They asked respondents to make a single rating, with the extent to which the cause reflected something about their spouse at one end "versus something about themselves, other people, or the circumstance" (p. 44) at the other end of the dimension. Attributing a spouse's negative behavior to oneself probably has very different implications from attributing the spouse's negative behavior to outside circumstances. The former attribution is a self-blaming explanation whereas the latter absolves the couple of responsibility and places it on outside factors. Thus, combining these two attributions at a single end of the rating scale probably obscures meaningful psychological differences in the respondent's explanations.

Fincham and O'Leary's scale has some assets that are not present in the DAI. It may turn out that assessing controllability is important. For example, if the respondent believes that the spouse could not control some negative behavior, he or she may be more forgiving of the spouse. Also, by asking how the respondent would behave in response to the spouse's behavior, the clinician can look for patterns of how the respondent's attributions might be related to the respondent's subsequent behavior. At times the clinician may focus on altering inappropriate or distorted attributions; however, the clinician also might need to focus on counterproductive behavioral responses that follow from certain attributional patterns.

Partner Observational/Attributional Questionnaire (POAQ; Baucom, Wheeler, & Bell, 1984).

The POAQ has similarities to the other inventories; however, it relies on actual rather than hypothetical marital events. The specific spouse behaviors occurring within the marriage are examined by using a format adapted from the Spouse Observation Checklist (SOC; Weiss et al., 1973). For the POAQ, 102 behaviors were selected from the 408 items listed on the SOC to sample 25% of each of the SOC's 12 content categories. POAQ respondents are asked to check the behaviors their spouses have engaged in during the past 24 hours and to rate these events as having a positive, neutral, or negative impact. When the checked items are summed in each category, a measure of the number of positive, neutral, and negative spouse behaviors can be obtained for the 24-hour period.

The next part of the POAQ is almost identical to the DAI. The respondent lists one major reason for the spouse's behavior and then evaluates this reason on three attributional dimensions: (a) source (separate ratings for me, partner, and outside circumstances), (b) global/specific, and (c) stable/unstable. Attribution scores are obtained by averaging across the items rated as positive. Similar procedures are used for the neutral and negative scores, resulting in a total of 15 attribution scores (5 attribution × 3 affective states). Finally, the respondent rates on a seven-point scale how satisfied he or she has been with the marital relationship during the past 24 hours. This allows the clinician to relate daily marital satisfaction to frequencies of various behaviors and attributions for those behaviors. Because the amount of time that couples spend together and the behaviors that occur vary from day to day, relying on data from a single day can produce an atypical set of responses. Therefore, whenever possible, the clinician should obtain at least several consecutive days of data which would include both weekdays and weekends because patterns of behavior are often different for those two time periods.

Baucom et al. (1984) found that the attributions from the POAQ correlated with marital adjustment as expected. That is, couples with higher levels of satisfaction attributed positive behaviors to their partners and themselves and saw the causes as both global and stable. Considering attributions for negative behaviors, the correlations were in the opposite direction. Furthermore, the findings indicated that daily marital satisfaction could be predicted much better when both the frequencies of behaviors and attributions for those behaviors were considered, compared to predictions based on the frequencies of behaviors alone. These findings confirm cognitive theory that one must be attuned not only to how people behave, but also to how they interpret those behaviors if the individual's level of satisfaction is to be understood.

Marital Attitude Survey (MAS; Pretzer et al., 1985) (See Appendix).

All of the preceding questionnaires employ a common format of having a respondent provide a cause for some behavior and then rating that cause on several attributional dimensions. The resultant scores are in terms of these dimensions, and the above findings suggest that this approach has yielded useful results. However, the scores from these inventories lose the actual content of the attributions. As mentioned earlier, the *content of the situation* being assessed may need to be taken into account. In addition, the *content of the attributions* may be important. As Pretzer et al. (1985) point out, "My wife is mean because she is a crabby person" and "My wife is mean because she doesn't love me" might both be classified as involving global, stable attributions. Yet they might have quite different impacts on the respondent, e.g., anger versus sadness, respectively.

The MAS was developed to assess the specific content of attributions for marital problems, resulting in the following subscales: attribution to one's own behavior, partner's behavior, one's own personality, partner's personality, partner's malicious intent, and partner's lack of love. The MAS includes two additional subscales based on self-efficacy theory (Bandura, 1977): (a) the extent to which the respondent believes that the couple has the *ability* to change, and (b) the degree of improvement in the relationship which the respondent believes the couple *will* make. The MAS consists of 74 statements, and the respondent rates each statement on a five-point Likert scale ranging from "strongly agree" to "strongly disagree." Thirty-nine of the items are scored on the eight attribution subscales.

The subscales have alpha coefficients ranging from .93 to .58, the lower coefficient for attributions to one's own behavior. Existing validational evidence for the MAS is positive. As predicted, level of marital adjustment is negatively correlated with attributing problems to the partner's behavior and personality and to the partner's malicious intent and lack of love. Overall, 40 of 44 correlations between the MAS and related marital and cognitive phenomena were significant as predicted (Pretzer et al., 1985).

Because the MAS has a rather different format and different focus from the above scales, a combination of one of the above scales and the MAS would allow the clinician to focus on both attributional dimensions and the content of the attributions. For example, a respondent who has attributed a partner's negative behaviors to lack of love on the MAS and who has viewed the attributions for the partner's negative behaviors as stable on the DAI is presenting a rather hopeless, helpless picture, and the clinician must have concern about whether the respondent will be motivated to improve the relationship. This can be examined further by noting the respondent's score on the MAS subscale focusing on the expected improvement in the relationship.

Daily Record of Dysfunctional Thoughts (DRDT; Beck et al., 1979).

All of the above strategies are rather structured techniques in which the respondent makes ratings on five- or seven-point scales. A more open-ended technique which asks the respondent to record his or her thoughts during specified emotional states was originally devised for use with depressed clients. Because it is a useful approach for gathering information about an individual's cognitions during day-to-day life, it is typically employed during the course of therapy. The DRDT includes columns for providing a brief, concrete description of an event, a verbatim record of the associated automatic thoughts, and a description of the resultant emotional state(s). We also commonly ask spouses to add an additional column to the DRDT, in which they briefly describe their behavioral responses associated with their cognitive and emotional responses to their partner. The latter data are important for determining the reciprocal patterns of cognition, affect, and behavior that occur between two spouses. Thus, the DRDT provides an opportunity to obtain information about cognitions in specific situations soon after the events. The DRDT is discussed more fully in Chapters 7 and 9.

Interview

In addition to the information about attributions gained in the preceding self-report inventories, a great deal of information regarding attributions can be obtained from the initial and other interviews with the couple. Whereas the inventories provide little information regarding the appropriateness of the attributions, the interview provides the clinician with information more relevant for making this determination. First, the spouses often spontaneously provide important attributional information when they are discussing the history of their marital relationship. Following is an excerpt from the marital history component of an initial interview.

Therapist: Mary, what is it about Bill that attracted you to him?

Wife: I think the way he talked to me was a big part of it. He used to say such nice things to me. He complimented me a lot and made me feel good about myself.

Therapist: Is he still that way?

Wife: Oh, he is still a good talker, for sure. In fact that is one of our main problems. He goes out and does whatever he wants, and then when I ask him about it, he always has such a nice explanation. He is so believable, and me being so gullible, I believe him again and again. But he doesn't really care about me; he just cares about himself. I just can't live with his lies any more.

In this example, the wife has suggested that the reasons for her husband's unacceptable behaviors and subsequent lies are his self-centered focus and lack of concern for her. Consequently, the clinician heard early in the initial interview one of the major attributional themes that characterized this wife's perceptions of her husband's behavior: that he is self-centered and really does not care about her any longer. One of the goals of the clinician in this context will be to assess the appropriateness of these attributions. After being attacked as the husband was in this example, most spouses will feel the need to defend themselves. Consequently, directly asking the husband if he agrees that he is self-centered and only cares about himself is unlikely to provide useful information.

There are several strategies for obtaining both spouses' attributions for the husband's behaviors. First, the couple needs to become specific in terms of what behaviors are being discussed. In the above example, the specific behaviors of concern to the wife are unclear. Without this specificity, the couple is left to make broad, sweeping generalizations that are difficult to evaluate in terms of appropriateness of attributions. Second, seeking the partner's attributions for his or her behavior should not be attempted soon after the partner has been attacked by the spouse. At that time, the attacked partner is likely to feel most defensive and either blame the spouse or withdraw. Consequently, the clinician times the discussion of attributions for a period when the two partners are not upset with each other. At the same time, the clinician must acknowledge the concerns raised by the spouse. In the above situation, the clinician attempted to accomplish these goals with the following response:

Therapist: You seem to be feeling pretty uncared for right now, and that appears to be hurting you a lot. I think that is really important, but let me suggest that we hold off a bit before discussing your current problems. If we could, let me try to get a better sense of how your relationship developed. I think that will give me a context to consider when we start looking at your current concerns. Mary, you were saying . . .

To lessen the impact of blame on the partner, the clinician can ask the spouse to clarify other factors that have contributed to the problem. At the same time, the clinician should realize that additional solicited attributions are not spontaneous and may not have occurred to the person without the clinician's eliciting them. However, if the clinician prompts and pulls for other attributions and the person cannot give any, then the clinician is obtaining information about that person's openness to considering other factors that may influence the situation and the possible simplistic manner in which that person explains problems.

Although spontaneous attributions can occur at any point in the marital history, attributions for negative events are likely to occur particularly as the couple describes different problematic times in their marriage or major shifts in the relationship. Thus, when asked, "When did you first think you two were experiencing significant difficulties in your marriage?" couples often describe the situation and attempt to explain why the problems arose. Similarly, when couples are discussing major shifts in the relationship, attributions are frequently given to clarify those shifts. Thus, the following circumstances are likely to elicit spontaneous attributions: (a) when the couple married; (b) when there were school or job changes; (c) when children were born, and so forth. If the spouses describe problems or relationship shifts at these times but do not offer attributions, the clinician can ask them why they think the problems arose or the relationship shifted as it did.

Because relationship problems are of such salience to distressed couples, they are likely to focus on these issues when presenting their marital history to the clinician. However, how couples explain the more positive times in their marital history and the more enjoyable aspects of their relationship also should be addressed. If a couple does not spontaneously offer such information, the clinician can inquire. Below is an example from an initial interview.

Therapist: It sounds like during these first five years there have really been some rocky times. What would you see as the best years or months during this time period?
Wife: I think probably the year we moved to Arizona was *our* year.
Therapist: What made that year stand out as good?

Wife: Well, we were far away from our parents. We were finally on our own without someone telling us what to do. And with Joe's change in job, we had enough money to make it on our own. But then the job didn't work out. We moved back here . . .

Therapist: Let's look at that time period in more detail. For you, what aspects of your relationship were most satisfying?

In the above example, the therapist first elicited the most positive time period for the couple and focused on the wife's attributions for why this time period was enjoyable. Next, the therapist began to focus on specific aspects of the relationship that were positive and would then proceed to explore attributions for these specific aspects of the relationship. Among couples who are experiencing less anger and hostility, focusing on these positive aspects of the relationship can become a rewarding experience.

However, exploring attributions even for positive events can lead to arguments and hurt feelings, and the clinician must control such interactions. For one thing, some distressed spouses are willing to say little positive about the partner or the relationship. This may arise for any of several reasons. First, the spouse may have focused so much on the negative aspects of the relationship and the partner that he or she really perceives very little that is positive (Epstein, 1985b). Or the spouse may perceive positive aspects of the relationship and the partner but be unwilling to acknowledge them overtly. Many distressed spouses view themselves as being in a battle with their partners, and their philosophy is that you do not say nice things about your enemy. Instead, their interaction is typified by negative reciprocity in which negative statements from one spouse increase the likelihood of negative statements from the other. Not only is withholding positive statements about the partner not rewarding the partner, but such interactions also can be quite punishing, and this appears to be the goal of many angry spouses.

The clinician might respond to such statements in at least two ways. First, he or she can continue to search for more positive aspects of the past. If the clinician perceives that the spouse is somewhat dedicated to remembering the relationship as negative, he or she can probe for more positive times by lowering the demand on the spouse. That is, rather than questioning for times when the relationship was really good, the clinician can ask for times when things were not as bad.

If such efforts fail, he or she will still want to bring closure to the interaction without simply acknowledging that everything has always been terrible. Such a conclusion would only bolster the sense of hopelessness that the couple might be experiencing. At such times when the spouse is unable or unwilling to acknowledge positive aspects of the relationship, the clinician can inform the couple that difficulty seeing the positive aspects of the relationship is typical of many distressed couples and that treatment will help them recognize positive events which do occur as well as increase the frequency of positives and decrease negatives.

Discussion of current relationship concerns.

From the couple's marital history, the clinician is able to gain a good understanding of each spouse's explanation for why their relationship has developed as it has. During the discussion of current relationship concerns, he or she hopes to obtain a specific statement of current concerns and attributions given for those areas of difficulty. As discussed in Chapter 5 on assessment of behaviors, this portion of the interview is structured around responses to the Dyadic Adjustment Scale (DAS) and the Areas of Change Questionnaire (A-C). The clinician's first task is to obtain a clear, specific statement of the individual's concerns. Following this, he or she turns to a clarification of the individual's attributions for the problem area. The DAS and A-C differentially focus on concerns about the relationship versus individuals and, thus, provide an opportunity to observe attributions for relationship difficulties, the partner's behavior, and one's own behavior.

More specifically, many items on the DAS focus on how frequently the couple disagrees about specific aspects of the relationship, but the questions focus on neither person's behavior. Thus, the clinician might ask the husband to explain why he thinks the couple frequently disagrees about leisure time and activities. The clinician should be alert to whether the individual focuses on his or her own contributions to the problem area or chooses to blame the spouse only. Again the clinician can attempt to isolate patterns across content areas. A reasonable inquiry follows:

Therapist: So you believe that you and Jean frequently differ on demonstrations of affection and by that you mean that you would like to hug and kiss more often than she would. What is your explanation for this difference that you two are experiencing?

If the person cannot identify attributions, then the clinician can ask about his or her feelings or emotional reaction. Once a person expresses sadness, anger, frustration, and so forth in some situation, often it is possible to clarify the thoughts, including attributions, that are related to those feelings. If more than one emotion is involved, the specific thoughts related to each emotion should be determined. Gaining access to a person's thoughts via the person's feelings is a strategy which is often successful.

The A-C also offers an opportunity to clarify attributions for areas of concern but focuses on individuals' behavior. Because Part I specifically focuses on desired changes in the partner's behavior, the attributions will be for the partner's behavior. Just as during the marital history portion of the session, this is an occasion when one spouse may become defensive if blamed by the partner. The clinician wants to avoid an interaction between the spouses that involves blaming and counterblaming. Again, in part this can be accomplished by having the spouse who is discussing the problem speak to the clinician, not the partner. The partner is asked to listen during this time, with the opportunity to speak later. Whereas this may avoid an immediate blaming/counterblaming interaction, the spouse who believes that he or she is being unjustly blamed might still become angry and resentful and want to defend him- or herself to the clinician. To allay this need to defend oneself, the clinician should introduce this phase of the session with a statement such as the following:

Therapist: Now, I realize that you two may perceive things differently. So when I hear one person's point of view, I take it for just that — one person's point of view on the issue. So if you see it differently, you don't need to be concerned that I have accepted the other person's position as some ultimate truth. I do want to hear what you both have to say, but while I am talking to one of you, I'd like the other person to listen quietly and overcome any temptation to jump in and defend yourself. You don't need to do that.

The clinician should also compare the two persons' attributions for a given problem. If one spouse has just blamed the other person, the person who has just felt blamed is unlikely to agree with the explanation if that explanation makes the person appear unreasonable or unfair. One way to minimize the defensiveness of the partner who is likely to believe he or she has been unjustly blamed is for the clinician to rephrase the attribution in a more neutral, socially acceptable way, that is, "depathologizing" the message. One specific strategy is to make clear that similar patterns occur in many distressed relationships. Note also the lack of perjorative terms in the clinician's response below.

Therapist: Bill, a minute ago Mary was saying that she would like to spend more time together at night. Her perception is that some nights you go out with your friends directly from work, and she doesn't know where you are. She is starting to think that the relationship focuses a lot on your needs. First, would you agree that you do go out some nights with your friends without telling Mary?

Husband: Yeah, once in a while, but not as often as she makes it sound.

Therapist: What is it about going out with your friends or not going home that you enjoy?

Husband: Well, I've just always enjoyed going out and having a good time. I've never been a homebody. And I like going out with my friends and having a beer.

Therapist: OK, so you see it that you have just always enjoyed going out and having a good time. How about Mary's belief that your marital relationship has somehow gotten focused on you? I know often in marital relationships, for one reason or another, the relationship does start to focus around one person's needs and preferences. Usually when that happens it is not necessarily that one person is trying to be selfish or anything. Perhaps one person is more forceful in the way he or she expresses things than the other, or sometimes it is just the circumstances. For example, when one person is in school, often the couple starts to focus on getting the student through school. Do you think your relationship is one where you two, for some reason, have started to focus on one of you?

Husband: I guess there is some truth to that. It is sort of like you were saying: I've always had a more outgoing personality than Mary. Until recently, she has just sort of kept quiet.

As is often the case, no clear determination of the appropriateness of the wife's attributions results from a brief interaction such as this. However, the therapist has learned that the relationship may be one in which the husband often has done what he wishes whereas the wife until recently has not made her desires clear. This information would be combined with much additional information to evaluate the appropriateness of the wife's attributions. This has important treatment implications. If her attributions seem significantly distorted in this area, then a major focus will be on helping her evaluate the situation more appropriately. If her attributions that her husband is primarily concerned about himself seem realistic, an early focus on these attributions in treatment can be disastrous. In the latter situation, helping the couple to engineer some needed behavioral change would have top priority.

Couple's interaction and communication.

During the marital history and discussion of current concerns, the clinician attempts to minimize the defensiveness between the two spouses as attributions are discussed. One major strategy to accomplish this goal is to have each spouse speak directly to the clinician. That is, there is not an extended conversation between the spouses during these phases of the interview. However, the clinician also is interested in how the spouses communicate with each other. Consequently, the clinician asks the couple to have several conversations with each other with different goals in mind. During these interactions, the clinician does not intervene, thus providing the opportunity to observe the extent to which the couple spontaneously makes attributions during their conversations, again noting consistencies and differences from any attributional patterns already noted from other assessment strategies.

First, as discussed in Chapter 5 on behavioral assessment, the couples are asked to select a relationship problem and reach a solution to it. The extent to which couples focus on attributions or explanations for the problem versus becoming solution-oriented is important. Whereas attempting to gain some understanding of the reasons for the problem can be of assistance in seeking reasonable solutions, some couples focus almost exclusively on attributions and rarely become solution-oriented. From a problem-solving perspective, this major focus on attributions is not facilitative. The clinician must realize that the instructions given to the couple might greatly influence the extent to which attributions are discussed. For example, the instruction, "State the problem and try to come to a solution" does not lead toward a discussion of attributions, whereas "State the problem, discuss your ideas and understanding of the problem, and try to come to a solution" directs the couple toward discussing attributions. Our preference is to use the former instructions and observe whether a couple chooses to include a discussion of causal explanations.

The clinician is interested not only in the amount of time spent discussing attributions, but also in the types of attributions made. This direct encounter between the spouses discussing a marital problem perhaps is the context most likely to promote defensive, self-serving attributions. Knowing that they are likely to disagree and that negative emotions are likely to arise, many distressed couples attempt to justify their behavior and positions and defend themselves from the partner's anticipated attack. Given the rapid development of negative reciprocity in couples' conversations (e.g., Gottman, Notarius, Markman, Bank, Yoppi, & Rubin, 1976; Margolin & Wampold, 1981), often only a single blaming attribution from one spouse is needed to spark an immediate escalation of defensive attributions from both persons. The speed, intensity, and degree of entrenchment shown for such defensive attributions are important for the clinician to note. Often spouses' clinging to blaming, self-serving attributions can serve as a major roadblock to successful problem solving. If the couple exhibits this pattern, then the clinician should intervene during treatment. For example, if the couple makes distorted attributions, the clinician's role will be to assist them in making the content of their attributions more realistic. If the partners express their attributions in destructive ways or are devoting too much attention to attributions, then during therapy the clinician will use communication and problem-solving skills to assist the couple in becoming more efficient problem solvers.

In Chapter 7, procedures for assessing spouses' abilities to express emotions are discussed in detail. Briefly, each person is asked to express his or her feelings on several topics: (a) something he or she likes about the partner; (b) something he or she would like to see changed in the partner; (c) something he or she would like to change in self. For each of these conversations, the couple discusses the topic without intervention from the clinician. Again during these interactions, attributions are often spontaneously provided. This choice of topics is useful because it takes the focus away from each spouse's discontent with the partner, which often is discussed at great length during assessment sessions. During the discussion of something the speaker likes about the partner, the clinician should be particularly alert to whether the speaker actually gives credit to the partner for the positive behavior or attribute. On many occasions, distressed spouses will in some way undermine the importance or value of this behavior or attribute which has been labeled as positive. For example, the positive act will be described as unstable or selfish, or questionable motives will be attributed to the positive behavior. At times the speaker suggests that the partner's positive behavior does not reflect on the couple's relationship, maintaining the perspective that even though the partner may have some redeeming graces, these positive qualities do not carry over to the marriage. Finally, the speaker may directly contaminate the discussion of something positive about the spouse by quickly altering the discussion to focus on negative behavior or characteristics of the partner. The following is an example of how a wife shifted from positive to negative and used this contrast to make the major attribution that her husband does not care much for her.

Wife: Well, I think you are a pretty good father to the kids. You're really affectionate with them, and I think they need that so much. I know I do. That's one reason why I can't understand why you are never affectionate with me. All I can figure is that you really don't care about me.

One potentially important function that a spouse can serve is to help the partner feel good about him- or herself, to help that person feel valued by others, and to realize his or her strengths and abilities. By observing how a spouse discusses the partner's positive behaviors and characteristics and the attributions for those behaviors, the clinician can begin to evaluate whether a spouse communicates in ways that are likely to erode the partner's self-esteem or enhance that partner's self-image.

A second task asks the individual referred to as the speaker to discuss something he or she would like to change in him- or herself. The spontaneous attributions offered during this discussion also can be valuable. One major issue for the clinician to note is whether the speaker assumes appropriate responsibility for his or her behavior and the person's belief that he or she can change in that area. Many distressed spouses offer numerous excuses for their undesirable behavior; perhaps most destructive are attributions suggesting that the partner makes it difficult or impossible for the speaker to change, that is, blaming, defensive attributions.

Therefore, this discussion presents an opportunity for the speaker to make attributions for his or her own undesirable behavior; in addition, the partner often offers attributions for the speaker's behavior. Perhaps most important, the clinician should evaluate whether the partner uses the speaker's admission of undesirable behavior as an opportunity to attack the speaker. Such a situation occurred during an initial evaluation session:

Husband: Well, I really would like to do more of my share of housework. I don't know why it is so hard for me to do it. I think maybe in part it is because when I grew up, my mother and sisters did all the housework. I wasn't accustomed to doing it, and as a result I just don't think about what needs to be done.

Wife: Why is it that it took us coming here for you to admit it? That's what I've been saying to you for years. You think you're too damn good to do housework. That's women's work.

When the partner responds with condemning attributions, it often decreases the speaker's willingness to take appropriate responsibility for his or her behavior. In essence, the clinician should evaluate the way in which spouses communicate attributions and responses to those attributions. This allows for isolation of any destructive communication patterns which make it difficult for either person to share reasonable causal attributions for various behaviors and marital events.

Holtzworth-Munroe and Jacobson (1985) have developed a coding system to rate attributions that couples make spontaneously during a discussion. Their coding system provides guidelines for determining whether a statement involves an attribution, as well as ratings on the following dimensions: locus, trait/state, stability, globality, positive or negative intentionality, and voluntariness. As with the other instruments for assessing attributions, this rating scheme is in the early validational phases. Also, similar to most behavioral coding systems, this coding system requires an amount of time that makes it impractical for routine clinical use. At present, it is primarily a research tool. However, becoming familiar with the coding system could help the clinician become more attuned to the couple's attributions in their conversations and assist the clinician in evaluating these attributions in a less formal manner.

The preceding methods for evaluating couples' attributions during their conversations have involved the clinician or some trained rater making formal or informal assessments of what the couple's attributions are, based on the couple's statements. However, the clinician also might wish to obtain the couple's own evaluation of their conversation. One seemingly important attributional dimension involves the perceived intent of a communication. An adaptation of a system developed by Markman (1979, 1981) can be used for the couple to evaluate intent on a positive-to-negative dimension. One person speaks at a time. After that speaker finishes talking, the speaker holds up one of three cards numbered 1 to 3 to indicate what the intent of the communication was, ranging from 1 for negative, 2 for neutral, to 3 for positive. Similarly, the listener holds up a card to indicate what the listener perceived the speaker's intent to be. (This approach varies from Markman's in that he instructs the listener to rate the impact of the message rather than what the listener believes the intent was.) Both cards are held up simultaneously toward the clinician and away from the partner. This procedure continues after each person speaks. This approach allows the clinician to observe the extent to which the two spouses concur or disagree regarding the intent of each person's communication. By listening to the conversation, the clinician also can take into account his or her own perception of the intent of the communication. It would be inappropriate to consider the clinician's judgment as a final criterion, but it is possible to observe whether one spouse seems to greatly distort the intent of the other's communication.

Utilizing Attributional Information

Consistencies versus inconsistencies in attributions.

The strategies discussed above provide numerous opportunities to obtain couples' attributions for marital events. One major task of the clinician is to take this wealth of information and synthesize it to aid in treatment planning. One aspect of this integrative process is dealing with seeming consistencies and inconsistencies in the data: These inconsistencies typically can be observed within a given assessment device, across assessment strategies, and across the two spouses. Within a single instrument such as a self-report measure of attributions, the respondent may vary in attributional ratings to different items. Whereas this could reflect measurement error or true inconsistency in the individual, the variability in responding may be more systematic. As discussed earlier, the respondent may have different attributions for different content areas of the relationship. Also, the seeming inconsistency can result from situational factors included in the events being explained.

However, there may be occasions when the pattern of responding seems inconsistent, contradictory, or uninterpretable to the clinician. In such situations, the respondent can be asked to help interpret the basis for his or her responses. The assessment procedure is not an excercise in which the couple provides information to the clinician who then assimilates the information and explains the couple's problems to the couple. Instead, the clinician and couple can view the assessment as a *joint* task in which they work together to arrive at a common understanding of the couple's strengths and weaknesses. For example, one wife responded to all but one of the communication-oriented items on the DAI by suggesting that her husband found her boring and did not want to talk to her. The clinician responded as follows:

Therapist: On this one questionnaire, you responded to several items in a way that suggested you believe that your husband doesn't talk to you often because he finds you boring. However, on this item about your communication, you seemed to have responded very differently. Would you take a look at your response and try to help me understand your thinking on that item?

Also, there often seem to be inconsistencies in attributions from one assessment strategy to the next. The clinician's task in this case, again, is to evaluate whether this seeming inconsistency provides important information about the spouse and the couple. For example, one pattern is for some spouses to be less blaming of their partners on self-report inventories than in their direct communication with their partners. Such a pattern might indicate that the couple has developed a destructive communication pattern in which the individual believes that he or she must defend him- or herself by attacking the partner when they have a conversation. Thus, such a pattern would suggest a need for communication training to help the couple express their explanations honestly without having to anticipate being attacked.

Also, the two spouses' attributions for the same event or situation often differ. Whereas no two spouses, either distressed or satisfied, will agree on their explanations for all events, when the two spouses have discrepant attributions for most marital events, cognitive restructuring to assist the couple in arriving at more agreed-upon explanations for the factors contributing to their problems and successes is appropriate.

Distorted attributions.

In general, cognitive restructuring also is appropriate when either or both spouses are significantly distorting their attributions. Assessing whether and whose attributions are distorted often is difficult, particularly during an initial assessment when contact with the couple has been somewhat limited. Nor should the clinician automatically conclude that if both spouses provide similar attributions for a problem, the attributions are appropriate. In fact, cognitive restructuring is typically needed when both spouses agree that one of them is to blame for most of their marital problems. In some relationships, both the husband and wife agree that one person is "bad," "emotionally disturbed," and so forth and blame the couple's problems on that individual. For example, some depressed persons with low self-esteem agree with their partners that the depressed person is the basis for the marital troubles. Even though some specific behavior from one person may have initiated a problem, both partners are almost always involved in the maintenance of the problem through their reciprocal influence on each other. This statement does not mean that the two partners are colluding to keep the problem alive or that both people are behaving with the intention of maintaining the problem. Instead, it means that no behavior occurs in isolation; both persons behave and intentionally or unintentionally affect the other partner's behavior. Thus, once cognitive restructuring is initiated with a couple, they are almost always able to clarify how both people contribute to any given problem to some degree.

On many occasions, it is unclear whether the attributions are distorted, but the attributions clearly do not facilitate therapeutic change. For example, one or both spouses may make stable attributions for a problem area. Whether or not a couple can or will change in a given area is often impossible for a clinician to predict; the clinician uses every appropriate strategy available and determines whether the couple changes.

However, as Bandura (1982) has demonstrated outside of the marital area, predictions that one will change often correlate highly with subsequent behavior change. Thus, stable attributions can become a self-fulfilling prophecy for couples that no change will occur. Consequently, cognitive interventions should be *considered* when an individual makes stable attributions for a problem area. At the same time, the clinician should not automatically assume that a stable attribution in a problem area is a signal for cognitive restructuring to produce more unstable attributions. If the spouse's perception that a given problem area is unlikely to change seems to be confirmed by other information, then acceptance of that reality is appropriate.

"Accurate," distress-enhancing attributions.

At times spouses make attributions for problem areas which seem destructive for the relationship; yet based on the partner's behavior or responses to the attributions, the spouse's attributions seem accurate or at least appropriate. For example, one wife explained that the reason she thought her husband played basketball several nights a week was because he found her boring. The husband responded that she was correct; he had found her boring for years, was ready to give up, and was considering terminating their relationship. He clearly confirmed her attributions, which did little to improve the relationship. What are the therapeutic implications of such situations?

If a spouse's negative, pessimistic attributions for a problem area seem realistic, then at least two intervention strategies are appropriate to consider on an immediate basis. First, the clinician might wish to focus on behavioral change to alter the realistically aversive situation. Second, if behavior change seems unrealistic, the clinician would probably focus on the couple's standards of how each should behave and what the relationship should be like. The goal would be to help the couple evaluate whether the problem area in its current form can be accepted by both persons and how they can expect it to influence their relationship in the future.

EXPECTANCIES

As spouses continue to interact with each other, they develop cognitions regarding patterns of behavior emitted by their partners, themselves, and the two persons as a couple. Based on these direct experiences and indirect learning through such processes as instruction from parents, friends, and others, they predict how each person and the couple are likely to behave in the future. Although no behavioral prediction is perfect, making such predictions is essential in order to guide behavior to maximize desired goals and to minimize expenditure of energy in unproductive ways. The clinician is concerned with predictions or expectancies that do not seem to conform to existing data or are likely to maintain a negative pattern of interaction between the spouses. For example, based on many years of a husband's consistent disregard for agreed-upon spending limits, his wife might logically conclude that he is unlikely to change his spending habits. However, clinging to this expectancy might greatly lower her motivation to discuss this problem and attempt to produce behavioral changes in this area. Thus, the clinician will be concerned with expectancies for which there are supporting data but which are counterproductive for therapeutic change, as well as being attuned to distorted expectancies.

Expectancy Self-Report Inventories

Two self-report inventories have been developed that are related to spouses' expectancies regarding their relationship. The Marital Attitude Survey (MAS; Pretzer et al., 1985) contains a subscale that assesses the respondent's prediction of the degree of improvement that the couple will make. Such an attitude is likely to be related to the individual's willingness to make efforts in marital therapy and therefore can alert the clinician to possible motivational problems.

Marital Agendas Protocol (MAP; Notarius & Vanzetti, 1983).

The MAP involves three types of assessment by each spouse. First, each spouse is presented with 10 areas of marital functioning that are frequent problems for couples (e.g., money, communication, sex). Each person rates how much of a problem he or she believes each area is in his or her marriage. In addition, each person evaluates how he or she believes the partner will rate each area. The second question is directly related to expectancies. Each person answers the following question for the 10 areas: "Out of every ten disagreements in each marital area below, how many do you believe you and your spouse resolve to your mutual satisfaction?" (p. 225). As phrased, this question is not a direct assessment of expectancies as the term is used in this text. That is, expectancies refer to predictions about the future; however, the MAP might be interpreted by respondents to refer to the frequency with which the couple has successfully resolved problems in the past. Thus, it might reflect a summary statement of past behavior rather than a prediction of future behavior. A simple wording change could focus the couple more directly on predicting future behavior. Still, the MAP as currently worded appears to have utility. Notarius and Vanzetti summed the "expectancy" scores across the 10 areas and found the scores to be significantly related to marital adjustment. In addition, for both males and females the scores were negatively correlated with the spouses' perceptions of negative behavior from their partners. (A third question on the MAP asks for who the respondent believes is responsible for unresolved disagreements in each of the 10 areas, thus providing information related to attributions.)

The MAP has provided a useful beginning for addressing couples' expectancies. As noted, these efforts can be expanded in at least three directions. First, as mentioned above, the questions need to be worded to focus directly on predictions about future behavior. Second, a wider range of relationship behaviors can be considered. For example, the Areas-of-Change Questionnaire asks for the amount of behavior change the spouse desires from the partner in 34 specific marital areas, such as finances. To assess expectancies, the respondent also could be asked to predict the likelihood that the partner will make those desired changes in the future. Each spouse also could assess the likelihood that he or she will make the changes desired by the partner. Thus, with minor additions to existing scales, it is possible to assess a spouse's predictions that he or she, the partner, and the couple will be able to make specific behavioral changes. Third, for research purposes, the MAP has employed an expectancy summary score across relationship areas. Whereas this is sufficient to address the research questions posed with the MAP thus far, for many clinical purposes it will be important to consider expectancies for each content area separately. Although data are lacking in the marital area, such information is probably important because it might serve as an index of the extent to which an individual is willing to make initial efforts to produce change in a given area.

Interview

Spouses also share important predictions during the marital history and discussion of current concerns. At times these predictions seem unsupported by the couple's current and past relationship. Such distorted predictions are harmful because they often result in behavior that is destructive for the relationship as well as creating negative affective states. One husband was unrealistically jealous of his wife and became outraged if she had conversations with other men at social gatherings or went out with groups of friends at lunch if men were included. His concerns were based on his prediction that she would leave him some day for another man. They both agreed that she had never threatened to do so or even shown significant displeasure with the relationship other than his jealous behavior. In further discussion, it became clear that his fears were based on his childhood experience when his mother unexpectedly left the family. He decided that he would never allow himself to be surprised in this way again; therefore, he remained alert to the possibility that his wife might leave. To accept that she planned to stay in the marriage would mean that he was once again vulnerable to an unexpected loss.

Couples also make their expectancies clear as they discuss the bases for their past behavior. That is, often an individual behaves in a given way because of predictions that he or she has regarding the effects of that behavior. Consequently, as the clinician hears the couple discuss important events from the past, or how they interact regarding problem areas, the clinician can ask each spouse what he or she believes the impact of each person's behavior would be.

Couples' interaction and communication.

As spouses attempt to problem-solve and express feelings, they frequently provide predictions for what is likely to happen in the relationship. For example, in responding to proposed solutions during problem solving, often one spouse will respond with concerns based on predictions of what is likely to occur if the solution is implemented. At times, information is provided to clarify that there is a reasonable basis for the prediction. Also as the discussion progresses, at times it is clear that there are few data on which to base the prediction. The spouse may even be explicit: "I just know you will behave that way. I don't have to have evidence from the past. After living with you this long, I know what you are like." Such attitudes inhibit the couple from attempting new solutions; therefore, during therapy the clinician should evaluate these predictions carefully. On other occasions as the spouses communicate with each other, the basis for a prediction is unclear. Although the clinician will probably not want to interrupt the discussion during the assessment, following the conversation the clinician can inquire about the basis for the prediction that the couple made in order to determine whether they have a tendency to make unsupported predictions.

In addition, the clinician should note how and when predictions are made. At times an individual communicates a prediction in order to influence the partner or to obtain a certain solution to a problem; in essence, the prediction can be used as an ultimatum or a bargaining tool. When one husband could not get his wife to agree to his proposed solution to a problem, he responded: "We may as well forget coming here; we aren't going to change. We'll never even reach a solution to this problem." Such uses of predictions are destructive because the partner often feels forced to comply in order to prove the prediction wrong.

Utilizing Expectancy Information

Understanding the basis for a faulty prediction can be important to the clinician in treatment planning. At times, the spouse might make an unmotivated logical error—the person takes existing information, integrates it, and reaches an unlikely prediction. That is, some persons do not appear to be skilled at using the ambiguous, complex behavior in interpersonal contexts in order to predict a person's behavior. However, on other occasions, the person's faulty prediction serves some purpose, such as using the prediction as a bargaining tool in the preceding example. In addition, predictions often serve a protective purpose. In an earlier example, in order to avoid being surprised by an important loss, the husband was willing to predict the loss of his wife on an ongoing basis. Understanding possible motivations for a poor prediction is important as treatment plans are developed. In the same example, if the clinician were merely to try to convince the husband that he had put the information together poorly in predicting his wife's leaving, the strategy would probably be unsuccessful because the husband's fear of an unexpected loss was not being addressed. The husband could more easily change his prediction if a strategy were developed to help him alleviate his fear of unexpected loss or at least help the couple devise a more adaptive way to deal with his fear of being surprised.

When an individual vacillates about predictions of marital events, one of two processes frequently is involved. First, the person may have a great deal of emotional conflict about an issue. Thus, a person who at one time predicts that a spouse is going to terminate the relationship and then predicts that the two will never separate is clearly troubled by the issue.

One of the two predictions may appear more realistic, with the opposite prediction being given for defensive purposes. The clinician should help clarify the likelihood of each prediction and understand the basis for the unlikely prediction. Second, a spouse may alternate between contradictory predictions because that person has difficulty interpreting interpersonal interactions and the partner's behavior, or the spouse is not effective in taking information from past behavior to predict future behavior. In such instances, the clinician helps the person focus on the important aspects of the couple's interaction, interpret that interaction appropriately, and then form realistic predictions based on the information.

Spouses' predictions of relationship events often develop over many years. At times these predictions develop even prior to the marriage. In an example given earlier, the husband reported that before he even met his wife, he assumed that if he ever got married, his wife would leave him. A problem with such predictions is that they are rather independent of the partner's behavior; thus, the partner can do little to alter these predictions. Whereas couples in such situations often benefit from marital therapy, such circumstances should raise the consideration of supplemental individual psychotherapy for the person making the faulty prediction. That is, if an individual has a number of fears and concerns not caused by the current relationship but these concerns are interfering with the relationship, then supplemental individual psychotherapy might be helpful. Marital therapy also would probably benefit the couple because their relationship is in a state of distress. The difficulty with employing only marital therapy in such instances is that when faulty predictions are based on one individual's need to protect him- or herself, there are often a number of long-term fears, old memories, and so forth which the person needs to process. Attempting this in marital therapy can result in the clinician's conducting individual psychotherapy while the partner listens. This issue of when to proceed with marital therapy, individual therapy, or some combination is a complex one with no available data to serve as guidelines; additional recommendations for decision making are provided in more detail in the intervention chapters.

ASSUMPTIONS

Just as with expectancies, no formal assessment devices have been developed to explore systematically the many assumptions that individuals might have related to marital functioning. In part, this probably results from a lack of clarification of the various categories of cognitions which are important to understand for a couple (Baucom et al., 1989). Thus, assumptions have rarely been discussed in attempting to understand couples' functioning. In addition, this lack of available instruments results from the extremely broad range of assumptions that would have to be addressed. Assumptions refer to an individual's conceptions of the characteristics of persons, objects, and events, that is, how that individual thinks the world actually exists (or what he or she *assumes* about the nature of the world and people). Consequently, there are almost an infinite number of assumptions that an individual might hold relative to a marriage, and assessing them systematically would be an overwhelming task. As a result, the primary assessment strategy has been based on the clinical interview during which the clinician listens for and probes for assumptions that appear to be erroneous or dysfunctional for the marriage.

Assumptions Self-Report Inventories

An initial attempt has been made to assess some rather global assumptions which have been noted clinically among maritally distressed spouses. Three subscales on the Relationship Belief Inventory (RBI; Eidelson & Epstein, 1982), which is discussed in more detail below, focus on assumptions about individuals and members of the opposite sex. First, one subscale assesses the extent to which an individual assumes that partners can change. Many distressed spouses enter therapy stating that people really do not change to any significant degree, and therefore they question the utility of intervention. A second subscale, entitled sex-role rigidity, assesses the extent to which the respondent assumes that the two sexes can ever really hope to understand each other and the extent to which their needs and desires are assumed to be different. The third subscale assessing assumptions focuses on the notion that disagreement is destructive; couples with this assumption attempt to avoid raising difficult issues for fear that they might experience a confrontation with their partners. Understandably, endorsing these three assumptions is negatively correlated with level of marital adjustment (Eidelson & Epstein, 1982). These three assumptions were selected for assessment because of their seemingly pervasive impact on the relationship. If a spouse believes that people do not change, that the relationship is in a state of distress but disagreement must not occur, and that spouses cannot even hope to understand each other, then a marked sense of futility regarding the marriage can be expected.

Interview and Couple's Communication

The primary approach to assessing spouses' assumptions is based on the clinical interview. As the history of the relationship and current concerns are discussed, many assumptions are made explicit or at least implied. These vary from general assumptions about the ways that relationships operate to very specific assumptions about the partner. For example, a wife might assume about her husband, "You are not very physically affectionate, and you don't express your feelings verbally. Therefore, I know you really don't want a close, intimate relationship." In this instance, the wife is assuming a correlation between emotional expression and desire for a close relationship which may or may not exist.

In this example, the wife was explicit in terms of the conclusion she reached based on a presumed correlation. However, clients are not always this explicit, and often basis for the conclusion is not provided. For example, the wife in this example might have said only, "Well, one of my major concerns is that Joe doesn't really want a close, intimate relationship with me." When presented with such a conclusion, the therapist's role is to explore the basis for it, including attempts to clarify any assumptions that the wife is making.

Therapist: I'm sure that it is really distressing to you to believe that. How do you know that Joe doesn't want to be close to you? Does he tell you that?

Wife: Well, not in so many words, but his message is clear. He almost never touches me, and he never tells me he loves me. In fact, he rarely tells me anything that he is feeling.

Therapist: So, you are assuming that these things automatically go together. People who don't show physical affection and who don't express feelings also don't want close relationships. Is that right?

Wife: Well, sure. That is pretty obvious, isn't it? I don't have to be a psychologist to figure that one out, do I?

Therapist: You may be right. In some people, those behaviors and desires do coincide, but not always. I've worked with a lot of people who really want to be close, but don't know how. So I'm not comfortable assuming that Joe doesn't want to be close until we have a lot more information and understanding. And then we may find that you are right, or maybe not.

Wife: OK, but if I behaved like he does, that is sure what I would mean.

In her last statement, the wife has implied another very general assumption which often leads to distress. This assumption takes various forms, such as, "If I behaved that way, here is what it would mean. Therefore, if my spouse behaves that way, it must mean the same thing." Another frequent form of the assumption is, "If I were in your situation,

I would want you to do this for me. Therefore, I assume you want me to do this for you. *And,* if you don't want me to do this for you, it means that something is wrong: you don't love me, etc." Somewhat the opposite of the assumption that males and females have different needs and can never hope to understand each other, this assumption states, "We are both alike. We have the same needs and behave in a given way for the same reasons. Therefore, in a given situation, I will behave toward you as I would want you to behave toward me. And I will understand your behavior according to what it would indicate if I were to behave that same way." Thus, in an attempt to be empathic, a spouse says, "I try to put myself in your place and think what I would want," again based on the assumption that spouses want the same thing in the same situation. Clearly, this strategy often fails and leads to much resentment. Instead, it is more adaptive for the individual to try to think of what the partner is like and what the partner as a unique individual needs in a given context. A great deal of cognitive restructuring with couples focuses on the uniqueness of individuals and the need to recognize and accept those differences rather than assuming either (a) that both partners are alike, want the same things, behave the same way, or (b) that individual differences mean that something is wrong with the marriage.

STANDARDS

The above cognitions focus on spouses' perceptions of what events occur, the relationships among events, why events occur, and what events are likely to occur in the future. All of these cognitions focus in one way or another on the spouses' views of the world *as it exists.* However, there is a distinct shift when focusing on beliefs or standards, for here attention turns to how a spouse thinks the world and people *should be.* In fact, one of the major cognitive difficulties occurs when there is a significant discrepancy between one's standards for how the world should be and one's view of how the world actually is.

In assessing spouses' standards, the same strategies discussed in the attribution section hold promise. That is, self-report inventories have been developed which focus on standards. In addition, during the initial interview with the couple, many of their standards become clear as their marital history and current problems are discussed. Finally, the spouses often share their standards with each other when they are asked to discuss various issues during the initial interview sessions.

There are various ways to informally classify spouses' standards. One category involves common "broad" standards, which are themes that can be used to unify many of the specific standards which spouses have in individual situations. Thus, "I (or you) must be perfect in everything and not make any mistakes" is a theme that underlies many specific standards. These more specific standards form the second category, and these are the standards that are typically presented by the couple. For example, one wife became angry any time her husband came home after their agreed-upon time and would say, "If you say you're going to be here at 5:30, I expect you to be here at 5:30, not 5:45, not 6:00."

Although concluding that she had strongly perfectionistic standards from this one instance would not be appropriate, other specific standards made clear that she did expect her husband never to make a mistake. However, she did not offer this broader standard spontaneously; each standard she provided was specific to the particular situation discussed. The different assessment strategies distinguish between these two categories of "shoulds." The self-report inventories are designed to assess the broader, theme standards whereas the couple typically offers situation-specific standards during discussion in the initial interview. Therefore, administering and scoring the self-report inventories prior to the initial interview can alert the clinician to broader themes to help explain some of the more specific standards usually raised by the couple during the interview.

Self-Report Inventories Focusing on Standards

An additional distinction in categorizing "shoulds" is whether they concern an individual (self or partner in this case) or a relationship. Self-report inventories have been developed to assess commonly observed standards for both individuals and relationships.

Irrational Beliefs Test (IBT; Jones, 1968).

The IBT, which consists of 100 items rated on a five-point scale, was developed to assess 10 irrational beliefs often discussed by Ellis (1962) within the context of Rational Emotive Therapy (RET). These 10 extreme standards involve the following themes: (a) demand for approval; (b) perfectionistic self-beliefs; (c) blame proneness; (d) low frustration tolerance; (e) emotional irresponsibility; (f) anxious overconcern; (g) problem avoidance; (h) dependency; (i) helplessness; (j) seeking perfect solutions. The focus of these standards is on individuals, both self and others. Thus, from this instrument, the clinician can obtain an indication of whether the respondent holds certain common unrealistic standards for him- or herself and others, such as a spouse.

A brief glance at the IBT makes apparent that the items do not discuss marriage at all. Thus, one must not assume that atypically high scores are indicative of marital discord, although Ellis and Harper (1975) suggest that adherence to these standards affects marital satisfaction as well as other life experiences. For example, holding the standard that "I must be perfect or fully competent in all important areas" can detract from a marriage in a number of ways. First, some persons focus this concern primarily on their profession and spend the great majority of their waking hours at work. This does not leave them with adequate time to devote to a marriage or family. Such spouses have great difficulty "finding" even 10 or 15 minutes to devote to therapy homework to improve their marriages. Some women who endorse this standard believe they must be a superprofessional, superwife, supermother, and thus become too superexhausted to enjoy any of these roles. Second, persons who believe that they must be great achievers often do not value leisure because they do not view themselves as accomplishing anything at such times. Third, persons who believe that they must be perfect frequently believe that they must portray this image to their spouses. That is, they are uncomfortable expressing self-doubts or sharing failures with their spouses; thus, they rob themselves of the opportunity for comfort and support from their spouses during difficult times. Consequently, there are a number of ways in which this one extreme standard can detract from a marriage, but the clinician cannot assume any of these complications. Instead, knowing that a respondent holds a certain extreme standard, the clinician can become alerted to possible implications for the marriage.

Relationship Beliefs Inventory (RBI; Eidelson & Epstein, 1982) (See Appendix).

Whereas the IBT focuses on standards about individuals, the RBI deals with standards about relationships. The RBI consists of 40 items comprising five subscales: (a) disagreement is destructive; (b) mind reading is expected; (c) partners cannot change; (d) sexual perfectionism; (e) sex-role rigidity (i.e., the two sexes are different and can never hope to understand each other). The RBI was based on unrealistic relationship themes which the scale constructors had frequently observed in distressed couples. The RBI was not intended to reflect "shoulds" only, but two of the subscales do reflect standards from this perspective. More specifically, the standards (a) that partners should know what the other person wants and is thinking, and (b) that sexual encounters should always rate an 11 on a 10-point scale, both involve expectations of how a relationship should be, yet are almost impossible to fulfill. Eidelson and Epstein (1982) found that all RBI subscales correlated significantly in the negative direction with marital adjustment; similarly, the pattern of correlations between the RBI and IBT subscales was generally as expected (Epstein & Eidelson, 1981). Alpha coefficients for the subscales have ranged from .81 to .72 for the disagreement-is-destructive and the sexes-are-different subscales, respectively.

Interview

While discussing their marital histories, individuals often make clear how they believe their spouses should behave, think, and feel as individuals as well as what the relationship should be like. These issues most often arise when standards are violated; thus, spouses frequently clarify their standards when discussing problems. One husband clarified some of his major standards during the history portion of the initial interview:

Husband: I know it's hard to believe, but we had never discussed what she would do about her job once we had kids. I just assumed she would stay home with them. But once she got pregnant and we discussed it, she made it clear there was no way she was giving up her job. And the battles haven't stopped since then. I don't know; I just don't think it's right. I don't want our children raised by strangers. I think they need a parent at home during the day. Women can take those kinds of breaks in their careers; men can't.

In this example, the husband stated his standard that a parent should be home with the children during the day. It would be inappropriate to classify this standard automatically as unrealistic for a given couple. Unrealistic standards are those which are impossible or highly improbable to fulfill, or if fulfilled they bring distress to one or both partners or are destructive to the relationship. If both spouses viewed it as important for a parent to be home with the children during the day, they might very successfully make such an arrangement.

Therefore, standards can become a problem for the couple in at least two ways. First, the two spouses' standards may both be reasonable but different from each other. Some individuals cling rigidly to their standards, with little willingness to deviate from them or consider other ideas. If two individuals view their standards as absolute, then contrasting standards can result in marital discord, even if each standard is reasonable in content. In such cases, the clinician's primary role will be to help the couple view these standards as preferences and then to reach some compromise solution through problem solving.

Second, standards can become problematic if the person's standards are unrealistic, as defined above. In the latter instances, the clinician's goal is to alter the content of these standards. Consequently, in the preceding example, if the husband believed that his wife should always put her family first and disregard her own preferences and needs, this would be detrimental to the wife's personal well-being. Consequently, the clinician would work toward having the husband reevaluate this standard.

However, as spouses frequently note, what seems realistic to one person can seem absurd to another person. A judgment is clearly involved in labeling a standard too extreme. In most cases, the clinician does not attempt to force a spouse to alter a standard against that person's will. Instead, the clinician isolates standards, discusses possible problems caused by such standards with the couple, and together with the couple decides what standards to attempt to alter. The criterion to use during assessment is whether a standard about the individuals or the relationship seems to be contributing to the marital distress.

In the previous example, the husband volunteered how he thought the wife should behave. Obviously, this does not always occur, but if the clinician wants to know an individual's standards, this information can usually be obtained through the Socratic method of questioning.

Wife: Then about a year after we got married, I got depressed for the first time, I mean really depressed.
Therapist: What do you think caused that?
Wife: Well, he just changed so much that first year. When we were going together, he would go out of his way to do things for me, to try to make me happy without my ever asking him to. Then after we got married, he seemed to stop.
Therapist: When he stopped doing things to make you happy, what did you do?
Wife: After a while, I got depressed.
Therapist: But did you let him know what you would like him to do?
Wife: No, I figured I didn't need to. From the days we went together, it was clear he knew how to make me happy. So if he wasn't doing it after we got married, I figured he didn't want to.
Therapist: Well, would you be willing to ask Joe to do things or tell him what you would like?
Wife: I guess so, but to me that will just ruin it if I have to ask him each time I want him to be nice to me. I want him to do things on his own.

From this excerpt, the clinician began to wonder whether the wife believed it was appropriate for her to express her own needs and whether she expected her husband to mind-read. Further information confirmed that the wife held these standards. At the same time, it is critical not to overinterpret available information. Relative to the above example, many persons want their spouses to initiate caring, thoughtful behaviors without being asked to do so; such self-initiated behavior frequently is interpreted as a sign of love. The clinician's concern was whether the wife clung so strongly to this standard that she was unwilling to express any needs or preferences, even when it became clear that her husband was not providing what she wanted. In an attempt to isolate unrealistic standards, clinicians at times exaggerate what their clients have said, conceptualizing the clients' standards in a more extreme manner. The clinician should not expect to identify an extreme standard at the core of every marital problem; such an assumption is clearly unrealistic on the clinician's part.

During the discussion of current problems in the initial interview, spouses again frequently clarify how they believe the individuals should behave and what the relationship should be like. These are handled no differently from how standards are discussed in the marital history portion of the interview.

Couples' interaction and communication.

As couples problem-solve and express emotions with each other, they frequently express what they think should occur. In observing the couple's communication, the clinician should have two major foci: (a) the way that standards are communicated and (b) the content of the standards.

The communication of "shoulds" often occurs during problem solving when the spouses are proposing solutions to their concern. Some therapists attempt to have couples remove the word "should" from their vocabularies. Whereas we believe that position is somewhat extreme, one concern arises when spouses state almost all proposals to solutions or rejections of proposals in terms of "should" and "should not." That is, "should" and "should not" often have a moral connotation of being right or wrong. If the couple is merely stating preferences, then phrasing them in terms of "shoulds" can turn the discussion needlessly into a moral discussion or at least give a proposal an unfair impact by suggesting that the partner is bad if he or she does not agree. Consequently, the clinician monitors the frequency with which spouses express their desires or preferences as "shoulds"; if it is excessive, then communication training can typically help the couple state preferences in a different way. However, if a spouse is not merely stating a preference but is attempting to communicate a value, a standard, or the appropriate way for things to be, then using the word "should" is appropriate. Thus if a spouse said, "I believe we should try to be good models for the children on how to express affection," the speaker should not be castigated for using that "dreadful" word. Still, the spouses can be sensitized to the word "should" so that they can clarify to themselves and their partners what the standard is that they are endorsing and evaluate whether or not they wish to maintain this standard.

Difficulties also arise when spouses for some reason do not make their standards clear when communicating with each other. One husband openly espoused and acted on the standard that they should have an open marriage in which sexual relationships with other persons were acceptable, with the addendum that this was clearly the enlightened way to live in the twentieth century. It seemed clear to the clinician that the wife wanted a monogamous relationship, but she was embarrassed and fearful of presenting this traditional standard. Instead, she found one practical reason after another why an open marriage would not work, at times distorting the description of their home life and frustrating her husband. Thus, the clinician should evaluate whether one or both partners have difficulty expressing standards and the reason for the difficulty. As Sager (1976) points out, individuals may not clearly understand their own standards.

The content of the standards discussed as the couple communicates during a session also is important; however, the clinician's goal at this point is no different than earlier in the session. That is, the focus will be on (a) whether either partner expresses extreme or unrealistic standards or (b) whether both partners' standards seem reasonable but merely conflict.

Utilizing Standards

Consistencies versus inconsistencies in standards.

Just as with other cognitions, seeming inconsistencies in standards arise within a given assessment strategy, across strategies, and across spouses. One of the major reasons for variability shown by an individual in terms of "shoulds" appears to be the lack of clarity and/or the ambivalence that individuals have regarding their own standards. That is, although individuals do seem to operate on a set of standards for how people should behave, most people have not crystallized those standards. As the clinician asks questions, those "shoulds" may become illuminated. However, as the person hears them and contemplates them, he or she may be uncomfortable with the "shoulds," recognize that they seem unrealistic, and alternate between rejecting and accepting the standards. This vacillation is a normal aspect of clarifying one's own ideas. Thus, when a spouse seems confused about his or her own standards or conflicted about some recognized "shoulds," then cognitive intervention to clarify the standards is appropriate.

Also, difficulty can arise when the two spouses' standards clash, even though neither standard seems unreasonable. In such cases, the clinician evaluates whether these "shoulds" involve mere preferences or moral values. In the former case, problem solving with compromise is called for. Asking people to compromise their moral values is more difficult, but the two spouses may need to compromise their behaviors even though their values do not shift.

Major clashes in moral values and standards of what is important in a marriage and in individuals also provide one realistic basis for considering terminating a relationship. In such relationships, even when the two persons compromise behaviorally, they both often have a sense of not being fulfilled, of continuously questioning their spouses' standards, and of sensing that the marriage is a consistent struggle. All, or almost all, marriages require effort and compromise from both persons to be successful, but this is different from viewing life as a struggle with someone who has vastly different values and standards as to what life should be like. At the same time, some individuals are willing to reconsider and alter a moral position after examining both the advantanges and disadvantages of it.

Unrealistic standards.

When either or both spouses have unrealistic standards, cognitive restructuring to alter these standards in a more reasonable direction is appropriate. In evaluating whether a standard seems realistic, the clinician must take into account (and later, help the couple to do so) the particular individuals involved in the marriage. That is, a standard might seem quite realistic for most couples, but given the persons involved and the relationship history, the standard may be quite unreasonable. For example, one husband held the standards that spouses should be good friends, should share their sorrows and joys with each other, and should spend much of their time interacting with each other and with their friends. These standards, in fact, overlapped with the therapist's views about marriage and appeared to incorporate a reasonable set of values. However, the wife came from a troubled family and had experienced a difficult childhood. She had always been somewhat of a loner and had rarely shared her feelings with anyone. Whereas helping the wife share more with the husband seemed appropriate for therapy, she was very unlikely to ever meet his standards and develop the type of relationship that he believed marriages should embody. In essence, the clinician must ask not only whether a standard seems unlikely in the abstract, but also whether these particular persons can meet each other's standards.

In addition, the clinician must not conclude that standards are reasonable because both persons have similar standards. In fact, shared unrealistic standards can be the basis for much marital distress. For example, both members of a couple clearly believed that disagreeing with each other was inappropriate and that expressing anger was a sign of immaturity. For a number of years, they had experienced a satisfying marriage while maintaining these standards. However, when the husband encountered a major career setback resulting in an undesirable change of location for the family, their standards suddenly became a handicap, and resentments were expressed indirectly and destructively. The clinician helped the couple recognize that their standards were too absolute, providing them with little opportunity for sharing negative feelings and differences of opinion.

SELECTING ASSESSMENT STRATEGIES

As in the behavioral area, it is not possible to incorporate all of the assessment strategies discussed in this chapter. Therefore, the clinician must be selective in deciding on assessment approaches. We rely heavily on the interview sessions for obtaining information about the couple's cognitions, using the guidelines described above. In part this is because the couple makes many of their cognitions apparent during the sessions. When their cognitions are not apparent, careful questioning from the clinician often is needed to uncover their important thoughts, again making the interview session valuable. Most self-report measures of cognitions are in the early validational phases, yet they can offer information which can then be pursued with the couple. Therefore, it might be helpful to select one attributional measure to administer to the couple, along with the RBI, which taps some important assumptions and standards. As mentioned in the previous chapter, if the spouses seem to be selectively attending to what events occur, then the SOC can be used to more formally assess this difficulty. Also, if the couple seems particularly pessimistic about change, then using the adapted version of the A-C which asks for expectancy of change can clarify specific aspects of the relationship where the couple believes change will and will not be difficult to obtain. In addition to data gathered prior to initiating treatment, the clinician maintains an ongoing cognitive assessment during the therapy sessions using many of the techniques described above as well as strategies suggested in Chapter 9. Of particular use for ongoing assessment is the Daily Record of Dysfunctional Thoughts, which allows for monitoring of cognitions outside of the sessions.

SUMMARY AND CONCLUSIONS

The preceding discussion makes clear that there are numerous ways to obtain information about spouses' cognitions. As when assessing any psychological domain, the findings will not always be consistent. In part, this may reflect an imperfection in existing assessment techniques. However, this seeming inconsistency is not always measurement error but can be helpful in understanding the couple. Attempting to resolve the meaning of this inconsistency is a major task for any clinician. Also, when a spouse makes negative statements about the partner or the marriage, it is not an automatic call for cognitive restructuring, nor are positive statements about the spouse or the marriage routinely reinforced. What is at times difficult but important to evaluate is whether the cognitions, either positive or negative, are significantly distorted and interfering with the couple's relationship. If so, then the clinician should seriously consider employing the cognitive restructuring techniques discussed in Chapter 9.

7

Assessment of Affect

As described in Chapter 4, there are four aspects of affect that the marital therapist needs to assess in order to understand the nature of a couple's problematic interactions and to plan interventions for reducing the couple's distress. These include: (a) the amount and intensity of positive and negative emotions experienced by each partner; (b) the degree to which the spouses are aware of their emotions, can differentiate various emotions, and can identify cognitive and behavioral events that elicit their emotional experiences; (c) inadequate and dysfunctional expression of emotion; and (d) the degree to which particular affective states (e.g., anger, depression, anxiety) interfere with the couple's adaptive functioning. This chapter describes strategies and procedures for assessing each of these four aspects of affect in marital and similar intimate relationships.

In contrast to the well-developed procedures available for assessing couples' behaviors (Chapter 5) and the rapidly developing methods for assessing marital cognitions (Chapter 6), there are as yet few systematic measures and procedures available for assessing affective components of marital relationships. This relative lack of standardized self-report questionnaires, interview procedures, and behavioral observation systems exists in spite of the fact that marital therapists (e.g., Margolin, 1983) have noted the importance of including affect in one's conceptualization of relationship problems. Consequently, marital therapists and researchers currently must use affect measures that are somewhat limited in scope, and they must rely heavily on interviews to elicit the necessary emotional data from spouses. Nevertheless, through the use of available question-naires, behavioral observations, and careful interviews, the therapist can identify emotions that should be targets of therapy with distressed spouses. The following is a description of methods that can be used in the assessment of marital affect.

THE AMOUNT AND INTENSITY OF POSITIVE AND NEGATIVE AFFECT

This section describes three strategies for assessing the amount and intensity of positive and negative affect experienced by each member of a relationship. These methods include (a) measures of global marital satisfaction, (b) reports of satisfaction associated with specific daily events in the relationship, and (c) behavioral observation of spouses' affective responses to each other's moment-to-moment actions.

Measures of Global Marital Satisfaction and Positive Affect

There are a number of self-report questionnaires available that can provide an overall index of the degree of marital pleasure versus distress experienced by an individual. For some of these measures the distress scale constitutes the entire questionnaire, whereas for others it is one of several subscales in a questionnaire assessing a variety of aspects of marriage. Some of these questionnaires clearly tap the emotional component of marital satisfaction, whereas others appear to assess cognitive and behavioral components of dissatisfaction (e.g., degree of disagreement between spouses) as much as affect.

Dyadic Adjustment Scale (DAS; Spanier, 1976).

As noted in Chapter 5, the DAS is a widely used self-report inventory of adjustment in marriage and similar intimate relationships. For the purpose of assessing global marital distress, one might use the total DAS score, but it is important to note that the total scale includes items that tap dimensions other than affect. For example, the 13 consensus items measure the degree to which the individual reports agreement versus disagreement between the spouses concerning aspects of the relationship such as handling of family finances, recreation, religious matters, friends, decision making, and household tasks. In addition, the five cohesion items assess the frequency with which the partners engage in discussions and activities together. Although a couple's consensus, cohesion, affectional expression, and satisfaction are interrelated aspects of marital adjustment, as reflected by the very high internal consistency coefficient of .96 found for the total DAS (Spanier, 1976), the clinician who is especially interested in the affective quality of a relationship may want to focus on the 10-item satisfaction subscale. However, in general clinicians should exercise caution in using DAS subscale scores, because Spanier's original (1976) DAS factor structure has been replicated by Spanier and Thompson (1982) but not by Sharpley and Cross (1982).

In Spanier's (1976) factor analysis of the DAS, the single item (#31) that asks the respondent to rate his or her happiness in the relationship on a seven-point Likert scale had a high commonality of .76, and Sharpley and Cross (1982) found that this item had a correlation of .86 with the DAS total score (corrected item-total correlation). Consequently, item 31 might be used by itself for a quick screening for level of distressed affect.

Marital Satisfaction Inventory (MSI; Snyder, 1981).

As described in Chapter 5, the MSI contains 11 subscales that cover a variety of aspects of marriage. Of relevance for the assessment of the overall affective quality in a relationship is the Global Distress subscale, which includes items measuring a spouse's degree of unhappiness with his or her marriage. However, Fredman and Sherman (1987) note that the Global Distress scale includes items assessing the respondent's level of commitment to the relationship (e.g., "I am thoroughly committed to remaining in my present marriage"), as well as those directly tapping unhappiness. Consequently, the latter items would seem to provide the best indication of emotional distress. The MSI has the advantage of providing not only a measure of overall distress, but also information concerning other areas of the marriage that might become targets of treatment.

Marital Happiness Scale (MHS; Azrin et al., 1973; Bornstein & Bornstein, 1986).

This brief questionnaire asks the respondent to report his or her degree of happiness concerning each of 11 areas of marriage (e.g., household responsibilities, rearing of children, social activities, money, communication, sex) using a 10-point scale ranging from "completely unhappy" to "completely happy." The last item assesses general happiness, in a manner similar to the single "happiness" item on the DAS. Bornstein and Bornstein (1986) stress the utility of the MHS in providing a rapid assessment of spouses' distress.

General Happiness Rating Scale (Terman, 1938).

This is a single item with which the respondent indicates how happy his or her marriage is, on a six-point scale ranging from very unhappy to very happy. It has been found to correlate highly (.88) with the Locke-Wallace Marital Adjustment Scale and to be a sensitive measure of change due to marital therapy (Hahlweg, Schindler, Revenstorf, & Brengelmann, 1984).

Positive Feelings Questionnaire (PFQ; O'Leary, Fincham, & Turkewitz, 1983).

This questionnaire was developed to assess positive affect that spouses experience regarding a variety of aspects of their interactions (e.g., touching each other, kissing, being alone with each other, understanding, sitting close to each other). The authors note that such positive feelings are not equivalent to overall marital satisfaction, which includes a cognitive appraisal of the relationship. They note that the PFQ's correlation of .70 with the Locke-Wallace Marital Adjustment Test reflects only a 49% overlap in variance, and that a major difference between the two measures is that more than half of the Locke-Wallace items assess the couple's degree of agreement or disagreement about marital matters, not their emotional responses to each other.

For each of the 17 PFQ items, respondents rate their feelings on a positive to negative continuum. O'Leary et al. (1983) reported that the scale had high internal consistency (alpha = .94), and that all of the items significantly differentiated groups of clinic and nonclinic couples. In addition, there was evidence of construct validity, including significant correlations of .40 with Navran's (1967) Primary Communication Inventory and .40 with spouses' self-reported commitment to their relationship.

Summary.

All of the preceding self-report scales assess aspects of marital distress and can differentiate clinical from nonclinical couples. Such measures tend to correlate highly with one another, although there often is a notable degree of unshared variance (e.g., between the Locke-Wallace scale and the Positive Feelings Questionnaire). The limited overlap seems to be due at least in part to the fact that the questionnaires assess a variety of affective, cognitive, and behavioral aspects of marital distress, and the degrees to which those components are represented in the various scales differ. For the clinician or researcher who is primarily interested in obtaining a measurement of overall positive versus negative *affect* in couples' relationships, it is important to select a scale that is specifically designed to tap that dimension (e.g., the PFQ), or to examine the subscales and items of the more multidimensional instruments that focus on emotion.

Because single happiness-unhappiness items (e.g., item 31 of the DAS; the General Happiness Scale) tend to correlate highly with longer marital satisfaction scales, many clinicians rely on the former as an index for determining the emotional distress level of their client couples. This practice seems to be reasonable, especially when the clinician (or researcher) wishes to keep a test battery as brief as possible. However, scales such as the DAS also allow one to compare clients' scores to established norms, and their multidimensional nature can help provide a more detailed assessment of a couple's relationship.

Reports of Satisfaction Associated with Specific Events

Although it is helpful to obtain spouses' reports of their overall levels of distress, a cognitive-behavioral approach to marital treatment necessitates that the clinician identify situational variation in each partner's emotions concerning the relationship. Although it is possible that an individual might have some degree of negative emotion at all times when he or she is interacting with the partner or thinking about the partner, most often the level of negative affect varies from situation to situation, and the individual might experience some neutral or even positive feelings at times. When the therapist and couple's goals are to identify and modify factors contributing to distress, and to maximize pleasing interactions, it is crucial to identify variations in the spouses' emotions as well as the cognitions and behaviors associated with pleasant versus unpleasant emotions. For this purpose, the therapist needs to use measures that provide logs of emotions experienced in different situations during a couple's daily life. The following are some instruments that can produce this information.

Marital Satisfaction Time Line (MSTL; Williams, 1979).

    Spouses use this instrument to record the quantity and quality of the time they spend together each day in any setting. The instrument is set up as a grid, by which a day is broken into 15-minute periods. Each spouse independently rates the quality of each period spent together, using a five-point scale ranging from very pleasant to very unpleasant. Williams (1979) noted that there may be important discrepancies in the quality ratings that two spouses give to particular shared experiences, for example, with one person rating them as pleasant and the other as neutral or unpleasant. Williams found that partners are not always aware of such discrepancies. Because the spouses also are asked to make notations about the nature of the activities engaged in during the shared time, the therapist can gather a wealth of information from this instrument. For example, Williams found that the time line records of distressed couples revealed a much lower overall ratio of pleasant to unpleasant time than did the time lines of nondistressed couples. When this is the case, couples can be aided in scheduling more pleasurable shared time into their daily lives. However, in order to accomplish this goal, it is important to know whether there are certain activities that are pleasant for one spouse but not for the other. The time line records allow the therapist to identify which specific activities are pleasant, neutral, or unpleasant for each spouse, taking into account idiosyncratic preferences of each individual. However, a limitation of the time line approach is that it tends to identify shared pleasing and displeasing activities (e.g., "We went to a movie together") and may not elicit specific positive and negative actions that each partner exhibited during that period that made it a pleasant or unpleasant experience for each spouse. The clinician may subsequently need to make a detailed inquiry during a therapy session in order to pinpoint the specific aspects of a shared activity that elicited particular emotions from each spouse.

Spouse Observation Checklist (SOC; Weiss & Perry, 1983).

    Although the SOC is used primarily as a means of identifying problematic *behaviors* in a couple's relationship, it can be used in a manner similar to the marital time lines in determining the overall degree of distress in a relationship. As described in Chapter 5, each spouse is asked to record the occurrence of specific pleasant and unpleasant behaviors, on a daily basis. For the purpose of assessing the affective quality of the relationship, the clinician can compute the percentage of pleasing behaviors that are reported by each partner. Because each spouse notes not only which behaviors occurred but also categorizes each as pleasing or displeasing, the SOC can help reveal whether spouses may be experiencing "sentiment override" (Weiss, 1980). In other words, some distressed spouses have such a global negative cognitive set concerning their partners that they interpret as negative many partner behaviors that the average person would be likely to experience as positive.

As noted in Chapter 2, several studies have demonstrated that SOC ratings are correlated with spouses' levels of marital satisfaction, but low rates of interspouse agreement about marital behaviors have led investigators such as Elwood and Jacobson (1982) to caution researchers and clinicians that the SOC should be interpreted as a self-report measure rather than an index of actual behavior. Although this means that therapists need to obtain other, more objective measures of couples' behavioral interactions, it does not lessen the value of the SOC for the cognitive-behavioral marital therapist. The SOC provides data about which behaviors each spouse perceives and whether each behavior is experienced as pleasing or displeasing. Any information that the SOC elicits concerning subjective processes in marital interaction is of prime interest in a cognitive-behavioral approach.

Weekly Activity Schedule (Beck et al., 1979).

Beck and his associates use this instrument in individual cognitive therapy of depression, based on the observation that depressed people commonly are physically and socially inactive. It consists of a grid in which the client records the activities in which he or she engages during each waking hour of each day of the week. The client also is instructed to rate the degrees of mastery and pleasure experienced during each activity, on 0-to-5 scales. Activity schedules can be used both for obtaining a baseline assessment of an individual's activities and associated levels of pleasure and for modifying a pattern of inactivity by scheduling new activities each day.

Weekly activity schedules can be used in marital therapy in a manner similar to Williams' (1979) time lines. The therapist can ask both members of a couple to log their activities independently, and then the therapist and couple can examine the logs to identify (a) the overall frequency of pleasant shared activities, (b) specific pleasurable activities that could be increased, and (c) discrepancies in the degrees of pleasure that the two spouses experience during particular activities. One advantage that activity schedules have over the marital time lines is that the former instrument allows spouses to record all of their daily activities, shared and unshared, thus providing a broader view of each person's range of mood states. The additional data about each person's experiences independent of the partner may reveal some patterns that have important treatment implications. For example, it may become clear that a spouse experiences very little pleasure from *any* work or leisure activity, and in this case the therapist would be wise to conduct an assessment of possible depression (that may or may not be linked to the individual's marital distress). As another example, an activity schedule may reveal that both spouses enjoy a particular activity with other people but never engage in it with the partner. The therapist then can inquire about the reasons why the spouses do not share that activity. Some distressed couples have such busy schedules that they have very little time set aside for shared pleasurable activity, a problem that clearly detracts from their marital satisfaction. In some cases it has been possible to increase marital satisfaction solely by helping couples problem-solve ways to schedule more joint pleasant activities.

Daily Record of Dysfunctional Thoughts (DRDT; Beck et al., 1979).

As described in Chapter 6, this instrument is another means for having spouses keep records of their cognitions and emotions that are elicited by particular situations. In contrast to Williams' (1979) time lines and Beck et al.'s (1979) Weekly Activity Schedules, the client does not keep an ongoing record of his or her daily activities, but instead makes written entries when clinically significant experiences occur. For example, a therapist might instruct spouses to use DRDTs to describe any situations involving their partners (including thoughts about the partner when the other person was not present) that elicited any unpleasant emotions, or those that elicited either pleasant or unpleasant emotions, or even those that elicited only a more specific emotion such as anger. No matter how the therapist decides to structure the use of the DRDT, it is the client's task to write concrete descriptions of the relevant situations, the associated cognitions, and the concomitant emotions (with intensity ratings ranging from 1 to 100). Therapists who wish to identify links between marital interactions and spouses' emotional states should request that clients record situations associated with as wide a range of pleasant to unpleasant emotional experiences as possible. As noted earlier, an advantage of the DRDT is that it simultaneously provides data about situational stimuli, cognitions, and emotions; however, it also requires that clients be socialized somewhat into the cognitive model and that they develop some skill at monitoring their cognitions. Consequently, the DRDT is less likely to be used for initial assessment of spouses' affective states than it is for ongoing assessment during therapy.

Videotape recall sessions.

Gottman and Levenson (1985) developed another method for obtaining spouses' self-reports of fluctuations in their emotional states during marital interaction which may be too cumbersome for clinical practice but still is worth noting. They asked each spouse to return separately to their laboratory and to review videotapes of their interactions with their partners. While reviewing the tapes, spouses indicated changes in their affect, using a dial (thus providing a continuous recording). The levels of positive versus negative affect measured in this manner discriminated distressed from nondistressed couples, discriminated between high- and low-conflict taped interactions, agreed significantly with affect ratings that objective coders made regarding the same taped interactions, and exhibited agreement between spouses. In addition, the patterns of autonomic nervous system arousal assessed during the original marital interaction and during the videotape recall session were correlated significantly.

Although Gottman and Levenson's methodology may not be practical for the practicing marital therapist, their basic procedure of asking spouses independently to provide videotape feedback about fluctuations in their emotional states is feasible for the clinician who has videorecording equipment available. Although it would be more disruptive to the client's recall experience than Gottman and Levenson's method to stop the tape periodically and inquire about his or her emotions at those points, the clinician still could obtain more moment-to-moment affective data with this procedure than by asking spouses to recall their overall responses at the end of a therapy session.

Summary.

The instruments described above that are available for the assessment of emotional states associated with specific marital events represent variations on a theme; that is, they are different methods by which spouses can log the quantity and quality of their daily interactions. The SOC provides the most structure by listing sets of potentially pleasing and displeasing marital behaviors; the time lines and Weekly Activity Schedule elicit the most extensive coverage of a couple's shared and unshared daily activities;

and the DRDT potentially produces the most detailed information about links among spouses' behaviors, specific cognitions, and emotions. Any of these instruments can be useful to the marital therapist in the assessment of affect in a couple's relationship.

Behavioral Observation of Marital Affect

Among the behavioral coding systems that have been developed for identifying problematic and constructive dyadic interaction patterns, the categories for coding affect have been limited. Furthermore, the affect codes sometimes are combined with other behaviors that do not seem to be direct measures of emotion, in order to produce summary categories. The following is a summary of how the major behavioral coding systems address the assessment of emotion.

Marital Interaction Coding System (MICS; Hops, et al., 1972; Weiss & Summers, 1983).

As noted in Chapter 5, this system has been used extensively in marital research to identify behaviors that differentiate distressed from non-distressed couples, and as a measure of behavioral marital therapy outcome (Weiss & Summers, 1983). It includes summary categories for coding both verbal and nonverbal behaviors: problem solving, positive verbal, positive nonverbal, negative verbal, and negative nonverbal. Within the categories, some of the codes tap pleasant and unpleasant emotions, whereas others do not specify any affect. For example, the positive (MICS +) codes include Agree, Approve, Assent, Attend, Humor, Smile/Laugh, and Positive Physical Contact (Weiss, 1984). The code Assent easily might reflect a cognitive agreement, rather than any expression of pleasant emotion. Similarly, the negative (MICS −) codes include those such as Turn Off (nonverbal gestures of displeasure, disgust, and disapproval) as well as codes such as Disagree and Deny Responsibility, which might not be expressed with any affect. Thus, summary codes do not identify the degrees of positive and negative affective expression per se. Furthermore, the summary codes do not differentiate *which* positive and negative emotions they may reflect (e.g., whether a high frequency of negative behaviors reflects anger, disgust, or depression).

The latest revision of the MICS (MICS-III; Weiss & Summers, 1983) uses several nonverbal Affect Carrier Codes (e.g., Positive Physical Contact, Smile, Turn Off) to focus on spouses' affective responses; these codes can occur singly or modify other behavioral codes (e.g., Agree plus Positive Physical Contact). Consequently, the MICS-III may be more helpful than earlier versions of the MICS for identifying degrees of emotion experienced by spouses. The MICS was developed to assess constructive and problematic communication behavior during marital problem-solving interactions (Weiss & Summers, 1983); thus, it was not intended as a measure of affect per se. However, its nonverbal affect codes can provide useful guidelines for therapists' behavioral observations of their clients.

Couples Interaction Scoring System (CISS; Gottman, 1979).

Using the Affect Code (AC) of the CISS, an observer rates spouses' nonverbal behaviors (facial expressions, voice, body position, and gestures) as positive or negative. The guidelines for nonverbal coding include specific examples of positive and negative behaviors in each nonverbal "channel" (e.g., examples of negative facial expression include "frown," "angry face," and "disgust"). These nonverbal behaviors are coded separately from the content of the spouses' verbal messages. Gottman, Notarius, Markman, Bank, Yoppi, and Rubin (1976) found that except for the "agreement" code, the verbal content codes do not discriminate distressed from nondistressed couples well on their own; however, when verbal content codes are combined with nonverbal affect codes, the CISS provides strong discrimination of the groups. Notarius et al. (1983) conclude that the communication of affect involves an *interaction* between verbal content and nonverbal cues, such that both are needed to convey emotional states accurately. Familiarity with the CISS facial, voice, body position, and movement cues can be quite useful to the clinician in assessing levels of spouses' positive and negative emotion.

Kategoriensystem für partnerschaftliche Interaktion (KPI; Hahlweg, Reisner, Kohli, Vollmer, Schindler, & Revenstorf, 1984).

The KPI is similar to the CISS in that for each verbal response that is coded, the accompanying nonverbal behavior is coded as positive, neutral, or negative. The guidelines for coding nonverbal behaviors are the same as those used by Gottman (1979), including a primary emphasis on facial expression, followed by voice tone (if the facial cues are unclear) and body cues (if neither facial expression nor voice quality seems to differentiate the valence of the message's emotional quality). As is the case with the CISS, the authors of the KPI report good levels of interrater reliability for these nonverbal codes. Thus, the KPI can be used to assess the overall levels of positive and negative affect expressed during marital interactions.

Assessment of "expressed emotion."

Brown, Birley, and Wing (1972) first used the term "expressed emotion" (EE) to describe a combination of hostility, criticism, and emotional overinvolvement exhibited by relatives of hospitalized schizophrenics. Expressed emotion has been rated from interviews with these relatives (Brown et al., 1972; Vaughn & Leff, 1976a, b) and coded from actual family interaction (Doane, West, Goldstein, Rodnick, & Jones, 1981). Goldstein (1987) has noted the difference between the negative *attitudes* and emotions tapped by EE interviews with patients' family members and negative affective *behaviors* assessed from actual patient-family interactions.

The Camberwell Family Interview (CFI; Brown et al., 1972; Vaughn & Leff, 1976a, b) is conducted with individual family members of an identified patient, in order to assess the impact of the patient's symptoms on family life. Each family member's expressed emotion concerning the patient is rated in terms of both the verbal content and voice qualities (e.g., tone) communicated as the individual describes the patient's behavior. The rating criteria include critical comments (particularly disapproval and dislike), hostility (criticism of the person rather than his or her actions), dissatisfaction with the patient's behaviors, warmth (a positive factor), and emotional overinvolvement. However, the EE index derived from the CFI places most weight on the criticism, hostility, and overinvolvement criteria. Magaña et al. (1986) developed criteria for rating expressed emotion from a five-minute audiotaped sample of a family member's comments about a patient. This "short form" for rating EE was highly correlated with EE ratings from the CFI when the two measurements were made within two weeks of each other.

Doane (Doane et al., 1981) developed an Affective Style coding system, used by observers to code positive and negative emotion expressed behaviorally by family members toward each other as they engage in a problem-solving interaction. Doane's system includes codes for personal criticism, supportive statements, guilt induction, critical intrusiveness, and excessive noncritical intrusiveness. Relatively benign criticisms (e.g., "I didn't like it when you left the room in the middle of our conversation") are distinguished from harsh generalized attacks (e.g., "You are the most selfish person I know"). Harsh criticisms and guilt-inducing statements are given the greatest weight in categorizing family interactions as "negative affective style."

Level of expressed emotion has been found to predict the onset of schizophrenic symptoms among high-risk adolescents and the relapse of symptoms among schizophrenic patients (Brown et al., 1972; Doane et al., 1981; Goldstein, 1987; Vaughn & Leff, 1976a, b; Vaughn, Snyder, Jones, Freeman, & Falloon, 1984). High EE also has been found to be associated with relapse among depressed and manic patients (Hooley, 1987). Hooley notes that high-EE relatives, particularly spouses of patients, tend to be rated high in expressed emotion mainly on the basis of their critical rather than their overinvolved attitudes. Consequently, there seems to be a considerable degree of overlap between expressed emotion and marital distress.

Hooley and Hahlweg (1986) found that depressed individuals whose partners were rated high in EE had significantly lower Dyadic Adjustment Scale scores than those whose partners were low in EE. The relationship between the partners' EE levels and their own marital distress remains to be explored. Hooley (1987) notes that high EE ratings can reflect either critical comments that a partner intends as constructive (attempts to motivate a psychiatrically symptomatic partner to make positive changes) or hostile criticism from a frustrated partner who is retaliating for the symptomatic partner's "misbehavior." Thus, it seems likely that high EE and marital distress overlap, but that a fairly nondistressed spouse can be rated high in EE. In other words, there seems to be a difference between high-EE *behavior* and the subjective emotions and attitudes involved in marital distress. Consequently, it may be useful to assess both expressed emotion and marital distress, especially when a member of a couple exhibits symptoms of a disorder such as depression.

The assessment of expressed emotion would not be relevant for understanding marital and family relationships if EE rated from relatives' comments about a family member was not related to the manner in which the relatives actually interacted with that person. In fact, a number of studies have demonstrated that family members rated high in EE when interviewed about a patient exhibit more negative verbal and nonverbal behavior (including nonverbal expressions of negative emotions) toward that individual (Hahlweg et al., 1987). In return, the recipients of high levels of EE tend to respond in a defensive, self-justifying manner. Ratings of EE clearly tap a characteristic that contributes significantly to marital and family interactions which can escalate conflict and distress.

Coding of specific affects from physical features versus judgments by cultural informants.

Gottman and Levenson (1986) note that two major approaches to the coding of affective behavior have developed. First, with recent developments in psychophysiological methods, it is now possible to measure specific aspects of behavior such as voice qualities and muscular movements involved in facial expressions which are associated with particular emotional states. In addition, Ekman and Friesen's (1978) Facial Action Coding System can be used to identify specific visible facial movements. However, Gottman and Levenson (1986) note that such methods only code nonverbal aspects of affective communication, and that in marital interaction the verbal content also conveys a great deal of emotion. In addition, they stress that the communication of emotion involves the interactive *combination* of verbal and nonverbal information, and that much emotional information is communicated in ways that vary from one culture to another. Therefore, an alternative method for coding affective behavior is to use "cultural informants" who have expertise in identifying specific emotions in couples' marital interactions. Gottman and Levenson now use a combination of cultural informant coding of "emotional moments" and coding of specific facial expressions using the Facial Action Coding System. Although these methods (particularly the coding of physical features) are not likely to be practical for the marital therapist, clinicians can improve their skills at identifying and differentiating nonverbal cues of emotion by studying the coding systems.

Summary.

Behavioral observation methods for assessing marital affect are important because spouses' self-reports of their emotions can be limited by a number of factors, such as a tendency to respond in a socially desirable manner, or a lack of awareness of one's own emotional states. Also, some self-report questionnaires ask respondents to summarize their emotions concerning long sequences of marital interactions, relying on retrospective accounts and an "averaging" of various emotions that occurred during a particular period. Behavioral coding allows one to identify when a particular emotional response occurred during a sequence of behavioral interactions between spouses, and thus to isolate its specific cause (and effect).

Although the behavioral coding systems described above have been valuable in marital research, most of them require too much time and expense to be useful in clinical practice. However, as noted previously, the clinician may be able to adapt these methods to his or her practice and use more simplified versions in order to be able to collect some behavioral data to supplement clients' self-reports about their emotions.

Identifying Varieties of Positive and Negative Emotions

Although it is important to obtain an assessment of the overall level of positive versus negative affect experienced by each spouse, it is equally important to identify the specific emotions that the clients are feeling. As described in Chapter 10, the therapist's interventions will vary according to whether a spouse's primary emotion is anger or depression or jealousy, for example. Consequently, the clinician should use methods that assess a variety of emotions, as well as overall marital satisfaction. Measures described earlier, such as Williams's (1979) marital time lines and versions of Beck et al.'s (1979) Weekly Activity Schedule and Daily Record of Dysfunctional Thoughts, can be used to log fluctuations in the types of emotion experienced. Similar data can be collected during clinical interviews with the spouses, in which the therapist inquires about varieties of emotions that the couple experience. In addition, the clinician can administer some other questionnaires assessing particular affective states such as depression, anger, and anxiety (which are described later in this chapter) in order to determine current levels of these emotions.

SPOUSES' RECOGNITION OF EMOTIONS AND THEIR DETERMINANTS

In order to determine the degree to which each spouse is aware of his or her emotions and the events (partner behaviors, own cognitions) that elicit them, the clinician must rely on the clients' self-reports. A number of the questionnaires and interview procedures described previously can be used for this purpose.

Written Logs of Emotions

When spouses keep daily logs of their activities and moods such as Beck et al.'s (1979) Weekly Activity Schedule, or when they are instructed to use Beck et al.'s (1979) DRDT to record marital situations and cognitions associated with a range of both pleasant and unpleasant emotions, the therapist is likely to find that some individuals report a rich variety of emotions whereas others do not. It is important to examine both the *variety of emotions* that an individual reports and the degree to which he or she is able to tie the emotional states to particular eliciting events. Some spouses can list a range of emotions that they felt during a day or week but cannot identify their antecedents. Other spouses can report events that occurred in their marriages but have difficulty identifying what, if any, emotions they experienced at those times. Because cognitive-behavioral treatment methods rely on clients' abilities to link behavioral, cognitive, and affective aspects of marital interaction, it is important to determine each spouse's ability to make such discriminations early in one's assessment of a couple. When spouses lack a high level of such awareness, some of the therapist's initial interventions must be focused on increasing this ability. Techniques for increasing spouses' awareness of their emotions and their determinants (e.g., discriminating physiological and behavioral cues of emotional arousal and their association with life events) are described in Chapter 10.

   It is important when assessing awareness of emotions to differentiate between a spouse who reports few emotions owing to a lack of awareness of mood states and an individual who, in fact, has limited emotional responses to marital (and perhaps other) events. In the former case, interventions for enhancing awareness of emotions would be most appropriate, but in the latter case the question becomes whether it is useful or desirable for the person to experience more frequent, intense, or varied emotions within his or her marriage. One fairly common situation in which this issue arises is when one spouse is upset that the partner does not experience and discuss emotions as much as he or she does. The therapist is faced with evaluating the extent to which it is appropriate to work toward increasing the partner's emotionality within the marriage. Some of the factors involved in this evaluation include the following. First, it is crucial to determine whether the less emotional partner defines his or her level of affect as a problem and wants to modify it. In addition, the therapist must evaluate the *degree* to which the less emotional partner would have to increase emotionality in order to satisfy the other person. As discussed earlier (Chapter 3), couples often experience a cognitive process of "polarization" in which they magnify the extent of actual differences in their characteristics and therefore believe that they or their partners would have to make major changes in order for them to be compatible. However, it is our experience that when a less (or more) emotional spouse makes even a small but noticeable change in his or her level of affect during marital interactions, the partner often becomes significantly more satisfied. In other words, the spouses do not need to become equal in the realm of affective responsiveness, but they each need to perceive that the other individual *can* relate to them in their preferred mode and *wants* to do so at times (i.e., the partner is not an alien being and cares about their preferences).

Second, it is important to identify whether the other spouse's desire for a more emotional partner in fact represents a different underlying issue (e.g., he or she interprets the partner's lack of emotion as a lack of caring or love) that might be addressed in another manner (e.g., by helping the partner to communicate caring and love for the spouse clearly in other ways; by helping the person who feels unloved to expand his or her definition of loving behavior). These aspects of assessment require an inquiry into the cognitions that both spouses have regarding the experience and expression of emotion in the marriage.

In summary, when a therapist asks spouses to keep written logs in order to assess the degree to which each person is able to recognize his or her emotions and their determinants, it is important to examine whether they are able to describe a variety of emotions and to specify the events (e.g., partner behaviors and their own interpretations of those behaviors) that seem to elicit the emotions. In addition, when an individual lists few emotional responses to the partner, it is important to (a) ask whether this is typical of his or her emotions regarding the partner, (b) probe for emotional experiences that the individual may have neglected to report (first in a nondirective manner, but then with more specific questions about particular emotions if the open-ended questions fail to yield affective data), and (c) inquire about the range and intensity of emotions that the person experiences in other life situations such as work and leisure activities with friends.

A Weekly Activity Schedule may itself reveal that an individual does experience a variety of emotions in other settings but is relatively emotionally "turned off" when with his or her partner. When this is the case, the therapist will need to explore its causes, including cognitions that may inhibit the experiencing of emotion. For example, some spouses who have been disappointed and hurt by their partners experience cognitions such as "I won't let him hurt me again. I just won't let myself feel anything." Some other spouses are more concerned with their own ability to maintain emotional stability and have cognitions such as "If I get emotional, I'll lose control and go crazy." Consequently, these individuals actively suppress affective experiences. Therefore, when structured record-keeping forms are used to evaluate the degree to which an individual is able to recognize his or her emotional responses and their determinants, it commonly is necessary to "flesh out" the assessment with some skillful interviewing.

Clinical Interviews

In addition to using interviews in the manner described above for refining the data collected with written logs, the marital therapist can use clinical interviews in a number of other ways to determine each spouse's ability to recognize emotions and their causes. First, when a spouse reports that he or she has been upset about the marriage *in the past*, the therapist can ask the individual to specify what kinds of upsetting feelings were involved and what occurred in the marriage that seemed to elicit such feelings. Responses may range from a clear specification, such as "I repeatedly became angry when he made promises to share the work load around the house and then went off with his friends," to a vague description, such as "I just found myself happy at work but unhappy at home, but I don't know exactly what I felt or what went on at home that caused it."

Second, the potential errors involved in retrospective reports when spouses are requested to remember situations and emotions from the past can be avoided if the therapist monitors the spouses' apparent mood states during their interactions in the office and inquires about them. At various points when the therapist suspects that a spouse may be having emotional responses to the events in the session, he or she can ask about the spouse's immediate mood. Again, some individuals will readily report a particular affect, whereas others may only be aware of a global positive or negative quality to their moods, and still others may report no emotion even when the therapist observes some nonverbal cues commonly associated with emotion (e.g., facial expressions).

When a spouse does report an emotional state, the therapist then can inquire about the factors that the individual believes elicited it, using open-ended questions such as "What was going on at that moment that seemed to set off that sad feeling you had?" More specific questions can be used to guide the client in identifying behavioral events and cognitions that influenced his or her mood. For example, if the client has difficulty identifying what elicited sad feelings during a marital interaction, the therapist might say, "I noticed that your face looked sad when you two were discussing your plans for the upcoming holiday. Was there something about that discussion, or your thoughts about it, that seemed to lower your mood?" By conducting this type of inquiry from time to time during conjoint marital therapy sessions, the therapist can get a sense of each spouse's ability to pinpoint factors that may be contributing to pleasant and unpleasant emotions.

Partners as participant observers.

Spouses also can serve as sources of data about each other's emotions and their determinants. For example, when one husband reported that he often felt irritated around his wife, but that he was not sure what it was about her that bothered him, his wife responded, "Well, I've sure noticed that you get irritable whenever I ask you to change your daily routine. If it doesn't go just the way you are used to, you become miserable." Although it is possible that a partner's perceptions about such causal factors can be inaccurate attributions, the therapist can propose that the partner has suggested an interesting hypothesis that should be checked out. Whether or not the partner's hypothesis was valid, the exploration of alternative causes for the spouse's emotional state is likely to help the latter individual develop an ability to monitor and differentiate determinants of emotions.

Cognitions that impede recognition of emotions and their determinants.

As was described in Chapter 4 and earlier in this chapter, it is important to identify any cognitions that may inhibit the awareness of emotions. When a spouse expresses thoughts that experiencing emotions within the marriage is dangerous or undesirable, the therapist should conduct a more extensive cognitive assessment, in order to determine whether these cognitions are tied to firmly held assumptions or standards about individual functioning and relationships. For example, using a series of questions, one therapist elicited a husband's basic standard that "a man is not supposed to spend his time being emotional; his mind should be on other things, like figuring out what needs to be done to fix a problem." The therapist needed to address this man's sex role standards before it would be fruitful to attempt to increase his monitoring of fluctuations in his emotions.

Another example of a stable cognition that can reduce an individual's tendency to monitor determinants of emotional states is the common assumption described in Chapter 4 that emotions are always caused directly by events and are not mediated by cognitions.

Thus, as has been emphasized previously in this book, it tends to be artificial to try to assess emotions, cognitions, or behaviors independent of the other two components of marital interaction. In practice, when assessing affect a therapist also will assess particular types of cognitions and behaviors that influence the experience and expression of emotion. In vivo interviews while spouses are interacting in the therapist's office provide a major source of data about the interplay of the three factors.

Spouses' affective vocabularies.

An individual's failure to report a variety of emotions can stem at least in part from a limited vocabulary for describing emotions. Such a deficit sometimes stems from growing up in a family where emotions were discussed infrequently. Whatever its source, it involves a restricted number of emotional descriptors, which are likely to be associated with a restricted number of personal constructs (Kelly, 1955) for differentiating various emotions. For example, some clients are not familiar with the distinction between anxiety and depression, in terms of knowing any of the symptoms that tend to define the two syndromes.

Thus, it is important to encourage spouses to describe their emotions as fully as possible, using any words that occur to them. Partners' affective vocabularies also can be assessed by showing them a list of positive and negative emotions (see Table 10-1) and asking them to (a) define the terms as best they can, and (b) indicate which terms best describe their emotions in particular marital situations.

DEFICITS AND EXCESSES IN THE EXPRESSION OF EMOTION

The manner in which spouses communicate their emotions to one another has been a central concern of marital therapists and researchers, and some form of emotional expressiveness training tends to be included in most behaviorally oriented treatment approaches (see Chapter 4). Problems in the expression of emotion that typically are focused on in therapy include both (a) behavioral *deficits* such as lack of open, direct, specific statements of feelings and (b) behavioral *excesses* such as criticisms, interruptions, put-downs, and other aversive modes of communicating negative feelings (e.g., Baucom, 1985; Baucom & Lester, 1986; Emmelkamp et al., 1984; Hahlweg, Schindler, Revenstorf, & Brengelmann, 1984; Stuart, 1980). Consequently, the assessment procedures used to gather data about a couple's emotional expressiveness should cover both the constructive behaviors that are not occurring to a sufficient degree and the dysfunctional behaviors that can escalate marital conflict and distress. The following are some measures that are useful in collecting such data.

Partner Reports

There are a number of self-report scales available with which spouses describe the quality of emotional expression in their relationships. In general, the items on these questionnaires tap the individual's perceptions of the partner's verbal and nonverbal expression or the communication of the couple as a unit. For the most part these questionnaires do not differentiate between the expression of emotions and the expression of attitudes, opinions, and other cognitions. However, they can give the clinician a sense of how two partners perceive each other's overall communication process, and interviews with the couple can help identify whether the behaviors reported on the questionnaires describe the expression of emotions per se.

Verbal Problems Checklist (VPC; Chavez et al., 1981).

Chavez et al. created a 27-item self-report version of Carter and Thomas's (1973) observational coding system that includes behaviors assumed to be problematic in marital communication. In the self-report version, each spouse rates the frequency with which his or her partner exhibits each of the behaviors, using a five-point scale ranging from "never" to "always." Total scores on the VPC have been found to be highly correlated with marital distress (Chavez et al., 1981; Epstein et al., 1987), but not with observer ratings of couples' communication (Haynes, Chavez, & Samuel, 1984).

Epstein et al. (1987) cautioned that scores on self-report communication scales such as the VPC can be influenced by spouses' idiosyncratic cognitive appraisals of their partners' behaviors. For example, ratings of a partner's expressiveness on VPC items such as "talks too little," "criticizes you in an unhelpful manner," "asks too many questions," and "fails to express emotions" can be highly subjective and therefore influenced by the rater's own standards about relationships. Consistent with this idea,

Epstein et al. (1987) found that spouses' scores on the VPC were significantly correlated with their scores on two measures of problematic marital cognitions: the Relationship Belief Inventory (Eidelson & Epstein, 1982) and the Marital Attitude Survey (Pretzer et al., 1983). Furthermore, multiple regression analyses indicated that a significant amount of the statistical relationship between the VPC and the Dyadic Adjustment Scale was accounted for by the relationship that each of those measures had with the cognitive measures. Consequently, when using self-report marital communication scales it is important to take into account that the spouses' responses probably represent a combination of accurate perceptions of each other's expressive behaviors on the one hand and subjective cognitive appraisals on the other hand.

A factor analysis of the VPC (Epstein et al., 1987) revealed three factors for each sex: critical/defensive, withdrawn, and submissive for females who were rating males and critical/defensive, withdrawn/submissive, and dominant/controlling for males who were rating females. Because the factors were not highly intercorrelated and were related differentially to measures of marital cognitions and satisfaction, it seems useful to compute subscale (factor) scores rather than using only a total score on the VPC. In clinical practice, a therapist is likely to obtain more information that can be used in planning specific therapeutic interventions by examining spouses' responses to each VPC item.

Marital Satisfaction Inventory (MSI; Snyder, 1981).

This questionnaire, which was described previously, includes an "affective communication" subscale. That subscale consists of a variety of item content, including the degree of affection expressed in the marriage, the degree of empathy and understanding received from the partner, and the degree to which the partner discloses emotions. Consequently, a spouse's score on "affective communication" can alert the therapist to a problem in this area, but identifying the specific nature of the deficit or excess in the expression of emotion will necessitate further inquiry.

Barrett-Lennard Relationship Inventory (RI; Barrett-Lennard, 1962).

This scale originally was designed to assess clients' perceptions of the degree to which their therapists provided the facilitative therapeutic conditions (level of regard, empathy, congruence, and unconditional regard) proposed by Rogers (1957). Subsequently, the 64 items comprising these four subscales have been applied with a variety of intimate relationships, including marriages. For example, Epstein and Jackson (1978) found that couples given group communication training exhibited a significant increase in spouse-rated empathy on the RI compared to a waiting-list control group, whereas couples in an interaction insight group showed no increase in empathy compared to the group receiving no treatment.

Schumm, Bollman, and Jurich (1981) constructed a much briefer (13 items for husbands and 15 items for wives) version of the RI, which includes three factors: empathic understanding, level of regard, and congruence. The level of regard items (e.g., "My husband [wife] feels a deep affection for me") tend to tap positive emotion, and the congruence items (e.g., "My husband [wife] expresses his [her] true impressions and feelings with me") tend to assess open expression of emotions. However, some items on each subscale seem to measure cognitions rather than emotions (e.g., "My husband [wife] respects me as a person"). Consequently, given the information available regarding the construct validity of either the original 64-item RI or the short form, the clinician must interpret scores on these scales with care, especially noting how spouses respond to the items most clearly measuring the emotions that individuals perceive their partners to be expressing.

Spouses' ratings of their partners on the empathy subscale of the RI can help assess the degree to which couples have deficits in the listening skills (especially reflective listening) considered to be a major aspect of effective communication (see Chapter 4). However, if an individual is rated low in empathy by his or her partner, it is important to observe samples of the couple's communication and to assess whether the former person actually lacks the listening skills outlined by writers such as Guerney (1977), or whether the latter person is failing to notice or acknowledge the partner's good listening.

Emotional empathy.

For the purpose of assessing the expression of affect, it is important to note that the items of the RI empathy subscale do not differentiate clearly between the cognitive understanding component of empathy and the extent to which the listening spouse empathically experiences some degree of the partner's emotions (i.e., emotional empathy). Empathy researchers have emphasized the distinction between cognitive understanding and emotional empathy, and there has been considerable empirical support for the idea that altruistic behavior and the inhibition of aggression are facilitated when an individual experiences an empathic sharing of another person's emotional or physical pain (Eisenberg & Miller, 1987; Feshbach, 1987; Miller & Eisenberg, 1988).

Reviews of empathy research (e.g., Eisenberg & Miller, 1987) indicate that the self-report scale most widely used to assess emotional empathy is the questionnaire developed by Mehrabian and Epstein (1972). Although this scale measures emotional empathy as a trait, rather than as a response in particular situations, and it was not intended specifically for use in marital assessment, it is a brief (33-item) instrument that can be used to identify whether spouses have notable deficits in emotional sensitivity to other people. Items such as "People around me have a great influence on my moods," "I become more irritated than sympathetic when I see someone's tears," "I like to watch people open presents," and "It is hard for me to see how some things upset people so much" clearly assess a variety of affective (and even cognitive) aspects of empathy. Further research clearly is needed to develop methods for assessing emotional empathy in the marital context, both as a general disposition and as a response to a partner in specific situations.

Personal Assessment of Intimacy in Relationships (PAIR; Olson & Schaefer, undated; Schaefer & Olson, 1981).

This scale includes a six-item subscale for each of five types of intimacy: emotional, social, sexual, intellectual, and recreational. It also includes six items from Edmonds' (1967) marital conventionalization scale, which assesses a spouse's tendency to describe his or her marriage in a socially desirable manner. For each area of intimacy, each spouse reports both his or her expected (desired) degree of intimacy and the degree of intimacy that he or she receives in the relationship. Thus, the PAIR is useful for revealing discrepancies between desired and experienced intimacy. The subscales have exhibited modest internal consistency and some evidence of construct validity. The PAIR scale is included here as a possible measure of inadequate and dysfunctional expression of emotion, because its items appear to measure both (a) the process of intimate interaction and (b) the spouses' subjective appraisals of the degree of intimacy in their relationship. In the emotional intimacy subscale, the items "My partner listens to me when I need someone to talk to," "I can state my feelings without him/her getting defensive," and "My partner can really understand my hurts and joys" describe the quality of the communication process between the spouses. The items "I often feel distant from my partner," "I feel neglected at times by my partner," and "I sometimes feel lonely when we're together" appear to tap the affective tone of the relationship. The other subscales of the PAIR do not appear to assess affect.

A discrepancy between expected and experienced emotional intimacy might be due to a variety of factors, such as (a) actual deficits in intimate marital interactions, (b) the perceiver's selective inattention to or memory of intimate interactions, or (c) unrealistic standards concerning the nature and degree of marital intimacy.

Behavioral Observation

A number of the behavioral coding systems described earlier (MICS, CISS, KPI) can be used as clinical guidelines when a therapist is attempting to identify whether spouses have deficits or excesses in the expression of positive or negative emotion. Therapists also can use Carter and Thomas's behavioral coding version of the Verbal Problems Checklist (Carter & Thomas, 1973; Thomas, 1977) for this purpose. However, many of the coding categories in the VPC do not clearly address the expression of emotion per se. On the other hand, the VPC includes many behaviors that can *impede* effective communication of emotion (e.g., topic content avoidance, singsong speech, poor referent specification). As is the case with the other behavioral coding systems, when using the VPC it is important to differentiate between negative versus positive (i.e., destructive versus constructive) communication behaviors and expressions of negative versus positive emotion.

In Guerney's (1977) Verbal Interaction Task, one spouse is asked to take the role of speaker and to express his or her "feelings" about a topic (likely to include both cognitions and emotions) while the other spouse is asked to listen and to help the partner express those feelings. After four minutes, the spouses exchange roles. During each spouse's first turn in the speaker role the topic is to be something that he or she would like to change about the self; during the person's second turn as speaker the topic is something that he or she would like to see changed in the partner.

A couple's communication during the Verbal Interaction Task then can be coded according to Stover, Guerney, Ginsberg, and Schlein's (1977a) Self-Feeling Awareness Scale (SFAS) and Stover, Guerney, Ginsberg, and Schlein's (1977b) Acceptance of Other Scale (AOS). The SFAS is an eight-point scale for rating the degree to which a speaker has expressed important feelings in subjective terms. The coding unit is each statement by the person that occurs between two statements by the partner. A high score is given when the speaker states his or her own feelings (particularly emotions) in clear, direct terms (e.g., "I get angry when you interrupt me"). Moderate scores reflect abstract comments about the self, as well as social conversation, and low scores reflect aspects of communication that fail to disclose the speaker's feelings (e.g., making suggestions to influence the partner, rejecting the listener's ideas, giving directions, attacking or praising the self or partner without owning one's feelings).

The eight-point AOS is used to rate the degree to which the listener focuses on the speaker's content and verbally reflects the speaker's deepest feelings in an empathic manner. Moderate scores are given to listener responses that paraphrase some aspects of the speaker's message but miss the basic feelings, and low scores are given when the listener directs the exchange (e.g., with advice, social conversation, disagreement, and criticism).

Detailed guidelines for coding speaker and listener behavior are provided by Guerney (1977). High interrater reliability has been found with both the SFAS and the AOS. Guerney also describes some validity evidence for each rating scale. The SFAS and AOS are restricted in scope to the assessment of feeling expression and empathic listening, in contrast to coding systems such as the MICS, CISS, and KPI which tap other behaviors such as problem solving. However, they provide clear sets of guidelines for identifying deficits in the communication skills emphasized by Guerney (1977) and many other behaviorally oriented marital therapists, and they focus on the communication of emotion.

Dyadic behavioral patterns.

Researchers who study marital communication increasingly have coded *sequences* of behaviors exchanged by spouses in addition to simple frequencies of constructive and problematic acts (Gottman, 1979; Revenstorf et al., 1984). This approach takes into account systems theory concepts of circular causality and "positive feedback" whereby there is an escalating exchange of negative or positive behavior. Revenstorf et al. (1984) found that distressed couples exhibited a higher probability of negative escalation than did nondistressed couples, suggesting that nondistressed couples do have negative exchanges but are able to "exit" from them more effectively than distressed pairs.

Consequently, when assessing a couple's expression of negative and positive emotion, therapists should look at the sequential pattern. Thus, when a wife voices her anger by criticizing her husband's basic personality, it is important to look at the husband's behaviors that precede and follow her remark. It may be that she attacks him only after he has "disqualified" her less aggressive expressions of her feelings (e.g., he may give replies such as, "You are really mixed up and don't know what you feel"). In this case, the therapist may have observed an escalation of aggressiveness by the wife when she perceives that unaggressive expression of her emotions is ineffective. In order to help such a couple alter their problematic manner of expressing emotions, the therapist must take into account how each spouse's affective communication influences and is influenced by the other's. Any of the behavioral coding systems described in this chapter can be used to identify problematic sequences between spouses. Similarly, Guerney's (1977) guidelines for empathic listeners (e.g., communicate acceptance and respect even when you disagree, do not give advice, do not voice judgments about what the expresser says) can be used to identify sequences in which one spouse's manner of expressing emotions is influenced by the manner in which the other responds to the expression.

Cognitions that impede constructive expression and listening.

As noted above and in Chapter 4, spouses' dysfunctional expression and listening regarding emotions in their relationship may be based on choice rather than skill deficits. Spouses who express few emotions may be inhibited by standards that it is inappropriate to discuss negative (and even positive) emotions, or they may have expectancies that their partners will react negatively if they express their emotions. On the other hand, spouses who use aversive means of expressing negative affect (e.g., insults, threats) may hold an assumption such as "Only 'strong' statements are taken seriously by other people." Similarly, a spouse who argues rather than listens empathically to a partner's feelings may be capable of better listening in other situations (e.g., with co-workers) but may hold an assumption such as "There is always a winner and a loser in a conflict, and I must gain the upper hand in order to avoid defeat." Thus, a comprehensive assessment of deficits and excesses in the communication of emotion should include the identification of any cognitions that affect each spouse's choices among alternative means of expressing affect or responding to the emotions expressed by a partner.

The context of emotional expression.

Particular situations can influence the manner in which an individual expresses emotions or listens to a partner's feelings. Some couples attempt to discuss anger just at the times when they are most aroused, and this can lead to verbal or physical aggression. Consequently, clinicians who work with couples who have difficulty expressing anger in a constructive manner (e.g., Neidig & Friedman, 1984) help them to identify environmental factors (e.g., noise, alcohol, distracting tasks) that increase stress. Marital therapists need to take into account the contexts in which couples attempt to share affective material. At times, spouses may be better able to use constructive expressive and listening skills that they already possess if therapists help them to create an environment conducive to good communication. Therefore, therapists should collect information about the situations in which couples typically discuss emotions concerning their relationships, noting whether there seem to be particular situations that have been more conducive to effective communication than others.

EMOTIONS THAT INTERFERE WITH ADAPTIVE FUNCTIONING

This section describes methods for assessing several types of emotion that have the potential to interfere with constructive marital interaction: anger, depression, anxiety, and jealousy. These emotions are not necessarily problematic; their disruptive influence tends to depend on their intensity and the abilities that both members of a couple have to cope with them. The following discussion is not intended to be a comprehensive review of methods for assessing each of the emotions, but rather a survey of some measures that can be used fairly easily for initial identification of dysfunctional mood states. If such an initial screening indicates that the functioning of one or both spouses is impaired by particular emotional responses, further assessment should be conducted, and appropriate referrals for assessment should be made if the marital therapist lacks expertise in this area. Furthermore, when a thorough assessment reveals a significant problem involving an affective state such as depression, the marital therapist is faced with clinical decisions regarding (a) whether or not he or she has the expertise to treat problems such as clinical depression and (b) whether a spouse's dysfunctional affect is best treated in the context of marital therapy, separately but concurrently with marital therapy, or prior to marital therapy. Although clinicians frequently voice various preferences among these treatment options, there are as yet no empirical findings that address the issue. The most common clinical guideline for treating an affective problem in individual therapy before pursuing marital treatment is that conjoint work is unlikely to be productive if emotional states impede spouses' abilities (a) to take a collaborative attitude toward resolving marital conflicts, (b) to think objectively, and (c) to learn and practice new ways of interacting with each other. In particular, it is important to determine whether a spouse's anger leads to verbal or physical abuse, and whether clinical levels of depression essentially immobilize a spouse physically and cognitively or produce significant suicidal risk.

Anger

Self-report inventories.

Conflict Tactics Scales (CTS; Straus, 1979). This self-report questionnaire was developed to assess the degrees to which couples use particular constructive and problematic means of handling conflicts. Spouses report the frequencies with which they and their partners exhibit various responses during marital conflict. The CTS contains subscales for reasoning, verbal aggression, and violence; Fredman and Sherman (1987) note that the verbal aggression subscale includes nonverbal behaviors and might be better labeled "symbolic aggression." The CTS is primarily a measure of the ways in which spouses *express* anger, rather than an index of the levels of their anger. For example, it includes items such as "stomped out of the room or house (or yard)," "slapped the other one," and "insulted or swore at the other one."

Conflict Inventory (CI; Margolin, Fernandez, Gorin, & Ortiz, 1982). The CI is similar to the CTS in terms of asking each spouse to report how often he or she and the partner exhibit particular constructive and problematic behaviors during marital conflicts. The CI also asks spouses to indicate how often they would like the self and the partner to exhibit each behavior, as well as how often the partner would like them to exhibit the behaviors. Thus, the CI is intended to reveal not only how the spouses tend to handle conflict, but also how satisfied they are with their patterns of conflict management (i.e., actual versus preferred behaviors). The CI includes subscales for problem solving, aggression, and withdrawal. As is the case with the CTS, the items of the CI (e.g., "insult partner," "take out anger elsewhere," "hit, push, slap") tend to assess the mode of anger expression rather than the level of anger.

Anger Checklist (Margolin, Olkin, & Baum, 1977). This is a clinical instrument (with no available reliability and validity data) with which spouses can log situations that angered them and indicate which of 79 specific reactions were components of their anger responses. The anger symptoms are divided into the following categories: (a) somatic cues (e.g., rush of adrenaline, clenched jaw, muscles tightened), (b) feelings (e.g., hurt, numb, afraid, enraged, rejected), (c) actions (e.g., pacing, yelling, throwing objects, foot stomping, slapping, punching), (d) thoughts (e.g., "I hate you," "Get out of my life," "You've got no right to. . ."), and (e) angry words (e.g., threats, name calling, sarcasm). The respondent also is asked to rate the intensity of his or her anger during the incident, on a six-point scale ranging from "barely angry" to "most intense anger ever experienced." Jacobson and Margolin (1979) suggest that the Anger Checklist can be used to report on one's own or a partner's anger responses, although it is not possible to monitor most of a partner's somatic and cognitive cues.

Because the Anger Checklist breaks anger responses down into the above components, it can be a good source of clinical data for a cognitive-behavioral approach to the assessment and treatment of couples' anger. However, many of the items easily could reflect emotions other than anger. For example, somatic items such as rush of adrenaline, unable to relax/sleep, clenched jaw, muscles tightened, and upset/acid stomach can reflect anxiety as much as anger. Many of the feelings items (e.g., hurt, numb, afraid, rejected, helpless, depressed, guilty) clearly refer to emotions other than anger. Similarly, some actions items (e.g., crying, avoidance/staying away from partner) and thoughts items (e.g., "I don't want to deal with this") may be associated with emotions other than anger.

The seeming lack of discriminant validity does not mean that the Anger Checklist cannot be used in the assessment of spouses' anger. Clients' responses to the scale may reveal that their somatic, emotional, cognitive, and other reactions at the times when they experience anger include not only anger but also other states. For example, a spouse's responses across several anger incidents might reveal that he or she has many somatic cues of tension, feels rejected and fearful as much as angry, withdraws more than expressing anger directly, and has cognitions involving escape rather than confrontation. This pattern suggests that the individual's tendency to withdraw from conflict may be due to a high level of anxiety regarding possible negative consequences of open conflict with the partner. Thus, data from the Anger Checklist can be used to generate hypotheses about factors influencing spouses' idiosyncratic experiences and expressions of anger.

Semantic Differential Scales. Margolin et al. (1988) assessed spouses' affective responses following problem-solving discussions by asking them to rate their emotions on nine seven-point bipolar scales. Three of the scales comprised an index of anger: angry–calm, out of control–in control, and hurtful–compassionate. Physically aggressive husbands scored significantly higher on the anger index than did verbally aggressive and withdrawing husbands, but wives in the three groups did not differ in reported anger. In clinical practice, semantic differential scales provide a simple means of assessing levels of anger and other emotional states; yet one must be cautious in considering the validity of brief semantic differential instruments in differentiating various affective states.

Anger Log (Neidig & Friedman, 1984). The Anger Log is similar in format to Beck et al.'s (1979) DRDT. It includes columns for recording (a) date/time, (b) anger-eliciting incident, (c) anger level (0–100), (d) automatic thoughts during and after the incident, and (e) outcome. The "outcome" column includes any actions that the individual took, as well as any consequences of behaving in that manner (e.g., "I yelled, and my husband stopped nagging me"). The reason for asking the client to report consequences in the outcome column is to identify any effects that may be reinforcing problematic ways of expressing anger (Neidig & Friedman, 1984). The Anger Log is a useful tool for measuring spouses' anger, including its antecedents and consequences, especially within a cognitive-behavioral framework. It integrates the assessment of affect with the measurement of problematic cognitions and behaviors. In regard to identifying levels of anger that might impede spouses' abilities to collaborate in resolving marital conflicts, Anger Logs can be used to determine whether a spouse is experiencing "sentiment override" (Weiss, 1980), whereby he or she responds with anger no matter what positive or negative behavior the partner exhibits. When this seems to be the case, the Anger Logs also may reveal whether there are particular cognitions (e.g., extreme standards for partner behavior; attributions of blame for marital problems) that produce consistent anger regardless of the partner's current behavior.

Behavioral observation.

Behavioral coding systems such as the MICS, CISS, and KPI include categories for differentiating positive from negative responses, and both the CISS and KPI provide coding of nonverbal behaviors assumed to reflect positive and negative affect, but none of these systems differentiate specific emotions such as anger. Gottman and Levenson's (1986) coding of affect through a combination of specific nonverbal features and judgments of "cultural informants" has been a promising method for differentiating anger from other emotions, but their methods are much less practical for clinical practice than for research.

Living in Familial Environments (LIFE; Arthur, Hops, & Biglan, 1982; Hops et al., 1987). The LIFE is a behavioral coding system that does include the differentiation of affects. Messages exchanged by family members are coded in terms of both verbal content and quality of affect. The LIFE affect codes include happy, caring, irritated, dysphoric (depressed), sarcastic, and whining. In terms of reliability, Hops et al. (1987) found kappas at the .6 level for each of the six affect codes. Those investigators combined the irritated and sarcastic codes to form an index of "aggressive affect." The evidence obtained with the LIFE system demonstrates the potential for coding behavioral expressions of anger, but once again, at present such a coding system probably is too cumbersome and time-consuming for clinical practice. However, marital therapists who study a system such as LIFE are likely to refine their abilities for assessing anger and other emotions when observing marital interactions.

Depression

Given the growing evidence that depression is influenced by marital interaction patterns, it is important to assess both the individual spouses' levels of depressive symptoms and the antecedents and consequences of depressive behavior within the couple's interactions. The following are some measures that can be helpful in that regard. When assessing depression, it is important to distinguish between the variety of cognitive, behavioral, affective, somatic, and motivational symptoms that comprise a depressive syndrome (Beck, 1972; Leber, Beckham, & Danker-Brown, 1985) and the affective component of depression per se. Some of the instruments described below focus on depressive affect, whereas others cover a wide range of depressive symptoms.

Another caution concerning the assessment of depression concerns limitations in the discriminant validity of existing depression measures. There is considerable empirical evidence that methods for assessing depression have difficulty differentiating depression from other negative states such as anxiety (Dobson, 1985; Lipman, 1982; Mountjoy & Roth, 1982).

Consequently, therapists who use the instruments described below should consider the possibility that high depression scores may reflect other psychological states and should attempt to conduct a "differential diagnosis" of spouses' expressed affect.

Self-report inventories.

Several self-report depression scales are available, and these scales vary considerably in the degree to which they assess the affective component of depression, as opposed to other symptoms (e.g., self-criticism, appetite disturbances). Consequently, the clinician's choice of an instrument should be based on a decision about the range of depressive symptoms that he or she wishes to assess.

Beck Depression Inventory (BDI; Beck et al., 1979). The BDI includes 21 items measuring affective, cognitive (including suicidal ideation), behavioral, and physical symptoms. Its reliability and validity are well documented, and it has been used extensively in research and clinical practice. The BDI takes only a few minutes to complete and can be administered repeatedly over the course of therapy to monitor changes in depressive symptoms. An apparent limitation of the BDI is that it tends to have moderate correlations with self-report anxiety scales (Shaw, Vallis, & McCabe, 1985). It is not clear to what degree such correlations (also found between other depression and anxiety measures) are due to impure measures or to actual overlap of symptoms in depression and anxiety. This is an issue currently receiving a great deal of attention by researchers. Until more information is available regarding the discriminant validity of the BDI, it would be wise for clinicians to assess spouses' levels of both depression and anxiety and to try to differentiate the two types of affect as best possible through detailed interviews.

Depression Adjective Checklist (DACL; Lubin, 1967). The DACL includes positive and negative adjectives that were found to discriminate between clinically depressed psychiatric patients and normal control groups. The scale has exhibited good reliability and correlates highly with patients' global self-ratings of depression. However, the DACL taps only the affective component of depression, and therapists who use it must supplement it with an assessment of other depressive symptoms. Furthermore, it has not demonstrated good discriminant validity in differentiating depression from other psychiatric syndromes (Shaw et al., 1985).

Minnesota Multiphasic Personality Inventory depression scale (Scale 2) (Hathaway & McKinley, 1951). The MMPI depression scale is a 60-item, true-false, self-report measure. The items were selected based on a contrasted-groups approach. Most of the items were derived by comparing patients in a depressed phase of a bipolar disorder with normal individuals. However, some nondepressed persons scored high on this initial depression scale; therefore, the item responses of a group of these nondepressed individuals were compared with those of the depressed patients in order to isolate items that differentiated these groups. Eleven items were selected in this way, and these serve as somewhat of a "correction factor," such that truly depressed persons score higher on these items. The 60 depression scale items have been clustered in many different ways, based on factor analytic studies as well as investigators' intuitive impressions. The most commonly used subjective clustering by content areas (Harris & Lingoes, 1955) clarifies the nature of the set of items: subjective depression, psychomotor retardation, complaints about physical functioning, mental dullness, and brooding. Whereas the first three subscales are consistent with the concept of depression, the last two subscales appear to be less central to the construct.

Test-retest reliability coefficients are typically .80 to .90 for one-month intervals, and .40 to .50 for periods up to one year. This decrease in temporal stability over longer time periods would be expected for an affective disorder that fluctuates over time. Evidence for the construct validity of the scale is somewhat mixed. It typically correlates about .50 to .60 with psychiatric ratings of depression (Endicott & Jortner, 1966; Nussbaum, Wittig, Hanlon, & Kurland, 1963; Zuckerman, Persky, Eckman, & Hopkins, 1967). Scale 2 also typically correlates significantly with the BDI, although the magnitude of that correlation fluctuates a great deal (e.g., .41 [Seitz, 1970] to .75 [Nussbaum et al., 1963]). Whereas Scale 2 demonstrates moderate correlations with psychiatric ratings of depression, Zuckerman et al. (1967) found that Scale 2 correlated even higher with psychiatric ratings of manifest anxiety. As Zuckerman et al.'s findings point out, this difficulty is not focal to MMPI Scale 2. Differentiating between depression and anxiety is difficult with self-report scales, checklists, self-descriptions, and psychiatric ratings.

Daily Mood Rating Form (Lewinsohn & Arconad, 1981). At the University of Oregon Depression Research Unit, depression is assessed with a number of self-report measures, including the DACL, the MMPI, and this simple 9-point scale ranging from "very happy" to "very depressed." The instructions to the Daily Mood Rating Form ask the client to report how "good" or "bad" he or she felt during each day. Although the scale provides a quick index of distress, its lack of specificity limits its ability to differentiate depressed affect from other mood states; consequently, it should not be used as the sole index of depression.

General Well-Being Schedule (U.S. Public Health Service, 1977). Stuart (1980) uses the General Well-Being Schedule to assess depression in marital therapy clients. The four items of the scale that assess cheerfulness versus depression focus on emotional and cognitive symptoms, with no measurement of somatic and behavioral symptoms. Stuart (1980) notes that the scale has moderate (.5 to .6) correlations with other depression scales. Despite its limitations in covering the range of depressive symptoms and providing differentiation of depression from other affective states, the General Well-Being Schedule depression subscale can be useful for monitoring mood fluctuations, particularly if it is used in conjunction with other measures of depression.

Daily Record of Dysfunctional Thoughts (DRDT); Weekly Activity Schedule (Beck et al., 1979). Both of these instruments can be used to assess fluctuations in depressed mood as a function of external events and the individual's cognitions. Spouses can be asked to pay particular attention to recording incidents that elicit depression. Both measures can help identify whether spouses' depressed moods are relatively restricted to marital interactions or are elicited by a wide range of life events. As noted earlier, competent use of the DRDT requires practice on the client's part, so it is used for ongoing assessment during therapy rather than as an initial measure of depression.

Clinical interviews.

Proficient use of clinical interview schedules for assessing depression generally requires that the clinician receive some training. Consequently, if a marital therapist lacks expertise in the administration of these structured interviews, he or she should refer clients as needed to colleagues who have such expertise in the assessment of depression.

Hamilton Rating Scale for Depression (HRSD; Hamilton, 1960). The HRSD includes 17 items designed to tap severity of depression in patients already diagnosed as depressed (Shaw et al., 1985). Because Hamilton did not provide detailed interview guidelines, the data generated with the HRSD have varied considerably from one interviewer to another. Criteria for rating symptoms as severe are ambiguous, and the scale has only moderate internal consistency; however, there has been consistent evidence of high interrater reliability (Shaw et al., 1985).

Although the HRSD has been shown to differentiate depressed from nondepressed psychiatric patients and normals, it has not discriminated well between depression and anxiety (Riskind, Beck, Brown, & Steer, 1987). Consequently, Riskind et al. refined both the HRSD and the Hamilton scale for anxiety, shifting anxiety items from the depression scale and shifting depression items from the anxiety scale. The revised Hamilton scales have exhibited better discriminant validity than the original measures.

Schedule for Affective Disorders and Schizophrenia (SADS; Endicott & Spitzer, 1978). The SADS is a detailed interview guide for surveying psychiatric symptoms used in the differential diagnosis of depression, schizophrenia, anxiety, and personality disorders. It assesses both current symptoms and psychiatric history. Data from SADS interviews lead to diagnoses according to Spitzer, Endicott, and Robins' (1978) Research Diagnostic Criteria (RDC) for depression. Alternatively, the data can be used to define an individual's diagnosis according to DSM-III-R (American Psychiatric Association, 1987), which has similar but somewhat different diagnostic criteria. The highly structured SADS interview is intended for use by highly trained clinical diagnosticians. Consequently, marital therapists who are not well versed in psychiatric diagnosis can study the SADS as a guide for identifying levels of psychopathology that require systematic assessment by a clinician who specializes in this area.

Behavioral observation.

In addition to assessing an individual spouse's depressive symptoms by questionnaire and interview, it is important for the marital therapist to observe the couple's interactions during assessment and therapy sessions. As in the dyadic assessment of anger described previously, the purpose of this behavioral observation is to identify behaviors of one spouse that serve as antecedents and consequences for the other's depressive symptoms. For example, a therapist may observe that a spouse tends to exhibit more depressive symptoms after the partner has been hostile and critical, or that the partner tends to pay much more attention to the depressed person when that person expresses more symptoms.

Anxiety

Self-report inventories.

Beck Anxiety Inventory (BAI; Beck, Epstein, Brown, & Steer, 1988). There are several brief self-report scales available for assessing anxiety. Although instruments such as Zung's (1971) *Self-Rating Anxiety Scale* and the "state" version of Spielberger, Gorsuch, and Lushene's (1970) *State-Trait Anxiety Inventory* have high correlations with each other and other indices of anxiety, they do not differentiate well between anxiety and depression. Consequently, Beck et al. (1988) developed the BAI based on the ability of its 21 items to discriminate patients diagnosed with anxiety disorders from those diagnosed as depressed. The BAI items include cognitive, somatic, and behavioral manifestations of anxiety. The scale has high internal consistency and test-retest reliability, and it has exhibited good discriminant validity in its correlations with other indices of depression and anxiety, as well as in its ability to differentiate anxious from depressed individuals.

Daily Record of Dysfunctional Thoughts; Weekly Activity Schedule (Beck et al., 1979). Both of these instruments can be used to assess the frequency and severity of anxiety associated with particular events and cognitions. Procedures for using these logs are the same as those described earlier for assessing anger and depression.

Clinical interviews.

Hamilton Anxiety Rating Scale (HARS), revised version (Riskind et al., 1987). The revised version of the HARS, which includes items with demonstrated ability to differentiate individuals with anxiety disorders from those with depression, can provide a brief screening for severity of anxiety symptoms such as anxious mood, tension, fears, somatic cues, and cardiovascular symptoms. However, it lacks clear criteria for severity ratings, and it does not lead to any differential diagnoses of various anxiety disorders.

DSM-III-R (American Psychiatric Association, 1987). The clinician can use the DSM-III-R criteria as a guide for diagnosing a variety of anxiety disorders (e.g., agoraphobia, social phobia, post-traumatic stress disorder, generalized anxiety disorder). The DSM-III-R diagnostic criteria for anxiety disorders are based on empirically derived sets of symptoms, including autonomic nervous system arousal (e.g., increased heart rate or palpitations, shortness of breath, trembling, nausea, dizziness, chest pain), negative cognitions (e.g., thoughts of impending dangers), and behaviors intended to avoid threatening situations (e.g., restricted travel by an agoraphobic person; repetitive, stereotyped behavior by an obsessive-compulsive individual). It is important for marital therapists to be alert to anxiety symptoms (e.g., panic attacks, rumination about possible dangerous future events) that can impede spouses' marital interactions. The antecedent events and consequences that one spouse may provide for instances of the other's anxiety symptoms also can be assessed through interviews and observation of the couple's behavioral interactions during therapy sessions.

As is the case with depression, if a marital therapist's screening of spouses' affective states indicates the presence of problematic levels of anxiety and the therapist lacks expertise in the assessment and treatment of anxiety disorders, appropriate referrals should be made.

Jealousy

Of the types of affect that can influence marital functioning, the least work has been done on the assessment of jealousy. The relative absence of measures of jealousy seems to be due at least in part to the complexity of the phenomenon. As noted in Chapter 4, jealousy has been defined as a combination of anxiety and anger (Constantine, 1976, 1987; Jacobson & Margolin, 1979). Thus, it does not seem to be a "pure" emotion that is easily measured with a unidimensional scale.

Self-report inventories.

Self-Report Jealousy Scale—Revised (Bringle, Roach, Andler, & Evenbeck, 1979). This scale includes 25 items describing situations that may elicit an individual's jealousy. A factor analysis resulted in the items being divided into three subscales: minor romantic (e.g., "At a party, your partner hugs someone other than yourself"), nonromantic (e.g., "Your best friend suddenly shows interest in doing things with someone else"), and major romantic (e.g., "Your partner has sexual relations with someone else"). During the development of this scale, some respondents did not think that the word "jealous" should be used to describe their responses to the situations, so the authors replaced it with "upset," and the five-point response scale ranges from "pleased" to "extremely upset." Consequently, although the Self-Report Jealousy Scale—Revised has good internal consistency and correlates significantly with measures of constructs theoretically related to jealousy (e.g., low self-esteem, anxiety, low life satisfaction), it is unclear what kind(s) of unpleasant affect it is tapping. Clinicians and researchers should exercise caution when using the scale to measure jealousy.

Given that marital jealousy has been conceptualized as comprised of a combination of anxiety and anger associated with the perceived threat that one will lose the affection or interest of one's partner, it often is helpful to use *DRDTs* (Beck et al., 1979) or *Anger Logs* (Neidig & Friedman, 1984) to assess it. A therapist can ask spouses to record incidents that made them "feel jealous" or can ask them in a less directive manner to record all upsetting marital events (which then can be surveyed for those that involve anxiety and/or anger associated with cognitions involving loss of the partner).

Clinical interviews.

In terms of clinical interviews, the therapist can probe for the cognitive, affective, and behavioral components of jealousy whenever spouses report reactions that seem to reflect it. In a similar manner, the therapist can observe spouses' responses to each other during therapy sessions and can probe for jealousy whenever one spouse appears to be upset after the other has described any thoughts, actions, or plans that involve interests or activities that do not involve the partner. It also is important to gather self-report and observational data regarding the antecedents and consequences that a spouse provides for a partner's jealous responses. For example, it may become clear that a spouse becomes jealous after the partner makes comments about feeling trapped in the relationship. Similarly, the couple's interactions during therapy sessions may reveal that the nonjealous spouse may be much more solicitous of the jealous partner when the latter is exhibiting jealous symptoms than at other times. Information about each spouse's history of jealousy in other relationships, as well as his or her current jealous reactions in situations outside the marriage (e.g., with friends), is important for making clinical decisions regarding individual therapy.

INTEGRATING AFFECTIVE DATA

Due to the scarcity of standardized measures of affect in the context of marriage, the clinician must rely heavily on clinical interviews. Although it is helpful to administer the Dyadic Adjustment Scale as a measure of global distress, particularly because the DAS also identifies areas of conflict in the relationship, the therapist still must conduct a careful inquiry in order to determine the degree to which an individual's distress involves emotional responses. Because some spouses do not volunteer information about particular affective experiences (e.g., anger, depression), it is important that the therapist ask about these if a couple does not mention them.

Furthermore, a measure of global distress is a summary index that does not reveal the range of marital situations that elicit unpleasant affect. A spouse's low score on the DAS might be due to unpleasant emotional experiences across most interactions with the partner, or to heavily weighted unpleasant experiences in only a few situations. Consequently, the clinician must collect data about possible fluctuations in the types and degrees of emotion that each spouse experiences in various interactions with his or her partner. Much useful information about situation-specific emotional responses can be obtained through careful interviewing, but such retrospective reports by spouses during assessment interviews are susceptible to error (selective or inaccurate recall). Consequently, it is desirable to supplement interview data by having spouses keep logs of pleasant and unpleasant marital interactions for at least a few days. When a therapist is using a cognitive-behavioral approach to marital treatment, use of DRDTs (Beck et al., 1979) is efficient, because it permits collection of data about both emotional states and cognitions in various situations.

Both clinical interviews and DRDT logs can be used to identify the varieties of emotions (e.g., anger, depression, anxiety, jealousy) experienced by each spouse. When the initial data suggest that a spouse may experience degrees of a particular affect (e.g., depression) that may be dysfunctional for either individual or marital functioning, it is important that the clinician pursue a more focused evaluation in that area. For example, if it appears that the degree of anger or the manner in which it is expressed is a problem for a particular couple, it is useful to supplement the clinical interview with measures such as Straus's (1979) Conflict Tactics Scales, Margolin et al.'s (1982) Conflict Inventory, or Neidig and Friedman's (1984) Anger Log. Similarly, further screening for depression can be done quickly with the Beck Depression Inventory (Beck et al., 1979), and the Beck Anxiety Inventory (Beck et al., 1988) can provide screening of anxiety symptoms. Appropriately trained clinicians can conduct more refined assessments of specific affective disorders and anxiety disorders with systematic interviews (e.g., using DSM-III-R criteria). Spouses' low levels of marital satisfaction, as well as deficits in their affective expression and empathic listening skills, should be evaluated in light of any evidence of dysfunctional levels of affect such as clinical depression.

Although behavioral observation coding systems such as the MICS, CISS, and KPI are too complex for use in clinical practice, it is important to integrate self-report (interview and questionnaire) data with some direct observation of spouses' affective states, expressiveness skills, and empathic listening skills. Guerney's (1977) Verbal Interaction Task (VIT) provides a brief sample of a couple's communication skills and also an opportunity to observe verbal and nonverbal cues of their positive and negative affect when discussing desired changes in the self and partner. Therapists who are familiar with coding systems such as the MICS also can identify instances of other types of constructive and destructive communication that may occur during the VIT. On the one hand, the couple's behaviors during the VIT may be more restricted in range than their interactions at home (which may be tapped better by interviews and behavioral logs), but on the other hand, the live interactions in the therapist's office may reveal affective responses and affective communication deficits that the clients failed to identify in their self-reports.

In addition to using a structured interaction such as the VIT, which is focused on particular affective communication skills, the therapist has repeated opportunities to observe the *process* of a couple's behavioral interactions during their unstructured discussions during therapy sessions. Whether using Stover et al.'s (1977a, b) Self-Feeling Awareness Scale and Acceptance of Other Scale or behavioral categories from systems such as the MICS, the therapist focuses on the types of affect communicated and the constructive or destructive ways in which the affect is communicated.

As illustrated in this chapter, the assessment of affect realistically cannot be isolated from the assessment of behavioral and cognitive aspects of a couple's interactions. The degrees of various positive and negative emotions experienced by each spouse are likely to be influenced by specific aspects of the behaviors exchanged by the couple, as well as by their cognitions about those interactions. Consequently, in order to derive a clear conceptualization of the affective quality of a couple's relationship, the clinician must not only integrate information from questionnaires, interviews, and behavioral observations of the spouses' affect, but also interpret these data in light of the assessment information concerning the couple's behavioral patterns (Chapter 5) and cognitions (Chapter 6).

Epilogue:

Feedback to Couples Regarding Assessment

In order for a skills-oriented approach to marital therapy to be successful, it is important for the therapist and the couple to have a common understanding of the couple's problems and relationship strengths, a common set of goals, and an agreed-upon set of strategies for trying to attain those goals. After the clinician has obtained the relevant information discussed in the preceding assessment chapters, it is appropriate to provide feedback to the couple regarding the clinician's conceptualization of their relationship and appropriate treatment. This is important for at least three reasons. First, although the couple has provided the information on which the assessment is based, at times of stress couples often have difficulty putting their problems in perspective. Thus, the feedback can provide a much needed framework for understanding their difficulties. This alone can be very important to the couple because the framework provides a sense of clarity and, at times, hope for how changes can be brought about. Second, the feedback provides information about the types of interventions that the therapist envisions. This information allows the couple to make an informed decision about whether or not they wish to participate in treatment. For example, some couples may come to treatment believing that they will talk with the therapist for an hour a week and that their relationship should improve. They might be quite surprised to learn that they will be asked to engage in a number of activities outside of the sessions, and some spouses might not be willing to make that level of commitment to the intervention. Third, the feedback to the couple can help to build a collaborative relationship between the therapist and the couple which takes a certain form. The therapist does not attempt to assume the role of a wizard, a guru, or a "blank screen." Instead, the therapist wishes to transmit the message, "Here is what I see happening in your marriage. Based on what you told and showed me, these look like the major problems in your relationship, and to address these specific problems, here are some specific interventions which I hope will have the following effects." In essence, the therapist models a clear, specific form of communicating to the couple which encourages them to be open with each other and with the therapist. These specifics are discussed and mutually agreed upon, so that the couple has a sense of participating in the design of the treatment rather than having it imposed by an authority figure.

The feedback to the couple after the data-gathering phase need be neither formal nor lengthy. In most cases, it can be accomplished in 15 to 25 minutes, depending on how complex the situation is and how verbal the couple is. Some clinicians prefer to set aside a separate session explicitly for this purpose; they find that they are more effective if they accumulate all of the information that they have been provided and attempt to integrate it before discussing it with the couple. Other clinicians are comfortable providing feedback to the couple at the end of a data-gathering session, without an opportunity to contemplate the information at length. Regardless of this issue of timing, certain principles should be incorporated into the feedback.

First, the feedback should be integrative in several different respects. One aspect of this integrative process is the joint presentation of cognitive, affective, and behavioral components of the relationship. That is, the clinician need not systematically discuss each of the cognitive variables, followed separately by a discussion of each behavioral strength and weakness, and so forth. Instead, typically a few major issues create difficulty for a specific couple. The couple is likely to understand the feedback more clearly if it is focused around these issues. Within this context, the clinician can discuss the relevant cognitions which the spouses have in that area, how those cognitions influence emotional reactions, and how behavior understandably results from the person's thoughts and feelings about the situation. Often consistent cognitions, emotions, and/or behavioral patterns cut across different content problems, and the clinician then comments on these patterns when appropriate.

The feedback is integrative also in terms of focusing on the relationship. There clearly are two individuals involved, and their specific contributions to the problems need not be ignored, although the therapist must be careful not to blame one person. (One of the most frequent reasons that couples provide for changing marital therapists is the belief that the therapist aligned him- or herself with one spouse.) This deemphasis on blaming one person can be accomplished if the therapist describes how both people contribute to a given problem or set of problems and how this results in a repeated pattern of interaction in their relationship.

The couple often can accept the clinician's understanding of the current problems more easily if the presenting complaints are integrated with historical and developmental patterns. Often the presenting complaints in isolation appear strange, abnormal, and are embarrassing to the couple. Without attempting to decrease the couple's motivation for working on important issues, the clinician can help the couple to understand how their problems have arisen from their learning histories. This may include a discussion of (a) how they interacted early in their relationship and sowed the seeds of current problems, (b) a specific event that was a turning point in their relationship, or (c) early interaction patterns in their families of origin which resulted in certain cognitions about relationships and established early behavioral patterns. When viewed from this learning perspective, many concerns that are originally attributed to hostility or lack of love on the partner's part can start to be conceptualized as a more understandable outgrowth of earlier behavior, cognitions, and emotions.

The feedback also should integrate a discussion of the couple's strengths and weaknesses. When seeking marital therapy, most couples are quite problem-oriented and do not focus on the positive aspects of their relationships. Helping them to see this balance of positives and negatives is one aspect of conceptualizing their relationship. This does not mean distorting the couple's relationship or reframing negative aspects of the marriage in a positive way merely to give the couple hope. Instead, the therapist remains attentive to strengths of the relationship and helps the couple to see the positive aspects of their marriage.

Finally, the feedback should be integrative from the perspective of clearly relating presenting complaints to treatment interventions. Some of these links might be quite obvious to the couple. Thus, if the couple has complained that they routinely argue when they try to resolve problems, then problem-solving training will appear as a logical intervention to them. However, if they complain that they do not feel close to each other, it may not be apparent to them why learning to express emotions to each other is an appropriate intervention. Thus, the therapist would want to explain how sharing emotions is one major behavior that can lead to a feeling of closeness between individuals. Again, rather than proclaiming to the couple that these are the interventions to be followed, the therapist describes how these strategies perhaps can be of help and solicits the couple's input on the issues.

Frequently, the couple has concerns about some of the interventions or the general approach taken, and these concerns must be discussed. For example, couples or individuals who have had previous interventions from more psychodynamic perspectives may voice concerns that the interventions appear to be too surface-level or trivial and do not attend to the "real problems." Also, the couple's expressed concerns can draw the therapist's attention to aspects of the couple's problems and concerns which he or she has misunderstood, and the couple's point of view often can lead to an altered treatment plan. Intervention strategies are much more likely to be followed and trusted if they are consistent with the couple's understanding of their difficulties.

In addition to being integrative, the feedback to the couple should be specific. Thus, specific communication problems are discussed, and disruptive behaviors outside of the session are pinpointed. Similarly, the particular cognitions that lead to difficulty are clarified to the extent possible. The therapist does not describe the cognitions to the couple as distorted, because such statements would probably lead the couple to become defensive. However, the therapist can discuss how these thoughts can contribute to the couple's difficulties and suggest that the couple will be asked to reconsider these thoughts during treatment. Similarly, the spouses' emotional reactions are discussed in an integrative fashion with their behavior and cognitions. Spouses' difficulties with differentiating and labeling emotions, their concerns about expressing specific emotions, and their experiences with specific disruptive emotions are discussed. As mentioned above, when these specifics are discussed, the therapist also assists couples in seeing patterns that integrate these specific behaviors, cognitions, and emotions.

Below is a small portion of the feedback to a couple:

Therapist: You have given me a lot of information, and that has been very helpful in my gaining an understanding of you. There are several key issues which you mentioned to me that I believe we will want to address in our sessions. First, you both said that you felt that you have really grown apart from each other, that you don't feel close, and really don't know each other very well any more. From what I can tell, that didn't happen because of maliciousness or a lack of love from either of you. Instead, like so many couples, it developed gradually over time without your realizing what was happening. Bill, you grew up in a very achievement-oriented family where you were taught to do your very best and to provide well for your family. You have been trying to do that in your job, and as a result with those demands,

demands of the children, church commitments, and various civic interests, you have ended up spending little time with Helen.

Helen, you have been developing a full-time career and trying to be mother to three children, as well as assisting your sick mother. And as a result, you simply run out of time and energy.

From what I understand, you both believe that you should do all these things and that your own pleasure should come last. You have considered time with your partner to be part of your own pleasure, and therefore you make little time for each other. I believe that you said you sometimes spend about 10 minutes talking about the events of the day after the children go to bed, and that is about all during the week. You go out for an evening as a couple about once a month. So you are really spending very little time together as a couple. I think that your commitment to your children, your emphasis on doing a good job in your professions, and your giving to various organizations are all positive, but they have resulted in an unbalanced marriage. You, as a couple, have taken low priority. It is hard to feel close to someone when you spend little time talking to the person and don't do enjoyable things together.

Therefore, we are going to need to give you higher priority as a couple, find times for you to have together when you can get to know and enjoy each other. That will probably include setting time aside to talk to each other on a regular basis before you are exhausted at night and giving you more time out as a couple. In order for you to feel good about doing those things, I think we will need to examine your belief that you should come last, and that to give yourself priority as a couple is selfish. Right now you feel guilty when you say no to the children or the church in order to do something for yourself as a couple, and I don't want to perpetuate those bad feelings. What are your thoughts about my understanding of your not feeling close to each other and some of the changes I was suggesting?

SECTION III

INTERVENTION

This section discusses a myriad of intervention strategies for addressing the behavioral, cognitive, and affective components of marital distress. Although any specific intervention is likely to impact all three of these domains, separate chapters are devoted to each of these areas, because most interventions are targeted to promote changes primarily in one domain. In addition, the clinician must have guidelines for when to select a given intervention strategy, when to shift from one intervention to another, and how to make such shifts. Consequently, a fourth chapter focuses on ways to integrate the various intervention strategies. Throughout these intervention chapters, it is stressed that cognitive-behavioral marital therapy is not a set of routinely applied techniques; instead, it involves a number of decisions made by the clinician based on the characteristics of the particular couple receiving intervention. Many of these decision points are discussed, and guidelines are provided for individualizing treatment for the specific couple. More so than with other theoretical approaches, behavioral and cognitive-behavioral marital therapists have emphasized evaluating the effectiveness of their treatments. Consequently, the final chapter discusses the empirical status of the field, with primary emphasis on the clinical implications of the research findings.

Chapter 8 discusses various behavioral interventions for altering communication and noncommunication behaviors. Some of these interventions call for teaching the couple new skills, whereas other strategies merely involve the couple's agreeing to behave in different ways based on their specific needs. A major focus of this chapter involves teaching the couple to resolve problems and improve their communication while problem solving. In addition, a number of issues involving the role of the therapist (e.g., controlling the session tempo, deciding when to intervene, avoiding power struggles with clients) are discussed.

Chapter 9 covers a number of intervention strategies for addressing a couple's dysfunctional perceptions, attributions, expectancies, assumptions, and standards. These interventions include ways to: (a) introduce the concepts of inappropriate and distorted cognitions; (b) build skills for identifying dysfunctional cognitions; and (c) test and modify dysfunctional cognitions. In addition, the chapter includes discussion of strategies for addressing cognitions about the partner or the relationship which are negative but appear to be reasonable or accurate. Finally, both spouses may have cognitions that appear reasonable, yet the cognitions of the two persons are incompatible with each other (e.g., reasonable but incompatible standards). The chapter provides recommendations for assisting in such instances.

Chapter 10 focuses on ways to assist couples with affective difficulties. These strategies include helping couples to: (a) label emotions and understand the bases of their emotional reactions; (b) express emotions more adaptively; and (c) alter dysfunctional levels of emotions, such as anger, depression, jealousy, and anxiety. Whereas the primary treatment targets discussed in this chapter are the spouses' affects, the interventions are primarily behavioral and cognitive. That is, the therapist attempts to change the spouses' affects by asking them to behave differently toward each other and think differently about their relationship. This approach is possible because the cognitive-behavioral model involves a basic assumption that behaviors, cognitions, and emotions are interrelated.

Chapter 11 describes the integration of behavioral, cognitive, and affective intervention strategies discussed in the previous chapters. This integrative approach includes guidelines for (a) developing an overall treatment plan; (b) sequencing various intervention strategies; and (c) shifting intervention strategies and revising treatment plans. The chapter emphasizes when and how to shift among strategies that focus on behavior, cognition, and affect.

Chapter 12 presents a discussion of the empirical status of the intervention approaches described throughout the book. Most of the studies to date have focused on altering couples' behavior and overall marital adjustment. These investigations of the effectiveness of BMT have addressed a number of specific issues: (a) the effectiveness of BMT versus wait list and other control conditions; (b) the relative effectiveness of various BMT treatment components; (c) the impact of varying other BMT treatment parameters, such as single therapists versus cotherapists; (d) the magnitude of BMT effects; (e) the prediction of specific couples' responses to BMT; and (f) the application of BMT to specific target populations. More recently, attempts to alter couples' cognitions have been addressed, and the results of these initial studies are evaluated. Beause the integration of empirical findings and sound clinical practice is essential in order for the field to continue to progess, implications of therapy outcome studies for clinical practice are discussed.

8

Modification of Behavior

The goals of BMT are to assist couples in behaving in more positive and less negative ways by employing two major categories of intervention strategies. First, couples are given assignments to behave differently in specific ways in their day-to-day lives without receiving training in specific skills. The second category of behavioral interventions involves skills training. In many cases, couples have not learned to communicate with each other effectively, or their communication has deteriorated. Intertwined with this difficulty, many distressed couples have difficulty attempting to resolve problems, seemingly being unaware of or unable to accomplish the steps needed to reach an agreeable solution; other couples experience difficulty effecting agreed-upon behavior changes. Thus, much time is devoted to skills training in communication, problem-solving, and behavior change strategies.

INCREASING POSITIVE AND DECREASING NEGATIVE NONCOMMUNICATION BEHAVIOR

One of the major goals of BMT is to help couples behave toward each other in more positive ways and less negative ways. This goal underlies all of the BMT treatment procedures to be discussed, but some interventions are aimed explicitly at increasing positive and decreasing negative day-to-day marital behavior, based simply on various instructions to do so. These strategies seem particularly helpful when spouses report or the therapist

251

observes that they make little effort to please the other person. Similarly, when spouses frequently feel irritated with their partners' day-to-day behaviors, then decreasing negatives becomes important. These techniques are not intended for major areas of conflict in which the couple will need to negotiate behavior changes. In essence, clinicians working with distressed couples become aware that many distressed spouses make little effort to be nice to their partners. The message from the clinician is that "If you want to be happier in your marriage, try being nice to each other." Whereas this may seem naïve for many of the complex issues confronting the couple, these techniques do not constitute the entire treatment. They are devoted to helping the couple start thinking about making efforts to please the other person and changing the atmosphere of the relationship by altering small, frequent behaviors.

One strategy involves having each spouse complete the Spouse Observation Checklist (SOC) nightly, describing the partner's behavior for the past 24 hours. As discussed in Chapter 5, each spouse uses the SOC to describe which of 408 marital behaviors his or her partner exhibited and then rates each behavior as positive, neutral, or negative. At the beginning of therapy, the clinician should get a baseline of behaviors. Therefore, each spouse can be instructed to complete the form nightly, perhaps for a week, and not to share this information with the partner. These completed forms are returned to the clinician, who calculates the mean number of positive, neutral, or negative behaviors occurring daily. This information is shared with the couple, and the partners are asked to increase positive behavior and decrease negative behavior by some percentage during the following week. How much to ask the couple to change must be based on the individual couple, their initial level of various behaviors, amount of time spent together daily, level of motivation for change, and so forth. The degree of change requested should be set to maximize the likelihood that the couple will experience success with this assignment. Arbitrarily deciding that all couples should double their positives or cut negatives in half will doom some couples to failure.

A second strategy used to increase positive behaviors is referred to as "love days" (Weiss et al., 1973; Wills et al., 1974) or "caring days" (Stuart, 1980). Although there are numerous variants of this procedure, we ask partners to alternate days and do something nice for the other person on that day. This positive behavior need not involve some major effort or major expense; such major positive acts are unlikely to be maintained over time. Therefore, couples are encouraged to engage in positive behaviors which they could realistically continue within their marriage on an intermittent basis. Because one frequent complaint of spouses is that they often feel taken for granted, each person also is encouraged to be alert to positive behaviors shown by the partner. Appreciation should be made obvious, by either a verbal "thank you," some demonstration of affection, or some reciprocal act. Thus, love days can serve as an opportunity to build positive reciprocity into the relationship.

The spouses are encouraged to perform acts of caring which will focus on the preferences of the particular couple and individuals involved and which will bring pleasure. For example, spouses who feel distant from each other and who spend little time together would be encouraged to select acts that would provide for more togetherness. Conversely, if one of the couple's difficulties is that they do almost everything together during nonwork hours and one or both is feeling smothered, then an appropriate act of kindness would be one that would promote individuality. Thus the husband might wash the dishes for his wife so she can retire to the bedroom alone to read. Whereas the specific behaviors are to be decided upon by the couple, the therapist can be helpful in pointing out general guidelines, such as spending more or less time together.

Although the idea of caring days is appealing, it is not universally successful when applied. Occasionally, both spouses cooperate for the first few days, but one spouse then fails to continue with the activities. In response, the partner likewise either stops participating or continues but feels angry and/or hopeless. There are numerous reasons why a person may not comply with this assignment. First, the individual may cling to the belief that he or she should not have to make special efforts, because the relationship should be "naturally" satisfying to both partners. Under such circumstances, the therapist needs to help the client alter this attitude. The therapist's goal is to help the client see the need for special effort, especially given the state of the relationship. Hopefully each person has characteristic behaviors which bring pleasure to the partner, but rarely is that alone enough to sustain a gratifying relationship. Most people seem to want a partner who is thoughtful, and thoughtful means thinking about how to behave in order to bring happiness to others. Thus, planned positive behaviors are reinterpreted to the client as ways of showing that one cares and is willing to make an effort to improve the relationship.

Second, a spouse may be unwilling to engage in acts of kindness if he or she is angry toward the partner. Thus a couple may be enjoying caring days until they have an argument in the middle of the week and then cease to carry out their acts of caring. It is not atypical for couples to have disagreements and arguments; the concern is with the extent to which the couple allows an argument to infiltrate other areas of their lives for a long time period. By means of various communication skills, couples are taught how to respond to negative affect in a way that will not disrupt their lives on an ongoing basis.

Whereas the above reasons for lack of compliance with caring days involve certain attitudes which interfere with the person's seeking to make efforts to please the partner, other persons are motivated to change but have difficulty thinking of what to do to please the partner. Although this can be interpreted as an excuse for not really trying, some spouses are so distant from each other and it has been so long since either person has made an effort to please the other that they simply cannot think of how to make the other person happy during the day. Therefore, spouses at times return to a therapy session saying, "I tried, but I just could think of only one or two things to do during the week. I don't know what to do to make her happy any more. My mind just went blank." Such individuals typically have spent little time recently being attentive to their partners. They might not require an attitudinal shift but do need a shift in attention toward thinking about ways to satisfy their partners. Other related treatment strategies have been devised to assist in accomplishing this goal.

The "cookie jar technique" is a strategy for helping an individual who cannot think of small positive acts to perform for the spouse (Weiss & Birchler, 1978). If the wife cannot think of ways to please her husband, he can write down on separate pieces of paper a number of small acts that would bring him pleasure. Then he places these pieces of paper in a jar or container. Whenever the wife cannot think of things to do to please her husband, she can go to the jar and remove a slip of paper. Spouses are encouraged to spend some time trying to decide on activities before going to the cookie jar, so that each individual will become accustomed to focusing cognitively on what to do to please the partner.

Another treatment strategy similar in structure and purpose to the cookie jar technique is the *wholistic contract* (Stuart, 1980). As used in this volume, the term *contract* refers to an agreement with an explicit set of contingencies for completion and noncompletion of an agreement. In this sense, the wholistic contract is not a contract because there are no contingencies included. In the wholistic contract, each person makes a list of perhaps 10 to 20 activities in which the partner could engage to bring pleasure to the person. The partner agrees to engage in a specified number of these at some point during the next week. However, the partner does not state which specific activities he or she will enter into or exactly when during the week these acts will occur. These guidelines are intended to provide suggestions for how to please the other person, but they also include choices as to which specific acts will occur and the timing for those behaviors. This sense of choice and freedom is important to some people who engage in the acts, so that they do not feel they were forced into activities against their will. This sense of volition also can be beneficial to the person receiving the act of caring, because it increases the sense that the partner acted voluntarily and wanted to bring pleasure, thus increasing its significance at times. As will be discussed later in this chapter, one of the concerns that has been raised about behavioral contracts is that their legalistic nature can serve to alter the meaning of the behavior included in the contract.

The above techniques focus on one *individual* behaving in certain ways to bring pleasure to his or her partner. However, there are frequent occasions when it is important to alter the *couple's* behavior, for example, when they report that they engage in few pleasurable activities together. For some couples, having children ends their life as a viable dyad because most free time is focused on either the children's needs or family activities. Whereas the family unit is not to be minimized, it is important for most couples to maintain some sense of being a couple as well. For other couples, little time is spent with the spouse in pleasurable activities, either as part of the family or as part of the couple. These latter couples typically have become distant from each other, and each has built an independent world for him- or herself.

When the couple spends little time together enjoying themselves, increasing the number of pleasurable or leisure activities together is appropriate. As a result, early in therapy couples often are asked to engage in more pleasurable activities together. Typically, couples agree with the importance of such activities for the welfare of their relationship. However, this does not mean that they immediately increase the number of enjoyable events which they share. For many couples, there is an awkwardness as they struggle and acknowledge that they have difficulty thinking of what to do together. Under such circumstances, the therapist might suggest that the couple think back to things they once did together and enjoyed. Also, activities that one person currently enjoys can be altered to include the partner. Frequently when one person has a hobby or area of knowledge, that person is quite willing to share information and teach the partner about that area. Table 8-1 includes a list of joint activities that couples have reported they enjoy together. Such a list can be given to couples to spur their thinking if they are having difficulty arriving at joint activities.

TABLE 8-1
Joint Activities for Couples

Taking a walk	Going to a concert
Going to a movie or play	Attending a lecture
Going out for dinner	Going to a ballgame
Bicycling	Having a picnic
Playing golf or tennis	Hiking
Playing board games or cards	Preparing a special meal
Going bowling	Taking photographs
Working on a joint hobby	Going dancing
Taking a class	Jogging
Going to a park	Sitting outside
Having a cookout	Staying overnight at a hotel
Camping out	Listening to music
Playing musical instruments	Going sailing
Shopping	Going out for dessert
Working together on the computer	Working in the garden or lawn
Going to a museum	Going to the zoo
Working on a household project	Visiting friends or relatives
Studying the family genealogy	Preparing a photograph album
Going bird watching or star gazing	Working on a community project
Visiting the library	Reading together

Whereas the couple should take primary responsibility for deciding what they wish to do together, some guidelines from the therapist might prove to be helpful. This can be particularly useful if one spouse complains that he or she does not enjoy activities in which the partner engages. The therapist might respond as follows:

Therapist: That actually turns out to be a problem for many couples who are unhappy with their relationships, but I don't think that means that you two will have to stay apart from each other. One thing that I think is important is for each of you to learn to take pleasure in the other person's happiness. Even if some activity isn't inherently fun for you, I would like to suggest that you give it a try and see if you can enjoy it by watching the other person have fun. See if you can enjoy yourself by interacting with the other person and sharing that other person's pleasure. Sally, for example, I know the idea of going to the farm with Jim and helping him plow the fields doesn't sound like fun to you. But if you were to go, what could you or he do to make it more fun for you?

Wife: Well, as I said, that is really not my idea of fun. I'll get bitten by a lot of bugs and get hot and sweaty. But in answer to your question, I like to read, so I could take a book and try to find some shade.

Thus, in this example the therapist tried to have the wife think of suggestions to make the activity more inherently pleasurable for her while attempting to direct her focus toward sharing her husband's joy. Just as the focus of caring days is on small events, the general recommendation for increasing leisure time activities is on inexpensive, relatively brief events. Many couples, in their burst of initial enthusiasm for therapy, schedule major events together and seem to enjoy them. However, neither their finances nor their amount of free time allows them to continue such activities. The goal of this procedure is to help couples to start including the partner in leisure activities on an ongoing basis. This is best accomplished when smaller events which require little planning, money, and time can be incorporated into the couple's life.

In the use of the preceding strategies, as with all of those discussed in this book, only those are selected which are pertinent to helping a couple achieve a certain goal. Consequently, the therapist does not routinely begin with love days, and so forth. Instead, based on the initial evaluation and the resulting conceptualization that the therapist has of the couple, those procedures are selected which will assist the couple to reach the desired goals.

PROBLEM-SOLVING AND RELATED COMMUNICATION TRAINING TECHNIQUES

The preceding techniques promote behavior changes without teaching the couples any specific skills. On the other hand, the problem-solving and communication techniques about to be discussed have a major skill orientation. Virtually all distressed couples come to therapy with concerns they have been unable to address successfully. Problem-solving skills have the goal of helping couples learn how to successfully resolve areas of conflict for themselves. However, whether the couple successfully navigates these problem-solving steps is in part related to how they communicate with each other. Frequently couples are moving successfully through the problem-solving steps until one spouse expresses something in a way that angers the partner. That partner reciprocates with a negative comment, and the situation quickly escalates into an argument. With communication training, such arguments can be decreased in frequency, intensity, and duration.

Communication can be divided into two major categories in addition to social chitchat. These are (a) expression of emotion and related thoughts, and (b) problem-solving-oriented communication. With most couples, these two kinds of communication are taught separately. There are no empirical data bearing on the issue, but our experience is that asking couples to express their feelings about a highly emotional issue during problem solving often results in the spouses' becoming flooded with feelings and losing a solution orientation. In essence, it seems necessary for many couples to keep their feelings in check during problem solving in order to maintain the cognitive focus needed to reach a successful resolution to a difficult issue. After couples are proficient in both types of skills, they are given opportunities to see whether they can successfully integrate the two during a given conversation. If they can, they are taught to use one or both sets of skills as needed during a conversation. If they encounter frequent difficulties, then they are encouraged to keep the two processes separate.

As somewhat of a related issue, couples also encounter difficulties when one is attempting to problem-solve and the other is attempting to express emotions. This difficulty was exemplified by one couple in which the wife complained that her husband would not talk to her about the problems she was having at work. As he explained, "Why should I talk to her? I have little control over what happens at her job, and when I offer a solution for what she might do, she rarely seems to want to hear my suggestions." However, as his wife clarified, she really was not asking him to try to solve her problems. Instead, she just needed someone to talk to, some way to ventilate her feelings. Although both were attempting to communicate in a constructive way, they both felt frustrated with the conversation without knowing why.

Consequently, couples are taught to communicate to each other what they want from the communication through cues that orient each other to what is about to transpire. For example, a desire to problem-solve could easily be expressed as, "Could we talk for a few minutes? I'd like your help in trying to reach a solution to a problem." Similarly, a request for expression of emotion could be stated, "Would you talk with me for a few minutes? I am so frustrated, and I just need to get it off my chest." If the couple experiences no difficulties in coordinating the purpose of the conversation, then there is no need to develop a more explicit cue system. However, when couples do have this difficulty, then helping them develop a way of focusing each other on the goals of the conversation can be helpful.

The strategy described below is purposely somewhat simple in conceptualization, so that it can be used by a wide range of couples. However, couples often find the strategy to be much more difficult when they try to apply it to one of their own problems. Because applying these steps involves learning a new way of communicating for almost all couples, beginning with relatively minor problems is recommended. As couples deal with highly emotional problems, they become absorbed with their feelings and the content of the problem. Within this context, they tend to pay less attention to the problem-solving steps. Therefore, it is important that they be skilled in these steps before attempting difficult issues so that the steps will be almost automatic to them.

However, at times there are significant problems that require immediate resolution before the couple is well trained in problem solving. In such cases, the therapist simply provides additional guidance to the couple as they attempt to resolve the issue. On other occasions, couples become frustrated dealing with minor issues even though they understand the rationale for the approach. The therapist must then make a decision, attempting to achieve a balance between maintaining the couple's enthusiasm for treatment on the one hand and providing them with optimal conditions for learning skills and having success experiences on the other hand. If the therapist proceeds with more major problems and the couple is successful in addressing the issues, then the therapist can acknowledge how well the couple is progressing with the skills. If the couple is not successful, the therapist can still reinforce them for their effort to confront difficult issues in their relationship, but can point out that probably it was premature to address the issue so early in therapy. It is important to help the couple realize that progress on the issue will still be possible after they have had more practice with the problem-solving steps.

Problem-Solving Steps

Table 8-2 is the set of guidelines given to couples as the steps of problem solving are explained to them. It is useful to provide a loose-leaf notebook for each couple to organize the guidelines, examples, and homework sheets used during treatment.

Statement of the problem.

The first step in problem solving involves stating the problem. Although this may appear obvious, many couples attempt to resolve an issue without clarifying with each other what the issue is. Lack of a clear statement of a problem is one of the major impediments to successful problem resolution. Couples are asked to state their concerns in terms of the *behaviors* which are currently occurring or not occurring that are of

TABLE 8-2
Guidelines for Problem Solving

1. Clearly and specifically state what the problem is
    a. Phrase the problem in terms of behaviors that are currently occurring
       or not occurring
    b. Break large, complex problems down into several smaller problems,
       and deal with them one at a time
    c. Make certain that both people agree on the statement of the problem
       and are willing to discuss it
2. Discuss possible solutions
    a. Stay solution-oriented; your goal is not to defend yourself, decide who
       is right or wrong, or establish the truth regarding what happened in
       the past
    b. Your goal is to decide how to do things differently in the future
3. Decide on a solution that is agreeable to both of you
    a. Do not accept a solution on which you do not intend to follow
       through
    b. Do not accept a solution that you believe will make you angry or
       resentful
    c. If you cannot find a solution that pleases both partners, suggest a
       compromise solution
    d. State your solution in clear, specific, behavioral terms
    e. After agreeing on a solution, have one partner restate the solution
4. Decide on a trial period to implement the solution
    a. Allow for several attempts of the new solution
    b. Review the solution at the end of the trial period

concern to them. Implied in this guideline is that the statement of the
problem is to be as specific as is realistic. Consequently, if a wife states that
her concern is that when they go to parties, she feels unloved by her
husband, she is asked to state what he does or does not do at parties that
makes her feel bad. A more appropriate statement might be that when they
attend a party, she is unhappy that he leaves her alone with people whom
she does not know well. At times couples will comment that the problem
is not a behavior but an attitude. They are asked to state the problem in
terms of what behaviors or absence of behaviors indicate that attitude. Thus,
although it may not be universally possible to state all concerns in terms
of behaviors, the vast majority can be stated in that manner.

In an attempt to be specific, couples at times may redefine problems
in terms of some specific behavior which is only obliquely related to the

actual concern. When this occurs, the couple may reach a satisfactory solution to the stated problem but feel disappointed that they have not really addressed their concern. This again points out the importance of an appropriate statement of the problem.

Some couples experience difficulties in problem solving because they do not differentiate among the concepts "behaviors," "thoughts," and "feelings." Thus when they are asked to state the *behaviors* that occur, they may express their thoughts or feelings. At such times, alternative wording and examples from the therapist can be of assistance. "What is it that your husband *does* or *doesn't* do when you are at a party that makes you feel unloved? Is it that he stays with you but does not talk to you during conversations? Does he make negative comments about you to other people?" Another, more concrete way of communicating what is desired in terms of behaviors is to use the image of a movie screen. "If we were watching a movie screen, describe what we would actually *see* on the screen that is of concern to you. Or what would be absent from the screen that would concern you?"

When spouses learn the concept of specifying behaviors, they often state the problem in terms of some behavioral solution which they desire. For example, in the above scenario, the wife might state the problem as, "When we go to parties, I would like for you to stay with me and not leave me to talk to other people." The difficulty with such a statement is that it greatly biases the direction in which solutions will be sought. If the partner agrees to deal with the problem as stated above, many times he or she feels obligated to accept the solution offered in the statement of the problem. Therefore, couples are asked not to state a proposed solution in the statement of the problem.

Another important guideline involves breaking large, complex problems down into several more specific problems that can be approached one at a time. When couples have attempted to resolve multifaceted problems in the past, they have often felt overwhelmed by them. Without training, as the couple attempts to deal with one aspect of the problem, they soon start discussing another aspect of the problem without reaching a resolution to the first issue addressed. The couple's discussion drifts from one aspect of the problem to another without any sense of progress. Consequently, couples are encouraged first to define the problem, break it down into subproblems if appropriate, and attempt to resolve one subproblem at a time.

Couples also are asked to state the problem in a way that minimizes blaming one of the two people. Couples are more successful at reaching solutions if they are working on a problem that is perceived as a *joint* problem in which they both are invested. When one person is blamed, spouses have a tendency to focus their energy on defending themselves and deciding who is at fault rather than working as a team to reach a mutually satisfying resolution. Consequently, rather than stating, "You are not doing your part to keep clothes, newspapers, and glasses picked up from the den," a more helpful statement of the problem might be, "I am unhappy because at the end of the day, there are often clothes, newspapers, and glasses still in the den." Avoiding displeasure with the partner's behavior is not always possible or even preferable, because it could result in a lack of clear communication and disguise the true nature of one person's concerns. However, stating the problem in a way such that it does not needlessly single out one person is an important goal.

Couples at times raise the issue of whether or not to discuss a problem if one person is not concerned about the topic. For example, a husband might state, "Well, I'm not really unhappy about it. As far as I am concerned that is not *our* problem, that is *your* problem." The couple is told that any issue that involves the two of them or the relationship and which is of concern to either person is an appropriate issue for discussion. Although one person might not be displeased with the current status of an issue, if the other person is unhappy then the problem area quite likely will have an impact on their relationship.

The above statement does not mean that either person should be forced to deal with a particular problem at a specific time. Spouses quite appropriately state that they are not in the frame of mind to tackle a particular problem at a certain time. Each individual should respect the other partner's decision not to deal with a problem at a particular time. If one partner routinely refuses to discuss a particular problem, however, intervention from the therapist may become necessary. This may be as simple as asking the person to agree to a time when he or she would be willing to discuss the problem, or a discussion with the therapist may be needed in order to better understand why the person resists discussing the issue.

Once the spouses have stated the problem in a clear, specific, behavioral manner, they are instructed to make certain that both people are willing to discuss the problem as stated. Otherwise one person may not really want to discuss the problem but not directly offer that information. This lack of desire to reach a resolution to the problem often becomes somewhat obvious as the problem solving proceeds, and the less enthusiastic partner has difficulty suggesting alternative solutions and finds drawbacks to every alternative suggested by the spouse. Because the couple might spend quite a while clarifying the statement of the problem, it can be exasperating to decide after that point that the problem will not be discussed any further at that time. However, couples typically have difficulty knowing whether they want to address an issue until it is clearly stated. This is not always the case, though. For example, at times spouses know that they do not want to discuss anything that is related to their household budget at a given time. When this is the case, there is no reason to continue working to state the problem before making clear that the problem will not be addressed at that time.

Consideration of alternative solutions.

The next step is for the couple to generate alternative solutions to the problem. Because couples seem more likely to continue with treatment procedures that are more natural and less artificial for them, an attempt is made to make this phase of the process as much like everyday interactions as is possible. More specifically, the couple is instructed that one of them is to propose a solution that is preferable and to get the other person's reaction to it. Almost always, this initial proposal is not acceptable to the partner. At this point, the partner often responds with a different solution, which again is unacceptable to the first person. The couple's task is to continue seeking alternative solutions until they find one that is acceptable to both people.

During this process, couples typically arrive at one of three types of solutions. First, in the minority of instances, couples arrive at solutions that delight both partners. Second, some solutions represent a compromise between the desires of the two people. Although most couples will pay lip service to the importance of compromise, some couples have great difficulty even offering compromise solutions, much less agreeing to a compromise. As described in Chapter 2, as some couples search for solutions, they become stalemated, with each person advocating a different solution and neither willing to budge from his or her position. A closer look reveals that what frequently happens is that the husband, for example, offers a solution which the wife rejects. The wife then offers a solution which the husband rejects. He responds by restating his initial solution and tries to convince his wife that his solution is preferable. Similarly, she responds with her initial solution, advocating its strengths. The couple continues in this manner until they decide that the process is fruitless, and they terminate the conversation. The difficulty occurs when they repeat the same solutions. The focus then becomes who will give in to the other person.

After hearing and rejecting a solution two times, rarely is one person truly convinced by the other person that this is the best solution. With couples who repeatedly have this difficulty, the therapist might ask that neither person offer the same solution more than twice for a given problem. After that, other solutions must be sought. One approach is a compromise, but the therapist might need to give concrete, specific instructions in helping the couple arrive at compromise proposals. The couple can be instructed to take the solution offered by the husband and the solution offered by the wife and attempt to put them together so that some of the preferences of both people are included in the solution. This may prove to be more effective than merely telling the couple to "compromise."

The approach suggested above for generating solutions is one in which the couple proposes one solution at a time and evaluates its merits. Another approach is to have the couple *brainstorm* alternative solutions; the couple lists numerous alternatives with encouragement to include creative ideas, even ideas that may at first seem implausible. Also, these various alternatives are not to be evaluated as they are first proposed. After all alternatives are mentioned, then the couple goes back and evaluates them one at a time. The purpose of this strategy is to help the couple be creative in thinking of innovative solutions to problems. This strategy also can be helpful in avoiding the types of stalemated situations mentioned above. That is, if the husband and wife typically each select and cling to a single solution, brainstorming can help the couple to generate alternative solutions. Also, a modified form of brainstorming in which the partners alternately provide possible solutions without evaluating them can be of assistance with couples in which one partner typically dominates offering the solutions. The more silent partner is forced to offer solutions, and the way the other partner responds to those alternatives is assessed.

The compromise solution described above includes elements of both people's desires within the one solution. However, there are times when alternatives are dichotomous, and the couple either acts or does not act. For example, the couple may disagree on whether to move to a different state to take a new position that has been offered to one of them. Although compromises can be proposed for how the current decision will interact with future decisions, the decision of whether to move or not at present is dichotomous. Under such circumstances, a compromise is probably not the most fruitful way to approach the issue. One person's preferences will be satisfied in the solution and the other person's will not. Compromise within a given solution is not the universal way to deal with different preferences.

Various strategies can be employed to help couples who face such difficult dilemmas. One approach is to help the couple clarify whether they have any guidelines or would like to develop any guidelines as to who should have prominent decision-making power in certain aspects of the relationship. There is no research to suggest that couples must share equal decision-making power in every aspect of their marriage. For example, the couple might decide that each person has the freedom to make a decision about his or her own career changes as long as it does not involve changing residences, in which case both people must agree to the move. If a couple has had difficulties with dichotomous decisions in the past, then it might be helpful to discuss strategies for such situations, even if the couple is not facing such decisions at present; often it is easier for the couple to decide what guidelines they believe are fair if they are not currently facing a decision that will be affected by the guidelines.

A second approach to helping couples when they confront dichotomous decisions is to have each person rate independently the importance of the decision to him or her. For example, the couple can be told that each person should rate the importance of the outcome on a scale from 1 to 10, with 10 being of the utmost importance and 1 being of no interest to the person. Each person decides privately the rating that he or she would give to the outcome and then announces this rating to the partner. Whoever has rated the solution as more important makes the final decision. This strategy relies on honesty and trust, because without further guidelines, it would be possible to rate every solution as a 10; thus, it will not be successful with all couples.

A third approach is to point out that compromise does not always occur within a given solution but rather occurs across several solutions. That is, many couples deal successfully with such situations by establishing an informal quid pro quo system across time. They operate on the assumption that if we do what you want to do regarding this solution, then at some point in the future when we face another dichotomous situation, we will adopt my solution. This approach again requires trust and is a rather general expectation for how the relationship will proceed. If the couple believes that they can operate successfully with this type of understanding, then it is perhaps worth a try. However, if the attempt appears unsuccessful, then greater structure and clarity regarding how solutions to various problems will interface will probably be needed. Behavioral contracting, which will be discussed later in the chapter, is an example of how this structure can be made more explicit.

Adopting a final solution.

Couples will not find solutions to all problems which will make both partners joyous. However, the solution must be feasible and at least acceptable to both partners. Otherwise, even if both partners agree to the solution, the future of the solution may be doomed. At times, partners agree to solutions primarily to end the conversation without the intention of actually implementing the solution. Obviously, the lack of follow through is likely to create difficulties for the couple. On other occasions, individuals intend to and do implement the solution but greatly resent it. These negative feelings then result in additional problems for the couple. Third, at times spouses intend to carry out the solution but do not because the solution was not reasonable in the first place. For example, one wife did not enjoy having sexual intercourse with her husband. However, had it not been for concerns raised by the therapist, she would have agreed to have intercourse with her husband every night, including engaging in various acts that she found unpleasant. Consequently, couples should reflect for a moment to consider exactly what they are agreeing to do.

Similarly, once the couple has reached agreement on a solution, they are asked to restate the solution in order to ensure that they have agreed to the same resolution. On numerous occasions, couples believe they have agreed to a solution, but when one person restates the solution they find that they had different understandings of the solution. This misunderstanding can be minimized if the solution is worded in clear behavioral terms, analogous to the statement of the problem.

As couples restate their solution, they should also consider whether extenuating circumstances have been taken into account. For example, often couples derive solutions that are intended for weekdays, but they do not consider what will happen on the weekend when they are on different schedules. This process can be assisted by having the couple "walk through" the solution and note points where different circumstances might make the solution inappropriate. The therapist might comment, "Why don't you imagine that you are in that situation. Think through each step of the solution and see if there are any circumstances in which the solution as you have stated it won't work well."

Selecting a trial period.

After the couple has agreed upon a solution, they are asked to agree upon a trial period during which they will implement the solution. A trial period serves several functions. First, couples are encouraged to consider creative solutions as they problem-solve, and they may adopt solutions that they have never attempted before. Not surprisingly, some of the solutions that couples adopt are not successful. The adoption of a trial period for implementing the solution gives each partner the opportunity to opt for another solution once the trial period is completed. Some couples have a fear of change, and making the trial period time-limited can lessen this fear of change. Second, the trial period provides an automatic time when the solution is reviewed. If couples have been attempting a solution without great success, at times the partners will discontinue the solution without any further discussion of how the problem is to be handled in the future. The end of the trial period serves as a reminder to the couple that they are to assess the success of a solution and decide whether to continue with the solution or problem-solve to reach a new solution.

Third, a trial period often allows couples to be more flexible and compromising in their adoption of solutions. That is, if each person believes that the solution being selected is permanent, then frequently each person adopts the strategy of making sure that he or she is getting as much as possible from the solution. If the couple begins to reach an impasse on solutions, the therapist can remind them that they are agreeing to a trial solution for a period of time which they will determine. If after that trial period, either person is unhappy with the solution, then they will seek a new solution to the issue. The couple is encouraged to try new solutions, in order to be creative in their approach to addressing old issues. A therapist might give a couple the following message:

Therapist: In reaching solutions to problems, I don't want you to worry about whether or not you have reached the absolute "best" solution. What I want you to do is to decide upon what looks like a reasonable solution to you, and I am going to ask you to implement that solution for a trial period only. If a solution does not work, then we will talk about it and try to understand what about the solution was unsatisfactory. Often that will give us some ideas about what the next solution might be in order to better address both of your needs.

A trial period includes two dates: a date when the solution will first be implemented, usually the current date, and a date when the solution ends and is reevaluated. Deciding on the length of the trial period is a function of at least two factors. First, the frequency with which the solution is likely to be implemented must be considered. Thus, if the solution is likely to occur only once every two weeks, then a trial period of only one week would be inappropriate. New solutions and resulting behaviors are often awkward initially, and the couple should make enough attempts at implementing the solution so that initial discomfort from engaging in new behaviors can be minimized before the solution is reevaluated. On the other hand, so many attempts at using the solution should not occur that the couple feels saddled with a solution that is clearly unacceptable to them after several trials. As a rough guideline, couples frequently have selected a two-week trial period for solutions that are likely to be implemented on a daily basis. Second, the length of the trial period is influenced by the comfort that the two partners have with the solution. On occasions, one partner is willing to attempt a solution that he or she is very unsure of but sees as worthy of an attempt. Understandably, the uncertain spouse may request a short trial period.

Couples vary a great deal in the extent to which they comply with the solutions they reach and whether or not they review their solutions on or near the end of the trial date. In fact, some couples' major problem is a lack of follow-through on agreed-upon solutions, although the actual problem-solving process proceeds rather smoothly. This lack of compliance may result from several factors. First, a noncompliant spouse may have agreed to a solution that he or she really opposed. This issue can be handled by stressing one of the major principles of problem solving: spouses do not agree to solutions that are unsatisfactory to them. It may be necessary to teach some spouses that it is acceptable to disagree with their partners, through the use of cognitive restructuring techniques discussed in Chapter 9.

Second, spouses might not comply with a solution to a specific problem because they are upset with their partners about other issues. Such concerns can be handled by teaching the couple to express their emotions about areas of concern and problem-solve about them if appropriate. Third, some persons seem to have a rather disordered style and have difficulty meeting obligations in various aspects of their lives. That is, there may not be anything focal to the relationship that is greatly influencing the individual's behavior in this regard. A given individual might have difficulty meeting obligations in almost any marriage in which he or she would be involved. In the latter case, the couple can benefit from techniques that provide more structure and order to their lives. Such couples might be instructed to choose one night a week during which they look back through their agreements which are filed in a notebook and review the solutions that are nearing the end of the trial date. The therapist also can assist by reviewing with the couple at the beginning of sessions various solutions that have been accepted and by determining the status of those solutions. Finally, the couple can be asked to problem-solve about strategies that will assist them in complying with solutions and reviewing previous solutions.

Communication Training

Focusing on a couple's communication is central to almost every type of marital therapy currently in practice. The behaviorist uses a skills-oriented approach to teach the couple clearer, more specific, nondestructive ways of communicating. In communication training, at least two major issues must be decided. First, the content of the communication to be taught must be specified. As noted in Chapter 2, although numerous investigations have been conducted to isolate what specific forms of communication differentiate distressed from nondistressed couples, the results of these studies are rather inconsistent. Most investigations do indicate that distressed couples engage more in what the researcher has defined as negative communication and less in positive communication. Yet from one study to the next, the specific positive and negative communication behaviors that differentiate between distressed and nondistressed couples vary. Therefore, the field is not at a point where it can be stated on an empirical basis that couples should communicate in some specific ways but not in other ways. (See Baucom and Adams [1987] for a review of the findings on marital distress and communication.) Consequently, the therapist must rely on clinical observations of what appears to be useful to couples as they attempt to resolve problems.

Second, the *strategy* used for teaching communication skills to couples must be specified. There exists a continuum for the degree to which the couple is presented systematically with a list of specific communication guidelines to be followed and avoided. In the more systematic approach, a couple might be taught one specific type of communication, and practicing that communication might be the focus for that session. The following session might focus on a different communication skill, with efforts at practicing that particular skill. In this way, the sessions build in a predetermined manner, with one skill being taught after another. This approach requires that the communication skills be determined ahead of time. This strategy has been employed successfully in teaching relationship enhancement (RE) communication skills to dyads (Guerney, 1977). The systematic approach to teaching RE skills has been possible because a limited number of skills (two major skills) are taught to the couple. At the other extreme is an approach in which the therapist teaches the couple communication skills as they become relevant in the couple's interaction. That is, the therapist has in mind a wide range of behaviors which may be constructive or problematic for a couple as they attempt to resolve problems. As the couple engages in problem solving, the therapist points out the positive aspects of the couple's interaction as well as problem areas that arise. This approach is based on the logic that there are almost an indefinite number of types of communication in which the couple can engage; the therapist's role is to build on the couple's strengths in communicating and to help them alter problematic aspects of their communication. This less systematic, more individualized approach has been used extensively in BMT, and several of the larger treatment outcome studies in the United States have followed this strategy (e.g., Baucom, 1982; Jacobson, 1978a). An intermediate strategy is for the therapist to provide a brief set of helpful communication guidelines for problem solving and then to watch for the many idiosyncratic aspects of the couple's communication as they interact with each other.

The present approach to communication training during problem solving involves this more intermediate approach. Providing couples with a brief list of guidelines helps to increase the likelihood that they will have a satisfying interaction. In addition, it lessens the anxiety that some couples experience if they know that their communication is being monitored but they have no initial guidance as to what constructive communication involves. A list of communication guidelines that might be given to couples is provided in Table 8-3.

Communication to establish one's current desires and preferences and one's role in previous interactions.

"I" statements. Among the facilitative behaviors, couples are encouraged to use "I" statements. That is, each person is asked to speak for him- or herself, stating what that person thinks or feels. Correspondingly, spouses are discouraged from "mind reading" or speaking for the other person. Even if the spouse is accurate in mind reading, many partners resent having others speak for them. When a person is interested in the partner's position on an issue, he or she is encouraged to ask the partner for his or her views rather than speaking for that person. At times, spouses find this guideline to be artificial because the two persons recently have discussed the issue. On such occasions, the person speaking first can state that in a recent conversation he or she understood the partner to take a certain position and then ask whether he or she understood and remembers correctly. For example, the husband might say to his wife, "You know, we

TABLE 8-3
Communication Guidelines While Problem Solving

Communication to establish one's current desires and preferences, and one's role in previous interactions

1. Speak for yourself
   a. Use "I" statements
   b. No not mind read what your partner thinks, feels, or wants — ask instead
2. Express your desires, preferences, and needs clearly and directly
3. Volunteer to accept responsibility for your previous behaviors that have contributed to problems; do not focus on blaming and finding fault with your partner

Communication to acknowledge one's partner

1. Use nonverbal communication to express listening and concern
   a. Make eye contact
   b. Avoid vague and negative nonverbal communication, such as eye rolls, sighs, crossing your arms, turning away from your partner
2. Reflect on or paraphrase important thoughts and feelings that your partner expresses
3. Acknowledge positives about your partner
   a. Comment on something your partner has done to assist with the problem in the past; express appreciation for your partner's efforts
   b. Tell what aspects you like about your partner's proposed solution, even if other aspects of the solution are undesirable to you
   c. Express thanks or appreciation when your partner compromises or agrees to aspects of the solution that are important to you
4. Do not interrupt while your partner is speaking
5. Do not use broad, general, unchangeable traits to describe your partner (or yourself)

Communication to assist in staying appropriately solution-oriented

1. Focus your communication on the future and what you can do to make changes in the problem area
   a. Do not focus on the past
   b. Do not dwell on trying to establish the "truth" of what happened and did not happen in the past
   c. Avoid the use of absolute or exaggerated terms such as "always" and "never" in discussing past behaviors and events
2. Do not get sidetracked by discussing other concerns, even if they are related to the problem
3. Do not use indirect or inappropriate strategies to obtain the solution you desire
   a. Do not attempt to obtain your solution by making your partner feel guilty for not going along with the solution — "poor me"
   b. Do not attempt to make your partner feel stupid or illogical for not seeing things your way
   c. Do not use implied or explicit warnings, threats, or ultimatums as way of forcing a solution on your partner

discussed this just last night, and I understood you to be saying that the reason you don't like me to go out immediately from work is that when I get home, I am too tired to talk. Is that correct?" Not infrequently one spouse does tend to speak for the other, and this contributes to a dominant-submissive relationship in which the more submissive partner rarely expresses his or her views. In addition, when one partner speaks for the other, it sets the stage for them to argue about whether the person indeed did or did not make the statement or feel a certain way. This diverts the couple's attention from the task at hand, to reach a resolution to the problem being discussed.

Expression of desires. Similarly, each person is encouraged to express to the partner what he or she wants, desires, or needs regarding the problem being discussed. Many spouses need permission and encouragement to state what they would like. Some persons have become so focused on pleasing the spouse and other family members that they rarely seem to consider their own needs. Other spouses are aware of what they would like but are reluctant to voice their preferences for various reasons: (a) the individual is ignored or punished for raising preferences, or (b) the person believes it is wrong to state what one wants. When a therapist notes that one spouse rarely proposes solutions or the solutions proposed focus primarily on the other person's desires, then some time should be spent trying to understand the basis for this pattern. For example, if the person feels punished by the partner for stating his or her preferences, then the communication or other behaviors contributing to this sense of punishment need to be isolated and possibly altered.

Fault finding. As described in Chapter 2, many couples inappropriately spend large amounts of time attempting to decide who is at fault for problems. Negative reciprocity is a robust phenomenon among couples, and when spouses feel attacked, they frequently counterattack or withdraw. Rather than attempting to blame the partner, it often assists problem solving when one partner acknowledges that certain of his or her behaviors have contributed to the problem in the past. If a spouse voluntarily accepts partial responsibility for negative interactions, then the partner has little need to blame that person because responsibility has already been accepted. Frequently, if one spouse acknowledges his or her contribution to a problem, reciprocity prevails, with the other partner also acknowledging partial responsibility. The goal is not to determine whose fault the problem is; yet, an acknowledgement of partial responsibility often frees the couple to then focus on changing behavior for the future.

Communication to acknowledge partner.

Eye contact. A supportive attitude toward the partner during problem solving helps develop a collaborative set between the spouses, and this type of communication can be facilitated in many ways. For example, the nonverbal behavior of the couple is important. Couples are taught to make eye contact with each other because many people seem to feel that it creates a greater sense of closeness between the partners. This impact of eye contact was made clear in a distressed couple in which the husband felt rather detached from his wife and was uneasy being close to her. When encouraged by the therapist to make more eye contact, he commented that it did indeed create a greater sense of closeness, and he was not sure whether he wanted that closeness. He clarified further that whenever he had something important to discuss with his wife, he called her on the telephone from work to discuss it rather than having the uneasiness created when she looked at him in person.

Similarly, occasional head nods are another way of indicating to the speaker that he or she is being heard. Body posture also is important. Sitting back with one's arms crossed tends to create a sense of distance between the two spouses, whereas sitting up straight or leaning forward while the other speaks can demonstrate a desire to listen and understand. What is important is that each person feels that he or she is being listened to and taken seriously. Thus, if a spouse rarely makes eye contact, that will be discussed by the therapist. Likewise, if one spouse stares at the other with little movement and little affect, thereby creating an angry or detached atmosphere, those nonverbals also will be discussed. Consequently, there is no standard list of relevant nonverbal behaviors which is to be followed; instead, any nonverbal behavior that the therapist believes is disrupting or not optimizing the communication should be discussed with the couple.

The extent to which nonverbal behaviors are consistent with verbal behaviors must be considered because discrepant verbal and nonverbal communication is often a source of confusion for couples. Many a spouse comments that when he or she asks the partner what is wrong, the partner responds in an angry or dejected way, "Oh, nothing." Similarly, when agreeing on a solution in problem solving, one partner may respond in an angry tone of voice, "Fine. If that's what you want, then that is fine with me." Rather than giving these indirect messages of distress or disapproval, spouses are encouraged to be explicit about their negative feelings.

Reflections. The cooperative, supportive attitude that shows respect for the partner's perspective also can be facilitated through a number of other communication skills. One of the most important of these is the timely use of reflections or paraphrasing the speaker's thoughts and feelings. Because the use of reflections is discussed at length in Chapter 10, it will not be considered here in detail. Reflections can serve several useful functions in problem solving. First, reflections indicate that the individual has been listening, and most persons appreciate knowing that they have been heard. Thus, reflections can show a respect that the other person's ideas and feelings are valued. This is particularly important in problem solving when the two persons frequently disagree with each other on a course of action to pursue. Therefore, spouses are taught to reflect the other's proposed solutions, particularly if they are about to disagree or offer a counterproposal. Second, in order to reflect, the person does have to listen. Frequently, one spouse will stop listening to the other after hearing only a few words and either will wait for the other to stop talking or will interrupt the speaker. By deciding to reflect, the listener focuses on the other's message. Third, reflections slow down the communication process. Thus arguments that escalate rapidly can be tempered or avoided at times through the use of reflections. Finally, reflections clear up misunderstandings because inaccurate reflections can be corrected.

Based on the above considerations, couples are taught to reflect each other's messages on the following occasions. First, when one person feels unheard or misunderstood, the other can reflect that person's expressed thoughts and feelings. Second, when the listener is not certain that he or she understands what the other has said, the listener can reflect and then receive feedback from the partner about whether the perceived message was accurate. Third, the therapist can teach a couple who has difficulty listening to each other to do so more effectively by practicing reflecting. Fourth, spouses are asked to reflect when the partner has said something "important."

During problem solving, the statement of proposed solutions is one such important communication. Similarly, expressions of deeply felt emotions are important; therefore, spouses are asked to reflect most strong emotions expressed by the partner.

Because reflection of affect can lead to more affect, spouses are taught to reflect affect in a certain way during problem solving. The feelings are first reflected, followed by an additional statement designed to return the discussion to a solution-oriented focus. Thus a husband might reflect, "When I come home late and don't feel like talking to you, you feel sort of depressed and unimportant. Let's see if we can figure out some way that I can feel like I have some time to myself but without making you feel bad." Finally, any time that either person thinks the conversation is moving too rapidly or is in some way becoming confused or getting out of hand, the person is encouraged to reflect in order to slow the conversation and to bring greater focus to what is being said.

Interruptions. Reflections are based on the assumption that the listener is attending to the speaker and has a primary focus on trying to understand what the speaker is saying. As noted in Chapter 2, interruptions can have both constructive and destructive impacts on the communication process. The theoretical and empirical literature offer differing views on the adaptiveness or inappropriateness of interruptions. Interruptions have at times been described as adaptive, in that they indicate an informality and flexibility in the communication. Similarly, communication research does not indicate consistently that distressed spouses interrupt each other more than do nondistressed spouses (Baucom & Adams, 1987). In part, this divergence of thought about interruptions may result because interruptions occur at different times and serve different functions. For example, interruptions occur when one person is in the midst of a statement, and the partner breaks in to present his or her own ideas. Another instance often referred to as an interruption is when one person has paused momentarily and the other person begins to speak. Although data are lacking on the issue, it is likely that the latter situation is less distressing to the speaker. Also, the *content* of the interruption may influence its impact. If the husband is speaking and his wife interrupts him to disagree with him, he is likely to feel cut off and displeased. However, if in her interruption she provides an empathic ending to a sentence he was struggling to complete, then his reaction may not be nearly as negative. Also, if she interrupts to provide him with important information which may change his views or feelings, he might appreciate the additional information. Thus, labeling interruptions as all good or all bad is probably an oversimplification. Because distressed couples may have difficulty differentiating between constructive and problematic types of interruptions, they are encouraged not to interrupt each other. If one person does wish to speak before the other is finished, the couple is advised to develop some sort of agreed-upon nonverbal signal, such as slightly raising the index finger, to let the speaker know that the listener wishes to add something or is having trouble understanding or continuing to listen.

Acknowledging positives. Because couples are dealing with a problem area that most likely has been discussed previously with little success, they have a tendency to behave negatively toward each other during the problem-solving interaction. It is important to teach couples to comment to each other when they do have a positive reaction to what the other has just said or how the other behaves in the problem situation. Thus, if one person offers a solution which the partner does not find totally acceptable but which has some positive elements, the partner is encouraged to comment on those aspects of the solution that he or she likes. If the proposed solution does sound good to the partner, rather than saying, "I'm willing to do that," the partner might say, "That is a good idea. Let's give it a try." Similarly, if one person has conceded on an important aspect of the solution, the partner might show appreciation for the other's willingness to accept the solution: "I really appreciate your willingness to try this solution. I know it means some extra work for you which is not much fun." This discussion has focused on showing appreciation and acknowledgment regarding proposed solutions. However, the same principle applies for any partner behaviors noted during the actual problem solving and those which are related to the problem area when it occurs outside of the session.

Trait labels. There are some communications that seem particularly likely to occur at certain stages of the problem solving process. As mentioned earlier, a couple's statement of their problem should be specific and behavioral. Although all types of vagueness are to be discouraged, the use of negative trait labels in describing the spouse is to be particularly discouraged. Thus, the statement of a problem that the partner is lazy around the house is not only unclear, but the spouse being discussed is likely to be offended. Describing the particular behaviors of concern not only is clearer and probably will assist when various solutions are being considered, but the description of the specific behaviors typically seems less condemning than trait labels. Whereas spouses might use trait descriptions at any time, this communication is frequent when spouses initially state a problem.

Communication to assist in staying appropriately solution-oriented.

Focusing on the past. The above discussion suggests that during problem solving couples are encouraged to avoid attempting to reconstruct the past to establish exactly what did and did not happen or to attribute blame. However, this is not meant to suggest that couples should under all circumstances avoid a discussion of specific past events while problem solving. The issue really involves the *purpose* for discussing the past. If the goal is in some way to make the partner look bad, then the discussion is to be avoided. At times a discussion of the specific events surrounding a problem area can be useful if the couple is attempting to gain a clearer understanding of previous instances of the problem so that they can evaluate possible changes to incorporate into a solution. Again, the key is for the couple to maintain a solution-oriented focus. Thus, after listing the various behaviors that occurred during some specific occasion, the spouses should automatically ask each other, "What can we change to make this better in the future?" With some couples this is successful. For other couples, once they begin discussing specific past events, they routinely become upset with each other and lose their problem solving orientation. If it becomes apparent that a couple is taking a great risk by discussing such situations, they are encouraged to avoid detailed discussion of specific past events. Instead, they are asked simply to talk about how they want to behave in the future. Thus, certain types of communication may create a high probability of discord for some couples, whereas other couples can handle the same communication quite successfully. After a number of unsuccessful attempts at helping a couple communicate in a certain way, the therapist might conclude that a particular couple can be better helped by being taught to avoid particular types of communication.

Establishing the truth. Another communication guideline in this same vein is that the couple should avoid attempting to establish the truth of what happened or did not happen during past events unless these facts are needed to arrive at a solution. For example, while trying to decide when to have dinner so that it will be hot with everyone present, the couple may get into a disagreement regarding what time the husband arrived home the previous evening. In most cases, the couple could decide when to have dinners without coming to a resolution of what time the husband came home the previous evening if both agree on a time when they can be home in the future.

Always and never. One particular type of communication often leads couples into a disagreement about how past events have occurred—the use of the terms "always" and "never." Thus, when a husband tells his wife that she *never* asks him about his day, his wife is likely to respond with a list of times when she did ask him. The conversation is likely to continue with an unproductive disagreement about whether she did or did not ask him about his day on a given occasion. Consequently, couples are advised to avoid the use of extreme terms such as "always" and "never" because they are rarely accurate and tend to create arguments. Instead, they are taught to tell the partner that some behavior does not occur as frequently as they would like or occurs infrequently.

Sidetracking. Once the couple begins considering alternative solutions, a frequent communication difficulty is that they become sidetracked onto other issues and lose their solution focus. At times this is apparent if the second issue is minimally related to the first. However, it is more difficult when the couple raises issues seemingly related to the originally stated problem. For example, while discussing the husband's difficulty getting ready on time for work in the morning, the wife may mention that she thinks he stays up too late at night and therefore cannot get out of bed in the morning. Changing bedtime might be an effective way to alleviate the original problem, so the therapist might allow the couple to continue with the discussion of bedtime. The message to the couple is that if they do not need to deal with the issue that they just brought up in order to resolve the originally stated problem, they should discuss it later.

Power plays. Understandably, each spouse is invested in having his or her preferred solution accepted. Unfortunately, some spouses have learned maladaptive ways to persuade the partner to accept solutions. For example, some spouses need to be taught to be assertive rather than aggressive in interacting with their partners. As noted in Chapter 2, whereas assertiveness involves expressing one's opinions, feelings, or preferences directly without attempting to force compliance from the partner, aggression involves various strategies to *force* the partner to comply.

These coercive attempts take several forms. Some partners attempt to overpower the other, using either implied threats or the strength of their personalities. One wife typically pointed her index finger at her husband and glared at him when she proposed a solution. Although the threat was not made explicit, the husband certainly perceived that in some way he would be punished if he did not accept her solution. Whereas different persons may use different strategies to get their messages across, the essence of the threat is, "Either accept my solution, or you will be punished."

Other spouses do not threaten, but they overpower their partners through other means. For example, often one spouse is more verbally fluent, can think faster, has a more logical mind, or has a stronger, more confident voice than the other spouse. The partner simply cannot hold his or her own in a logical debate. The latter person often gives in during problem solving when feeling confused or overwhelmed, even though he or she does not find the solution acceptable. As one husband stated, "Well, I guess I don't really like it, but I can't come up with any good reasons for not going along with it. Every reason I give, she shoots down." Under such circumstances, it is important to point out to the couple that the best solution is not necessarily the one that seems most rational or logical. The goal of problem solving is to adopt a solution that will satisfy both partners to the extent possible. Each person's feelings are an essential aspect to consider in the solution, and one's feelings and preferences frequently are not the result of logic.

When spouses agree to solutions because they feel overpowered in the problem-solving process, difficulties often result which may or may not be obviously related to the issue discussed. In one couple, the husband typically gave in to his wife's superior logic and agreed to her solutions. However, after their discussions he would disregard the solution and do what he wanted. This was the only strategy he knew to use in order to feel that he had some power in the relationship. As Epstein et al. (1978) point out, this can be viewed as a form of passive aggression: The individual does not express his or her feelings, desires, or preferences directly, but the person still attempts to force his or her solution on the partner. Whereas the discontent with the solutions was rather obvious in the above example, other spouses follow through with the agreed-upon solutions but experience significant resentment and anger which is not expressed in the context of the original problem. Instead, the anger is expressed in other situations, without any understandable basis.

Therapists also must intervene actively when spouses respond to feeling overwhelmed by their partners' coercive efforts by disrupting the problem-solving process. For example, when one wife felt coerced into accepting a solution she did not like but could not logically rebut, she began to cry and disrupted the process. The husband, an emotionally unexpressive person, detested this "outburst" and typically would terminate the conversation. The couple's pattern was discussed with them, and the husband was shown how his demand for logic was an important contributor to their negative cycle. The wife was taught to be appropriately assertive and to disagree verbally when she did not like his solution, and the husband was taught to accept her concerns whether or not they were based on what he considered to be the most logical approach.

Guilt induction. Another destructive strategy used to obtain compliance with a proposed solution is "to guilt" the partner into accepting a solution. Again, this type of communication can take many different forms. Among the arguments typically encountered are statements carrying the following messages: "If you really love me, you can show me by doing what I want you to do"; "I did something that you wanted in the past, so you should do this now for me—you aren't being fair"; "I am willing to accept your solution, but it will be an unbearable hardship on me—wouldn't it be better to do it my way?" Common among these appeals is the suggestion that you should do what I want, or you are a bad or unloving person.

Whereas it is appropriate for a couple to discuss fair play and reciprocity while addressing a problem, if guilt induction is a predominant approach for attempting to induce compliance from a partner, then the issue needs to be raised by the therapist. The therapist should point out how the pattern reduces the recipient's sense of freedom to prefer a different solution to a problem. As with the other forms of coercion described above, therapists can use basic skill training procedures to help spouses substitute assertive requests for guilt induction. Many individuals appear to choose aggressive responses owing to a variety of cognitive factors (e.g., a standard that "things must go my way or I can't stand it"; or an expectancy that "if I don't push for what I want, people will take advantage of me"). Consequently, it is important to assess whether spouses' guilt induction and other forms of coercion are influenced by cognitive factors as well as their behavioral skills, and to combine skill training and cognitive restructuring as appropriate.

The above guidelines focus on speaking for oneself and allowing the other person to do the same. The atmosphere that the therapist is attempting to create is one in which the spouses recognize that in addition to being a couple, they are individuals who perceive the world in their own unique ways. The goal is for the couple to recognize these individual differences and decide on a way to handle the problem area so that they will be more satisfied in the future.

Behavioral Contracting

At times during problem solving, couples agree to make behavioral changes but are then unsuccessful in actually implementing the changes. Behavioral contracting involves the use of contingencies to assist couples in making behavioral changes. Thus, a spouse may be rewarded or punished according to whether that person behaves in some agreed-upon way. The use of contingencies in bringing about marital changes has been part of BMT since Stuart (1969) published his original multiple case studies. However, as contracting became more widely used by researchers and clinicians, concerns began to surface. Some couples complained about the seeming rigidity of the approach; others were dissatisfied that it placed the couple's willingness to behave positively toward each other within the context of reward and punishment rather than love or altruism. Some couples found that changes produced through contracting were less rewarding because the partner's changes now seemed motivated by a desire to get something in return. Phrased differently, concerns arose that when behaviors seemingly came clearly under the control of contingencies, then the attributions for those behaviors were different, and the behaviors might lose their value. However, as discussed in Chapter 12, treatment outcome data indicate that at least some couples do respond well to contracting. Clinical experience indicates that contracting can be particularly helpful when couples experience difficulty complying with agreed-upon behavior change. That is, the contingencies can serve as an additional incentive to change behavior. In addition, the presence of the rewards and punishments can serve as a reminder to behave in a certain way. Thus, contracting provides increased structure to couples needing such assistance. Consequently, although contracting is unlikely to be used with all couples or for the duration of treatment with any single couple, it involves a set of treatment strategies with which the therapist should be familiar.

Technical aspects of contracting.

Quid pro quo contracts. Quid pro quo contracting (qpq) can best be viewed as two problems, one selected by each spouse, which are solved and which then have their solutions woven together in the following manner: If husband does "X," then wife does "Y." If wife does "Y," then husband does "X." If husband does not do "X," then wife *need* not do "Y." If wife does not do "Y," then husband *need* not do "X." That is, in qpq contracting, each person agrees to make a behavior change, and the partner's behavior change is the reward for changing one's own behavior. For example, the wife may agree to pick up her clothes each night, and the husband agrees to prepare breakfast each morning. If she picks up her clothes one night, he must prepare breakfast the next morning. If he prepares breakfast one morning, she must pick up her clothes that night. However, if he does not prepare breakfast one morning, she is not required to pick up her clothes that night. Similarly, if she does not pick up her clothes one night, he is not required to prepare breakfast the next morning.

Qpq contracting can be taught to couples by having each spouse select one problem area in which he or she would like to see the partner change. The couple then problem-solves for each of the two problems, one at a time. After a solution is reached for each problem, the two solutions are woven together as described above. One difficulty couples encounter is that their contracts can become complex in order to seem equitable. In order to simplify the contracts, several guidelines should be considered. First, the contingencies can be simplified if the behaviors chosen to focus upon in the two problems occur with somewhat equal frequency. If the two behaviors do not occur with equal frequency, at times one behavior can be handled in multiples. For example, the couple might decide that if the wife mows the lawn on Saturdays, the husband will wash the dishes each night (7 washings for 1 mowing). They must then decide how many dish washings missed allow the wife to skip mowing the lawn, and so forth.

Second, the contingencies can be simplified if the two behaviors being considered are of relatively equal magnitude of importance. Again in the above example, the couple might decide that preparing breakfast and picking up clothes are similar in magnitude of importance and effort required. Arranging contingencies becomes more complex if one of the two behaviors is much more valued or more difficult to accomplish. Consequently, a couple would be cautioned against attempting to work out a contract in which the wife agrees to clean up nightly in the den for a few minutes in return for the husband agreeing to spend several hours daily painting the house.

Third, the contingencies are easier to carry out if the solutions to the two problems are simple and involve change on only one person's part in each solution. Thus, if the husband agrees to prepare breakfast three days a week and the wife prepares it four days a week, this solution to preparing breakfast might be difficult to integrate with the wife's also agreeing to pick up her clothes at night as the solution to the second problem. In this example, the couple might simply wish to form a contract concerning breakfast preparation because the solution involves behavior change on both persons' parts. This example points out that qpq contracts need not always involve two distinct problems. At times the solution to a single problem will involve behavior change from both partners, and they may wish to specify contingencies within the one problem area. In fact, this type of contract is favored by many couples because it involves a clear sense of compromise.

Qpq contracting can become more effective if the couples understand (a) the types of problem content well suited to contracting; (b) the characteristics of the solution that are important; and (c) ways of using the contingencies effectively.

Clinical experience strongly suggests that behavioral contracts of all types are most successful with instrumental, task-oriented behaviors. In essence, contracting is one way for spouses to decide which person will be responsible for which chores. However, contracting need not be limited to chores. For example, one husband agreed to stop cursing in return for a desired behavior change from his wife. Most important, couples should be advised to refrain from contracting for sex, affection, or any other behavior that is rewarding because it is spontaneous, motivated by love or caring, or derives its major meaning from the internal motivation of one or both partners.

Second, the *types of solutions* accepted in contracting can affect the success of the contract. An important aspect of the solution is that the solution should involve *behavior* that is under the control of the person who agrees to make some change. One wife agreed to lose 3 pounds a week in exchange for her husband walking a mile each day to get exercise. Although quite specific, this contract had two difficulties. First, losing weight is not a behavior per se; it is the result of a series of behaviors. Instead, she might agree to limit her caloric intake to 1,200 calories a day as her part of the contract. The second problem with the contract highlights another important characteristic of the solutions that are included in contracting. The solution that involves behavior change for the wife in qpq contracting should not be some behavior which she is internally motivated to engage in without the contract, or which is clearly for her personal well-being. Otherwise, if the husband does not fulfill his part of the contract, she is in a difficult position. If she continues to diet regardless of whether or not he walks, the contract is for all practical purposes defunct. However, if she does not diet in response to his not walking, she is avoiding a behavior in which she wants to engage and which is beneficial to her. Good faith contracts described below might be more appropriate for providing added incentive for behavior changes that the person wants to make but for some reason is having a difficult time achieving.

Appropriate use of contingencies is also important to successful contracting. The use of contracting *cycles* is essential for maintaining behavior change in qpq contracting. One cycle is defined by one complete set of behaviors as outlined in the contingencies. If the couple has agreed that the husband will prepare breakfast one day in exchange for the wife's picking up her clothes one night, a cycle consists of one breakfast preparation and one clothes pickup. Use of contracting cycles is important in order to provide the couple with a way of reinstituting the behavior changes after one person has not met his or her part of the contract one time. After the contract is out of operation for one complete cycle, it should resume. Therefore, if the husband does not prepare breakfast one morning, the wife need not pick up her clothes that night. That completes one cycle, and the husband is to resume preparing breakfast the next morning.

Spouses at times ask whether they should automatically not fulfill their part of the contract if the partner has violated the contract. That is, if the husband does not prepare breakfast one morning, does this mean that the wife should definitely not pick up her clothes? Although data are lacking on this issue, our impression is that the wife in this circumstance might well pick up her clothes in order to benefit the relationship. By picking up her clothes when the husband has failed to prepare breakfast, she can show him that she is doing her part because she wants to improve the relationship, not merely because she wants breakfast prepared. However, continuing to pick up her clothes if her husband consistently failed to prepare breakfast would in essence terminate the contract. Also, if the wife preferred never to pick up her clothes when her husband did not prepare breakfast, this is acceptable because it is within the confines of the contract.

Some couples comment that they do not wish to be in marriages in which the only reason that the partner behaves in some positive way is to get something in return. Such a marriage would, indeed, be sterile. Contracting is not offered as a means of resolving all marital difficulties. However, contracting can be helpful when the couple is having difficulty changing behavior, because the other person's behavior change can serve as both a reminder and a motivator to change one's own behavior. In addition, the therapist can recommend to the couple that once the new behaviors seem to be well established, they may wish to formally terminate the contract and evaluate whether they are able to maintain the agreed-upon changes.

Good faith contracts. One of the potential difficulties with qpq contracts is that if one spouse does not conform to the contract, then two behavior changes that might benefit the relationship are in danger of being cancelled, because the other partner might no longer maintain his or her behavior change either. The good faith contract circumvents this problem. In the good faith contract, a given partner agrees to make a behavior change, but the reward is not a desired behavior change from the partner. Instead, the reward is typically something that does not involve the other partner's behavior. Consequently, if the husband agrees to clean off his boots after working in the garden, he might receive strawberries on his cereal in the morning, something which he considers a special treat. The wife might also agree to make some behavior change, but her reward would be unrelated to whether her husband cleans his boots or not. Whereas quid pro quo contracts make one person's behavior change the reward for the other partner's behavior change, good faith contracts separate the contingencies for the two spouses' behaviors.

At present, there are no data demonstrating that one of the two contracting strategies discussed thus far is superior to the other. However, clinical experience suggests several circumstances when the good faith contract might be preferred. First, if one partner continuously fails to follow through with quid pro quo contracts, this results in the loss of two potentially constructive behavior changes for the couple. In this instance, the partner who has been following through with the quid pro quo contract can be encouraged to continue to engage in the behavior change through the development of a good faith contract for that person alone.

Second, some couples appear to be too enmeshed. That is, perhaps almost all of their attention and behaviors focus on joint activities. Given such a couple, the therapist probably would not want to recommend quid pro quo contracts for behavior change because they accentuate interdependency of behavior. Good faith contracts would more likely be the intervention of choice because the contingencies are developed to focus on rewards for an individual independent of the other person's behavior. On the other hand, quid pro quo contracts would be the intervention of choice when a major concern is that the couple is already operating so independently of each other that they are experiencing a lack of closeness or a lack of sense of relatedness.

Third, good faith contracts are appropriate when one partner wishes to make a given behavior change but is having difficulty achieving the change. For example, a husband may decide that he wishes to go on a diet but has been somewhat unsuccessful with it in the past. As noted in the section on quid pro quo contracts, this type of behavior change is not best handled within such a contract. In that circumstance, if his wife should not follow through with her part of the contract, then the husband will either continue with the diet (and over time, in essence, negate the contract) or else give up his diet, which he desires and which is good for his health. A simple solution would be to form a good faith contract for his dieting. The reward might serve as the additional incentive that he needs in order to follow through with the diet. Not only does this approach alleviate the concerns about the contingencies discussed above, but the good faith contract emphasizes personal responsibility because the partner's behavior is not an integral part of the behavior change. Increased personal responsibility might be important in helping to promote behavior changes in some spouses.

One of the potential difficulties of good faith contracts is that they rely on external reinforcers; that is, the reward is not a requested change in the partner's behavior. Consequently, heavy reliance on good faith contracts results in the need for numerous external reinforcers. A number of couples have commented that they begin to run out of reasonable reinforcers. Most of the reinforcers that spouses select involve either time or money, both of which are in limited supply. As a result, a number of reinforcers that are selected are rather small, and on a purely economic basis they would not suffice to entice the person to make a behavior change. Consequently, it is important not to present the notion of reinforcers to couples as a form of payment for making the behavior change. Instead the therapist should emphasize to the couple that they will be agreeing to make behavior changes in order to improve the relationship. As somewhat of a *bonus* and a *reminder*, they will receive an additional small reward during good faith contracting.

The development of a good faith contract is relatively simple. The couple problem-solves on some issue using the guidelines of problem solving discussed earlier. They then discuss and agree on a reinforcer for the behavior change(s). If both persons have agreed to make behavior changes as part of the solution, then the couple selects reinforcers for both persons.

Wholistic contracts. Stuart (1980) introduced a third type of contract, termed the wholistic contract, in an attempt to overcome some of the concerns raised about attributions resulting from contracting as discussed above. Stuart's goal was to provide a strategy which would encourage couples to make desired behavior changes and to expect to get something in return, but which would increase the sense of freedom, volition, and choice in the act. Wholistic contracts involve having each person make a list of perhaps 10 or so behavior changes that he or she would like to see the partner make during the next week. Each spouse makes a separate list for the partner. Then each person agrees to make perhaps five of these changes some time during the following week. However, the individual does not state which five of the behaviors will be followed or exactly when during the week the behaviors will occur. Each person expects that the partner will follow through with the agreement, but there is no explicit contingency for keeping or not keeping the agreement. By giving each person the choice of what behaviors to exhibit and when to engage in them, personal choice and motivation are emphasized.

Again there are no data to direct the appropriate use of wholistic contracts, but clinical experience provides some direction. One primary differentiation between wholistic contracts and the other two forms is the amount of structure implicit in the interventions. Good faith contracts and qpq contracts are very structured, providing exact expectations of behavior and the precise contingencies. Many couples are disorganized and have difficulty arranging schedules, getting tasks accomplished, and monitoring time. The increased structure of good faith and qpq contracts may be useful to these couples. Members of other couples do not have difficulty with a lack of structure but have gradually drifted away from attempting to please the other person. For these latter couples, drawing their attention to behavior changes that their partners would like them to make and the intermediate structure of wholistic contracts may be sufficient to promote behavior change.

A part of the structure provided by good faith and quid pro quo contracts is the explicit contingencies provided for behavior change. Couples who are extremely angry and distrustful of each other at times want to see exactly what they will receive in return for their behavior changes. These same couples often feel that the partner has not been "fair" in terms of who gets what out of the marriage and have a desire to make sure that from this time forward, agreements are fair. Because the partners are agreeing to specific contingencies in good faith and quid pro quo contracting, they are at times able to achieve a sense of fairness about the agreement. With wholistic contracts, more distressed, distrustful couples may be concerned that the partner will attempt to select the easiest changes listed and make minimal behavior changes. Consequently, Stuart agrees that wholistic contracts are most likely to be successful with less distressed couples who still have an element of trust, good will, and motivation in their marriage.

Presenting contracting to couples.

As alluded to throughout this section, contracting has the potential to be seen by couples as either a cold, legalistic approach to resolving problems or a structuring strategy to assist them in making difficult behavioral changes. In part the couple's reaction is likely to be influenced by the therapist's attitude toward contracting and the way in which it is presented. To begin with, contracts can be presented to the couple as "behavior change agreements" rather than as contracts. The term "contract" with its tie to the legal profession can have a negative connotation to some people. Second, rather than emphasizing the tit-for-tat nature of quid pro quo contracting or the supremacy of the external reward in good faith contracting, the therapist can emphasize the usefulness of the strategy in providing reminders and some additional incentives in helping the couple to remember to carry out the changes they have agreed to make. The following is an example of the way in which contracting might be presented to a couple.

Therapist: You have been practicing problem solving for several weeks now and you have gotten pretty good at the skills. You have also had some success at carrying out some of the agreements you have reached. At the same time, as you have told me, it has been hard to carry out some of the agreements, and at times you haven't. What I want to do now is teach you a technique to help you carry out the agreements that you make because they seem really important in improving your marriage. I refer to this approach as "change agreements," and it is really an extension of problem solving. In change agreements you will problem-solve like you always have, and now we will add some additional reminders and incentives to help you carry through with your agreed-upon solution. Let me explain the mechanics of just how this type of change agreement works. [This would be followed by a discussion of the mechanics of one type of contracting or change agreement.]

    I have found that change agreements are helpful for several reasons. First, the extra bonus you receive for making your behavior change can serve as a reminder to continue making that change. I believe that when you leave here with an agreement, you do intend to carry it out. But I also know that you have often gotten into a habit of behaving differently, and at times it is hard to remember to behave in the new way. Hopefully when you receive the bonus reward for making your behavior change, it will ring a bell to remind you to keep it up.

    Second, the bonus reward not only can serve as a reminder but also as some additional incentive to make your behavior change. At times you are agreeing with your partner to make some difficult changes because you believe this will help your marriage. I think that is great, and I hope that you both recognize and appreciate the effort that is required to make these changes on both sides. Well, if we can make that task a little easier for you, then I think that is also fine. There is nothing wrong with giving each other some encouragement by rewarding each other for making difficult changes. Remember, that is one of our major philosophies here: that you will both probably be a lot happier if you build more rewards into your lives with each other. I personally don't think that needs to take away from the importance of a spouse's internal motivation to please the other person. If you can make a difficult behavior change to improve the marriage and get an additional bonus for yourself, then I think that is a wonderful system. You don't have to be a martyr to prove your love or concern for the other person.

    Third, providing a reward can often make problem solving an easier task. Let's face it. There are a number of issues you need to resolve which involve solutions that are unpleasant: understandably neither of you looks forward to the behaviors that may be needed to resolve the problem. For example, I've seen couples go through long discussions about who is going to clean the bathroom, and they come up with all sorts of wonderful justifications for why they shouldn't be the ones to do it. Basically, what it comes down to is that many people just don't like to clean the bathroom. Often this type of long discussion can be short-circuited if each person sees that in return for engaging in this type of undesirable behavior, he or she will receive some type of meaningful reward. That may not always be possible, but when you can provide something which the person enjoys in return or allow the person to avoid something else unpleasant, then I think you will be working to make your lives together more enjoyable.

At the same time, behavior change agreements are not intended to be used to resolve all issues. [At this point the therapist might discuss the importance of spontaneity in the relationship, the pitfalls of change agreements with affection and sex, etc.]

THERAPIST INTERVENTIONS IN BEHAVIORAL MARITAL THERAPY

The preceding discussion describes some of the major therapeutic strategies to employ in assisting couples as they attempt to make important behavioral changes. In order to accomplish these goals, the therapist's behavior is quite important. The therapist must understand general guidelines for how to intervene with a couple, when to intervene, how to control the tempo of the session, and how to avoid battles and power struggles with the spouses. Whereas teaching the couple to follow certain communication guidelines might sound like a somewhat mechanical task, sensitively relating to the couple and dealing with the above issues as well as others is essential to quality treatment. The latter statement might well be made about any treatment, but in a skills-oriented approach the structure provided can easily seduce the therapist into believing that a focus on the skill guidelines is all that is needed. Most therapists in training can learn the technical skills, but attending to the issues discussed below can often mean the difference between a productive and unproductive session. Although these guidelines are presented within the context of focusing on behavior changes, the guidelines apply to skills-oriented interventions in general, whether focusing on behavior, cognition, or affect.

How to Intervene

While the couple is problem solving, the therapist is listening and waiting to intervene, perhaps to point out something positive about their interaction or to assist if the couple interacts inappropriately. The intervention can be viewed as consisting of three phases: the initiation of the intervention, the intervention proper, and the termination of the intervention. It is possible for the therapist to be skilled in some of these phases but not the others, leading to a less than optimal intervention. Therefore, attention must be paid to all three phases.

Often the couple is talking when the therapist decides to intervene. The initiation of the intervention, therefore, involves interrupting the couple. As discussed previously, people typically do not like to be interrupted. This seems to be particularly true when they are discussing an issue of importance, as is often the case during problem solving. Consequently, interrupting the couple must be handled sensitively. To prepare the couple for the therapist's interruptions, to clarify that the couple is to minimize interrupting each other, and to make the interruption the least disruptive possible, an introduction such as the one that follows can be given prior to the couple's first attempt at problem solving. An abbreviated reminder might be given before subsequent sessions if needed.

Therapist: My role while you are problem solving is like that of a coach. That is, you will be talking to each other, and I will be listening to you. Occasionally I will stop you to point out some things that I think you are doing well in communicating with each other so that you can do them more often. Also when you start to get into difficulty in your communication, I'll stop you and point it out so that you can learn what communications you need to change. Although I'll be interrupting you, I'll ask you not to interrupt each other while you are talking with each other. Also, I know that when people get involved in talking about an issue, at times they are not aware that I am trying to stop them. When I want you to stop for a moment, I'll just raise my hand a little bit like this. If you don't see it, I'll call your name, and if you would stop your conversation at that time, it would be helpful. I don't want to have to shout or talk over either of you. Does that sound O.K. to you?

Consequently, part of the ease of interrupting the couple can be accomplished by establishing the therapist's role and agreeing on a signal for the couple to stop talking. When possible the therapist wants to make a smooth, nonabrasive entree when providing the couple with feedback. Beginning therapists, in an eagerness to terminate an aversive interaction between the spouses, often enthusiastically shout, "Stop!" Such a pronouncement typically stops the couple, jolts them in fact, and is not needed. If the couple does not notice or respond to a nonverbal cue or their names being called, then a stronger intervention is appropriate, perhaps even calling "Stop." However, the therapist does not wish to be any more assertive or disruptive than necessary. There are no specific words that are to be used; what is important is for the therapist to develop a smooth, easy way of initiating the intervention.

Once the therapist has halted the couple's interaction, the content of the intervention is important. When the purpose of the intervention is to provide skills training, then the intervention should label the specific communications that are important at the moment. If the therapist finds a specific communication to be nonproductive, he or she will typically label the communication, clarify why it is not helpful (at least the first few times the communication is noted), and ask the spouse to phrase the communication differently, perhaps providing examples. Thus the therapist might intervene as follows:

Husband: You never come up with ideas about where we can go out on the weekend. Why is it always up to me to decide?

Therapist: Bill, let me suggest that you try to stay away from words like "never" and "always." As I mentioned to you, my concern is that those types of words often create a sense of defensiveness in the other person. There is a real pull for Jean now to think of a time when she did think of what to do on the weekend. The danger is that you two will get in a disagreement over that and lose your focus on the major issue of how to decide what to do on the weekends. Try to restate your concern, this time leaving out the absolutes "always" and "never."

Pointing out the specific communication or problem-solving skill is important if the couple is to internalize the principles. Consequently, the therapist does not simply want to lead the couple through the problem solving without pointing out specific principles. Such a strategy might be effective in resolving a particular problem but does not teach a couple skills. This approach to problem solving is referred to as "traffic copping" because it resembles a policeman directing traffic to get the job done but without any attempt at teaching the motorists any skills. The next time they are at the intersection, the policeman is once again needed. Thus if a couple has drifted "off track" while problem solving, the therapist does not want to say:

Therapist: Mary, what were you saying earlier about making a list of possible places you might go on the weekend?

This intervention would successfully return the couple to the topic of discussion, but it has not pointed out to the couple that they got sidetracked and that they should try to avoid doing so in the future.

The specificity of the feedback is also important. If the couple is to alter specific behaviors, they need to know what those behaviors are. Beginning therapists often are aware that one spouse has said something inappropriate but cannot clarify or label the specific behavior. As a result, they may respond, "Bill, you are getting pretty negative with Mary. That is just going to make her defensive." Bill may know what he is to change, but he may not know. The therapist is to model clear, specific communication. At the same time, there are likely to be occasions when even the most experienced therapist considers the interaction dysfunctional but is unable to clarify the specifics that are involved. In such circumstances, the therapist can ask for the couple's help in clarifying the specifics of the interaction:

Therapist: Let's take a look at the interaction that just took place between the two of you. I'm not sure what the specifics were, but it seemed to me that in some subtle way you were trying to give each other a hard time. Did it strike you that way? [Yes.] Help me figure out specifically what you do in those instances to give each other a hard time. Bill, what was it you were doing?

Through such requests, the therapist models that one need not be all-knowing and that it is acceptable to ask for help. Also the spouses are being asked to monitor themselves, which again is important for internalizing changes that are needed in communication. Third, at times when an individual verbalizes what he or she does to bother the partner, continuing to engage in that behavior becomes too transparent and it decreases. (The examples provided above all focus on interventions for specific communications. Additional interventions will focus more broadly on the *system* of interaction displayed by the couple. These issues are discussed later in this chapter.)

After the therapist clarifies the communication skill or problem-solving step to be addressed, the final phase of the intervention is to return the couple to problem solving. The therapist can help the couple by suggesting where in the interaction they should resume. Thus, if the spouses have become emotionally aroused and have begun talking rapidly, somewhat loudly, and simultaneously, the therapist not only cautions them about interruptions but also might suggest to them how to continue their conversation:

Therapist: You've started interrupting each other. Not only does that make it hard to hear what the other has to say, but it can give the other person the sense that you don't want to hear his or her thoughts. Try to make sure that you wait for the other to finish before you start to speak. Mary, why don't you tell Bill what your concern was with trying to decide at the last moment about where to go out to eat?

When to Intervene

Because the spouses are interacting with each other on a continuous basis during the session, the therapist has numerous opportunities to intervene, and some judgments must be made regarding when to intervene. One general guideline (which has exceptions) is to intervene in early therapy sessions whenever the therapist becomes aware that one person is beginning to communicate unproductively or is not following problem-solving guidelines. That is, the intervention comes immediately in order to halt a negative chain of interactions. This is particularly important for couples who are angry with each other and who have a tendency to escalate rapidly into arguments. The message that the therapist is sending is that these types of communication are not acceptable. Early in therapy, a primary focus is given to increasing positives and eliminating negatives in order to improve the atmosphere of the relationship.

At the same time, negative communication cannot be avoided totally in the real world, and teaching the couple to respond productively when one's partner has communicated negatively is important. Couples are not provided with this opportunity if the therapist intervenes each time one spouse communicates negatively. Therefore, the therapist discusses the notion of negative reciprocity with the couple and points out the importance of both persons' being willing to respond to a negative communication in either a positive or neutral way. In order to allow the couple to practice this interaction, the therapist may wish not to intervene when one spouse communicates negatively so that the response of the partner can be monitored. The therapist should comment on this interaction *sequence* rather than focusing on only one partner's communication.

There are other reasons why a therapist may not wish to intervene immediately following each negative communication. First, if the therapist has intervened frequently with one spouse, that spouse may start to feel that he or she is being singled out or treated unfairly. If the therapist believes that it is important to intervene but is concerned that numerous recent interventions were directed to that spouse, the therapist can make the feedback less personalized to that one spouse. That is, the therapist can comment that the *couple* has a tendency to interact in a certain way. For example, in one session the therapist had frequently stopped the husband's speech. When the husband began to try to make his wife feel guilty, the therapist responded:

Therapist: Let's stop for a moment. I've noticed a pattern that both of you show. When either of you suggests a solution that involves the other person doing more work, that other person often starts pointing out how he or she is overloaded already. For example, just now, Sam, you were telling Cathy how... And last week, Cathy, when Sam was suggesting that you help out with the dishes, you...

Second, providing input on numerous types of negative communication can flood the couple or one spouse. Consequently, if the therapist decides that there is a major communication problem interfering with the couple's interaction, during a given session, the therapist might focus primarily on that specific form of communication, attending to other communication concerns only when necessary to maintain the proper atmosphere in the session.

When to provide feedback on positive interactions is somewhat more complex. Whereas immediate feedback is helpful from a learning standpoint, the intervention from the therapist also interrupts the interaction. If the spouses have been having a difficult time interacting positively with each other and then begin to do so, the therapist runs the risk of interfering with that more positive interaction by interrupting the process. Therefore, the therapist might not want to stop the couple and comment each time some positive interaction occurs. This is also true if the spouses are saying something tender or affectionate to each other. At such times, the clients probably do not want to be interrupted to have their skills commented upon. In order to avoid disrupting a positive interaction but still provide feedback, one strategy is to delay input on positive interaction. One opportunity to provide this feedback is when the couple has started to become negative or to experience communication difficulties. This does not interrupt a positive interaction and also makes the input on the negative communication easier to hear because it is coupled with some positive input.

Another opportunity to provide positive as well as negative feedback is after the couple has completed problem solving. At that point, a few minutes can be spent summarizing specific strengths and problematic aspects of the interaction that just occurred. It is often helpful to ask the spouses' to comment first, so that they can evaluate themselves. Following the couple's commentary, the therapist can add additional input about points that the couple overlooked.

These suggestions do not imply that feedback on positive interaction should never be provided immediately. Indeed, we provide a great deal of immediate positive feedback to the couple. This is particularly important for a spouse who has been receiving a large amount of negative feedback and needs to know when he or she is doing well. If the therapist is not concerned that his or her interaction will either halt a positive chain of interactions or disrupt a special moment for the couple, the feedback can be given immediately.

Controlling the Session Tempo

Couples come to sessions in various moods which influence the pace and atmosphere of the session. At times marital therapists will comment after a session that the couple was so slow in speech and flat in affect that the therapist was about to fall asleep. On the other end of the spectrum, couples may enter a session so angry that they speak rapidly, and the therapist is exhausted by the end of the session from trying to keep the interaction under control. Although a certain amount of this variability is unavoidable, the therapist can influence the tone and tempo of the session to make it more productive and enjoyable, or at least less aversive. There are two major strategies for accomplishing this goal: (a) commenting to the couple about some major pattern that appears to be influencing the interaction negatively and (b) adapting one's own behavior to influence the couple's tempo. First, if the couple speaks very rapidly, then the therapist can comment on this as a communication pattern. Each person can be asked to speak more slowly and pause before the other begins speaking. If the communication is proceeding slowly because one or both partners appear to be making little effort, are slumped in the chairs, and are not attending, the therapist can comment on the specifics, noting to the couple how this seems to be impeding the interaction.

The therapist's own tempo can affect the couple to promote the types of changes desired. If the couple appears tired or is moving through the process slowly, the therapist can set a more energetic pace through his or her own rate of speech, energy in his or her voice, and body language. If the pace of the session is slow, the therapist might sit up straight or lean forward, speak with enthusiasm, and set a positive tone by giving frequent reinforcement to the couple. Similarly, if the couple is experiencing an escalation of negative emotions, the therapist can set a more cognitive tone by stopping the couple and rationally analyzing the communication process that is occurring. Whereas these strategies can be helpful in establishing an appropriate tone and tempo for the session, they must not be relied on too heavily. A major tenet of the skills training approach is for the therapist to train the couple in communication so that the therapist becomes dispensable. Therefore, it is important that the therapist make the couple aware of and able to monitor the tone and tempo of their interactions, so that they can become proficient in producing the needed changes.

Avoiding Battles and Power Struggles with the Couple

Thus far, almost total attention has been paid to the relationship between the two spouses. However, the relationship between the spouses and the therapist also is very important. At times, one or both spouses will begin to struggle with the therapist for various reasons. If the couple is confronting a difficult issue and one of the partners feels threatened, one way of avoiding the issue is to argue with the therapist about the usefulness of the procedures. Some spouses feel the need to control interpersonal interactions and resent the therapist's position of authority. Other spouses become angry with their partners during the session but direct that anger toward the therapist because it feels safer than directing it at the partner. Conversely, some spouses will attempt to align the therapist with themselves in an attempt to disrupt the therapist's relationship with the partner. Skillful management of these situations is important if the therapist is to acknowledge couples' legitimate concerns yet not become embroiled in heated debates with the spouses.

If spouses are questioning the appropriateness of the therapeutic strategies seemingly as a way to deflect attention away from the issues being discussed, the therapist's role is to respond to the particular complaint and then make it as easy as possible for the couple to address the content issue that is being avoided. For example, one husband commented to the therapist as the couple was approaching a solution which he did not like but which seemed equitable:

Husband: This whole thing really strikes me as stupid. This problem-solving approach of yours is really simple-minded. You can't just deal with the complicated issues which we have in this way like you are dealing with some question of which shoe to put on first. It just won't work.

Therapist: I know it does seem difficult to resolve some of the issues with which you are struggling. You do have complex problems you are confronting, and you are dealing with one of those right now. I sense that you are about to adopt a solution that you are unhappy with. Remember that one of the major rules of problem solving is that you don't accept a solution that you really don't like. Don't put yourself in that awkward spot.

Dealing with spouses who need to control the session and who resent being given input is a challenge for the therapist. One husband entered the initial evaluation session, opened his briefcase, took out pen and paper, and kept notes throughout the entire session. From the beginning of therapy, he made numerous attempts to establish himself as "in charge" of the sessions, and he debated the therapist on almost every therapeutic guideline. This controlling, argumentative style also typified his interaction with his wife. Whereas the therapist might be tempted to show the person "who the boss is," such efforts usually tend to intensify the power struggle. Because control is important to such persons, the therapist should offer interventions in ways that stress the choice aspect of the person's changing his or her behavior. In response to the husband mentioned earlier in the chapter, who made numerous protests about eye contact with his wife, the therapist responded:

Therapist: I can understand that you don't want to look at your wife all the time when you are speaking. I don't really want to *suggest* that. For you, you can think more clearly when you are looking away. I'm simply *recommending* that you try to look at each other occasionally. For most people, it has the effect of making them feel closer. So if you want to try to feel closer while you are talking to each other, that is one thing *you might choose* to try. But that is clearly up to you. What I will try to do is to point out things that I think might be helpful in changing your communication to achieve certain goals. What I hope is that you will experiment with some of those changes and decide for yourself whether that helps.

Another frequent strategy exhibited by spouses is to attempt to align themselves with the therapist in an attempt to make the partner look bad. In a skills-oriented approach, this often occurs when the therapist has intervened to comment on the unproductive behavior of one spouse. In such circumstances, the partner may respond, "See, I've been telling you for years that you do that to me, and you have been denying it. Now will you admit it?" Or, stated similarly to the therapist, "Exactly, he does that all the time.

It drives me crazy. I wish you could get him to stop it." Clearly, in such circumstances the therapist wants to be certain not to alienate one partner and align with the other partner. When this type of situation occurs, the therapist might respond:

Therapist: I hope I can help you both change a number of aspects of your communication. Because we have been able to pinpoint one of those areas that might be useful for Bob to focus on doesn't mean that he is the bad guy here. You both are doing things that contribute to the difficulty you are having communicating with each other. What I hope is that as we discover those specifics, you both will be willing to attempt to interact with each other in different ways. Bob, try to tell Kay again what . . .

In the above excerpt, the therapist did not back off from the intervention in order to make Bob feel better. Nor did he use the complaint from Kay as additional leverage to get Bob to change. Instead the therapist matter-of-factly commented that this will be one area for Bob to work on and that they both will have several areas to address in their communication patterns. He made certain not to blame Bob, but rather focused on the shared interactive aspects of the communication. Finally, rather than continuing to debate the issue, the therapist returned the couple to the problem solving.

Common to many of the interventions above are the following elements: (a) acknowledging the spouse's concern; (b) empathizing if it does not place blame on one partner; (c) providing information about how the concern fits into the therapeutic goals and specific skills to be learned; (d) returning the couple to the task at hand; (e) not arguing with the person about his or her position.

SUMMARY

In this chapter, behavioral interventions have been isolated. In reality, however, the spouses' behaviors both influence and are influenced by related cognitions and emotions. Consequently, the clinician also must be attuned to these cognitions and emotions. At times, specific interventions will be needed to address these important phenomena, and Chapters 9 and 10 describe such therapeutic strategies. Chapter 10 also includes a discussion of additional behavioral interventions which focus on the expression of emotions, along with listening skills. In addition, Chapter 11 describes how the clinician can attempt to integrate therapeutic strategies for dealing with relevant behaviors, cognitions, and emotions.

9

Modification of Cognition

Although this chapter focuses on the modification of cognitive processes that contribute to marital discord and distress, in actual clinical practice a therapist works simultaneously with the relationships among cognitive, behavioral, and emotional components of dysfunctional marital interaction. As noted earlier, these three components can influence one another reciprocally, and maximal therapeutic impact is likely to occur when the treatment addresses all three. For the purpose of clear presentation, this chapter focuses on a description of cognitive restructuring procedures, but it also notes points at which a therapist would be likely to include other interventions intended to influence behaviors or emotions more directly. The details of those interventions are described in Chapters 8 and 10.

TARGETS OF COGNITIVE RESTRUCTURING

The goal of cognitive restructuring is to modify cognitive phenomena that distort spouses' experiences of their interactions, increase their distress about their marriage, and induce them to behave in destructive ways with each other. As described in Chapter 3, these phenomena include any biased *perceptions* of stimuli (external or internal), *attributions* about determinants of marital problems, *expectancies* about probabilities that particular events will occur in one's relationship under certain circumstances, *assumptions* about the characteristics of spouses and intimate relationships, and *standards* about how close relationships "should" be.

For example, through the cognitive distortion of "selective abstraction" (Beck et al., 1979) a husband may have a biased *perception* of the way his wife treats him. He may notice only the critical comments his wife made during a discussion and fail to notice that for the first time in months she had taken the initiative to approach him and say, "There are some things I have been unhappy about, but I really want to work them out smoothly with you because I care about our marriage." Alternatively, the man may in fact perceive his wife's positive behavior but discount its significance by means of an *attribution* that she acted that way "only because she wanted to get my attention so that she'd have another chance to blast me with criticism." His attribution might be correct, but it also might be quite inaccurate and based on an "arbitrary inference" (Beck et al., 1979).

Similarly, this man may have an *expectancy* that any time he voices his opinions to his wife she will almost certainly respond with anger and criticism. Because he finds these anticipated responses aversive, he chooses to avoid self-disclosure with his wife. However, there are at least two ways in which this expectancy may be inaccurate: (a) if the frequency with which his wife would react negatively is significantly lower in general than he estimates it, or (b) if he has failed to differentiate particular circumstances when she is highly likely to be critical (e.g., when he begins a conversation with a criticism of her) from those situations when she is unlikely to respond negatively. In the first case, the man's overall probability estimate is inaccurate, and in the second case he has not developed accurate conditional probability estimates.

In terms of *assumptions*, the man in this example may be upset about his marriage because he assumes that open conflict between partners is a sure sign of serious problems in their relationship. Whatever the source of this assumption may have been (e.g., the "vivid" experience of growing up in a family troubled by chronic parental arguments and obvious marital dissatisfaction), once he has assigned his own marriage to the category "a relationship in trouble," he is likely to assume that a variety of other characteristics also fit the marriage. As we noted in Chapter 3, it is likely that the man's assumptions about correlations among characteristics and events in his marriage will shape many of his attributions and expectancies about the marriage.

This husband's distress also may be elicited by the failure of his marriage to meet his personal *standards* about how a "good" marriage should be. For example, he may be angry with his wife because he believes that in a good marriage the spouses should provide unqualified support of one another. Furthermore, he may go so far as to evaluate it as "terrible" or "intolerable" for one spouse to criticize the other, thereby intensifying his negative emotional response to the violation of his standard.

As discussed previously, it is often the particular *combination* of two spouses' standards that produces problems in a relationship. For example, one person's standard that disagreement should be avoided can itself create communication and problem-solving difficulties for the couple, but the degree of distress in the relationship may be even more intense if the other spouse holds the standard that a marriage is the one setting in life where one can really "let your hair down" and disclose all thoughts and feelings. Consequently, it is important to consider as treatment targets both the individual standards of the two parties and the interaction of the two individuals' standards.

As described in the earlier chapter on cognitive assessment, the selection of particular types of cognitions as targets for treatment is an ongoing process throughout the course of therapy. Although there often are common themes in the cognitions each spouse experiences during a variety of distressing marital interactions, his or her range of idiosyncratic perceptions, attributions, expectancies, assumptions, and standards can be substantial. Consequently, the therapist and each client must collaborate continually in identifying the relevant cognitions in each disturbing marital interaction. One cannot assume that the cognitive treatment targets identified during the initial assessment period will be the appropriate targets throughout therapy.

GOALS OF COGNITIVE RESTRUCTURING

At the broadest level, the major goal of the restructuring process is to identify and modify aspects of each spouse's cognitions (perceptions, attributions, expectancies, assumptions, and standards) that produce dysfunctional emotions and behaviors during marital interactions. Central in this process are procedures whereby evidence is collected to determine how valid or reasonable each individual's cognitions about the relationship are. When the evidence indicates that an individual's perceptions, attributions, expectancies, and assumptions about an event in his or her marriage are accurate, and that his or her standards about the nature of an intimate relationship are realistic, the focus of therapy is likely to shift toward modifying other aspects of the marital interactions (e.g., the couple's problem-solving skills) rather than cognitive restructuring. However, when the evidence indicates that a spouse's cognitions are biased or unrealistic, the goal of cognitive restructuring procedures is to substitute more appropriate cognitions. It is assumed that much marital distress is due to events that most clear-thinking individuals would find displeasing, but that a significant proportion of the distress in many discordant marriages is due to some degree of cognitive distortion. Cognitive-behavioral marital therapy is intended to help spouses identify cognitive components of their marital problems and modify these in a systematic manner.

It is a premise of a cognitive-behavioral approach to therapy that people typically do not question their own thinking. As noted earlier, an individual's stream-of-consciousness thoughts tend to occur in a reflexive manner and are quite plausible to the individual. The perceptions, attributions, expectancies, assumptions, and standards reflected in these "automatic thoughts" (Beck et al., 1979) constitute the individual's reality at that moment. In addition, even when another person uses logic and data to challenge an individual's basic assumptions and standards about the nature of relationships, these usually are such longstanding parts of the individual's life philosophy that they are resistant to change. Consequently, the cognitive-behavioral marital therapist's approach to testing the validity and reasonableness of cognitions may make sense to many clients but still will seem foreign to them in practice. For some others, the whole concept of questioning one's thinking may seem repugnant. The therapist must be prepared to "socialize" clients into this approach, providing a clear and convincing rationale for cognitive restructuring and providing some reassurance to those individuals who are skeptical or threatened by its concepts.

TEACHING COUPLES THE COGNITIVE MODEL

The concept of cognitive distortion and the rationale for cognitive restructuring often are more difficult to convey to distressed marital partners than to clients who have sought therapy for more individually oriented problems such as depression and anxiety. Whereas the depressed person often recognizes the existence of persistent negative thinking as part of the depressive syndrome (Beck et al., 1979) and welcomes methods for counteracting it, distressed spouses often attribute their upset to the interactions they have with their partners and blame the partner for the problems (Baucom, 1987; Fincham, 1985; Pretzer et al., 1985). Some unhappy spouses may react initially to the idea that cognitions may be distorted or unreasonable by saying, "You must think I'm imagining all these problems!" The therapist then has the job of walking the fine line between assuring the client that his or her identification of real problems is not being dismissed and, on the other hand, introducing the idea that cognitive distortion can occur and can impede spouses' abilities to notice and build on whatever positive aspects exist in their relationship.

It generally is helpful to introduce the basic rationale of cognitive-behavioral marital therapy to a couple before starting any systematic cognitive assessment or treatment. However, it may be much easier to do so if the therapist already has conducted an initial assessment of the couple's presenting problems and thus has some data from their reports to illustrate a description of the cognitive model for them. For example, if in the course of describing one of their recent fights one member of a couple contradicts an inference the other made, the therapist can use this material to raise the idea that perceptions and interpretations of events can be subjective and should be tested. The following illustrates this process.

Husband: I had been out playing softball with friends and had told Julie that I'd be home before dark. The game went on longer than I expected, and then people hung around talking afterward. When I pulled my car into the driveway, it had been dark for a while. I knew that Julie must be furious, because all the lights in the house were out except one upstairs in our bedroom. When I walked into the bedroom and asked her why she didn't leave a light on for me downstairs, she just blew up and said that I only think of myself.

Wife: Well, what did you expect when you didn't even say hello and started grilling me about the lights?

Therapist: Bob, what was it that you figured had Julie so upset with you at the time?

Husband: That I was late and hadn't kept my word.

Wife: No, Bob, I was upset at the way you charged into the room and started questioning me about the lights. You usually end up playing later than you think you will, so I figured you'd be late and planned to get some chores and reading done.

Husband: Then why were all the lights off if you weren't angry about the game?

Wife: When I decided to read in bed it was still light out, and I got involved in the book and didn't even realize it had gotten dark!

Therapist: Julie, were you upset with Bob for being late?

Wife: No. I don't like his staying out late, and we've had arguments about being on time in a variety of situations, but I've gotten used to the softball routine and just make other plans for myself. I was actually having a nice time reading.

Therapist: So, Bob, were you assuming that the lights were off downstairs because Julie was angry with you for being late and left them off because of that?

Husband: Yes. She locked me out of the house once when I was late.

Wife: Now wait a minute! You know that was different! That time you . . .

Therapist: (interrupting): Well, I think this is a good example of something we look at very closely in this kind of marital therapy. What seems to have happened is that the two of you had very different interpretations about what was going on between you, and each of your views got you pretty upset with the other person. Bob, you arrived at home and automatically assumed that the lights being out meant that Julie was angry at you and left them off intentionally. Certainly, that was one possible reason for their being off, but Julie has described an alternative reason. You may have been more likely to assume that it was intentional because of a past event which you remembered that seemed similar. You walked into the bedroom expecting trouble, and your questioning Julie about the lights seems to have followed from what you assumed was going on between the two of you. However, Julie, you have said that you were not angry with Bob until he questioned you about the lights. At this point you both were upset and got into a shouting match.

This type of sequence of events occurs frequently when couples fight. When one person assumes that he or she knows what the other person's behavior means, the assumption may be accurate, but when it isn't, the person still gets as upset as if it were true. Bob, based on what Julie has said, you may have had much less to worry about when you got home than you assumed. Unfortunately, that got lost in the midst of the fight the two of you got into. Also, it seems that your assumption was based on a prior experience, but at this point I don't have enough information to tell how it was similar and how it might have been different. What is important in this kind of therapy is for both of you to develop a new habit of "second guessing" your assumptions. Many of them may turn out to be valid, but if any of them are invalid it is important to be aware of that, because that knowledge can prevent fights from developing. Cognitive-behavioral marital therapy is designed to help you take an approach to marital problems somewhat similar to the approach a scientist takes to answering questions. The basic approach is to gather evidence to discover which of your views about problems that occur in your relationship are accurate or reasonable, and which may not be the most accurate or reasonable ways to interpret what you see happening. Then your approach to solving a problem will be based on a clear picture of what is contributing to the difficulties between the two of you.

The above is one example of how a therapist could introduce some concepts from the cognitive model by using illustrative material from a couple's own interactions. The last extended description by the therapist may seem to be a monologue that would lose clients' attention, but the therapist could break the presentation into segments, asking for questions and reactions from the couple. However, the above example does represent the type of content that is useful when a therapist initially presents a couple with a basic rationale for the cognitive component of cognitive-behavioral treatment.

When a therapist first introduces concepts of the cognitive model by means of such personal illustrations, it is important that the examples include inappropriate cognitions (e.g., inaccurate perceptions or attributions) on the part of *both* spouses. In the above example, it is possible that the husband will interpret the therapist's comments as singling him out as the identified patient. The therapist should try to find examples where both parties have made perceptual or inferential errors that can be noted. Early in therapy, when the spouses may be quite sensitive to the issue of who is to blame for their marital problems, using only one person's material to illustrate the model can be problematic. We also consider it prudent to avoid challenging either partner's basic assumptions and standards at this point, because doing so before the therapist has built clients' confidence in the cognitive model and methods can elicit quite a bit of defensiveness.

In addition to presenting clients a general theoretical rationale for cognitive-behavioral procedures, it often is helpful to identify the major types of cognitive phenomena that will be the foci of the couple's treatment. Brief descriptions of the characteristics of perceptions, common forms of causal attributions, expectancies, assumptions, and relationship standards can be given, and it might even be noted that recent research has linked these variables with marital distress. At this point in therapy, it is less important that clients remember all of the details about the cognitive model than that they understand the basic concept of cognitive mediation. However, presentation of the more detailed material may increase the credibility of the approach for some individuals.

The socialization of clients into the cognitive-behavioral treatment approach involves not only presenting a theoretical rationale, but also providing information about the general "philosophy" of this approach (i.e., a skeptical and empirical approach to the assumptions all people make about life events). Furthermore, it is important to prepare clients for the degrees of structure and directiveness characteristic of the treatment. For example, in terms of structure, the therapist commonly notes that sessions usually begin with the setting of an agenda and that the couple is expected to spend additional time working on their relationship between sessions by completing "homework" assignments. The therapist explains that a typical session agenda includes a brief review of the couple's past week, a check on their current emotional states, review of their homework assignment from the last session, selection of one or more issues for discussion during the current session, collaboration between the therapist and couple on the design of a new homework assignment, and feedback from the couple about their reactions to the session.

Concerning directiveness of the treatment, the therapist commonly tells the couple that unlike some approaches to therapy, in cognitive-behavioral marital therapy the therapist often will make direct comments and suggestions to them. It is stressed that it is *not* the therapist's intention to tell them what to do, and that all suggestions are offered in a collaborative spirit. The therapist explains that it is his or her role to act as an expert consultant who provides input they can use in testing their own cognitions and exploring alternative ways of viewing events in their relationship.

Some clients initially are concerned that a treatment labeled "cognitive-behavioral" will not deal with the very unpleasant emotions they are experiencing in their relationship. One possible therapist response to such a concern is as follows:

Therapist: In fact, this approach to working with marital problems places a lot of importance on the emotions you are feeling. It is called "cognitive-behavioral" because it focuses on how the many emotions that spouses experience when their marriage is not going well can be influenced significantly by the behavioral patterns in the couple's interactions, and by the ways in which the two people interpret each other's behavior. I would like you to pay close attention to your emotional reactions to the events in your relationship, because these will be important cues about the specific things going on in the marriage that mean a lot to you. We then can determine what changes in the way you two behave toward each other would create a more satisfying relationship. We also can identify whether there are times when you have become upset or dissatisfied owing to a misunderstanding or misinterpretation of your spouse's behaviors. The end goal of the cognitive-behavioral procedures is to form a relationship that is a source of more pleasant emotions for both spouses.

Another concern raised by some clients is that the procedures of cognitive-behavioral therapy will not alter what they perceive as their partner's ingrained personality traits. Of course, such attributions are one of the major targets of this therapy, and having the client raise this issue at the outset of treatment provides the therapist's first opportunity for cognitive restructuring. However, it is our experience that it is risky to challenge this type of attribution too strongly before establishing rapport and a working relationship with the clients. On the other hand, one cannot ignore the client's concern, because people who make trait attributions can experience a sense of helplessness and hopelessness about solving their marital problems (Doherty, 1981a; Pretzer et al., 1985) and might even drop out of treatment.

One strategy that often is useful in alleviating a client's initial concern that this therapy will not address what seem to be longstanding traits is to first acknowledge that the spouses indeed have described some distressing persistent patterns in their interaction. Then the therapist introduces the idea that many couples are able to make changes in such patterns that are extensive enough to raise their marital satisfaction significantly. This does not entail changing either partner's basic personality, but it does mean working consistently for a period of time to alter the specific aspects of marital interaction that have been upsetting. Because many clients who speak of problematic personality traits also expect interminable treatment, it also is helpful to propose a time-limited therapeutic contract (e.g., three months), followed by a review of progress and a decision about further therapy. By setting this type of contract, the therapist communicates to the couple that there is reason to believe that some changes will be evident within a fairly short time.

ROLE OF THE THERAPIST

The goal of a cognitive-behavioral marital therapist is not only to modify cognitions that are producing spouses' current distress, but also to teach the couple specific skills for identifying and modifying dysfunctional cognitions in the future. The preventive aspect of this approach is quite important. Consequently, the therapist assumes the roles of consultant and teacher, providing expert information and observation, on the one hand, and developing the spouses' own cognitive-behavioral skills, on the other hand.

Both aspects of the therapist's role require at least a moderate degree of activity and directiveness. As noted earlier, the therapist at times gives brief lectures about principles, concepts, and techniques of this type of therapy. The couple is given handouts such as those included in this chapter (Figure 9-1, Table 9-1, Table 9-2), as a further means of presenting didactic material. As the therapist introduces each component of cognitive restructuring (e.g., identifying one's stream-of-consciousness "automatic thoughts," testing the validity of an attribution, evaluating the reasonableness of a standard), he or she generally gives a brief didactic presentation, models the appropriate skill, and coaches the spouses in practicing the new skill during the session. When clients have demonstrated some proficiency at using a new cognitive skill during a session, the therapist helps them design a homework assignment in which they will practice the skill further.

It is likely that the degree of therapist activity and directiveness during these skill-building procedures will vary according to each couple's initial skill level and the ease with which they learn the new concepts and techniques. One should also monitor clients' reactions to therapist directiveness; that is, some people want a considerable amount of guidance from a therapist and others want more autonomy. Thus, the therapist must make clinical decisions in each marital case, varying the degree of directiveness in terms of the therapist's own preferred style, the clients' abilities to function on their own, and the clients' preferences.

When the therapist notices that a spouse's perception or interpretation of his or her partner's behavior is faulty, or that the person seems to be applying an unrealistic standard to his or her relationship, it may be tempting to engage in a debate with the client about "the facts." However, our experience is that such debates generally are ineffective in producing cognitive change, and they may establish an adversarial relationship between the therapist and client. Consequently, the therapist tends to be more effective by adopting a *collaborative* relationship with the couple, guiding them toward taking a close, objective look at the evidence concerning the appropriateness of a particular cognition but allowing them to draw their own conclusions from the data. At times when they seem to draw the "wrong" conclusion, the therapist may be better off waiting until another opportunity arises to challenge a similar cognition than forcing the issue with the present cognition. Over time, a collaborative therapeutic relationship may make clients more open to input from the therapist.

INTERVENTION STRATEGIES

To date there are no research data available to identify whether there is an optimal sequence of cognitive and behavioral interventions for marital problems. Also, as noted earlier, the cognitive-behavioral therapist continually monitors the ongoing interactions of a couple for instances of perceptual distortions, inferential errors, and unrealistic assumptions and standards and tends to intervene to modify these as they occur, on an ad hoc basis. However, in our clinical experience we have found that there is a sequence in which the cognitive restructuring procedures of cognitive-behavioral marital therapy tend to unfold most logically and smoothly.

As described earlier, the therapist's first task is to elicit a description of presenting problems from a couple, and to assess the degrees to which inappropriate cognitions and behavioral excesses and deficits seem to contribute to those problems. The second task involves the socialization of the couple into the cognitive-behavioral model in the manner described above. Because our therapeutic approach depends so much on collaboration between the couple and therapist, we devote as much time as is necessary to teaching couples basic concepts (e.g., the general cognitive mediation model; important types of potentially problematic cognitions such as attributions) and illustrating those concepts for the couple with material from their own interactions, particularly the "here and now" interactions that occur during sessions. We typically review basic principles with couples periodically during therapy to consolidate their learning and to prepare them for the introduction of additional concepts and procedures.

The major intervention strategies in a cognitive-behavioral approach involve training spouses to be attuned to their cognitive processing of events in their relationship and skilled at testing the validity or appropriateness of their cognitions. We tend to begin by building spouses' skills for identifying and modifying their own stream-of-consciousness cognitions ("automatic thoughts" in Beck's model) at a generic level. In other words, our initial goal is to increase a couple's awareness of *any* thoughts (and visual images in many cases) that are associated with their emotional and behavioral responses to events in their relationship. Some clients already are introspective and attuned to these cognitions, whereas others need some degree of guidance in noticing them.

When spouses have demonstrated an ability to monitor their cognitions, we then move toward helping them identify instances of perceptions, attributions, expectancies, assumptions, and standards in their stream-of-consciousness thinking. It is our experience that all five types of cognition can be identified in the ongoing thoughts of most spouses. Sometimes an individual will express a cognition such as an attribution quite directly when describing his or her automatic thoughts (e.g., "I was angry when he didn't say hello to my brother, because I could tell that he was ignoring him on purpose"). However, at times a therapist needs to probe for an upsetting cognition through a Socratic inquiry. For example, in the above situation the woman initially might only report, "I was angry when he didn't say hello to my brother, because my brother was standing right in front of him!" Open-ended questions by the therapist, such as "What was it about seeing your brother standing right in front of Jim and seeing Jim not say hello that made you angry?" often can elicit the "bottom line" upsetting thought, such as an attribution concerning the spouse's negative intentions.

For some clients, perceptions, attributions, and expectancies are more accessible cognitions than assumptions and standards. In other words, it is our experience that quite a few individuals are not as aware of their broad, longstanding assumptions and standards about characteristics of people and relationships as they are of their perceptions, attributions, and expectancies. Perhaps this is due to the fact that many of the latter forms of cognition are specific to the here-and-now events in the couple's interaction, whereas assumptions and standards often are global schemata that the individual applies to people and relationships in general. At times it is only through examination of repetitive themes in a person's automatic thoughts in a variety of situations regarding the partner that a therapist and client can deduce the individual's basic assumption or standard that has elicited distress in all of those situations. Also, unless a spouse has expressed an assumption or standard quite clearly, without sampling his or her thoughts regarding upsetting marital events in a number of situations, the therapist runs the risk of making inaccurate inferences about the specific nature of the client's assumptions and standards. There is a danger that once a therapist (or client) has made a premature and inaccurate inference about the content of a particular assumption or standard, new data that are inconsistent with the identified theme may be ignored. The result may be misdirected efforts toward modifying an assumption or standard that is not, in fact, one of the central determinants of the person's marital distress.

The following are descriptions of the major procedures used during the sequence of cognitive restructuring in our work with distressed couples. They are presented in the order typical of the course of treatment.

Building Skills for Identifying and Modifying Cognitions

A therapist might introduce the concept of stream-of-consciousness cognitions or "automatic thoughts" (Beck et al., 1979) in the following manner.

Therapist: As I described earlier, it isn't simply the ways that spouses behave toward one another that make them upset, but also it is what those behaviors *mean* to each person. Two people's spouses might behave in exactly the same way, but one recipient might be much more upset about the behavior because of what it means to that person. We all interpret each other's behaviors, and these interpretations occur almost instantaneously. In cognitive-behavioral therapy, the thoughts that occur in this instantaneous and unplanned manner are called "automatic thoughts." When we have automatic thoughts, they seem highly plausible; in other words, our thoughts about our relationships seem quite accurate and reasonable to us at the time. Our emotional reactions to another person, as well as the way in which we behave toward him or her, depend on how our automatic thoughts portray the situation. For example, a person who believes that his or her spouse did something hurtful intentionally may be more likely to feel angry and seek revenge than someone who interprets the partner's behavior as accidental.

When automatic thoughts are accurate and reasonable, they allow a person to "size up" a situation quickly and respond appropriately. However, automatic thoughts often can be inaccurate, even when they seem to be true. When a person's automatic thoughts about a spouse are inaccurate, they can lead the person to be quite upset with the spouse and to behave in a very negative manner that is not appropriate to the actual situation. Also, some automatic thoughts may involve unreasonable standards that a person is setting for his or her relationship. For example, it may be unreasonable for a person to believe that spouses should *never* disagree with each other, because it is highly unlikely that any relationship could live up to that standard. Consequently, as long as the individual clings to such a belief, he or she will be upset about his or her relationship. In cognitive-behavioral marital therapy, it is crucial for each spouse to become aware of the automatic thoughts he or she has about events in the marriage and to separate the accurate and reasonable ones from those that are inaccurate or extreme.

Monitoring one's automatic thoughts may not be as easy as it sounds. Because automatic thoughts occur so quickly, you may not always be aware that they are flitting through your mind. However, with some practice it is possible to spot their occurrence. A very useful cue that you probably are experiencing some automatic thoughts is to notice when either your emotions or your behavior toward your spouse has shifted. For example, if during a conversation with your spouse you suddenly notice that you feel irritated or that you are speaking more loudly and rapidly, this often indicates that you have interpreted the other person's behavior in a manner that is getting you upset. At this point, it is important to notice what automatic thoughts were running through your mind at the time. They are likely to reveal what your spouse's behavior meant to you, and therefore why you became upset.

Again, a long didactic description such as this may be presented in segments, with the therapist periodically asking the couple whether they have any questions and even asking them questions about the basic concepts to ensure that they have understood the material. Because the process of monitoring automatic thoughts is new to most clients, it usually is necessary to present the above concepts a few times during therapy, until it is clear that both spouses understand them and are applying them.

A didactic presentation on automatic thoughts can be aided by the use of illustrative handouts, such as the cartoon in Figure 9-1. Most couples see some humor in the cartoon but also quickly grasp the idea that the

Figure 9-1. *Example of cognitive and behavioral factors in a couple's interactions.* Conceived by James L. Pretzer and drawn by R. Robert Robinson, Jr. Reprinted with permission.

depicted wife's upset, as well as the conflict that is likely to follow, is influenced by her inaccurate interpretation of her husband's behavior. Couples also commonly note that the spouses in the cartoon seem to have different standards for defining caring behavior (a good introduction to the concept of relationship standards) and that this upsetting event might not have occurred if the couple communicated more directly (a good opportunity to emphasize the value of the expressiveness training component of this therapy).

We typically spend a few sessions helping spouses identify the automatic thoughts they had during recent upsetting events that occurred outside the therapy office, as well as those that occur during their marital interactions in the office. We coach them in noticing when their moods and behavior change in response to something the other person said or did, and in monitoring any thoughts and visual images they experienced at that time. If an individual states, "I didn't *think* anything; I just *felt* upset," we ask the person to describe the "feelings." Often clients initially do not distinguish between thoughts and emotions, and their descriptions of feelings frequently include cognitive content.

After the therapist and couple have spent time in sessions practicing identifying each spouse's automatic thoughts, the couple is assigned homework in which each partner independently monitors his or her automatic thoughts during marital interactions that occur at home. Each spouse is to keep a written log of situations that elicited either positive or negative emotions, using forms such as the Daily Record of Dysfunctional Thoughts (DRDT; Beck et al., 1979).

Introducing the concepts of cognitive distortions.

Once a couple has been taught about the basic characteristics of automatic thoughts, it is helpful to introduce them to the common information-processing errors that Beck and his associates (Beck & Emery, 1985; Beck et al., 1979) have argued produce the distortions in automatic thoughts. A therapist can describe the distinction between the *content* of an automatic thought and its *logical structure*. The clients can be given brief descriptions of cognitive distortions such as arbitrary inference, selective abstraction, and dichotomous thinking, perhaps with a handout (see Table 9-1) that provides definitions and examples of each distortion. We have found that it is less important that couples memorize the list of distortions than that they become sensitized to the potential for such distortion in their own thoughts. Knowledge about systematic cognitive distortions often helps couples adopt an orientation toward examining how valid or reasonable their thoughts about their relationship are. Again, there is no clear evidence regarding when the optimal time may be for introducing information about cognitive distortions, but our clinical experience suggests that information overload is less likely to occur if the therapist waits to provide didactic material about distortions until spouses seem adept at monitoring and reporting their automatic thoughts.

TABLE 9-1
Cognitive Distortions

The following are several ways in which individuals may distort information when thinking about events in their lives, including aspects of their marriage. Improving a marriage requires that one take as realistic a view of the relationship's strengths and problems as possible. Consequently, it is important that spouses be able to identify instances when their thoughts about their relationship are distorted.

ARBITRARY INFERENCE: This involves drawing a conclusion that is not based on clear evidence. An individual may draw such an arbitrary conclusion either

(continued)

TABLE 9-1 (*continued*)

when there is no evidence available, or in the face of evidence that contradicts the conclusion.

Example: When Ted told Joan about an argument that he had with a co-worker, she joked about the "crazy" people in his office. Ted made an arbitrary inference that Joan's joking reflected a lack of respect for his concerns about his job. Later, Joan was able to tell Ted that she had joked in an effort to cheer him up.

SELECTIVE ABSTRACTION: This involves focusing one's attention on only some aspects of a situation, while failing to notice other aspects. The individual concludes that the noticed aspects represent the nature of the situation.

Example: Cheryl became angry at Tom when she saw his list of proposed guests for their upcoming party, because he had omitted an old friend of hers. When she concluded, "You didn't take my needs into account when you made that list," she overlooked the fact that he had listed a number of her business associates whom he hardly knew.

OVERGENERALIZATION: This occurs when an individual draws a broad conclusion based on a limited number of incidents. The individual assumes that what held in those isolated incidents holds in general, in other situations.

Example: When Mary chose to work on a project for her job all day Sunday instead of taking Bob up on his suggestion to spend the day together, Bob concluded that he could not count on Mary to put much effort into their relationship.

MAGNIFICATION AND MINIMIZATION: This involves either exaggerating or minimizing the significance of an event. The individual is either overestimating or underestimating the importance of the event.

Example: When Susan and Sam had an argument about her parents, Susan concluded that their marriage was falling apart (magnification). Although Susan appeared upset for the rest of the day, Sam did not ask her about her feelings because he had concluded that the fight was of little consequence and that "it will all blow over" (minimization).

PERSONALIZATION: With this distortion, the individual concludes that events are related to himself or herself, when this is not the case.

Example: When Stan walked into the living room and Doris appeared irritated when he asked her a question, he concluded that she was upset with him for some reason unknown to him. In fact, she was irritable because she had been thinking about how her boss had failed to acknowledge her contribution to a project at work that day.

DICHOTOMOUS THINKING: This involves viewing aspects of the world in all-or-nothing terms. The individual fails to see "shades of gray" between two extreme opposite positions. One common sign that spouses are engaging in dichotomous thinking is when they describe each other with terms such as "You *always*..." and "You *never*...."

Example: Laura and George frequently argued about their different opinions about how children should be disciplined. During these arguments, Laura thought (and expressed to George) her view that "he doesn't know *anything* about teaching children how to behave. If we don't do it my way, the children will be totally out of control."

EMOTIONAL REASONING: The individual who engages in emotional reasoning equates subjective personal experiences such as emotions with facts. In general, the person's line of thinking is "If I *feel* as if something is so, it must be so."

Example: Vince and June had been married for several years, and Vince increasingly noticed that he felt a lack of warmth and sexual feelings for June. Based on these feelings, Vince concluded that he must have fallen out of love with June and that he no longer was emotionally involved with her. However, further exploration with the couple revealed that they both had heavy work schedules and tended to overlook the importance of sharing time alone together on a regular basis. When the couple experimented with scheduling time together doing things that they used to enjoy sharing, Vince found that he still felt much affection for June but had to find ways of coping with his anxiety about getting his work done.

These definitions of cognitive distortions are based on those presented in Beck et al. (1979) and Burns (1980). The present examples focus on how the distortions can influence spouses' responses to aspects of their relationships.

Introducing the concepts of perceptions, attributions, expectancies, assumptions, and standards.

Once a couple is familiar with the cognitive model of relationship problems and the "automatic" nature of thought processes, usually after a few sessions, the therapist can describe the five major types of cognition commonly associated with problems in marital interaction. The initial didactic presentation concerning *perceptions* can include a description of how people are unlikely to be able to notice all of the information available in a situation, and that if two people notice different aspects of the same situation they probably will have different reactions to it. In order to illustrate how people generally make incomplete observations of their environment, one can invoke examples of how people who have witnessed an incident such as an auto accident or a crime often cannot recall major characteristics of events

and people's appearances. This process also can be demonstrated to a couple by tape-recording them as they have a discussion in the therapist's office and then asking each partner to report memories of the discussion.
Discrepancies between the two individuals' perceptions of the same event can
be noted, and the tape can be replayed to test the accuracy of each person's
perceptions.

The therapist can introduce the concept of *attributions* by describing
how people seek to understand the causes of events that occur in their lives,
in order to make sense of the world and to allow them to predict events. This
description also can include a brief review of some of the major types of attributions that distressed couples tend to make about positive and negative
events in their marriages (i.e., a summary of the research described in Chapter
3 concerning global-specific, stable-unstable, and self-versus-partner blame
attributional dimensions, as well as attributions about malicious intent and
lack of love).

Whenever possible, it is helpful to illustrate particular problematic attributions with material from the couple's own relationship. For example, in
the situation described earlier where the husband arrived home late and concluded that his wife left the house lights off intentionally, the therapist could
discuss the attributional process as follows.

Therapist: Bob, it is my understanding that when you saw that the lights were
off downstairs you concluded that Julie left them off intentionally. Is that
what you concluded?

Husband: Yes, I did. Especially because she has acted that way before. A few weeks
earlier, she locked me out of the house when I was late getting home from
work.

Wife: Yeah, but that was after you made a specific promise to be home in time
to go to that political meeting I wanted to attend, and you showed up two
hours late!

Therapist: Bob, what is it that you conclude about Julie when you think about
how the lights were off this time and she locked you out the other time?

Husband: What I conclude is that she's a vindictive person.

Therapist: Do you mean that she takes revenge whenever you do something she
dislikes or just on occasion?

Husband: She does it consistently. That's the kind of person she is.

Therapist: Bob, it seems that you were making two kinds of attributions about
Julie's behavior that were very upsetting to you. First, you saw that the lights
were off and attributed that to an intentional choice on Julie's part. Second,
you attribute that behavior to a stable personality trait of "vengefulness,"
so you don't see it as varying from situation to situation. Your seeing that
trait in Julie may make you more likely to see events such as the "lights out"
situation as intentional on her part. What is important here is to find out

how accurate your attributions about the causes of her behavior were. If it is true that Julie left the lights off intentionally, then we need to deal with her reasons for doing that. However, if she left them off by accident, as she has stated, then it was your attribution about her intentions that got you upset, rather than her actual intentions or behavior. Similarly, if it is true that Julie *always* acts in a vengeful manner owing to a personality trait, I can see how you would be concerned that you are dealing with an ingrained pattern that could be difficult to change. However, if in fact Julie has acted in a vengeful manner only on occasion and has responded in a different way at other times when you were late, this suggests that we need to figure out what goes on between the two of you that leads to the problems in certain situations. In other words, attributions about malicious intent make most people pretty angry, and attributions that a spouse has negative personality traits tend to make people feel hopeless about improvement. Each of you needs to identify what attributions you make about the causes of each other's behavior and to test how accurate each attribution is. It often can be a relief to discover that a negative attribution you have about your partner is not accurate, or not the most reasonable explanation for the events that have occurred.

Similarly, the concept of negative *expectancies* can be introduced by describing how people tend to make predictions about the ways their partner will respond in particular situations. The therapist can explain that accurate expectancies allow people to prepare for events in daily living and to make choices about how they will behave, based on the consequences that are likely to result from alternative behaviors. However, when a person's predictions are inaccurate, his or her choices and behaviors are likely to be inappropriate. It is helpful to illustrate this point with examples, both hypothetical and from the couple's own experiences.

The concept of *assumptions* can be introduced by describing how people, based on their life experiences, develop ideas about how particular characteristics of individuals and relationships are associated with other characteristics. Rather than attempting to convey this concept at an abstract level, the therapist can illustrate it with concrete examples, such as an individual assuming that the more outgoing a person is the less anxiety that person tends to have about meeting new people. It can be noted that such assumptions develop from a variety of sources, including direct observation of people, models presented in the mass media, and verbal instruction from other people such as parents.

Next, the therapist can note that many of a person's assumptions can be quite accurate reflections of the world (in terms of both the direction and magnitude of the assumed correlation between two characteristics), but other assumptions may be inaccurate. This point can be illustrated with a variety of examples that will be obvious to most people. For example, clients generally readily see that a person who assumes a strong positive correlation between an individual's height and his or her ability as a basketball player is failing to take into account that some tall people may lack coordination and some short people may have good coordination.

The therapist then might return to the earlier example of an assumption about a strong correlation between outgoing behavior and absence of social anxiety. At this point, it is useful to ask clients whether they can think of situations in which an anxious person still might behave in an outgoing manner, or in which a very calm person might act reserved. Clients usually have little trouble imagining major exceptions to the basic assumption. Then, the therapist can stress that even those assumptions that initially may seem quite plausible should be examined carefully, because they may have major limitations that were not apparent at first glance.

In addition, the therapist may describe how all people develop "scripts" about sequences of events that normally occur in particular situations, and how individuals tend to be surprised and often upset when events do not unfold according to the script. Concrete examples from everyday life (e.g., the sequence of events that occur when people eat in a restaurant, including the typical behaviors of the host or hostess, the diners, and the waiters or waitresses) are helpful for illustrating this concept. Again, it usually is easy for clients to see how people (including themselves) have many such internalized scripts, and how they could become quite confused if events did not fit their assumptions (e.g., if in a restaurant the waiters did not take meal orders but all sat down at one of the empty tables and started playing cards).

It also is stressed to clients that spouses commonly have developed sets of scripts about typical behaviors of partners in a close relationship, and that their behaviors toward one another are likely to be guided by such assumptions. It is important to note how the accuracy of such assumptions as estimates of typical sequences of events between spouses in particular situations can vary significantly, so that a person might behave in an inappropriate manner if his or her script for role behaviors in a situation differs from the scripts of other people who are involved in the interaction. A concrete example of this point is the situation where a visitor to another culture behaves as would be appropriate at home and offends his or her foreign hosts by unwittingly violating a social custom of their culture.

Relationship *standards* can be introduced as concepts about how a relationship "should" be, which a person has learned through a variety of life experiences, and by which he or she conducts his or her marriage or evaluates the quality of the marriage.

TABLE 9-2
Common Dysfunctional Relationship Standards

1. Spouses should be able to sense each other's needs and thoughts as if they could read each other's mind.

2. One should be a perfect sexual partner.

3. In order to demonstrate his/her love, a spouse must (do X).

4. Over the course of a relationship, being in love should feel like (some version of "the bells ringing").

5. You do not have to be polite to your partner, as you would be to an acquaintance, friend, or stranger.

6. In a close relationship, spouses should meet all of each other's needs.

7. A person is fully responsible for maintaining his or her spouse's happiness in life.

8. Spouses should be completely supportive of all of each other's ideas and actions.

This list is not intended to be comprehensive. There are many other unrealistic standards that people may apply to their relationships. Because real-life intimate relationships are unlikely to meet any of these standards, spouses who believe in them commonly are distressed about their marriages.

A didactic presentation about standards can be illustrated with examples of common unrealistic standards about intimate relationships, such as those included in Eidelson and Epstein's (1982) Relationship Belief Inventory (see Chapter 5) and other such standards listed in Table 9-2. Many distressed couples have little difficulty seeing the relevance of standards to their problems, especially because they often enter therapy complaining about discrepancies between their basic philosophies regarding the nature of a satisfactory marriage. However, spouses often are much less likely to see their own standards as unrealistic than to see those of their partner as extreme and problematic.

Building skills for identifying assumptions and standards.

Although it is fairly common for an individual's stream-of-consciousness automatic thoughts to include statements of basic assumptions and standards, it also is not unusual for these schemata to be much more implicit in a client's thinking. The thoughts of which a spouse is aware may include only a fragment of a standard (e.g., the conscious thought "You just don't let someone tell you what to do" may be a fragment of a standard, "A person who lets others tell him what to do is not a real man"). One's automatic thoughts also may be logical extensions of basic assumptions and standards rather than statements of the schemata themselves (e.g., the thought "She can't tell me what to do!" may be an extension of the above standard about masculine behavior in relationships). In either case, identification of the standard itself requires that either the individual or another person such as a therapist needs to conduct a Socratic inquiry to identify the standard or assumption tied to the stream-of-consciousness thoughts.

Because the therapist's assessment of assumptions and standards depends primarily on the couple's self-reports, the spouses typically begin to learn how to identify their own basic standards by observing the therapist's procedures and collaborating with the therapist in the assessment process. This learning process may proceed faster if the therapist describes the assessment procedures to the couple explicitly.

As described in Chapter 6, some common unrealistic assumptions and standards that affect marital functioning can be identified with standardized questionnaires, but often members of a couple have idiosyncratic assumptions and standards. The most common method used by cognitive-behavioral therapists and taught to clients for identifying an individual's schemata when they are not expressed directly in the person's automatic thoughts involves extracting repetitive themes from the automatic thoughts associated with marital events that elicit negative affect. In other words, the spouses are taught to collect logs of automatic thoughts from upsetting situations concerning their marriage and to look for themes that appear to represent broad assumptions about the nature of spouses and relationships, or standards regarding the qualities of a good versus a bad relationship.

For example, one husband brought several Daily Record of Dysfunctional Thoughts forms to a session and announced that he had noticed that he tended to become most angry with his wife in situations when she questioned decisions he had made on his own (e.g., regarding the color of a new shirt he bought, his decision to stay up late watching a TV movie when he had to wake up early for work the next morning). He also noticed that his automatic thoughts in those situations included a repetitive concept that could be summarized as "She is not a loving wife because she does not validate me." Any one automatic thought did not necessarily include such a statement, but the husband deduced the theme from the overlapping content of the thoughts elicited by several incidents that had angered him. The therapist then coached him in wording the common theme as a standard or "rule" that he held about marriage: "In a good, loving marriage, the spouses accept each other as they are and consistently express their support for each other."

Some clients quickly become adept at identifying their underlying assumptions and standards, but many others need a good deal of practice before they can do so on their own. Because the identification and modification of unrealistic assumptions and standards is a central component of cognitive restructuring, the therapist should provide each spouse whatever practice and encouragement are needed to achieve competence with these skills.

Testing and modifying cognitions.

After the spouses have become familiar with the concept of automatic thoughts, have learned to differentiate the five types of cognitions that will be the foci of our treatment, and have developed some skill at monitoring their own thoughts, the therapist can proceed to train them in methods for testing the validity or reasonableness of these cognitions and modifying inappropriate ones. One's clinical decision regarding the proper time to begin training a couple in techniques for modifying cognitions must strike a balance between two factors: (a) confidence that the spouses are adept at identifying their thoughts accurately enough to provide appropriate cognitive "data" to serve as treatment targets, and (b) concern that some modification of distressing cognitions takes place early enough in therapy to provide encouragement for distressed couples. In some cases, the need to produce a cognitive shift early in therapy may necessitate that a therapist introduce procedures for testing the appropriateness of perceptions, attributions, expectancies, assumptions, and standards as soon as it is clear that spouses understand the nature of such cognitions. Early therapy sessions then are devoted to identifying *and* examining the validity and reasonableness of particularly upsetting thoughts that spouses have about one another. As stressed above, such a procedure should be conducted with great caution, in order to avoid restructuring efforts directed toward cognitions that were not assessed accurately.

The goals of cognitive restructuring are to improve each spouse's skills at gathering data for testing how valid and reasonable his or her perceptions, attributions, expectancies, assumptions, and standards concerning relationship events are, and to modify those cognitions that contribute to repetitive destructive sequences of interaction between the partners. The following are specific procedures for accomplishing these goals.

Reducing perceptual errors. Perceptual errors, particularly when an individual abstracts only some of the information from a situation and fails to notice other important information, can be reduced by instructing and coaching spouses in being more systematic and thorough "scanners." When it becomes clear that a spouse is overlooking relevant information in his or her perceptual field, it is helpful for the therapist to stress the importance of gathering all the information that is available for understanding one's marital interactions. A couple can be given opportunities to practice participant observation by holding discussions during therapy sessions and receiving videotape or audiotape feedback to test their memories of their interactions. Another way of increasing spouses' sensitivity to variations in the events that occur in their relationship is to ask them to keep written logs of daily events at home, and then to review the logs with them during therapy sessions, noting the broad range of behaviors exhibited by each partner. The Spouse Observation Checklist described in Chapter 6 in the context of behavioral assessment can be quite useful in this regard, because it requires each spouse to notice whether or not the partner exhibited each of an extensive list of positive and negative behaviors. Williams's (1979) "marital time lines" technique also can increase spouses' appreciation of the subjectivity in their appraisals of marital events, because each partner is asked to rate the subjective quality of time spent together as a couple, in 15-minute periods, as well as the specific events during each period that contributed to the level of pleasure or displeasure he or she experienced. When the therapist has the couple compare their ratings of a particular period of shared time, it often becomes clear that they had different subjective experiences. Furthermore, it may be evident that the two spouses had different experiences during a particular time period together because they attended to different events during that time and/or because the same events had different meanings for each of them. The therapist can use such evidence to emphasize that spouses must be aware of the potential for subjectivity and bias in perceptions of even seemingly mundane events.

Training spouses in expressive and empathic listening skills, a form of communication training described in detail in the next chapter, is another behavioral approach to increasing clients' sensitivity to the potential for perceptual errors. Each partner is taught two major sets of skills: (a) expressing his or her thoughts and emotions in a clear, direct, nonhostile manner, and (b) careful reflective listening that communicates one's understanding of the other's expressed messages. Not only do these procedures improve a couple's communication, but they also make the spouses better observers of their own marital interactions.

Exercises such as these are not intended to produce obsessive self-monitoring or "spectatoring," but rather a sharpening of observational skills among spouses who tend to have perceptual biases.

Logical analysis of cognitions. Once one has determined the accuracy of an individual's perceptions, the appropriateness of the inferences he or she makes from perceptual data can be tested by means of logical analysis. Using a Socratic approach, the therapist guides the client toward discovering the logic or illogic in his or her own thoughts about perceived events. For example, one husband attributed his erectile dysfunction to a lack of sufficient "effort" on his part. The following exchange occurred in the therapy session.

Therapist: What were your automatic thoughts last night when you started making love and noticed that you only got a partial erection?

Husband: I thought, "Here we go again! I'm not getting aroused. Why the hell can't I just concentrate on what we're doing and make this work? I'm really inadequate."

Therapist: That's a nice job of paying attention to the specific thoughts you had. Now I think we should take a close look at what you assumed was causing the problem. You had the thought "Why can't I just concentrate and make this work?" Were you assuming that when it comes to sexual arousal a person can "make it happen" through a conscious effort?

Husband: Yes, I was assuming that.

Therapist: Well, from what you know about sexual arousal, do men tend to get erections by deciding that now is the time to get one and then by concentrating on doing so?

Husband: No. Usually you get them when you aren't even thinking about it. You think about something sexy or see something sexy, and you suddenly notice that you are aroused.

Therapist: So, erections seem to be like a reflex that occurs when you are relaxed and focused on sexually interesting things?

Husband: Yes, I guess that's so.

Therapist: Then if that's true, does it make sense that you could "make an erection happen" by working at it?

Husband: It doesn't seem like that would work.

Therapist: Then the attribution you were making automatically about the cause of your erection problem, where you blamed yourself for not making it happen, doesn't seem to be appropriate, because it was based on an unrealistic assumption about sexual arousal.

Husband: No, it doesn't. I guess there must be some other explanation for it.

Therapist: Then let's think about what else might be contributing to the problem. Perhaps there are some hints about that in what you said are the conditions that tend to result in sexual arousal.

Another approach to the logical analysis of a spouse's thoughts is to coach an individual who has made a particular attribution about the cause of an event to think of *alternative explanations* for the event. The therapist begins by acknowledging that the original attribution is a possible explanation for the event, but then stresses that it is important to determine whether this is the most accurate or reasonable explanation. The therapist and both spouses then can "brainstorm" a list of other plausible causes, a process that may broaden both partners' views of causality in their relationship. The spouse who made the original attribution then may choose another explanation solely on logical grounds, or the therapist may guide the couple in testing the relative validity of the various alternatives by gathering evidence.

In a similar manner, the therapist can guide a client in the logical analysis of an expectancy, investigating whether the premises underlying a particular prediction "make sense." For example, one wife who had experienced a series of physical illnesses predicted that her husband would become disgusted by her and leave her. When the therapist inquired how she came to that conclusion, she replied that any man whose wife had suffered chronic illness would be likely to leave. However, when asked whether it made sense to her that only men whose wives were healthy stayed married, she said that the assumption seemed "silly." Further exploration of the wife's thoughts revealed that in fact *she* was disgusted with being sick and found it difficult to imagine how anyone would want to be with her. She accepted the importance of catching herself at "projecting" her own reactions and predicting that her husband would have the same responses to marital events.

Logical analysis can be used to determine whether an assumption or standard and its premises "make sense." For example, when one husband examined his standard that loving spouses should accept and support each other at all times, he concluded that this standard did not differentiate between accepting someone as a person and accepting all of that person's behaviors. He also concluded that the standard required expressions of support even when one firmly believed that one's spouse was risking his or her own welfare. Consequently, he decided that the standard did not appear to be a logical definition of a loving relationship; it clearly needed considerable qualification.

Gathering evidence to test cognitions. Evidence bearing on the validity or reasonableness of a cognition can be gathered from a variety of sources. The following are the major sources of evidence that we draw on when a spouse reports a thought which he or she assumes is valid and reasonable but which appears to the therapist to be inappropriate. The choice of which, and how many, of these sources of evidence to use with any particular client depends on the strength of the person's belief in the cognition (more contradictory evidence being needed to modify more firmly held beliefs) and the types of evidence that are most credible to each individual (e.g., some clients find in vivo experiences more persuasive than memories of past events). The order in which we describe the various sources of evidence below is merely one of convenience, and does not suggest a preferred sequence or hierarchy of interventions.

One source of evidence regarding the appropriateness of a cognition is for the therapist to ask a spouse to *recount the details of past experiences,* with the partner and in other relationships, that provide data about the accuracy of the current automatic thought. For example, one wife reported that her great distress about her marriage was associated with automatic thoughts that her husband "has *no* interest in our family or in helping me raise our children." When the therapist asked both of the spouses to describe a typical weekday in their lives, both noted that the husband awoke early and helped the children wash and dress for school, and also packed a lunch for each child, while the wife made everyone breakfast. He often worked quite late at a high-pressure job and brought home work a few nights per week. During a typical evening, he spent about half an hour playing with the children and reading them stories before they went to sleep. He then might work for another hour or two before talking or watching television with his wife.

After these details had been elicited, and the spouses agreed about them, the therapist asked the wife how this information "fit" with her automatic thought that her husband has *no* interest whatsoever in the family or in raising the children. She responded that it really was not accurate to say that he had no interest, and he did take on some of the child care responsibilities. However, she then added that he spent too much time with his work, often calling home to say that he would be working too late to be home for the family dinner. She said that she was stuck at home each day with the younger child who attended school for only half the day, and that she had to cope with two noisy kids for several hours each evening until her husband got home. The therapist helped the wife relate all of these facts to her initial automatic thought, and it became clear to the therapist and both spouses that the thought was not valid per se. However, its *theme* of disinterest and neglect indicated that her husband's behavior was not meeting her personal *standard* about what a caring husband and father does. The issue shifted from an inaccurate view that he was totally uninvolved to a conflict between the spouses' standards regarding what kind and amount of family involvement are satisfactory. The husband had been unwilling to accept his wife's original view that he did nothing, but the new focus on alternative forms of family involvement opened him to considering some negotiation about time management and scheduling.

The preceding example illustrates the importance of searching for the idiosyncratic meanings that each person attaches to the specific events in his or her marital interactions. It is not simply a matter of collecting data and dismissing an automatic thought as totally invalid. Often, the content of a distressing thought reflects some actual aspect of the relationship that the individual finds unpleasant. It is the therapist's responsibility to help the couple identify any distortions in their cognitions and then to work toward resolving the remaining problems.

A second rich source of evidence regarding the validity or reasonableness of cognitions is *in vivo marital interactions during conjoint therapy sessions*. A disadvantage of retrospective accounts of events and associated cognitions is that the accuracy of clients' memories will deteriorate over time. This is especially a problem in cognitive restructuring, because it is important to know the specific content of thoughts that have elicited particular dysfunctional emotional and behavioral responses in order to modify them effectively. In contrast, the thoughts that are elicited in each spouse by the other's behavior can be tapped immediately, and data regarding their appropriateness tend to be readily available in the session, particularly when the therapist routinely tapes sessions and can replay relevant segments.

Monitoring the process by which spouses escalate a fight during a session and providing them taped feedback about the sequence of events often helps them to take a more objective view of the causes of the fight. In the midst of an escalating argument, it is easy for each spouse to notice the aversive things that the other person is doing, but the participant-observer role can produce a perceptual bias in which one's own contribution to a problem is overlooked.

Another common process that occurs during arguments and which can be identified during conjoint sessions is a *polarizing* of the two parties' positions. For example, each time a particular couple discussed their respective standards about the proper way to raise their daughter each focused on the aspects of the other's approach that he or she believed are not in the child's best interest. The more that the husband heard his wife talking about sparing the daughter stressful life experiences at a fairly young age, the more he insisted that such an approach would leave the child unprepared for life's inevitable frustrations. In return, each time she heard him stressing that their daughter should be exposed to unpleasant experiences, she forcefully argued that childhood is a special time that a child should enjoy, and that early stresses can produce an anxious child. During each exchange of opinions during a therapy session (as well as at home), each partner perceived the other as taking a more extreme and inflexible stand and therefore felt a need to counter that position with a strong opposite stand. Although the spouses' initial views actually may have had some overlap, this "polarizing" process moved their perceived positions (and perhaps eventually their actual positions) further apart.

Members of a couple are unlikely to notice how such a "polarizing" process occurs during their interactions unless a therapist provides detailed feedback about the sequence of events in the escalation of their conflict. Viewing or hearing a tape of their interaction may shift the spouses' perceptions of the distance between their positions and alter their attributions about how the conflict intensified. They may now see the process as a *reciprocal* escalation that was based on their perceptions that their standards about the topic were polar opposites, and not as a unilateral escalation by one of them.

At times, the therapist can elicit a "re-creation" of cognitions that a couple had during an argument at home by asking them to discuss the incident with each other in the session. Then the thoughts can be tested in vivo. For example, one couple reported a recent distressing exchange about a party their 12-year-old daughter attended. During the therapy session, their discussion went as follows.

Wife: We'd been having a good week until then, but you've stayed in a bad mood since. Things have been more calm for the last day or so, but we never really resolved anything.

Husband: It didn't seem to me that any further discussion would do any good.

Wife: Well, what did you want me to do?

Husband: Look, the party was poorly planned. It was inappropriate for a party for twelve year-olds, with both boys and girls, to start at eight o'clock and go on until midnight, especially with little parental supervision.

Wife: I said she could go because there was going to be an adult in the house, and they are a very nice family. They wouldn't let anything go on that you should worry about. I still think you were being very old-fashioned about the whole thing!

Husband: That's just the kind of statement that made me not want to listen to you. I have a right as a father to use my judgment about what is good and what isn't for my daughter.

Wife: But if you had listened to me when I told you about the arrangements for the party you would have known that it was well supervised. You just tuned me out.

Husband: You went on in such detail and sounded so defensive that I really didn't want to hear it all.

Wife: I kept talking because I just wanted to get some response from you. You had been affectionate and friendly before that, but you withdrew.

Husband: All I heard from you were comments about how the party was OK and how I was being unreasonable. You made me irritated when you wouldn't listen to *my* concerns, as usual!

During this exchange, both spouses became visibly upset, and it was clear that they were reliving the original incident. Although their upsetting automatic thoughts may not have been identical to those that they experienced during the interaction at home, it is likely that the material was similar enough to be quite relevant for cognitive restructuring. The therapist could draw upon cognitions directly expressed by each partner (e.g., the husband's expectancy that no further discussion would be of use, or the wife's perception that her spouse had "tuned her out" and her expectancy that only persistent talking would elicit a response from him). In addition, the therapist could stop the exchange at any point and ask either person what thoughts were running through his or her mind. Because that process tends to disrupt the flow of the exchange, one might choose to wait until the couple had discussed the issue for a while and then ask them to report what their thoughts had been at various points. The success of the latter procedure in eliciting the spouses' cognitions accurately will be limited by deficits in recall; people often give retrospective accounts of what they think they "must have been thinking" rather than an accurate verbatim report. A compromise approach is to tape an uninterrupted exchange, stop the tape replay at particular points, and ask the spouses to report what their thoughts were at those points in the discussion. Even if some of the thoughts that they report are, in fact, influenced by the replay process, rather than those they experienced during the taping, the themes are likely to be comparable and quite relevant to the couple's distress.

A third source of evidence concerning the validity and reasonableness of cognitions is the *written logs and diaries* that cognitive-behavioral therapists commonly have spouses keep regarding their distressing interactions, with their associated automatic thoughts, emotions, and behavioral responses. As described earlier in this chapter and in Chapter 6 on cognitive assessment, Beck et al.'s (1979) Daily Record of Dysfunctional Thoughts is a convenient form for this purpose, because it provides columns for writing the date of an upsetting event, a brief concrete description of the event, the verbatim automatic thoughts, and the emotional response. The client also rates the degree to which he or she believed each thought at the time and the degree of each emotion's intensity, using 100-point scales. Again, given the interpersonal focus of marital therapy, addition of a column to the DRDT for the description of behavioral responses toward the partner is quite important.

When clients keep written logs or diaries over time, the therapist can ask them to record all interactions that are relevant to particular perceptions they have had about each other, or (if the behavior has a high base rate) at least to record a representative sample of such interactions. The written records then can serve as evidence regarding the perceptions. For example, if one spouse perceives the other as consistently preoccupied, the records may indicate that there have been some instances when that person in fact paid full attention to what the aggrieved partner was saying. In order to reduce the work involved in keeping fairly complete logs of particular types of interactions, the therapist may help spouses devise shorthand notations for recording the targeted incidents. For example, the person who believed that the partner was preoccupied need not write full descriptions of his or her attempts to talk to the partner, but instead could simply list dates and times when such efforts were made and brief notations regarding the outcomes (e.g., "Monday, 6 P.M.: I talked about my day at work; she watched the TV news and made no comment").

Another valuable use of written logs is the comparison of the cognitions, emotions, and behaviors that the two partners had during one of their interactions. For example, the differences in the attributions that they made about causes of the shared event can illustrate for the couple that personal inferences are quite subjective, and that there are usually alternative ways to interpret any marital interaction. At times the comparison increases spouses' empathy for each other, and at the very least it provides each party some data that can help explain the causes of the other's behavior.

A fourth source of evidence for testing the validity or reasonableness of cognitions involves *interviewing the couple regarding changes in their behaviors and perceptions of each other over the course of the relationship.* The information that the therapist initially gathered about the history of the couple's relationship, including their descriptions of the characteristics that attracted them to each other, can provide useful evidence for challenging negative trait attributions. Abrahms (1985) has described a "flip-flop" phenomenon in which an individual initially attributes a partner's behavior to a desirable trait but later attributes the *same* behavior to an undesirable trait. The partner might rightly complain, "I haven't changed," but the person who has experienced the interpretive shift does not see it that way.

The case of Sue and Frank illustrates such an attributional shift and how a therapist can intervene with it. The couple began dating exclusively in high school and married during college. They now were in their early thirties and had a nine year-old daughter. One of their major areas of conflict was how to save or spend money, and another was how to spend their leisure time. Sue complained that Frank had an "irresponsible" attitude about money, typified by what Sue called his "business schemes." Frank had a minor management position in a company, which provided a steady salary but limited opportunities for advancement. He often had ideas about business investments that would supplement his income, but Sue was uncomfortable with the risks involved in such ventures. Sue had a supervisory position in a government agency, and her salary was a little higher than Frank's. Frank complained that Sue was inflexible and unsupportive concerning his investment ideas.

With regard to leisure time, Frank complained that Sue did not know how to relax and have fun, because she resisted his plans for them to go dancing and to parties. Sue said that she did not mind socializing, but she complained that Frank acted like a "young man who hasn't settled down."

Both spouses clearly were attributing negative characteristics as causes of their partner's displeasing behaviors. The therapist then referred the couple to the descriptions each partner gave about the characteristics that attracted them originally to the other person. Frank had emphasized that he had liked Sue's "maturity, steadiness, caring, and willingness to stand up for what she believed." Sue had been attracted by what she labeled Frank's "humor, not taking himself too seriously, caring, and courage not to be a conformist." A further recounting of the therapist's notes from the earlier assessment indicated that the *behaviors* the spouses used to define the initial attracting qualities were quite similar to the behaviors they now attributed to negative traits. For example, Frank had seen "maturity" and "steadiness" when Sue had studied hard in school rather than spending time "hanging around" with other kids who did not care about getting an education. Now he saw similar behavior as "not knowing how to have fun."

After noting to the couple that some of their behaviors had remained fairly consistent but that their attributions about the behaviors had shifted markedly, the therapist emphasized that to a large extent it is one's perception of a spouse's behavior rather than the behavior itself that produces satisfaction or dissatisfaction. The therapist noted how each spouse had used the same behavioral evidence to support two opposite attributions, and suggested that they needed to reconcile the seeming discrepancies. Next, the therapist suggested that perhaps neither the old attributions nor the new ones represented complete and true explanations of each spouse's behaviors. Each spouse acknowledged that there were some positive aspects *and* some negative aspects to the other person's behavior, and that as the other's behavior became more unpleasant than pleasant over time, it was easy to attribute it to an enduring negative trait. Both spouses also acknowledged that the other still had positive attributes that originally had been attractive. This discussion led Sue and Frank to conclude that each of them sometimes behaved in ways that were pleasing to the other and sometimes behaved in ways that were displeasing, but that the changes in what they found displeasing were not due to changes in each other's personalities.

The next important step in this cognitive restructuring was for the therapist to guide the couple in exploring what factors other than hypothetical personality changes might have increased their displeasure with each other's behavior. Again, the developmental history of the relationship provided relevant evidence. Sue described how she seemed to enjoy Frank's playfulness and risk taking less once they "settled down" with a child and a house. She began to look to him more for security, and she felt anxiety when it appeared that his job provided limited earning potential and that he was willing to risk their savings on "business schemes." Clearly, her expectations concerning Frank's role in their relationship had changed during their developmental transition from a young couple to an established family with a child.

Similarly, Frank described how early in their relationship he had valued the efforts that both of them made toward bettering their lifestyle, but that he had expected that once they had achieved a "comfortable" standard of living they would relax and enjoy the fruits of their labor. He had perceived Sue as someone who was goal oriented but who would relax her efforts somewhat and enjoy life with him when they had achieved their basic goals. Frank also was somewhat frustrated by the limitations of his job and had decided that he needed to pursue other business ventures in order to be successful. Thus, the couple had experienced a developmental transition as a family *and* Frank was in the midst of a personal developmental transition regarding his career. As the spouses became aware during this discussion that their attributions about each other's behavior may have been shaped by changes in their expectations about their relationship, they both voiced an interest in negotiating some changes in their interactions that might meet their current preferences better.

In general, all of the methods we have described for collecting evidence to test the validity or reasonableness of people's cognitions use preexisting data, whether memories of past experiences or information about an interaction that recently occurred in the session. In contrast to these approaches, evidence also can be collected by means of a fifth method, *planned behavioral experiments*, in which the spouses interact in a preconceived manner and closely monitor the outcome. For example, one couple who had been married for 40 years had experienced increasing tension and fights. Over the years they had had a fairly traditional marriage, with George supporting the family and Claire staying at home to focus on raising the children. After the children were grown and had left the home, George continued to work long hours at his business, and Claire took a part-time job in a library. As they both approached retirement age, Claire became increasingly distressed that George did not provide much companionship for her. She had more personally rewarding experiences interacting with people at work than with George, and when she complained about this, George seemed to ignore her. By the time they entered marital therapy, Claire was convinced that George did not care about her and that he habitually failed to even listen to what she had to say.

Among the interventions used with this couple, the therapist described the basic concepts and procedures of emotional expressiveness training (see Chapter 10) and suggested that if they agreed to experiment with those skills they might learn how well or poorly they were functioning in terms of intimacy and communication. Although they both agreed to this plan, Claire was quite skeptical, stating, "I doubt he has any interest in this; he's got me tuned out." However, when the therapist instructed the couple in the expressive and listening skills, George expended obvious effort, and when he practiced the empathic listener role, he did a good job of reflecting back the thoughts and emotions Claire had expressed. As he did so, Claire began to smile. When the therapist inquired about her smile, she said, "He's really listening to me," and she described how good it felt to have George focus his attention on her. Certainly this exercise did not resolve all of the couple's difficulties, but it served as a behavioral experiment that contradicted Claire's perception that George had no interest in listening to her.

When a behavioral experiment is designed, it is important that both spouses acknowledge beforehand that they consider it a credible test of their cognitions. In the above example, George's performance during the emotional expressiveness training would have had little impact on Claire's view of him if she had discounted the validity of the experiment (e.g., "Sure he listened, but he only did it because you [the therapist] asked him to, and he doesn't care enough to pay attention to me on his own"). At times, one spouse discounts the other's behavioral changes during therapy only after the experiment is completed, by attributing the change to an undesirable cause not proposed when the experiment initially was planned. For example, after one wife displayed good empathic listening skills after emotional expressiveness training, her husband remarked, "Brenda has made sure that we practiced the communication exercises every day, and it dawned on me that this was a convenient way for her to divert our attention away from how she hurt me in the past and how I really can't trust her any longer." Although the wife seemed (to the therapist) to be making a sincere effort to rebuild trust in the marriage by improving the couple's communication skills, the husband interpreted her behavior in the context of his established negative view of her. If such discounting should occur following behavioral experiments, it is important for the therapist to challenge the negative attribution, using techniques such as logical analysis. When asked to consider alternative explanations for the spouse's behavioral change, some clients are open to the idea that even if their partner has not suddenly adopted a totally new way of behaving, he or she certainly had an opportunity to put minimal effort into the experiment but clearly did more than that.

Behavioral experiments can be used to produce evidence that an assumption or standard is unrealistic. For example, if a spouse assumes that disagreement is destructive to a relationship, a graduated series of experiments can be conducted wherein the individual tries expressing first mild and then moderate and major disagreements with the partner and observes the impact on the overall relationship.

In contrast to the above assumption, some spouses define marital intimacy in terms of uncensored self-disclosure, and their resulting lack of tact often produces considerable distress (Stuart, 1980). A therapist might counter this problematic standard by proposing a behavioral experiment in which the spouses systematically reduce their unbridled disclosure in graduated steps and monitor the subjective quality of the relationship over time. Their ratings of relationship quality should be designed to differentiate between initial anxiety about not knowing what the other may be thinking and overall satisfaction with the time they spend together.

When gathering evidence that either supports or contradicts *expectancies*, some extreme predictions (e.g., that the partner *always* will behave in a particular way) are fairly easy to challenge because it takes only one *credible* exception to disprove the rule. However, there are some situations when a spouse believes that he or she would find it highly aversive if the partner responded in a certain way *even once* (e.g., a husband anticipates that if he disagreed with his wife in public and she criticized him for that in front of other people, he would be humiliated). Consequently, the individual may make a concerted effort to avoid eliciting that response, that is, essentially engaging in phobic avoidance behavior. Fear of the anticipated aversive behavior thus reduces the person's motivation to seek any data concerning the actual probability of the event by means of behavioral experiments (e.g., in the preceding case, the husband was unwilling to try disagreeing with his wife about a minor issue at the next party they attended). The therapist then may need to rely on helping the individual gather more indirect evidence (e.g., memories of the partner's past behavior, observations of similar situations in other couples' relationships). Otherwise, in cases where spouses are willing to risk the occurrence of an event they have predicted, behavioral experiments can provide compelling evidence that some predicted unpleasant marital interactions in fact will not occur.

When examining the evidence regarding the degree to which an assumption or standard is valid or reasonable, it is important to pay close attention to historical material. Many assumptions and standards have been developed in the context of a person's experiences with past relationships, beginning with those that he or she had in the family of origin. It is crucial to help each spouse differentiate between evidence that a particular standard or assumption *was valid* in another relationship at an earlier time and evidence that it *is now valid* under current circumstances. A prime example is when an individual has a residual assumption that may have been at least moderately true when he or she was a young child relating to adults (e.g., "I cannot survive in this world without the support of [my parents]") but is unrealistic and dysfunctional in adult-adult relationships.

Spouses also can gather evidence concerning their assumptions and standards about marriage by observing the relationships of other couples they know, by participating in couples "support groups" and marital enrichment groups, and by reading literature that describes myths and realities of married life (e.g., Lazarus, 1985). Many couples also find it enlightening when a therapist points out how people are exposed to unrealistic ideas about relationships through popular love songs (e.g., the common theme that "I can't live without you"), novels, and movies. Contrasting such assumptions and standards with available data regarding "real-life couples" can underscore the unrealistic nature of the media portrayals of relationships.

When helping couples to evaluate the appropriateness of their basic assumptions and standards about intimate relationships, we also guide them in *assessing the utility* of those schemata. We define an assumption or standard's utility as the degree to which the advantages of adhering to such a schema outweigh the disadvantages. This concept is based on an assumption that a person continues to hold an assumption or standard over a period of time not only because core attitudes and beliefs tend to be resistant to change even in the face of contradictory evidence (as explained by cognitive consistency theories), but also because they are functional. Living one's life according to particular schemata often has identifiable benefits as well as costs. Consequently, one of our procedures for increasing spouses' motivation to alter their basic standards about the nature of good marital functioning is to assist them in identifying and comparing the advantages and disadvantages of their assumptions and standards.

For example, in one couple, the wife was quite distressed that her second husband had strained relationships with her children. When the therapist inquired why she thought this difficulty existed (looking for her causal attributions), she labeled her husband as an "uncaring, intolerant parent." Further inquiry revealed that she attributed such negative traits to him because she had a basic standard that parents should be loving and accepting of their children's personalities, and that she was applying this standard to the stepparent-stepchild relationship.

As noted by clinicians who work with stepfamilies (e.g., Visher & Visher, 1979), what makes this wife's standard particularly dysfunctional is that it requires members of stepfamilies to have the same bonds in their relationships (e.g., love, loyalty, respect) as those commonly found in well-adjusted nuclear families. However, as was the case with this particular family, simply living together often does not instantaneously produce close relationships among members of stepfamilies. The wife's standard that her new husband should relate toward her children as if he was their biological father was unrealistic.

When the couple's therapist discussed the wife's standard with her, she acknowledged that it contributed to her pessimism about improving their marriage. The therapist then spent time with the wife conducting a logical analysis of the standard and gathering a variety of evidence about its validity. Even though the wife was able to recount some stories about stepfamilies whom she had known who had difficulty adjusting to their new family structure, she still found her standard to be very appealing. The therapist then introduced the concept of the advantage-disadvantage balance that can affect adherence to a basic standard. The wife then dictated her wording of the standard, "Members of a successful stepfamily should have the same loving, intimate relationships as members of a close nuclear family," as the therapist wrote it on a blackboard. The therapist then constructed two columns on the board, one each for advantages and disadvantages of living according to the standard. It was stressed to the couple that the wife most likely had some good reasons for adhering to that standard, but that this procedure would make it clear if there actually were some disadvantages/costs that outweighed the advantages.

The listing of the standard's advantages and disadvantages was conducted as a "brainstorming" session, where the wife, husband, and therapist contributed whatever items came to mind for either category, without evaluating how important or trivial an advantage or disadvantage might be. The therapist only contributed to the list when the couple seemed to overlook an important advantage or disadvantage, or when the lists needed some additional breadth. The following were representative advantages and disadvantages of this wife's standard:

Advantages
1. gives one a sense of security that past losses (conflict and breakup of the first marriage) will not be repeated
2. makes life less unpredictable; one has a clear picture of the nature of family life
3. eliminates the need to work hard to understand and develop new patterns of relating (different from familiar nuclear family patterns)
4. tends to place the responsibility for problems on the newcomer to the family, the stepparent

Disadvantages
1. frustration and disappointment are highly likely, because stepfamily relationships require significant adjustments; strangers rarely develop intimacy quickly

2. can produce anger and depression (related to disadvantage #1)
3. discourages or impedes attempts to solve problems, because special stepfamily issues contributing to the problems are denied
4. reduces empathy that stepfamily members might have for one another's difficulties in adjusting to a new life situation

Weighing the advantages and disadvantages of an assumption or standard does not involve a simple counting of the entries in the two lists. Rather, the therapist asks the "owner" of the assumption or standard to rate the importance of each advantage and each disadvantage. Giving numerical weights to the entries probably is not necessary; we tend to place asterisks next to those the individual considers quite important, at most making distinctions among no asterisks, one, or two.

Based on these judgments, the spouse who holds the assumption or standard is asked his or her opinion about the relative costs and benefits of living by it. The therapist stresses that there certainly are some attractive advantages on the list, but most spouses tend to express a preference for eliminating what are often very distressing disadvantages. The therapist then states that the goal of analyzing the assumption or standard in this manner was not to try to convince the person to eliminate it entirely, and that to expect such a drastic shift in a longstanding schema probably is unrealistic, especially because of its advantages. Therefore, the next step in working with the assumption or standard is to *revise* it, constructing a new version that may retain some of the truly useful aspects of the original schema but will eliminate as many of the disadvantages as possible.

The therapist then coaches the spouse in "rewriting" the assumption or standard so that it becomes more realistic, less extreme, and less disadvantageous. Although the person's partner and the therapist may contribute suggestions about the wording of the revised schema, it is important that the holder of the original schema find the new wording palatable and compatible with his or her general way of "phrasing" ideas. In the preceding example, the wife constructed a revised standard that stated, "Members of a stepfamily are more likely to have satisfying relationships with one another when they are sensitive to each person's needs and difficulties in adjusting to the situation, when they make efforts to negotiate their differences, and when they work toward gradually building intimacy."

It is important to stress to the couple that devising such a revision of an old schema does not guarantee that the individual will actually believe the revision as much as, or more than, the original. The next important step is for the couple to devise behavioral experiments by which they can evaluate the validity or reasonableness and the utility of the revised assumption or standard. The therapist asks the couple to "set up behavioral experiments where you try living as if the new standard were true, and see what happens." With this particular couple, the therapist suggested that the experiments focus on application of the revised standard to specific aspects of the wife's presenting complaints, namely, her husband's strained relationships with the children from her first marriage. The husband agreed with the wife that his relationships with her children were problematic. The therapist said to the couple, "If you now approach the problem of Ted's strained relationships with Beth and Billy with the revised standard about stepfamily relationships, you need to set up an experiment that would demonstrate that standard." The spouses agreed that if they held to the new standard, they should be thinking of ways to improve Ted's relationships with the children, particularly strategies that take into account the needs of stepfamily members. The therapist supported their view that the revised standard was most consistent with a collaborative problem-solving approach to the problem and coached them through the steps of problem solving (see Chapter 8).

The spouses decided on specific strategies that Ted would use both to build greater intimacy with the children and to share the role of disciplinarian with Lisa. Lisa's specific role in the solution (e.g., helping to set up pleasurable activities Ted could share with the children; telling the children that she and Ted would be sharing in the setting and enforcing of rules for their behavior) also was specified. Both spouses agreed to communicate to the children that (a) Ted was not trying to replace their biological father, but rather cared to develop a different type of positive relationship with them, and (b) neither adult expected the children to suddenly feel close to Ted. Lisa also agreed to look for signs that Ted was making efforts to spend time with the children, rather than signs that he did or did not feel love for them.

In the final stage of the experiment, the couple attempted to implement their solutions at home and evaluated the results over a two-week period. Lisa was able to report that Ted was making an obvious effort to relate in a different manner with the children, and that the children had behaved more positively toward him as well. The experiment did not provide unqualified or conclusive evidence that the revised standard was more realistic than the wife's original standard, but it encouraged the couple to continue to experiment with living according to the revised schema.

Counteracting "pessimistic" schemata that impede change. Assumptions and standards that express pessimism about the potential for change in a relationship arise quite commonly in the early stages of marital therapy, as the spouses evaluate why they are sitting in the therapist's office and whether the effort is likely to be fruitful. If spouses' initial assumptions that their relationship cannot change are not modified somewhat in a timely fashion, the couple may either drop out of treatment prematurely or "resist" trying to make changes. Consequently, this particular assumption often must be identified and addressed quickly. It may not be necessary to produce a major modification in the assumption at the beginning of therapy in order to increase the spouses' motivation and optimism concerning change, but the therapist often will need to introduce an element of doubt in their minds about the assumption's validity. This may be accomplished with the techniques described earlier, and also at times by the therapist presenting a challenge to the couple. After listening to their expressions of pessimism, the therapist might make a statement (with a vocal tone that expresses some surprise and skepticism) with the theme "You two seem to think you are slaves to your past when it comes to. . . ." This particular labeling of their assumption tends to give it a negative valence (Who wants to be a slave?) and challenges them to see if they can establish "freedom" from the past. Of course, such a challenge must be presented to a couple in a tactful manner.

FOCUSING ON THE INDIVIDUAL
VERSUS THE COUPLE

Because it is important to modify the idiosyncratic cognitions of each spouse, there are times when the therapist will talk almost exclusively with one person. However, as illustrated in the preceding description of cognitive restructuring techniques, the therapist commonly involves the other spouse in the procedures. This creates more collaborative change efforts, increases the other spouse's empathy concerning the person's subjective experiences, allows the partner to provide information useful in testing the validity and reasonableness of the spouse's cognitions, and often has an impact on the partner's own cognitions as well. For example, when two spouses hold the same unrealistic standard, and therefore tend to reinforce each other's thinking, it can be useful to work on the standard with one person at a time, with the other just listening. This procedure can reduce input from one spouse that may impede the other's attempts to test the validity or utility of a standard. The use of conjoint sessions makes it possible for the therapist to address one spouse's standards indirectly when talking with the other spouse.

When two spouses have *complementary* unrealistic assumptions or standards, it is useful to work with both parties simultaneously, focusing on how each person provides data that seem to validate the other's schema. For example, one husband assumed that it is dangerous to the survival of a close relationship for the spouses to have arguments, and the wife assumed that if one is not careful one's needs will become controlled by and subjugated to those of a spouse. Based on his assumption, the husband tried to avoid overt conflict with his wife by cutting off discussions of their disagreements quickly and deflecting the conversations to other topics. The wife interpreted her spouse's behavior as support for her own assumption (i.e., she inferred that by not talking, he was protecting his own position and preventing her from asking for what she wanted), even though in reality the husband's avoidance blocked the fulfillment of *both* spouses' needs. In return, based on her own assumption, the wife tended to be highly vigilant for signs that her husband was "taking over" her life. This led her to challenge his suggestions about solutions to daily problems (e.g., where they should shop for new carpets) and made her quite anxious and angry whenever he made even mild critical comments about her. Given his own assumption about the dangers of conflict, the husband was quite distressed whenever his wife responded in this manner.

In order to deal effectively with such complementary assumptions or standards, the therapist can help each spouse identify not only the nature of his or her own schema, but also how the behavior of the partner (which follows from that person's own schema) tends to reinforce the assumption or standard. In other words, the therapeutic intervention focuses on the *interaction* and mutual influence between the two spouses' assumptions or standards and associated behaviors.

DEALING WITH INCOMPATIBLE STANDARDS

It is important to note that distress in a relationship can result from spouses' realistic but incompatible standards about their marriage, as well as from unrealistic standards. When the therapist determines that a dysfunctional interaction pattern between two spouses is based on a basic disagreement about standards for their relationship, and that both people's standards are reasonable, the focus then must shift to (a) whether the problem is partly one of intolerance for their differences (which can itself involve extreme standards), and (b) whether the couple needs assistance in negotiating a compromise. The latter problem calls for more direct behavioral intervention.

CONCLUSION

As noted earlier and illustrated in this chapter, when the cognitive-behavioral marital therapist conducts cognitive restructuring procedures, it is assumed that these will have an impact on spouses' emotions and behaviors, and also that emotional and behavioral changes can produce cognitive changes. Behavior change procedures such as those described in Chapter 8, as well as "behavioral experiments," frequently are used to test the validity and reasonableness of, and to modify, cognitions. In addition, in many instances the assessment of a couple reveals that their distress results primarily from actual aversive behaviors being exchanged, rather than from cognitive distortions. In such cases, the therapist tends to focus on behavioral interventions. However, given the complex ways in which cognitions, behaviors, and emotions are intertwined, it is important for therapists to be aware of cognitions that may impede spouses' acceptance of behavior change efforts (e.g., a spouse's discounting of a partner's new positive behavior as due to pressure from their therapist rather than the partner's sincere desire to improve the relationship). Thus, at any moment the cognitive-behavioral marital therapist may focus interventions on one of the three major components of marital functioning (cognitive, behavioral, and emotional), but he or she constantly is prepared to address the other two realms.

The next chapter describes methods for altering the amount and forms of emotion experienced and expressed in a couple's relationship. The discussion of these interventions once again underscores the reciprocal influences among spouses' cognitions, behaviors, and emotions.

10

Modification of Affect

Although emotions, cognitions, and behavior have been separated for the ease of presentation, the three are intimately related. In fact, our approach to altering emotions is based on cognitive and behavioral interventions. A wide range of treatment strategies is available, and the particular intervention chosen will depend on the specific goals that the therapist has in mind. First, some spouses have difficulty recognizing what their emotions are. In this case, the therapist's task is to help the individual learn to recognize and label emotions. These same individuals often are unaware of the bases of their affective states; thus, even if they are able to label a feeling, they do not understand why they are feeling the way that they are. They are unable to relate what they are feeling to environmental circumstances or to their cognitions. Second, the individual might be quite aware of his or her feelings but have difficulty expressing those feelings. In such cases, helping the individual to express feelings appropriately to others might be the intervention of choice. Third, one spouse might be experiencing emotions that are interfering with the adaptive functioning of the couple. Perhaps the individual is clinging to anger based on a series of events that happened many years ago, or the person expresses jealousy in a way that is punitive and restrictive of the partner. In such cases, the ultimate goal may be to alter these dysfunctional emotional states and related behavior. Thus, from a skills training perspective, there is no single way to intervene with "emotions": instead, the intervention must follow from the particular goals that the therapist and couple have in mind.

LABELING AND UNDERSTANDING EMOTIONS

Many individuals experience emotions at a vague, diffuse level. Without being able to label one's feelings clearly, it is difficult to understand oneself, recognize the impact of the other person's behavior on oneself, or communicate one's emotions. Therefore, assisting the individual in labeling emotions is important. Persons who have difficulty labeling feelings often have few affective words in mind. For that reason, providing such spouses with a list of feeling words can be helpful to them as they attempt to label feelings. Such a list, which can be shared with couples, is provided in Table 10-1.

Other strategies also can be employed to assist the individual in labeling emotions. Many people experience a state of physiological arousal or a subjective sense that something feels good or bad, but their labeling stops at that point. In part, this is because they do not attempt to put the emotion in the context from which it derives. Thus, the therapist can assist the individual in labeling the emotion by teaching the person to recall the situation that led to the emotion. At first the therapist may provide the cues, but eventually the therapist will want to teach the individual to provide this function for him- or herself.

Therapist: O.K., let me try to help you figure out the feeling you are having. If I understand, it is a negative feeling, and it is related to the plans that you and Sarah had for Friday evening. Is that right?

Husband: Yeah, that is pretty much it. It was a pretty bad evening overall, but I can't figure out the exact feelings I was having.

Therapist: One thing that a lot of people find is that their feelings become clearer if they go back through what happened in some detail. So, without attempting to put the blame on Sarah, let's think back to Friday night. Why don't you give me the setting for what happened?

Husband: Sure, we decided that Friday night was a time we were just going to relax together at home. Sarah was going to stop on the way home and pick up some Chinese food so we wouldn't have to cook or clean up much after dinner. Well, I got. . .

Therapist: How did you feel when you thought about that evening?

Husband: Well, I felt good. I was looking forward to it, to being alone with Sarah, and to having an incredibly hard work week behind me.

Therapist: O.K., you felt good, but more specifically what was the emotion?

Husband: I'm not sure. Maybe excited and relieved that the week was over but also apprehensive because I didn't know how the evening would go.

Therapist: O.K., as you remember it, what happened that evening?

Husband: I got home a little early and had decided to try to make the evening special. I had bought some flowers and had them on the table. I had

TABLE 10-1
List of Feeling Words

Negative Moods

Depression/Dejection

Sad	Bored
Blue	Gloomy
Helpless	Grim
Hopeless	Low
Miserable	Rejected
Worthless	Hurt
Discouraged	Sorry
Unhappy	

Anxiety/Tension

Shaky	Tense
Restless	Nervous
Anxious	Fearful
Panicky	Insecure
Terrified	Frightened
Bashful	Shy
Worried	Confused

Fatigue

Exhausted	Listless
Fatigued	Sluggish
Weary	Wilted
Lifeless	Tired

Anger/Hostility

Angry	Frustrated
Resentful	Spiteful
Bitter	Agitated
Furious	Critical
Disgusted	Enraged
Annoyed	Irritated
Mad	Outraged

Other Negative Mood States

Bewildered	Alone
Jealous	Upset
Ashamed	Guilty
Incompetent	Stupid

Positive Moods

Energy/Vigor

Active	Lively
Peppy	Vigorous
Energetic	Enthusiastic
Adventurous	

Happy/Joyful

Cheerful	Happy
Excited	Pleased
Amused	Hopeful
Delighted	Gay
Glad	Joyful
Thrilled	

Relaxed/Calm

Gentle	Peaceful
Calm	Relaxed
Contented	

Close/Warm

Loving	Warm
Devoted	Safe
Secure	Tender
Sexy	Turned-on
Close	Loved
Friendly	Affectionate
Whole	Sympathetic

Other Positive Mood States

Agreeable	Cooperative
Confident	Inspired
Lucky	Ambitious

showered and was waiting for her, and then I got this phone call. Sarah and her co-workers had left work early to get a couple of drinks. She asked me if I would like to come to the restaurant and join the group rather than having dinner at home. It was clear that was what she wanted to do. I didn't want to force her to come home, so I said fine.

Therapist: So you had decided to surprise her with a nice homecoming, and she asked you to eat with her friends instead. How did you feel when she asked you that?

Husband: I was *hurt.* I had come home early for a nice evening, and she was out drinking. It was a hopeless feeling, like here we go again. Someone or something always seems more important than me or us. . . .

In the above example, the therapist guided the client through the details of the evening, and he was then able to recall how he felt. Often it is easier for the client to label feelings if he or she focuses on the details of the situation rather than trying to remember some isolated feeling from several days ago. In addition, a spouse can learn to label the feelings more immediately as they occur in the environment. Using a format similar to the Daily Record of Dysfunctional Thoughts, the individual provides a brief, concrete description of the event, associated thoughts, and resultant emotions. The goal in this case is not to isolate dysfunctional thoughts but rather to clarify emotions.

The above strategies capitalize on the linkages between behavior, cognitions, and affect. Consequently, when a spouse cannot label affect, increasing the salience of the related behavior and cognitions can serve as a way of clarifying the emotion. Some spouses experience a related but different problem. They can label their emotions, but they do not relate the emotions to behaviors and cognitions. In such circumstances, the goal is to clarify whatever the client does experience and use this salient information to build the linkages with behavior and cognitions. For example, one husband recognized that he often was irritable on the weekends, particularly Sunday. He could suggest a number of reasons why he might be irritable, but he did not experience any sense of relationship between these factors and his irritability. First, the therapist asked the husband to describe the irritability, what it was like.

Husband: Well, it is like I don't want anybody bothering me. I have this feeling of doom that at any minute someone is going to come in and start making demands on me. At the same time, that doesn't make much sense because Tammy and the kids really make very few requests and demands on me.

Therapist: Fine, but the sense is that someone is going to intrude on your freedom and make demands on you, and that makes you feel irritable. You mentioned that there were several things going on that might contribute to your irritability. What are they?

After continued discussion, it became clear that the husband greatly disliked his job and had dreaded going back to work each Monday for years. Even though the link between his job and his irritability on Sundays made sense to him cognitively, subjectively he still did not experience the two as causally related. Therefore, the therapist asked the husband to think about his job the next Sunday, to consider the upcoming day and week, and to label his feelings. Also on Sunday, the couple was to share their feelings about the upcoming week. The husband completed this task and was able to clarify that his irritability was related to his dread of returning to an unpleasant job.

Finally, helping an individual label feelings and relate them to internal and external events is greatly facilitated by practice in expressing emotions. These communication skills, described below, are of extreme importance in the treatment of many distressed couples.

EMOTIONAL EXPRESSIVENESS TRAINING

Many couples are unable to express their emotions in a productive manner. Some individuals have particular difficulty expressing negative feelings, whereas others experience difficulty verbalizing positive, warm, or tender feelings. To assist in these communication difficulties, emotional expressiveness training (EET) is an appropriate intervention. (Actually, EET teaches spouses to express both emotions and related cognitions. Rarely would an individual express emotions without sharing the thoughts that accompany them.) However, some persons who do not express their emotions are not convinced of the appropriateness or usefulness of such communication. In such cases, individuals are very action-oriented and focus on solving problems and seeing tangible changes. Such persons usually delight in problem-solving training but are uncertain whether expressing emotions does much more than upset people and serve as an obstacle to progress. A typical response to such concerns is as follows:

Therapist: I agree that reaching solutions and resolving problems are an important part of life, and we are going to focus on problem-solving skills during our therapy. But learning to express emotions effectively also can be helpful to a relationship. Even in terms of reaching solutions, understanding each person's feelings and thoughts about an issue is important. Often solutions to a problem are not carried out appropriately. Sometimes that is because one person's feelings were not listened to and taken into account in reaching the solution. Then that person was angry and undermined the solution.

Also there is more to marital communication than just reaching solutions to problems. You mentioned that you don't feel very close to each other any more. Well, sharing thoughts and feelings seems to bring people close together. I know that it may be difficult and even embarrassing to share your feelings with each other. But I'd like to teach you how, and then you can decide whether it is a way of interacting with each other that you find rewarding.

Similarly, some individuals object to the specific guidelines included in EET training. A courtroom attorney had major concerns about communicating subjectively. His professional identity was built on establishing truth. Feelings and subjectivity were of no use. In responding, the therapist noted that the type of communication the client was describing often did contribute to one side's winning and one side's losing. Such is not the goal and is, in fact, to be avoided in most marital interactions because it makes the two parties adversaries rather than a team. Thus, there are appropriate contexts for different types of communication.

Role of the Therapist

EET is a communication training strategy, and the therapist assumes the role of teacher and coach, almost identical to the role played in problem solving and related communications training from a BMT perspective. In fact, some behavioral marital therapists teach EET as the first phase of problem solving (e.g., Hahlweg, Schindler, Revenstorf, & Brengelmann, 1984). Teaching EET to couples uses several different intervention strategies. First, there is a didactic component. The therapist explains the skills to be taught and how they are to be implemented by the couple. Handouts supplied in this chapter (Table 10-2) assist in this aspect of training.

Second, the therapist models these skills with the couple. One partner assumes the role of expresser or listener (explained below), and the therapist assumes the other role. The therapist then models the appropriate communication; if cotherapists are available, the two therapists can model the two roles for the couple and answer any questions.

Next, the couple attempts to implement the skills themselves. During this time, the therapist is a coach, commenting on the couple's appropriate use of skills and assisting them when they have difficulty. For example the therapist might comment after one spouse has expressed his or her feelings: "Will, that was much better. You really stayed subjective that time. You told Jill that this is merely how *you* saw it, your feelings, rather than the absolute truth. That is what we are after."

One major difference among therapists is the extent to which they model when one spouse has difficulty appropriately implementing a skill. Some therapists respond by modeling frequently, "Say this. You are really excited about our vacation. You really want to get away from writing that book." Other therapists try to isolate the difficulty, clarify any guidelines that seem to be problematic, and ask the spouse to try again. The intervention of choice depends on the stage of training and the ability level of the couple. The therapist does not want to overwhelm the couple with information at any given time or make the couple feel inadequate owing to repeated failures. Modeling is less demanding than asking the spouse to create his or her own response. In order to develop skills independent of the therapist, however, couples are asked to construct their own communication whenever possible based on feedback from the therapist. Other guidelines which were provided for the role of the therapist in discussing BMT are applicable for teaching EET skills also.

Expresser Skills

Once initial concerns about sharing feelings have been addressed, the couple begins EET training. One of the two basic sets of skills is referred to as expresser skills (Guerney, 1977). These communication skills are for the person who is expressing his or her feelings and thoughts. Table 10-2 summarizes these skills.

Subjectivity.

The first guideline focuses on expressing one's views subjectively, and not as absolute truth. The general atmosphere to be created by the expresser is, "This is how I *feel*; this is what I *think*. It may or may not agree with how other people feel or see the same situation, but this is my point of view." Often spouses argue over who is right and wrong. This tends to distract them from trying to understand the other person because they are focused instead on winning the argument. Keeping one's position subjective can help to avoid discussions about who is to blame.

TABLE 10-2
Guidelines for Expresser and Empathic Listener*

Expresser Skills

1. State your views *subjectively,* as *your own* feelings and thoughts, not as absolute truth.
2. Express your *emotions or feelings.* When talking about your partner, state your feelings about your partner, not just about an event or a situation.
3. When expressing negative emotions or criticisms, also include any positive feelings you have about the person or situation.
4. Make your statement as specific as possible, both in terms of specific emotions and thoughts.
5. Express your feelings and thoughts in a way that shows that you are aware of the impact your statement may have on your partner and that you understand and care about your partner's feelings.

Empathic Listener Skills

1. Show that you understand your partner's statement and accept his or her right to have those thoughts and feelings. Demonstrate this acceptance through your tone of voice, facial expressions, and posture.
2. After your partner finishes speaking, *summarize and restate* your partner's most important feelings, desires, conflicts, and thoughts.
3. Try to put yourself in your partner's place and look at the situation from his or her perspective in order to determine how the other person feels and thinks about the issue.
4. While in the listener role, *do not*:
    a. ask questions,
    b. express your own viewpoint or opinion,
    c. interpret or change the meaning of your partner's statement,
    d. offer solutions or attempt to solve a problem if one exists,
    e. make judgments or evaluate what your partner has said.

* These guidelines are based on recommendations presented by Guerney (1977).

Expression of feelings.

The second guideline is for the individual to express his or her emotions. Frequently couples do not differentiate between (a) their emotional reactions and (b) their thoughts. Whereas the spouses are encouraged to express their thoughts, the therapist encourages them to include their emotions as well. After receiving such encouragement, an individual may respond, "OK, I feel that you should come home when you say you are coming home." This is important information, but the person still has not made his or her emotional reaction explicit; instead, another thought was provided. Statements of the form, "I feel *that*..." typically are followed by a thought rather than an emotion.

One of the major purposes of expressing emotions is to help spouses feel closer to each other. This goal is accomplished in part by sharing one's thoughts and feelings about almost any issue; such disclosure assists in getting to know each other better. In addition, closeness can be facilitated by expressing feelings directly *about the partner* and the relationship, particularly when the emotion expressed is positive. The following is an intervention by a therapist which was oriented toward helping a couple focus on the tender feelings experienced during the previous week.

Wife: I really liked it when you washed the dishes before I got home Wednesday night. I was exhausted, and it was such a relief to get to come home and just relax. I really appreciate what you did.

Therapist: That's a nice expression of your feelings. You got across what it felt like for you to come home to that environment. It would be helpful, though, if you let Bill know how it made you feel about *him,* that he surprised you with doing the dishes. I know you appreciated that he did it, but what were your feelings for him?

Wife: I just felt really warm toward you. I felt like we were sort of back in our old partnership, and that felt so good. I guess I just love you and want to make this thing work.

Therapist: Nice, when something good happens, don't just let the other person know how you feel about the situation; let your partner know how you feel about him or her or the relationship. Is the difference clear?...

Underlying positives.

The third expresser guideline recommends that positive feelings also should be expressed whenever realistic. This is referred to as expressing underlying positives (Guerney, 1977). Although distressed couples are reluctant to acknowledge it, many negative feelings result when positive feelings are frustrated. Focusing on the positive feelings makes it much easier for the partner to hear the negative feelings. For example, a husband might be angry at his wife when she does not come home on time from work in the evening. Instead of arriving home at 7:00 as she had stated, she arrived at 9:00. He might have several feelings about the event. Most recognizable, he might be angry with her for not doing what she said she would do. Focusing on this feeling alone might result in an argument in which the wife tries to defend her actions. However, the husband also is likely to have been worried about her because she was so late, fearing that something might have happened to her. Having him express his concern about her safety could be helpful in emphasizing the care that still remained for her. However, when spouses are angry with each other, they seem unlikely to recognize or at least spontaneously acknowledge their more positive accompanying feelings. Therefore, the therapist initially may need to probe for the more positive feelings. The following is such an example:

Husband: I just feel incredibly bored and helpless with the whole relationship right now. We seem to have very little in common and don't even know each other.

Therapist: Your feelings of boredom and helplessness come through clearly. Remember we talked earlier about expressing underlying positives. I wonder what it is that you would like in the relationship. Why don't you express your feelings to Alice about that before she reflects?

Husband: Well, I'd like things to be more like they were the first couple of years that we were married. You know, we had fun together and enjoyed being with each other. I don't necessarily expect all that romance back again, but I would like for us to feel close again. . . .

The above example points out one very useful intervention for obtaining underlying positives even when the speaker is not currently experiencing positive feelings. The therapist always can ask the spouse to express how he or she *would want things to be in the future*. Thus, the therapist can ask for current underlying positive feelings if they seem to be present or focus on the positives the spouse would want for the relationship in the future. However, such feelings should not be contrived, or clearly they will lose their impact.

Specificity.

The fourth guideline calls for the speaker to be as specific as possible in his or her statement. Many persons routinely state that they "like, dislike, feel good, feel bad." For some of these persons, the difficulty in expressing a specific emotion results from not being able to label the emotion. For others, their affective state seems to be somewhat diffuse and undifferentiated, being primarily positive or negative in tone. In either case, the person can benefit from attempting to clarify his or her emotion. The therapist can help attain this increased specificity by asking the speaker to try to state more clearly what the emotion is, or if a label is hard to find, then merely to describe what the emotion is like. Similarly, the therapist can suggest that the speaker try to reexperience that emotion right now during the session, with the hope that this will make the emotion more accessible to expression. Providing a list of words that describe a variety of emotions, such as in Table 10-1, also can be useful in this process.

Empathy.

The speaker should try to put him- or herself in the listener's position to anticipate the impact that the expression will have on the listener. That is, the current communication skills are not meant to provide an opportunity for a speaker to crush the partner through harsh or cruel statements under the guise of "Well, I thought I was supposed to express what I felt." It is difficult to provide specific guidelines regarding what the speaker might profitably refrain from expressing. In part this will be a function of the particular couple and what they are comfortable sharing with each other. The general guideline is to be aware of the impact that a statement may have and not needlessly hurt the partner. If there is something negative that the speaker wishes to express, he or she should express it in the least destructive way possible. Thus, one way to show that the speaker cares about the partner's feelings is by choosing carefully what content to express. In addition, the speaker can demonstrate empathy when expressing something that may be painful for the partner to hear by commenting that the speaker can understand that it may be difficult: "I realize that it is hard for you to talk about your weight, but I think it is really interfering with my sexual attraction to you. I don't feel the excitement and desire that I have in the past."

Although these guidelines may seem numerous and somewhat difficult for the speaker to keep in mind when addressing the partner, in actuality they are not difficult for most speakers. Phrased succinctly, the guidelines ask the speaker to express his or her feelings in a subjective manner, being as specific and empathic as possible. In addition, when expressing negative feelings, the speaker should express underlying positives along with the negatives.

Empathic Listener Skills

The empathic listener has two different tasks. The first is to focus on what the expresser is saying while the expresser speaks. Second, the listener is to reflect the expresser's most important thoughts and emotions after the speaker has finished. These guidelines, developed by Guerney (1977), are presented more formally in Table 10-2.

Frame of mind.

The first guideline attempts to put the listener in the proper frame of mind for listening. It asks the listener to put him- or herself in the speaker's place to understand how the speaker thinks or feels about the issue. Many persons while listening are focused on evaluating the speaker and preparing a rebuttal; the first guideline attempts to set a different tone. The listener's role simply is to try to understand the speaker's position on the issue. While listening, the listener is asked not to evaluate or prepare a defense, just listen.

Empathy.

The second guideline is the heart of the communication aspect of the listener role. The listener is to show understanding and acceptance of the speaker, both while the speaker is speaking and while the listener is responding to the speaker. In large part, this can be accomplished nonverbally. While listening, the person's posture and facial expression convey much information. If the listener is leaning back with arms folded across his or her chest and is turned away from the speaker, then the speaker is unlikely to feel listened to and accepted. Similarly, if the listener's facial expression appears angry, bored, or cold and emotionless, then the speaker is not likely to feel accepted. Although any nonverbal cues carried to the extreme will be counterproductive, the listener generally is encouraged to face the speaker, sit somewhat erect, make eye contact, and adopt a facial expression that shows that he or she is interested in listening to the other person. When responding to the speaker, the same nonverbal cues are important, as is the listener's tone of voice. When reflecting the speaker's message, some listeners speak with a rather flat tone of voice as if they are repeating some message that they are trying to memorize. Clearly, this is not the goal; instead, the listener's tone of voice should emphasize the emotions expressed by the speaker.

After the speaker has finished speaking, the empathic listener is to reflect the speaker's most important thoughts and emotions. Many persons have difficulty with the listener skills; these difficulties are anticipated in the remainder of the guidelines which tell the listener what *not* to do. Thus the listener is not to ask questions, express his or her own thoughts and emotions, interpret the speaker's message, make suggestions for solving problems, or make judgments about the speaker's statements. Simply put, the listener merely reflects, with an emphasis on the speaker's emotions.

Some persons are awkward in reflecting a partner's messages, even when they understand the goal. Some individuals try to repeat the speaker's message word for word as if it were a memory test. The therapist can reinforce the person for reflecting but point out that the emotions and thoughts can be summarized. Usually the listener's reflection is considerably shorter than the speaker's original expression. The listener also can be encouraged to use his or her own words without changing the meaning of the speaker's message. Awkwardness in reflecting also occurs when the listener routinely begins the reflection in the same way. That is, some persons regularly state, "You feel...," or "You said...," or "I heard you say that you feel...." There is nothing wrong with these phrases when used on occasion, but if for nothing more than the sanity of a therapist who conducts several sessions a day, some variability is in order. The listener can reflect what the speaker said without any kind of introductory phrase: "It really hurt you when I didn't bake you a birthday cake this year. Even though you feel sort of foolish because you like to think things like that are mainly for kids, not having a cake made you feel unimportant and like you weren't worth the trouble to me."

On other occasions, listeners are resistant to reflecting what the speaker has said. The guideline asks the listener to show *understanding and acceptance* by reflecting. Some persons do not want to reflect because they think that a reflection signifies *agreement* with what has been said. Because they often do not agree with the speaker's statements or believe that the speaker should feel a certain way, they hesitate to reflect. An important distinction should be made to the couple between (a) agreement and (b) understanding and acceptance. Understanding simply means that the listener is aware of what the speaker is thinking and feeling, not that the listener agrees. Similarly, acceptance is meant to acknowledge to the speaker that, "I may or may not agree with what you just said, but I accept your right to take that position and feel that way." Thus a reflection is not meant to imply agreement. Instead, a reflection is a way of saying, "Here is what I heard you say, and I respect your feelings and thoughts."

Some couples are resistant to reflecting for other reasons as well. A complaint from some couples is that reflecting every time the other person speaks feels unnatural, and most people do not communicate that way with each other. As a result, the couples report that they reflect systematically when they are practicing their communication skills, but they are unlikely to do so otherwise. Even most therapists who value the role of reflections do not reflect every time the client speaks. Instead, reflections are used for particular therapeutic purposes. Therefore, once couples become adept at reflecting, they are taught particular occasions when it will be particularly helpful for them to reflect. However, in the early stages of skills training, they are asked to reflect after each speaker's statements.

Steps in Teaching Emotional Expressiveness Skills

Expressing positive feelings.

The initial attempts at using EET skills are aimed primarily at helping the couple become comfortable expressing feelings and reflecting. Therefore, each spouse is asked to assume one role, and the speaker expresses his or her feelings on some topic. In order to allow the couple to concentrate on the skills and not become negatively aroused, the initial topics discussed should be rather nonthreatening. Typically, couples are asked to restrict themselves to discussing issues about which they feel positive. The topic can focus on something that the partner has done recently that the spouse likes, some positive trait of the partner, something about the relationship that the speaker likes, something outside of the relationship but within the personal life of the speaker, or something outside of either individual's personal life.

Often distressed couples cannot or are unwilling to say something positive about their partners, so asking them to focus on something positive about their spouses can be counterproductive. The therapist must gauge the likelihood that such a request will be successful and direct the topic accordingly. Alternatively, the couple can be given the wide range of options listed above, making sure that the choices are presented in a way such that focusing on issues outside of the relationship is not perceived as an insult. The speaker expresses his or her feelings and thoughts on the topic chosen by the speaker, and the partner reflects. Distressed couples frequently begin expressing positive feelings but within a few moments drift into expressing negative emotions. Such instances provide the therapist with an opportunity to comment on how easily couples drift into discussing negatives without giving appropriate attention to the positive. On the other hand, some couples enjoy the instruction to express positive feelings to the partner. They have been deadlocked into negative interaction and rarely share anything positive with the other person. This exercise, in essence, gives them permission to do so.

The partner reflects the important feelings and thoughts of the speaker. If the reflection is inaccurate or contains significant omissions, then the speaker repeats the message. Also, if the speaker has more to express on the same issue, then he or she expresses again, followed by the reflection of the partner. The therapist may then invite the speaker to express positive feelings about other topics that come to mind. At this point, the interaction does not resemble a typical conversation because several unrelated issues are being addressed without any attempt at bridging the topics. The couple is clearly practicing skills. After several opportunities in the same role, the partners are asked to reverse roles.

Who is speaker first or second is not critical, but in some couples asking one partner to speak first can be useful. If the couple has numerous negative feelings that seem to dominate their relationship, then asking the person who seems more willing to say positive things to be the speaker first can help to break the negative interaction cycle. That is, some spouses convey the message "I'm not going to say something nice first. You be my guest." The therapist is wise to respect this message, although asking the same spouse to make positive statements first session after session can create or maintain a skewed interaction pattern that mirrors the couple's interaction outside of the session in which one spouse typically makes conciliatory efforts.

Changing roles.

After a few sessions when the couple has become more skilled in expressing and reflecting, the therapist might suggest that they select a positive topic to discuss and alternate roles on that one issue. That is, they are to have a conversation on a topic about which they feel positive. In order to accomplish this task, the couple needs to know how to change roles spontaneously. In most cases, this is easily accomplished. One person begins as the speaker and the other as the listener. After the listener reflects, the speaker may speak again, or they may change roles and the listener becomes the speaker. The important issue at this point in the training is for the listener always to reflect before becoming the speaker or before the original speaker speaks again. Thus the pattern is: speak, reflect, speak, reflect, etc.

Some couples do not need particular guidelines to decide whether to change roles or to resume the same roles after a reflection. They use cues employed in everyday conversation to recognize whether a person is finished or wishes to continue speaking after the reflection. However, there may be particular times when either the speaker or the listener wishes to change roles. If the speaker wants to hear the partner's views and feelings on a matter, the speaker can ask, "What do you think?"

At other times, the listener may want to become the speaker for any number of reasons. Guerney (1977) has outlined some of the more likely reasons that the listener may want to change roles: (a) if the listener has some information that might alter the speaker's understanding or feelings about a situation; (b) if the speaker is having difficulty continuing listening; or (c) if the speaker has repeated him- or herself several times and the listener seemingly has reflected the statement and feelings appropriately. On such occasions, the listener should reflect and then comment that he or she would like to speak, or speak directly after reflecting.

If the listener wants to speak while the speaker is still speaking (for example, to provide updated information which would change the speaker's perspective), the couple can develop some sort of nonverbal signal which does not interrupt the speaker but lets the speaker know that the listener has something useful to add. Below is such an example.

Husband: That really infuriates me that my mother did not send John a birthday present or even a card. She has always sent him something really nice, and he has come to expect it [wife raises index finger, an agreed upon cue]. What do you want?

Wife: It's really upsetting to you that mom seemed to have forgotten John's birthday. But actually she didn't. After you left, she called and wished him happy birthday. She had ordered him something personalized, and it just arrived two days ago. She said she mailed it immediately. I think it is something pretty special from the way she spoke. She said it is just like something that she and your father gave you when you were growing up.

The wife's signal was particularly well timed because it could help to minimize her husband's guilt for becoming upset with his mother due to a misunderstanding. Many people have found that raising an index finger is a somewhat nondisruptive yet recognizable way to inform the partner that the listener wants to speak.

At times the listener has difficulty continuing listening because the speaker talks at great length. Some speakers provide many details which are of little interest to the partner. Other speakers do not provide too many details but talk about many different issues before they let the listener respond. The result is a listener who does not want to listen. Many partners on the receiving end of this verbal barrage have learned how to make eye contact, nod appropriately, and say "um hum" without knowing what the speaker is talking about—a polite turnoff. In such cases, the therapist assists the speaker in changing this speaking style.

For the person who provides needless detail, the therapist can instruct the individual to pause, think of the main point, express that main idea with a bit of supporting information, and then stop. Also, the listener can be instructed to provide some nonverbal cue if the speaker is giving too many details.

Similarly, the person who talks about numerous issues can be helped to develop only one point at a time while speaking. We tell couples to speak in paragraphs, not chapters. That is, decide what the main topic is. Express that main idea and give no more than a few sentences before letting the partner reflect. Then if the speaker has more to say, continue after the reflection. At the same time, spouses differ in the amount of detail and number of topics that they like to share. When the therapist becomes aware of this, it should be spelled out to the couple as a difference in personal styles, so that neither is offended by the other's actions. Then the therapist attempts to help the couple learn some compromise stance on the amount of detail and number of topics discussed.

Finally, some persons repeat themselves even when the partner has accurately reflected the speaker's message. On some occasions, the speaker seemingly repeats him- or herself because the speaker believes some important point was not appropriately grasped, and he or she is attempting to make it clear. Second, the speaker may repeat in order to clarify the issue in his or her own head. Repetition can also occur when a person has such strong feelings about an issue that he or she feels a need to express them again. In such cases, the repetition is not intended primarily for the listener to understand the message as much as it is for the speaker to clarify for self or to emote. These reasons for repeating seem legitimate, and the repetition can be useful to the speaker. On the other hand, some persons repeat themselves for no apparent reason. Such a pattern can be frustrating for the partner, who may avoid conversations or suddenly vent anger from the frustration, much to the surprise of the speaker who thought they were having a fine conversation. In this instance, the therapist needs to point out the pattern to the couple and help the individual not repeat him- or herself.

Expressing negative feelings.

After the spouses are able to conduct conversations in which they express positive feelings and can change roles, the therapist might introduce expression of negative feelings. In the couple's initial attempts, the topic of the negative feelings might best be focused outside of the relationship, or at least restricted to more minor issues within the relationship. Again, the goal is to give the couple practice in using the skills before they become highly negatively aroused. After some practice expressing negatives on less threatening issues, the couple can begin expressing feelings about some of their more important concerns in the marriage.

Content of discussions.

At least three types of issues are profitable for the couple to address. First, couples might discuss their emotions and thoughts about happenings that occur on a day-to-day basis. These include specific events which occurred between therapy sessions and which the person has feelings about, either positive or negative. These events might be related to the relationship or not. Some couples complain that they have little to say to each other, or that their conversations are boring, focusing on who ate what for lunch that day. Helping these couples to express their feelings about local, national, and worldwide events can provide a source of stimulation. At the same time, commenting on minor occurrences in the relationship is important. Showing appreciation for small acts of kindness, complimenting the partner on routine behaviors, and so forth is helpful because major events do not happen to most couples daily. Similarly, expressing discontent about seemingly small issues is important if not overdone because it allows for clearing the air.

Second, expressing emotions and thoughts on the major issues that brought the couple to therapy is clearly needed. Whereas it might seem that couples would rush to do this, many couples do not. This can occur for at least two reasons. Some couples have a generally avoidant style and would prefer not to address difficult issues directly. Consequently, they will continue to focus on minor issues and must be encouraged to confront their major problems. Also, the format of the treatment can create a pattern in which couples do not focus on their major problems. Early in the skills training phase of EET, the couple is encouraged to deal with minor issues, think back to the day's or week's events, and express thoughts and emotions about what occurred. Consequently, this is what couples come to expect when they come to therapy. As a result, after several sessions of training in EET and being told that it is time to focus on more important issues, some couples respond that they cannot think of anything to talk about. Thus, the therapist needs to clarify that

TABLE 10-3
Topics About Which to Share Thoughts and Feelings[1]

1 . How do I feel about my lifetime goals?
2. You are my sweetheart because...
3. I enjoy listening to you talk about...
4. How are we teaching our children about sexuality? How do I feel about it?
5. In what way are you a mystery to me?
6. What is my most prized possession?
7. In what way am I afraid to grow old?
8. What special qualities do I admire most in you?
9. How would I feel and what would my life be like if you were to die?
10. How do I see you as a giving person?
11. How do I feel about the influence of my mother in my life?
12. How do I feel about the "me" I am and the "me" I want to be?
13. How do I feel when I avoid sharing something with you?
14. How do I feel when you praise me?
15. What did I enjoy most about last week?
16. Why do I want to stay married to you today?
17. How do I feel when we are intimate?
18. Why do I love you today?
19. How do I feel when you accept my feelings?
20. When do I feel closest to you?
21. How do I feel about planning for a romantic time together?
22. How do I feel when you touch me in public?
23. What about you do I find most attractive?
24. What do I really like about myself?
25. What do I really dislike about myself?
26. What can I change to improve our relationship? How do I feel about making those changes?
27. I like to look at you when... How do I feel telling you this?
28. What gift would I like to give one of our children?
29. How would I feel if our TV were to break?
30. I would really feel pampered if... How do I feel telling you this?
31. You help me to be a better person in the following ways. How do I feel about that?
32. What special qualities do I most admire in you?
33. When was the last time we did something crazy?

(continued)

---

[1]From Worldwide Marriage Encounter, *Love Is . . ., 1984* (pp. 1–12). St. Paul: Brown and Bigelow, Inc., 1984. Adapted by permission.

34. If I had my life to start again, what would I change?
35. How do I feel when you compliment me to others?
36. How do I want to spend our "golden years"?
37. Thoughts of our retirement days bring feelings of. . .
38. If I knew I were to die tomorrow, what would I do and feel today?
39. If I had to choose just one day to remember, I'd choose. . . because. . .
40. What do I need from you when I'm feeling crummy?
41. I would like people to think of me as. . . How does telling you make me feel?
42. What feeling do I find most difficult to reveal to you?
43. In what ways am I afraid to look ahead? Why?
44. If I could change one thing about me, I'd. . .
45. What quality as a parent do I most admire in you?
46. What was my greatest fear as a new bride/bridegroom?
47. What do I like most about our sex life? Why?
48. What kind of death frightens me most? Why?
49. What do I want most to be remembered for?
50. How do I feel in my bathing suit?
51. How am I becoming a better person because of you? How do I feel about that?
52. How do I feel having you to share special times with?
53. What needs of yours do I see me being able to help with?
54. What are my feelings when you tell me you need me?
55. What are my feelings about the way we spent last weekend?
56. What nice thing have I noticed about you this week and have not told you?
57. What are my feelings about the way our children respond to you?
58. How do I feel when you show your love for me in front of others?
59. What year of my life would I like to relive?
60. How do I feel when relatives visit?
61. What goals would I like to see us achieve in the next few months?
62. What are the thoughts and feelings I have about the birth of one of our children?
63. What can I do to make our relationship stronger?
64. What joys have our children given us?
65. How important are material things to me?
66. How do I feel when you listen to me?
67. How do I feel when someone hurts you?
68. How do I feel about part of our lives continuing on through our children?
69. What are my top priorities in our lives today?

(continued)

TABLE 10-3 (*continued*)

70. What hopes do I have for our children and what can we do to help them?
71. How do I feel about our religious lives and what values we are teaching our children?
72. How do I feel spending the rest of my life with you?
73. How do I feel when I think of one of our children dying?
74. How do I feel watching our children grow?
75. What do I like best about you?
76. When was the last time I saw myself as a failure? How did I feel then?
77. What excites me most about you?
78. What are the three closest moments we shared together?
79. How do I feel when we spend an evening alone together?
80. What one possession do I want most and can't have?
81. In what area of our relationship do I have the most control?
82. What do we have to be thankful for?
83. How can I put more romance in our marriage?
84. If I could take you anywhere, where would we go and what would we do?
85. How do I feel when you kiss me?
86. In what area do we as a couple need to grow?
87. What area is the hardest for me to share with you?
88. What is the nicest thing that happened to me this week?
89. What do I value most in life?
90. What is our favorite holiday memory?
91. You bring out the best in me when...
92. What is the most embarrassing time I can remember in my life?
93. What is the biggest mistake my parents made that I hope to avoid with our children?
94. I know I have a real weakness for...
95. When I am feeling depressed, I want you to...
96. Our family tradition which I value most is...
97. I know I can count on you to...
98. Whose good opinion is important to me?
99. I'm happy to be alive today because...
100. The most unfair thing that has even happened to me was... How did that make me feel telling you this?

---

a shift in mind set is appropriate, that the couple should start to deal with the important content issues that have been of concern to them. The therapist can have available to the couple a summary of the major concerns that they provided during the intake sessions and on the self-report inventories. This does not mean that the couple is restricted to this list. They may wish to share their reactions to events that occurred or emotions they felt during the week. Such a focus is legitimate, but the therapist must remain attentive that the couple is not avoiding discussing their major concerns.

Third, there are a number of "basic life issues" which many couples enjoy discussing. A list of possible topics for discussion is presented in Table 10-3. Many of these are issues that the couples would not think to discuss but help them get to know each other better and stimulate their thinking. For example, the question "What is my most prized possession?" often results in answers that are quite a surprise for the partner. Questions such as "In what way am I afraid to grow old?" can result in a very touching, emotional interaction. Typically, couples are given the entire list and choose topics for discussion. The use of this topic list is particularly helpful on occasions when the couple may need a break from addressing their major problems, when one partner states that during this session he or she would like to focus on something positive, or when the couple genuinely is having difficulty thinking of issues to discuss.

Selectively reflecting.

As noted earlier, in the initial stages of EET, the listener is taught to reflect each time the speaker makes a statement. However, our experience is that couples often do not do this except when they are practicing their skills. Therefore, we attempt to teach couples occasions when reflecting is particularly important. Couples are then encouraged to reflect at these particular times. Table 10-4 includes a list of situations in which it is particularly helpful to reflect. These occasions are based on the functions that are served by reflections. First, it is impossible to reflect accurately with any regularity unless the listener has been attentive to the speaker. Therefore, a reflection is a communication from the listener to the speaker that the listener heard what the speaker said. Consequently, whenever one spouse has been complaining that the partner does not listen or pay attention when they have a conversation, the partner can demonstrate that he or she is listening by reflecting often. Closely related, a reflection can be a sign of respect—indicating that the listener values what the speaker is saying. Therefore, any time the listener wants to demonstrate respect for the speaker's emotions and thoughts, a reflection can be useful. This might be needed on many occasions, but one particular instance is when the speaker has just said something with which the listener is about to disagree. The acceptance of the speaker's emotions and thoughts on the issue followed by a *subjectively stated* differing point of view can be quite effective in avoiding a needless discussion of who is right and who is wrong.

Third, reflections slow down the speed of the interaction. For distressed couples, interactions often move too rapidly, particularly when they disagree and want to make their point. Therefore, when the conversation is moving too quickly, a reflection phrased slowly can bring the conversation back to a more moderate pace.

Fourth, reflections can clarify misunderstandings because the speaker can make clear whether the listener correctly heard the communication. Consequently, the listener can reflect whenever the listener is not certain that he or she correctly understood the speaker's message. Even when the listener believes that he or she correctly understood the speaker, that may or may not be so. Many spouses will make statements to the effect, "I understand what you just said." However, when asked to reflect, their reflections involve significant distortions, additions, or omissions.

Fifth, reflections make the speaker feel understood and keep the focus on the speaker. As a result, reflections are helpful when one partner wants to keep the focus on the speaker, perhaps to help the speaker continue addressing an issue that is hard for the speaker to discuss. In addition, reflections can be helpful if one of the two members of the couple is rather quiet and withdrawn, as a means of drawing the quiet partner out.

TABLE 10-4
Occasions When It Is Important to Reflect the Speaker's Message

1. When the speaker thinks the responder does not listen to what the speaker says.
2. When the responder wants to show respect for what the speaker has said; this is particularly important when the responder plans to disagree with the speaker.
3. When the interaction is moving rapidly, and the responder wants to slow the conversation.
4. When the speaker has said something of importance, and the responder wants to ensure there is not a misunderstanding.
5. When the responder wants to keep the focus on the speaker.
6. When the speaker has expressed negative feelings; reflection or some other response of acknowledgment is appropriate after the speaker has expressed positive feelings.

Finally, reflections can bring about a sense of closeness between the speaker and responder when the responder shows empathy for what the speaker has said. This closeness is particularly emphasized when the speaker has expressed deeply felt emotions. An acceptance of these feelings can make the speaker feel understood, validated, and trusting of the listener. Therefore, reflections are particularly useful when the speaker has just shared important feelings with the listener.

Alternatives to reflecting.

At the same time, the automatic response to hearing deeply felt emotions is not necessarily to reflect. Generally, reflections to negative emotions are quite effective. However, other responses seem more appropriate to certain positive emotions which have included complimentary, tender, or loving comments about the listener; at such times reflections may seem somewhat awkward and unresponsive. What is important is for the listener to *acknowledge* the speaker's message in a way that will make both people feel good about the interchange.

For example, if a wife says to her husband, "You know, I really love you. We have such a fun time together when we go out," he can respond in various ways. First, he could reflect, making a statement such as "You had a great time tonight and that makes you realize how much you love me." This statement would then probably be followed by an expression of his own feelings. Second, he could reciprocate immediately, and in so doing make clear that he understood the message from his wife: "Thanks, you are pretty neat yourself. And I agree, it is great when we just take a night off and play. I feel so rejuvenated." Third, he could affirm his wife's statement or show appreciation: "Thanks for saying that. I need to know that you love me and enjoy being with me." Fourth, he could develop an interesting conversation based on the compliment: "Yeah, I had a fun time also. I've noticed that when it is just the two of us, I am a lot less shy...." Several couples have commented that reflecting feelings of love and tenderness feels more distancing when they want to reciprocate. Consequently, couples are encouraged to choose among the above types of options as well as other responses that they might think of, using a guideline of acknowledging the speaker's feelings in some way and being honest in one's own response. If the husband in the above example did not enjoy the evening, he might respond with a reflection or a statement of appreciation for his wife's comment.

DEALING WITH DYSFUNCTIONAL
EMOTIONS

Learning to label, express, and reflect emotions is of great benefit to many couples. These skills are of particular use in dealing with changing day-to-day feelings which arise. However, for some couples, there are protracted, recurrent, and/or intense emotional responses which are disruptive to the relationship. The goal in such circumstances is to reduce or eliminate these emotional states. Often, expressing these feelings to the partner is a first step in dealing with these emotions. However, at times, expressing the feelings to the partner does not sufficiently modify the individual's mood. On such occasions, additional interventions are needed.

Anger

Anger based on previous events.

In a substantial number of couples, one person harbors extreme anger, either (a) as a result of some event or set of events that have occurred in the past, or (b) in response to current circumstances. Anger based on events from the past presents a special difficulty for the therapist and the couple because the behavior is no longer present and cannot be altered. An unlimited number of events can result in such feelings, but several common ones dominate couples' concerns: (a) one partner had sexual affairs during an earlier time in their marriage; (b) one partner physically or verbally abused the other in the past; (c) one partner using alcohol or other drugs to excess; (d) one partner was left uninvolved in the marriage and leaving the other with most of the responsibilities for children and family, along with ignoring the emotional needs of the other. If these behaviors are still occurring, then interventions can focus on altering the behaviors or attempting to change the emotional response to the behaviors. However, if these behaviors have already terminated, then the couple and therapist have the task of dealing with the residual feelings from the painful events. The spouse who has changed his or her negative behavior is in the awkward position of having made a difficult behavior change which has been requested numerous times by the partner, only to find that it is not enough. The partner does not welcome him or her back to the marriage with open arms. Instead, the partner who was abused is angry and resentful. (Although rarely is one partner solely the victim and the other the culprit, in order to have some label to refer to the partners, the one who has perpetrated the negative behaviors will be referred to as the abuser, and the partner will be referred to as the abused. These labels are being applied broadly and are not meant to be restricted to physical abuse.) The partner who was abusive does not know what to do to improve the relationship and will often state, "It doesn't seem to matter what I do. Nothing helps. How can I change what is already done?" The partner who was abused is likewise in an awkward, uncomfortable position. He or she is furious about what happened, but the behavior is now absent. The transgressor is trying to improve the relationship, but the abused does not know what to do with the anger. As a result, it comes out in unproductive, unpredictable ways.

Many of the interventions for dealing with anger from the past have a cognitive focus. One major focus has to do with the concept of forgiving and forgetting. Many people are taught that they are to forgive for transgressions; however, this is difficult to do depending on the meaning that is given to "forgive." The therapist can help to clarify what might and might not be reasonable in such instances:

Therapist: Sue, you were clearly hurt a lot by the affair that John had, and I don't think that that memory will actually disappear from your brain. I anticipate that you will always be aware that it happened, just like you continue to be aware of other major events that happened in your life. So I don't think you are going to actually forget it. Then there is the issue of forgiveness. Many people take forgiveness to mean that what you did is accepted as O.K. Again, I think that is unreasonable to ask. John violated what you both viewed as a major trust in your relationship, and, Sue, you have said that that is not O.K. It was not acceptable to you when he did it, and I doubt whether it will ever be acceptable to you. However, that does not mean that you have to stay locked up with all the anger. Sue, I hope you can say after a while, "I don't like what you did. It hurt me a lot. However, I do want things to work, and I'm willing to see what we can do from this point forward to make our relationship better." But I don't expect you to be able to say that right now. We have some work to do before we'll be at that point.

There are three major elements to the above message: (a) the abused will not actually forget what happened; (b) the behavior will never be acceptable; (c) in spite of the past, the couple can decide to build on their relationship, starting in the present, and not continue to punish the abuser for the past. Helping the couple to adopt reasonable expectancies and standards is important. Otherwise the abused is likely to hold onto the anger as a way of saying that he or she is justified in feeling negative about what happened.

Whereas establishing reasonable standards in this area is needed, adopting the standards often is not enough to alleviate the problem. In order to be of assistance to the couple, the therapist must understand what the abused partner is experiencing.

The "Three R's": Cognitive components of anger. As mentioned in Chapter 4, Schlesinger (1984) and Schlesinger and Epstein (1986) have noted three desires often experienced by an abused individual. These concern themes of (a) retribution, (b) restitution, and (c) refuge. Skills-oriented therapists often assume that distressed couples want to make positive changes in their relationship and are only impeded by skill deficits. However, this clearly is not always the case, particularly in the circumstances currently being discussed. One person has been greatly hurt and wants the other person to be punished in return. The message from the abused is "If you think you can do what you did to me, then come in here, say you are sorry, and expect me to go along happily, forget it. You hurt me badly, and you are going to pay for it." Some partners express this message explicitly, but others are indirect because they have been taught that revenge is immature. Therefore, they offer legitimate reasons for responding negatively to almost everything the abuser says and does. Attempting to problem-solve on other issues at this point in therapy is often disastrous because the abused finds no solution acceptable or is displeased with the way that the partner implements the solution.

This desire for *retribution* or revenge is difficult to deal with as long as it is covert. In fact, the clinician should wonder whether there is unresolved anger if one spouse has continual difficulty not blaming the partner regarding various relationship issues, has difficulty accepting any solutions (even those that he or she initially proposed), and finds almost any behavior change from the spouse to be of little consequence. The first task for the clinician is to help make the focus of the anger explicit. Next, the clinician legitimizes the anger, while not taking sides between the partners. Then the clinician points out that, because of the anger, the abused spouse is punishing the partner. Helping to make the discussion of the punishment concrete can make the angry partner recognize the impact of his or her behavior on the relationship. Also, asking the angry partner to become specific regarding what methods he or she believes are needed to punish the partner to make things even, and how long it will take to do so, can at times make the angry person see major drawbacks for clinging to the anger for long time periods.

Therapist: Bill, it seems that you really felt abused by Helen and have been angry for a long time. I can understand that, and it also seems that you have not been able to find a very satisfactory way of dealing with those angry feelings. I'd like to help you with those because I know it isn't pleasant spending most of your time being upset. Also, it seems to be pretty miserable for Helen, and that may be in part what you want. Let's try to figure out exactly what you need to do so that you will feel that you have gotten your feelings out. It would be nice if we could do something rather concentrated and get it over with. Do we need to have a session in which you just tell Helen everything that you have been feeling and have her sit there quietly without responding? Helen, could you do that if it meant that you could then get on with your marriage? Or do you need to do something else? Also, let's see how long you think you will cling to your anger. Some people hold onto this anger for weeks, some for months, and some even for years. Given your style, what do you think we can expect? Your anger is legitimate and understandable, but you do need to realize that as long as you cling to it, we have little chance of improving your marriage. I'm not trying to put all the responsibility on you because Helen's drinking has really created problems for the two of you. But you need to realize the implications of what you are doing.

In response to the therapist's request that the client identify means for expressing his or her anger, most clients respond that they do not know. Most come to recognize that because they were hurt so badly and perhaps for so long, it would require a set of extremely hostile acts to express their feelings in some satisfactory manner. It is important that the angry spouse sees the anger as under his or her control and *chooses* to give it up. Most angry spouses become even more upset if they perceive that someone is telling them that they have no right to feel what they feel or that they must now give those feelings up. It is much better for the angry party to perceive that he or she chose to give up the feelings.

Closely related to the desire for retribution, the abused spouse often wants *restitution:* "Before things will be O.K. between us, I expect you to make up for what you did to me. I expect payment, and I expect a lot." The problem is that in most cases, almost nothing that the partner does is enough. The angered spouse rejects the attempts of the partner to provide restitution, giving the message that "That is not adequate." After a period of time, the abuser is likely to become discouraged and/or angry and stop making efforts.

Many spouses attempt restitution after they have exhibited some negative behavior. Thus, asking for some degree of restitution is unlikely to seem extreme to many spouses; it is woven into the very fabric of relationships to provide something positive after someone has experienced negative events. However, the transgressor's efforts at restitution are usually oriented toward "making the other person feel better and showing that one cares." This is different from attempting to balance the books by providing an equally extreme positive behavior for every negative behavior that occurred. Thus, it is the *degree* of restitution and the idea that in some way one can make up for what was done that is unrealistic in many of these cases.

Third, the abused partner often wants *refuge* from the other, some form of protection from the possibility of a repeat of the aversive behavior. The refuge sought is often a psychological one in which the abused becomes detached emotionally from the partner and withdraws behaviorally. The abused protects him- or herself by becoming less vulnerable to further pain from the partner. It is as if the abused were saying, "You have hurt me greatly in the past, and I cannot tolerate that pain again. You are going to have to prove to me in some way that it will not happen in the future." The partner often is aware of this message and makes great efforts to "prove" his or her reformation. Again, however, almost any behaviors offered as evidence are insufficient. Following the same line of intervention, the therapist can inquire of the abused what the partner can do to *prove* his or her change. Again, rarely is a set of behaviors outlined which the abused views as sufficient evidence. The therapist might then respond in the following manner:

Therapist: I think you are right—there is nothing that George can do to suddenly prove to you that he won't have another affair. Such evidence simply does not exist. Trust is something that develops over time, and right now it is not there. I think you will grow to trust him as you two continue in the relationship, and you observe that he does not have other affairs. And, Mary, it is understandable if you feel reluctant at times to take chances and allow yourself to become vulnerable to George again. However, gradually it will become important for you to take some chances. If you hang back consistently, you won't have those critical opportunities you need to interact and rebuild a new relationship and sense of trust. That is, you build trust as you relate to each other in a trusting way and find that it works.

There is a clear logic in the strategies just described. In each instance, the therapist asks what specific behaviors would provide for adequate retribution, restitution, and refuge. Typically, the abused is unable to list such behaviors, and the therapist clarifies that such behaviors do not exist. The couple's task is not to undo or make up for what has been done. However, merely making clear to the abused that he or she cannot have what he or she wants would be somewhat less than gratifying to a person who is angry and feels cheated in the relationship. So what options are available for dealing with the angry feelings?

First, the couple is encouraged to express whatever feelings they have about the event(s). If the transgressor did behave inappropriately, he or she is encouraged to acknowledge that without justifying his or her behavior. One of the least painful ways of handling some negative interaction is to state with honesty, "I messed up. I'm sorry for what I did. I know that it hurt you, and I'll try not to do it again." Such an apology might not lay the issue to rest, but accepting responsibility for behaving negatively is often quite helpful in restoring good feelings to the relationship.

Next, the couple is asked to analyze the relationship and each person's behavior to see how each contributed to the situation in which they were involved. This is not for the purpose of attributing blame, but rather to enable the couple to understand more fully how their behaviors are interrelated. Consequently, it is helpful for each person to speak for him- or herself in describing what he or she did that contributed to the problem area, in order to avoid cross-blaming. This intervention is not to be confused with blaming the victim. A person who physically abuses another or has an extramarital relationship must take responsibility for the decision to act in that way, but those behaviors do occur in a context. Attempting to understand that context and how changes in each person's behavior can alter the situation can give a couple a sense of hope and control over what has appeared in the past as hopeless. For example, a husband might be quite angry because his wife hit him on numerous occasions. As they explore the events of the past, they might become aware of a certain pattern of behavior that can be changed.

Finally, understanding each person's behavior and how the two persons' behaviors are interrelated prepares the couple for problem solving on how to behave toward each other in the future and how they can break the chain of behaviors that have led to the negative behavior in the past. Thus the intervention strategies are likely to include cognitive restructuring, emotional expressiveness, and problem-solving techniques.

Anger based on current events.

Current aspects of the relationship also can contribute to intense and frequent anger from one or both spouses. The mere experience of anger is not cause for intervention; however, if one or both spouses are angry a great deal of the time or the experience of anger is extremely intense, intervention should be considered. Similarly, anger might result in disruptive behaviors such as shouting matches, prolonged withdrawal, and/or physical abuse; again, such experiences call for intervention.

No single intervention or set of interventions is appropriate for attempting to lower high levels or frequent expressions of anger because anger can serve a number of functions for the individual and is influenced by a number of factors. Consequently, intervening on anger within a marital relationship requires an understanding of the roles served by anger and the factors influencing anger for a given individual.

A number of investigators and theoreticians have pointed to the importance of cognitive factors in anger and other emotions (Burns, 1980; Deschner, 1984; Ellis, 1977; Neidig & Friedman, 1984; Novaco, 1975, 1976, 1978; Schachter & Singer, 1962). Ellis (1977) has suggested four irrational cognitions that he conjectures lead to an anger response:

1.   "How awful or terrible that you treat me like this!"
2.   "I can't stand your unfair behavior!"
3.   "You should not act in that unacceptable manner toward me! You must treat me fairly!"
4.   "Because of your unacceptable behavior, you deserve punishment and are a rotten person!"

These statements actually can be collapsed into two major components. First is an emotional response based on the belief that the individual has been treated unfairly (Burns, 1980). Second, a behavioral response is initiated based on the belief that people who are unfair should be punished. Consequently, as Neidig and Friedman (1984) point out, anger and anger responses are at times motivated by a sense of moral righteousness, that such injustices should not go unpunished. To the extent that anger responses are based on the above logic, then cognitive interventions are in order. First, the individual can be asked to examine the evidence that the partner has really been so unfair. Perceiving the partner as unfair is strengthened by focusing only on the partner's negative behavior. Helping the couple to recognize that both persons engage in behaviors that contribute to the problem area can be useful in altering the perception that the partner has been terribly unfair. Even if the angry spouse concludes that the partner has been unfair, the issue of whether or not the partner is allowed to make mistakes can be addressed. Finally, a discussion of the pros and cons of punishment as a response for a wrong-doing can be initiated.

Not only is anger motivated through a sense of self-righteousness, anger can also help to maintain a sense of control and mastery (Neidig & Friedman, 1984). That is, anger can be experienced as an attempt not to give up. Many spouses comment that if they do not get angry, then they are helpless; their partners only respond when the person speaks in an angry tone of voice or behaves in an angry manner. Consequently, as noted in Chapter 4, anger responses are frequently reinforced when a partner alters his or her behavior in response to an expression of anger from the spouse (Novaco, 1976). Such couples clearly need assistance in learning other strategies for obtaining a sense of control and obtaining desired behavior changes. Problem-solving training can be of assistance if the request is for behavior change in various areas. Rosenbaum and O'Leary (1981) found that abusive husbands were relatively unassertive in their interactions with their partners; in such instances, the therapist will need to focus on assertive communication during the problem-solving sessions. On other occasions, the goal of the angry spouse is to obtain an emotional response from the partner by escalating the level of emotional arousal in the interaction. In such circumstances, emotional expressiveness training can assist the couple as an alternative strategy for expressing emotions.

Third, expression of anger can mask other emotions such as anxiety, fear, intimacy, or a sense of vulnerability with which the individual is uncomfortable (Neidig & Friedman, 1984). The person might avoid these other emotions because he or she believes that the partner will find them unacceptable or because the person him- or herself fears these emotions. Through emotional expressiveness training, the therapist can help the person search for emotions that underlie the anger.

As should be evident, anger responses are influenced by internal factors such as cognitions and physical states, for example, fatigue. Also, the experience and expression of anger are influenced by external factors such as the spouse's behavior and work stresses. In addition to the strategies discussed above, other interventions have been developed based in part on the source of the anger. These interventions include relaxation training, time out, stress inoculation training, social support networks, and conflict containment skills. A discussion of all of these strategies is beyond the scope of this work; for an in-depth discussion, the reader is referred to Neidig and Friedman (1984), Deschner (1984), Hansen (1982), Stuart (1980), and Novaco (1975, 1978).

Depression

Both depression and marital distress are frequent in our society, and, as noted earlier, their joint occurrence is greater than would be expected by chance. One major issue is whether such couples require any "special" or additional interventions compared to other distressed couples. At present the data are conflicting in this area. Sher, Baucom, and Larus

(1988) found that depressed/maritally distressed couples demonstated as much *change* as other couples receiving cognitive/behavioral marital therapy; however, because they began at a lower level of marital functioning, they were still more distressed at the end of treatment. Similarly, Jacobson, Schmaling, Salusky, Follette, and Dobson (1987) have indicated that couples experiencing both disorders need marital therapy but also individual therapy to optimize treatment for the depression. On the other hand, Beach and O'Leary (1986) have presented pilot data demonstrating that behavioral marital therapy is effective for treating both marital distress and depression.

Most likely the proper combination of treatments will vary from couple to couple. Although there are no data bearing on this issue, marital therapy alone may be sufficient when the depression primarily stems from marital difficulties. In such cases, making changes in the marriage might result in a decrease in the depression. However when the depression is related to a number of factors outside the relationship, it is likely that additional individual therapy for the depression is warranted. Even in the latter case, marital therapy is likely to be beneficial to the couple to assist with their marital problems; in addition, the couple needs to become skilled in handling the individual's depression.

An appropriate starting point for the treatment of depressed/maritally distressed couples is with marital therapy. In some cases, this proves to be sufficient. In other instances, complications arise. Some couples make the behavioral and cognitive changes that seem to be indicated to improve the relationship and increase the happiness of each spouse. Still, the depressed member remains depressed, and this continues to impact the marriage. After a reasonable amount of time and sustained effort by the couple, the individual is referred for individual psychotherapy to deal with the depression. In most instances, an attempt is made to provide cognitive/behavioral individual therapy in order to maintain consistency with the marital treatment, and owing to the evidence regarding its effectiveness in treating depression (Sacco & Beck, 1985).

On other occasions, the individual is so depressed that he or she is unable or unwilling to take part in the cognitive and behavioral interventions that are the essence of the marital treatment. In addition, the nondepressed spouse is so concerned about worsening the depression that he or she is extremely reluctant to make requests of the depressed partner. Often, the marital therapy resembles individual therapy focusing on the individual's depression, only with the partner present. If the individual becomes the focus of marital therapy, then the treatment plan should be reconsidered. In such cases, the clinician must decide whether individual therapy and marital therapy should continue concurrently or whether the depressed member should undergo individual therapy and wait until that person becomes more stabilized and functional before resuming marital therapy.

In dealing with cases in which one person is depressed, an important issue becomes how to address the depression without identifying that individual as the patient and the cause of the marital distress. The therapist can discuss with the couple that both people have individual and relationship needs and that at certain times, one person may experience significant distress when those needs are not being met. As a relationship skill, the couple is informed that it is important that they learn how to assist each other during difficult times for one or both persons. Also, the depressed person can be told that he or she seems to have concerns in addition to the marriage, which might be discussed most fruitfully alone with a therapist.

A number of patterns seem to be typical among maritally distressed couples with one depressed member. Being prepared for these patterns can sensitize the clinician to issues that probably will need to be addressed. In terms of cognitions, the couple's attributions for the depression and their marital discord must often be considered. Some couples prefer to see the depression as biologically based, and in so doing avoid responsibility for making efforts to improve the marriage and to assist the individual. Their hope is that if the person receives antidepressant medication, then all will be well. Whereas there is no need to negate evidence that there does seem to be a biological component to some depressions, the therapist must help the couple to recognize the maladaptive behavioral patterns and cognitions that will maintain their current difficulties.

Among other couples, the all-or-none thinking of the depressed person results in a maladaptive attributional pattern for explaining the marital distress. Some depressed persons have very low self-esteem, feel guilty, and blame themselves for the marital difficulties. In such instances, both persons are likely to label the depressed person as the patient and the cause of the marital distress. Again, there is no need to deny that the depression may be contributing to the marital discord, yet it is important to help the couple see how both members are contributing to their current difficulties. For other depressed persons, assuming this responsibility for the marital problems would be too devastating; therefore, as a result of their dichotomous thinking, they blame their spouses. The therapist must be careful in working with such couples when attempting to alter the attributions of these persons. At times they seem to conclude, "Well, if you are telling me that it is not my partner's fault, then it must be my fault." This "flip-flop" phenomenon then results in a worsening of the depression. In essence, blaming the partner can serve as a coping strategy that minimizes blaming oneself within the context of all-or-none thinking.

Communication among maritally distressed couples with a depressed partner seems to be particularly dysfunctional (e.g., Biglan et al., 1985; Sher et al., 1988). There is a great deal of mutual criticism between the depressed person and the partner. At present it is unclear how this negative cycle develops within distressed couples, but interaction studies outside of the marital literature provide some insight. One explanation is that the depression results from the critical behavior of the partner. However, studies involving depressed persons interacting with strangers suggest that interacting with a depressed person can engender negative interaction and feelings (Coyne, 1976; Gotlib & Robinson, 1982). The partners of depressed persons complain that the depressed individual makes implicit and explicit requests for support and reassurance. When the partner attempts to provide such support, he or she perceives the depressed person as rejecting the reassurance. This rejection alienates the partner, and the depressed person complains of being unloved. Consequently, the communication patterns of these couples are likely to require extensive intervention.

Jealousy

Jealousy is often described as a sign of immaturity and as involving a loss of control over one's own feelings and behavior. As a result, many individuals are unwilling to acknowledge their jealous feelings, although the feelings are readily apparent. This is unfortunate because feelings of jealousy need not imply something negative about the person who experiences this emotion. As noted in Chapter 4, in terms of a marital relationship, jealousy involves an emotional response consisting of fear of loss of the partner to another individual or activity (e.g., a job). Consequently, jealousy can include some positive elements which the therapist might point out to the couple. The jealous person typically is indicating that the partner is valued; in addition, the jealous individual typically is making clear that he or she does not want to lose the partner and wants assurances from the partner that he or she is loved, valued, and desired.

Thus, jealous feelings per se need not be viewed as pathological, just as feeling depressed, angry, or anxious at times is not pathological. However, feelings of jealousy clearly can become detrimental to the relationship and the individuals in several ways. First, the emotional experience can become so intense that it is extremely unpleasant for the jealous person. Closely related, feelings of jealousy can preoccupy the individual and interfere with other activities. Also, the jealous person can behave in ways that clearly are maladaptive for the relationship. However, when jealousy becomes a problem in the relationship, the source of the difficulty does not always reside within the jealous person alone. Indeed, often the interaction pattern of the couple creates and/or maintains the jealous feelings and behavior of one spouse. In fact, at times, the partner behaves in ways to evoke jealous responses from the other individual.

Consequently, in working with the issue of jealousy, it is important to understand the basis for the emotion and the behavioral responses. Considering the affective state, it is useful to differentiate between rational and irrational jealousy. Rational jealous feelings involve a fear that one is in some way losing one's partner, and there seem to be legitimate bases for this concern. Under such circumstances, the most likely intervention is problem solving to help the couple decide how to alter the circumstances that are leading to one partner feeling threatened in the relationship. In addition, if one partner is interested in an outside relationship, the couple must decide whether they wish to make changes in their own marriage to improve its value or whether a separation is preferable.

At other times, however, the experience of extreme or frequent feelings of jealousy seems more maladaptive. Frequently, these feelings result from perceptions and cognitions that the person is experiencing, and uncovering the specific cognition becomes important in providing interventions. In terms of perceptions, the jealous person may become attuned to the positive comments and behaviors that the partner shows toward other persons and ignores the partner's loving behavior toward the jealous individual. Clearly, one intervention in this case would be to redirect the person's focus to become aware of the positive behaviors of the spouse toward the jealous person. Often these skewed perceptions result from related cognitions, such as faulty attributions for the partner's behavior. Thus, if a partner spends time with members of the opposite sex at a party, this is attributed to a lack of love. When such attributions are made, it is important to explore other possible causes for the behavior and to hear the partner's explanation. Although the highly jealous person is unlikely to accept alternative explanations immediately, the goal is to make the person at least aware of other possible interpretations.

In addition, jealous feelings often result from questionable expectancies. Some persons become convinced that their partners are going to leave them or at least have affairs with someone. Frequently, these predictions are based on overgeneralizations from the person's earlier life. For example, a husband may have been abandoned in a previous marriage, and he may conclude that his current wife will do the same thing. Such expectancies might serve a useful function. First, the prediction serves to provide predictability so that he will not be surprised again; thus, it serves to protect him from an unanticipated negative event. Second, by expressing his jealous feelings, he may elicit assurances from his wife which alleviate his anxiety for the moment. Jealous feelings based on a questionable expectancy also may result from previous experiences within the current relationship. For example, the wife may have had an affair earlier in the marriage when the husband believed that everything was fine with the marriage. As a result, he now believes that he has no useful cues to tell him whether the relationship is going well or whether his wife is likely to become involved with another man. Pointing out that there are no indications that the wife is considering becoming involved with someone and seems happy in the marriage is of marginal assistance because the husband believes that she had an affair under similar positive circumstances in the past. The therapist must help the couple see how the current circumstance is different from the past one. Also, the expectancy that one's spouse is going to leave or become romantically involved with other persons can result from an overgeneralization of a childhood experience. Some persons whose parents were divorced develop negative views of the opposite sex (e.g., Hetherington & Parke, 1979) and make predictions such as "If my father left my mother and me, then my husband is extremely likely to leave me." Based on this childhood experience, the person can develop a generalized insecurity in relationships with members of the opposite sex and develop negative expectancies (Hetherington, 1972; Kelley, 1981).

These attributions and expectancies also may be related to distorted and dysfunctional assumptions about members of the opposite sex, oneself, relationships, and correlations among various behaviors and events. For example, a wife may develop the generalized persona for males that men are almost always interested in having sex with an attractive female and will have an affair with one if they can. When such assumptions become evident, the therapist should want to ask the wife to examine evidence supporting and refuting her assumptions. In addition, the pros and cons of acting on this belief can be discussed. Finally, asking the wife to behave based on an alteration of this belief and monitoring the impact can be useful in such instances. Assumptions about the self also can contribute to the development of jealous feelings and behavior. Some jealous persons question how lovable they are and whether other people find them appealing. Often such views are indicative of broad self-doubts and insecurities which extend beyond the marriage. Although continued marital therapy is needed to assist the couple in dealing with such attitudes, such general self-doubts are an appropriate basis for considering additional individual psychotherapy.

Questionable assumptions about the correlations among various behaviors and emotions also can lead to feelings of jealousy. For example, a husband may assume a strong correlation between finding members of the opposite sex attractive and having an affair. As with the preceding examples, examining the evidence pro and con regarding such an assumption and planned behavioral experiments to behave in ways consistent with altered assumptions are appropriate interventions. In particular, it is important to help spouses differentiate between emotions and behavior and recognize that certain emotions do not always lead to wish-fulfilling behavior.

Feelings of jealousy also arise from extreme, unrealistic standards and harsh evaluations when those standards are not followed. As noted in Chapter 3, a whole series of beliefs related to how one should get needs met within a marital relationship can contribute to jealousy: (a) that an individual should be able to meet all of his or her spouse's needs; (b) that one should not be attracted to other persons of the opposite sex, or (c) that caring about other persons means that the spouse is loved less. In addition, the evaluation of situations in which the partner violates such standards also can create feelings of jealousy. Telling oneself that it is awful for the partner to dance with other persons, that one cannot stand it when such events occur, and that the partner should be punished, all can result in extreme emotions and related maladaptive behaviors. These extreme standards should be addressed in the same manner as other extreme standards discussed in Chapter 9.

Jealous behavior also serves several functions which must be understood. One goal of much jealous behavior is to punish the partner who is viewed as violating some standard. Thus, leaving a party early because the partner is talking to members of the opposite sex is a way of telling the partner to stop showing so much attention to others. Such persons have learned to use punishment to stop their partners from engaging in undesired behaviors. Teaching such persons problem-solving skills and more appropriate behavior change strategies can be of assistance in such instances.

The second goal of jealous behavior is to prompt statements of caring from the partner. Thus, statements that the partner no longer loves the jealous person might be an attempt to obtain reassurance from the partner. In moderate degrees and with moderated frequencies, such behaviors might not be problematic. However, frequent crying spells and repeated requests for assurances that one is loved can drive the partner away. Teaching the partner to provide unsolicited acts of caring can decrease the need for the frequent requests. Also, teaching the jealous person other ways to ask for attention and caring and to monitor and limit inappropriate jealous behavior is essential.

The use of emotional expressiveness skills is often called for because some jealous persons state that the only time the partner responds with any intense feelings, either positive or negative, is when they get into an argument about relationships with other people. Thus, some jealous behavior is directed toward purposely provoking the partner to have an intense emotional reaction. When such motivation becomes apparent, teaching the couple other ways to ask for and provide support and caring becomes a major treatment goal.

Extreme feelings of jealousy often are accompanied by high levels of arousal, and the subsequent jealous behavior may be an attempt to moderate this uncomfortable level of arousal. This pattern is similar to the cycle described in physical abuse in which there is a gradual increase in tension, followed by abuse, and then a honeymoon period after the emotions have been expressed. Strategies such as relaxation training can be of assistance to lower the level of arousal. However, such strategies will not always be successful, and the couple needs additional strategies for responding when one person is experiencing extreme jealousy. If it is apparent that the couple cannot sit at that time and problem-solve or express feelings in an adaptive manner, then instituting a time-out procedure to separate them might be helpful. Still, the jealous person may need assistance in alleviating the high level of arousal. Various strategies such as vigorous physical exercise and thought stopping can be considered in such instances.

Anxiety

Although there are likely to be multiple sources of anxiety, several are particularly pertinent within the marital context. First, as Seligman (1975) has suggested, individuals often experience anxiety when significant events in their lives are unpredictable. Thus, a wife may become quite anxious, being uncertain whether her husband will remember an important dinner engagement with her employer. Second, individuals seem to become anxious when they believe that negative events are likely to occur, thus experiencing a sense of impending threat or danger. Consequently, many couples who experience unsatisfactory sex lives have developed routine aversive interaction patterns regarding their sexual behavior when they get into bed. As that time approaches, they anticipate a negative interaction and experience significant anxiety. As these two bases for anxiety point out, expectancies for future behavior are central to our understanding of anxiety.

Third, some anxiety seems to be conditioned to particular stimuli, even though those stimuli no longer are related to aversive experiences. Therefore, a woman who was physically and/or sexually abused as a child may experience anxiety when her husband touches her, even though she rationally knows that he has always behaved in a tender, loving manner toward her and that she loves him. That is, she can rationally predict that their physical interaction will be pleasant, but that does little to alleviate her anxiety when he touches her. She has an automatic response over which she experiences no control.

Just as when considering jealousy, it is useful to differentiate between rational and irrational anxiety. Thus, it is reasonable to experience a certain amount of anxiety if important future events truly have little predictability or appear likely to become negative. However, anxiety can be viewed as more irrational when dysfunctional cognitive processes are involved. First, there may be multiple cues in the environment which make prediction possible or likely, but the individual either is not attuned to those cues or does not use that information in a meaningful way to make predictions. For example, a husband might have great concern that his wife will leave him. His wife might be behaving in numerous ways that indicate her love and commitment to him, yet he does not perceive those actions or does not use that information to arrive at the conclusion that she is likely to stay with him. Therefore, the perceptual process of selective attention and the reasoning process based on relevant information can be of central importance in dealing with anxiety. When one spouse is anxious about the marriage or the partner and this anxiety appears to result from inattention to relevant information or poor reasoning using this information, then cognitive intervention to assist the individual in becoming aware of the information and how to use it to reach conclusions is relevant. Thus, if the husband is concerned that his wife may leave but this seems unlikely, the therapist might give the husband an assignment to write down all the caring, loving behaviors in which his wife engages during the week as well as her behaviors that suggest she might leave the marriage. This information can then be discussed during the next session to help the husband develop appropriate expectancies. As he relates some of the behaviors that indicate to him that his wife might leave, it may become relevant to discuss the attributions that he gives for some of these behaviors, because he might interpret behaviors that she intended to be positive instead as signs that she no longer loves him. If, however, the data do indicate that important events in one partner's life are highly unpredictable or are predictable but likely to be negative, then behavioral intervention to change the couple's or partner's behavior is appropriate. Thus, if a husband often does not come home for dinner and does not notify his wife, then she may have a legitimate basis for concern that he will not arrive on time for dinner with her employer. In such an instance, coming to some agreement regarding his being home for dinner or notifying her will probably be of more assistance than a cognitive intervention.

Cognitions at times also lead to anxiety based on extreme standards and evaluations of those standards. Thus, individuals who believe that "I should be able to predict everything that my spouse does and everything that happens in my life" are likely to experience frequent anxiety. Similarly, individuals who evaluate negative events in an extreme way such that "It is *awful* if my spouse displeases me or things do not happen as I wish" are likely to become anxious as they predict ways in which their partners will not behave as they wish. In such instances, helping individuals to alter extreme standards and extreme evaluations when standards are violated can be of great assistance in alleviating anxiety.

Finally, there are circumstances which have led to conditioned anxiety in the past. In such instances, the individual or couple needs to experience similar situations in a positive context to alleviate the anxiety. Again, behavioral interventions are of paramount importance here. Thus, if physical touch has been associated with negative experiences in the past, anticipating touch can result in anxiety, regardless of what one rationally knows. Numerous behavioral interventions for sexual dysfunctions are based on a graduated set of steps to experience previously aversive interactions in a more positive way. Sensate focus exercises (Masters & Johnson, 1970) consist of a series of experiences involving nondemanding, physical pleasuring between the partners. Similarly, LoPiccolo and LoPiccolo's (1978) treatment for inorgasmic females involves a series of graduated steps to become comfortable with one's body in a non-anxiety-producing setting.

As with the other negative and dysfunctional emotions, anxiety can be approached in a number of ways. When the information confirms that important aspects of a couple's life are unpredictable or aversive, then behavioral intervention to alter these ways of interacting is appropriate. Similarly, when anxiety has become conditioned to certain circumstances, a graduated, in vivo process of helping the partner become comfortable in previously anxiety-producing situations is called for. However, when there are important cognitive processes at work which distort the individual's or couple's experience of their interaction, then cognitive interventions are necessary. Therefore, when the individual is omitting important information or using that information inappropriately such that the person believes that he or she can make no predictions or the predictions are unnecessarily negative, then these cognitive processes must be addressed to alleviate the anxiety. Similarly, when the individual expects almost all facets of life to be predictable or routine negative experiences to be awful and overwhelming, then anxiety is likely to result. In such instances, helping the individual to develop more realistic standards and appraisals when those standards are violated can be of assistance.

As should be apparent, dealing with dysfunctional emotions is a complex process that involves a clear understanding of the cognitive and behavioral bases for the emotional reactions. At various times, all of the strategies discussed in this volume can be employed to assist with dysfunctional emotions based on the logic that emotion are intimately related to cognitions and behavior. Yet, any clinician who has worked with couples with the intense emotions described here knows that alleviating or decreasing these affective states often is a slow, arduous process. The person might have learned these affective responses over many years, and the couple often has developed patterns of interaction that support these responses. However, a careful analysis and persistent effort by the couple with the clinician's support can produce striking changes and lead to significant increases in individual as well as couple functioning.

11

An Integrated Approach to Skills-Oriented Marital Therapy

A skills-oriented approach to working with couples offers a number of specific interventions from which the therapist may choose. Consequently, a major issue confronting the therapist is how to make appropriate choices in order to be maximally helpful to a particular couple. Actually, this rather broad choice of appropriate treatment interventions includes a number of more specific issues to be addressed. First, the therapist must decide which major skills are to be a focus in therapy. For example, will the couple need emotional expressiveness training, will assistance in problem-solving training be of help to the couple, and/or will interventions be needed to address the couple's underlying standards? Second, and related to the development of a broad treatment plan, the *sequencing* of different skills must be decided upon. For example, if the therapist concludes that the couple needs emotional expressiveness training and problem-solving training, which should come first for this particular couple? A single answer does not seem to apply across couples, so some rationale must be developed in order for therapy to be maximally effective. Third, and still related to the development of an overall treatment plan, the therapist must decide whether interventions in addition to marital therapy are necessary. A question raised by many therapists is whether one or both spouses should be in individual psychotherapy, and whether individual and marital therapy should continue simultaneously or whether one should precede the other.

The above issues all relate to the development of an overall treatment plan which the therapist might have in mind by the end of the initial

384

assessment period. However, in most applied settings, therapy does not then proceed in a linear, uninterrupted fashion with one form of skills training following from another. Instead, the therapist might find it appropriate to shift from some behavioral intervention to a focus on cognitive factors during the middle of a session. Likewise, the therapist might plan that for a given session, the couple will practice their problem-solving skills. However, the couple might have had an argument on the way to the session, and it becomes obvious that one or both persons are unwilling to begin with problem solving owing to their intense anger. In such a context, the plans for the evening might shift in focus to a discussion of what the meaning of the interaction was to the couple, or they might be encouraged to express their feelings to each other. Thus, not only are there shifts in the focus during a given session, but also the entire session may take on a different focus from what was originally intended. Also, there are times when the therapist might be tempted to change the focus of a session, but it would be more beneficial to continue with the current focus. Guidelines are needed to suggest when changes in focus might be helpful and when the current focus of the session should be retained.

DEVELOPING AN OVERALL TREATMENT PLAN

The first task facing the clinician is to decide which major sets of intervention strategies, that is, cognitive, affective, and/or behavioral, are needed in order to assist the couple. The earlier assessment chapters provide numerous strategies for evaluating whether a couple or individual is experiencing difficulty in any of these various areas. If so, then the corresponding general category of interventions is likely to be employed with the couple. That is, if (a) a couple complains of numerous content problems (e.g., handling household chores) in their relationship, (b) a couple indicates that they have difficulty sitting and talking about their problems in a productive fashion that leads to resolutions, and (c) behavioral observation of the couple indicates poor problem-solving and related communication skills, then the therapist will want to include problem-solving/communication training for the couple. In some cases, both members of the couple seem to lack skills in an area; however, for some couples, one spouse is relatively proficient, but the other is not. In order for the couple to function effectively, it is important that both members have at least a minimum of skills. Therefore, if either member of the couple is experiencing difficulty in an area and it appears to be problematic for the couple, then intervention is appropriate in that area.

Conformity with Skills-Oriented Procedures

At least two cautions are necessary in considering the preceding guideline. First, there are no data to indicate that the specific communication skills taught in the skills-oriented approach or that the steps recommended in problem solving are necessary for a couple to function efficiently or be satisfied with the relationship. There are probably many happily married couples who do not immediately produce a clear, specific behavioral statement of a problem they are addressing and then proceed with the remaining problem-solving steps. Similarly, many couples are probably satisfied with the way they share emotions with each other, although reflection of the partner's feelings and thoughts rarely occurs. The skills recommended in this text have been shown to be helpful to many distressed couples. However, that does not mean that these are the only acceptable ways for couples to interact with each other or the only adaptive cognitions that they may have about their relationship. Consequently, there may be no need to intervene simply because the couple is not doing it the "right" way.

However, this does not mean that the therapist automatically complies with the couple's perceptions and suggestions. For example, the couple might indicate that they are satisfied with the way they express emotions; yet one of their major concerns might be that they feel distant from each other and do not experience a sense of caring from the other. The therapist's observation might be that the couple attempts to avoid sharing feelings and that this avoidance contributes greatly to their presenting complaints. In this instance, the therapist might recommend that they attempt to resolve the presenting complaint through emotional expressiveness training. Therefore, the therapist must continue to rely on his or her expertise and knowledge of marital distress in order to make treatment recommendations, even if the couple does not initially see the need for such interventions.

Conformity with Therapist Values

The above discussion advises the therapist to be cautious in recommending a particular intervention when the couple seems to be functioning adequately in an area, even though they are not conforming to the specific guidelines that the therapist typically recommends to couples. Similarly, the therapist must be cautious in recommending a particular intervention when the couple does not conform to the therapist's values regarding the form that marital relationships should take. The skills-oriented approach assumes that the various skills and ways of thinking about the relationship which have been discussed are adaptive for couples. Although there is a certain degree of latitude for differences among couples, the approaches described in this volume have the tendency to promote an egalitarian relationship. When observing a couple, the therapist must be cautious not to assume that any relationship that is not largely egalitarian in nature is maladaptive and that shifts are needed to promote an egalitarian relationship. Thus, the therapist must not assume that the dominant-submissive aspects of a relationship are the basis of a couple's marital discord. Instead a more thorough evaluation of the particular couple's problems and strengths is needed. Similarly, some couples might not value certain skills that the therapist values. For example, many men do not value or wish to express a great deal of emotion to their wives. If the lack of expression of feelings creates a difficulty for the couple, then it must be addressed. Otherwise the therapist should avoid imposing his or her values of what a relationship should be like.

Based on the initial assessment data, the therapist in collaboration with the couple determines which broad areas of intervention to include in a therapy plan. In some cases, the therapist might conclude that a single broad domain of intervention, such as behavioral, will be sufficient to aid the couple. However, more likely than not, the therapist is likely to conclude that most couples have difficulties in the cognitive, affective, and behavioral areas. That is, the majority of couples come to therapy because of problems they have been unable to resolve successfully. Thus, most couples seemingly could benefit from some form of problem-solving training and related communication training. Similarly, a large number of couples have difficulty expressing their feelings to their partners in an adaptive manner. As noted previously, Geiss and O'Leary (1981) found that communication problems were the most frequent presenting complaint of couples coming to marital therapy. Consequently, a focus on both types of communication training is common with many distressed couples. Similarly, by the time that many couples seek therapy, they have developed attitudes toward each other and the relationship which are maladaptive and which merit direct attention. Therefore, in the majority of cases the therapist is likely to be confronted with a couple who would benefit from interventions that focus on all three areas to some degree.

SEQUENCING INTERVENTION STRATEGIES

Client Concerns

There are a number of factors to take into account in deciding which intervention to introduce first. Perhaps the most important guideline follows from the longstanding clinical recommendation to "start with where the client is." More specifically, intervention is likely to begin with the couple's presenting complaints which have been defined in a specific manner during the initial assessment. This usually means that initial interventions are likely to focus on behavioral changes or on teaching the couple emotional expressiveness skills. Although couples initially arrive with distorted cognitions, rarely do they complain about having those cognitions (except, perhaps, to point out that the other person has a negative attitude). Instead, it is the clinician who is likely to believe that the cognitions need to be altered. Although the clinician might be somewhat successful in assisting the couple to reconceptualize their problems from a cognitive perspective and thus begin with a major focus on cognitive restructuring, our experience with this type of strategy has been less than optimal in most cases. In research contexts in which couples have received a number of weeks of cognitive restructuring as the initial intervention, the clients have found the interventions to be useful but often have said that they wanted to move on to changing the behaviors that were distressing to them when they first came for therapy. Thus, an initial focus is directed toward helping to alleviate the negative behaviors and/or expression of aversive emotions that are troubling the couple and to increase positive interaction in these same domains. Subsequently, cognitive interventions are interwoven as they become relevant and more palatable to the spouses within the context of these other interventions.

This initial focus on behavioral and/or emotional expressiveness training is helpful for several reasons. First, because these are more likely to be the complaints of the couple, immediate attention to these areas helps to make the couple view the therapist as attentive to their needs. Second, this focus can help to reduce the stress that spouses feel from their negative interaction patterns. Third, concrete changes can serve as a basis of hope for the couple that they can improve their relationship.

Issues Requiring Immediate Attention

There are a number of other factors to consider in making decisions regarding the skills to focus on first in treatment. At times there are issues that require immediate attention, and in such instances the skills chosen will be selected to assist the couple in dealing with those issues. For example, the wife of one couple was uncertain whether she wanted to remain in the marriage. Whereas it is not atypical for at least one partner to be unsure about the future of the relationship, this particular wife was uncertain and confused enough about what she wanted that she was unwilling to agree to work in therapy to try to improve the relationship. Instead she first needed to clarify her goals regarding the marriage. In this instance, the therapist believed that immediately focusing on behavioral interventions to improve the marriage was premature because the wife was unlikely to make meaningful efforts to bring about the improvement. Instead the clarification of her own thoughts and feelings regarding the future of the relationship, as well as hearing those of her husband, seemed appropriate and best handled through emotional expressiveness training. On the other hand, another young couple came to marital therapy with their life somewhat disarrayed. They were both in school, had little time together, had financial problems compounded by the birth of their first child, and had reached little resolution regarding how the many required household chores in their lives would be handled. The hopelessness, frustration, and anger brought about by these unresolved daily issues called for an immediate focus on problem-solving training. Finally, one husband was harboring long-term anger toward his wife for an affair she had had several years previously. Although both spouses also had several complaints about their current interaction, the therapist concluded that little progress could be made until some resolution occurred regarding the affair. Therefore, the initial sessions focused on emotional expressiveness training to assist the couple in developing better communication skills to share their feelings and thoughts about the affair and its impact on the relationship, with the intention of including a major focus on cognitive issues as the couple began their discussion of the affair. Thus, there will be numerous occasions in which the spouses have clear needs to focus on certain issues, either in order to express their feelings or to try to understand themselves or their partner better; to resolve certain problematic aspects of the relationship; or to alter some maladaptive cognitions early in therapy. In such instances, the issue and the goal for dealing with the issue will dictate the initial interventions to choose.

Whereas the above guideline suggests that the initial intervention is likely to focus on behavioral or affective concerns, this is not always the case. There are occasions when cognitive interventions seem to be needed immediately. This is particularly true when the couple enters therapy with maladaptive cognitions which would make behavioral change difficult or minimize the effects of behavioral change and affective expression. For example, one couple entered therapy for treatment of the husband's premature ejaculation, as well as other problems. The wife attributed his premature ejaculation to a desire on his part to frustrate her sexually and anger her. Thus, she viewed his rapid ejaculations as purposeful and intended to bring her pain. Based on numerous pieces of information, the therapist concluded that the wife's attributions were erroneous and that a discussion and understanding of the etiology of premature ejaculation from a behavioral perspective would be important before attempting to promote behavioral change in their sex lives. Otherwise the wife probably would continue to look for evidence that her husband was attempting to frustrate her and would interpret difficulties during the treatment as intentional on her husband's part.

Skill Level

Another consideration in sequencing interventions is whether a couple will be able to master the skills successfully at a given point in therapy. For example, one couple requesting therapy had always experienced significant difficulty *expressing* positive emotions toward each other. However, by the time they sought treatment, they not only had difficulty expressing positive emotions toward each other, but they also *experienced* few positive emotions toward each other. Instead, both experienced primarily feelings of anger. Consequently, focusing initially on expression of positive emotions would have failed. Beginning therapists at times contribute to increased hopelessness and anger among couples by asking one spouse to express positive emotions toward the other when that person is aware of few positive feelings that could be expressed. Such spouses need to learn to track the positive behavior of their partners and thus have positive emotions to express. Therefore, behavioral interventions are often helpful in creating a more positive relationship environment before the couple is trained in expressing positive emotions. An important guideline for the duration of therapy is to arrange the sequencing of skills and issues discussed within those skills in a manner that will provide the couple with maximally successful experiences.

Moderating Affective Tone

In determining what will be maximally helpful to a couple, one guideline is to begin with interventions that will restore or help to create a moderate affective climate within the relationship. For example, some couples enter therapy with very strong emotions that are displayed in a maladaptive manner, with loud arguments and unproductive attempts to discuss their problems. An early goal for such couples is to moderate the level of emotion so that there is less tension in the relationship. At present there are no research data regarding the best way to accomplish this goal, and rationales can be made for beginning with a focus on emotional expressiveness training or behavioral interventions. If the couple is expressing their feelings inappropriately, then EET with its focus on expressing feelings more productively might seem logical. At the same time, EET clearly focuses couples on their emotions, many of which will be extremely negative in this case. With an increased focus on their affective state, some couples have extreme difficulty expressing their strong emotions in a moderate manner. In such cases, a focus away from emotions and toward the more logical steps of problem solving can often redirect the energies of the couple and provide them with a strategy for interacting with each other less emotionally. Thus clinical experience suggests that couples in which one or both spouses have strong negative emotions and significant difficulty expressing their feelings in a moderate fashion often benefit from behavioral interventions initially.

There are also many couples who avoid expression of emotion and approach their relationship and marital problems in an unemotional, intellectual manner. Such couples often present with a sense of boredom and lack of closeness in their marriage. These couples are very comfortable with the intellectual way in which they can approach problem solving and cognitive issues. Although problem-solving steps and related communication skills often are helpful to such couples, such an approach does little to help the couple feel closer and experience a sense of vitality in the relationship. For that reason, it is preferable to begin by using EET skills with such couples. For some couples, the notion of expressing emotions is so threatening that beginning with this intervention can precipitate an early termination of therapy. In instances in which the therapist believes that EET skills cannot be presented slowly enough to the couple that they can successfully employ them, then behavioral interventions can serve as an appropriate beginning point.

SHIFTING INTERVENTION STRATEGIES

In EET training, spouses are taught both expresser and responder skills. Once both these skills are mastered, the couple needs to learn guidelines for alternating between the various roles. These guidelines fall under two general categories: (a) when to make role shifts and (b) how to make shifts. Similarly, the therapist needs a set of guidelines to assist in moving from one intervention strategy to another, and these guidelines also can be viewed from the perspective of when and how to make such shifts.

When to Make Intervention Shifts

There are likely to be an indefinite number of occasions when it is appropriate to make a shift in the intervention strategies being employed with couples. Whereas many of these situations are idiosyncratic, there are still a number of broad guidelines to assist the therapist in deciding when to shift therapeutic interventions. As mentioned earlier, therapy is most likely to begin with some behaviorally oriented skills training or emotional expressiveness training. A major question becomes when to shift to a more explicit cognitive focus.

Shifting to cognitive interventions.

One circumstance in which the therapist might consider inititating a cognitive intervention is when the couple continues in some way to "get off track" in the behavioral/EET training, and the couple's difficulty does not seem to result from a skills deficit. Often this results from an important cognition which interferes with the couple's proceeding with the task at hand. In such circumstances, the therapist probably will want to shift the focus to clarify whether there is such a cognition and then make an appropriate cognitive intervention.

For example, one couple was problem-solving regarding the husband's desire to spend some evenings with his male friends without his wife. He had clarified for her that he enjoyed spending time with her, but that he also valued his male friendships and at times liked just "being with the guys." However, as they considered various alternative solutions, the wife continued to ask for explanations of why he wanted to spend some evenings with his male friends. Her continued questioning had the effect of disrupting their solution-oriented focus. The therapist had made appropriate interventions to assist them in problem solving, and previous training suggested that the wife was capable of following the problem-solving steps. Thus, the therapist concluded that her current behavior did not result from a skills deficit, but instead her husband's request had a certain meaning which was troubling her and which needed to be addressed directly. The therapist's hunch was that she viewed her husband's request as a statement that he did not love her as much as he used to, and to grant his request would be tantamount to encouraging him to withdraw from her and the family. Thus, the therapist temporarily suspended the problem-solving process and shifted to a focus on attributions, or what the request meant to the wife.

Closely related to becoming sidetracked, the therapist may wish to shift to a more cognitive focus when the couple becomes blocked or stalemated during BMT or EET training, and the difficulty does not result from a skills deficit. For example, during EET the responder may decide not to reflect the partner's thoughts and emotions but instead inject his or her own reaction or interpret the speaker's statements. Whereas this could result from a skills deficit, at times it clearly does not. Instead the responder is having an emotional reaction to the speaker's statement, with accompanying cognitions which are interfering with being reflective. One strategy for handling this situation would be to ask the couple to switch modes soon, so that the responder could speak. However, at other times the therapist might be aware of a pattern of maladaptive cognitions which is being activated. The therapist might wish to make these implicit cognitions more explicit and then focus on them directly rather than having the couple continue with their EET discussion. Therefore, the therapist would shift to a cognitive intervention.

These same blocks occur during BMT training at various points. Occasionally the couple will problem-solve and nearly arrive at a final solution, but they find themselves unable to compromise on some final aspects which would lead to a satisfactory solution. In some instances, this is because either the content of the compromise or the mere act of compromising would have some unacceptable meaning to the partners. When compromise solutions are rather obvious, but the couple refuses to discuss or accept them, then this may be an indication that their attitudes toward problem solving or the meaning of the content of the solution need to be addressed from a cognitive perspective. Similarly, during problem solving, the couple may arrive at a solution that one person had originally desired. Yet, once the partner agrees to the solution, the individual finds the solution unacceptable. It may be that the individual has thought through the solution more carefully and now finds it unacceptable for legitimate reasons. In other instances, that person rejects the solution because of the way the partner presented it, or because of the meaning it has acquired during the discussion. Again, when this appears to be the case, a direct focus on the cognitive issues involved may be helpful.

The above examples focus on instances in which one or both spouses are displeased with some aspect of their behavioral interaction owing to their cognitive perspectives. However, there are other circumstances in which the spouses are willing to accept some solution or are expressing some idea that they both view as legitimate, yet the therapist has concerns about related cognitions which appear to be detrimental to the functioning of the couple. In one couple, the wife was clinically depressed, and both the husband and wife agreed that her not carrying out household tasks was the basis for their marital problems. During problem solving, almost all of the solutions focused on her assuming increasing responsibilities. The therapist was concerned with the way in which both spouses had labeled the wife as the patient. Although the wife's depression was certainly contributing to the marital discord, there were pronounced destructive interactive patterns that the couple was ignoring. Thus, the therapist believed that it was essential to help the couple rethink the bases of their marital problems and seek solutions that involved changes on both spouses' parts.

At times the therapist might wish to shift to a cognitive focus after conducting behavioral interventions in order to help spouses develop realistic expectancies about how they are likely to behave as a couple in the future. Clearly, not all interventions are successful in helping a couple make behavioral changes in the directions they would wish, or the changes achieved are only minimal. When sustained effort has been made to assist the couple in making desired changes but it becomes apparent to the therapist that changes in that area appear unlikely for the foreseeable future, then the therapist might wish to focus on realistic expectancies with the couple. That is, the therapist might wish to discuss with the couple what they probably can expect from each other in this particular area based on their past relationship plus minimally successful therapeutic efforts. This approach becomes particularly helpful when couples ask, after a number of weeks of therapy, whether the therapist thinks they should stay together or divorce. That final decision involves a value judgment about the way a person wants to live his or her life, and rarely is the therapist in the position to make that value judgment for another individual. However, based on the information available, the therapist can help the couple evaluate what they can realistically look forward to in the marriage.

Therapist: I know that deciding whether or not to continue with your marriage is an extremely important decision for the two of you. I'm not going to make a recommendation to you one way or another, and there is a reason for that.

Deciding whether or not to stay married involves a lot of value judgments about what you want for your life individually, what you want from your marriage, your ethical position regarding divorce, how you feel about divorcing with children, and so on. And I am not in a postion to make those judgments for another person. But what I can do is to try to help you realistically evaluate what your relationship is like and what you might expect for the near future. We have worked on a number of specific areas, and you both seem to agree that we have made progress on several of them. For example, . . . However, you still differ significantly in the degree to which you want to share and do share thoughts and emotions with each other. Sally, you are a much more private person than Bill, and I think you two need to acknowledge this difference. When things are going pretty well between you, you are better able to share emotions with each other. However, when you start to have difficulties with each other, you have different reactions to the stress. Bill, you start to feel abandoned, want to share more emotions, and try to initiate those discussions. Sally, when you are feeling badly toward Bill, your response is to withdraw; Bill then feels more abandoned and tries to initiate expression of emotions. You feel suffocated and withdraw more.

We've tried various strategies to help you break this cycle, but overall they haven't been very successful. So, based on what you both are comfortable with and what we've seen happen here, I think that at least for the foreseeable future, unless some unexpected change takes place, you can expect that this will continue to be a somewhat rocky area for you. I think it also is important for you to realize that this doesn't mean that the other person doesn't love you or wants to make you miserable. You simply have different ways of handling interpersonal stress, and that has led to a lot of misery in the past. What do you think? Given the other aspects of your marriage that have improved, is this an area that you think you can tolerate as you continue to look for better ways to handle it? Or is this aspect of your marriage so important and so unsatisfactory that when put within the context of your entire relationship, you feel you would most benefit from ending the marriage?

The occasions discussed thus far for shifting from interventions focusing on behavior and affect to cognitive interventions have focused on changes that are likely to occur during a session while skills are being taught or practiced. However, there also are occasions when the therapist is talking with the couple, not in a skills training mode, but the discussion reveals that a shift to a cognitive intervention is appropriate. Such opportunities frequently arise at the beginning or end of a therapy session. At the beginning of a session, the therapist is likely to inquire how the couple's week has gone and/or how their homework assignments have progressed. During this discussion, one or both spouses may make statements that indicate the need for a cognitive intervention. For example, a wife might make attributions for her husband's behavior which seem to fit into her attribution that he behaves in order to purposely disappoint her:

Wife: Basically, he did it again. He followed through on what we had discussed we would do during the therapy session for the first four or five days of the week. Then, when he had me believing that maybe this time he really was going to change, Monday he worked late, and we didn't have any time to sit and talk. He basically set me up to get my hopes up again, and then he let me down like he always does.

In this instance, the therapist thought that it was important to question the wife's attributions because there seemed to be a number of other feasible explanations for the husband's behavior, and the wife's explanation fit into a negativistic pattern which was becoming more clear during the course of therapy. This discussion occupied the remainder of the session, and the intended BMT session was delayed until the following week. Thus, sometimes the therapist alters the plans for the entire session rather than merely shifting the focus for a few minutes.

At the end of a therapy session, either the therapist may inquire about or the couple may spontaneously offer a reaction about the session that just transpired. Occasionally, these comments surprise the therapist because they will reflect discontent with the session or the way that a particular issue was discussed or resolved, when the therapist thought that the clients were satisfied with the session. This difference in perspective is often related to some cognition(s) the spouses had concerning what occurred during the session; however, the cognitions were not evident during the session. In order to be of assistance to the couple, the therapist needs to spend time addressing these concerns from a cognitive perspective. Unfortunately, therapists often do not solicit clients' reactions to sessions, so this type of information and the opportunity for intervention is lost.

Shifting to interventions focusing on behavior or emotions.

There also are a number of circumstances when the session has had a cognitive focus, and the therapist decides that a shift to interventions focusing on behavior and/or emotions would be more appropriate. One circumstance for making such a shift is when the couple has been focusing on some cognition in therapy, and a spouse has been able to consider thinking about a problem or behavior differently. However, rarely are such single discussions sufficient to consolidate a different set of cognitions concerning a problem area. In addition, behavior consistent with the new cognitions is often needed to reaffirm them. For example, one couple was experiencing a number of difficulties in their sexual relationship. Among these was the problem of how and when to let the partner know that one person wanted to make love. The husband liked the idea of raising the issue with his wife in the morning to make plans for making love that evening. He believed that he would enjoy the anticipation, and it would add excitement to an otherwise somewhat monotonous day. However, without ever trying this approach or discussing it with his wife, he was convinced that she would find it to be too rigid. After a discussion during a therapy session, the wife expressed that she also found the idea rather appealing. The husband was willing to consider that perhaps his initial expectancies were inaccurate, but he clearly needed behavioral evidence to confirm that she was not attempting to avoid having sex with him. Consequently, the couple problem-solved on the least anxiety-producing and most pleasurable timing for them to suggest making love and decided to adopt the husband's proposal. Their experiences were then used in later sessions to address the husband's cognitions as well as to improve the behavioral aspects of their sex life.

On other occasions, behavioral changes are not necessary to confirm cognitive shifts, but they can serve as examples of "good faith efforts" to please the other person. The husband in one couple made frequent business trips, and at the end of his trips his wife would pick him up at the airport to bring him home. On the trip home from the airport, the husband was often quiet. The wife's attribution for his behavior was that he did not enjoy being around her and would rather still be on his trip. During a therapy session, he clarified that this was not at all how he felt. Instead, by the time she picked him up at the airport, he typically was exhausted and felt that he could relax around her. In addition, he was usually tired of work and did not want to talk about it anymore; because she typically focused on problems that had developed while he was gone, he did not want to discuss issues she brought up either. Instead, he used the ride home from the airport as a time to "decompress." Finally, he reminded her that he generally was a much quieter person than she was. He assured her that he looked forward to returning from his trips to be with her, and he loved her a great deal. After hearing his point of view, she understood the reasons for his quiet behavior and could say that she logically believed that it was not because he did not love her. She agreed that she would remind herself of why he was being quiet, but any attempt on his part to show that he understood her preferences and wanted to make her happy would certainly make it easier for her. The husband agreed to try to rest on the plane and talk with her on the way home, particularly if they could focus on the positive things that had occurred while he was gone.

This type of situation is not uncommon. When two people differ greatly in style and preferences, one person can perhaps come to understand the bases for the other person's behavior and accept its meaning cognitively. In spite of this new understanding, the partner still states that the spouse's behavior hurts because it is so unrewarding to him or her. In such instances, changes in the spouse's behavior can be helpful in providing assurances of caring to the partner. When cognitive interventions have provided new understanding or a different way of thinking about an issue, but one spouse continues to be displeased owing to individual differences in preferences, then shifting to a behavioral intervention to promote realistic behavioral change is important.

The instances given above involve shifting from a cognitive focus to a behavioral focus in order to provide behavior changes to make the new cognitions more meaningful and/or solidified. In addition, frequently after a cognitive intervention, the couple is ready for a behavioral change in their relationship because the previous roadblocks to behavior change have now been removed by the cognitive intervention. For example, one couple held the standard that spouses must continue to be almost totally independent of each other and not look to the other for help or assistance. They had translated this standard into a lifestyle that was inefficient and miserable for both of them. Each person cooked his or her own meals, and because it was difficult to prepare two meals at once, they rarely ate at the same time at home. Each person did his or her own laundry because it was important to demonstrate self-sufficiency. The two spouses actually liked each other and enjoyed each other's company; their rather extreme standards for a relationship merely made it difficult for them to have an identity as a couple and created unmanageable work loads for each person. Once the therapist helped them to focus on their extreme standards and to see that assisting each other did not mean that each person had to lose his or her personal identity, the couple was eager to make behavioral changes to improve their life. These behavioral changes served not so much as evidence that their old cognitions were faulty; the couple accepted that their relationship standards were extreme. They then wanted to effect behavioral changes to make life more pleasant together.

The example given above involves a couple's making a cognitive shift and therefore being eager to make behavioral changes in line with their new way of thinking about a situation. However, on other occasions, the couple and therapist have considered a particular cognition, and one or both spouses decide to retain a cognition the therapist views as maladaptive for their relationship. In such instances, the therapist will probably want the couple to experience the affective and behavioral implications of the belief. Thus, a shift away from the cognitive focus is then appropriate.

For example, during the early phases of problem solving, the therapist found that a husband was quite unwilling to compromise on solutions. Skills-oriented instructions proved unsuccessful, and the therapist had shifted to a cognitive focus. After a brief discussion, the husband readily acknowledged that he believed that he should not have to compromise, that as an individual he should have the right to do what made him happy. The therapist encouraged a logical analysis of not making compromises within a marriage, and the husband concluded that he simply did not believe that he should make compromises. This was the first time that he had made explicit that he was unwilling to compromise with his wife. Previously, he had merely justified his position as being the one that he felt was best for the marriage. The therapist believed that this was a critical factor in the couple's distress and that the husband must realize the major impact that such a position had on the marriage. First, the therapist shifted to EET and asked the wife to express to her husband her feelings about the standard that he had made explicit. She expressed the anger, hurt, and sense of hopelessness that she experienced. Then the therapist shifted to a behavioral focus involving problem solving. The therapist asked the couple to note the implications of the husband's unwillingness to compromise during problem solving. They were able to recognize that the problem solving was painful and typically ended with a stalemate or with the wife resentfully giving in to the husband's demands. The couple also considered how well the solutions were implemented. Although some of the solutions were implemented effectively, the wife resisted following through on some of them or was angry, even though behaviorally she contributed to the solutions. In spite of this accumulation of information, the husband maintained that he should not have to compromise with his wife on disagreements. When faced with the reality of their situation, the wife decided that she did not want to continue to live in that type of marriage, and she divorced her husband.

Finally, a shift from cognitive restructuring to some form of communication training is essential when couples are unable to communicate effectively with each other. Again, for research purposes we have attempted cognitive restructuring as a separate treatment component before couples have received communication training. In such instances, it is at times difficult for couples to share their thoughts effectively with each other and/or the therapist. Teaching the couples some fundamentals of effective communication can greatly facilitate the exchange of important information regarding cognitions that the couple needs to process.

In summary, there are a number of occasions when a shift from cognitive restructuring to interventions focusing on behavior or emotion can be productive: (a) when behavioral changes are needed to confirm new beliefs; (b) when behavioral changes serve as "good faith reminders" of new beliefs; (c) when the couple wants to make behavioral changes to be consistent with new ways of thinking about themselves and the relationship; (d) when one or both spouses have clung to problematic beliefs and the affective and behavioral implications of those beliefs need to be clarified; and (e) when communication skills are needed to facilitate the exchange of ideas while discussing important cognitions.

When Not to Shift Interventions

Although shifting from one major type of intervention strategy to another often can greatly benefit the course of therapy, continual shifting among interventions is likely to be unproductive in several circumstances. The therapist must at times show restraint and continue the current intervention. At least three broad factors should be considered before deciding to shift intervention strategies: (a) the effect that timing a shift in interventions will have on the treatment; (b) the content that might be elicited with a shift in interventions; and (c) the basis for the couple's difficulty with the current intervention.

Timing.

Several issues related to timing must be considered in deciding to shift intervention strategies. Perhaps most fundamental, the therapist would not want to shift to another intervention strategy if it will break the flow of a productive session. For example during EET or BMT, the couple may be proceeding nicely, but during the course of their discussion one spouse may raise a cognition that the therapist believes is maladaptive for the relationship. The therapist may be tempted to break in at that point and shift to a cognitive intervention. Making such a decision is at times difficult, but a general guideline is that if the couple can proceed successfully without the shift in intervention, then continue with the current intervention strategy. Otherwise therapy is likely to consist of a number of aborted attempts to proceed with issues from a given perspective. Most couples come to therapy with a great deal of difficulty in proceeding from beginning to end with tasks such as problem solving on an issue or expressing thoughts and emotions about the issue. A major goal for such couples is to teach them to stay on task and complete what they have undertaken. This is done from a skills-oriented perspective, and learning applicable skills becomes much more difficult if the therapist frequently interrupts the process to shift to another intervention. As the couple practices new ways of interacting during the session, they may become confused as to whether they should be attempting such shifts themselves at home. Consequently, frequent shifts and interruptions from an initial focus are consistent with many couples' skill deficits and serve them poorly in learning to complete a task.

Also related to timing, the two spouses in a couple often progress with learning various skills at different rates. For example, frequently one spouse will master expressing emotions and thoughts from an EET perspective rather quickly while the partner is struggling to learn and implement the skills. Teaching the partner who is experiencing more difficulty can become rather laborious and not immediately rewarding for either the couple or the therapist. Under such circumstances, the therapist may rationalize that it would benefit the couple more to move on to other interventions rather than continue with the frustation of working with the slower spouse. Whereas there are circumstances in which this logic might hold (e.g., so as not to produce discouragement in a couple who already feels hopeless), in general both spouses should have a minimally acceptable skill level before leaving an intervention strategy on a long-term basis.

Another concern related to timing is the inadvisability of shifting to new intervention strategies just before a break in therapy, such as those resulting from vacations or holidays. This recommendation is based on a more general logic for individual as well as marital therapy—not to initiate difficult issues for clients just prior to a break because the therapist will not be available to assist in crises that might result from entertaining new and difficult issues. For example, one couple had difficulty expressing negative feelings to each other without having major arguments. The therapist had asked the couple to express negative feelings to each other using EET skills, but then the therapist became ill. During the three-week interlude that ensued, the couple continued to attempt to express negative feelings to each other at home with little success. Without corrective action, the spouses were quite alienated from each other by the time that therapy resumed. In this instance, the break was unplanned, but the result was the same.

Content.

   A second major reason that the therapist might not want to shift to
another intervention strategy is the content that would result from doing
so. In most cases, this can be considered another instance of the appropriate
timing for shifting interventions. There may be occasions in which a shift
to a particular intervention is likely to evoke emotions and thoughts that
are not productive for the couple at a given time. For example, one spouse
might experience feelings of hopelessness and perceptions that the couple
cannot change whenever he or she thinks about their past relationship.
The therapist may have worked rather effectively with the couple through
problem solving to promote some meaningful behavioral changes which
have occurred for only a short time period. The therapist might be tempted
to shift to a cognitive focus to address the husband's attributions that the
couple cannot change because there is now evidence to the contrary.
However, to do so after only a short period of behavior change might
refocus the husband on feelings of hopelessness and attempts on his part
to minimize the changes that have occurred. Unless the attributions are
interfering with behavior change or the meaning given to such change,
the therapist might build on the behavior changes until they appear rather
stable and the husband is clearly pleased with the relationship before
addressing the attributions. Consequently, the therapist must recognize
that through decisions to shift or not shift intervention strategies to address
an issue from a certain perspective at a given time, the skills-oriented
marital therapist is not a neutral party, but rather helps to shape the
direction in which the couple's relationship is likely to move.

Basis for difficulty.

   Third and finally, the therapist might shift intervention strategies
when the couple is experiencing difficulty with the current intervention,
and there is some salient issue that could be addressed effectively through
a different intervention. At times this is appropriate, but at other times
continuing with the current intervention can be more productive. In part
this decision is based on the reason that the couple is having difficulty with
the current intervention. One couple rarely was able to complete a
problem-solving task by arriving at an agreeable solution. When they
disagreed on a solution, the wife would often break into tears and refuse
to continue. The therapist supportively encouraged her to reinitiate the
problem-solving process, but without success.

The therapist had a number of options in handling the situation. The wife was having a strong affective response, and the therapist might believe that her strong experience of emotions was interfering with her ability to maintain a problem-solving focus. In that case, the therapist could shift to EET to have the wife express her emotions. After this affect was expressed and the husband had shown acceptance of his wife's feelings, the couple could return to problem solving. Or if the therapist believed that the wife had some maladaptive cognitions which needed to be addressed before the couple continued with problem solving, the therapist could shift to a cognitive intervention to attempt to clarify the wife's thoughts and then try to modify them. Following the cognitive modifications, the couple could again return to problem solving. As a third alternative, the therapist might consider the wife's crying as a manipulative or maladaptive communication aimed at disrupting the problem-solving process if the wife did not like the solution under consideration. In this case the therapist might not shift intervention strategies but rather intervene on a communication level, teaching the wife how to introduce and advocate for alternative solutions which were more acceptable to her. At times the therapist will be unable to determine the basis for the observed pattern. In such circumstances, the therapist might point out the pattern to the couple and ask for their assistance in clarifying the basis for it, perhaps mentioning the alternative interpretations which the therapist was considering. However, based on the assessment of the above case, the therapist concluded that the husband in the couple had a strong, confident way of expressing his opinion. He was more verbally articulate than the wife, was very logical in his arguments, and the wife could find little basis for not agreeing with his proposed solutions, although she often did not like them. Consequently, the therapist concluded that the only way that the wife could find to avoid accepting his logical solutions which she did not like was to cry and disrupt the problem-solving process. Therefore, the therapist intervened on a problem-solving/communications basis to help the wife disagree with her husband and propose her own solutions, and to assist the husband in respecting his wife's preferences, regardless of whether or not her proposed solutions withstood a rigid logical scrutiny. This intervention contained cognitive restructuring components as the therapist helped the couple recognize that the basis of a good solution is not necessarily the one which appears most logical; however, this did not involve a shift away from the problem-solving process.

In essence, during a behavioral intervention, the therapist must decide whether important cognitions and/or emotions are interfering and therefore must be addressed before behavioral progress can be attained.

Alternatively, the affect or cognitions may be offered by a spouse as a distraction to impede behavioral progress, but the content of the affect and cognitions need not be addressed. Of course, the same distinction applies when the couple is addressing an issue from a cognitive or emotional perspective. In fact, sophisticated clients come to recognize what types of behavior, affect, and cognition are likely to catch the therapist's attention and may offer one of these as "bait" to distract or disrupt a therapy session that is difficult for them. For example, the husband in one couple had difficulty expressing his emotions. From a cognitive perspective, the couple had discussed during therapy that based on the husband's childhood with parents who were threatened by emotions, he expected that he would be rejected by people if he expressed how he truly felt. He came to realize that whereas his parents may have rejected him, he was overgeneralizing and that his wife provided strong evidence to the contrary, demonstrating that she valued and would accept his emotional expression. Next, the therapist began teaching the couple EET skills to allow the husband to practice this new way of interacting with his wife and to provide evidence for him about whether he would be rejected for expressing his feelings. In spite of his new realizations, expressing his feelings was still difficult for the husband owing to a lack of practice. Therefore, on many occasions when he was attempting to share his emotions with his wife, he would stop and attempt to shift the session back to a cognitive focus by making statementes such as the following: "You know, on some level I must still be clinging to the belief that I am going to be rejected if I tell Anne how I feel because I just can't do it. Or maybe there is some other expectancy that I have which we haven't figured out yet which is getting in my way. Something is stopping me, and I'm not sure what it is."

In the above statement, the husband made a strong bid for the therapist to return to a cognitive focus which was much more comfortable for him. However, the therapist believed that no other major cognition needed to be addressed at that time and that the new experience of expressing his emotions was simply frightening for the husband. From the therapist's perspective, the husband needed behavioral data to evaluate whether he would be rejected; therefore, he continued with the EET intervention:

Therapist: I think that you are right, that in some way you do still fear that you will be rejected by Anne if you tell her how you feel. By discussing your expectancies, we hope to clarify what they are and to start to challenge them. But in most cases, that is not enough. You need to see firsthand what does happen when you share your emotions with Anne rather than just imagining what will happen. I know that it is somewhat frightening for you, but let's give it a try just briefly and then we will evaluate how it went. Bob, you were starting to tell Anne how you feel when one of your fellow workers compliments you on your work. Continue with what you were telling her.

In summary, on numerous occasions, the therapist should be cautious before shifting intervention strategies. These include instances in which shifting intervention strategies would: (a) break the flow of a session that is productive; (b) bring up a difficult issue just before a prolonged break in therapy; (c) move the couple to a new focus before both spouses have obtained minimal proficiency in the skills currently being taught; (d) direct the couple's attention to an issue or way of addressing an issue that would be destructive for therapy at that time; and (e) allow one spouse to avoid dealing with the current material of the session by offering a thought, emotion, or behavior that could distract the session. This is not meant to be an exhaustive list but rather a list of examples to clarify that often there is great value in restraint and continuing to proceed with a current intervention. Throughout the session, there are likely to be statements and behaviors from the couple which alert the clinician to the numerous interventions that are likely to be of benefit at some point during therapy. Just as marital therapy provides an ongoing set of choices for the couple, likewise the clinician is continually presented with a series of choices regarding whether to continue with a current intervention or to change to a new strategy. No formula for making such decisions can be given, but hopefully the above considerations can assist the clinician as these difficult choice points arise.

How to Shift Interventions

Shifting from one intervention strategy to another is simple if the therapy has been focusing on one type of intervention strategy for a number of weeks, and the therapist and couple agree that it would be beneficial to begin focusing on other skills. A couple may have practiced EET skills for several weeks, and then it is time to introduce problem solving to the couple. In such a case, the therapist clarifies for the couple the circumstances under which EET skills are likely to be of most use and then introduces problem-solving/communication training. That is, in this circumstance there is an understandable end point in teaching one set of communication skills, and another set of skills is begun.

The transition is more complex when the therapist decides to shift intervention strategies during the middle of a session for only a short time period. The primary guideline under such circumstances is to make clear to the couple that the therapist is recommending a shift in strategy. In this way, the spouses do not become confused as to what is happening and whether this seemingly new approach is or is not a part of the skills they have been using. During a problem-solving session, one couple became deadlocked in considering solutions, with each person clinging to one solution. The therapist believed that the difficulty arose from conflicting standards about the roles that husband and wife should take at home when both have full-time jobs outside of the home. Consequently, the therapist recommended that the couple shift momentarily from problem solving to considering standards, with the hope that later in the session they would be able to resume problem solving.

Therapist: You do seem to have gotten stalemated in considering alternative solutions. Remember, our usual approach is to continue to look for other possible solutions until you find one that is agreeable to both of you. However, I'm going to suggest that we break from our problem-solving process for a few minutes because I think there are some ideas about who should do what around the house that you have not made explicit. And I think those ideas may be getting in your way. If the two of you have different standards for what your roles should be, then it will be hard to reach solutions at times. So, if we shift for a few minutes and try to clarify what you think your roles should be at home given that you both work full-time, it may help us come up with some solutions. I hope we can come to some agreement about roles that you will both be comfortable with, and then we can translate those into specific behaviors, as in the problem we've been working on tonight.

Actually, the manner in which a transition is made to another intervention for a short time will probably be influenced by at least two factors: (a) whether the couple has already learned the skills in the area that is to become the new focus and (b) whether the therapist believes that the new intervention area will become a major focus in therapy. Relative to the first issue, at times the couple has already learned several sets of skills, and during a session the therapist might decide to shift from one set of skills to another. In this circumstance, little explanation of the skill is needed, merely an explanation for why the therapist is recommending that a shift occur.

Therapist: We've been working on this problem for a long time tonight, and you are having more trouble than usual coming up with possible solutions. Diane, you seem pretty upset with Jack about something, and I'm not sure what it is. I wonder if your being upset with Jack is making it hard to focus on this problem. If so, you can be aware of your upset feelings and try to keep them out of your way while we reach a solution to this problem. Or if your feelings are just too strong, we can switch from problem solving for a while and have you express your feelings to each other through EET. Remember, it really does not give problem solving a reasonable chance to succeed if you attempt it when you are so upset about something else that it continues to intrude on the problem you are trying to deal with. Give me your thoughts as to which direction we should move in—either continuing with the problem solving or expressing your feelings about what is bothering you.

In the above example, the couple was already trained in EET, so the therapist could raise the possibility of shifting to that set of skills. However, on some occasions the therapist will want to shift to a set of skills that the couple has not yet learned. In that case, the therapist's behavior is likely to be influenced by whether or not he or she believes that the new skills to be addressed will become a significant aspect of therapy in the future. That is, the therapist may be focusing on BMT skills and decide that a cognitive intervention would be helpful at present, but the therapist has not presented the cognitive model to the couple at this time in therapy. If the therapist believes that significant cognitive restructuring will be needed with the couple during therapy, this might be used as an opportunity to introduce the cognitive model and then proceed with the cognitive intervention. Whereas this introduces the cognitive model and helps the couple relate it to behavior and emotions on an issue that makes clear the importance of cognitions, breaking the BMT for such an introduction to the cognitive model is somewhat disruptive to the BMT process. If the therapist does not believe that cognitive restructuring will be a significant part of therapy, then he or she may choose to provide only a brief, informal explanation of the role of cognitions as they apply to this problem and then soon resume with the BMT. The example above focusing on problem solving and standards for roles around the house for a dual-career couple followed this more informal strategy.

In essence, when shifting from one set of skills to a different focus, the therapist can use this shift to begin teaching a new set of skills. Alternatively, the therapist can make the shift in focus in order to remove a block or aid the processing of an issue, but without attempting to teach new skills. In the latter case, the therapist frequently acts as a "traffic cop" directing the couple through the new skills. As another example of this traffic cop strategy, the therapist may have been working with a couple from a cognitive perspective, and the husband has agreed that his standards are unrealistic in a given area. Consequently, he has agreed to moderate those standards. This shift in standards will be accompanied by behavioral changes so that the couple can evaluate the effects of these altered standards. Therefore, some type of agreement for behavioral change related to the standards is appropriate. If the couple has not yet learned problem-solving skills, the therapist could introduce the skills, and then the couple could problem-solve. Or, the therapist could help the couple problem-solve by directing them through the process without introducing skills:

Therapist: O.K., let's think about what that might mean about the way that you two get the children ready in the morning. Jim, if I understand you correctly, you are willing to shift your standards that Sue be solely responsible for getting the children ready for school. What would you both think would be reasonable about who takes responsibility for what in the mornings in terms of the kids? Let's reach some sort of temporary solution, try it out for a while, and then we can evaluate how it is working. How do you think you can break down the responsibilities for the children in the morning?

The decision to teach new skills with the shift in focus is therefore related to two factors. If the new focus is likely to be a major thrust of therapy, then the therapist might want to use the opportunity to begin teaching the new skills. However, if the new, temporary focus is unlikely to be employed extensively in therapy, then teaching the new skills may not be an effective use of time. Instead, the therapist's active directing of the couple through the process may be more appropriate. Second, the extent to which introducing the new skills will interrupt the initial focus of the session must be considered. Therefore, if the therapist believes that it is critical that the couple complete problem solving on a particular issue during the session, diverting attention by introducing the cognitive model or EET guidelines may be counterproductive. Again, the therapist might choose under this circumstance to help the couple deal with any necessary cognitive or affective components that must be addressed in a more informal way. The therapist leads the couple through the necessary cognitive or affective aspects of the problem and quickly returns to problem solving.

It is hoped that the complexity of the cognitive-behavioral approach to marital therapy has become obvious. Too often the term "complex" is used as a euphemism for confused or unclear, and we do not mean unclear in that sense. Although the cognitive-behavioral approach to marital therapy will continue to evolve, numerous guidelines currently exist to help direct the therapist in making decisions regarding the interventions of choice, their sequencing, and ways to alternate among the various treatment strategies. The complexity lies in the nature of the phenomenon under consideration. Gone are the days when we believed we could present a routine set of behavioral skills rather uniformly to all couples and expect the couples' marriages to improve. Instead, it is critical that we evaluate each couple's particular strengths and weaknesses and decide how the various interventions at our disposal would be best applied and adapted to meet that couple's particular needs.

12

Empirical Status of Cognitive-Behavioral Marital Therapy

As should be apparent from the previous chapters, conducting a skills-oriented approach to marital therapy involves a great number of decisions on the part of the therapist. Thus, when a therapist or researcher notes that a couple received 10 weeks of problem solving and communication training, something is known about the overall skeletal framework of the sessions. However, little is known about how the guidelines for these intervention strategies were adapted for this particular couple, how the therapist attempted to pace intervention for the couple, how often the therapist reinforced the couple for their constructive communications, what the therapist said and did during the third session when the couple returned without their homework, and so forth. In the preceding discussions of marital therapy, we have tried to address these and many other issues which the therapist confronts while conducting skills-oriented marital therapy. Yet, the recommendations and suggestions offered have not been researched on any level of detail. Consequently, the detailed guidelines proposed must remain as recommendations based on clinical experience. Existing outcome studies only attempt to clarify whether overall treatment procedures such as problem-solving training, with the many decisions involved within it, are effective in aiding distressed couples.

The following review of outcome studies is restricted to controlled outcome investigations that focus on evaluating various aspects of cognitive-behavioral marital therapy for the treatment of marital discord. Thus, subjects must be assigned to treatment in a random or nonbiased manner;

the appropriate comparison groups must be included in the investigation to answer the questions being addressed; well-developed outcome measures must be employed; and the treatment must be described in some detail such that the content of therapy sessions is ascertainable and replicable. In addition, the length of treatment and the therapists must approximate what might be expected in actual clinical settings and training facilities; otherwise the applicability of the findings to the clinician is questionable.

In an attempt to be scientific and empirical, outcome investigators have often conducted treatment evaluation studies which for one reason or another are limited in their implications for clinical settings. As mentioned earlier, one set of limiting factors might be the length of treatment employed or the training of the therapists involved in the study. In addition, the method for assigning couples to treatment can lead to questionable generalizability to the clinical context. In all of the marital outcome investigations to be discussed, couples were randomly assigned to treatment when various treatments were being compared. This follows sound scientific practice, but it addresses a particular kind of question only. Randomly assigning couples to various treatments asks the question of whether one form of treatment is superior to another when the characteristics of the particular couple are not taken into account. This information is important early in the empirical exploration of a treatment procedure to determine whether the treatment approach seems to hold any promise for a broad range of couples. Once this question has been answered in the affirmative, then other questions arise, such as which couples seem to respond most favorably to a given treatment, and whether certain couples respond differentially to various treatments. These questions have not yet been the focus of any outcome investigations, and these issues have only been touched upon as a sideline in investigations designed to explore other issues. However, these later questions become the major ones that clinicians address when they confront a couple in a clinical context. That is, knowing this couple's history, their current concerns and ways of interacting with each other, their ways of processing what occurs in their marriage, and so forth, what treatment interventions seem most appropriate?

Addressing these issues awaits the next generation of investigations. Consequently, the reader must be cautious in interpreting the findings of the following studies. If two different treatments are compared in an outcome study by randomly assigning distressed couples to those treaments, and the findings indicate no significant differences between the two treatments in affecting change, the results suggest that neither treatment is superior overall in assisting a heterogeneous group of distressed couples. However, the study was not intended to address and does not answer whether certain couples respond better to one treatment than the other. Understanding this issue is important because many outcome studies have this design and these results. Unfortunately, many persons have read the outcome literature and concluded, "When I treat a distressed couple, it really doesn't matter which treatment I use because they all are about equally effective." On the contrary, for that particular couple one form of treatment might be much more appropriate than another; this issue simply has not been addressed empirically in most cases. This is not to say that the current findings are meaningless. Many important issues have been addressed, as will become apparent. Still, the one critical issue "of which couples for which treatment" is yet to be explored in much more detail.

EFFECTS OF BEHAVIORAL MARITAL THERAPY

Each theoretical approach to treating marital discord postulates that certain variables are important and even critical in assisting distressed couples. These variables then become the specific targets of intervention, with the assumption that along with change on these variables, the couple's marital adjustment is likely to improve. In order to test this logic, it is critical to evaluate whether the treatment has resulted in a change on these specific variables with corresponding change on marital adjustment (Baucom, 1983). BMT posits that these critical variables are communication and noncommunication behaviors. In treatment outcome investigations, this focus has typically been translated into evaluations of (a) attempts to communicate while resolving relationship problems and (b) couples' presenting complaints of specific behaviors they would like to see altered in the marriage. Thus, it is important to evaluate whether BMT is capable of promoting change in these areas and whether such changes are related to changes in marital adjustment. In order to evaluate this relationship most directly, correlations between (a) communication and noncommunication behavior change and (b) change in marital adjustment need to be determined. Unfortunately, such correlations are unavailable in existing studies; consequently, it is possible to evaluate only whether changes were produced on specific variables viewed to be important and whether changes in marital adjustment occurred in the same treatment conditions.

BMT Versus Wait List and Nonspecific
Control Groups

One of the first questions typically posed in evaluating a treatment is whether the intervention is more effective than (a) no treatment at all and (b) treatments that would not be expected to be effective. Consequently, a number of outcome investigations have included a waiting list (WL) and/or nonspecific control group. Although there are some exceptions (O'Farrell, Cutter, & Floyd, 1983; Turkewitz & O'Leary, 1981), the findings indicate that, overall, BMT is more effective than a WL in decreasing negative communication among couples. However, examination of the same investigations indicates that altering positive communication among distressed couples is more difficult. Only one investiagator has consistently reported increases in positive communication for BMT relative to WL and nonspecific control groups (Jacobson 1977, 1978a), and since then he has questioned the utility of his results based on the coding system employed (Jacobson, 1984a). Some investigators have found inconsistent or mixed results in altering positive communication (Baucom, 1982; Baucom & Lester, 1986; Mehlman, Baucom, & Anderson, 1983; O'Farrell et al., 1983), whereas others have found BMT to be no more effective than a waiting list in increasing positive communication (Hahlweg, Schindler, Revenstorf, & Brengelmann, 1984; Snyder & Wills, 1989; Turkewitz & O'Leary, 1981).

What are the clinical implications of this pattern of findings? First, basic research findings indicate that distressed and nondistressed couples are much more consistently discriminated by negative communications than positive communications, again with many studies finding no consistent differences between the two groups when positives are considered (see Baucom & Adams, 1987, for a review). Thus, the treatment investigations might be effective in helping distressed couples approximate the behavior of nondistressed couples by decreasing negative communication.

Why is it that BMT is more effective in decreasing negatives than increasing positives? This probably results from two factors. First, the negative communication is often quite aversive and catches the clinician's attention quickly, thus leading to immediate intervention. Also, as discussed in the BMT treatment chapter, at times the therapist is so pleased to see the couple interacting positively with each other that he or she does not want to interrupt to comment on the communication. Frequently this might lead to no reinforcement from the therapist for positive communications. The second reason for the increased treatment effectiveness for negative communication is that one is attempting to *decrease* the negatives whenever they occur, and it is easy to point them out and ask the couple to alter the communication. However, *increasing* the positive communication is apparently more difficult. Many of the positives that the clinician might want the couple to use are communications that need to arise somewhat spontaneously. That is, most couples would probably feel inappropriately manipulated if asked to smile at the partner or accept responsibility for some difficulty if he or she did not believe that he or she was responsible. The therapist can make recommendations for the couple to interact with certain positive behaviors when they seem appropriate, but these are somewhat difficult to engineer. However, the negative communications can almost always be commented upon and thus decreased.

Therefore, if the clinician wishes to meaningfully increase positive communication, thought must be given to at least two areas. First, the clinician must be certain to reinforce positive communications when they occur and not be seduced by the more dramatic negative communications displayed by distressed couples. However, this reliance on reinforcing naturally occurring positive communications may not be optimally effective if the positives occur at a very low rate among some distressed couples. For such couples, the clinician's task becomes how to more naturally include a focus on positives while communicating. For example, the couple might be taught to point out what they like about the partner's proposed solution, even if the solution needs some changes overall. The seriousness of not consistently increasing positive communications among distressed couples is unknown, but the clinician will probably work with many couples who display few positive communications. In such instances, the clinician must keep in mind that BMT, as typically described and used, is not optimal for such purposes.

In terms of altering presenting complaints and requests for behavioral change, 9 of 11 studies employing a WL demonstrate the superiority of BMT (Baucom, 1982; Baucom & Lester, 1986; Boelens, Emmelkamp, MacGillavry, & Markvoort, 1980; Ewart, 1978a; Hahlweg, Schindler, Revenstorf, & Brengelmann, 1984; Jacobson, 1984a; Johnson & Greenberg, 1985; Mehlman et al., 1983; Snyder & Wills, 1989), with only Girodo, Stein, and Dotzenroth (1980) and O'Farrell et al. (1983) finding no differences. In addition, Azrin et al. (1980) and Crowe (1978) found BMT to be superior to nonspecific control conditions in altering specific presenting complaints.

The above findings might lead the clinician to conclude that BMT interventions are the path to pursue if one is interested in altering various specific complaints and behaviors of the couple. However, with rare exceptions, the investigations have provided a summary score across presenting complaints, such that it is difficult to evaluate whether BMT is more effective in producing some behavioral changes than others. Bennun (1985a, b), in an investigation exploring the relative effectiveness of conjoint BMT, group BMT, and treatment of one spouse, divided the presenting complaints of couples into various content categories. He found that couples with the following categories of complaints responded to BMT: (a) communication; (b) sexual behavior; (c) household-domestic concerns; (d) child-care issues; (e) "behavior change," including such issues as timekeeping, tidiness, cleanliness; (f) violence; (g) finance-work; (h) decision making; and (i) extended family. However, couples with the following categories of complaints did not respond to BMT: (a) jealousy; (b) dependency; (c) psychopathology of one spouse; and (d) care and nonsexual affection. These latter categories seem to involve the care, concern, and ways of demonstrating these feelings which spouses experience, as well as individual psychopathology. Margolin (1978) has raised concerns that BMT may not be optimally designed for concerns involving passion, play, and other issues that are not easily negotiable. Bennun's findings, although they are in need of replication, lend credence to these concerns. BMT is clearly oriented toward negotiating changes, and the clinician can have some confidence that such treatment procedures are effective in producing behavior changes that are voluntary and can be agreed upon, at least in a significant portion of couples presenting for therapy. However, when the couple's concerns are more focused on being cared for, issues of possessiveness, and closeness and dependency, then the clinician might need to consider alternative or supplemental treatment strategies. As will be discussed later, the affective and cognitive treatments described in this book appear to produce some of these needed changes.

A final question of importance regarding the effectiveness of BMT relative to WL and nonspecific treatments is whether BMT, with its ability to produce the specific changes outlined above, also is more effective in increasing marital adjustment. Using self-report measures such as the DAS and MAS, 11 of 14 investigations have demonstrated the superiority of BMT over WL treatment (see Baucom and Hoffman [1986] for a more detailed discussion). However, the effectiveness of BMT compared to nonspecific treatments (interventions that provide attention but omit the assumed active ingredients of treatment) is much more uncertain. Azrin et al. (1980) found differences favoring BMT, but Jacobson (1978a) found differences on only one of two measures. Crowe (1978) found no differences at posttest, but BMT was superior during some of the follow-up periods.

The superiority of BMT over WL conditions in increasing marital adjustment is probably due to the fact that very few maritally distressed couples show meaningful improvement during a several-month waiting period. Combining the results across three outcome studies, Jacobson, Follette, Revenstorf, Baucom, Hahlweg, and Margolin (1984) found that only 14% of distressed couples showed reliable improvement (beyond that expected based on the reliability of the measurement instruments) during a waiting period. This finding in itself should caution clinicians not to suggest to couples that they wait and see if they improve because such improvement is rare, at least during a several-month period. Yet, the lack of clear superiority of BMT over nonspecific conditions in improving marital adjustment is of concern. These findings could mean that simply having the couple come for treatment and discuss their concerns without teaching them any skills or without attempting to change any specific variables viewed as important within existing theories of marital discord may be as helpful to some couples as teaching them the skills involved in BMT. Where BMT seems to excel relative to these comparision conditions is in altering many of the specific behaviors focused upon in treatment, particularly negative communication and behaviors that can be negotiated and voluntarily changed.

Relative Effectiveness of BMT Components

BMT typically does not consist of a single treatment component. Although different clinicians and investigators may implement treatment differently, attempts to teach couples (a) problem-solving and communication skills and (b) some form of contracting or behavior exchange principles often are included. Given the above findings that BMT does produce a number of meaningful changes in couples, an appropriate question to address is whether certain treatment procedures are responsible for couples' gains. This issue has been addressed in a number of different ways. For example, Jacobson (1978a) compared two behavioral treatments, each involving problem-solving and communication training, but one including good faith contracting and the other including quid pro quo contracting in order to evaluate whether one form of contracting was superior to the other. Ewart (1978a) employed communication training followed by either (a) goal setting without contingencies, (b) good faith contracting, or (c) quid pro quo contracting. Emmelkamp, van der Helm,

MacGillavry, and van Zanten (1984) used a crossover design in which one treatment included contracting followed by communication training, and the other treatment included communication training followed by contracting. This design enabled the investigators to evaluate the changes occurring within each treatment component and to compare the order in which the treatment components occurred. Baucom (1982) used a component study to compare the relative effectiveness of (a) problem-solving and communication training followed by quid pro quo contracting, (b) problem-solving and communication training alone, and (c) contracting alone. Finally, Jacobson (1984a) conducted an investigation similar to Baucom's with the exception that a behavior exchange component without contingencies was employed rather than quid pro quo contracts. With rare exceptions, the findings across these investigations were that BMT is effective in assisting couples, but there is little basis to conclude that any single treatment component is superior overall to the other or to a multiple component treatment. The one contrary result was Jacobson's (1984a) finding that couples receiving behavior exchange only showed more deterioration at follow-up.

Thus there has been no success in isolating "the active ingredient" in BMT. All of the treatment procedures investigated thus far seem to help some couples, but none of the specific components have been shown to help all couples. This conclusion also applies to behavioral contracting. Liberman, Levine, Wheeler, Sanders, and Wallace (1976) questioned whether behavioral contracting would be of use if not preceded by communication training, and Jacobson (1978b) raised concern that contracting might actually be detrimental to couples because it might change important attributions for spouses' behavior. However, the data consistently support that contracting can produce meaningful behavior changes, even without communication training, and further that contracting can be presented in a way that couples find enjoyable and valuable (Baucom, 1982; Emmelkamp et al., 1984; Ewart, 1978a).

Given the above findings, the clinician should give consideration to problem solving, communication training, and contracting when a couple has specific behavioral changes that are the focus of intervention. At present, there are no data suggesting when one intervention is likely to be more effective than another. This more detailed evaluation of the treatment procedures is warranted because clinical observation indicates wide variability in response to the various procedures. For example, at least two different types of couples seem to find contracting to be a valuable experience and profit from it.

First, couples who are extremely alienated from each other, who are angry toward each other, and who are mistrustful of each other seem to benefit from contracting. Such couples often are unwilling to make behavior changes primarily for the happiness of the other person or for the well-being of the relationship. On the contrary, they often feel abused and mistreated in the relationship. Contracting, with its clarification of the rewards that one receives for behavior change, promotes a sense of fairness, that neither spouse will take advantage of the other; in particular, quid pro quo contracting may help such couples. The second type of couple who appears to respond well to contracting is one in which one or both persons are rather self-oriented. Again, contracting makes clear what each receives for making changes in his or her behavior.

Whereas contracting might be appealing to both types of couples, the therapist might question whether the use of these techniques merely reinforces some of the attitudinal and behavioral patterns that warrant change in the couple. This might be true, but contracting can be a useful strategy to help the couple to change early in treatment while these maladaptive thoughts and behaviors persist. Then, subsequent interventions with the couple might alleviate the need for contracting. In reality, some couples never seem to get beyond this point of mistrust or self-centeredness, and for those couples contracting might continue to be a behavior change strategy that they employ long-term. Again, these observations are only speculative at present, so the clinician must experiment in order to gain further clarification about which couples respond to which BMT interventions.

Effects of Altering Other BMT Parameters

In addition to exploring the most effective treatment components of BMT, investigators have evaluated other aspects of treatment that might alter effectiveness. This has included an examination of the number of therapists present, whether one or both spouses are treated, the number of couples present, and whether delaying treatment alters the effectiveness of BMT.

Mehlman et al. (1983) examined whether having two therapists present was more effective than a single therapist. The results indicated that both formats were effective in producing communication changes, behavior changes, and increases in marital adjustment, but there were no differences in effectiveness between the two treatment formats. This finding is important for clinicians because it suggests that a cost-effective strategy of only one clinician per couple is warranted. At the same time, it must be recognized that the clinicians in the investigation were rather experienced when they treated these couples, having each treated between 20 and 30 couples with BMT. Thus cotherapy might still be more effective for inexperienced therapists, but such data are unavailable. Also, the results of this study must not be generalized beyond BMT. Therapists might play very different roles in marital therapy from other theoretical orientations, and cotherapy might still prove beneficial in those cases. In addition, Epstein, Jayne-Lazarus, and DeGiovanni (1979) found that couples shifted the verbal dominance patterns in their communication (i.e., whether the male or the female spoke more) toward the patterns modeled by their male-female cotherapist teams. Therefore, cotherapists might be helpful in assisting couples with particular needs where such shifts are appropriate.

Another cost-effective way to present BMT is to conduct it in a group format. In the largest controlled outcome study of marital therapy to date, Hahlweg, Schindler, Revenstorf, and Brengelmann (1984) compared BMT in a conjoint format with BMT in a conjoint group format. In both instances, BMT was successful in reducing presenting complaints, altering communication, and increasing marital satisfaction. However, conjoint BMT was superior to conjoint group BMT in improving the couple's report of relationship problems and happiness with the relationship. Bennun (1985a, b) also compared the relative effectiveness of conjoint and conjoint group BMT. In addition, he included a condition in which only one spouse received behavioral treatment focusing on the marital problems. Which spouse was included was based on the request of the referring agent or by having the couple decide which spouse would benefit most from treatment. The results indicated that all three treatments were effective in producing changes in presenting complaints, a self-report of communication, and marital adjustment. However, there were no significant differences among the treatments at the end of therapy or at follow-up. A closer look at the data revealed that the changes occurred most rapidly in the conjoint BMT condition, with the couples showing the majority of their change by the sixth week of treatment, whereas couples in the other two conditions continued to exhibit improvement until the end of the 10-week sessions.

These findings suggest that conjoint group BMT can be an effective, cost-efficient format for delivering treatment. However, the combined results of the two studies suggest that the effects of BMT might be somewhat diluted by the use of a group format. Hahlweg found the magnitude of change to be greater with conjoint BMT, and Bennun found that the changes occurred more slowly within the group format. Thus, some caution must be exercised in implementing group conjoint BMT, but the overall results indicate that it is a viable treatment format alternative when conditions necessitate, perhaps owing to a lack of therapist availability.

The results with regard to treating a single spouse call for a re-evaluation of some of the assumptions regarding the most effective way to treat distressed couples. Skills-oriented approaches along with other theoretical approaches have assumed that the most effective way to assist a couple is to have both spouses present. In teaching skills, working with both persons who will be implementing the skills seems only logical. However, the results of Bennun's work cannot be ignored. On many occasions, owing to difficult work schedules, and so forth, it is not feasible for both spouses to participate in therapy. Many therapists turn such couples away stating that without both persons present, little can be accomplished. Also, one spouse often contacts the therapist, and the partner is unwilling to come to treatment owing to fear, beliefs that no intervention is needed, and so forth. Bennun's couples were not couples in which one spouse refused to come for treatment, but his findings do raise the question of whether such couples can be assisted by the presence of the spouse desiring intervention. Although replication of these findings is in order, the ability to improve the marriage by directly intervening with only one spouse should encourage the clinician to explore intervention modalities other than conjoint marital therapy for improving marital discord.

Finally, Mehlman et al. (1983) investigated whether delaying treatment significantly altered the effectiveness of BMT. Waiting lists are often a necessity in many clinical contexts, but it has been unclear whether being asked to wait before receiving treatment decreases response to treatment, perhaps because of decreased motivation or additional destructive interaction during the waiting period. Also, many treatment outcome investigations include a waiting list condition for design purposes. Thus, it is important to evaluate the effects of being placed on a waiting list. Mehlman's findings indicate that there are no significant differences in the effects of BMT treatment, whether treatment is provided immediately or after waiting for 10 weeks. These results applied to requests for behavior change, communication, and marital adjustment. Consequently, it appears that placing most couples on a waiting list for this time period is not detrimental to their eventual response to treatment. However, this conclusion may not apply to couples who are experiencing an intense marital crisis.

Magnitude of BMT Effects

The above investigations have evaluated the effectiveness of BMT by the use of traditional inferential statistical procedures which allow conclusions regarding whether the various treatment group means are different from one another. However, such procedures alone provide little information about how large and meaningful the effects of treatment are. More recently, the magnitude of change has become of increasing interest to outcome investigators because it is important to ask whether marital therapy is improving highly distressed marriages but leaving them still distressed, or whether treatment results in many happy marriages. One approach that has been employed to address this issue is Smith and Glass's (1977) recommendations for conducting a meta-analysis of the results across studies. Hahlweg and Markman (1983) conducted such an analysis to evaluate the effect size of treatments based on the results of 17 BMT outcome investigations. The effect size is equal to the mean difference between the treated and control groups on a given dependent variable after therapy, divided by the standard deviation of the control group. That is, it indicates the number of standard deviations that a treatment group is above the mean of the control group. Hahlweg and Markman found that for the 81 measures included in the 17 studies, the average effect size for BMT was .92. Assuming a normal distribution, this means that on the average a couple receiving BMT was "better off" than 82% of the couples placed on a wait list or who received a nonspecific treatment. Furthermore, the effect size was similar for both self-report and observational data and remained rather constant during follow-up periods.

Nevertheless, examination of the effect size does not clarify whether the changes produced are clinically meaningful. One way to approach this issue is to ask whether couples have moved from the distressed to nondistressed range on the variable of interest. Using a cutoff score of 100 on the MAS and 97 on the DAS to diffferentiate between distressed and nondistressed couples (the optimal empirically derived scores for distinguishing between distressed and nondistressed couples), only 5 of 10 studies found that the mean of the couples treated with BMT was above the distressed/nondistressed cutoff at posttest (Jacobson, 1977, 1978a, 1984a; O'Farrell et al., 1983; Snyder & Wills, 1989). The remaining five studies have marital adjustment test scores in the distressed range at the end of treatment (Baucom, 1982; Ewart, 1978b; Liberman et al., 1976; Mehlman et al., 1983; Turkewitz & O'Leary, 1981). In addition, two other studies not presenting mean scores indicate that BMT did not increase marital adjustment more than a WL condition. These findings provide strong evidence that a significant number of couples are still in the distressed range at the end of treatment.

Further evaluation of this issue has focused on the percentage of couples who are no longer distressed by the end of treatment (Jacobson & Follette, 1985; Jacobson, Follette, & Revenstorf, 1984; Jacobson, Follette, Revenstorf, Baucom, Hahlweg, & Margolin, 1984). These investigators re-evaluated outcome investigations earlier conducted by Baucom (1982), Hahlweg, Schindler, Revenstorf, and Brengelmann (1984), Jacobson (1984a), and Margolin and Weiss (1978) and found that 35% to 40% of couples treated with BMT were in the nondistressed range at the end of treatment. This evaluation also required that any changes occurring were not within the range that might be due to error measurement in the assessment devices.

These findings are rather sobering and should caution the clinician that short-term BMT of 10 to 14 sessions is unlikely to result in the majority of couples' being in the nondistressed range at the end of treatment. This could be due to several reasons. First, BMT as practiced in these outcome investigations has had a rather narrow focus of intervention, and perhaps broadening the interventions to include a focus on cognitive and affective factors would be of benefit. Second, the treatment may be too short for many couples. For example, Snyder and Wills (1989) offered a longer version of BMT (averaging 19 sessions) and found that 55% of the couples joined the ranks of the nondistressed. Thus the description of BMT as a short-term treatment of 10 to 14 weeks is descriptive of the treatment in most outcome investigations but may not represent the optimal length of treatment for the couple in an applied setting. Third, some other theoretical orientation may be more appropriate for some distressed couples, but this couple-by-treatment interaction has rarely been assessed. Finally, marital adjustment may not increase for some couples regardless of the type or length of intervention. Some spouses simply do not like or value each other and do not want to live together or make significant efforts at improving the relationship, in spite of their request for assistance. Unfortunately, no outcome investigations have reported whether BMT or other forms of treatment have helped couples make reasonable decisions to terminate their relationships.

Predicting Response to BMT

Given that BMT is not a panacea, it is important to evaluate who benefits most from this approach to treatment. One focus has been to investigate the demographic characteristics of persons responding to BMT, but the results in this area have been somewhat mixed. Several studies have found that younger couples respond more favorably to BMT than do older couples (Baucom, 1984; Hahlweg, Schindler, Revenstorf, & Brengelmann, 1984; Turkewitz & O'Leary, 1981). However, Bennun (1985b) found such a relationship in predicting only one of three dependent measures and concluded that no demographic variables served as reliable predictors of response to treatment. Jacobson, Follette, and Pagel (1986) found no relationship between age and response to treatment. Similarly, Crowe (1978) found no correlation between age and response to BMT but did report that less educated couples responded more favorably to BMT.

In addition to demographic variables, interest has focused on both relationship variables and individual psychological characteristics of the spouses in predicting response to therapy. Basic research has indicated that communication is one major way in which distressed and nondistressed couples differ. As a result, it is possible that distressed couples who differ in their styles of communication or degree of dysfunctional communication may respond differently to treatment. As expected, Hahlweg, Schindler, Revenstorf, and Brengelmann (1984) found that couples who had self-reports of greater communication satisfaction prior to treatment showed greater changes in marital happiness in response to BMT. At the same time, couples who showed more negative communication as rated by coders demonstrated greater response to BMT in the same study. Thus, self-report and actual observation of communication predicted response to treatment in the opposite direction. Similarly perplexing, Baucom and Mehlman (1984) found that couples who demonstrated more positive communication according to outside ratings at the end of therapy actually were more likely to divorce during the follow-up period. Although further research in this area is clearly needed, the results to date indicate that quality of communication—either prior to treatment or at the end of therapy—is not an intuitive measure of how the couple is likely to fare.

One implication of these findings is that therapists must not lose confidence in the potential of treatment to help a couple simply because they present with extremely disordered communication patterns such as destructive arguments, blaming, and so forth. No findings indicate that such couples are less responsive to treatment than other couples. This is in keeping with our observation that it is extremely difficult to predict which couples will respond to treatment based on their level of overt distress and disordered communication at a given point in time. For some couples, extreme anger, frustration, and hopelessness can be overcome somewhat easily in spite of the disordered communication that such couples at times present. At the same time, other couples with these same reactions and communications are well entrenched in their patterns and do not change as easily.

However, the degree to which the couple has taken steps toward divorce or seriously considered divorce appears to be an important factor in response to treatment. These actual behavioral steps and related thoughts probably are an index of remaining commitment to the marriage, and the less committed couples respond less well to treatment in a number of ways. Such couples are more likely to drop out of treatment (Ewart, 1978b), show less change in marital adjustment at the end of treatment (Beach & Broderick, 1983; Ewart, 1978b; Hahlweg, Schindler, Revenstorf, & Brengelmann, 1984), and are more likely to divorce during follow-up periods (Crowe, 1978). Still, some other findings diverge from this pattern of results. Jacobson et al. (1986) found no relationship between steps taken toward divorce and response to BMT.

The steps taken toward divorce may also be related to the emotional climate of the relationship, and Hahlweg, Schindler, Revenstorf, and Brengelmann (1984) found that the quality of affection in the marriage prior to treatment was more closely related to response to treatment than how the couples handled conflict. When a couple reported a lack of tenderness between them, when sexual intercourse was infrequent, and when the wife reported a lack of togetherness prior to treatment, then the couple was unlikely to report marital happiness at the end of treatment. These findings are in keeping with Bennun's results that couples with these types of concerns do not seem to respond as well to BMT. Thus, characteristics may predict that the couple would not respond well to any form of treatment because the commitment and tenderness are no longer present, or the findings may indicate that such couples do not respond well to treatment because BMT is not the optimal treatment for addressing these issues. At present these interpretations cannot be differentiated, but in either case, such couples do not seem to respond well to BMT.

To a large extent, marital therapists have focused on the relationship as the client in marital therapy. As a result, much of the attention has been given to isolating relationship variables that might predict response to treatment. However, in a much-needed return to a balanced position, renewed attention is being given to how characteristics of one individual might influence the course of treatment. Along this line, investigators have started to explore whether normal personality characteristics are related to treatment response. Not surprisingly, several investigations have demonstrated that the sex roles of the spouses (i.e., levels of masculinity and femininity) and the match between the sex roles of the two spouses are related to the couples' levels of marital adjustment (Antill, 1983; Baucom & Aiken, 1984; Burger & Jacobson, 1979; Elliott, 1986; Kurdek & Schmitt, 1986; Murstein & Williams, 1983). As a result, Baucom and Aiken (1984) also explored whether response to BMT was related to sex roles. They found that if the wife was high on femininity prior to treatment, then both wife and husband reported a greater increase in marital adjustment at the end of treatment. The measure of femininity (Baucom, 1976) included an emphasis on expressing and experiencing emotions as well as value given to interpersonal relationships. Jacobson et al. (1986) attempted to replicate this finding. Whereas they found that the wife's femininity was correlated with both pretest and posttest levels of marital adjustment, it was not correlated with change in marital adjustment. However, they did find personality characteristics of the two partners that predicted response to treatment. Couples consisting of highly independent husbands and highly affiliative wives were less likely to respond to BMT. These may be the same types of wives who in the Hahlweg et al. study reported a dissatisfaction with the level of closeness in the relationship.

In addition to investigations of individual functioning which lies within the normal domain, some attention has been given to individual psychopathology as a predictor of response to treatment. Emmelkamp (1985) has reported that spouses with a heterogeneous group of individual disorders respond more poorly to BMT and cognitive marital therapy. However, Jacobson et al. (1986) found that depression prior to marital therapy was a positive prognostic sign for response to BMT. These results, which might seem discrepant, can perhaps be resolved by findings from Baucom and Sher (1986) indicating that couples with one depressed member responded well to skills-oriented therapy as described in this book, but couples in which one or both spouses had other psychiatric disturbances did not respond as well to treatment.

Overall, there are almost no variables that have been shown to be consistent predictors of response to BMT. At present the inconsistency in the findings might be due to a number of factors, including different characteristics of the samples, different measures, and different ways of implementing BMT in the various investigations. In spite of the inconsistencies, certain trends emerge. A number of studies indicate that couples who are more seriously considering or taking steps toward divorce are less likely to benefit from BMT. Also, findings suggest that when the couple has less affection, closeness, and good feelings between them they are less likely to benefit from treatment. Both of these trends could be interpreted to mean that more severely disturbed couples respond less well to treatment. Also, it appears that characteristics of the individual spouses are important in response to treatment, but much more research is needed in this area before strong conclusions are reached.

Applying BMT to Target Populations

As mentioned earlier, one major focus that treatment outcome investigations must take is to become increasingly clear in describing who is receiving treatment and which couples respond to treatment. One strategy to accomplish this is to target treatment to particular populations and evaluate its effectiveness. Research in BMT is beginning to take this approach, primarily focusing on couples in which one member has some type of diagnosable individual disorder.

Given the great frequency with which depression and marital discord overlap, it is understandable that investigators have begun to evaluate the effectiveness of BMT with maritally distressed couples in which one spouse is depressed. Beach and O'Leary (1986) have presented preliminary findings on a small sample of 10 such couples with depressed wives who were assigned to either BMT, individual cognitive therapy for the depressed wife, or a waiting list condition. The findings indicate that none of the wives receiving treatment were depressed at the end of therapy or at three-month follow-up. Also, wives in both conditions showed clear increases in marital adjustment at the end of therapy and at follow-up. However, the results further demonstrated that the wives receiving BMT evidenced more rapid and greater gains in marital adjustment than the wives receiving cognitive therapy. In a follow-up study based on a much larger sample size, Beach, Sandeen, and O'Leary (1987) found similar results. Wives in both treatment conditions demonstrated significant decreases in depression at the end of treatment, but BMT was superior in decreasing marital distress.

Although depression was not the focus of these other two investigations, the frequency of its co-occurrence with marital distress has allowed for evaluating the effectiveness of BMT with couples with this joint problem. As mentioned earlier, Jacobson et al. (1986) found that the presence of depression was actually a positive prognostic sign for a couple's response to BMT. Baucom and Sher (1986) did not find that depression predicted a better response to treatment compared to couples with marital distress only. However, depressed couples did show as much change on marital adjustment as maritally distressed couples in which neither partner was depressed. Complicating the picture somewhat was the finding that couples with one depressed spouse were more maritally distressed initially than other couples, so that equivalent change still meant that these couples were more distressed on an absolute level at the end of therapy. This is important because Baucom and Mehlman (1984) have found that it is the absolute level of functioning at the end of treatment rather than the amount of change during therapy which is important for the future functioning of the couple. Baucom and Sher also found that BMT was successful in significantly lowering the depression level among depressed spouses.

Thus, findings to date are rather consistent in indicating that couples with one depressed member respond to BMT, in terms of both increasing marital adjustment and decreasing depression. These findings are important to the clinician in treatment planning and prioritizing. The results suggest that one parsimonious approach is to attempt marital therapy with such couples.

O'Farrell, Cutter, and Floyd (1985) also have demonstrated the effectiveness of BMT with alcoholics. They placed couples in which the husband was an alcoholic into one of three conditions: (a) a conjoint-group BMT format; (b) a conjoint-group interactional format; or (c) a WL control group. Among other findings, the results indicate that BMT was more effective than the other two conditions in (a) increasing marital adjustment and (b) improving observed problem-solving communication and overall positive communication at the end of treatment.

Thus, the findings to date indicate that BMT is successful in treating two rather difficult populations, couples with alcohol-related problems who have been excluded from most outcome studies and maritally distressed couples in which one spouse is also depressed.

Effectiveness of BMT Versus Other Treatment Approaches

Another major focus in the evaluation of any therapeutic intervention is its effectiveness relative to other available treatments. As a result, BMT has been compared to a number of other theoretical orientations, including: (a) a communications training approach which emphasizes the emotional expressiveness and listening skills discussed in this text (Girodo et al., 1980; Hahlweg, Revenstorf, & Schindler, 1982; Turkewitz & O'Leary, 1981); (b) cognitive restructuring (Emmelkamp et al., 1988) and cognitive restructuring plus BMT as described in the preceding chapters (Baucom, 1985; Baucom & Lester, 1986); (c) a systems approach (Boelens et al., 1980;

Emmelkamp et al., 1984); (d) a group interaction approach (Liberman et al., 1976; O'Farrell et al., 1983); (e) a group analytic approach with a present focus (Crowe, 1978) and an insight-oriented approach (Snyder & Wills, 1989); and (f) an experiential approach (Johnson & Greenberg, 1985). Hahlweg and Markman (1983) conducted a meta-analysis of BMT versus other treatment approaches and concluded that there were no significant differences in the magnitude of changes produced by these different strategies, although there was a tendency for BMT to produce more stable follow-up changes. These results of the meta-analysis are consistent with the findings in most of the individual investigations noted above: BMT and the other theoretical approaches are successful in producing significant increases in marital functioning, but rarely are differences found among the various treatment conditions.

At the same time, there have been some exceptions to the above pattern which merit notation. First, Hahlweg et al. found that BMT offered in either a group conjoint or conjoint format was more successful than communication training with an emotional expressiveness focus when the latter was offered in a conjoint-group format. These findings were in terms of altering presenting complaints, selected aspects of communication, and marital adjustment. Second, O'Farrell's work with alcoholics has been described above. He and his colleagues found that when BMT was offered in a conjoint-group format, it was more effective than a group interaction approach in altering some positive communication and marital adjustment. Third, Johnson and Greenberg (1985) compared BMT with an experiential approach that used Gestalt and client-centered techniques to clarify negative interaction styles between spouses and to uncover affect that underlies such interaction styles. They found that the experiential approach was more effective than BMT at both posttest and eight-week follow-up in increasing marital adjustment and decreasing presenting complaints.

As noted in the introduction to this chapter, caution must be exercised in concluding that the various theoretical orientations are likely to be equally effective in working with a particular couple. In all of the studies mentioned in this section, couples were randomly assigned to treatment, and all outcome studies to date show large variability in response to treatment. That is, some couples seem to respond well to most of the treatments, but some couples do not respond well to particular treatments. Unfortunately, there is little understanding of which couples benefit from which treatment approaches. Also, the findings that are exceptions to the general pattern of no meaningful differences between treatments must not be overgeneralized. In no cases have attempts been made to replicate these findings in even a second investigation. In addition, although all of the investigations that found meaningful differences seem to have been conducted in a scientifically sound manner, in each case the treatment receiving favorable results was consistent with the theoretical orientation of the principal investigator. Whether alternative treatments are conducted with as much enthusiasm or competency is an important issue which future investigations need to assess more fully.

EFFECTS OF OTHER COMMUNICATION TRAINING APPROACHES

Exactly where to draw the line between BMT and other skills-oriented approaches is unclear, but consistent with the framework of this text, communication skills such as emotional expressiveness training seem worth differentiating from skills such as communicating in order to problem-solve. To date, at least five investigations have focused on distressed couples and compared non-problem-solving communication training to a WL condition (Ely, Guerney, & Stover, 1973; Epstein & Jackson, 1978; Girodo et al., 1980; Hahlweg, Schindler, Revenstorf, & Brengelmann, 1984; Turkewitz & O'Leary, 1981). The combined findings from these investigations suggest that these communication strategies can sucessfully teach the specific communication skills on which they focus; however, they seem to have little effect on marital adjustment. Because most of these couples were treated in a conjoint-group modality, and Hahlweg et al.'s findings suggest that communication training in a conjoint modality does increase marital adjustment, it is difficult to disentangle the effects of the skills being focused on from the treatment modality employed. However, based on the findings to date, the clinician should be cautious in using these communication treatments with distressed couples in a group setting (Beach & O'Leary, 1985).

Baucom (1985) has found that emotional expressiveness training in combination with BMT does result in increases in marital adjustment. Also important to one of the specific goals of emotional expressiveness training, this combination of treatment approaches resulted in an increase in reported closeness, trust, and intimacy between the spouses.

In one of the few investigations that has attempted to clarify which couples respond to which type of treatment, Turkewitz and O'Leary (1981) evaluated whether the age of the couples affected their response to BMT versus a communication approach emphasizing empathy training. Their findings indicated that older couples responded better to the communication treatment, and younger couples benefited more from

BMT. Although the basis for this finding is uncertain, given that BMT has a major strength in helping couples structure roles in terms of the accomplishment of tasks, it may be that such concerns are more typical of younger couples earlier in their married life. However, clinical observation suggests that many older couples seek treatment because they sense that the relationship has become dull, or they have become distant or devoid of intimacy over the years. Communication training focusing on increasing empathy may be what these relationships need.

Communication training also has been compared to other treatment approaches, and the results indicate no significant differences between treatments in altering marital adjustment. However, the approaches teaching a particular skill at times are understandably superior in effecting changes on that skill. Thus, Epstein and Jackson (1978) found that a treatment focusing on assertiveness skills was superior to an insight approach in altering assertive requests. Similarly, Jessee and Guerney (1981) found that treatment focusing on emotional expressiveness training was superior to a Gestalt approach in altering self-reports of communication. Also, Epstein, Pretzer, and Fleming (1982) demonstrated that a communication approach was not as successful as a cognitive approach in altering couples' attributions and unrealistic standards. In combination, these findings suggest that there are a number of ways to increase the marital adjustment of a couple, but if specific skills are needed, then the clinician should clearly focus treatment on the particular skills that are lacking in the couple.

EFFECTS OF COGNITIVE AND COGNITIVE-BEHAVIORAL APPROACHES

At present there are at least five investigations exploring the effectiveness of cognitive-behavior therapy with couples. Three of these studies have implemented a cognitive restructuring treatment in isolation without other treatment techniques in combination (Emmelkamp et al., 1988; Epstein et al., 1982; Huber & Milstein, 1985). In addition, two other investigations have explored whether BMT could be strengthened by adding a cognitive restructuring component to it (Baucom, 1985; Baucom & Lester, 1986). To a great extent, these investigations have focused on spouses' attributions and standards, although Epstein et al. looked at distorted cognitions more broadly. Taken together, the results of these investigations do indicate that cognitive restructuring in isolation and in combination with BMT is capable of producing meaningful cognitive changes in couples, particularly regarding unrealistic relationship standards. Most of the studies did not include a measure of attributions because no well-validated instruments were available at the time. Overall, these treatments also have been effective in increasing marital adjustment. However, consistent with findings presented earlier on BMT, the evidence indicates no meaningful differences between cognitive restructuring and BMT in altering marital adjustment. Also, although Epstein et al. (1982) found that cognitive restructuring was more successful than a communication approach in altering problematic relationship standards, other findings indicate no differences between cognitive restructuring and BMT in effecting similar cognitive changes (Baucom, 1985; Baucom & Lester, 1986; Emmelkamp et al., 1988).

Huber and Milstein (1985) focused on additional outcome variables which are focal to intended impacts of cognitive restructuring. That is, one reason to attempt to change the couple's attitudes is to increase their belief that therapy can help them (i.e., increase positive expectancies); similarly, cognitive restructuring hopefully will encourage couples to try to improve their relationships, an assumption that must not be made simply because couples are in treatment. They found that their rather brief cognitive therapy not only produced striking increases in marital adjustment, but compared to a WL condition, it also significantly increased couples' predictions that therapy would benefit them and increased their desire to improve their relationships.

Thus, the findings to date are somewhat encouraging that cognitive therapy is of assistance to couples. Cognitive restructuring can improve marital adjustment and results in meaningful cognitive changes which have been shown to be of importance. In addition, it appears to promote the kind of attitudinal changes that can prepare the couple for other interventions such as BMT. Again, couples have been randomly assigned to conditions in those studies which compare cognitive restructuring to other treatment approaches, and this lack of matching of treatment to couples' needs could help to explain the basis for a lack of differences between treatment conditions in several of the studies. Thus, lack of treatment differences could result from other factors as well. In order to combine cognitive restructuring with other treatment interventions, the number of cognitive sessions has been limited, at times from three to six sessions. This is probably too few sessions to expect meaningful cognitive changes which will significantly impact the marriage. Indeed, Baucom (1985) found that only three cognitive sessions resulted in very inconsistent cognitive changes, whereas six sessions produced more consistent changes, although six sessions are still probably too few.

Also, none of the studies to date have attempted to integrate cognitive restructuring with other treatment approaches, such as those discussed in Chapter 11. Instead, in an attempt to isolate the contributions of cognitive restructuring to treatment outcome, it either has been used as a total treatment or as a treatment component presented sequentially with other skills-based treatment components. In addition, most of the focus in outcome investigations has been on attributions and standards, with little attention given to selective attention, expectancies, and standards. Investigations are needed which intervene on all of these cognitive variables and which assess the impact of treatment in each of these cognitive domains. Thus, although much work remains, the results thus far indicate that if the clinician notes significant cognitive factors that are contributing to the marital difficulty or preventing the successful implementation of other treatment strategies, cognitive restructuring should be given careful consideration.

CONCLUSIONS

The findings to date provide considerable support for the types of interventions discussed in this volume. BMT is effective in producing behavior change in targeted areas, particularly those areas that are under voluntary control and rather instrumental in orientation. Similarly, it is effective in decreasing negative communication between couples, although its success in increasing positive communication is much less consistent. Devising ways of increasing couples' positive communication with each other while problem solving is an important area for therapists and investigators to continue to focus on. Also, BMT is effective in increasing marital adjustment for many couples, although the short-term nature of the treatment in most outcome studies leaves many couples improved but still in the distressed range of marital adjustment. As O'Farrell et al. (1985) report, many couples believe that longer treatments are needed, that they are just beginning to make significant progress on difficult aspects of their relationship when the therapy terminates. There are no data indicating that longer treatment for couples is superior, but in many cases clinical observation indicates that it appears warranted. BMT may have its major weakness in promoting a sense of warmth, closeness, and tenderness among spouses. However, this is a major goal of emotional expressiveness training, and some data suggest that BMT in combination with such training does result in significant gains in the couples' sense of closeness, trust, and sharing. Also, cognitive restructuring appears to produce some of the attitudinal changes which help to prepare the couple for other interventions. Consequently, there is increasing empirical support for a broad-based skills-oriented approach which takes into account cognitive, behavioral, and affective components of marital interaction.

Appendix:
Marital Assessment Scales

DYADIC ATTRIBUTION INVENTORY

Directions:

Please try to vividly imagine yourself in the situations that follow. If such a situation happened to you, what would you feel would have caused it? While events may have many causes, we want you to pick only one — the one *major* cause if this event happened to you. Next we want you to answer some questions about the cause and the situation.

Below is an example to clarify what you are to do:

Example:

YOUR PARTNER FORGETS TO BUY YOU A BIRTHDAY GIFT.

a. Write down the one major cause: *My partner is preoccupied with work as usual.*

b. To what extent is the cause due to each of the following:
(1) Me (**M**); (2) Partner (**P**); (3) Outside circumstances (**OC**)? (Rate all 3.)

Not at all   Totally
due to: due to:

M   1 ② 3   4   5   6   7
P   1   2   3   4   5 ⑥ 7
OC 1   2   3   4 ⑤ 6   7

c. In the future when you are with your partner will this *cause* again be present?

Will never   Will always
again   1   2   3   4   5 ⑥ 7   be present
be present

d. Is the *cause* something that just affects your partner's forgetting to buy you a birthday gift, or does it also influence other areas of your relationship?

Influences   Influences all
just this   1   2   3   4   5 ⑥ 7   situations in our
particular   relationship
situation

e. How important would this *situation* be if it happened to you?

Not at all   Extremely
important   1   2   3   4 ⑤ 6   7   important

f. If your partner behaved as described above, how would you feel?

Extremely   Extremely
bad   1 ② 3   4   5   6   7   good

In the above example, the person gave the major cause as being the partner's preoccupation with work (Question a). In Question b, the person felt the partner's preoccupation with work was mainly due to something about the partner and also outside circumstances. In Question c, the person stated that the partner would continue to be preoccupied with work in the future, and in Question d indicated that preoccupation with work influences many situations in the relationship. It is important to notice that Questions b, c, and d ask about the *cause,* in this case "work preoccupation"; Questions b, c, and d *do not* ask about the situation itself, in this case "forgetting to buy you a birthday gift." Therefore in answering Questions b, c, and d, always refer back to the cause you have written in for Question a. Questions e and f do ask about the *situation* itself. The person has responded in Question e that it would be somewhat important if the partner forgot to buy a birthday gift, and in Question f the person indicated feeling pretty bad if the partner forgot the birthday gift. Make sure you understand these instructions before you complete the questionnaire.

In some of the situations below, your behavior and your partner's behavior are described. Respond to the questions in term of your *partner's* behavior only, not your behavior.

1. Your partner appears to be pleased when you say how glad you are to be with him or her.*
2. Your partner does not respond when you reach out to take his or her hand.
3. Your partner declines taking a walk with you.
4. Your partner comes up and hugs you.
5. Your partner does not appear to be listening as you describe how angry you are with him or her.
6. Your partner tries to break a long-term habit that has been annoying you.
7. Your partner compliments you on the way you handled a difficult situation that has been bothering the two of you.
8. Your partner fails to respond when you try to discuss what you hope the two of you can accomplish over the weekend.
9. Your partner agrees to keep up with the monthly bill payments.
10. Your partner criticizes you on the way you have been handling your agreed-upon responsibilities.
11. Your partner refuses your sexual advances.
12. When you come home, you find that your partner has cleaned and neatened the house.
13. Your partner volunteers to help you when you are extremely busy.
14. Even though it is important to you that your partner look neat, your partner neglects his or her physical appearance.
15. Your partner goes out and spends money that had been set aside for savings.
16. Your partner does not ask for you opinion about a problem that needs to be solved and will affect both of you.
17. Your partner works with you on a project.

*In presenting the inventory to couples, each item (1-24) would be followed by questions a-f. They are omitted here to conserve space.

1 8 . Your partner listens attentively as you explain the problems you are having getting a household appliance repaired.

19. Your partner has trouble verbally telling you that he or she loves you.

20. Your partner clearly explains to you the steps needed to complete an important family or couple's task.

21. Your partner satisfies your current sexual desires.

22. Your partner does not complete his or her agreed upon household chores.

23. After agreeing to notify the other person when one of you is going to be late, your partner does not call to tell you he or she will be late.

24. Your partner asks to talk to you about something that is troubling him or her about your relationship.

MARITAL ATTITUDE SURVEY

Please circle the number which indicates how much your agree or disagree with each statement this week, using the rating scale below:

Rating Scale:
   1 = Strongly agree; 2 = Agree somewhat; 3 = Neutral;
   4 = Disagree somewhat; 5 = Strongly disagree.

1 2 3 4 5   1. When we aren't getting along I wonder if my partner loves me.

1 2 3 4 5   2. My partner doesn't seem to do things just to bother me.

1 2 3 4 5   3. If we were more healthy physically we'd get along better.

1 2 3 4 5   4. My personality would have to change for our relationship to improve.

1 2 3 4 5   5. If we had more money we would have a better marriage.

1 2 3 4 5   6. We could improve our relationship if we tried.

1 2 3 4 5   7. My partner intentionally does things to irritate me.

1 2 3 4 5   8. I think my partner could do something to help us get along better in the future.

1 2 3 4 5   9. I don't think I can do much to make things better between us.

1 2 3 4 5 10. Even if my partner's personality changed we still wouldn't get along any better.

1 2 3 4 5 11. I don't expect our relationship to improve any.

1 2 3 4 5 12. I don't think my partner could do anything to improve our relationship.

1 2 3 4 5 13. I don't think I'll ever be a better spouse than I am now.

1 2 3 4 5 14. It seems as though my partner deliberately provokes me.

1 2 3 4 5 15. I don't think my partner and I share responsibility for how our relationship goes.

1 2 3 4 5 16. If my partner did things differently we'd get along better.

1 2 3 4 5 17. I doubt that my partner will change for the better.

1 2 3 4 5 18. My partner's personality would have to change for us to get along better.

1 2 3 4 5   19. Any trouble we have getting along with each other is because of the type of person I am.

1 2 3 4 5   20. I don't think that the things I say and do make things worse between us.

1 2 3 4 5   21. Even if we were more healthy physically our relationship wouldn't be any better.

1 2 3 4 5   22. I don't think there's much my partner can do to cause fewer problems between us.

1 2 3 4 5   23. Any problems we have are caused by the things I say and do.

1 2 3 4 5   24. If we had different friends our relationship would be about the same.

1 2 3 4 5   25. I don't think our marriage would be better if my partner was a different type of person.

1 2 3 4 5   26. Even if my personality changed, my partner and I still wouldn't get along any better.

1 2 3 4 5   27. Even if our religious beliefs were more similar, that wouldn't improve our relationship.

1 2 3 4 5   28. The way my partner treats me determines how well we get along.

1 2 3 4 5   29. I don't think that my partner and I each contribute to any problems we have with each other.

1 2 3 4 5   30. Whatever problems we have are caused by the things my partner says and does.

1 2 3 4 5   31. My partner and I would get along better if it weren't for the type of person he/she is.

1 2 3 4 5   32. Problems between my partner and me aren't just his/her fault or just my fault, we both have a part in them.

1 2 3 4 5   33. My partner doesn't intentionally try to upset me.

1 2 3 4 5   34. (If you have children) If we didn't have children we'd get along better.
             (If you don't have children) If we had children we'd get along better.

1 2 3 4 5   35. When things aren't going well between us I feel like my partner doesn't love me.

1 2 3 4 5   36.   Our friends make a big difference in how our relationship goes.

1 2 3 4 5   37.   I couldn't do anything to improve our relationship if I tried.

1 2 3 4 5   38.   Stress from work influences how we get along.

1 2 3 4 5   39.   I think that our relationship will improve.

1 2 3 4 5   40.   I probably could do something to help us get along better.

1 2 3 4 5   41.   I think my partner and I each contribute to any problems we have with each other.

1 2 3 4 5   42.   Even if we had more money, our relationship wouldn't get any better.

1 2 3 4 5   43.   I don't think my partner will ever improve upon the way he/she is.

1 2 3 4 5   44.   I think my partner and I share responsibility for whatever problems come up between us.

1 2 3 4 5   45.   I think I will treat my partner better in the future.

1 2 3 4 5   46.   Our relatives don't influence our relationship.

1 2 3 4 5   47.   (If you have children) Our children have little to do with how we get along.
(If you don't have children) Our not having children has little to do with how we get along.

1 2 3 4 5   48.   Whatever difficulties we have are not because of the type of person I am.

1 2 3 4 5   49.   I think our relationship is going to get better in the future.

1 2 3 4 5   50.   What difficulties we have don't lead me to doubt my partner's love for me.

1 2 3 4 5   51.   If it weren't for our relatives we would have a better marriage.

1 2 3 4 5   52.   When things are rough between us it shows that my partner doesn't love me.

1 2 3 4 5   53.   Even if work was less stressful, our relationship wouldn't improve.

1 2 3 4 5   54.   If I did things differently my partner and I wouldn't have the conflicts we have.

1 2 3 4 5   55. I think my partner will make positive changes in the future.

1 2 3 4 5   56. My changing how I act wouldn't change how our marriage goes.

1 2 3 4 5   57. I'm sure that my partner sometimes does things just to bother me.

1 2 3 4 5   58. Even when we aren't getting along, I don't question whether my partner loves me.

1 2 3 4 5   59. I think my partner upsets me on purpose.

1 2 3 4 5   60. Our religious beliefs lead to problems between us.

1 2 3 4 5   61. I don't think I will change for the better in the future.

1 2 3 4 5   62. When my partner isn't nice to me I feel like he/she doesn't love me.

1 2 3 4 5   63. I think my partner will treat me better in the future.

1 2 3 4 5   64. When we have a problem, my partner could do something to make things better between us.

1 2 3 4 5   65. I'm certain that my partner doesn't provoke me on purpose.

1 2 3 4 5   66. I don't think it's possible for us to handle problems that come up better than we do now.

1 2 3 4 5   67. I think I will make some positive changes that will make things better between us.

1 2 3 4 5   68. Even when we have problems I don't doubt my partner's love for me.

1 2 3 4 5   69. I don't think that our relationship is likely to improve.

1 2 3 4 5   70. The things my partner says and does aren't the cause of whatever problems come up between us.

1 2 3 4 5   71. I could do something to make our relationship better.

1 2 3 4 5   72. There is no way for us to improve this relationship.

1 2 3 4 5   73. Our relationship could be better in the future.

1 2 3 4 5   74. I doubt that my partner deliberately does things to irritate me.

MARITAL ATTITUDE SURVEY
SCORING KEY

Note: Underlined items are reverse-keyed, as follows:

$$1 = 5; 2 = 4; 4 = 2; 5 = 1$$

Reverse the respondent's answers on these items before computing sums for the MAS subscales.

Subscale Items

PERCEIVED ABILITY OF COUPLE TO CHANGE RELATIONSHIP

   6   66   72   73

EXPECTANCY OF IMPROVEMENT IN THE RELATIONSHIP

  11   39   49   69

ATTRIBUTION OF CAUSALITY TO OWN BEHAVIOR

  20   23   54   56

ATTRIBUTION OF CAUSALITY TO OWN PERSONALITY

  4   19   26   48

ATTRIBUTION OF CAUSALITY TO SPOUSE'S BEHAVIOR

  16   28   30   70

ATTRIBUTION OF CAUSALITY TO SPOUSE'S PERSONALITY

  10   18   25   31

ATTRIBUTION OF MALICIOUS INTENT TO SPOUSE

  2   7   14   33   57   59   65   74

ATTRIBUTION OF LACK OF LOVE TO SPOUSE

  1   35   50   52   58   62   68

Note: The remainder of the 74 items have been included for the development of additional subscales. Until further validational work has been completed, these items are not scored.

RELATIONSHIP BELIEF INVENTORY
(Roy J. Eidelson and Norman Epstein, 1981)

The statements below describe ways in which a person might feel about a relationship with another person. Please mark the space next to each statement according to how strongly you believe that it is true or false for you. *Please mark every one.* Write in 5, 4, 3, 2, 1, or 0 to stand for the following answers.

    5: I *strongly* believe that the statement is *true*.

    4: I believe that the statement is *true*.

    3: I believe that the statement is *probably true*, or more true than false.

    2: I believe that the statement is *probably false*, or more false than true.

    1: I believe that the statement is *false*.

    0: I *strongly* believe that the statement is *false*.

_____ 1. If your partner expresses disagreement with your ideas, s/he probably does not think highly of you.

_____ 2. I do not expect my partner to sense all my moods.

_____ 3. Damages done early in a relationship probably cannot be reversed.

_____ 4. I get upset if I think I have not completely satisfied my partner sexually.

_____ 5. Men and women have the same basic emotional needs.

_____ 6. I cannot accept it when my partner disagrees with me.

_____ 7. If I have to tell my partner that something is important to me, it does not mean s/he is insensitive to me.

_____ 8. My partner does not seem capable of behaving other than s/he does now.

_____ 9. If I'm not in the mood for sex when my partner is, I don't get upset about it.

_____ 10. Misunderstandings between partners generally are due to inborn differences in psychological makeups of men and women.

_____ 11. I take it as a personal insult when my partner disagrees with an important idea of mine.

_____ 12. I get very upset if my partner does not recognize how I am feeling and I have to tell him/her.

_____ 13. A partner can learn to become more responsive to his/her partner's needs.

_____ 14. A good sexual partner can get himself/herself aroused for sex whenever necessary.

_____ 15. Men and women probably will never understand the opposite sex very well.

_____ 16. I like it when my partner presents views different from mine.

_____ 17. People who have a close relationship can sense each other's needs as if they could read each other's minds.

_____ 18. Just because my partner has acted in ways that upset me does not mean that s/he will do so in the future.

_____ 19. If I cannot perform well sexually whenever my partner is in the mood, I would consider that I have a problem.

_____ 20. Men and women need the same basic things out of a relationship.

_____ 21. I get very upset when my partner and I cannot see things the same way.

_____ 22. It is important to me for my partner to anticipate my needs by sensing changes in my moods.

_____ 23. A partner who hurts you badly once probably will hurt you again.

_____ 24. I can feel OK about my lovemaking even if my partner does not achieve orgasm.

_____ 25. Biological differences between men and women are not major causes of couples' problems.

_____ 26. I cannot tolerate it when my partner argues with me.

_____ 27. A partner should know what you are thinking or feeling without you having to tell.

_____ 28. If my partner wants to change, I believe that s/he can do it.

_____ 29. If my sexual partner does not get satisfied completely, it does not mean that I have failed.

_____ 30. One of the major causes of marital problems is that men and women have different emotional needs.

_____ 31. When my partner and I disagree, I feel like our relationship is falling apart.

_____ 32. People who love each other know exactly what each other's thoughts are without a word ever being said.

_____ 33. If you don't like the way a relationship is going, you can make it better.

_____ 34. Some difficulties in my sexual performance do not mean personal failure to me.

_____ 35. You can't really understand someone of the opposite sex.

_____ 36. I do not doubt my partner's feelings for me when we argue.

_____ 37. If you have to ask your partner for something, it shows that s/he was not "tuned into" your needs.

_____ 38. I do not expect my partner to be able to change.

_____ 39. When I do not seem to be performing well sexually, I get upset.

_____ 40. Men and women will always be mysteries to each other.

SCORING OF RELATIONSHIP BELIEF INVENTORY
RBI Subscales:
D = Disagreement is destructive
M = Mindreading is expected
C = Partners cannot change
S = Sexual perfectionism
MF = The sexes are different

Scoring Key

1. D +	2. M −	3. C +	4. S +	5. MF −
6. D +	7. M −	8. C +	9. S −	10. MF +
11. D +	12. M +	13. C −	14. S +	15. MF +
16. D −	17. M +	18. C −	19. S +	20. MF −
21. D +	22. M +	23. C +	24. S −	25. MF −
26. D +	27. M +	28. C −	29. S −	30. MF +
31. D +	32. M +	33. C −	34. S −	35. MF +
36. D −	37. M +	38. C +	39. S +	40. MF +

Compute a total for each subscale as follows:

For positively keyed items, leave the subject's response as is.

For negatively keyed items, reverse the response scale, as follows:

Subject's response	becomes	Score
5		0
4		1
3		2
2		3
1		4
0		5

Then compute the sum for the 8 items on the scale.

References

Abelson, R. P., Aronson, E., McGuire, W. J., Newcomb, T. M., Rosenberg, M. J., & Tannenbaum, P. H. (Eds.) (1968). *Theories of cognitive consistency: A sourcebook.* Chicago: Rand McNally.

Abrahms, J. L. (1985). Personal communication.

Abramson, L. Y., Seligman, M. E. P., & Teasdale, J. (1978). Learned helplessness in humans: Critique and reformulation. *Journal of Abnormal Psychology, 87,* 49–94.

American Psychiatric Association (1987). *Diagnostic and statistical manual of mental disorders* (3rd ed.—Revised). Washington, DC: American Psychiatric Association.

Antill, J. K. (1983). Sex role complementarity versus similarity in married couples. *Journal of Personality and Social Psychology, 45,* 145–155.

Arias, I., & Beach, S. R. H. (1987). The assessment of social cognition in the context of marriage. In K. D. O'Leary (Ed.), *Assessment of marital discord* (pp. 109–137). Hillsdale, NJ: Lawrence Erlbaum Associates.

Arkowitz, H., Holliday, S., & Hutter, M. (1982, November). Depressed women and their husbands: A study of marital interaction and adjustment. In N. S. Jacobson (Chair), *Depression and intimate relations.* Symposium presented at the annual meeting of the Association for Advancement of Behavior Therapy, Los Angeles.

Arthur, J. A., Hops, H., & Biglan, A. (1982). *LIFE (Living in Familial Environments) coding system.* Unpublished manuscript, Oregon Research Institute, Eugene.

Azrin, N. H., Besalel, V. A., Betchel, R., Michalicek, A., Mancera, M., Carroll, D., Shuford, D., & Cox, J. (1980). Comparison of reciprocity and discussion-type counseling for marital problems. *American Journal of Family Therapy, 8,* 21–28.

Azrin, N. H., Naster, B. J., & Jones, R. (1973). A rapid learning-based procedure for marital counseling. *Behavior Research and Therapy, 11,* 365–382.

Bach, G. R., & Wyden, P. (1968). *The intimate enemy.* New York: Avon.

Bandura, A. (1977). *Social learning theory.* Englewood Cliffs, NJ: Prentice-Hall.

Bandura, A. (1982). Self-efficacy mechanism in human agency. *American Psychologist, 37,* 122–147.

Barlow, D. H. (1986). Causes of sexual dysfunction: The role of anxiety and cognitive interference. *Journal of Consulting and Clinical Psychology, 54,* 140–148.

Barnett, L. R., & Nietzel, M. T. (1979). Relationship of instrumental and affectional behaviors and self-esteem to marital satisfaction in distressed and nondistressed couples. *Journal of Consulting and Clinical Psychology, 47,* 946–957.

Barrett, T., & Mizes, J. S. (1985, November). *Combat level and social support in the development of post-traumatic stress disorders in Vietnam veterans.* Paper presented at the annual meeting of the Association for Advancement of Behavior Therapy, Houston, TX.

Barrett-Lennard, G. T. (1962). Dimensions of therapist response as causal factors in therapeutic change. *Psychological Monographs, 76,* 1–36.

Baucom, D. H. (1976). Independent masculinity and femininity scales on the California Psychological Inventory. *Journal of Consulting and Clinical Psychology, 44,* 876.

Baucom, D. H. (1982). A comparison of behavioral contracting and problem solving/communications training in behavioral marital therapy. *Behavior Therapy, 13,* 162–174.

Baucom, D. H. (1983). Conceptual and psychometric issues in evaluating the effectiveness of behavioral marital therapy. In J. P. Vincent (Ed.), *Advances in family intervention, assessment, and theory* (Vol. 3, pp. 91–117). Greenwich, CT: JAI Press.

Baucom, D. H. (1984). The active ingredients of behavioral marital therapy: The effectiveness of communication/problem-solving training, contingency contracting, and their combination. In K. Hahlweg & N. S. Jacobson (Eds.), *Marital interaction: Analysis and modification* (pp. 73–88). New York: Guilford Press.

Baucom, D. H. (1985, November). Enhancing behavioral marital therapy with cognitive restructuring and emotional expressiveness training. In N. S. Jacobson (Chair), *Cognition and marital therapy: Current research.* Symposium presented at the annual meeting of the Association for Advancement of Behavior Therapy, Houston, TX.

Baucom, D. H. (1987). Attributions in distressed relations: How can we explain them? In S. Duck and D. Perlman (Eds.), *Heterosexual relations, marriage and divorce* (pp. 177–206). London: Sage.

Baucom, D. H., & Adams, A. (1987). Assessing communication in marital interaction. In K. D. O'Leary (Ed.), *Assessment of marital discord* (pp. 139–182). Hillsdale, NJ: Lawrence Erlbaum.

Baucom, D. H., & Aiken, P. A. (1984). Sex role identity, marital satisfaction and response to behavioral marital therapy. *Journal of Consulting and Clinical Psychology, 52,* 438–444.

Baucom, D. H., Bell, W. G., & Duhe, A. (1982, November). *The measurement of couples' attributions for positive and negative dyadic interactions.* Paper presented at the annual meeting of the Association for Advancement of Behavior Therapy, Los Angeles.

Baucom, D. H., Epstein, N., Sayers, S., & Sher, T. G. (1989). The role of cognitions in marital relationships: Definitional, methodological, and conceptual issues. *Journal of Consulting and Clinical Psychology, 57,* 31–38.

Baucom, D. H., & Hoffman, J. A. (1986). The effectiveness of marital therapy: Current status and application to the clinical setting. In N. S. Jacobson and A. Gurman (Eds.), *Clinical handbook of marital therapy* (pp. 597–620). New York: Guilford Press.

Baucom, D. H., & Lester, G. W. (1986). The usefulness of cognitive restructuring as an adjunct to behavioral marital therapy. *Behavior Therapy, 17,* 385–403.

Baucom, D. H., & Mehlman, S. K. (1984). Predicting marital status following behavioral marital therapy: A comparison of models of marital relationships. In K. Hahlweg & N. S. Jacobson (Eds.), *Marital interaction: Analysis and modification* (pp. 89–104). New York: Guilford Press.

Baucom, D. H., Sayers, S. L., & Duhe, A. D. (1987, November). *Attributional style and attributional pattern among married couples.* Paper presented at the annual meeting of the Association for Advancement of Behavior Therapy, Boston.

Baucom, D. H., & Sher, T. G. (1986, November). *Response to treatment and communication patterns among depressed and nondepressed maritally distressed couples.* Paper presented at the annual meeting of the Association for Advancement of Behavior Therapy, Boston.

Baucom, D. H., Wheeler, C. M., & Bell, G. (1984, November). *Assessing the role of attributions in marital distress.* Paper presented at the annual meeting of the Association for Advancement of Behavior Therapy, Philadelphia.

Beach, S. R. H., & Broderick, J. E. (1983). Commitment: A variable in women's response to marital therapy. *American Journal of Family Therapy, 11,* 16–24.

Beach, S. R. H., Jouriles, E. N., & O'Leary, K. D. (1985). Extramarital sex: Impact on depression and commitment in couples seeking marital therapy. *Journal of Sex and Marital Therapy, 11,* 99–108.

Beach, S. R. H., & O'Leary, K. D. (1985). Current status of outcome research in marital therapy. In L. L'Abate (Ed.), *The handbook of family psychology and therapy* (pp. 1035–1072). Homewood, IL: Dorsey Press.

Beach, S. R. H., & O'Leary, K. D. (1986). The treatment of depression occurring in the context of marital discord. *Behavior Therapy, 17,* 43–49.

Beach, S. R. H., Sandeen, E. E., & O'Leary, K. D. (1987, November). *Treatment for the depressed, maritally discordant client: A comparison of behavioral marital therapy, individual cognitive therapy, and wait list control.* Paper presented at the annual meeting of the Association for Advancement of Behavior Therapy, Boston.

Beck, A. T. (1972). *Depression: Causes and treatment.* Philadelphia: University of Pennsylvania Press.

Beck, A. T. (1976). *Cognitive therapy and the emotional disorders.* New York: International Universities Press.

Beck, A. T., Brown, G., Steer, R. A., Eidelson, J. I., & Riskind, J. H. (1987). Differentiating anxiety and depression: A test of the cognitive content-specificity hypothesis. *Journal of Abnormal Psychology, 96,* 179–183.

Beck, A. T., & Emery, G. (1985). *Anxiety disorders and phobias: A cognitive perspective.* New York: Basic Books.

Beck, A. T., Epstein, N., Brown, G., & Steer, R. A. (1988). An inventory for measuring clinical anxiety: Psychometric properties. *Journal of Consulting and Clinical Psychology, 56,* 893–897.

Beck, A. T., Rush, A. J., Shaw, B. F., & Emery, G. (1979). *Cognitive therapy of depression.* New York: Guilford Press.

Bennun, I. (1985a). Behavioral marital therapy: An outcome evaluation of conjoint, group and one spouse treatment. *Scandinavian Journal of Behaviour Therapy, 14,* 157–168.

Bennun, I. (1985b). Prediction and responsiveness in behavioural marital therapy. *Behavioural Psychotherapy, 13,* 186–201.

Berscheid, E. (1983). Emotion. In H. H. Kelley, E. Berscheid, A. Christensen, J. H. Harvey, T. L. Huston, G. Levinger, E. McClintock, L. A. Peplau, & D. R. Peterson, *Close relationships* (pp. 110–168). New York: W. H. Freeman.

Bienvenu, M. J. (1970). Measurement of marital communication. *The Family Coordinator, 19,* 26–31.

Biglan, A., Hops, H., Sherman, L., Friedman, L. S., Arthur, J., & Osteen, V. (1985). Problem solving interactions of depressed women and their husbands. *Behavior Therapy, 16,* 431–451.

Billings, A. (1979). Conflict resolution in distressed and nondistressed married couples. *Journal of Consulting and Clinical Psychology, 17,* 368–376.

Birchler, G. R. (1986). Alleviating depression with "marital" intervention. In A. Freeman, N. Epstein, & K. M. Simon (Eds.), *Depression in the family* (pp. 101–116). New York: Haworth Press.

Birchler, G. R., Weiss, R. L., & Vincent, J. P. (1975). Multimethod analysis of social reinforcement exchange between maritally distressed and nondistressed spouse and stranger dyads. *Journal of Personality and Social Psychology, 31,* 349–360.

Bland, K., & Hallam, R. S. (1981). Relationship between response to graded exposure and marital satisfaction in agoraphobics. *Behaviour Research and Therapy, 19,* 335–338.

Boelens, W., Emmelkamp, P., MacGillavry, D., & Markvoort, M. (1980). A clinical evaluation of marital treatment: Reciprocity counseling vs. system-theoretic counseling. *Behavior Analysis and Modification, 4,* 85–96.

Bornstein, P. H., & Bornstein, M. T. (1986). *Marital therapy: A behavioral-communications approach.* New York: Pergamon Press.

Bothwell, S., & Weissman, M. M. (1977). Social impairment four years after an acute depressive episode. *American Journal of Orthopsychiatry, 47,* 231–237.

Bradbury, T., & Fincham, F. (1987). Affect and cognition in close relationships: Towards an integrative model. *Cognition and Emotion, 1,* 59–87.

Bringle, R., Roach, S., Andler, C., & Evenbeck, S. (1979). Measuring the intensity of jealous reactions. *Catalogue of Selected Documents in Psychology, 9,* 23–24.

Brown, G. W., Birley, J. L. T., & Wing, J. K. (1972). Influence of family life on the course of schizophrenic disorders: A replication. *British Journal of Psychiatry, 121,* 241–258.

Brown, G. W., & Harris, T. O. (1978). *Social origins of depression: A study of psychiatric disorder in women*. New York: Free Press.

Buglass, D., Clarke, J., Henderson, A. S., Kreitman, N., & Presley, A. S. (1977). A study of agoraphobic housewives. *Psychological Medicine, 7*, 73–86.

Burger, A. L., & Jacobson, N. S. (1979). The relationship between sex role characteristics, couple satisfaction, and couple problem-solving skills. *American Journal of Family Therapy, 7*, 52–60.

Burns, D. D. (1980). *Feeling good: The new mood therapy*. New York: William Morrow.

Camper, P. M., Jacobson, N. S., Holtzworth–Munroe, A., & Schmaling, K. B. (1988). Causal attributions for interactional behaviors in married couples. *Cognitive Therapy and Research, 12*, 195–209.

Carter, R. D., & Thomas, E. J. (1973). Modification of problematic marital communication using corrective feedback and instruction. *Behavior Therapy, 4*, 100–109.

Chambless, D. L., & Goldstein, A. J. (Eds.). (1982). *Agoraphobia: Multiple perspectives on theory and treatment*. New York: Wiley.

Chapman, L. J., & Chapman, J. P. (1969). Illusory correlation as an obstacle to the use of valid psychodiagnostic signs. *Journal of Abnormal Psychology, 74*, 271–280.

Chavez, R. E., Samuel, V., & Haynes, S. N. (1981, November). *Validity of the Verbal Problems Checklist*. Paper presented at the annual meeting of the Association for Advancement of Behavior Therapy, Toronto.

Christensen, A., & Nies, D. C. (1980). The Spouse Observation Checklist: Empirical analysis and critique. *American Journal of Family Therapy, 8*, 69–79.

Christensen, A., Sullaway, M., & King, C. (1983). Systematic error in behavioral reports of dyadic interaction: Egocentric bias and content effects. *Behavioral Assessment, 5*, 131–142.

Coleman, R. E., & Miller, A. G. (1975). The relationship between depression and marital maladjustment in a clinic population: A multitrait-multimethod study. *Journal of Consulting and Clinical Psychology, 43*, 647–651.

Constantine, L. L. (1976). Jealousy: From theory to intervention. In D. H. L. Olson (Ed.), *Treating relationships* (pp. 383–398). Lake Mills, IA: Graphic Press.

Constantine, L. L. (1987). Jealousy and extramarital sexual relations. In N. S. Jacobson and A. S. Gurman (Eds.), *Clinical handbook of marital therapy* (pp. 407–427). New York: Guilford Press.

Cooper, J., & Fazio, R. H. (1984). A new look at dissonance theory. In L. Berkowitz (Ed.), *Advances in experimental social psychology* (Vol. 17, pp. 229–266). New York: Academic Press.

Costa, L. A. (1981). The effects of a Marriage Encounter program on marital communication, dyadic adjustment, and the quality of the interpersonal relationship. (Doctoral Dissertation, University of Colorado-Boulder). *Dissertation Abstracts International, 42*, 1850A.

Coyne, J. C. (1976). Depression and the response of others. *Journal of Abnormal Psychology, 85*, 186–193.

Coyne, J. C., & Gotlib, I. H. (1983). The role of cognition in depression: A critical appraisal. *Psychological Bulletin, 94*, 472–505.

Coyne, J. C., & Gotlib, I. H. (1986). Studying the role of cognition in depression:

Well-trodden paths and cul-de-sacs. *Cognitive Therapy and Research*, 10, 695–705.

Crowe, M. J. (1978). Conjoint marital therapy: A controlled outcome study. *Psychological Medicine*, 8, 623–636.

DeGiovanni, I. S., & Epstein, N. (1978). Unbinding assertion and aggression in research and clinical practice. *Behavior Modification*, 2, 173–192.

Deschner, J. P., (1984). *The hitting habit: Anger control for battering couples*. New York: The Free Press.

Doane, J. A., West, K. L., Goldstein, M. J., Rodnick, E. H., & Jones, J. E. (1981). Parental communication deviance and affective style: Predictors of subsequent schizophrenia-spectrum disorders in vulnerable adolescents. *Archives of General Psychiatry*, 38, 679–685.

Dobson, K. S. (1985). The relationship between anxiety and depression. *Clinical Psychology Review*, 5, 307–324.

Doherty, W. J. (1981a). Cognitive processes in intimate conflict: I. Extending attribution theory. *American Journal of Family Therapy*, 9 (1), 5–13.

Doherty, W. J. (1981b). Cognitive processes in intimate conflict: II. Efficacy and learned helplessness. *American Journal of Family Therapy*, 9 (2), 35–44.

Doherty, W. J., McCabe, P., & Ryder, R. G. (1978). Marriage Encounter: A critical appraisal. *Journal of Marriage and Family Counseling*, 4, 99–107.

Doherty, W. J., & Walker, B. J. (1982). Marriage Encounter casualties: A preliminary investigation. *American Journal of Family Therapy*, 10 (2), 15–25.

Dryden, W. (1985). Marital therapy: The rational-emotive approach. In W. Dryden (Ed.), *Marital therapy in Britain* (Vol. 1, pp. 195–221). London: Harper & Row.

Duck, S. (1977). *The study of acquaintance*. London: Saxon House.

Eaves, G., & Rush, A. J. (1984). Cognitive patterns in symptomatic and remitted unipolar major depression. *Journal of Abnormal Psychology*, 93, 31–40.

Edmonds, V. (1967). Marital conventionalization: Definition and measurement. *Journal of Marriage and the Family*, 29, 681–688.

Eidelson, R. J., & Epstein N. (1982). Cognition and relationship maladjustment: Development of a measure of dysfunctional relationship beliefs. *Journal of Consulting and Clinical Psychology*, 50, 715–720.

Eisenberg, N., & Miller, P. A. (1987). The relation of empathy to prosocial and related behaviors. *Psychological Bulletin*, 101, 91–119.

Ekman, P., & Friesen, W. V. (1978). *Facial Action Coding System*. Palo Alto, CA: Consulting Psychologists Press.

Elliott, M. J. (1986). *Relationships between sex role type and marital satisfaction*. Unpublished honors thesis, University of North Carolina, Chapel Hill, NC.

Ellis, A. (1962). *Reason and emotion in psychotherapy*. New York: Lyle Stuart.

Ellis, A. (1976). Techniques of handling anger in marriage. *Journal of Marriage and Family Counseling*, 2, 305–316.

Ellis, A. (1977). The nature of disturbed marital interactions. In A. Ellis & R. Grieger (Eds.), *Handbook of rational-emotive therapy* (pp. 170–176). New York: Springer.

Ellis, A. (1986). Rational-emotive therapy applied to relationship therapy. *Journal of Rational-Emotive Therapy*, 4, 4–21.

Ellis, A., & Grieger, R. (Eds.). (1977). *Handbook of rational-emotive therapy*. New York: Springer.

Elwood, R. W., & Jacobson, N. S. (1982). Spouses' agreement in reporting their behavioral interactions: A clinical replication. *Journal of Consulting and Clinical Psychology, 50,* 783–784.

Ely, A. L., Guerney, B. G., & Stover, L. (1973). Efficacy of the training phase of conjugal therapy. *Psychotherapy: Theory, Research, and Practice, 10,* 201–207.

Emmelkamp, P. (1985, August). *Communication skills training and cognitive therapy.* Paper presented at the annual meeting of the European Association for Behavior Therapy, Munich, West Germany.

Emmelkamp, P., van der Helm, M., MacGillavry, D., & van Zanten, B. (1984). Marital therapy with clinically distressed couples: A comparative evaluation of system-theoretic, contingency contracting, and communication skills approaches. In K. Hahlweg and N. S. Jacobson (Eds.), *Marital interaction: Analysis and modification* (pp. 36–52). New York: Guilford Press.

Emmelkamp, P. M. G., van Linden van den Heuvell, C., Ruphan, M., Sanderman, R., Scholing, A., & Stroink, F. (1988). Cognitive and behavioral interventions: A comparative evaluation with clinically distressed couples. *Journal of Family Psychology, 1,* 365–377.

Endicott, N. A., & Jortner, S. (1966). Objective measures of depression. *Archives of General Psychiatry, 15,* 249–255.

Endicott, J., & Spitzer, R. (1978). A diagnostic interview: The Schedule for Affective Disorders and Schizophrenia. *Archives of General Psychiatry, 35,* 837–844.

Epstein, N. (1981). Assertiveness training in marital treatment. In G. P. Sholevar (Ed.), *Handbook of marriage and marital therapy* (pp. 287–302). New York: Spectrum.

Epstein, N. (1982). Cognitive therapy with couples. *American Journal of Family Therapy, 10* (1), 5–16.

Epstein, N. (1985a, August). *Cognitive-behavioral marital therapy in the treatment of depression.* Paper presented at the annual meeting of the American Psychological Association, Los Angeles.

Epstein, N. (1985b). Depression and marital dysfunction: Cognitive and behavioral linkages. *International Journal of Mental Health, 13* (3–4), 86–104.

Epstein, N. (1986). Cognitive marital therapy: Multi-level assessment and intervention. *Journal of Rational-Emotive Therapy, 4,* 68–81.

Epstein, N., & Baucom, D. H. (1988). Outcome research on cognitive-behavioral marital therapy: Conceptual and methodological issues. *Journal of Family Psychology, 1,* 378–384.

Epstein, N., DeGiovanni, I. S., & Jayne-Lazarus, C. (1978). Assertion training for couples. *Journal of Behavior Therapy and Experimental Psychiatry, 9,* 149–155.

Epstein, N., & Eidelson, R. J. (1981). Unrealistic beliefs of clinical couples: Their relationship to expectations, goals and satisfaction. *American Journal of Family Therapy, 9* (4), 13–22.

Epstein, N., & Jackson, E. (1978). An outcome study of short-term communication training with married couples. *Journal of Consulting and Clinical Psychology, 46,* 207–212.

Epstein, N., Jayne-Lazarus, C., & DeGiovanni, I. S. (1979). Cotherapists as models of relationships: Effects on the outcome of couples' therapy. *Journal of Marital and Family Therapy, 5,* 53–60.

Epstein, N., Pretzer, J. L., & Fleming, B. (1982, November). *Cognitive therapy and communication training: Comparisons of effects with distressed couples.* Paper presented at the annual meeting of the Association for Advancement of Behavior Therapy, Los Angeles.

Epstein, N., Pretzer, J. L., & Fleming, B. (1987). The role of cognitive appraisal in self-reports of marital communication. *Behavior Therapy, 18,* 51–69.

Epstein, N., & Williams, A. M. (1981). Behavioral approaches to treatment of marital discord. In G. P. Sholevar (Ed.), *Handbook of marriage and marital therapy* (pp. 219–286). New York: Spectrum.

Ewart, C. K. (1978a, August). *Behavior contracts in couple therapy: An experimental evaluation of quid pro quo and good faith models.* Paper presented at the annual meeting of the Association for Advancement of Behavior Therapy, Toronto.

Ewart, C. K. (1978b, November). *Behavioral marriage therapy with older couples: Effects of training measured by the Marital Adjustment Scale.* Paper presented at the annual meeting of the Association for Advancement of Behavior Therapy, Chicago.

Falloon, I. R. H., Boyd, J. L., & McGill, C. W. (1984). *Family care of schizophrenia.* New York: Guilford Press.

Feshbach, N. D. (1987). Parental empathy and child adjustment/maladjustment. In N. Eisenberg & J. Strayer (Eds.), *Empathy and its development* (pp. 271–291). New York: Cambridge University Press.

Fichten, C. S. (1984). See it from my point of view: Videotape and attributions in happy and distressed couples. *Journal of Social and Clinical Psychology, 2,* 125–142.

Fincham, F. D. (1985). Attribution processes in distressed and nondistressed couples: 2. Responsibility for marital problems. *Journal of Abnormal Psychology, 94,* 183–190.

Fincham, F. D., Beach, S. R. H., & Baucom, D. H. (1987). Attribution processes in distressed and nondistressed couples: 4. Self-partner attribution differences. *Journal of Personality and Social Psychology, 52,* 739–748.

Fincham. F. D., Beach, S. R. H., & Nelson, G. (1987). Attribution processes in distressed and nondistressed couples: 3. Causal and responsibility attributions for spouse behavior. *Cognitive Therapy and Research, 11,* 71–86.

Fincham, F. D., & Bradbury, T. N. (1987). The impact of attributions in marriage: A longitudinal analysis. *Journal of Personality and Social Psychology, 53,* 510–517.

Fincham, F. D., & O'Leary, K. D. (1983). Causal inferences for spouse behavior in maritally distressed and nondistressed couples. *Journal of Social and Clinical Psychology, 1,* 42–57.

Floyd, F. J., & Markman, H. J. (1983). Observational biases in spouse observation: Toward a cognitive/behavioral model of marriage. *Journal of Consulting and Clinical Psychology, 51,* 450–457.

Foy, D. W., Donahoe, C. P., Carroll, E. M., Gallers, J., & Reno, R. (1987). Post-traumatic stress disorder. In L. Michelson and L. M. Ascher (Eds.), *Anxiety and stress disorders: Cognitive-behavioral assessment and treatment* (pp. 361–378). New York: Guilford Press.

Foy, D. W., Resnick, H. S., Sipprelle, R. C., & Carroll, E. M. (1987). Premilitary, military, and postmilitary factors in the development of combat-related posttraumatic stress disorder. *Behavior Therapist, 10,* 3–9.

Fredman, N., & Sherman, R. (1987). *Handbook of measurements for marriage and family therapy.* New York: Brunner/Mazel.

Friedman, A. S. (1975). Interaction of drug therapy with marital therapy in depressive patients. *Archives of General Psychiatry, 32,* 619–637.

Friedman, J. M., & Chernen, L. (1987). Sexual dysfunction. In L. Michelson and L. M. Ascher (Eds.), *Anxiety and stress disorders: Cognitive-behavioral assessment and treatment.* New York: Guilford Press.

Geiss, S. K., & O'Leary, K. D. (1981). Therapist ratings of frequency and severity of marital problems: Implications for research. *Journal of Marital and Family Therapy, 7,* 515–520.

Girodo, M., Stein, S. J., & Dotzenroth, S. E. (1980). The effects of communication skills training and contracting on marital relations. *Behavioral Engineering, 6,* 61–76.

Glick, B. R., & Gross, S. J. (1975). Marital interaction and marital conflict: A critical evaluation of current research strategies. *Journal of Marriage and the Family, 37,* 505–512.

Goldfried, M. R., & Robins, C. (1983). Self-schema, cognitive bias, and the processing of therapeutic experiences. In P. C. Kendall (Ed.), *Advances in cognitive-behavioral research and therapy* (Vol. 2, pp. 33–80). New York: Academic Press.

Goldstein, M. J. (1987). Family interaction patterns that antedate the onset of schizophrenia and related disorders: A further analysis of data from a longitudinal, prospective study. In K. Hahlweg and M. J. Goldstein (Eds.), *Understanding major mental disorder: The contribution of family interaction research* (pp. 11–32). New York: Family Process Press.

Gotlib, I. H., & Robinson, L. A. (1982). Responses to depressed individuals: Discrepancies between self-report and observer-rated behavior. *Journal of Abnormal Psychology, 91,* 231–240.

Gottman, J. M. (1979). *Marital interaction: Experimental investigations.* New York: Academic Press.

Gottman, J. M., & Levenson, R. W. (1985). A valid procedure for obtaining self-report of affect in marital interaction. *Journal of Consulting and Clinical Psychology, 53,* 151–160.

Gottman, J. M., & Levenson, R. W. (1986). Assessing the role of emotion in marriage. *Behavioral Assessment, 8,* 31–48.

Gottman, J. M., Markman, H., & Notarius, C. (1977). The topography of marital conflict: A sequential analysis of verbal and nonverbal behavior. *Journal of Marriage and the Family, 39,* 461–477.

Gottman, J., Notarius, C., Gonso, J., & Markman, H. J. (1976). *A couple's guide to communication.* Champaign, IL: Research Press.

Gottman, J., Notarius, C., Markman, H., Bank, S., Yoppi, B., & Rubin, M. E. (1976). Behavior exchange theory and marital decision making. *Journal of Personality and Social Psychology, 34,* 14–23.

Gottman, J. M., & Porterfield, A. L. (1981). Communicative competence in the nonverbal behavior of married couples. *Journal of Marriage and the Family*, 4, 817–824.

Gray-Little, B., & Burks, N. (1983). Power and satisfaction in marriage: A review and critique. *Psychological Bulletin*, 93, 513–538.

Greenwald, A. G. (1980). The totalitarian ego: Fabrication and revision of personal history. *American Psychologist*, 35, 603–608.

Guerney, B. G., Jr. (1977). *Relationship enhancement*. San Francisco: Jossey-Bass.

Hahlweg, K., & Markman, H. J. (1983, December). *The effectiveness of behavioral marital therapy: Empirical status of behavior techniques in preventing and alleviating marital distress.* Paper presented at the annual meeting of the Association for Advancement of Behavior Therapy, Washington, DC.

Hahlweg, K., & Markman, H. J. (1988). Effectiveness of behavioral marital therapy: Empirical status of behavioral techniques in preventing and alleviating marital distress. *Journal of Consulting and Clinical Psychology*, 56, 440–447.

Hahlweg, K., Nuechterlein, K. H., Goldstein, M. J., Magaña, A., Doane, J. A., & Snyder, K. S. (1987). Parental expressed emotion attitudes and intrafamilial communication behavior. In K. Hahlweg and M. J. Goldstein (Eds.), *Understanding major mental disorder: The contribution of family interaction research* (pp. 156–175). New York: Family Process Press.

Hahlweg, K., Reisner, L., Kohli, G., Vollmer, M., Schindler, L., & Revenstorf, D. (1984). Development and validity of a new system to analyze interpersonal communication (KPI: Kategoriensystem für partnerschaftliche Interaktion). In K. Hahlweg & N. S. Jacobson (Eds.), *Marital interaction: Analysis and modification* (pp. 182–198). New York: Guilford Press.

Hahlweg, K., Revenstorf, D., & Schindler, L. (1982). Treatment of marital distress: Comparing formats and modalities. *Advances in Behavior Research and Therapy*, 4, 57–74.

Hahlweg, K., Schindler, L., Revenstorf, D., & Brengelmann, J. C. (1984). The Munich marital therapy study. In K. Hahlweg and N. S. Jacobson (Eds.), *Marital interaction: Analysis and modification* (pp. 3–26). New York: Guilford Press.

Hamilton, M. (1960). A rating scale for depression. *Journal of Neurology, Neurosurgery, and Psychiatry*, 23, 56–61.

Hansen, J. C. (Ed.). (1982). *Clinical approaches to family violence*. Rockville, MD: Aspen.

Harris, R. E., & Lingoes, J. C. (1955). *Subscales for the MMPI: An aid to profile interpretation*. Mimeographed materials. Department of Psychiatry, University of California.

Hathaway, S. R., & McKinley, J. C. (1951). *The Minnesota Multiphasic Personality Inventory manual*. New York: Psychological Corporation.

Hathaway, S. R., & McKinley, J. C. (1967). *The Minnesota Multiphasic Personality Inventory manual*. New York: Psychological Corporation.

Haynes, S. M., Chavez, R. E., & Samuel, V. (1984). Assessment of marital communication and distress. *Behavioral Assessment*, 6, 315–321.

Haynes, S. N., Follingstad, D. R., & Sullivan, J. C. (1979). Assessment of marital satisfaction and interaction. *Journal of Consulting and Clinical Psychology*, 47, 789–791.

Heider, F. (1958). *The psychology of interpersonal relations.* New York: Wiley.

Heins, T. (1978). Marital interaction in depression. *Australian and New Zealand Journal of Psychiatry, 12,* 269–275.

Hetherington, M. (1972). Effects of father absence on personality development in adolescent daughters. *Developmental Psychology, 7,* 313–326.

Hetherington, E. M., & Parke, R. D. (1979). *Child psychology: A contemporary viewpoint.* (2nd ed.). New York: McGraw-Hill.

Hinchliffe, M. K., Hooper, D., & Roberts, F. J. (1978). *The melancholy marriage: Depression in marriage and psychosocial approaches to therapy.* New York: Wiley.

Hof, L., Epstein, N., & Miller, W. R. (1980). Integrating attitudinal and behavioral change in marital enrichment. *Family Relations, 29,* 241–248.

Hof, L., & Miller, W. R. (1981). *Marriage enrichment: Philosophy, process, and program.* Bowie, MD: Brady.

Holtzworth-Munroe, A., & Jacobson, N. S. (1985). Causal attributions of married couples: When do they search for causes? What do they conclude when they do? *Journal of Personality and Social Psychology, 48,* 1398–1412.

Hooley, J. M. (1985). Expressed emotion: A review of the critical literature. *Clinical Psychology Review, 5,* 119–139.

Hooley, J. M. (1986). Expressed emotion and depression: Interactions between patients and high versus low EE spouses. *Journal of Abnormal Psychology, 95,* 237–246.

Hooley, J. M. (1987). The nature and origins of expressed emotion. In K. Hahlweg and M. J. Goldstein (Eds.), *Understanding major mental disorder: The contribution of family interaction research* (pp. 176–194). New York: Family Process Press.

Hooley, J. M., & Hahlweg, K. (1986). Interaction patterns of depressed patients and their spouses: Comparing high and low EE dyads. In M. J. Goldstein, I. Hand, and K. Hahlweg (Eds.), *Treatment of schizophrenia: Family assessment and intervention* (pp. 85–95). Berlin: Springer-Verlag.

Hooley, J. M., Orley, J., & Teasdale, J. D. (1986). Levels of expressed emotion and relapse in depressed patients. *British Journal of Psychiatry, 148,* 642–647.

Hops, H., Biglan, A., Sherman, L., Arthur, J., Friedman, L., & Osteen, V. (1987). Home observations of family interactions of depressed women. *Journal of Consulting and Clinical Psychology, 55,* 341–346.

Hops, H., Wills, T. A., Patterson, G. R., & Weiss, R. L. (1972). *Marital Interaction Coding System.* Eugene: University of Oregon and Oregon Research Institute.

Howes, M., & Hokanson, J. (1979). Conversational and social responses to depressive interpersonal behavior. *Journal of Abnormal Psychology, 88,* 625–634.

Huber, C. H., & Milstein, B. (1985). Cognitive restructuring and a collaborative set in couples' work. *American Journal of Family Therapy, 13*(2), 17–27.

Hudson, B. (1974). The families of agoraphobics treated by behavior therapy. *British Journal of Social Work, 4,* 51–59.

Jacobson, N. S. (1977). Problem-solving and contingency contracting in the treatment of marital discord. *Journal of Consulting and Clinical Psychology, 45,* 92–100.

Jacobson, N. S. (1978a). Specific and nonspecific factors in the effectiveness of a behavioral approach to the treatment of marital discord. *Journal of Consulting and Clinical Psychology, 46,* 442–452.

Jacobson, N. S. (1978b). A stimulus control model of change in behavioral couples therapy: Implications for contingency contracting. *Journal of Marriage and Family Counseling, 4,* 29–35.

Jacobson, N. S. (1984a). A component analysis of behavioral marital therapy: The relative effectiveness of behavior exchange and communication/problem-solving training. *Journal of Consulting and Clinical Psychology, 52,* 295–305.

Jacobson, N. S. (1984b). Marital therapy and the cognitive-behavioral treatment of depression. *Behavior Therapist, 7,* 143–147.

Jacobson, N. S., Elwood, R. W., & Dallas, M. (1981). Assessment of marital dysfunction. In D. H. Barlow (Ed.), *Behavioral assessment of adult disorders* (pp. 439–479). New York: Guilford Press.

Jacobson, N. S., & Follette, W. C. (1985). Clinical significance of improvement resulting from two behavioral marital therapy components. *Behavior Therapy, 16,* 249–262.

Jacobson, N. S., Follette, W. C., & McDonald, D. W. (1982). Reactivity to positive and negative behavior in distressed and nondistressed married couples. *Journal of Consulting and Clinical Psychology, 50,* 706–714.

Jacobson, N. S., Follette, W. C., & Pagel, M. (1986). Predicting who will benefit from behavioral marital therapy. *Journal of Consulting and Clinical Psychology, 54,* 518–522.

Jacobson, N. S., Follette, W. C., & Revenstorf, D. (1984). Psychotherapy outcome research: Methods for reporting variability and evaluating clinical significance. *Behavior Therapy, 15,* 336–352.

Jacobson, N. S., Follette, W. C., Revenstorf, D., Baucom, D. H., Hahlweg, K., & Margolin, G. (1984). Variability in outcome and clinical significance of behavioral marital therapy: A reanalysis of outcome data. *Journal of Consulting and Clinical Psychology, 52,* 497–504.

Jacobson, N. S., & Margolin, G. (1979). *Marital therapy: Strategies based on social learning and behavior exchange principles.* New York: Brunner/Mazel.

Jacobson, N. S., McDonald, D. W., Follette, W. C., & Berley, R. A. (1985). Attributional processes in distressed and nondistressed married couples. *Cognitive Therapy and Research, 9,* 35–50.

Jacobson, N. S., & Moore, D. (1981). Spouses as observers of the events in their relationship. *Journal of Consulting and Clinical Psychology, 49,* 269–277.

Jacobson, N. S., Schmaling, K. B., Salusky, S., Follette, V., & Dobson, K. (1987, November). *Marital therapy as an adjunct treatment for depression.* Paper presented at the 21st annual meeting of the Association for the Advancement of Behavior Therapy, Boston.

Jacobson, N. S., Waldron, H., & Moore, D. (1980). Toward a behavioral profile of marital distress. *Journal of Consulting and Clinical Psychology, 48,* 696–703.

Jessee, R. E., & Guerney, B. G. (1981). A comparison of Gestalt and relationship enhancement treatment with married couples. *American Journal of Family Therapy, 9,* 31–41.

Johnson, S. M., & Greenberg, L. S. (1985). Differential effects of experiential and problem-solving interventions in resolving marital conflict. *Journal of Consulting and Clinical Psychology, 53,* 175–184.

Jones, R. G. (1968). *A factored measure of Ellis' irrational belief system, with* personality and maladjustment correlates. Unpublished doctoral dissertation, Texas Technological College.

Jones, E. E., & Davis, K. (1965). From acts to dispositions: The attribution process in personal perception. In L. Berkowitz (Ed.), *Advances in experimental social psychology* (Vol. 2, pp. 219–266). New York: Academic Press.

Jordan, T. J., & McCormick, N. B. (1987, April). *The role of sex beliefs in intimate relationships.* Paper presented at the annual meeting of the American Association of Sex Educators, Counselors and Therapists, New York.

Kaplan, H. S. (1974). *The new sex therapy: Active treatment of sexual dysfunctions.* New York: Brunner/Mazel.

Kaplan, H. S. (1979). *Disorders of sexual desire.* New York: Brunner/Mazel.

Kelley, H. H. (1967). Attribution theory in social psychology. In D. Levine (Ed.), *Nebraska symposium on motivation* (Vol. 15, pp. 192–238). Lincoln: University of Nebraska Press.

Kelley, H. H., Berscheid, E., Christensen, A., Harvey, J. H., Huston, T. L., Levinger, G., McClintock, E., Peplau, L. A., & Peterson, D. R. (1983). *Close relationships.* New York: W. H. Freeman.

Kelley, J. B. (1981). Observations on adolescent relationships five years after divorce. In S. C. Feinstein, J. G. Looney, A. Z. Schwartzberg, & A. D. Sorosky (Eds.), *Adolescent psychiatry: Developmental and clinical studies* (Vol. 9, pp. 133–141). Chicago: University of Chicago Press.

Kelly, G. A. (1955). *The psychology of personal constructs.* New York: Norton.

Klerman, G. L., Weissman, M. M., Rounsaville, B. J., & Chevron, E. S. (1984). *Interpersonal psychotherapy of depression.* New York: Basic Books.

Koren, P., Carlton, K., & Shaw, D. (1980). Marital conflict: Relations among behaviors, outcomes, and distress. *Journal of Consulting and Clinical Psychology, 48,* 460–468.

Kurdek, L. A., & Schmitt, J. P. (1986). Interaction of sex role self-concept with relationship quality and relationship beliefs in married, heterosexual cohabiting, gay, and lesbian couples. *Journal of Personality and Social Psychology, 51,* 365–370.

Kyle, S. O., & Falbo, T. (1985). Relationships between marital stress and attributional preferences for own and spouse behavior. *Journal of Social and Clinical Psychology, 3,* 339–351.

L'Abate, L. (1977). *Enrichment: Structured interventions with couples, families, and groups.* Washington, DC: University Press of America.

L'Abate, L., & McHenry, S. (1983). *Handbook of marital interventions.* New York: Grune & Stratton.

Lazarus, A. A. (1985). *Marital myths.* San Luis Obispo, CA: Impact.

Leber, W. R., Beckham, E. E., & Danker-Brown, P. (1985). Diagnostic criteria for depression. In E. E. Beckham and W. R. Leber (Eds.), *Handbook of depression: Treatment, assessment, and research* (pp. 343–371). Homewood, IL: Dorsey Press.

Lederer, W. J., & Jackson, D. D. (1968). *The mirages of marriage.* New York: Norton.

Lester, M. E., & Doherty, W. J. (1983). Couples' long-term evaluations of their Marriage Encounter experience. *Journal of Marital and Family Therapy, 9,* 183–188.

Lewinsohn, P. M., & Arconad, M. (1981). Behavioral treatment of depression: A social learning approach. In J. F. Clarkin and H. I. Glazer (Eds.), *Depression: Behavioral and directive intervention strategies* (pp. 33–67). New York: Garland STPM Press.

Ley, R. (1987). Panic disorder: A hyperventilation interpretation. In L. Michelson and L. M. Ascher (Eds.), *Anxiety and stress disorders: Cognitive-behavioral assessment and treatment* (pp. 191–212). New York: Guilford Press.

Liberman, R., Levine, J., Wheeler, E., Sanders, N., & Wallace, C. J. (1976). Marital therapy in groups: A comparative evaluation of behavioral and interaction formats. *Acta Psychiatrica Scandinavica, 266,* 1–34.

Lipman, R. S. (1982). Differentiating anxiety and depression in anxiety disorders: Use of rating scales. *Psychopharmacology Bulletin, 18,* 69–77.

Locke, H. J., & Wallace, K. M. (1959). Short marital-adjustment and prediction tests: Their reliability and validity. *Marriage and Family Living, 21,* 251–255.

LoPiccolo, J., & LoPiccolo, L. (1978). *Handbook of sex therapy.* New York: Plenum Press.

Lubin, B. (1967). *Manual for depression adjective check lists.* San Diego, CA: Educational and Industrial Testing Service.

Lumpkin, W. C. (1981). The relationships of marital communication and marital adjustment with self-esteem and self-actualization. (Doctoral dissertation, University of New Orleans, 1981). *Dissertation Abstracts International, 42,* 2883A.

Magana, A. B., Goldstein, M. J., Karno, M., Miklowitz, D. J., Jenkins, J., & Falloon, I. R. H. (1986). A brief method for assessing expressed emotion in relatives of psychiatric patients. *Psychiatry Research, 17,* 203–212.

Margolin, G. (1978). A multilevel approach to the assessment of communication positiveness in distressed marital couples. *International Journal of Family Counseling, 6,* 81–89.

Margolin, G. (1981). Behavioral exchange in happy and unhappy marriages: A family cycle perspective. *Behavior Therapy, 12,* 329–343.

Margolin, G. (1983). Behavior marital therapy: Is there a place for passion, play, and other non-negotiable dimensions? *Behavior Therapist, 6,* 65–68.

Margolin, G., Fernandez, V., Gorin, L., & Ortiz, S. (1982, November). *The Conflict Inventory: A measurement of how couples handle marital tension.* Paper presented at the annual meeting of the Association for Advancement of Behavior Therapy, Los Angeles.

Margolin, G., Hattem, D., John, R. S., & Yost, K. (1985). Perceptual agreement between spouses and outside observers when coding themselves and a stranger dyad. *Behavioral Assessment, 7,* 235–247.

Margolin, G., & Jacobson, N. S. (1981). Assessment of marital dysfunction. In M. Hersen & A. S. Bellack (Eds.), *Behavioral assessment: A practical handbook* (pp. 389–426). New York: Pergamon Press.

Margolin, G., John, R. S., & Gleberman, L. (1988). Affective responses to conflictual discussions in violent and nonviolent couples. *Journal of Consulting and Clinical Psychology, 56,* 24–33.

Margolin, G., Olkin, R., & Baum, M. (1977). *The Anger Checklist.* Unpublished inventory, University of California, Santa Barbara.

Margolin, G., & Wampold, B. E. (1981). Sequential analysis of conflict and accord in distressed and nondistressed marital partners. *Journal of Consulting and Clinical Psychology, 49*, 554–567.

Margolin, G., & Weiss, R. L. (1978). Comparative evaluation of therapeutic components associated with behavioral marital treatments. *Journal of Consulting and Clinical Psychology, 46*, 1476–1486.

Markman, H. J. (1979). The application of a behavioral model of marriage in predicting relationship satisfaction for couples planning marriage. *Journal of Consulting and Clinical Psychology, 47*, 743–749.

Markman, H. J. (1981). Prediction of marital distress: A 5-year follow-up. *Journal of Consulting and Clinical Psychology, 49*, 760–762.

Markman, H. J. (1984). The longitudinal study of couples' interactions: Implications for understanding and predicting the development of marital distress. In K. Hahlweg & N. S. Jacobson (Eds.), *Marital interaction: Analysis and modification* (pp. 253–281). New York: Guilford Press.

Markman, H. J., Floyd, F. J., Stanley, S. M., & Jamieson, K. (1984). A cognitive-behavioral program for the prevention of marital and family distress: Issues in program development and delivery. In K. Hahlweg and N. S. Jacobson (Eds.), *Marital interaction: Analysis and modification* (pp. 396–428). New York: Guilford Press.

Markman, H. J., & Poltrock, S. E. (1982). A computerized system for recording and analysis of self-observations of couples' interaction. *Behaviour Research Methods & Instrumentation, 14*, 186–190.

Markus, H. (1977). Self-schemata and processing information about the self. *Journal of Personality and Social Psychology, 35*, 63–78.

Masters, W. H., & Johnson, V. E. (1966). *Human sexual response.* Boston: Little, Brown.

Masters, W. H., & Johnson, V. E. (1970). *Human sexual inadequacy.* Boston: Little, Brown.

Mathews, A. M., Gelder, M. G., & Johnston, D. W. (1981). *Agoraphobia: Nature and treatment.* New York: Guilford Press.

Mehlman, S. K., Baucom, D. H., & Anderson, D. (1983). Effectiveness of cotherapists versus single therapists and immediate versus delayed treatment in behavioral marital therapy. *Journal of Consulting and Clinical Psychology, 51*, 258–266.

Mehrabian, A. (1972). *Nonverbal communication.* Chicago: Aldine Atherton.

Mehrabian, A., & Epstein, N. (1972). A measure of emotional empathy. *Journal of Personality, 40*, 525–543.

Meichenbaum, D. (1977). *Cognitive-behavior modification.* New York: Plenum Press.

Michelson, L. (1987). Cognitive-behavioral assessment and treatment of agoraphobia. In L. Michelson and L. M. Ascher (Eds.), *Anxiety and stress disorders: Cognitive-behavioral assessment and treatment* (pp. 213–279). New York: Guilford Press.

Michelson, L., & Ascher, L. M. (1987). *Anxiety and stress disorders: Cognitive-behavioral assessment and treatment.* New York: Guilford Press.

Miller, P. A., & Eisenberg, N. (1988). The relation of empathy to aggressive and externalizing/antisocial behavior. *Psychological Bulletin, 103,* 324–344.

Miller, S., Nunnally, E. W., & Wackman, D. B. (1975). *Alive and aware: Improving communication in relationships.* Minneapolis, MN: Interpersonal Communications Program.

Milton, F., & Hafner, J. (1979). The outcome of behavior therapy for agoraphobia in relation to marital adjustment. *Archives of General Psychiatry, 36,* 807–811.

Mountjoy, C. Q., & Roth, M. (1982). Studies in the relationship between depressive disorders and anxiety states. *Journal of Affective Disorders, 4,* 127–147.

Murphy, D. C., & Mendelson, L. A. (1973). Communication and adjustment in marriage: Investigating the relationship. *Family Process, 12,* 317–326.

Murstein, B. I., & Williams, P. D. (1983). Sex roles and marriage adjustment. *Small Group Behavior, 41,* 77–94.

Navran, L. (1967). Communication and adjustment in marriage. *Family Process, 6,* 173–184.

Neidig, P. H., & Friedman, D. H. (1984). *Spouse abuse: A treatment program for couples.* Champaign, IL: Research Press.

Nisbett, R., & Ross, L. (1980). *Human inference: Strategies and shortcomings of social judgment.* Englewood Cliffs, NJ: Prentice-Hall.

Noller, P. (1980). Misunderstandings in marital communication: A study of couples' nonverbal communication. *Journal of Personality and Social Psychology, 39,* 1135–1148.

Noller, P. (1981). Gender and marital adjustment level differences in decoding messages from spouses and strangers. *Journal of Personality and Social Psychology, 41,* 272–278.

Noller, P. (1982). Couple communication and marital satisfaction. *Australian Journal of Sex, Marriage and Family, 3* (2), 69–75.

Noller, P. (1984). *Nonverbal communication and marital interaction.* New York: Pergamon Press.

Notarius, C. I., & Markman, H. J. (1981). The Couples Interaction Scoring System. In E. E. Filsinger and R. A. Lewis (Eds.), *Assessing marriage: New behavioral approaches* (pp. 112–127). Beverly Hills, CA: Sage.

Notarius, C. I., Markman, H. J., & Gottman, J. M. (1983). Couples Interaction Scoring System: Clinical implications. In E. E. Filsinger (Ed.), *Marriage and family assessment: A sourcebook for family therapy* (pp. 117–136). Beverly Hills, CA: Sage.

Notarius, C. I., & Vanzetti, N. A. (1983). The Marital Agendas Protocol. In E. E. Filsinger (Ed.), *Marriage and family assessment: A sourcebook for family therapy* (pp. 209–227). Beverly Hills, CA: Sage.

Novaco, R. W. (1975). *Anger control: The development and evaluation of an experimental treatment.* Lexington, MA: Lexington Books.

Novaco, R. W. (1976). The functions and the regulation of the arousal of anger. *American Journal of Psychiatry, 133,* 1124–1128.

Novaco, R. W. (1978). Anger and coping with stress: Cognitive behavioral interventions. In J. P. Foreyt & D. P. Rathjen (Eds.), *Cognitive behavior therapy: Research and applications* (pp. 135–173). New York: Plenum Press.

Nussbaum, K., Wittig, B. A., Hanlon, T. E., & Kurland, A. A. (1963). Intravenous nialamide in the treatment of depressed female patients. *Comprehensive Psychiatry, 4,* 105–116.

O'Farrell, T. J., Cutter, H. S., & Floyd, F. J. (1983). *The class on alcoholism and marriage (CALM) project: Results on marital adjustment and communication from before to after therapy* (Tech. Rep. No. 4-1). Brockton, MA: Brockton/West Roxbury Veterans Administration Medical Center.

O'Farrell, T. J., Cutter, H. S., & Floyd, F. J. (1985). Evaluating behavioral marital therapy for male alcoholics: Effects on marital adjustment and communication from before and after treatment. *Behavior Therapy, 16,* 147–167.

O'Leary, K. D., Fincham, F., & Turkewitz, H. (1983). Assessment of positive feelings toward spouse. *Journal of Consulting and Clinical Psychology, 51,* 949–951.

O'Leary, K. D., & Turkewitz, H. (1978). Marital therapy from a behavioral perspective. In T. J. Paolino & B. S. McCrady (Eds.), *Marriage and marital therapy: Psychoanalytic, behavioral and systems theory perspectives* (pp. 240–297). New York: Brunner/Mazel.

Olson, D. H., & Schaefer, M. T. (undated). *PAIR: Personal Assessment of Intimacy in Relationships, procedure manual.* St. Paul, MN: Family Social Science, University of Minnesota.

Patterson, G. R. (1982). *A social learning approach to family intervention. Vol. 3. Coercive family process.* Eugene, OR: Castalia.

Pretzer, J. L., Epstein, N., & Fleming, B. (1985). *The Marital Attitude Survey: A measure of dysfunctional attributions and expectancies.* Unpublished manuscript.

Pretzer, J. L., Fleming, B., & Epstein, N. (1983, August). *Cognitive factors in marital interaction: The role of specific attributions.* Paper presented at the World Congress of Behavior Therapy, Washington, DC.

Raush, H. L., Barry, W. A., Hertel, R. K., & Swain, M. A. (1974). *Communication, conflict and marriage.* San Francisco, CA: Jossey-Bass.

Resnick, P. A., Welsh, B. K., & Zitomer, E. (1979, August). *Revising the Marital Interaction Coding System: Extension and cross validation.* Paper presented at the annual convention of the American Psychological Association, New York.

Revenstorf, D. (1984). The role of attribution of marital distress in therapy. In K. Hahlweg and N. S. Jacobson (Eds.), *Marital interaction: Analysis and modification* (pp. 325–336). New York: Guilford Press.

Revenstorf, D., Hahlweg, K., Schindler, L., & Vogel, B. (1984). Interaction analysis of marital conflict. In K. Hahlweg & N. S. Jacobson (Eds.), *Marital interaction: Analysis and modification* (pp. 159–181). New York: Guilford Press.

Rholes, W., Riskind, J. H., & Neville, B. (1985). The relationship of cognitions and hopelessness to depression and anxiety. *Social Cognition, 3,* 36–50.

Riskind, J. H., Beck, A. T., Brown, G., & Steer, R. A. (1987). Taking the measure of anxiety and depression: Validity of reconstructed Hamilton scales. *Journal of Nervous and Mental Disease, 175,* 474–479.

Robinson, E. A., & Price, M. G. (1980). Pleasurable behavior in marital interaction: An observational study. *Journal of Consulting and Clinical Psychology, 48,* 117–118.

Rogers, C. R. (1957). The necessary and sufficient conditions of therapeutic personality change. *Journal of Consulting Psychology, 21,* 95–103.

Rosenbaum, A., & O'Leary, K. D. (1981). Marital violence: Characteristics of abusive couples. *Journal of Consulting and Clinical Psychology, 49,* 63–71.

Rotter, J. B. (1954). *Social learning and clinical psychology.* Englewood Cliffs, NJ: Prentice-Hall.

Rounsaville, B. J., Weissman, M. M., Prusoff, B. A., & Herceg-Baron, R. L. (1979). Process of psychotherapy among depressed women with marital disputes. *American Journal of Orthopsychiatry, 49,* 505–510.

Sacco, W. P., & Beck, A. T. (1985). Cognitive therapy of depression. In E. E. Beckham & W. R. Leber (Eds.) *Handbook of depression: Treatment, assessment, and research* (pp. 3–38). Homewood, IL: The Dorsey Press.

Sade, J. E., & Notarius, C. I. (1985). Emotional expression in marital and family relationships. In L. L'Abate (Ed)., *The handbook of family psychology and therapy* (pp. 378–404). Homewood, IL: The Dorsey Press.

Sager, C. J. (1976). *Marriage contracts and couple therapy: Hidden forces in intimate relationships.* New York: Brunner/Mazel.

Schaap, C. (1984). A comparison of the interaction of distressed and nondistressed married couples in a laboratory situation: Literature survey, methodological issues, and an empirical investigation. In K. Hahlweg and N. S. Jacobson (Eds.), *Marital interaction: Analysis and modification* (pp. 133–158). New York: Guilford Press.

Schachter, S., & Singer, S. E. (1962). Cognitive, social, and physiological determinants of emotional state. *Psychological Review, 69,* 379–399.

Schaefer, M. T., & Olson, D. H. (1981). Assessing intimacy: The PAIR inventory. *Journal of Marital and Family Therapy, 7,* 47–60.

Schank, R., & Abelson, R. P. (1977). *Scripts, plans, goals and understanding: An inquiry into human knowledge structures.* Hillsdale, NJ: Lawrence Erlbaum.

Schlesinger, S. E. (1984, August). *3 R's in the marital treatment of alcohol abuse.* Paper presented at the annual meeting of the American Psychological Association, Toronto.

Schlesinger, S. E., & Epstein, N. (1986). Cognitive-behavioral techniques in marital therapy. In P. A. Keller and L. G. Ritt (Eds.), *Innovations in clinical practice: A source book* (Vol. 5, pp. 137–156). Sarasota, FL: Professional Resource Exchange.

Schumm, W. R., Anderson, S. A., & Griffin, C. L. (1983). The Marital Communication Inventory. In E. E. Filsinger (Ed.), *Marriage and family assessment: A sourcebook for family therapy* (pp. 191–208). Beverly Hills, CA: Sage.

Schumm, W. R., Bollman, S. R., & Jurich, A. P. (1981). Dimensionality of an abbreviated version of the Relationship Inventory: An urban replication with married couples. *Psychological Reports, 48,* 51–56.

Segraves, R. T. (1982). *Marital therapy: A combined psychodynamic-behavioral approach.* New York: Plenum Press.

Seiler, T. B. (1984). Developmental cognitive theory, personality, and therapy. In N. Hoffmann (Ed.), *Foundations of cognitive therapy: Theoretical methods and practical applications* (pp. 11–49). New York: Plenum Press.

Seitz, R. (1970). Five psychological measures of neurotic depression: A correlation study. *Journal of Clinical Psychology, 26,* 504–505.

Seligman, M. E. P. (1975). *Helplessness: On depression, development, and death.* San Francisco: W. H. Freeman.

Seligman, M., Abramson, L. Y., Semmel, A., von Baeyer, C. (1979). Depressive attributional style. *Journal of Abnormal Psychology, 88,* 242–247.

Sharpley, C. F., & Cross, D. G. (1982). A psychometric evaluation of the Spanier Dyadic Adjustment Scale. *Journal of Marriage and the Family, 44 ,* 739–741.

Shaw, B. F., Vallis, T. M., & McCabe, S. B. (1985). The assessment of the severity and symptom patterns in depression. In E. E. Beckham and W. R. Leber (Eds.), *Handbook of depression: Treatment, assessment, and research* (pp. 372–407). Homewood, IL: Dorsey Press.

Sher, T. G., Baucom, D. H., & Larus, J. M. (1988). Communication patterns and response to treatment among depressed and nondepressed maritally distressed couples. Manuscript submitted for publication.

Sloan, S. Z., & L'Abate, L. (1985). Intimacy. In L. L'Abate (Ed.), *The handbook of family psychology and therapy* (pp. 405–427). Homewood, IL: Dorsey Press.

Slusher, M. P., & Anderson, C. A. (in press). Belief perseverance and self-defeating behavior. In R. C. Curtis (Ed.), *Self-defeating behaviors: Experimental research and practical implications.* New York: Plenum Press.

Smith, M. L., & Glass, G. V. (1977). Meta-analysis of psychotherapy outcome studies. *American Psychologist, 32,* 752–760.

Snyder, D. K., (1979). Multidimensional assessment of marital satisfaction. *Journal of Marriage and the Family, 41,* 813–823.

Snyder, D. K. (1981). *Marital Satisfaction Inventory (MSI) manual.* Los Angeles: Western Psychological Services.

Snyder, D. K., & Wills, R. M. (1989). Behavioral versus insight-oriented marital therapy: Effects on individual and interspousal functioning. *Journal of Consulting and Clinical Psychology, 57,* 39–40.

Snyder, D. K., Wills, R. M., & Keiser, T. W. (1981). Empirical validation of the Marital Satisfaction Inventory: An actuarial approach. *Journal of Consulting and Clinical Psychology, 49,* 262–268.

Spanier, G. B. (1976). Measuring dyadic adjustment: New scales for assessing the quality of marriage and similar dyads. *Journal of Marriage and the Family, 38,* 15–28.

Spanier, G. B., & Filsinger, E. E. (1983). The Dyadic Adjustment Scale. In E. E. Filsinger (Ed.), *Marriage and family assessment: A sourcebook for family therapy* (pp. 155–168). Beverly Hills, CA: Sage.

Spanier, G. B., & Thompson, L. (1982). A confirmatory analysis of the Dyadic Adjustment Scale. *Journal of Marriage and the Family, 44,* 731–738.

Spielberger, C. D., Gorsuch, R. L., & Lushene, R. (1970). *STAI manual.* Palo Alto, CA: Consulting Psychologists Press.

Spitzer, R. L., Endicott, J., & Robins, E. (1978). Research Diagnostic Criteria: Rationale and reliability. *Archives of General Psychiatry, 35,* 773–782.

Stover, L., Guerney, B. G., Jr., Ginsberg, B., & Schlein, S. (1977a). The Self-Feeling Awareness Scale (SFAS). In B. G. Guerney, *Relationship enhancement.* San Francisco: Jossey-Bass.

Stover, L., Guerney, B. G., Jr., Ginsberg, B., & Schlein, S. (1977b). The Acceptance of Other Scale (AOS). In B. G. Guerney, *Relationship enhancement.* San Francisco: Jossey-Bass.

Straus, M. A. (1979). Measuring intrafamily conflict and violence: The Conflict

Tactics (CT) Scales. *Journal of Marriage and the Family, 41,* 75–88.

Stuart, R. B. (1969). Operant interpersonal treatment for marital discord. *Journal of Consulting and Clinical Psychology, 33,* 675–682.

Stuart, R. B. (1980). *Helping couples change: A social learning approach to marital therapy.* New York: Guilford Press.

Terman, L. M. (1938). *Psychological factors in marital happiness.* New York: McGraw-Hill.

Thibaut, J. W., & Kelley, H. H. (1959). *The social psychology of groups.* New York: Wiley.

Thomas, E. J. (1977). *Marital communication and decision-making.* New York: Free Press.

Thomas, E. J., Walter, C. L., & O'Flaherty, K. (1974). A verbal problem checklist for use in assessing family verbal behavior. *Behavior Therapy, 5,* 235–246.

Thompson, J. S., & Snyder, D. K. (1986). Attribution theory in intimate relationships: A methodological review. *American Journal of Family Therapy, 14,* 123–138.

Turk, D. C., & Speers, M. A. (1983). Cognitive schemata and cognitive processes in cognitive-behavioral interventions: Going beyond the information given. In P. C. Kendall (Ed.), *Advances in cognitive-behavioral research and therapy* (Vol. 2, pp. 1–31). New York: Academic Press.

Turkewitz, H., & O'Leary, K. D. (1981). A comparative outcome study of behavioral marital therapy and communication therapy. *Journal of Marital and Family Therapy, 7,* 159–169.

U. S. Public Health Service (1977). *A concurrent validational study of the NCHS General Well-Being Schedule.* Hyattsville, MD: USDHEW Publication No. (HRA) 78–1347.

Vaughn, C. E., & Leff, J. P. (1976a). The influence of family and social factors on the course of psychiatric illness: A comparison of schizophrenic and depressed neurotic patients. *British Journal of Psychiatry, 129,* 125–137.

Vaughn, C. E., & Leff, J. P. (1976b). The measurement of expressed emotion in the families of psychiatric patients. *British Journal of Social and Clinical Psychology, 15,* 157–165.

Vaughn, C. E., Snyder, K. S., Jones, S., Freeman, W. B., & Falloon, I. R. H. (1984). Family factors in schizophrenic relapse: Replication in California of British research on expressed emotion. *Archives of General Psychiatry, 41,* 1169–1177.

Vincent, J. P., Cook, N. I., & Messerly, L. (1980). A social learning analysis of couples during the second post-natal month. *American Journal of Family Therapy, 8,* 49–68.

Vincent, J. P., Friedman, L. C., Nugent, J., & Messerly, L. (1979). Demand characteristics in observations of marital interaction. *Journal of Consulting and Clinical Psychology, 47,* 557–566.

Vincent, J. P., Weiss, R. L., & Birchler, G. R. (1975). A behavioral analysis of problem solving in distressed and nondistressed married and stranger dyads. *Behavior Therapy, 6,* 475–487.

Visher, E. B., & Visher, J. S. (1979). *Stepfamilies: A guide to working with stepparents and stepchildren.* New York: Brunner/Mazel.

Watzlawick, P., Beavin, J. H., & Jackson, D. (1967). *Pragmatics of human communication.* New York: Norton.

Weiss, R. L. (1978). The conceptualization of marriage from a behavioral perspective. In T. J. Paolino & B. S. McCrady (Eds.), *Marriage and marital therapy: Psychoanalytic, behavioral and systems theory perspectives* (pp. 165–239). New York: Brunner/Mazel.

Weiss, R. L. (1980). Strategic behavioral marital therapy: Toward a model for assessment and intervention. In J. P. Vincent (Ed.), *Advances in family intervention, assessment and theory* (Vol. 1, pp. 229–271). Greenwich, CT: JAI Press.

Weiss, R. L. (1984). Cognitive and behavioral measures of marital interaction. In K. Hahlweg & N. S. Jacobson (Eds.), *Marital interaction: Analysis and modification* (pp. 232–252). New York: Guilford Press.

Weiss, R. L., & Aved, B. M. (1978). Marital satisfaction and depression as predictors of physical health status. *Journal of Consulting and Clinical Psychology, 46,* 1379–1384.

Weiss, R. L., & Birchler, G. R. (1978). Adults with marital dysfunction. In M. Hersen & A. S. Bellack (Eds.), *Behavior therapy in the psychiatric setting* (pp. 331–364). Baltimore: Williams & Williams.

Weiss, R. L., Hops, H., & Patterson, G. R. (1973). A framework for conceptualizing marital conflict, a technology for altering it, some data for evaluating it. In L. A. Hamerlynck, L. C. Handy, & E. J. Mash (Eds.), *Behavior change: Methodology, concepts and practice* (pp. 309–342). Champaign, IL: Research Press.

Weiss, R. L., & Margolin, G. (1977). Assessment of marital conflict and accord. In A. R. Ciminero, K. S. Calhoun, & H. E. Adams (Eds.), *Handbook of behavioral assessment* (pp. 555–602). New York: Wiley.

Weiss, R. L., & Perry, B. A. (1983). The Spouse Observation Checklist: Development and clinical applications. In E. E. Filsinger (Ed.), *Marriage and family assessment: A sourcebook for family therapy* (pp. 65–84). Beverly Hills, CA: Sage.

Weiss, R. L., & Summers, K. J. (1983). Marital Interaction Coding System-III. In E. E. Filsinger (Ed.), *Marriage and family assessment: A sourcebook for family therapy* (pp. 85–115). Beverly Hills, CA: Sage.

Weiss, R. L., Wasserman, D. A., Wieder, G. R., & Summers, K. (1981, November). *Subjective and objective evaluation of marital conflict: Couples versus the establishment.* Paper presented at the annual meeting of the Association for Advancement of Behavior Therapy, Toronto.

Weissman, M. M., & Paykel, E. S. (1974). *The depressed woman: A study of social relationships.* Chicago: University of Chicago Press.

Wessler, R. A., & Wessler, R. L. (1980). *The principles and practice of rational-emotive therapy.* San Francisco: Jossey-Bass.

Wieder, G. R., & Weiss, R. L. (1980). Generalizability theory and the coding of marital interactions. *Journal of Consulting and Clinical Psychology, 48,* 469–477.

Williams, A. M. (1979). The quantity and quality of marital interaction related to marital satisfaction: A behavioral analysis. *Journal of Applied Behavior Analysis, 12,* 665–678.

Wills, T. A., Weiss, R. L., & Patterson, G. R. (1974). A behavioral analysis of the determinants of marital satisfaction. *Journal of Consulting and Clinical Psychology, 42,* 802–811.

Worldwide Marriage Encounter. *Love Is . . . , 1984* (pp. 1–12). St. Paul: Brown and Bigelow, 1984.

Zanna, M. P., & Cooper, J. (1976). Dissonance and the attribution process. In J. H. Harvey, W. J. Ickes, and R. F. Kidd (Eds.), *New directions in attribution research* (Vol. 1, pp. 199–217). Hillsdale, NJ: Lawrence Erlbaum.

Zuckerman, M., Persky, H., Eckman, K. M., & Hopkins, T. R. (1967). A multitrait multimethod measurement approach to the traits (or states) of anxiety, depression and hostility. *Journal of Projective Techniques and Personality Assessment, 16,* 543–547.

Zung, W. W. K. (1971). A rating instrument for anxiety disorders. *Psychosomatics, 12,* 371–379.

Name Index

Subject Index

Ability to change, in attribution assessment, 169

Absolute terms, avoidance of, 41

Abstraction, selective, 68, 82, 314

A–C, *see* Areas-of-Change Questionnaire

Acceptance, in EET, 354

Acceptance of Other Scale (AOS), 225, 226, 241

Acceptance of the Other, 40

"Accurate" attributions, 183

Acknowledgment
of partner, communication for, 40, 273–276
of positives, 275–276
of speaker's message, 365

Adaptive functioning, emotions that interfere with, 106–124, 228–239

Affect(s), *see also* Emotion *entries*; Feeling *entries*
assessment of, 201–241
behavioral observation in, 210–215
interplay of behavior and cognition and, in marital interaction, 5–16
jealousy and, 119–120
modification of, 342–383
negative, amount and intensity of, 92–95, 202–215
of partner, spouse's expression of affect and, 15
positive
amount and intensity of, 92–95, 202–215
measures of global marital satisfaction and, 202–205
specific, coding of, from physical features versus judgments by cultural informants, 214

Affective Communication (AFC), 152

Affective data, integration of, 239–241

Affective factors
in marital dysfunction, 91–124
in marital interaction, 14–16

Affective responses, in partner, spouse's behavior and, 12

Affective states, of spouse, and own cognitions and behaviors, 14–15

Affective Style, 212

Affective tone, moderating of, 390–391

Affective vocabularies, of spouses, 220

Aggression, 41

Agoraphobia, marital dysfunction and, 116, 118

Agreement
in EET, 354
on what behaviors are, 159

Alternative explanations, for event, 324

Alternative solutions, consideration of, 263–265

Always, as term, 40, 41, 277–278, 315

Ambivalent reactions/responses
depression and, 113
jealous behavior and, 123–124

American Psychiatric Association, 119, 236, 237

Anger, 107–112, 229–232
based on current events, 371–373
based on previous events, 366–371
cognitive components of, 368–370
dealing with, 366–373
decision to commit to, 98
dysfunctional
characteristics of, 107–109
sources of, 110

Anger Checklist, 230–231

Anger Log, 231
in jealousy, 239, 240

Anxiety, 115–119, 236–238
dealing with, 381–383
effects of, on marital intreraction, 117–119
as response to relationship problems, 115–117

Appropriateness
of behaviors, 157
of cognitions, 48
of emotions, standards about, 99–100

Appropriate solution-orientation, communication to assist, 276–280

Arbitrary inference, 79, 313–314

Areas-of-Change Questionnaire (A–C), in assessment
of behavior, 136–138, 153
of cognition, 174, 175, 185, 200

Assertion
aggression versus, 41
skills for, anger and lack of, 111

Assessment
of affect, 201–241
of behavior, *see* Behavior, assessment of
of cognition, 158–201
of "expressed emotion," 212–213
feedback to couples regarding, 242–246
marital, scales for, 433–444
of marital problems, implications of interplay of behavior, cognition and affect for, 16
strategies for, selection of, 199–200
of utility of schemata, 335

Assumptions, 13, 47, 49–57, 66, 68
assessment of, 188–191
building skills for identifying, 320–321
about emotions and their causes, 98–99
functions of, 52
inappropriate, development of, 56–57
introducing concept of, 315, 317–318

471

Beliefs, 47; *see also* Standards
Blame, attributions of, 110–111
BMT, *see* Behavioral marital therapy
Bonus, in contracting, 286
Brainstorming, 264, 336

Camberwell Family Interview (CFI), 212
Caring, statements of, jealous behavior to
    prompt, 380
Caring days, 252–254
Causal attributions, 84
Causes of human behavior, assumptions on,
    54–55
Center for Cognitive Therapy, xi
Change(s)
  ability for, in attribution assessment, 169
  of behaviors
    of couple, interview regarding, 329–332
    skills for, 44–45
  in depressed couples, 374
Changing roles, in EET, 356–358
CISS, *see* Couples Interaction Scoring System
Clarity, of messages, 31–32
Client concerns, sequencing and, 388
Clinging, to partner, 95
Clinical implications, of research on
    constructive and destructrive
    communication, 38
Clinical interviews, *see* Interview(s)
Clinical practice, problematic and constructive
    forms of communication identified in,
    39–42
Coding, of specific affects, from physical
    features versus judgments by cultural
    informants, 214
Cognition(s)
  and affect, interplay of behavior and, in
    marital interaction, 5–16
  assessment of, 158–201
  dysfunctional, multiple, case example of,
    87–88
  that impede listening, 106
    and constructive expression, 227
  that impede recognition of emotions and
    their determinants, 219–220
  of individual, and own emotions and
    behavior toward partner, 13
  jealousy and, 119, 121
  logical analysis of, 323–325
  as mediators of couples' social exchanges,
    23–24
  modification of, 299–341
    building skills for identification and,
      310–339
    dealing with incompatible standards in,
      340–341
    focusing on individual versus couple in,
      339–340
    intervention strategies in, 308–339
    role of therapist in, 307–308

testing and, 321–339
of partner, *see* Partner, cognitions of research
    on, status of, 88–90
of spouse
  about marriage, own behavior and, 12
  and own cognitions concerning marital
    interaction, 13
  testing of, gathering evidence for, 325–338
Cognitive approaches, and cognitive-
    behavioral, effects of, 430–432
Cognitive-behavioral marital therapy, empirical
    status of, 410–432; *see also* Behavioral
    marital therapy (BMT)
Cognitive complexity, and awareness of
    emotions, 96–97
Cognitive components of anger, 368–370
Cognitive distortions, 78–84
  introducing concepts of, 313–319
Cognitive factors
  influencing jealousy 119, 121
  in marital dysfunction, 47–90
  in marital interaction, 13–14
Cognitive interventions, shifting to, 392–396
Cognitive model, teaching of, to couples,
    302–307
Cognitive restructuring
  goals of, 301–302
  targets of, 299–301
Cognitive view, of marital distress, 47–49
Collaborative relationship, of therapist with
    couple, 308
Command aspect of message, 41–42
Communication
  to acknowledge partner, 40, 273–276
  to assist in staying appropriately solution-
    oriented, 276–280
  constructive, *see* Constructive
    communication
  destructive/problematic, *see* Destructive/
    problematic communication
  to establish one's current desires and
    preferences and one's role in previous
    interactions, 270, 272
  evaluation of in behavior assessment,
    143–153
    insiders', 149–153
    outsiders', 144–149
  and interaction, *see* Couple interaction,
    and communication
  quantity of, 30–35
Communication guidelines, while problem
    solving, 271
Communication skills, 29–42
Communication training approaches/
    techniques, 269–280, 429–430
Comparison level, and marital satisfaction, 23
Complementary unrealistic assumptions or
    standards, 340
Compromise on solution, 43–44
Conflict Inventory (CI), 229–230, 240